Psychiatrist
of America

Psychiatrist of America

The Life of Harry Stack Sullivan

HELEN SWICK PERRY

The Belknap Press
of Harvard University Press
Cambridge, Massachusetts, and London, England 1982

Library of Congress Cataloging in Publication Data
Perry, Helen Swick.
Psychiatrist of America, the life of Harry Stack Sullivan.

Includes bibliographical references and index.
1. Sullivan, Harry Stack, 1892–1949.   2. Psychiatrists
—United States—Biography.   3. Psychologists—United
States—Biography.   4. Sociologists—United States—
Biography. I. Title.   [DNLM: 1. Psychiatry—Biography.
WZ 100 S95P]
RC339.52.S87P37   616.89′0092′4 [B]   81-7066
ISBN 0-674-72076-8   AACR2

The horses' heads on the title page were
designed as a personal symbol for Sullivan
by his friend John Vassos

for
Stewart E. Perry
Arthur J. Rosenthal

and in memory of
Mary Ladd Gavell (1919–1967)
Eunice Swick Tertell (1916–1981)

Contents

CONTENTS

Illustrations

ILLUSTRATIONS

Credits

Special thanks are extended to the following for providing photographs for this book: Dorothy Blitsten, 26; Brooks (photographers, Bethesda, Maryland), 28; Mary Fargo, 2, 15, 16, 17, and (with Maude Doing), 25; Vaughan E. Fargo, 31; Jane (Sullivan) Kenific, 9; John Kofler (photographer, Washington, D.C.), 29; Loretta Macksey, 14; Gertrude (Sullivan) Nash, 8 (from an unidentified Utica, N.Y., newspaper) and 30 (photographer, Walter F. Wright, Norwich, N.Y.); Dorothy Stack, 3, 7, 10, 11, 12, and 13 (photograph by Michael Leo Stack); Helen and Lillian Stack, 1, 5, and 6; James Inscoe Sullivan, 4, 19 (photograph by Harry Stack Sullivan), 21, 22, 23, 24, and 27 (photograph by Margaret Bourke-White); William Alanson White Institute of Psychiatry, Psychoanalysis, and Psychology, 18 and 20 (photographer, Underwood, Washington, D.C.). The map was prepared by Robert Forget.

CHENANGO COUNTY

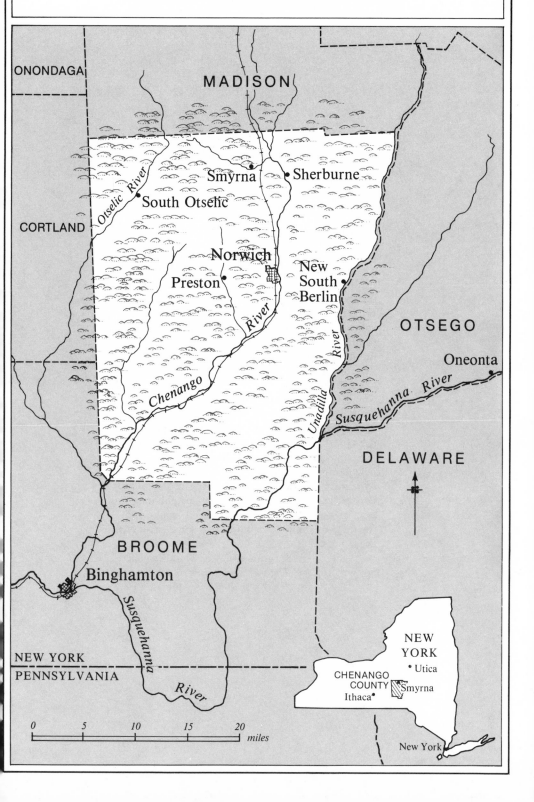

ONONDAGA

MADISON

CORTLAND

Otselic River

Smyrna

Sherburne

South Otselic

Norwich

Preston

New
South
Berlin

OTSEGO

Chenango River

Unadilla River

Oneonta

Susquehanna River

DELAWARE

BROOME

Binghamton

Susquehanna River

NEW YORK
PENNSYLVANIA

0   5   10   15   20
                          miles

NEW
YORK

• Utica

CHENANGO
COUNTY
Ithaca •

Smyrna

New York

Biography usually fails to integrate its subject person with the significant others who facilitated and handicapped his durable achievements as a contributor to culture history, and rarely indicates whence came his skills and limitations in the interpersonal relations which made his contribution effective. A survey of at least the near past and present of the culture-complex which he influenced is required to validate this sort of biographical data, to give it dependable psychiatric or social psychological meaning. The phenomenon of Freud without its setting in the contemporary society of Vienna has been followed by the phenomena of Freud's evangelists and Freud's detractors, also without sensitivity to the nuances of cultural differences within the major context of the Western world.... Any person is to a great degree a function of his past interpersonal history, the immediate present, and the well- or ill-foreseen neighboring future. Any people is an interlocking dynamic network of a great many contemporary persons, each with past, present, and neighboring future with considerable identities and similarities—roughly equaling the culture—and some significant differences.

—Sullivan, review of Ruth Benedict's
The Chrysanthemum and the Sword
in *Psychiatry* for May 1947

Prologue

I KNEW Harry Stack Sullivan for three years before his death in 1949. My first glimpse of him was as a teacher in the Washington School of Psychiatry, lecturing to a large group of students in a meeting room at the old Wardman Park Hotel in Washington, D.C. In that same year, I took the job of managing editor for his journal, *Psychiatry*. The journal office was in downtown Washington, and Sullivan's combined home and office was well out on Bradley Lane in Bethesda, Maryland, so that many of my contacts with him were by telephone and by notes back and forth on manuscripts submitted for publication to *Psychiatry*. Yet we had many meaningful encounters face-to-face. Sometimes, for instance, I would be summoned out to his house to bring a particular monograph that he was in urgent need of, or some galley proof that could not wait for the regular mail service; and we gradually got acquainted.

I remember distinctly my first visit, walking up to the house from the end of the jitney bus line that ran once an hour from Wisconsin Avenue out Bradley Lane. The house sat well back from the road, on quite an incline. The early summer foliage was already deep and dark, so that the great trees and thick underbrush of the Maryland countryside almost hid the house. The house itself was brick, solid and comfortable, a colonial-style house in the Williamsburg tradition. The front yard was landscaped with rocks and many varieties of day lilies—pale lemon, dark cinnamon, various shades of tawny orange—through which at a reckless rate dashed what seemed to me to be an army of cocker spaniels, seemingly intent on tearing me limb from limb, were it not for the intervening and perilously slender wire fence. Someone rescued me from the doorway, calling off the dogs: "General" (named after the Canadian psychiatrist General Brock Chisholm), "Blondie," and others whose names I do not remember.

I remember the house as elegant and eccentric, beautiful and strange. The large living room in which Sullivan held sway during the last years of his life was in the west part of the house, looking out toward the still un-spoiled countryside near the Potomac River and the Great Falls area. The molding around each small window pane was painted Chinese red—something I have never seen in any other house, save years later in the kitchen of the farmhouse in which he grew up. In either winter or summer—against the bleak great trunks of giant oaks and the occasional deep snow of a Maryland winter, or against the dark and vivid greens of late summer—this red tracing around the small window panes was strik-ing and exciting. In the room itself, there was a grand piano and Chinese hangings and statuary, many of them museum pieces. The main motif was of horses. The room was dark with rich and varied art objects, but the windows and the countryside outside lightened and softened it. Paradox-ically enough, this elegant room had passages cut in the doors for the dogs, and they wandered in and out of the rooms and the house at will. I remember a spot of linoleum in the kitchen where the dogs were allowed to sharpen their claws until the bare wood beneath was worn down by their urgent clawing.

After my first visit to his house, I knew that I was working for a culti-vated man of genius—sensitive, perceptive, but shy and tense. I myself was much too shy and overwhelmed to observe more sharply what it was that impressed me about him and the house. I suppose that it was the first time I had ever been in the house of a famous person, and by 1946 it was clear that Sullivan had become a world figure.

Curiously enough, although I did not know the full extent of it for fif-teen years, we had roots in common, and I think that we must have had some quick recognition of this. My father, a government scientist, had grown up as a farm boy in western New York State and had managed to win a state scholarship to Cornell University in Ithaca. Sullivan, coming from a farm in south central New York State, had also won a state schol-arship, although he had attended Cornell for less than a year. The teach-ers in the primary and secondary schools in New York State who taught my father and mother belonged to the same tradition as the teachers who taught Sullivan. Out of this, I think, we had a common exposure to a transplanted New England literary tradition as it came to a belated and less brilliant flowering in New York State. Both of us had some interest in finding the exact word and a tendency to cling tenaciously to a word that suited us, whether or not it suited someone else. One of our more serious differences on literary style developed around his use of a semicolon. I once suggested that an exclamation mark would be more appropriate in one of his sentences; he was adamant, but I continue to think that I was right.

At the time that I knew him, I was not aware of any dimensions of commonality. I had gotten the job because Sullivan wanted, as he said, a "good A.B." as a managing editor. I had had quite a lot of writing experience, had earned my living as a writer, but I had never edited anything but a college publication, and I had only limited knowledge of the printer's world. I was only a novitiate in the world of psychiatry, just beginning to study at the Washington School of Psychiatry. I was in the course of a personal psychoanalysis—an intensive personality study, as Sullivan called it—and this he considered a requirement for my job.

Since I had a new and demanding job and was in the process of reviewing and changing my own life, I had little time or inclination to puzzle about the personal life of this brilliant man for whom I was working. I vaguely knew that his background was Irish-American and Catholic, and that he came from humble beginnings. But this information seemed remote and distant to me, and I did not really begin to examine it in the light of the man for whom I worked. After his death in 1949, I began the editing of Sullivan's posthumous papers; and again I was immersed in trying to keep abreast of the task, in trying to learn enough to do a reliable job. The man and his beginnings would interest me from time to time; an occasional student would ask me about Sullivan as a person, and I sometimes fantasied writing some kind of a memoir of my brief relationship with him.

But in the spring of 1961, my interest in Sullivan and his beginnings abruptly changed. I was preparing a book of Sullivan's writings for publication by the Foundation he had helped to establish; and I had titled the book *Schizophrenia as a Human Process,* with the approval of the appropriate committee. In my proposed introduction to the book, I mentioned the fact that Sullivan himself had been hospitalized with a schizophrenic break—a fact that seemed particularly germane to the contents of the book. To my amazement, the committee of Sullivan's colleagues who passed on my work objected to this statement, doubting its reliability. One day, years before, when I had been driving Sullivan home after a meeting at St. Elizabeths Hospital in southeast Washington, he had told me that he was glad that no electric shock or lobotomy had been prevalent at the time he was growing up; he had been ill and hospitalized with schizophrenia, he said, and his case might have been treated so drastically that he would have ended up his life as a vegetable. Over the years, other people had commented to me about Sullivan's early schizophrenic break, and I had presumed that it was established and reliable information.

When I was challenged by Sullivan's colleagues on this crucial fact, I felt that I must 'prove' it. It was either right or wrong; it was essential to know dates and places, to establish what had happened. So it was that on the morning of April 18, 1961, I set out from Boston on a one-car electric train, crossing Massachusetts to Albany and on down to Binghamton, New York, having made some contacts with people in nearby Chenango

County where Sullivan was born and raised, in the hope of establishing a fact, nothing more. The train ride took all day, with stops at every small station along the way. The light was gray, the clouds were wintry and sullen; spring comes more slowly to that part of the world than along the coast. Somewhere in the midst of that journey, I began to sense that my task was changing. Near evening, after a drafty, cheerless day, I scribbled on a piece of paper I found in my pocketbook: "Evening falls like a Hardy novel—sad, with brave little lights. This is mid-April, the farms of central New York. This train might be fifty years ago—it has gone backward. I feel this loneliness through me, but it is real and edgy and existence."

Twenty years later, I still have not definitely established the place, the time, the circumstances of Sullivan's illness and hospitalization, although I have other information that establishes the fact itself that he was hospitalized at least once. But that first trip did establish something else far more important. Out of the ground, out of the faces of neighbors, friends, and relatives, his past began to emerge; and this child growing up in a lonely and isolated way began to be as real to me as my own childhood.

My vision of this book in the beginning was limited—to order the biographical facts on the life of the American psychiatrist who had made significant contributions to the social sciences and who had evolved the theory of interpersonal relations. As I worked for almost two decades piecing together the scattered material that I could find on his early life and studying the social values of the time and place in which he grew up— measuring all of this against the scope of his contributions—I began to understand that I was actually engaged in the study of the network of circumstances and people that produced a major American thinker in the first half of the twentieth century. By the same token, I began to contemplate the strange eddies in the stream of American life that spell out creative living or defeat for any of us. At times I felt appalled by the pattern that seemed to emerge—that only with deprivation and loneliness could anyone in America break with the emphasis on being conventionally successful. That need for success is not a simple materialistic grind, as it is often portrayed, but the pressure and the desire to prove, in this diversified, democratic society, that one's own forebears are as good as anybody else's; that regardless of the country of origin—either recent or remote— each person has the right and the capacity to be successful. Yet this need for success is so demanding of human resources and time that there are too few hours left to make the journey meaningful. Whether advantaged and success-ridden or disadvantaged and despairing, all too many of us still live out our lives in "quiet desperation."

Sullivan did not believe that such travail, such waste is a necessary part of life. In a truly democratic sense, he began to take seriously the third part of the "inalienable rights" spelled out in the Declaration of Independence—"the pursuit of happiness." Happiness for him was not a frivolous concept; it meant the living of a productive, creative existence in meaningful relationships with others. Nor could a science of interpersonal relations "ignore such dynamic factors as strivings towards truth, beauty, and humanity," as he wrote in 1939.[1] The first and most important task was to begin to achieve some consensus between people of good will as to the meaning of life. I once heard him say that perhaps this beginning consensus lay implicit in the sight of a newborn baby and the wish on the part of most people throughout the world that that baby would somehow have a good life.

He began his work with trying to solve the riddle of young adolescents who all too often were threatened by the possibility of schizophrenic terror in the paralyzing conflict between the urgent need for sexual expression and the definition imposed by the society for maintaining self-esteem. Out of his early work in the 1920s in mental hospitals, he posited the ubiquitousness of an "archaic sexual culture" and spelled out the need for sexual reform.

When he began private practice in New York City in 1931, he discovered that his task had widened; the waste of human abilities was more chronic than he had anticipated. He discovered that privileged people were often caught on the flypaper of their own ability to use stereotypes as a way of avoiding the anxiety of learning a new and better way of living; often their preoccupations had some monetary success so that they were unwilling to give up their formulae; and they moved from one sticky situation to another, with no hope of release for happier and more productive work.

Beginning in the late 1930s, Sullivan was able to observe American youth within an even wider social and racial dimension. In 1939 he made his first trip into the deep South to study black youth mainly in rural communities, followed by a study of black youth in Washington, D.C. White America had stereotypes about black people that had no relationship to reality, he thought: "[The Negro people] deserve to be observed as they are, and the blot of an American interracial problem may thus gradually be dissipated."[2] Later as a consultant for Selective Service during World War II, he had an opportunity to see a cross section of young males in America, all too many scarred by inadequate health care and poor education, imperfectly equipped by family and society to participate in the work of a wartime civilian army. He felt anew the vast work to be done in setting up a more adequate social system for equipping the young for life.

Yet all of these tasks paled before the impact of Hiroshima: "The bomb that fell on Hiroshima punctuated history," he reported in late 1945.[3] Even more haste was required if mankind were to survive at all, for there had to be enough informed, well-intentioned people in the very next generation to join in a "cultural revolution to end war." He was ill and frail by then, and only three more years of life were left to him; but he tackled this greatest of all tasks with the ardor of a young and vigorous man. Most of his psychiatric colleagues did not encourage him in this final endeavor; but his Canadian counterpart, G. Brock Chisholm, grasped its nature and importance, so that they moved together in their consensus that we must find a way to have more knowledge about raising children. It was Chisholm who officially authored the most dramatic expression of the task, but it was without any doubt a collaborative statement:

We have learned to raise pigs and cows and horses, even to grow flowers and vegetables, in ways that make them of greater service to mankind. If your son is going to raise pigs for a living he goes to a college for three or four years to study under experienced teachers. But if he is merely raising children he commonly learns nothing; nor appreciates, even dimly, that there is anything that he has to learn. Surely the rearing of children is greatly more important, and more complicated, than the raising of pigs. Within the possible expressions of human nature are the personalities of a Caligula or a Franklin Roosevelt, a female guard at Belsen Camp or a Florence Nightingale, a Hitler, or, almost, a Christ. Is it not important to us which we produce? Is not this the great problem facing our generation?[4]

Together Chisholm and Sullivan began to move towards a psychiatry of peoples in which parents, teachers, and members of various disciplines and professions throughout the world would begin the enormous task of collecting data on the raising of children who would become creative, productive people.

Chisholm's examples of human personality are presented in the form of extremes of creative and destructive forces in society. But the rural county in which Sullivan grew up—Chenango County of south central New York State—had its own gradations of violence and productivity, less extreme, but just as real. I shall deal with the violence later on in the book; but here I want to mention two other children, varyingly productive as adults, who were growing up in Chenango County at about the same time as Sullivan and whose lives will be partially documented in this book. One of them, the cultural anthropologist Ruth Fulton Benedict, came from a comfortable Anglo-Saxon Protestant background; by contrast, Sullivan himself had four Irish Catholic grandparents, all of whom emigrated from Ireland during the potato famine in the middle of the nineteenth century. Partly because of differences in religious affiliations and social class, Benedict and Sullivan never had occasion to know each other in their growing-up years, although they collaborated as adults.

The other child, Clarence Bellinger, lived on the farm next to Sullivan's childhood home. Like Benedict, Bellinger came out of a WASP background; but there were crucial differences in living experience between these two representatives of the dominant society of that time and place, so that Bellinger, like Sullivan, was an outsider. Again, by contrast with Benedict, Bellinger was a close friend of Sullivan's for an important part of their growing-up years. In adult life, neither Bellinger nor Sullivan ever married, and both became psychiatrists—a seeming coincidence of some magnitude in that small rural area. Though Bellinger was for many years head of the Brooklyn State Hospital in New York, his life and work were insignificant by comparison with either Benedict's or Sullivan's, so that he was indeed a "poor caricature" of what he might have been, as Sullivan has described the fate of all of us in a damaging society. With the exception of the founders of the Mormon religion, Benedict and Sullivan are the only two people with roots in Chenango County (to my knowledge) who became known throughout the world, and whose writings have been translated into many languages.

I have suggested in this book some of the dimensions of the differences in the lives of these three children—differences that emerged not from genes but from the differing strands of experience that determined the patterning of three lives in the same time and place. In Sullivan's adult life, there are echoes of these early days in the interpersonal relationships that he was able to make, or unable to achieve. I have used these early lives and experiences—and indeed the lives and experiences of several of Sullivan's colleagues, particularly Edward Sapir—as a way of illuminating his own life. In a sense, they are mirrors by which I can try to reflect for the reader who and what he was as a nexus of interpersonal relationships.

The raw data for much of Sullivan's theory of interpersonal relationships came out of the rural life of Chenango County in the first half of the twentieth century as surely as Freud's theory came out of Vienna in the preceding half century. It was the human experience as Sullivan observed it around him in his growing-up years—at home, at school, and in the local newspaper accounts of the troubled lives of other people in that setting—that informed his theory and gave it the dimension of an American experience. As surely as Walt Whitman's *Leaves of Grass,* or Theodore Dreiser's *Sister Carrie,* or Sherwood Anderson's *Winesburg, Ohio,* or Willa Cather's *My Ántonia,* Harry Stack Sullivan's interpersonal theory is an American product, raised to the level of science and art through the lonely search and brilliant observation of a boy growing up in Chenango County at the turn of the century.

⇜ 1 ⇝

The First Moon

The infant seeing for the first time the full moon,
reaches for it. Nothing transpires. He utters a few
goos and nothing transpires; then he starts to cry in
rage, and the whole household is upset. But he does
not get the moon, and the moon becomes 'marked'
unattainable.

—Sullivan, *Conceptions of Modern Psychiatry*

THE first moon that the child saw was in the little town of Norwich,
New York—county seat for Chenango County, with its remote,
wooded, rocky farmland in the Appalachian foothills, and its all too brief
stretch of prosperous farms and small New England-like villages mainly
clustered along the beautiful Chenango River valley. The child, who became Harry Stack Sullivan, was born on Sunday, February 21, 1892, at
his parents' home on Rexford Street, then as now thought of as the Irish
part of Norwich. No name for the child appears on the birth certificate,
only the parents' names—Timothy Sullivan and Ella M. Stack Sullivan—and the name of the attending physician, Dr. B. J. Ormsby.

In the week before the baby was born, the weather had been so icy that
the trains had had trouble getting through the valley, and in the week
after there had been an early thaw and the sap in the maples had begun to
run. The thaw was deceptive, for February, March, and even part of
April are bitterly cold in that part of the world. The mother must have
known about February weather there, for she had been born in the
County thirty-nine years before and had spent most of her life on a remote
farm in the foothills near the village of Smyrna, about twelve miles north
of Norwich, where the winters are so severe that "the dogwood never
blooms." Timothy, too, was a native of the County, born almost thirty-
five years before in the township of New Berlin, about six miles east of
Norwich in a more accessible area.

The parents, Ella and Timothy, had reason to fear that February was
not a good month for the birth of a child. Old-timers believed that babies

less than six months old when summer came would not have a good chance to live through the first summer; and indeed the graveyard markers of those years would seem to bear out this sad prediction. Timothy and Ella had already buried two babies, both boys, in the Catholic cemetery in Sherburne twelve miles up the valley. Both children had been born in February, one in 1888 and the other in 1890; and each time the baby had died in convulsions before the first autumn leaves had fallen. Now Ella at thirty-nine had another February baby.

On the Thursday before the child's birth, the daily newspaper in Norwich carried on its front page a story of the daughter of an Irish lord in Belfast who had killed her child. However upsetting such a story might be for a woman about to bear a child, there was nothing novel about it for readers of the Norwich *Sun.* Suicides of distraught, lonely farm women, who took their children with them, were not uncommon in and around Norwich. The pioneers who had come in to the County from New England to the east and from the Susquehanna valley to the south had more than a speaking acquaintance with tragedy. After the advent of the Irish into the County in the 1840s—usually brought in to help build the canals and the railroads—the interest of the old settlers had shifted to the foreign-born, almost as if it were a relief to find affliction in other kinds of people living in distant lands or newly come from them. Eventually the legend grew among the old settlers that the foreign-born had imported the tragedies and ruined the promised land, but it was a legend that no one believed: the face of tragedy was too well known in almost every family. Eventually, the omnipresence of tragedy in that part of the world would find a strange immortality in Theodore Dreiser's *An American Tragedy,* for the young girl murdered in his story had her real counterpart in a child growing up in the County at the same time as Harry Stack Sullivan.

As one reviews the history of this part of the world, and of the land across the sea from which all four of Harry's grandparents had come, there is an almost overpowering sense of inevitability about his destiny, as if both his loneliness and his wish for productive living for all of mankind were already recorded in a book of doom before he drew his first breath. For the first sixteen and a half years, the compass of his life was very small. It all lay in the same county. Before he was three, he moved from the relative metropolis of Norwich, where about five thousand people lived, to the farm where his mother had grown up, on the edge of the village of Smyrna, which held in its hills no more than three hundred men, women, and children.

Smyrna was twelve miles from Norwich by the milk train, but by horse and wagon it was a harder, longer way. First one went twelve miles north and a little east up the Chenango River valley, slow and tranquil in the summer, fierce and blustery in the winter. At Sherburne, the wagon would turn left, heading west into the hills for four miles, moving slowly up and down for a net rise of 150 feet, until one reached the village of Smyrna. Another mile and a half past Smyrna and 250 feet higher in the hills over the village, was his grandmother Stack's house. From the third to the seventeenth year of life, the child lived in this farmhouse, seeing little of the world beyond the farm and the village: he went to school in the village; occasionally he went to visit his older cousin, Leo Stack, in South Otselic, fifteen miles southwest of Smyrna; he went to the library and to church in Sherburne; sometimes he visited his grandmother Sullivan, who lived with his bachelor uncle on the Sullivan farm just west of Norwich at Preston; and after he began school, he went each September with his parents to Norwich to buy clothes and school supplies. But the moon that he saw was still a Chenango County moon, and he would learn that much more than the moon was unattainable for him, for he was the only Irish Catholic boy in the village school district. Now as then, the remote hamlet is apt to be frightened of the stranger in its midst and to withdraw from him.

The Rexford Street house in Norwich where he was born could not have formed an important part of his memory—he was between two and three when he left—but it too had its own reflection in the development of his life. The house, small, framed, and ugly, still stands, a few rods from the railroad tracks. Although it is only a mile from the pleasant square that forms the center of the town, the distance is greater than the mileage would suggest. It was this distance from the wrong side of the railroad tracks to the comfortable houses of middle America that the child grown to manhood would understand so well, so that the lonely, frustrating journey through Chenango County would haunt his life and would give new depth and meaning for him to what all the great American writers had written about, from Thoreau to Walt Whitman, from Theodore Dreiser to Eugene O'Neill, from Willa Cather to Sherwood Anderson—of the American dream and its erosion by reality.

Like the artist in Willa Cather's short story, "The Sculptor's Funeral," the child grown to manhood—admired and treated as a sage throughout much of the Western world—would never find much understanding of his work in the towns that had dominated his first sixteen years: Norwich, Sherburne, and Smyrna. In 1967, eighteen years after his death, at a time when his books were read more avidly by university students than ever before, a story appeared in the Norwich *Sun* which began, "Who was Dr. Harry Stack Sullivan?" The question of renaming the Chenango County Mental Health Clinic had come up before the Board of Supervisors, and the director of the clinic, who had contact with the larger world, had made a motion that the clinic might be named after Harry Stack Sullivan.

The motion was quietly tabled after one supervisor indicated that the present name was good enough. A decade later, after considerable discreet education of the Board of Supervisors, the clinic was renamed after Sullivan. This lack of understanding existed throughout the County. Here and there, distant relatives or old neighbors remarked on the importance of the man and of the implicit honor to be found in the fact that his schooling up to college had all taken place in this small rural community, that his reading had mainly come from a library in the County. But such remarks were made quietly, so as not to intrude on the generally held belief that as a child in the district school he had been too smart for his own good, that he had brought disgrace to the village and to the County by some of his youthful failings, that nothing good had ever happened to him after he left the County, that the evil world, so far removed from the tranquil center of rural virtues and Horatio-Alger values, had somehow ruined his early teachings in the County—that, in fact, evil had eventually triumphed over rural goodness, although the nature of that evil never becomes explicit.

To some extent, he was affected by this personification of himself throughout his life, and it seemed as if he shifted his name around from time to time to accommodate his hopes and his fears. His name appears, through the years, on various documents, first as Harry Francis Stack Sullivan, with the Francis added at the time of his confirmation in his thirteenth year; then for a while as H. F. Sullivan, for the boy of seventeen in the outside world had somehow violated the hopes of his mother and her family for Stack greatness, and the name Stack disappeared for about six years; then later as H. Stack Sullivan, a surgeon in Chicago; and finally as simply Harry Stack Sullivan. But the Francis was never entirely lost. In a network of Irish fancy and mysticism, the man, grown famous and perhaps even more lonely, held on to that early identity, from the years when he could not—by family edict, or nonverbal sanction, or self-imposed exile—aspire to the proud name of Stack. On hundreds of his official letters, written during the last twenty years of his life, his full name, Harry Stack Sullivan, is typed in below the complimentary closing; and the scrawled signature, or initials, seems at first to be Harry *S*. Sullivan, or H. *S*. S. Only after one begins to learn something of his early life does the middle initial begin to look at times like an *F* for Francis. Then one feels sharply the power of that initial, the return symbolically to the years when the tight grip of the Stack tradition of greatness had been loosened, however painful the freedom.

This power of a name—the young boy's pride in the destiny of the Stacks and his fear that the Sullivans did not quite measure up his mother's family—dominated much of his growing-up years. Yet the differences between the Stacks and the Sullivans were minimal by comparison with their similarities, and eventually the child grown to adulthood would understand this and use it as a central thesis for his theory. To understand these similarities and artificial differences one must seek another beginning for this story. The child was born in 1892, but his story began between 1845 and 1849, in Ireland where "the great hunger," as Cecil Woodham-Smith has named it, led to the violent uprooting of families and their often tragic adjustments in a new country.[1]

It was the west and the southwest of Ireland that felt hardest the terrible pain of hunger during the potato famine, and it was from these two sections of Ireland, both in Munster Province, that Sullivan's paternal and maternal grandparents fled—his mother's people from County Clare on the west coast and his father's parents from County Cork, farther south. He was, as he once noted, "a blend of Southern Irish from Counties Cork and Clare."[2] Both sides of the family were Roman Catholic, which meant that officially they could not own land after the enactment of the Penal Laws of 1695. In 1829 the Catholic emancipation theoretically changed this restriction on the owning of land, but by then most families were too destitute to be able to purchase land, so that most Irish people who fled the country during the years of the great famine were still renters.

Yet there were exceptions to this rule of thumb. One such exception was found in the Stack family, who had come into Ireland from England at the beginning of the fourteenth century; by the sixteenth century they were Irish in all particulars, including opposition to the English, but they still thought of themselves as landed gentry. By contrast, the Sullivans belonged to one of the ancient Gaelic families loosely designated as septs; traditionally these families had long since lost all their property because of the staunchness of their religion, as well as long opposition to the English. Both the Stack and the Sullivan families sent members to America, fleeing the great famine. Yet even people harassed and destitute seek points of invidious comparison—standards for being "better than" someone else also in trouble, as Sullivan came to term that act of comparison.[3] Thus the Stacks in Chenango County still claimed descent from landed gentry, and the Sullivans claimed moral superiority because they had *not* been landed. Out of such differences, real or imagined, the distant past became cogent for this child born in 1892.

Ella Stack's Family

> Consider an only surviving child of a proudly pro-
> fessional maternal family not yet recovered from the
> reduction in status that attended on grandfather's
> emigration—among the mythological ancestors of
> which is the West Wind, the horse who runs with the
> Earth into the future.
> —Sullivan, "Towards a Psychiatry of Peoples"

THE child's mother and her family were the important figures as he
was growing up. His grandfather Stack died before he was three
years old, so it was probably his mother who told him about Michael
Stack's coming to this country and of the mythological ancestors of the
Stacks. He clung to that story, and as an adult he adopted the horse as a
symbol of himself. Thus he became at times his own fairy-tale ancestor,
who would pick up the challenge from the distant past in Ireland and run
with the Earth into the future.

At times the myth of Stack splendor would become too much for him
under his mother's watchful eye; as an adult he would mourn the fact that
" 'her son' was so different from me that I felt she had no use for me except as a clotheshorse on which to hang an elaborate pattern of illusion."[1]
Yet he fluctuated between the tight clutch of the legend and the periods
of freedom when he would shed the illusions from the clotheshorse and
become the horse of the West Wind again.

He never quite made up his mind about his mother. Eventually he
would understand that the reason he never knew his father during his
growing-up years was that his mother kept him apart from his father. He
would only come to know his father when he was well past thirty years of
age and his mother had died; even then he could not judge objectively his
mother's explanations of his father. She had told him that the men in the
Stack family had always chosen the professions of educator, or lawyer, or
doctor, or priest until she had married his father; and even as an adult

Sullivan accepted this definition, without looking hard at the reality. Certainly by the time his father and mother were married in 1885, neither of her two brothers nor any of the Stack cousins of that generation had distinguished themselves in a professional way, although all of them were ambitious and eager to move on into the larger world. Yet his mother was right enough about there being a difference between the aspirations of the Stacks and the prosaic lives of his father's family. He would mention the Stack family myth near the end of his life and equate it with the myth that particular cultures had—for good or for evil. Myths, he said, are "dreams that satisfy the needs of many."[2]

The more formal history of the Stacks in Ireland and before did not interest Ella and her child as much as the myths, but they knew that long story too, as did most of the Stack descendants. In 1964 Neil Stack, a grandson of one of the first settlers, assembled a family history, listing all the descendants of the two Stack cousins that came into Chenango County at the time of the famine. The story begins in true Irish fashion with a review of the origin of the Stacks in France, England, and Ireland—of kings and battles, land granted and land stolen—a proud family history that parallels the history of Ireland from 1066 onward. Thus there was a castle in Normandy, now in ruins, owned by the De Staques, who fought bravely in the Norman invasion, changed their name to Stack, and were rewarded with land grants in Counties Kerry and Clare in Ireland. The story is full of the exploits and accomplishments of the Irish Stacks in general and of particular persons who served in the Irish Brigade, or as bishops in the Roman Catholic Church. There is even mention of a sixteenth-century Stack from County Clare who abandoned his church; he raised a son who became a distinguished figure in the early days of Trinity College in Dublin, which eventually became a Protestant stronghold in Ireland. "To our knowledge," Neil Stack writes, "there has never been a member of the family with an unsavory reputation. All have been held in high esteem [as] respected members of their community."[3]

Ella's father, Michael, was not the first Stack to arrive in Chenango County. James and his older brother Thomas Stack, Michael's first cousins, were the original settlers, probably in 1845, the first year of the great famine. In 1849, Michael followed. Thomas remained a bachelor and died at a relatively early age; thus he largely disappeared from the family annals. But James and Michael, who were both born in 1816 in Milltown Malbay, prospered in the new country, married, and raised families. For over twenty years, James's eleven children and Michael's four lived in and around Smyrna, and those of school age attended the village school. They were probably the only Irish Catholic children in the school, and they clung together as if they were brothers and sisters. Fifteen years after Sullivan's death, several of James's granddaughters still spoke of their third cousin Harry as if he were a brother or a nephew; their actual contacts with him as an adult had been minimal, but their interest in his doings and their concern for his soul were still strong.

No picture of Harry's grandfather, Michael Stack, exists, but a tintype of the first James Stack, taken in this country when he was about fifty, reflects his encounter with famine, probably at an early age. His face is rugged and strong, yet the jawbone is tortured and the flesh hangs loosely, almost unattached, as if the famine had made inroads on the basic bone structure. In 1821, when both James and his cousin Michael were five years old and living in Milltown Malbay, they were undoubtedly affected by their first experience with famine. In that year and the succeeding one the potato failed completely in the west of Ireland, where almost no other food was available. In particular, the jawbones of children were often affected permanently by famine. In all, there were twenty-four recorded failures of the potato crop by 1851.[4]

Family legend has it that the two brothers, James and Thomas, set sail from Spanish Point on the wild west coast of Ireland, near their small native town of Milltown Malbay. In the days of the great famine one could not always wait for a day in May to set sail, and at almost any other time of the year, a sudden squall can descend upon these waters. Three times, James's granddaughters report, the small sailing vessel set out, and twice it was driven back to the coast by stormy winds before it finally managed to move out across the Atlantic. Throughout the legend of the Stacks, three is a magic number, as it is in much of Christendom. Thus there were originally three Stack brothers, each of whom was given a mountain in County Kerry because of his participation in the Norman Conquest; and, true enough, a current map of Ireland carries the name "Stack's Mts."

The name "Spanish Point" as the point of embarkation carries its own legend of the past and of the elaborately mottled history of Ireland. In 1588 part of the Spanish Armada went down along this tortuous coast, within sight of the great castle-like Cliffs of Moher. Along the coast there are still legends about the fate of the sailors on the Armada, and four hundred years have not dimmed the drama of that event. Some Irish people say that no Spanish sailors escaped the dictate of the hated English government that all the sailors must be killed. Others are sure that some sailors were sheltered by the inhabitants at the risk of their lives, and that these sailors took Irish maids for wives, who bore them children with Spanish faces.

Certainly Sullivan himself had some special interest in Spain. When he first went to Europe in 1928 for a fleeting visit, he made a special effort to go to Spain, and he subsequently bragged to his kinfolk of this trip, so that he must have felt that his going to Spain had a magical meaning for them as well. He was fascinated with Ireland, too, but he never got there. Perhaps like some other Irish-Americans he had an uncanny dread of ever visiting Ireland, as if the reality could only destroy the dream—as if some tragic affinity of inherited homesickness would capture and hold him in this island of so much magic.

What brought the first Stacks from Spanish Point to Chenango County in particular is not known. Most Irish people who came to the United States during the famine years stayed in the big cities; only about ten percent went to small towns or agricultural communities. But as early as 1837 there were Irish in Sherburne, where the Stack brothers first went before moving on to Smyrna.[5] The presence of a few Irish immigrants in the general area was undoubtedly the link through which later immigrants found their way from Ireland to Sherburne and Smyrna.

Most Irish immigrants arriving in central New York State settled along the river valleys, where the canals and the main railroads were being built. As the immigrants got off the boats in New York City, company representatives would hire them for "a few cents" a day and pay for their transportation to the areas in which work was in progress.[6] But it is safe to assume that the two Stack brothers came on their own, without benefit of employer, arriving first in Sherburne. James was a blacksmith by trade and thus had a marketable skill, an uncommon occurrence in the west of Ireland during that period. By 1850 James was married to Bridget O'Rourke, also from Milltown Malbay, and they were living in Smyrna, where James was both farmer and blacksmith. The O'Rourkes, members of a Gaelic sept and traditionally devout Catholics, were related to the great Irish liberator Daniel O'Connell.

Michael's career in the new country began somewhat differently from that of James. According to family legend, Michael, who was the same age as James and also from Milltown Malbay, had been educated for the priesthood in Ennis. He was thirty-three when he left for America, so his commitment to the church may have been more than that of a novitiate, although a family history reports that he "never took the orders." Generally Stack descendants speak of Michael's departure from the church as a "disgrace," and several are quick to note that Michael did not know his future wife, Mary White, who also came from Milltown Malbay, until he arrived in this country. The implication is that his decision to end his church career before he came to America was at least not prompted by a clandestine arrangement with his future wife.

The White family, like the Stacks—and unlike the O'Rourkes—belonged to the Anglo-Irish tradition, and members of one branch of the family were landed proprietors in County Clare. Thus James and Michael married into quite different traditions—a sensitive area for most Irish families during the trials of the famine years and the transition to the new country. Indeed, James Stack's family was more nearly like Timothy Sullivan's than Michael's in their devotion to the church; and the church-going habits of Michael's descendants were always under sharp

1. James Stack, blacksmith, the first Stack in Smyrna

2. The old blacksmith shop in Smyrna

3. Harry's grandmother Mary White Stack

4. The Smyrna farm at the turn of the century

scrutiny by the descendants of James. Some disapproval is implicit in the family's statement that Michael and Mary were "double cousins," which means that the families had done some in-marrying. Catholic priests in Ireland sometimes granted dispensations for such marriages in order to protect the holdings of those Irish Catholic families, mainly with Anglo-Irish names, who had managed to hold on to property under the stern rule of English landlords. These intricate differences were reflected in Stack ambivalences about the English. Thus one of James's granddaughters reported angrily that the English landlords had gradually taken away most of the property once owned by the Stacks; but later she described admiringly Harry's appearance at a family wake: "He was a real English gentleman—or rather Irish."

Partly because of Michael's termination of his church career when he came to America, and partly because Smyrna was so far by horse and buggy, or by foot, from the town of Sherburne, where the Catholic mission from Hamilton maintained a monthly visitation in this early period, Michael became in part at least a "heritage Catholic"; that is, he retained an identification with the religion, but his practice was minimal. Only one child in the two original Stack families eventually "turned" Protestant—Michael's oldest boy, Ed—but the fear was omnipresent. The idea that the less observant religious pattern of Michael's family explained some of the sadnesses of Harry's life would be voiced eventually by both Stack and Sullivan cousins and by other Irish Catholic families in the County; even Protestant neighbors in Smyrna felt that Michael's family did not attend church often enough. One neighbor mentioned the fact that Michael was in such poor standing with the Roman Catholic Church when he died in 1894 that the family had to make a good many frantic excursions to see the priest and "pay up" before a proper burial could be arranged. By contrast, James's move back to Sherburne in the 1870s made it possible for his children to maintain closer contact with the Irish Catholic community there, which early began to establish its own church.

The myth of the Stacks seems somehow at variance with the reality of Michael Stack's life in this country, as it emerges from various documents. His accomplishments in a new land were considerable. His "loss of status" in coming to a new land, as described by Sullivan, seems more ephemeral than real. He had lost the status of priesthood, but he was a canny and respected farmer on a rocky bit of land, acquiring 108 acres, piece by piece, by 1887. He and his wife came to Smyrna sometime in the early 1850s. Their first child, Harry's mother, was born there in 1853 and named Ellen Mary, which became Ella Mae in the style of the new country. Four more children were born to Michael and Mary in the next sixteen years: Edmund James (Ed) in 1856; John Bartholomew in 1857; Margaret Ann in 1864, usually called Maggie in the early years; and a baby, born in 1869, who was named after his father and survived only one day.

By the time Maggie was born, Michael had clear title to 80 acres of farmland on the west hill above the village, and he had already made arrangements for his farm to be included in the village school district when it became necessary to decrease the size of that district as the population of the village expanded. The Common School records for 1862 report that part of the village school district was to be transferred to a country school district "excepting and reserving therefrom five acres from the East side now owned by Michael Stack." This gerrymandering meant that Michael's children—and eventually his grandson Harry—could go to the educationally superior village school rather than to the nearby country scool. Given the educational aspirations of the Stacks and Michael's priestly training in Ireland, part of the credit for this arrangement must go to his political astuteness; he may even have paid an extra fee, officially or unofficially, for this privilege. By the time of the redistricting, James and Michael each had two children of school age who were already attending the village school, so the village may have agreed to keep the Irish Catholics together and not scatter them throughout the township.

This redistricting was a crucial fact of life for Ella and her child. To state its net effect psychologically and educationally would be as complicated as to decide the effect of busing on a particular child today. For Ella as a schoolgirl, it meant that she, as well as her brothers and her sister, had close contact with James's numerous children; thus these second cousins formed a rather numerous and solid block—an island of comfort and support—in the small village school, which did not include high school. By the 1870s, when James moved his family to Sherburne, a dozen Stack children had attended the village school, eight of James's and four of Michael's.

There is a curious confirmation of the impact of the closeness of these cousins. According to James Stack's granddaughters, Harry had an even more pronounced Irish accent than his mother. This can be explained in part by Harry's lack of access to contemporaries as a child. In American society, the peer group usually determines the child's accents; first-generation children of immigrants are particularly dependent on the peer group in school to teach them the nuances of pronunciation and slang—usually an abrasive process. Michael's and James's children could share their unhappy and alienating experiences in the inadvertent use of County Clare language and gestures at school; thus much of the pain of acculturation was minimized and the process facilitated. James's children were more advantaged than Michael's by living in the village proper and participating in its life. By the time Harry began school, shortly before the turn of the century, he was the only Irish Catholic child in the school; he did not participate at all in village life; and his grandmother Stack, who spoke like people from the west of Ireland, had a more important part in his learning of language than his own more acculturated mother.

As one reviews the lives of this first generation of children, it becomes clear that Ella Stack had a more restricted life than any other child in the two families. Born in Smyrna on January 14, 1853, she was the first child to survive in either family and to make the thrust into the non-Irish world. When she began school in Smyrna, there was no other Irish Catholic child there; within a couple of years, two of James's sons were in school with her; and by the time she had been in school for three or four years, her own brother Ed and James's oldest daughter, Mary, were also attending school. They all had their lessons in the same room for a year or so, before Ella moved into the room for the older students. But all the younger children leaned on her, just as her mother relied on her at home to take care of the younger children. A year after her brother Ed was born, another brother, John, was born. She became the unofficial guardian of each child in turn—her own brothers and her cousins—as they came to the Smyrna school. Thus she early came to be called "Big Ella," only partly to distinguish her from other Ellas in the family.

Although Mary was four years younger than Ella, they became fast friends as the first daughter in each family. At that time, farm families were peculiarly dependent on the oldest girl. The farm chores kept the boys busy in the summer and in the late fall, and they were sometimes kept out of school during the harvest season; but on a dairy farm, a girl was busy helping out on the farm in all seasons. Mary's father was both blacksmith and farmer, so she had many of the same duties as Ella.

As the years went by, James had four more daughters and four more sons. Ella knew all of them, but it was only her girl cousins who had a shared concern with Ella about what they would do when they finished school. Neither her mother, who still spoke Gaelic most of the time, nor Cousin James's wife, Bridget, could provide her with any idea of a career, except as a wife and mother.

In the beginning there was a built-in importance for Ella in being needed at home. She was past eleven years old when her only sister, Margaret Ann, was born; she would always have a special feeling for Maggie, whom she undoubtedly cared for as a baby. When Ella was sixteen her mother became pregnant again, and since Ella had completed all the schooling available in Smyrna, she probably took over most of the chores for her mother during that pregnancy. This boy baby died when he was one day old, and in a way that must have been a relief as well as a sadness for Ella.

The role of being the big girl in the family began to pall when Ed, her younger brother, got a job as a teacher in the nearby country school at seventeen. Ella was just as qualified as Ed to teach in the country school, but Ed, as a male, was not needed as much on the farm in the winter. Good students in the village school were usually selected to teach in the district schools; Michael Stack's children were all good students, and at one time or another three of them, all except Ella, would earn their living as teachers. At about the same time that Ed started teaching school, Cousin James moved his family to Sherburne, and Ella was more alone than ever. By then John and Maggie were both in the village school. When John was seventeen he went away to Brockport Normal School; four years later he graduated from there with honors, the first of Michael's children to have any advanced education. In the meantime, Ed had given up teaching and had gone to Wisconsin to try his hand at a business; he was there only a year, but when he came back he got his own farm, near his father's, and tried farming for a couple of years before marrying "Little Ella" Noonan and acquiring a hotel in the village of South Otselic.

In 1880, when Ella was twenty-seven years old, she was still "at home," as noted by the United States census taker. Mary, James's oldest daughter, was listed in the same census as a "servant" in one of the Yankee families in Smyrna. All the others were beginning to move out into the larger world. Cousin James also had a daughter Ellen, called "Tall Ella," who was clerking in a store in Norwich. His second oldest boy, Bartholomew, was away studying law, and Mary's small cash income undoubtedly helped to pay for that schooling. Unlike Ella, all of James's daughters had Irish Catholic friends in Sherburne. And they were beginning to plan on getting away from home, and eventually most of them did.

Occasionally Big Ella, too, would get away from home for a day or two and have an exciting time with these girl cousins. There is a photograph of Big Ella with two of James's daughters and Ed's new wife, probably taken in Norwich in the early 1880s. But such excursions were costly of time and money, and these commodities were precious in the continuing plans in both families for the boys to achieve in the larger world in a way commensurate with the glory of the Stacks.

So the years dragged on for Ella. In the spring of 1885, Ed and Little Ella had their first child, Michael Leo, the first grandchild in either family. By then Big Ella was thirty-two years old. This had been the year of truth for many Stacks; Michael himself liked to say that he was thirty-two when he married, but in truth he was that age when he left the seminary in Ireland. If one were not married by then, according to Stack legend, marriage was unlikely; indeed, this was true in much of Ireland after the great famine.

The family's excitement over Ed's baby must have moved Big Ella closer to the idea of marrying. She did not know any eligible men, certainly none as exciting as her own brother Ed. Most of the Irish Catholic

5. *Ella M. Stack, shortly before her marriage*

6. *Margaret Stack, about 1890*

7. *The cousins. Left to right: standing, Ella Noonan Stack ("Little Ella") and Ella M. ("Big Ella," Harry's mother); seated, James Stack's daughters, Ella C. ("Tall Ella"), Lucy, and Elizabeth*

8. *Harry's grandmother Julia Galvin Sullivan*

9. *Judge William H. Sullivan*

men that she met at church in Sherburne were workers on the railroad or farm laborers. Late in the year, she decided to marry Timothy Sullivan, one of the farm laborers, who was working either on her father's farm or on a nearby farm. Her family felt that she was marrying beneath her, but she had a clearer idea by then of the dismal alternative—staying on the farm forever.

For seven dreadful years, she would manage to escape from the farm. But in the end she would come back—the only one of the fifteen children of the original Stack families who would spend most of her life on a farm.

❧ 3 ❧

Timothy Sullivan's Family

His father's had been a large family, and the two eldest children, Timothy and Michael, had to take over
support and direction of the household when their
father was killed in an accident. The men of his
mother's family had traditionally chosen the professions of educator, lawyer, doctor, or priest until Ella
Stack married Timothy, who was by this time a
skilled workman and who later became a farmer.
                    —Sullivan's description of his parents in
                                   Current Biography, 1942

THIS solitary mention of his father's family represents both Sullivan's
lack of knowledge about that side of the house and some distortion
of the facts. When Timothy married Ella, he was not a "skilled workman" but a farm laborer in Smyrna. Moreover, the "two eldest children"
were in fact John, eighteen years old at the time of the accident, and Timothy, seventeen; Michael was fifth in order and eleven years old.

Sullivan's account of the professional accomplishments of the men in
his mother's family undoubtedly reflects his mother's myth of Stack
greatness. At the time that she married Timothy, the men in her family
were not nearly so far along in their careers as Sullivan reported; indeed,
their final careers only measured up to this legend in at best two instances. Her father was a farmer; Cousin James was a blacksmith and
farmer; true, her two brothers had both taught school, but only John had
any training past the village common school. Cousin James's sons had
begun to move out into the larger world and would eventually earn their
livings in diverse and interesting ways; but only one son, Bartholomew,
could be termed a true professional; he began as a lawyer, but after he
passed the bar, he was trained as a priest. One of James's oldest sons became a foreman in a cigar factory; another son was one of the best

cheese-makers in the state, having received some training at Cornell University; still another began as a dispatcher for a railroad company and eventually became an officer in a utility company; and two of the sons were printers for newspapers. In summary, the category of "educator" was filled only by John; the category of "doctor" would have to wait for another generation, unless one includes a distant Stack cousin who came as a physician from County Clare to Smyrna in 1878 and practiced there for two years before disappearing; and the categories of "lawyer" and "priest" were lumped together in the person of Bartholomew. Yet in one particular the legend was correct: the possibility of movement into the professions was omnipresent in the thinking of the Stack family; but Timothy and his brothers had more limited aspirations, largely determined by the past history of the family and by their father's accident.

Both of Timothy's parents, William Sullivan and Julia Galvin, came from Munster Province, the traditional home for the O'Sullivan and the O'Galvin septs, William Sullivan having been born in 1825 in Fermoy, and Julia Galvin in 1821 in Ballyvourney. The very term "sept" implies an attachment to the land in a given locality of Ireland and a loyalty to the Catholic religion that survived the trauma of the English laws against Catholicism. Sullivan is the third most common name in Ireland; in the 1950s, eighty percent of the Sullivans in Ireland still lived in Counties Cork and Kerry. The Galvins, smaller in number, came traditionally from County Clare. There was an ancient aristocracy implied in these old Gaelic names, and their arms and histories were revered in Ireland.

However proud the tradition of these families, most of them who left Ireland during the famine years were renters and more impoverished than other Irish emigrants of the same period. Their unwillingness to accede to the English rule had gradually impoverished them; they had lost ownership of the land and were without power and influence. For the most part, the landlords in Munster Province had English and Norman names. Since most of the families with Gaelic names no longer owned land, even the word "landlord" could arouse bitterness in them. During the long history of the Penal Laws, there had been other failures of crops, and starving Irish countrymen were periodically offered watery soup from the English-controlled food distribution centers only if they declared themselves, however temporarily, to be Protestant. Those who accepted were called "soupers," a term of extreme opprobrium that was again used, more symbolically, during the years of the great flight from Ireland.[1] Although the Anglo-Norman families had joined with the sept families during the Elizabethan wars and had themselves remained loyal to the Catholic faith—or even if Protestant had allied themselves with the Irish—the famine years aroused the old suspicion that the families with Anglo-Irish names had managed to retain property through some unacceptable influence. So the old historical divisions between surnames began again and still survived in the new country, where some families got ahead faster than others.

Against this background, William Sullivan, twenty-three years old, his younger sister, Bridget, and his brother Patrick, then only fourteen years old, left County Cork in 1848. By various family records, Patrick came first and the others followed shortly. "Without a friend in this country and almost without a dollar in his pocket [Patrick Sullivan] started out in life," according to his obituary notice.[2]

There is little doubt that it was the construction of the railroad through the valley that brought the Sullivans to central New York State and that they arrived, all of them, almost penniless and were hired as they left the boat in New York City. That people would arrive penniless in this country in 1848, with no friends or relatives to pave the way, suggests the extreme conditions then existing in the south and west of Ireland. In 1847, the continued blight of the potato crop and the increasing threat of starvation had been further intensified by the appearance of what was loosely called "famine fever."[3] Before the famine fever broke out, these country people were reluctant to leave their ancestral homes. Woodham-Smith reports that after pestilence appeared, "the people, terrified and desperate, began to flee a land which seemed accursed. In a great mass movement they made their way, by tens of thousands, out of Ireland. . . . Yet they did not leave fever behind; fever went with them, and the path to a new life became a path of horror."[4]

It was in this time of mass terror that William Sullivan and Julia Galvin, who became his wife, left Ireland, probably on the same boat. Whether they were married at sea or after they arrived is not known. According to Galvin family lore, Julia left Cork at twenty-seven as the wife of another man, whose name is unknown, and as the mother of an infant son. The sailing vessel was caught in an Atlantic storm, and an epidemic broke out among the passengers. Julia's husband and baby died in this epidemic and were buried at sea. In those days of terror, when sailings took place at any time of year, storms often lengthened the voyage to as much as thirteen weeks. When Julia finally arrived in port, her eyes were still so swollen from weeping that she could not see. Either before landing or shortly afterwards, Julia married William. In those bitter days, the death of husband and child were not incompatible with a prompt remarriage. Although Julia's brother Allen and her sister Johanna also arrived at about the same time, it is doubtful that any of them felt able at that juncture to offer any financial support to Julia. Thus William Sullivan represented survival for the widow in the new country.

For eight years after their marriage, no children were born to the couple. Perhaps Julia was so depleted by the events of the voyage that she could not conceive, or there may have been miscarriages or infant deaths.

Not until 1856, when Julia was thirty-five years old, was their first child born, a son. The second son, Timothy, Harry's father, was born in the following year. Six more sons were born in fairly rapid succession, although two survived only briefly. In 1868 their only daughter, Ellen, was born. Three years later, the last child, a son, was born. Seven of these children were born after Julia was forty years old; she was fifty when she had her last child in 1871. By then, William and Julia had been in this country for twenty-three years, but they had acquired no farmland. For all these landless refugees from the famine, the acquiring of land was of the greatest importance; yet most of them were so physically emaciated and impoverished when they landed that they settled in the slums of the port cities, where they stayed. Obviously William was sturdy enough to be hired at the dock. He and Julia continued to hope that they would be able to buy some farmland, but William was still working as a laborer on a railroad gang when he died, and it had not been easy to save up any money. Winters were more severe in Chenango County than in Ireland, so that work on the tracks was sometimes halted by heavy snows; and when the work was canceled, so were the wages.

On June 9, 1874, the family's hopes for getting ahead were abruptly shattered by William's accidental death while he was working near Norwich on the tracks of the Delaware, Lackawanna, and Western Railroad. The newspaper account of the accident reflects the status of the two Irishmen who were killed that day:

On Tuesday afternoon a frightful accident occurred near this village, by which two laborers were instantly killed, viz.: Thomas Cox, who lived near the Catholic Church, on Pleasant street, and William Sullivan, who resides about a mile above Wood's Corners, on the King Settlement Road. Both belong to the track gang of the D.L. & W.R.R. and were at work on that road near the residence of Marmaduke Wood, about two and a half miles north of this village. The instrument of their destruction was the locomotive attached to a special train which left Binghamton early in the afternoon for Utica. The facts, as near as we can learn them, are as follows:

The track hands had all received notice the day previous of the intended passage of the train and were on the look-out for it. Soon after three o'clock an alarm was heard by them, and the train was announced by one of the hands. On looking up, however, it was discovered [to] be a coal train on the Midland, which runs parallel and about one hundred feet from the D.L. & W.R.R. at that point. The men at once turned to their work again, Cox and Sullivan with their faces to the north. Scarcely had the coal train passed them before the lightening special came upon them, its small noise being drowned by that of the passing coal train. The foreman and one or two others of the gang who were at work about fifteen or twenty rods south of them saw the train and got out of its way, and tried to alarm the others and succeeded with all but these two. The engineer sounded the alarm whistle and rang the bell when about fifteen rods from them, but before they could get off both were struck, one thrown to the right and the other to the left and instantly killed. They were horribly crushed and mangled. The legs and necks of each were broken, as well as the skulls and many other bones also. The survivors of the party at once went to them and the train stopped and backed up to where they were, and Superintendent Thompson gave orders to have the bodies taken care of, and then proceeded on his journey. The foreman of the gang took them to their residences.

The train was running upwards of forty miles an hour, and we can not see that any one was really to blame except the injured men themselves, though we can't see the necessity of running specials through our village, or any other, as it was at that fearful rate. A more fearful accident might have occurred at any one of the dozen crossings in our village, running as it was at a time when trains did not usually pass and were consequently unexpected.[5]

The last paragraph tells of the nativism already developing in the County, and of the low esteem in which "foreigners" were held by the very people who had imported them. An inquest produced no new findings. It seems doubtful, given the particular slant of the article, that any restitution was made by the railroad company to the widow.

Since William died intestate, Julia at fifty-three signed a petition to the judge for the County of Chenango for formal disposition of property, listing eight "infant" children and stating that the entire estate did not exceed $150. The children's ages as listed on the petition were as follows: John, eighteen years old; Timothy, sixteen; Willie, fourteen; Jeremiah, thirteen; Michael, twelve; Frank, eight; Ellen, six; and Edward, or Edwin, three.

The petition is signed in a clear, bold handwriting with the name "Joulia" Sullivan, as the widow of William. This version of her name, which does not appear anywhere else, doubtless indicates her unfamiliarity with English spelling at that time. She spoke Gaelic throughout her life, and what education she had received in Ireland would have been in the illegal "hedgerow" schools, usually taught in Gaelic. These schools, often established by devout Irish Catholic families who refused to allow their children to attend the state Protestant schools, had as their teachers priests who had been trained, again illegally, on the Continent. The level of scholarship was usually high, and the classes were often held literally in ditches alongside the roads, hidden by the hedgerows. Julia's brother Allen, who knew both Gaelic and Latin, had gone to such a school, and it is probable that Julia went with him, since girls and boys often went to these schools together.[6]

Michael Stack and William Sullivan, Harry's two grandfathers, had come to the County within a year of each other. By the time of William's death, Michael had already purchased about a hundred acres for a total of $1640 in cash. If William had lived, that difference might have been minimized over the years, for his brother Patrick raised a family that fared much better than William's in the New World. But Julia's fatherless children never completely recovered from William's accident. Julia herself never acquired a farm, even though she tried desperately to extract from each son a commitment to this goal.

Each of Julia's sons, in turn, was sent out by her to work as a laborer or servant for some farmer, with the expectation that his small wages would build toward her goal of owning a farm. But each son, in turn—with one exception—married and was burdened with other commitments, after which she tended to write that son out of her life. In effect, Julia would then promote the next child to the status of eldest and pin her hopes on him. In the census of 1880, Michael, then seventeen and the fifth living son but the oldest still at home, is entered on the report as being twenty-two, which was actually Timothy's age for part of that year. Since Timothy was working away from home, no adjusted age for him had to be recorded, but it is safe to assume that he was still contributing and had become the oldest child in Julia's mind. Finally, in 1885, Timothy married as well, but Michael never escaped. Local records show Julia at eighty-one still living with Michael, then thirty-nine, on a dairy farm in Preston that he leased. He thus had a farm, but it was not his—or his mother's.

This system of writing off the children who no longer contributed to the household is echoed in Harry's own version of his father's family: he reports that Timothy as the eldest child had to take over the "support of the household" at the time of his father's accident; and this story was obviously used by Ella to explain Timothy's humble position in life. In fact, Timothy had been out of school long before his father's death and was already working as a farm laborer at seventeen. In the end, only Timothy and Michael were accepted by Julia as sons, and Ella Stack went along with this myth. This definition is also echoed in the recollection of Margaret [Normile] Hannon, a second cousin of Harry's on the Galvin side of the house. She reports that she was *amazed, simply amazed,*" to learn years later that her great-aunt Julia had been survived by six sons, "only three of whom I had ever heard of." Julia's children were without money, prestige, or education, Margaret Hannon reports. Even Julia's brother blamed her for the plight of the boys; she wanted her own bit of land, and she wanted them to work it for her. She had no ambition for her sons other than to see them "big enough to hold a hoe and strong enough to use it," according to her own brother. Her daughter, Ellen Sullivan Crandall (also called Ella), eventually got away from her mother, too, and earned enough money working in Norwich to go to Philadelphia and become a graduate nurse, without any encouragement or help from her mother.

The fate of Julia's sons—their inability to get ahead in this country—is illustrated by their life patterns as compared to those of the Stack cousins of the same generation. All but one of Julia and William Sullivan's sons remained on the land for the rest of their lives, and most of them ended their days without acquiring a farm; the youngest boy became a machinist. This pattern was related to the history of the families in Ireland, but some of it was an outcome of William's accident, which occurred before the family had begun to find its way into the American mainstream. The impact of the accident can be documented in part by comparing the record of William's family with that of his younger brother, Patrick, who began a second branch of the family in America.

One of Patrick's sons, William H., became a respected lawyer in Norwich, eventually known throughout the state, and he was active in the state Democratic party. Although Will was not financially successful in a conventional sense, his reputation for even-handed dealing and his concern for the oppressed were remarkable. Of all the relatives on both sides of the family, the career of Timothy's first cousin, Judge Will Sullivan, most closely paralleled that of Ella Stack Sullivan's only child.

Another of Patrick's sons, Michael, who was considerably older than Will, would become successful by a different route. Both Michael and Will began their careers by working for one of the old Yankee families in Norwich, the Bissells, who had a fine house on the main street. But Michael eventually married the Bissells' daughter, Agnes, and he was soon the proprietor of a thriving shoe store, the superintendent of his own farm, and an ardent Republican.[7]

There is a general feeling in the County that the Sullivans did not measure up somehow to the Stacks. Both Stack and Sullivan cousins are reluctant to talk about this directly. In the presence of Stack cousins, a friend of theirs termed the difference as being that between "lace curtain" and "shanty" Irish. The Stack cousins withheld comment on this diagnosis, but they agreed that Harry was a Stack through and through and that this explained his genius. This sort of explanation of human behavior was eventually rejected by Sullivan himself in his cogent formulation of the one-genus postulate: "We are all much more simply human than otherwise, be we happy and successful, contented and detached, miserable and mentally disordered, or whatever."[8]

In the period when Sullivan was first beginning his career as a psychiatrist, he made a particular effort to have dinner with his cousin, Margaret Hannon, a granddaughter of Julia's brother, Allen Galvin. By then he was beginning to formulate this postulate, and he wanted to question her about his father's family; she was probably one of the few cousins that he knew at all on that side of the family, except for those he may have met at his grandmother Sullivan's funeral in 1908. Margaret Hannon's report of their conversation is reminiscent of Sullivan at his most Socratic, as he attempted to push his cousin to make some clear-cut statement about the Sullivan side of the family:

He was plying me with questions—all about our antecedents, what I knew about them. He started with whether or not I knew his own grandmother. I remembered her, but very slightly.... Did I ever know my grandfather [Julia's brother Allen]? No, he was dead many years before my mother married. What had I heard about him? Did I remember any of the other brothers and sisters? . . . He finally said to me, "Does it ever occur to you to question where we came from? For instance, there's myself" (Harry's modesty was always one of his more charming qualities— he went first), "there's you, and there's [another Galvin cousin who was a brilliant mathematician] . . . Wouldn't you say we were different?"

"Well, Harry, perhaps we're more fortunate."

"No, that doesn't answer the question at all! What has made it so? Look at my other first cousins. Lumps! Do you know them?"

"No, I really don't know them. I know them when I see them, but I don't know them."

"Lumps, lumps. Now, is it the Galvin? That can't answer everything. Their father had Galvin blood, too."

"Well, of course, they are my second cousins, not my first cousins, and they all live in the country, I simply don't know them."

"Well, I'm telling you. I don't know them. I've met them, I've seen them, I've talked to them, or tried to. But here we are, sprung from illiterates."

Well, my back stiffened. I said, "What do you mean, illiterates?"

"Your grandfather, my grandmother Julia, they could not read or write."

"Well," I said, "there is where you are *very* much mistaken as far as my grandfather is concerned. I cannot answer for your grandmother, but my grandfather could read and write Gaelic, and could read and write Latin."

"He could?"

"Yes," I said, "he *could.*"

"Where did he learn them?"

"In the hedgerow schools of Ireland."

He said, "I never knew that. Do you think my grandmother could?"

I said, "I have no idea. . . . But I do know that my grandfather was far from illiterate."

"All right. Then come back to us. What has made us different?"

"Well," I said, "your other cousins are living in the country. They are working very hard from dawn to dusk. They start work very young. Perhaps it's just a matter of environment."

And Harry clapped his hand on the table until the silver jumped. . . . "*That's* what I wanted to hear. *That's* the word I wanted you to come up with! . . . Well, how then do you account for the fact that I never left Smyrna until I went to college? Where do you fit environment into that?"

"Yes," I said, "you left Smyrna with every book you read, with every publication your Aunt Margaret sent you. You left Smyrna every time you got your nose stuck in a book. And you wouldn't speak to anyone, and you wouldn't permit anyone to speak to you."

And he said, "I wasn't very gracious to you that summer you came up to the farm, was I?" [Sullivan was then fifteen, and his cousin was almost eight.]

I said, *"Gracious? Harry, you were perfectly horrid!"*

And he smiled, a crooked little smile, and said, "Yup, just a horrid little boy."[9]

It was largely a "matter of environment" that differentiated the fates of the Sullivans and the Stacks. But the Sullivans too were "more simply human than otherwise." In retrospect, the matriarch Julia Galvin Sullivan becomes more magnificent than otherwise. She had a tenacious grip on life, holding her family together after William's death. When she died in 1908, Harry undoubtedly went to her funeral, and it may have been the only time he saw some of his uncles and cousins on his father's side, shadowy figures who virtually disappeared in the myths told him in his early years. But Julia's picture, which appeared with the obituary notice, is real.[10] She looks handsome, if tired. Her mouth is full, her eyes wide-set and appealing. She was a rugged woman, in "fairly good health" until five days before her death at eighty-seven. She had been vain about her age, which changed progressively downward on official records—until the death notice corrected it. Margaret Hannon remembers a cousin asking, "How old are you, Aunt Julia?" And Julia answered sharply, "Old enough."

According to the grave markers, Julia was four years older than her husband William. Her Stack daughter-in-law, Ella, was also four years older than her husband, and she too occasionally changed her age, always in the same direction as Julia—downward. They were alike, too, in their tenaciousness. Julia effectively determined that most of her sons would be farmers. And Ella Stack determined that her only son would *not* be a farmer.

⋈ 4 ⋊

Rexford Street

If a sibling died during the memory span of the patient, that may be quite significant, but it is also important to note those siblings who died before he can remember, because they might have been of particular significance to his parents and thus have a considerable effect on him.

—Sullivan, *The Psychiatric Interview*

SHORTLY after the beginning of the new year, 1886, the *Sherburne News* carried a notice of the marriage of Ella and Timothy: "Sullivan-Stack at St. Malachy's Church, in this village Dec. 30th 1885, by Rev. Father Cullen, of St. Patrick's Church, Norwich, Mr. Timothy Sullivan and Miss Ella M. Stack, all of Smyrna, N.Y." So began the life of Timothy and Ella as man and wife. Ella was less than a month away from being thirty-three years old, and Timothy was twenty-eight and a half. After the wedding, Ella and Timothy returned to the Stack farm.

Their first child, a boy, was born in Smyrna a little more than two years after the marriage, on February 8, 1888, and was named William Harold. On the birth certificate, Ella's age is given as thirty-two, although she was by then thirty-five. The birth of William was apparently followed in less than three months by a move to Norwich, for on April 8, William was baptized in St. Paul's Catholic Church in Norwich and the family is listed as living there at that time.[1]

In Norwich, Timothy worked for the Maydole Hammer Company, founded forty years before by David Maydole, the "mighty hammer-maker of Chenango."[2] Timothy probably began work as an unskilled laborer in the factory, but at some point he became a "skilled workman."[3] When the Sullivans moved to Norwich, there was a relatively large population of Irish people living east of the principal street in Norwich. Most of them worked either for the Hammer Company or for the Ontario and Western Railroad—Norwich was the main marshaling-yard for the Northern Division of that railroad.

The Sullivans lived in the Irish part of town, first on Mitchell Street and then on Rexford Street, both residences being near the railroad tracks. Their house on Rexford Street was the second one from the tracks; the first one was occupied by Mrs. Brown, a former Negro slave. The Browns had moved to Norwich after the Civil War and were well thought of in the community. They were not poor; Mrs. Brown's grown children had been caterers in New York City before coming to Norwich to live with their mother. On the other side of the Sullivans lived the Smiths, who belonged to an old Yankee family. Most of the other people who lived on Rexford Street were Irish and Catholic in origin, and as soon as the Smiths could afford it, they moved to another part of town.[4]

During this period, the Irish-Americans in Norwich were derogated almost as much as they were at the time of Timothy's father's death almost a generation before. A Norwich descendant of one of the early Yankee settlers reports that her father, as a young boy in the 1880s, was not allowed to go down to the Rexford Street area except on horseback, for fear that he would be stoned by the intoxicated Irish residents.

Both Sullivan houses in Norwich were also situated only two or three blocks from the abandoned canal that had once carried traffic between Binghamton and the Erie Canal at Utica. In the late 1880s a great epidemic of "black diphtheria" broke out in and around this area. The canal ditch had not been properly drained when it was abandoned some years before, and there were still great stagnant pools of water in holes along it, so that everybody blamed the canal in general for the epidemic. Although the same epidemic affected children who lived at some distance from the canal and in other parts of the state, the old Yankee settlers in Norwich were as ready as ever to blame the disease partly on the "foreigners" who lived in the Irish part of town. Rexford Street was hit especially hard by the disease, and the Irish-American families were bitter about the cesspools in the abandoned canal ditch. There is a legend in Norwich that five children were buried from Rexford Street in one day, all victims of diphtheria. The situation became so acute that people were afraid to go into a house where a child had died. In one instance, the body of a child on Rexford Street was displayed to mourning relatives and neighbors by tilting the open casket toward the front window.[5]

On September 20, 1888, the Sullivans' first-born, William, died in the house on Mitchell Street, at the age of 7 months and 12 days. His death was "due to cholera infantum," and he died in convulsions, as reported by Dr. Ormsby, who was used by the family in each succeeding crisis for as long as they were in Norwich. The baby was buried on the corner of James Stack's plot at St. Malachy's Cemetery—the only plot owned by either side of the family at that time. The baby was only distantly related to James Stack—a first cousin twice removed—but the bonds of the heart were particularly strong in this instance; James, too, had lost his first-born son in infancy.

On February 18, 1890, a second boy, Arthur Timothy, was born to Ella and Timothy, who now lived on Rexford Street. Again, the child did not live through the first summer. On August 1, after a five-day illness, he died in convulsions from "entero colitis"; he was buried beside the other baby. Sometime afterwards, Ella and Timothy erected a small marker bearing the names and ages of both babies under the heading, "Our Darlings." Although neither of these deaths as reported on the death certificates could be directly related to the diphtheria epidemic, the Sullivans, like other parents in distress over the death of young children, saw these losses as directly related to the conditions near the canal.

In the early summer of 1891, Ella became pregnant for the third time. Each pregnancy had begun at approximately the same time, whether by design or by chance, so that each of her three sons was born in February. But it was the third child who came closest to being born on a president's birthday, for this child, Harry, was born on February 21. In some curious manner, February 22 became a measure for Harry in evaluating his friends. Thus Clarence Bellinger, the only boy to become close to Harry during his growing-up years, was born on February 22; and Roscoe Hall, a particularly close colleague in Sullivan's adult years, was also born on February 22. Such coincidences were reinforced by the fact that each of the three was an only child, all became psychiatrists, and none of them married. Sullivan always had a particular interest in birth dates, and the coincidence of birth dates may have had a kind of magical meaning for him in building up an initial relationship.

On May 29, the new baby was baptized at St. Paul's as "Henricum Stack Sullivan," using a latinized form for Henry. But Henry was never used either formally or informally thereafter. He became simply "Harry."

At thirty-nine, Ella probably despaired of having any more children after Harry. One can imagine the care she bestowed upon this third and only surviving child, the aura of protectiveness that shielded him from any stray germ, the adoration in which he was held by his mother. Some of this feeling of needing to protect others clung to Sullivan all his life. At the same time, he had a curious ambivalence about the expression of sentiment. He tended to fluctuate sharply between being sentimental himself, like his mother, and fiercely unsentimental, so that those who liked him described him as kind and sympathetic, and those who disliked him described him as unpleasant and bereft of feeling. His impatience with sentiment was epitomized by his hatred of the color blue; he explained this aversion to one friend as being derived from his mother's use of the color on his baby clothes, which she preserved and exhibited proudly from time to time.[6] He told a colleague that he had an aversion even to sitting in a blue chair.[7] Blue was for him a hated color, imposed on him by his mother before he could protest.

Yet Ella's concern for Harry had its practical as well as its sentimental side. The alternatives to life on Rexford Street were already forming in her mind, reinforced by clear evidence of the effect of mere chance on what happened to people. In 1889, Ed's wife, Little Ella, had died when their son Leo was only four years old; and Maggie, then twenty-five and still living at home in Smyrna, had gone over to the Gothic House, Ed's prosperous hotel in South Otselic, to take care of the child. Although the move was envisioned as a temporary expedient, Maggie had stayed on, becoming more and more a part of the rather impressive social life of this all-Protestant village. Thus Ella's brother and sister were living in a world as different from hers as it was possible for her to imagine. Even more significant was the clear path for achievement that lay before her nephew Leo, seven years older than Harry; by the time Harry was born, Leo was already attending a Protestant Sunday school and playing with the children of the village elite. Everyone seemed to be moving except Timothy and his brothers. Two of his first cousins, Michael H. and Will, were already on the path to success, and their names often appeared in the local paper. And her own brother, Ed, who was a contempory of Timothy's, was referred to in the *Sun* as "Landlord Stack" when he came to Norwich on business. The only mention of Ella and Timothy that appeared in the *Sun* was always in connection somehow with her brother. In 1891, shortly after Ella became pregnant with Harry, the *Sun* reported that Ed and Maggie visited Ella on Rexford Street, doubtless to reassure her about this third pregnancy after two children had already died.

On October 23, 1893, the *Sun* reported that Timothy, Ella, and Harry, then twenty months old, had spent a weekend with Ed's family in South Otselic. It was an expedition of some importance at that period, particularly for the family of a Catholic workingman; since there was no Catholic church in South Otselic, the Sullivans had had to give up going to Mass on that Sunday. By the time of the visit to South Otselic, the full impact of the national depression had hit Norwich: unemployment was a real threat, and there was talk of a strike in one of the factories. Periodically the hammer factory would be closed, under the pretext of some holiday, but these were not paid holidays. It seems quite possible that not only Ella but also Ed and Maggie were trying to bring Timothy into a new orbit of mobility by the trip to South Otselic. Ed was already engaged in several lucrative businesses in and around South Otselic, including a livery stable, and it would have been reasonable for him to offer Timothy some job there or at the hotel. Or Timothy might have gotten a job at the Gladding Fish-Line Factory. Ed had a good business relationship with the factory owner, Ralph Brown, his only rival in the village. Brown was a descendant of the Gladdings, a Yankee family who had come into South Otselic from Connecticut early in the nineteenth century. The factory had been a successful national business since the middle of the century, and the village largely centered around the factory and Ed's hotel, where traveling salesmen stayed when they came to town. Brown and Stack were considered the wealthiest men in town, although Ed had not yet caught up with the Gladding family. They were also good friends, with many interests in common, including a good-natured rivalry about the racing ability of the horses they owned.

Ed had early come to grips with the problem of being the only Irish Catholic in the village by trying to separate his religious beliefs from his social and political life. He later made a public declaration on his philosophy about these matters in a book of biographical sketches of the "leading citizens" of the County. "In religious belief, [Edmund J. Stack] is a faithful member of the Catholic Church. Socially, he belongs to [three different units of the] I.O.O.F. [International Order of Odd Fellows]. In political belief, he adheres to the principles advocated by the Democratic party."[8] This separation of activities, obviously supplied by Ed, might be acceptable to heritage Catholics, but devout Catholics were dubious about it; both the Masons and the Odd Fellows were considered incompatible with membership in the Catholic Church at that time.[9] Yet this solution opened doors for Ed in his own village and in the County. Maggie could tell Ella of the esteem in which their brother and his son were held by Yankee neighbors. Leo was already playing croquet with the children of the best families in town, including Nina, the younger of Ralph Brown's two daughters. It was rumored that Nina and her sister would one day inherit half a million dollars each.

All of this Horatio-Alger story was beginning to unfold before the starved eyes of Ella as she watched from the lowly house on Rexford Street. For both Maggie and Ella, Ed's compromise with his religious training seemed only a superficial one, unrelated to his religious convictions. But Timothy Sullivan's view of Ed was considerably different. Timothy's dedication to his religion was complete; he did not argue about it, for he was a taciturn man, but he was firm and unmoving. The worldliness of Ed and Maggie seemed foreign to Timothy—a laborer, schooled in hard work, struggling throughout his life to earn a living against overwhelming odds. After a hard day's work, he was apt to have some hard cider with the men at the hammer factory. As the layoffs became more frequent, his need to find solace with his fellow workers became greater. He tended to get out of the house on those days when the factory was not running, and he was beginning to listen to the talk of the need for some kind of workers' organization; his cousin, Will Sullivan, a staunch Democrat like himself, was a leader in the rights of the working man.

In 1894 the depression worsened, and Ella, like other wives of the Irish workers around Rexford Street, was worried. She resented the atmosphere in which her son was being raised. Already the Italian immigrants had begun to move into the area not far from the Rexford Street house. They drank too much, like the other laborers in a period of uncertainty, and they had fights among themselves.[10]

Sometime during that summer, a series of upsets in the house on Rexford Street changed the pattern of life for Harry. The trouble centered about his mother, who had taken care of him until then. There is a mystery as to what exactly happened, but a general pattern of events establishes the time when Harry's grandmother Stack became a replacement for his mother.

◆§ 5 §◆

The Disappearance
of Harry's Mother

In my very early childhood it was discovered that I
was so repelled by spiders that the body of a dead
spider put at the top of the stairs would discourage
my ambulatory efforts, which had previously often
resulted in my falling downstairs. . . . This occurred
around the age of two and a half to four.
—Sullivan, *The Interpersonal Theory of Psychiatry*

In his lectures, Sullivan sometimes used—almost casually—the age of
thirty months as marking the beginning of childhood, and this is an
autobiographical reference to an important change in his "early childhood." In his more formal statement of developmental eras, he defines
childhood functionally, as beginning with "the appearance of the ability
to utter articulate sounds of or pertaining to speech."[1] Most children
would reach this stage long before the age of two and a half.

It was Harry's grandmother Stack who initiated him into a fear of spiders in his third summer of life, when his own mother, for whatever reason, was absent from the scene for an unknown period, perhaps until he
was four. As one reviews the transition for him from the practices of one
mothering person to those of another, it seems clear that the change itself
must have made the spider particularly terrifying. His dating of this first
encounter with the spider is oddly but characteristically detailed; the
event occurred, of course, long before he would have been able to pin-
point events by his age at the time. Thus he must have based his reporting
on his memory of concurrent events in the family that had occasioned the
use of new methods for taking care of him. It is because of these other
events that Sullivan can be so specific about when "it was discovered";
but he avoids saying *who* discovered this phenomenon.

Quite simply, it appears that Harry was moved to the Smyrna farm
house in the late summer of 1894, when he was two and a half. Less than
a month before the move his father had purchased the Rexford Street

house for $650, with only Timothy's name appearing on the deed, although both Ella's and Timothy's names appear on other civil and legal documents before and after this time. When the deed was negotiated, the hammer factory was again shut down temporarily, and Timothy was without income—a situation not unexpected in the midst of a nationwide depression. His unilateral decision to purchase the house during a shutdown may have reflected his frantic attempt to do something about Ella's growing despair, or indeed his action may have precipitated her upset.

In either case, someone had to take over the care of the child, and his grandmother Stack, at the busiest season of the year on a farm, took on the duty. She did not have time to dote on the child and follow him around all day, as Ella had done. A dozen times a day during the summer months she might have to go down the steep stairs into the cellar, where a cold spring bubbled up, to get supplies for the midday dinner for the help on the farm, or to store the eggs and butter that were sold for cash in the village of Smyrna. To keep the child from following her, she placed a dead spider at the head of the stairs. Ordinarily a child of thirty months can be partially controlled by spoken admonitions, but his grandmother's Gaelic words and gestures must have puzzled and frightened Harry, who was accustomed to the more acculturated accent of his parents. Indeed, his grandmother may have resorted to this practice because she could not make him understand what she was saying.

One can imagine the family explanation given to Harry as he grew older: *Your mother was very ill when you were two and a half, she wasn't well at all, so you went to live with your grandmother, and she took care of you. She used to put a spider at the top of the stairway going down to the cellar, and you were so deathly afraid of spiders you wouldn't go near the steps.* Stack cousins who were contemporaries of Harry's note that the use of the spider must have come from his grandmother Stack and the child-care practices of County Clare: the body of a small animal, such as a mouse or a large insect, was sometimes used to keep a child from falling into the fireplace, they report.

As to what happened to Ella and why, one can only speculate from the veiled references of relatives and neighbors, which indicate some kind of mental breakdown. Some say she tried to "harm" herself and Harry in the Rexford Street house, so she could not be left alone with him. Various cousins and neighbors report that grandmother Stack "raised" Harry and that he spoke as a child with even more of an accent than his own mother because he spent so much time with his grandmother. When one asks why Ella was not caring for her son, the answer is uneasy and evasive: "Oh, I suppose that Ella was helping Timothy on the farm." There is another story that she died when Harry was young and that Timothy remarried; but this rumor merely explains her disappearance and the probable change in her bearing when she reappeared.

Throughout the County, the mystery of exactly what happened to Ella appears and reappears; but the hills guard their secrets well, whatever they are, so the actual events may never be known. Ella's name does not show up in the records of nearby hospitals. She may have gone to her brother's hotel in South Otselic to be near her sister, Maggie, who was living there at this period; or she may even have gone up to the Smyrna farm with Harry and been relegated to the attic until she recovered.

Whatever Timothy hoped to accomplish by the purchase of the Rexford Street house, his plans were fated to be changed by subsequent events. In December of that year, Michael Stack died in the Smyrna farmhouse; and later in the same month the hammer factory, which had started up again, announced another unpaid "vacation" for its employees. Timothy seemed the obvious one to go back to the Stack homestead and run the farm. Michael's other children were involved with their own destinies by then: Ed was busy with his prosperous business in South Otselic; Maggie was caring for Ed's child; and John was living and working in New Haven. Mary Stack, Michael's widow, was already taking care of Harry, so that the family could be reunited under her aegis. On February 13, 1895, Timothy acceded to the pressure of circumstance and signed over his deed on the Rexford Street house to Ed Stack in return for $400, with Ed assuming a mortgage of $250 plus interest. On this deed the name of "Ellen M. Sullivan" reappears, so that she is now in agreement with the transfer, or at least competent to participate. The deed was signed in the presence of Timothy's first cousin, "Wm. H. Sullivan, Justice of the Peace." Symbolically, Will's participation represented some small triumph for Timothy in a swiftly deteriorating situation, for Will was becoming a power in the county and the state. In many ways Will was a counterpoint for the life-style of Ed Stack, since Will had gained a substantial measure of respect and success without turning Protestant or becoming a landlord.

In some such fashion, then, Timothy was elected to go back to Smyrna and run the farm. It was for him, at least, a fateful decision, for he became at a psychological level that tragicomic figure seen in the west of Ireland—*cliamhan isteach,* literally "son-in-law going in."[2] He had escaped his own mother and her need for owning land; but from now on, the same drive would dominate his own life as a son-in-law and a brother-in-law. For thirty-six years, from 1895 until his death in 1931, Timothy owned and farmed the land, but old-timers in Chenango County continued to refer to the property as "the Stack Farm."

It was on Harry's third birthday, February 21, 1895, that a formal legal document was drawn up in preparation for Timothy's taking over the Smyrna farm.[3] The date was not simply a coincidence; the move was undoubtedly seen by everyone involved as made in Harry's best interests and appropriately signed on his birthday. The document was signed by Mary Stack's four children, including John's wife, as parties of the first part, and by Timothy as the party of the second part. Ella, as a party of the first part, signed her name as "Ellen M. Sullivan" of Norwich.

In brief, under the terms of the contract Timothy acquired the farm in Smyrna by paying one dollar to the parties of the first part, with certain qualifications: in exchange for boarding Mary Stack for the rest of her life, for the further payment of $1,237.43 to the Stack children by March 1, 1900 (without interest if Mary Stack were still alive by that time), and for assuming a mortgage of $1,431 held by John Stack, the full and clear deed to the property would be given to Timothy on or before March 1, 1900. The document specified that Mary Stack's medical expenses were to be paid by her four children. In addition, 2,000 feet of hemlock flooring was to be purchased by the four children and drawn to the farm by Timothy. Timothy's duties were specified so precisely as to define him as less than trustworthy: he was to keep the buildings and fences in good repair; he was to keep the buildings insured against fire in a solvent insurance company; and he was "to work and properly cultivate three acres of hops on said farm until the delivery of the deed to him," and in general to carry out farm tasks "in a proper and workmanlike manner." In case Mary Stack should choose to live elsewhere, Timothy agreed to pay during her lifetime the sum of $74.25 per year for her room and board in another domicile. Ed Stack's name led off the list of legal signatures, followed by Timothy J. Sullivan, Ellen M. Sullivan, Mary Stack, Margaret A. Stack, John B. Stack, and Ella E. Stack (John's wife).

A few days later, on February 27, 1895, the Norwich *Sun* carried a notice in the Personal and Society column: "T. J. Sullivan of Rexford Street has removed to a farm near Smyrna." There is no mention of his family—his son or his wife—which is a significant omission for the *Sun.* It seems likely that in fact Timothy made the move alone. Whatever the exact sequence of events, it is clear that neither Harry nor his mother had been living in Norwich for some time.

For both Timothy and Ella, the move represented defeat and compromise. Yet the farm offered a measure of economic security that they did not have in Norwich; and the child could have the security of his grandmother's ministrations until his mother had fully recovered. For Timothy, the loss of parish life in Norwich, with its easy access to convivial drinking companions, turned him into a taciturn and withdrawn person. For Ella, the return to her childhood home placed her again under the domination of her mother and turned her into a "complaining semi-invalid with chronic resentment at the humble family situation," as her son would remember in adulthood.[4]

◆ 6 ◆

The Imprint of Chenango

There has never been a city in the whole county. In
the folds of the Chenango hills the shadows lie deep
and dark.
—Carl Carmer, *Listen for a Lonesome Drum*

F OR fourteen years, Harry was destined to live on the edge of Smyrna
village, one of the few hill villages in the County, with only occasional visits to the valley villages. But whether hill or valley, all of them
lay in Chenango County. As time went on, as his childhood and youth
unfolded, it would become clearer and clearer to him that something had
gone wrong in this part of the world, something that his relatives and
neighbors could not talk about in rational terms. Carl Carmer has termed
it a curse and has related it to the displeasure of God with the people of
Chenango County:

The story is that a man of God rode into the Chenango Valley and
tried to start a church there. He preached loud and he preached long but
he could not get the people to give him enough money to build the
church. So he mounted his horse and rode on. When he got to the top of
the ridge on the far side of Unadilla Creek, that marks the Otsego County
line, he turned back in his saddle, lifted a hand and cursed the land of the
Chenango. Never, he said, should people gather in the valley, it should
never hear the wheels of industry nor feel the happy prosperity of busy
cities, it should always dwell darkly in the displeasure of his God.[1]

Inevitably Carmer's legend gives a religious meaning to the curse, for
this remote part of the country still retains much of the religious fervor
that was brought in by the early settlers. Carmer feels that, despite the
curse, Chenango people live contentedly. But their contentedness is fragile and mixed with defeat and uneasiness, as they cling to their beautiful
hills and valleys; and a painful question is written on their faces, though it
is never quite expressed directly: *What went wrong?*

For something did go wrong between 1825, when the Erie Canal was completed, and the depression of 1894. The depression was but a punctuation point for the intervening years, for the decline of the dream had begun long before Timothy Sullivan moved to Smyrna in 1895. It was this decline and its aftermath that informed much of Sullivan's life and theory. As a result of the decline, a virulent nativism took root in the County—and particularly in Smyrna—so that Michael Stack's grandchild was ostracized in Smyrna as his children had never been. In the end Harry's isolation in growing up was his salvation, for in the traumatic adjustment that took place when he left Smyrna for college, he discovered that these hills, so soft and alluring in their natural beauty, contained people and values that were narrowing of the soul, entrapping of the mind. Other young people left the County for college and university and undoubtedly discovered the same thing. But many of these young people who were from old Yankee families and completely accepted in the community were bound by ties of loyalty to the very defeatism of the County as it had affected their own families and close friends; and they would have to struggle all their lives with an increasing sense of hopelessness and defeat, maintaining an uneasy equilibrium by disparaging anyone who managed to escape. Thus Sullivan's loneliness and isolation in growing up may have helped to free him from this sense of loyalty to the scenes and people of his childhood that might have entrapped him, too.

In the decline of Chenango County, which became more visible after the depression of 1894, Smyrna was hit more drastically than Norwich in certain ways. Although the economic depression was more pronounced in Norwich where the industry for the County was centered, Smyrna had much less access to the outside world, and a more serious social paranoia developed there. To describe this process adequately requires a brief look at the patterning of life in Chenango County as it had developed since its settlement by white people at the end of the eighteenth century.

The central part of New York State had as its first white settlers the people from the hill country of New England who pushed westward after the Revolutionary War in search of better farmland and more hope for their children. In a partly superstitious invocation of divine support for their worldly intentions, they exhibited a religious fervor that has caused central New York State to be identified as the "burned-over district," that is, the area in which the intensity of religious experience had the quality of a great fire.[2] Chenango County was a part of this phenomenon; the two chief founders of the Mormon religion, for instance, had roots in the County—Brigham Young had once lived in Smyrna township, and Joseph Smith had worked for a while in the southeast part of the County near Afton.

In such a new and beautiful land, the old problem arose as to the meaning of any personal failure. Did God subject the good and the just to special trials, as He did Job, and would He then reward these chosen victims in another world? Delayed reward seemed harder and harder to accept in this new land, where certain families were already establishing dynasties of wealth and well-being that had been denied them in Connecticut and western Massachusetts. In many ways, Heaven had become a poor second to the immediate prospects of grandeur and a new lifestyle. Yet there were inevitably failures that must somehow be explained and digested. Perhaps God was punishing a particular family for its indifference to His dictates, or for a failure in diligence. In some such way, individual failure was handled and the meaning of failure explained. It was only when individual failure turned into the failure of a region, or more particularly the failure of a particular county, that the meaning of the disaster became a more complicated problem.

Somewhere in the middle of the nineteenth century the fear began to spread that a whole region—Chenango County—was being punished, and a frantic effort was made to turn the tide. In part, the growing incidence of that fear can be measured by the denial of the fact that something was wrong. In the midst of the depression of 1894, the *Sun* continued to define the trouble as being somewhere else—in New York City, in Chicago, in any part of the country except Chenango County. Yet retrospectively, there were clear indices that in fact the County had failed a long time ago, although the farmers and townspeople had denied it for well over half a century.

The blunt truth was that the hills in Chenango County ran the wrong way for the building of canals and railroads. Three tributaries of the Susquehanna had carved their way through the County—the Unadilla at the eastern edge, the Chenango River through the most central part, and the Otselic River in the west. Flowing southward in the main, they formed pathways and hills that were at cross-purposes to the east-west flow of empire through New York State in the nineteenth century. When the County was first settled, the fact that its geographic axis was north and south did not seem a drawback for the development of the area. The early settlers did not view the foothills on each side of Chenango Valley as any handicap; most of them came by ox cart, persevering into these valleys with no thought that the hills were insurmountable. Indeed, the Allegheny foothills were not as high as the Berkshires in western New England. Here was beautiful land, with serene and wide valleys and picturesque Indian trails through the foothills where game and fish were plentiful.

In this postcolonial period small crafts and businesses flourished, and almost every village was surprisingly self-sufficient. There were several such points of hope in Chenango County. Norwich and Sherburne, located in the valley, and even the hill village of Smyrna had emerged in the early part of the century as self-sufficient communities that burgeoned and produced a feeling of contentment in their inhabitants. The Albany-Ithaca Turnpike, built in 1805, passed through the village of Smyrna; a stake driven in the center of the village marked the distance of 101 miles from Albany. From Smyrna westward over the hills to the Otselic Valley was a difficult but possible journey by stagecoach.

Early in the century there was a "flourishing academy" in Smyrna, although it was discontinued before the middle of the century. But the interest in better education for the children in that community continued, as it did in so many other transplanted New England communities, long after the township of Smyrna had begun to decline. A "social library" was organized in 1818 as a private enterprise, and when it was disbanded in 1845, 300 volumes were sold at auction. This library was later supplanted by a school library in the village, which in 1880 contained 200 books, so that in those years even the library facilities had begun to decline. Industries and trades survived longer than hope. In 1880, Smyrna's business enterprises included a hotel, two gristmills, a tannery, three blacksmith shops (one of which had a carriage shop), a harness shop, two shoe shops, six stores, a wagon shop, and a cabinet shop and undertaking establishment. Although the village had only about 350 inhabitants, the nearby farmers also depended on merchants in the village for supplies; thus the businesses continued mainly on their own momentum.[3] But after the disastrous fire of 1900 in Smyrna, when a good part of the main street burned, the village never really rebuilt. The fire was only a dramatic ending for what had ended some time since.

What happened in Smyrna was only an exaggeration of what went on throughout the County after the Erie Canal was completed in 1825. The Canal was built along the natural east-west passage from the Hudson to Lake Erie, first beside the Mohawk River and then over the great plain that lay north of the Finger Lakes. Thus the Canal found a natural east-west pathway only about fifty miles north of Norwich, but this fifty miles was crucial. Later, another important east-west passage would be found through Binghamton, some forty miles south of Norwich, penetrated by the Erie Railroad. It was these distances from the two great east-west passages that Chenango County could never overcome.

As soon as construction on the Erie Canal was begun in 1817, residents of Chenango County started to agitate for a north-south canal that would link with the Erie Canal. As early as 1823, a County newspaper editorialized on the importance of a canal along the Chenango Valley.[4] Twice the citizens of Chenango County had surveys done of the area at their own expense, to study the feasibility of a north-south canal; and finally in 1829, the state legislature authorized its own study to see whether the feed-in canal would have enough water and would be able to pay for itself at the end of ten years. In 1830, a state commission issued a negative report on the financial feasibility of such a canal. But this negative report was finally overridden, and in 1834, work began on the Chenango Canal. The County rejoiced, both when the work was begun and when the Canal was completed in 1836. But the Canal was never successful: "What growth the branch canal did bring largely preceded its completion," Whitney Cross reports.[5] By 1876 the Chenango Canal was abandoned, and by 1880 the Canal was *a literal stench* in the nostrils of those it once benefited."[6]

Yet the sturdy farmers, the craftsmen, and the few landed gentry in Chenango County did not give up easily. All around them were counties that were prospering under the great surge of transportation that made New York the Empire State in the nineteenth century, the crossroads between the eastern seaboard and the expanding western part of the country. Almost as soon as the Erie Canal was finished, various companies made plans to build railroads that would compete with the canal traffic. In 1839 the Syracuse and Utica Railroad opened for business, and the east-west railroad traffic began to expand rapidly, with the tracks following basically the Erie Canal route at first and finally culminating in the great network of the New York Central. The residents in all the small villages of Chenango County yearned to become a part of this newest growth.

After many preliminary starts and the construction of short railroad lines, willy-nilly, in the central part of the southern tier of counties, the New York and Oswego Midland Railroad was incorporated in 1866, in the hope that it would open up the whole area to the east-west commerce that was flourishing to the north and south. Under the enthusiastic and unscrupulous prodding of a promoter from New York City, the villages and towns in Chenango County—as well as other contiguous counties—raised money for this Midland Railroad. In the 1860s, Norwich village and township bonded itself for a half million dollars; Smyrna was bonded for $120,000, a prodigious amount for a village of 300 surrounded by a township of small dairy farms—and actually more than any other part of the County, except for Norwich and two other villages. By 1875 Chenango County had a railroad indebtedness of almost two million dollars, more than that of any other county in New York State except Otsego, directly east of Chenango County. By 1879 much of the Midland Railroad had to be abandoned; thereafter, certain parts of the road were in use only once a week during the summer and fall seasons to take care of the production of cheese factories on the line.

A local historian of the period, who had watched the promoter sell one of the villages on bonding itself for the railroad, called it "one of the rawest financial deals ever carried out in New York State." When it was all over, the original estimated cost had more than doubled, and a receivership followed. From the beginning, "insurmountable obstacles faced the engineers who surveyed the original line. Unlike the Erie [railroad] or New York Central, the road could not follow a river valley for hundreds of miles, but had to take the hard way across a series of river valleys and intervening mountains and hills that ran at right angles to the general direction of the road."[7]

Some index to the effect of the sense of failure in the County can be found in the figures for the United States decennial censuses between 1800 and 1900. In 1800, Chenango County already had a population of 16,087; by 1840, it had reached 40,785. In the following twenty years the population remained relatively stable, but after 1860 it began to decline steadily. While the shift from agrarian to urban living would eventually overtake many nearby farming areas, the change in Chenango came much earlier than in the counties that surrounded it—Delaware, Madison, Otsego, Cortland, and Broome. All these counties maintained or increased their populations until at least the last decade of the century. Broome County increased dramatically, largely because its main town, Binghamton, was located on the east-west axis of railroad development in the southern part of the state. In brief, Chenango alone showed an early and consistent decline in population, at least thirty years before the others.

Another significant index to the sense of failure in Chenango County in the nineteenth century is found in the decline of teachers' salaries there, as compared to other counties. By 1896, the County superintendent of schools reported that "the qualification of teachers in Chenango County is lower than in the rest of the state. As a result the wages are about one-third lower. There is a [decided] lack of professional spirit among the teachers of Chenango County."[8] In a county that had been settled early by people from New England farms and villages, with strong feelings about the importance of education, this represented a failure of some magnitude.

Retrospectively, it seems clear that by 1870 the economy of Chenango County was not significantly involved with the growing centers of industry all around it—Syracuse to the north and west, Utica to the north, Binghamton to the south. The direction of rivers and valleys had determined the sweep of industry and history, and Chenango County was as isolated in many ways as the Eastern Shore of Maryland, and considerably more isolated than it had been in the first half of the nineteenth century. As long as the turnpikes were a significant part of the development, the County could compete at the necessary level. With the Erie Canal, that competition became largely a hope. For a while that hope was sufficient, but as time went on, hope was changed into a frantic question: Where did the fault lie?

As the morale of the County ebbed, a defensiveness grew up. The children and grandchildren of the Yankee pioneers could not bear to blame themselves; here and there was a weakling who had descended from New England stock, and this could be accepted—there were always some failures, even in the best of families. But the widespread sense of failure that touched so many families, particularly in the last decade of the century, must have another explanation, they felt. As in so many other communities, people could find only one source for the failure of the land that had been kind to their forebears—it was the strangers who had come in and ruined everything. The strangers were the immigrants. Old residents of the County, who have long since established close relationships with individual Irish-American neighbors, still grieve over the fact that "the Irish came to build the railroads and never left."

Even today the major east-west highways are either north or south of the County, following the successful paths made by the canals and the railroads of an earlier period. Even though only small hills separate the County from the rest of the state, they are still sufficient to hold the rhythm of life firm and unchanging. One can see the County as protected and serene, a hideaway from the world of crime and strife. But in many ways, it is a trap. There is no easy way out; the same words and ideas have reverberated in the valleys and hills for a hundred years or more. So it is that the outsider, living there for a few weeks at a time, comes to understand all too well the stereotypes of the old Yankee settlers and to sense the treachery of the nativism that dwells—almost unnoticed—in all too many of us who trace our ancestors, however remote, back to the early American settlers.

Nor are crime and violence unknown in the valleys and hills of Chenango. The Horatio-Alger dream of "strive and succeed" has been more often frustrated than realized. This is as true for the old Yankees as it is for the Irish and Italians, the Syrians and the Greeks—whatever people were lured in long ago to work on the canal, on the railroads, in the knitting mills, or to pick hops in the summer months. The dream is still remembered and cited in a pure form; but the frustrations are deep and dangerous. So it is that there is a peculiar fascination with suicide and homicide; this fascination existed eighty years ago, and it exists today.

No small wonder that the hero of Dreiser's *An American Tragedy* worked in one of the Utica mills, and that the girl whose pregnancy betrayed his desperate search for success was in real life a girl living on a farm in South Otselic. Nor does it seem strange, once one understands the values of this remote, rural part of America, to know that a new religion had its roots here. This part of the country demanded hopeful and successful lives from its young, although the parents of each generation often lived lives of despair. Most of the young learned to despair like their parents, for their wings were firmly clipped by those who longed for them to fly; over time, they too learned to be loyal to the idea of clipping wings. A few dared to dream of leaving the County: some of them founded religions, others found their way to the electric chair or to the insane asylum. There were many dangers in trying to find a way out of the Valley—perhaps the most dreaded of all the dangers were isolation and utter loneliness.

7

The Growth of Nativism

> Up to some two decades ago [that is, ca. 1918], persons reared in certain Protestant communities had profound—early emergent—hatred of Catholics that approached, apparently exceeded, the intensity of their anti-Semitic attitudes.
> —Sullivan, "Anti-Semitism"

IN 1845, just before the first Stack settled in Chenango County, more than eighty percent of its population were born in the United States but *not* in New York State.[1] Thus the Stacks and the Sullivans came into a relatively new society, still trying to find its own meaning and to search out a way to make a good living within that part of the world. In this search, it was necessary to have the right kind of God on one's side, as evidenced by the many Protestant religious sects that flourished in this part of the burned-over district.

In 1858, there were enough Catholic families in and around Sherburne to purchase a church building and to support a mission from nearby Hamilton. This congregation, mostly Irish people, had a religion that, to the various Protestant sects in the area, was more foreign than they were to one another. The Seventh-Day Baptists, the Free Baptists, the Mormons, the Quakers—all had representation in the hills around Sherburne. Protestant neighbors knew the arguments that had split one group off from another; however heated the religious debates were, they were familiar. But the Catholics were foreigners by virtue of their religion. Michael Stack's accent and ways might be accepted by neighbors in a friendly manner but his religious affiliation was foreign and strange.

An 1862 history of Sherburne, commenting on the Catholic church that young Harry would attend thirty-five years later, illustrates the beginnings of nativism quite early in that part of the world: "There is not an American-born citizen, except their own children, united with them. It appears to be the policy of their Priests, to keep them isolated as much as possible from all religious or educational intercourse with the Protestant community."[2] The stereotypes about the Irish immigrants have remained amazingly constant for over a hundred years in the valley villages. A librarian in the County reported in the 1970s that the priests had been responsible for keeping the Catholics and Protestants separated from each other, using almost the same words as those given in the 1862 history of Sherburne.

By the time Harry was two years old—in the depression year of 1894—the specter of nativism had moved toward a different kind of reality in Norwich and the valley villages. It had become more focused and brutal, as it emerged in the *Sun,* the only daily paper in the County, then in its third year of publication. The *Sun* carried, mainly in boiler-plate stories, both national and international news; and as the depression deepened, these stories from outside the County fed into the growing fear that trouble could be imported from outside. In the beginning of that year, as reports of economic trouble throughout the nation appeared more and more frequently on the front pages of the *Sun,* there was a slight feeling of local euphoria. It seemed possible that Chenango County had simply had an earlier battle with depression—and had learned to deal with it—while the great cities, Chicago, New York City, Pittsburgh, and so on, were now having a more serious encounter with such problems. There was a sense of adolescent joy in having achieved maturity first and of being able to help out less fortunate people who had mistakenly opted for the big cities, far away from rural wisdom. Several pleas appeared in the *Sun* asking residents of the County to send food and clothes to the "poor people" in New York City.

Yet there was an ever-present danger that "others" might bring in to Chenango the disease of trouble from the outside world. As 1894 wore on and the news of a nationwide disaster increased, the suggestions as to how the trouble could be kept outside of Norwich grew apace. When it became apparent that some of the trouble had taken root in Norwich and had even existed in its midst for some time, the explanation for the trouble changed somewhat: now the trouble had been brought in by the "foreigners." Some such feeling for the Irish had been there for decades, of course, and showed itself in the story of the accident to William Sullivan, Harry's paternal grandfather; but it had usually been handled by an elaborate denial of the importance of the Irish—they were somewhat of a joke, good storytellers who spoke the "King's English" with a curious deviation. Still, they did know English, which was somewhat different from the real foreigners who came later—the Italians, the Syrians, the Russians, and so on.

The overt focus of local fears now settled on the non-English-speaking foreigners. Stories in the *Sun* on the dangers of foreigners had some of the same intensity as the religious fervor that had swept that part of the world fifty or sixty years before. The danger of the foreigner was equivalent to the earlier danger of Satan; it was an evil to be overcome.

These descendants of the early settlers saw themselves as God-fearing people who had followed all the rules for succeeding and had failed. They had wrestled with the evil in themselves to no avail; they had been punished over and over again for diligence, for their self-sacrifice in trying to bring commerce into their midst; yet other people in nearby counties had prospered. Now suddenly the answer became clear: the danger was in the outsiders.

In 1893, there had been 1,239 men, women, and children working in the factories of Chenango County; 687 of them were employed at the David Maydole Hammer Company, the Norwich Pharmacal Company, and the Silk Dye House, to name the main ones. The rest of the factory work force was in other Chenango Valley villages—Oxford, Sherburne, and Greene—and also in Bainbridge, which was in the Unadilla Valley.[3] It was of course these industrialized villages that first felt the depression. Various evasions were used by the factory owners to minimize the disaster; for example, wholesale layoffs at the hammer factory, where Timothy worked, were avoided by cutting down on the time and the wages for an individual worker.

On March 14, 1894, a series of news stories began in the *Sun* on a strike at the Silk Dye House in Norwich. Thirty weavers had walked out, demanding that wages be returned to what they had been before the summer shutdown, when they had apparently been cut by fifty percent. The owner-superintendent of the factory refused to bargain with the strikers, stating that he would not "recognize any union" nor did he "see any necessity for it here in Norwich." Shortly thereafter the owners of the factory brought in weavers from outside—more "underpaid paupers from abroad"—and paid them even more than the striking weavers were requesting, explaining that they did not object to the demands of the striking weavers but that they did not like to do business with union men. But the strike continued, and on April 6, the owners lodged a charge of conspiracy against two of the strikers—Benjamin Haefeli and Emil Amann—complaining that they had been conspiring "to stop the [workmen] who had taken the places of the strikers." Judge Will Sullivan appeared for these defendants with such foreign names, and he was able to have the charge dismissed on grounds of insufficient evidence. There was also some public sentiment for the strikers, and the *Sun* carried that too. On April 17, the paper carried a long letter to the editor in a "Public Forum" column, written apparently by an old Yankee, which evoked the Declaration of Independence, the founding principles of the Republic, the right of workmen to strike, and so on. One of the owners, in particular, came in for a great deal of criticism. In supporting the striking weavers, the writer of the letter also evoked the intense religious feeling in the district. And in his charge that one of the owners drank beer in the weaving room he reflected the temperance movement, which had a strong hold on many of the old Yankees in that area.

In the end, however, the strikers went back to work, on April 21, 1894—about five weeks after the strike had begun—accepting the same wages as before. Unions had no place in Norwich, it would seem. They only made the situation worse, and people with foreign names were the ones who made trouble. After this brief flare-up, labor union trouble seems to have largely disappeared from Norwich and environs. In a history of Norwich from 1914 to 1964, the city historian reports that "serious labor difficulties have been rare. The one most prolonged was the railroad shop strike of 1922. This resulted in favor of the company."[4]

There was trouble at the Maydole Hammer Company as well in 1894, but there was no strike. On July 28, 1894, the *Sun* reported that the plant would reopen after a "short vacation [which] has been thoroughly enjoyed by all the employees." Near the close of the same year, on December 16, the hammer factory was closed again, "for inventory"; it remained closed for almost a month. On January 5, 1895, the *Sun* announced that the hammer factory would reopen on January 11: "This will be good news to their many employees and also the merchants generally." Again, this was obviously an unpaid period for the employees. By the end of the next month, one of employees of the hammer factory, Timothy Sullivan, had removed himself from Norwich and begun farming in Smyrna.

The depth of the depression in Norwich itself was steadily denied during 1894, but the indices of its presence became clearer and clearer. In a psychological sense, they can be read in the increase in fears and in the rise of frantic explanations for the trouble. Early in the year, the bad news was mostly contained on the front page of the *Sun*—first the coal miners' strikes, then the Pullman strike, referred to as Deb's strike. The front page usually contained the national news in boiler-plate stories, systematically segregated from local news stories on the inside pages. By March, news of Coxey's Army of the unemployed, and its march on Washington, began to appear on both the front page and the inside pages. The front-page stories, emanating from various cities, were relatively factual, and often quasi-sympathetic to the Army. But the inside pages simultaneously began to carry hostile accounts of the probable impact of Coxey's Army on Chenango County; these stories made fun of the local contingent of the Army then gathering in Utica, with plans to march directly down Chenango Valley through Norwich on its way to join the Army in Washington, D.C.

At first these local stories stressed facetiously the value of this march through Norwich as a way of clearing the region of all the tramps and no-goods. Local farmers were warned by the *Sun* of March 27, 1894, to keep their chicken roosts and barns under lock and key. "When the army reaches Washington they will be received with open arms by Uncle Sam's regulars, and at once, either imprisoned, drowned in the Potomac or shot from the mouths of cannons à la the Sepoys in India in 1857." The *Sun* hoped that the company forming in the County would be as large as possible, so that all those undeserving people could get the Sepoy cure in Washington.

On the next day, the *Sun* suggested that so many people in Norwich were eligible for Coxey's Army that a game of chance would have to be played to see who would have the honor of joining: "The allotment [for Norwich] is 200 and as there are 500 out of work here the chances will be about one in two for whites, one to one for colored and one to three for dagos and others." The *Sun*'s admission that 500 (out of a population of 5,500) were out of work indicates that the situation had worsened significantly since the factory inspection in 1893, when 687 people were working in Norwich factories, not including other places of business. It is clear that there were few unemployed in 1893 as compared to 1894.

On April 9, the *Sun* reported almost approvingly that Commander Coxey had issued directions to his subalterns "to refuse all applications from foreigners of every description except colored gents. This will of course bar Dagos, Hungarians, Bulgarians, Magyars, Esquimaux and Poles and will [eliminate] the army of anarchists, highbinders and the worst class of criminals that have threatened the movement from the start with division, subtraction and failure. We are glad to note that the African race is thus honored by being allowed to join and have no doubt but that from this town the major part of the command will be recruited from this class." Noteworthy in the *Sun*'s reporting is the fact that the Irish-Americans are not singled out; in Norwich at least some of them had already achieved enough stature and influence to militate against open hostility. But there is a beginning hostility to the "African race"—a notable change for an area that was so firmly a part of the early Abolitionist movement. As early as 1860, the decennial census showed that there were 139 "free colored" living in Norwich; after the Civil War, a fair number of ex-slaves found their way into Norwich. Their acceptance in the community was reflected in the occasional proud reports in the *Sun* of the birth of "the first colored baby" in one village or another.

After such extensive coverage, it is significant that the *Sun* carried no information as to whether the Utica contingent ever marched through Norwich. On May 3, 1894, the *Sun* reported on the front page that Coxey had been arrested on the Capitol grounds in Washington, and that the March was over. However much the March had been presented as something abhorrent to Norwich and to Chenango County, there was no note of triumph over the denouement. By then some of the people in Norwich had begun to identify with the members of the Army, many of whom were much like themselves.

Yet this insight did not free the residents from a search for other sources for the trouble. In the midst of the stories on Coxey's March, "Jew pack peddlers" in Norwich came in for attack in the *Sun* for April 9: "Every cent paid to one of these brigands takes just so much out of our town, and makes our merchants, who do all in their power to help build up the town, so much poorer. . . . Beware of pack peddlers. Shun them. The majority of them are thieves, robbers, thugs, escaped convicts and murderers."

Itinerant farm labor also became the enemy during the depression, although it too had been a part of the County's labor force for many years. As the availability of this kind of labor increased and many unemployed men roamed the countryside looking for work, the harshness of the attitude toward the "tramps" was extreme. The local police officer, charged with the responsibility of ridding the village of these itinerant workers, put a sign on his door, "No tramps wanted in Norwich"; and all that were apprehended were sentenced to six months in the penitentiary. A number of people arrested had Irish names; the majority were young men in their twenties and thirties.

Even the hop pickers, who were traditionally needed in the County during the peak of the season, were issued warnings by the *Sun* in August of that year: "Norwich has no use for tramps and vagabonds and all who value their liberty and wish to rusticate a few days in the hop country had better give this town a wide berth." Obviously some of the hop-picking jobs were needed for local people that year, and a task once reserved for "tramps," women, and children had been taken over by many of the farmers for themselves.

As the year progressed, the pattern of denial and admission of economic trouble in the County became more and more irrational, so that within the same newspaper story both statements were made: the trouble exists outside of Norwich; the trouble exists here in Norwich as elsewhere. Yet as late as November of that year, the *Sun* published an article on "Prosperous Norwich," which stated that "in spite of the loud cry made in various sections regarding prevailing hard times and business depression the merchants of Norwich are all doing a prosperous business. Our factories and industries are all running and on full time. . . ." Yet the chant by then had become a meaningless litany. By January 11, 1895, the *Sun* admitted in a lead editorial that 1894 had been a terrible year: "On the whole, if we have come through 1894 with enough to eat and wear and a shelter over our heads, if no awful griefs have bowed us down and we have fairly good health, then, really and truly, we have much to be thankful for at the beginning of 1895."

There seems little doubt that during the depression years of 1893 and 1894, Norwich suffered economically and psychologically, and that this suffering called forth a virulent nativism. But there was a growing self-doubt and doubt of the system that represented a more insightful approach. Some of this insight was forced on Norwich residents by the reality of what was happening: they had immediate data on many different kinds of people, so that stereotypes were continually being overturned by events. There is very little evidence that Irish-Americans in Norwich were openly blamed for what was happening; there were too many Irish descendants who held positions of trust and responsibility in the community. On another dimension, some of Norwich's impending decline was masked. As the hill farms began to fail and people left them, there was a temporary increase of population and activity in Norwich, even as the overall population of the County was declining. In the midst of the worst depression year, Norwich could still remain somewhat hopeful, partly because there was some emergent correction of the social paranoia through the leadership of people like Will Sullivan.

No such correction existed in Smyrna. The nativist ideas from Norwich were carried daily into the hills around Smyrna by the *Sun,* which arrived only a day late from Norwich. There the ideas were nourished by very little else but fear and a rapidly declining economy. There was practically no contact with "foreigners" that might have modified attitudes; and there was relatively little leadership to combat the stereotypes. Here and there, a sane voice would be heard in the community around Smyrna. The principal of the village school, for one, would try from time to time to temper the stereotypes that clustered in the hills like bees around rotting apples.

But by and large, the nativism grew unchecked. It tended to focus on one family—the Sullivans who moved to Smyrna in the period of the depression. Earlier the Stacks had been tolerated, smiled over, endured. But the Sullivans were different. Timothy was related to Judge Sullivan, who was considered a dangerous radical. The Judge was also a leader in St. Paul's Roman Catholic Church in Norwich; and there were people in the hills around Smyrna who claimed that they knew people who had seen guns in the basement of St. Paul's. The people in Norwich came to know better about St. Paul's, but Smyrna would retain its opinion about Roman Catholics—forever, it would seem. One week after Ella Stack Sullivan's death in 1926, the Ku Klux Klan would burn a cross on St. Patrick's Day on a hill within sight of the Sullivan farmhouse; with her death, Timothy was probably the last Catholic left in the village. By then, there were already intimations that Al Smith was becoming too powerful nationwide; at the time of his presidential candidacy in 1928, Smyrna would become the center for Klan activity for the whole of Chenango County.

⊰ 8 ⊱

Two Chenango
Childhoods

> The rate of growth of personality through all these
> earlier phases is truly amazing. We realize this more
> and more as we begin to analyze the enormous num-
> ber of rather exquisite judgments which one uses in
> directing one's life in an incoherent culture among
> people with many specific limitations and individual
> abilities and liabilities.
> —Sullivan, *The Interpersonal Theory of Psychiatry*

BY a fortunate coincidence, there was another child growing up in Chenango County at about the same time as Harry Stack Sullivan— the cultural anthropologist Ruth Fulton Benedict; and she has written of her own childhood experiences more explicitly than Sullivan but in many of the same dimensions. So it is that the tantalizingly limited glimpses of Sullivan's childhood (before school) that appear in his published and un- published writings attain more depth and meaning when they are juxta- posed with Ruth Benedict's early life. They did not know each other until they were adults, for their families were separated by ethnic allegiances and social class, and by the geography of isolated farms and different communities within the arbitrary unity of the County. Thus they grew up in households as different as one can imagine, as Benedict once told a col- league.[1] Yet, as Sullivan was to emphasize so strongly in his theories, the accidents of different life experiences do not separate people from their common human heritage and common responses to the problems of growing up in "an incoherent culture." Although they were unknown to each other as children, the two found themselves in later life working together to find the underlying patterns that would make sense of the be- wildering, conflicting values and messages transmitted to the child by sig- nificant adults.

Until Harry started school, his only significant encounters were with adults, mainly women. His father was withdrawn and shy and busy all day on the farm. His Aunt Maggie was often a visitor in the household; for a short time, she taught in the country school nearby and lived at the farm. His own mother was a shadowy figure at best during the early years; it was his grandmother who was the continuous and important figure in his early life. In his writings he often mentions the role of a maiden aunt, of parents, and so on, but there are few references to a grandmother. In lecturing to a group of psychiatrists in training on some of the important areas to be watched in eliciting a life history from a patient, he once made a rather important reference to a grandmother: "Then I ask who, besides the parents, was chronically or frequently in the home in his first seven years. For example, if grandma—or a maiden aunt, or even the sheriff—was very frequently in the home during those years, this may leave a quite permanent effect.... Sorting out such data is truly impressive to a great many people. They may have actually forgotten that grandma was the one bright spot in the home in their first seven years, and are glad to be reminded of it."[2]

His reluctance to define his grandmother's importance to him, whether good or bad, may have stemmed from the usual attitude of an American child trying to overcome the foreign influence of the home environment, as he begins to attend school. Indeed at some basic level, Harry was probably ashamed of both his grandmother and his mother when he began to make contact with other children in the Smyrna school; his aunt Margaret was another matter, for she would eventually teach in the New York City school system. It was his grandmother's speech that set him aside in the Smyrna school; in 1964 there were still old-timers in the area who would imitate Harry's childhood brogue without being asked. Thus he was considered the child of immigrants instead of the grandchild, partly because there were no other Irish-American children in Smyrna. This he considered a problem peculiar to America: "These successive waves of immigrants have become the targets for the hostilities that have grown up in the people who have lived here longer. One group after another, they have been regarded more or less as public enemies. And their children have grown up with the dubious asset of being the children of public enemies, regarded by their confreres who have been one generation longer in America as being anything from somewhat human—but, of course, of foreign parentage—to definitely vicious ingredients of the school society."[3]

At home there were the conflicting values between his grandmother Stack's standards for behavior and his parents' admonitions. And his parents had different ideas one from another, in particular about the importance of attending church in Sherburne. Since Harry was an only child, these differences from one adult to another offered some serious handicaps. In his writings, Sullivan particularly takes note of the child of thirty months—his age when he came under the care of his grandmother Stack—as being handicapped by this kind of confusion: "Insofar as the authority figures are confusing to the child and insofar as the authority situations are incongruous from time to time so that, according to the measure of the child's maturing abilities and experience, there is no making sense of them—then, even before the end of the thirtieth month, let us say, we see instances in which the child is already beginning to suffer a deterioration of development of high-grade foresight."[4]

"The close friends of his childhood were the livestock on the farm," his colleague Clara Thompson reports. "With them he felt comfortable and less lonely."[5] He also usually had a dog; and one of his cousins describes the dog he had when he was about fourteen or fifteen as following Harry around the farm, completely attentive to his master.

Before he started school, his playmates were imaginary. In Sullivan's writings, published and unpublished, the child growing up on a lonely farm, without access to other children, is described as dependent on a rich fantasy life. Sometimes the fantasy life is so real that it becomes of great interest to the parents; this may result, as Sullivan reports, in "an exceedingly disturbing sort of experience. . . . without intending to communicate anything to the authority figures, the child may speak aloud, just because this is exercise of his vocal abilities and part of his imaginary play; the child's ideas, or rudimentary ideas, are picked up by the parent who hears this, and rewards or punishments, particularly the latter, are poured out on the child, to his quite profound mystification."[6]

His contacts with relatives outside his own household were for the most part intermittent and confusing. The Sullivan cousins lived too far away for any meaningful contact. Some of James Stack's children and grandchildren attended the church in Sherburne where Harry went with his parents. And Uncle Ed came to the farmhouse periodically, bringing his son, Leo, seven years older than Harry, and Leo's stepmother, Marcia Lamb, a vivacious, pretty woman who had a certain gift for sharp retorts and a realistic appraisal of people in the larger world. But this family was not a part of the church-going Stack family in Sherburne, and that too must have represented a mystery. The only other first cousins who came to visit were Uncle John's children, who lived in distant parts of the country and occasionally visited in the summer. But all these visitors became part of the myths that his mother and his grandmother told him about— the Stacks and their mission in life. There was never enough time to study these real people and match them against the legend, so they continued to endure as part myth, as part growing awareness that the myth did not fit the persons who appeared at the farm from time to time.

In later years, he sometimes pondered over his own lot in childhood, as if he were reviewing the case of a patient. The disguise is thin; he is talking about himself:

Now what is the case with the . . . only child on a rather large farm (not large enough to have tenants with children, but one that has quite a lot of country around it, which diminishes visits from other children) [who] grows up rather largely alone, excepting for other significant adults and occasional visits, which are such special occasions that they color the visitors. . . . If you see an uncle and aunt with the cousins—oh, every six or seven days [or] every two or three weeks, through the years—they're rather taken for granted and become subject to . . . as good an appraisal as one's already warped personality will permit. But if, on the other hand, this uncle and aunt and cousins show up only . . . [for] something like an annual visit . . . well, there is such an aura from the views of one's parents that [it] hides illuminating facts from the person, and one just has a mythology of these people that doesn't get itself reversed in a capable direction very much.

If, for example, one of the cousins is reputed to be a wonderfully good boy, and so on, and all one's experience with him is that he is a mean little bastard who gets one into all sorts of trouble, then the net result is a profound feeling . . . [of] "confusion," in the sense that one knows there's a big mistake in the business, but one doesn't know whether there is something wrong with oneself that calls out hostility in the cousin or whether the people who think he's wonderful are just deceived. One's feeling of security about one's judgment and particularly in dealing with the cousin, is very small.[7]

The "wonderfully good boy" in this account is probably Leo, who came oftener than the other cousins. In his retrospective account, Sullivan notes that there is an element of insecurity in having a "family visit thrust upon [such an isolated child], coupled with anger at being imposed on."[8]

Leo's widow, Nina, who was herself a childhood friend of Leo's, has described this early relationship: "[Leo] was always held up as a model boy to Harry. . . . I remember that Leo often spent several weeks in the summer with Harry on the farm. I do not remember that Harry ever stayed with Leo at the hotel in South Otselic though he may have visited there. I imagine the farm with hay-loads to ride, etc., had more glamour for small boys than the hotel."[9]

However much Harry resented Leo, it is obvious that throughout the rest of his life he tried to emulate him in a number of ways, so that there remained a "confusion" about Leo's values and standards. Leo's importance never faded for Harry. When Timothy Sullivan died in 1931 and the farmhouse was abandoned, Harry returned to his home in New York City with a picture of Leo at about the age of twelve, although apparently there were no pictures of himself at that age. Perhaps the Sullivans did not have much money for studio pictures, or it may be that Sullivan destroyed his own pictures and saved the one of Leo, dressed in finery and lounging almost opulently in one of the sitting rooms at his father's hotel at the time of his father's second marriage. At that time Leo was almost twelve and Harry almost five. At that age, a difference of seven years is very large indeed; yet it seems entirely likely that this was the only child that Harry saw much of in the years before he went to the Smyrna schoolhouse when he was five and a half.

Near the end of childhood the need for compeers arises, according to Sullivan, and even the isolated child, who has had little access to other than imaginary playmates, now begins to imagine real people as playmates:

As childhood progresses, a time is reached when there is very rapid acceleration of change in the character of fantasy; and this change is in the direction of burying, losing interest in, forgetting, or modifying what may in very early childhood have been truly incredibly fantastic imaginary playmates, and toward a direction of attempting to personify playmates very like oneself. . . . But even in the case of children who have grown up with no possibility of playing with other children, who are born on remote farms, or in other isolated places, this change in play or change in imagination appears. The child now begins to have rather realistic imaginary playmates, while before a great deal of his imaginary accouterments, his imaginary toys, and so on were strikingly fantastic.[10]

Ruth Benedict has written poignantly of her own imaginary playmate on another farm in Chenango County, and of the few moments of happiness that she treasured in childhood—usually by herself, for her sister, eighteen months younger, played only a small part in her "real life." As a child Ruth played a game about

the beautiful country on the other side of the west hill where a family lived who had a little girl about my age. This imaginary playmate and her family lived a warm, friendly life without recriminations and brawls. So far as I can remember I and the little girl mostly explored hand in hand the unparalleled beauty of the country over the hill. About the time I was five my mother thought I was old enough to stand the climb up the west hill, and one day I went up with her and my aunts. I had been promised that we'd go up to the top and look over. It was a long climb for my legs, and I was very hot and tired when at last we came to the edge of the pasture and looked down into the rolling hills beyond—and *Uncle George's farm.* Instead of the wonderland I'd pictured, it was all familiar and anything-but-romantic territory. We had driven through the ravine to Uncle George's every holiday since I could remember. And that was all. I never played again with my little playmate over the hill.[11]

The farm that was the important home for Ruth Benedict in her early childhood—she lived there for most of the period from the age of one until she was seven, and she spent her summers there for many years afterwards—belonged to her maternal grandparents, the Shattucks. Although the isolation of Sullivan and Benedict as farm children was significant for both of them, their isolation from each other was even more remarkable. Ruth's maternal grandparents were well-to-do for that time and place. They owned a proper valley farm, about three miles from the village of Norwich, with a substantial two-story house and well-maintained barns; the Stack farmhouse to which Harry would move when he was in his third year was a story-and-a-half structure set in the rocky soil of the hill country and surrounded by rickety outbuildings.

As one measure of the substantial position of the Shattucks in that community, the grandparents had sent at least two of their daughters—Bertrice, Ruth's mother, and Hettie—to Vassar College. This was the proper advanced study for the girl-children of prosperous people in New York State at that time. In due course, Ruth and her sister would also attend Vassar. At about the same time, Nina Brown from South Otselic would attend Vassar too and would subsequently marry Harry's cousin Leo.

For both Ruth and Harry, the mother's family was the important one; and each of these families had its own myths. Benedict's family myth was Old American and Shattuck. Both sets of Ruth's grandparents lived in Norwich in her childhood, but one set, the Shattucks, were insiders and the other set, the Fultons, were newcomers. This difference is reflected in Benedict's evaluation of her background, written in 1941, when she was already a renowned anthropologist.[12] On her mother's side, her Shattuck ancestors journeyed west from Connecticut to New York in 1799, she reports, "on a bob-sled, with a cow tied on behind to give milk for the babies. Six of [my] ancestors fought in the Revolution." It was this side of the family that was considered the elite of the County, for the Daughters of the American Revolution is still the most respected women's organization in the area. On Ruth's father's side, the Fultons did not qualify for this honor and were considered newcomers to the County—they had arrived there a half century or more after the old settlers. Benedict describes how her great-great-grandfather had come to the United States after the Revolution, fleeing from his home in Nova Scotia "because he dared to propose a toast to George Washington at a public banquet." But Ruth's grandfather, a physician, did not arrive in Norwich until 1876, bringing with him his English-born wife and family from Michigan; at that time, Ruth's father was nineteen years old and already slated to become a physician, so he did not tarry long in the County. Thus Ruth's father was a real outsider in the County.

When Ruth was born in 1887, her parents were living in New York City where her father was a successful surgeon. A year later, her family came back to Norwich to live with the Shattucks because of her father's mysterious illness; in December of that year, a second child, Margery, was born in Norwich; and three months later, Ruth's father died.

In 1892—the year that Harry was born—Ruth's mother took a job on the faculty of Norwich High School, and she stayed in town during the school week with her two children and an unmarried sister, returning to the farm for the weekends. Ruth was then five, and she began school in the town either in that year or the next. When Harry came of school age, he would go to the village school in Smyrna, rather than to the inferior country school. Thus each family, in its own way, made sure that the child received the best education available in each locality.

In 1894, when the depression was acute, both Harry and Ruth left Norwich; in both instances, economic factors had a bearing. But Ruth's mother left Norwich under more benign circumstances than Harry's parents; as reported in a headline in the Norwich *Sun* for July 19, 1894, "Mrs. Fulton" had acquired "A Better Position," teaching school in St. Joseph, Missouri, where she was to receive a salary of $1,000 a year, $400 more than she was earning in Norwich. In spite of the fact that Ruth Benedict describes her mother as almost a psychological cripple, it seems clear that Bertrice Fulton had a commendable need to be self-sufficient economically and a drive, unusual for women in that period, to emerge as a person in her own right in spite of her widowhood. Always accompanied by an unmarried sister, she continued to move around with her children, seeking a better job. After two years in St. Joseph, she got a job as a "lady principal of Pillsbury Academy" in Owatoma, Minnesota; thereafter she took a job as a librarian in Buffalo at a lower salary in order to have more job security.

Yet Chenango County remained the continuity for the Fulton family; and the children—and the mother if she could—returned there each summer. In the County, the definition of all this travel and success was an occasion for ambivalent speculation. Local people feel rejected by anyone who leaves the area permanently, particularly if he has been well educated and has a profession. Because the structure of the Valley geographically and socially is a closed circle, any news of its sons and daughters is a recurring story. Thus the various moves made by Ruth's mother as a widow in order to be productive and self-sufficient economically were carefully noted in the *Sun*. An atmosphere of keeping score pervades all conversations about wandering children of the "old families." What happened to them if they chose to remain in the outside world? Did they prosper? The answer is never an unqualified yes, since indeed each life ends in death—sometimes prematurely—and there are disappointments along the way.

The Fultons, like the Shattucks, were staunch members of the local Baptist church; but they were outsiders nonetheless. While the Shattucks are still mentioned by knowledgeable people in Norwich as the grandparents of Ruth Benedict, no one mentions the Fulton grandparents as having been residents of Norwich. This attitude toward the Fultons is expressed even in Benedict's autobiographical sketch. She mentions only one Fulton relative—an uncle of her father's of whom she felt frightened; she does not report that her father's family were living in Norwich during her childhood; and her close friend and colleague, Margaret Mead, also omitted this fact from her account and chronology of Benedict's life.[13]

Although Benedict glorified her dead father throughout her life, she seems to have had little meaningful contact with the living members of her father's family. It seems possible that the death of her father was somehow looked upon by both the Shattuck family and neighbors as some divine justice visited upon a family who had dared to aspire to fame and fortune beyond the County. In this context, Bertrice Shattuck Fulton's move into the larger world after her husband's death takes on a heroic character.

Various versions of Ruth Benedict's life, including her own, report that she grew up in poverty; but relatively speaking, this is misleading. She herself reports on a certain skimpiness in the household affairs after her mother took a more secure job in Buffalo at less money, so that they suffered a loss of income at the very time they began to know city people with a higher economic status than their own. But both Fulton girls went to private secondary school and to Vassar College on scholarships. Upon her graduation from Vassar Ruth went to Europe with some of her classmates, as was customary for the well-to-do college graduates of that day. Her first published work was an article for the *Sun* written in May 1910 describing her stay in Switzerland.

Different as were the childhoods of Benedict and Sullivan, his later theory on childhood would cover the unique experience of each. Sullivan's theory would be put together without knowledge of the patterning of Benedict's childhood, but he undestood how accidents of fate could color anyone's life. The differences may be large, but the reaction to these accidents in "career lines," as Sullivan termed the particular and individual chain of events that impinge upon a person, is human and therefore available for study. For example, death had an intense meaning for both Sullivan and Benedict, not alone from family history but from the nature of the society in which they grew up. Harry was guarded against death and sheltered by his family because of the reality of the childhood epidemics that had decimated the Sullivan family. Benedict has written specifically of her mother's grief over her father's death and of how it affected her. As Ruth grew older, she was told that her weeping mother had taken her to look at her father in his coffin and had told her to remember him. She did not remember the scene consciously, but she tended to feel that it explained her excruciating misery whenever she saw her mother weep: "Certainly from my earliest childhood I recognized two worlds, whether or not my knowledge was born at that tragic scene at my father's coffin—the world of my father, which was the world of death and which was beautiful, and the world of confusion and explosive weeping which I repudiated. I did not love my mother; I resented her cult of grief, and her worry and concern about little things. But I could always retire to my other world, and to this world my father belonged. I identified him with everything calm and beautiful that came my way."[14]

Death, which had a majestic beauty for the child, could be in itself puzzling and many-faceted.[15] Margaret Mead has reported that Ruth as a small child learned of the suicide of a "servant girl" on a neighboring farm and discovered that her Shattuck grandparents "condemned the girl out of hand"; but in the school, which her grandparents approved of, she read about the "noble Cato," who also committed suicide. "It did not make sense to her that suicide should be applauded among the ancient Romans and at the same time be execrated in [central] New York State. Yet if one tried to say this to the people one loved most in the world, they not only would not agree but would be hurt and shocked and alienated. The world was so ordered that one must at whatever cost live up to the ethical standards not of ancient Rome but of modern America."[16]

Some fifty years later, Sullivan would discriminate between normal grief and morbid grief as if he were writing about Ruth Benedict's mother or his own mother, who treasured the baby clothes of the lost children. He reports first on normal grieving:

The first day after the loss, since intimacies interpenetrate so much of life, it is almost impossible not to be reminded of the loss by any little thing— even the position of the saltcellar on the table, for instance. But each time this happens, you might say, the power of that particular association to evoke the illusion of the absent one is lessened. . . . Thus, immediately after a loss, the position of the saltcellar may be reminiscent to you of dear John, because it was always placed half-way between you and John. But the next time you see the saltcellar, you might become a little bored; its power to evoke dear John is diminished by the very fact that you have clarified the associational link with him. And so it goes: by erasing one tie after another, and releasing the personality to move on into life and seek satisfactions by cooperation or collaboration with other people, grief protects us from making a retreat. . . . The experience is, of course, an extremely painful one, but the pain diminishes day by day; fewer and fewer things have the power to evoke this erasing process, which I insist grief is.[17]

But a person who suffers from morbid grieving is not interested in erasing grief, Sullivan thought. His description fits the pattern of grief shown by Ruth's mother. Sullivan termed it "morbid," but it may have been a fairly common pattern for women in a period of history when it was difficult to be creative in any other way than through one's family and children:

Like all the other dynamisms of living, grief can be distorted into a horrible caricature of its function by certain complex operations. It becomes dangerous and destructive to the extent that the erasing function is abandoned and grief becomes an adequate mode of life. . . . Under those circumstances, the self, of course, is not engaged in erasing processes, for the self-system is solely concerned with the maintenance of security. That is,

*if the loss throws one terribly open to anxiety and to the loss of one's self-re-
spect and prestige in the community, the erasing action of the self will not
appear.* Instead, these associational links will become a preoccupation in
many ways analogous to any other substitutive process. . . . We find that,
instead of progressively losing its power to evoke tragic recollections, the
saltcellar is now surrounded by a very elegant doily, or is in some other
fashion enhanced and made a symbol, extravagantly fortified in its power
to evoke the lost one. [Emphasis mine][18]

At a fairly nonspecific level, Sullivan's theory would encompass the
social-class pressures of both childhoods, his and Benedict's. Both of
them were isolated children on the farm, in spite of the fact that both had
access to several adults, particularly during the summer months—hired
help and visiting relatives. Sullivan's isolation was intensified by the barriers of being thought of by neighbor children as foreign and Catholic.
Superficially, one might say that Ruth Benedict escaped such isolation;
indeed it was merely a more subtle isolation. Her sister, only a baby when
the father died, was never charged with the mission of remembering her
father, and with somehow making up to the mother for the father's death.
The mother was a successful career woman in a day when a married
woman with family resources available (as with the Shattucks and the
Fultons) did not make such an adjustment after widowhood, particularly
in rural America. As Ruth moved around from school to school in the
early years, there was seldom enough continuity to allow her to confide in
a special friend. And finally, Ruth Benedict had only her Shattuck grandparents' home as a shelter of continuity in her early years; that shelter in
itself emphasized her differences from the children in the surrounding
countryside. By the age of nine, she had traveled more than most adults
in Chenango County, and she, too, like Harry Sullivan, was an outsider.

The stresses of these two childhoods are only somewhat more intense
than those of any child growing up in America. But the isolation of both
children seems to have alerted them to the inconsistencies of the values
that were set before them. In a thinly disguised autobiographical note,
Sullivan writes of this knowledge and of the "exquisite judgment" required for the child to find his way around in an "incoherent culture."

A boy a little over five years of age for the first time observed his father's
penis, semi-erect, and hastened to the mother and maiden (maternal)
aunt with the report that "Daddy has a great big dickey, and it's made of
wood." The information proved extremely disconcerting to the auditors,
and his interest in other people's penes was dissociated. Within six
months, however, he, in company of some men, witnessed coitus of a bull
and a cow, and reported this interesting event to the self-same audience,
with a notably different reception. The aunt's reaction of shocked virtue
proved amusing to the mother, who refused to be chagrined. The juvenile

then prehended several personal facts, including the unwisdom of discussing such events with women. The dissociation was lifted, it now being necessary merely to suppress behavior (including speech) about such things when in the women's company.[19]

The aunt is his mother's unmarried sister Margaret. In the story about his father's penis, the boy is just past five, so the event took place in the period immediately following Harry's birthday on February 21. "Within six months," a bull was apparently brought to the farm for breeding purposes. In Chenango County, August (which is "within six months") is often considered the proper month for breeding, since the calf would then be born late enough in the spring so that it would have a better chance for survival in the hill country. Sullivan is obviously reporting on actual events. Thus his use of "six months" is again a clue to an autobiographical event, as "two and a half" was.

Like Harry, Ruth Benedict was exposed to trouble and upset at an early age, and this necessitated moving around and being cared for by various relatives. In order to achieve any temporary stability with an array of relatives, she had to be unusually perceptive of the inconsistent standards set for her by different adults in her immediate environment.

Benedict writes of "running away" to find her grandfather Shattuck in a distant field where he was haying, against the admonition of her mother who wanted her to stay in an elder patch near the farmhouse. On the way home from the field on the wagon, she confided in her grandfather that her mother did not know she had gone away from the elder patch. And her grandfather smiled and entered into a conspiracy of silence about her infraction of the rules, as long as her mother did not ask where she had been. But her mother did ask her subsequently, when her grandfather was not present, and she lied. Later in the evening, her grandfather asked her privately whether her mother had asked her whereabouts; and she lied to her grandfather and told him that her mother had not asked. She notes that it did not bother her to lie to her mother, but she had lied to her grandfather and "that was a different matter"; she reports that she could not eat any supper. Her grandfather was very important to her: "Life was more complicated than I had supposed, and somehow, somehow after that I must plan so that I wouldn't have to *lie to Grandfather.*"[20]

For both Ruth Benedict and Harry Stack Sullivan, Chenango County, with its precise but conflicting value systems, spurred them on to find answers in the larger world: Benedict seeking value systems of other societies as a way of understanding the incoherencies in her early family and community environment; Sullivan searching for the relation between outworn value systems and the sickness that infected gifted adolescents in the delicate transition from the early environment to the larger world. Many of the same tragedies all around them in the small world of Chenango County determined their interests in adult life; and for both of them school represented the first avenue toward larger ideas, broader horizons than those found in the home. Significantly, they would both spend the summer of 1948—the last summer of life for each of them—at a UNESCO conference in Poděbrady, Czechoslovakia, on "Childhood Education Towards World-Mindedness."

In both lives, the correction of the confusion of values had come from the world beyond the early family situation. For Harry, the main correction lay in the preadolescent era and the finding of a friend, a "chum" as he termed it. For Ruth Benedict, the correction probably was more urbane but also more lonely; by the time she was eleven and living in Buffalo, she had been exposed to a variety of school environments, but she does not seem to have found a close friend of her own age. This moving around had its own problems; and when she moved to Buffalo, her "ungovernable tantrums" increased for a while. Yet there must have been a personal stimulation, a meeting of people with wider vistas, that did not come to Harry until he left Smyrna in his seventeenth year.

An old-time resident of Norwich, who knew the Shattuck family well, once told me sympathetically that Ruth as an adolescent had a reputation for wearing unkempt clothes and being personally "unhygienic" when she was in Norwich in the summertime; the gifted young had a hard time in a town like Norwich, this woman thought. Harry, too, was thought of as queer and remote by Smyrna neighbors, although no one has ever commented to me on his personal appearance as being unkempt. Yet both Ruth and Harry found the intellectual stimulation that defined them as "gifted." The question of what "gifted" means haunted Sullivan's life and thought. All too often, he thought, the gifted were simply the ones who lucked through, who had not been crushed by the environment. For that he gave a lot of credit to the public school, which introduced the child—particularly the child or grandchild of immigrants—to a larger world. In part, he had lucked through; he would think that Ruth Benedict also lucked through. What were the ingredients that, however painfully, forced them out into another world, in search of larger and more consistent values? And was the warping, the agony, of that search necessary? For him, the movement from Smyrna to the larger world would almost end tragically, with mental confusion so obvious that he might have spent his life in a public institution. How was this to be avoided? Did society have to exact such risks for moving the young into productive adult life? And was it possible that all of us were potential geniuses, except for those who had suffered brain damage of some kind? None of us realize more than a small part of our human potential, he believed. It is foolish, then, to speculate on the measurement of the realized potential, when all of us are so definitely limited by the time and space into which we are born. This theme recurs in all of Sullivan's writings, as it does in Ruth Benedict's. He never engaged in speculation on the effect of heredity versus environment. Testing the intelligence of a child by devices contrived by a more advantaged denizen of another culture-complex made no sense to him. Time enough to look at the variables of heredity after the child had been freed from the crippling effects of poverty, restricting custom, limited schooling, accidents of geography, and the environing stereotypes. He understood this from his own life and from his observation of the lonely ones in the larger society.

On September 17, 1948, Ruth Benedict died in New York City, shortly after returning from the conference in Czechoslovakia; and Sullivan wrote of her death in an obituary that was published shortly after his own death. He ended the memorial piece with the almost wistful statement, "Ruth Benedict had come to be at home in the world."[21] He seemed to feel that in the end she had achieved a peace that he would never find. At the same time, there is an understanding of the fact that both of them had suffered alienation in their childhoods; he mentions in the same piece that Ruth Benedict had "finished secondary school in the Chenango Valley of upstate New York"—a correct statement of his own schooling rather than hers, for she had finished secondary school at St. Margaret's School for Girls in Buffalo. Yet the human paths by which both of them had attained some degree of world-mindedness went back to Chenango County, and in this there was coincidence enough to please his Irish fancy and inspire him to a slight exaggeration.

& 9 *&*
Going to School in Smyrna

> The maturation of the need for compeers ... ushers
> in what it seems best to call the *juvenile era,* which is
> particularly the period of formal education, as re-
> quired by law, in this nation at least.
> —Sullivan, *The Interpersonal Theory of Psychiatry*

U NTIL Harry began public school at the age of five and a half in the
village of Smyrna, one might say that he was living in an alien
world by comparison with the other children around him. His contacts
with people were limited to relatives who were still not assimilated into
the old Yankee society of Chenango County. Nor were there enough relatives in his daily life to offer any broad view of the various possible stages
of assimilation into American society. Going to school was the most
important transition so far in his life, for it forced him to look at the
farmhouse on the hill above Smyrna and its occupants in quite another
dimension. "This is the first developmental stage in which the limitations
and peculiarities of the home as a socializing influence begin to be open
to remedy," he writes.[1]

He was a small child for his age, slight and eager, with blondish curly
hair. He already knew how to read, being much more familiar with the
written word than the spoken one. His grandmother Stack, who spoke
Gaelic at least part of the time, still dominated the house on the hill, and
his own mother was apt to be quiet when Grandma Stack was around.
Yet it was his mother who took him to school that first day for registration. She was "all dressed up" for the occasion, and this was newsworthy
in the village. She usually came to the village dressed as a farm woman,
with a sunbonnet on her head; everybody knew that Ella Stack, as she is
still referred to, was Irish, and that was why she drove a two-wheeled cart
when she brought eggs and butter in to the village. To suddenly see her
looking like other mothers was so startling to the villagers that the memory of her appearance still lingers on.

The school in Smyrna, a two-story clapboard structure on one of the main streets of the village, was imposing by comparison with the one-room school houses in the country districts. By 1898 the village school included all grades from primary through high school, with the lower grades housed on the lower story and the high school on the upper. The pupils were almost entirely village children who lived in far more elegant houses than the small farmhouse on the hill. Their language was difficult for Harry to understand at times. And his own brogue, plus his preco-ciousness in knowing how to comprehend rather complicated words, made him an easy butt for ridicule by the village children.

Throughout his life, Sullivan considered himself more visual-minded than auditory-minded, and he sometimes found it difficult to avoid mis-pronouncing words. He related this difficulty to his early experience:

One of the first great embarrassments I had [was] in my own juvenile era. I had learned to read before I went to school, but apparently there are some very common words that never bumped into me in my private reading. And one day, in the second grade, I came in the primer or what-ever it was to the astonishing combination of letters t-o-g-e-t-h-e-r and it gave me pause. It was new. I hadn't seen it before. And I was encouraged by dear teacher, and so I said "to-get-her" and there were many guffaws from my colleagues. . . . What I've done since with many another word, usually without knowing it, arises from the fact that a good deal of my vocabulary was acquired from acquaintance with symbols of words before I heard them. That is somewhat exceptional, [but] it is not so ex-ceptional in isolated children. . . . You might have some difficulty [under-standing me] if I said "surruptuous" to you . . . but "surruptuous" was what I [once] produced as a string of [phonemes] for "surreptitious." I was a bit too lazy to struggle with all the syllables in the printed word. I had a perfect idea of what it meant, . . . but it took me . . . some thirty years to be sufficiently embarrassed at my condensation to get it right oc-casionally.[2]

He also had a curiosity about words, and a new word would invariably send him to the dictionary in search of an exact meaning. Sometimes this made his formal concepts sound austere and complicated to his col-leagues and students, and he would be criticized for the difficulty of his expression for almost all of his professional life. He had learned, perhaps from the early encounter with children in grade school, to disregard this kind of criticism at one level, even to act disdainful of it; but it effectively barred him from communicativeness at times, and kept him overly criti-cal of his own writings and reluctant to publish before many revisions had taken place.

He had an early interest in science and in learning the scientific names for animals, plants, fossils, and so on, and throughout his life he retained a delight in using words derived from Latin or Greek, sometimes to the consternation of his colleagues. He comments on this pattern in himself and its meaning:

One thing may be noticed which has a bearing on events in the juvenile era: this is simply that some people have a curious lack of facility for using the Anglo-Saxon. While it is practically impossible to talk English without using words derived from Anglo-Saxon, to some people words of Greek or Latin derivation seem to be much more attractive, more welcome, and more frequently used than their equivalents from the Anglo-Saxon. I, being one of these people, can tell you that a person may use words derived from Latin and Greek because Latin and Greek roots have been mixed up in the development of science. I started a science education very young, and was enamored of the precise reference which science had conferred on these Greek and Latin roots. That, however, doesn't explain those instances in which the use of the Anglo-Saxon becomes practically vestigial wherever a good Latin- or Greek-derived word can be used instead. If a person grows up in the home of a Latin or Greek professor, it probably isn't strange. But it is of great interest when a person has grown up in a situation in which there was no obvious reason for distrust of the Anglo-Saxon, and in which it was the prevailing form of English used, and yet goes through life thereafter using chiefly words derived from Latin and Greek. It may be that he found in the acculturation in school, and in the educational possibilities that opened to him there, something much more attractive than anything he had come to expect at home.[3]

Here, as elsewhere in his writings, Sullivan fails to spell out another set of variables in his attitudes about language—his ethnic and religious background. He does not, for instance, mention in this passage his familiarity with Latin words from attending church. Being Irish and Catholic in rural America at that time was tantamount to being an outsider; and while Sullivan was sensitive to the meaning of being an outsider in other ways, he nowhere describes the actual feelings of the child who is an outsider by virtue of his ethnic and religious identity.

For the first three years of school, Harry walked the mile and a half from the farmhouse to the village. His was the last house in the village school district on the road that led to South Otselic. The walk must have been a long and lonely one for a small child, and arduous coming home, when the way led mainly uphill. But he was eager for knowledge, and school was not a chore or an unpleasant destination. For a week or two each winter he was forced to stay home from school, since the roads were impassable after a heavy snowstorm.

He was a loner at school by all reports, and some of his ways of relating to other children were a mark of his lack of experience. In later life, he spoke humorously of one of these experiences, although there is a note of terror and wistfulness hidden in his account: "As a boy in grammar school, I had an illuminating experience with the hysterical possibilities. Having mixed a little red ink with a glass full of water, I was approached by a girl whom I disliked chiefly because of her remarkable cupidity. She had to know what it was; I said it was wine, and she had to have a drink of it. She thereon became most embarrassingly drunk. For fear of what might happen after the recess, I explained what it was. She thereon became poisoned. Not only did she defeat my efforts on her behalf for a half an hour, but then required the teacher's aid in surviving."[4]

The principal during the first seven years that Harry attended the village school, Professor Herbert W. Butts, was undoubtedly one of the most important figures in Harry's early life. He was a professor by acclamation, for his formal academic credentials were slim. In many ways he seems to have been a reincarnation of Bronson Alcott, the teacher-pedlar who was an innovator in Boston and Concord in the early part of the nineteenth century. Like Alcott, Mr. Butts took Christ as his mentor; once he had done this, he had the basic and eternal principles of pedagogy well in hand.

Herbert Butts was born in 1855 in New Berlin, the birthplace of Harry's father. He was a farm boy and, like Harry's father, one of a large and poor family, with nine children. He was taken out of school in peak periods of farm work, so that his education was sporadic. There was no public high school available to him, but like other good students in the County, he was granted a license to teach when he was eighteen. He began his career in North Norwich, where he ultimately earned the title of "Professor" for his diligence and scholarliness. When he had been teaching for about ten years, he attended summer school for two successive years to compensate for his lack of formal education, and earned a state certificate. For one term, he also went to school at Chautauqua, then an important source of inspiration and adult education for all of western New York.

When Harry had been in school for a year, a high school program was instituted, the first in Smyrna, and the program began to try to qualify for the statewide regents' examinations. Two teachers, Professor Butts and Lydia Antoinette Johnson, a talented and much loved teacher, were transferred from the lower grades (where every teacher taught all subjects to all the children) to the high school faculty. Mr. Butts remained principal of the whole school but also taught high school mathematics and history; Miss Johnson was responsible for Latin and German. Other teachers were recruited for other subjects. This change had a profound effect on Harry's educational opportunities.

Herbert Butts was an avowed Democrat in the Republican stronghold of Smyrna; he later became a Prohibitionist, which improved his standing in the village. But it was his political stand on issues other than prohibition that was important as an influence on Harry. In 1909, the superintendent of schools in Norwich wrote a long obituary on Butts in the *Sun* reviewing his values and the meaning of his life to other poor boys; part of this statement seems to anticipate Sullivan's own life: "In a number of Medical schools today, none but a college graduate can matriculate, and soon, it is believed, the poor boy will be barred out of the medical profession. Let us beware of the growing tendency of class distinction; it is un-American. Let us remember that we are all descendants of people of the Old World, and we know the reasons why they left their native land. They were outclassed in one way or another."[5] Within two years of the death of Butts, Harry would matriculate at the Chicago College of Medicine and Surgery, where only a high school diploma was required.

Professor Butts represented for Harry much of what Timothy Sullivan was not. It is obvious that Butts became an idol for Harry; he was probably one of the first men that Harry knew at all well outside of members of his own family—particularly his father and his Uncle Ed. His father was taciturn and shy, except when he drank too much of his own apple and raisin cider, and he showed little interest in Harry's education. Uncle Ed was beyond Harry's wildest hopes—a glamorous and successful figure, a high-stepper, and almost a Protestant. Professor Butts was modest, friendly, and scholarly; some people disagreed with his stand on various issues, but they respected him.

Many of Sullivan's colleagues described him as being exclusively one or another of these three kinds of characters: a withdrawn and cantankerous drunk; a somewhat pretentious high-stepper and sophisticate; the kindest, most considerate man who ever lived. Seldom did he show all three sides to the same person. Such reports seem puzzling and mutually exclusive until one examines the paucity of his early relationships with men and the sharp differences between them, so that the growing child found it difficult to pattern his own life after such dissimilar people. Yet the model set by Professor Butts was clearly the dominant influence on Sullivan.

In an autobiographical account, Sullivan tells about an early experience with Professor Butts: "In this isolated existence the boy showed a very early interest in physics, and almost as soon as he started to school the principal of the school, an old friend of his mother's, began taking him on high school geology excursions. Even on these early excursions he learned almost as much about human nature as about geology—learned, for example, that a certain diffidence was helpful when identifying structures and fossils unfamiliar to the older students."[6] That part of the County contained a good many fossils; indeed the red sandstone and limestone in the hilly area were more conducive to fossil collection than to farming. Near the schoolhouse, along Pleasant Brook, there was an exposure of the Hamilton shale from the Devonian period; and brachiopods and trilobites, marine fossils that were 300 million years old, were there for the finding. The first Stack settlers must have had knowledge of this kind of geologic formation, not too different from the soil and formations around Milltown Malbay, so that there was a kind of destiny in the child's interest in these geology trips.

Eventually these expeditions were taken over by Harry's teacher in the fifth, sixth, and seventh grades—Miss Mary E. Wedge, who later became Mrs. Lasher. She reports that Harry only *once* accompanied a group of older high school students on a geology trip that she supervised. Harry was still a grade school student at the time, and she did not think that his inclusion was fair to the other students, so she refused to allow him to go again. "It 'most broke his heart," she reported sixty years later. In general, she thought that Harry's intellectual accomplishments were a problem in the classroom: he was very uneasy; he wanted to answer all the questions; he would wave his hand wildly so that he would be called on. It would have been better, Mrs. Lasher thought, if Harry's I.Q. had been spread around to some of the other children: "He was just born too smart."[7]

Somewhere between these two accounts of the geology trips—Mrs. Lasher's and Harry's—there seems to be another story, but it is now hidden from view. Was it Professor Butts who began to take Harry on these trips, and was this privilege canceled after Professor Butts left his job at the Smyrna School about 1904, and Mrs. Lasher took over the geology trips? Or was fantasy mixed with fact in Harry's youthful mind, so that he fantasied that if Professor Butts had been running the expeditions he would have been allowed to continue? It is notable that these two accounts have survived, for it was Mrs. Lasher who reported on the trip to me, with no prompting; obviously the event or events had some importance in the annals of the Smyrna School. And it is clear that Smyrna considered Harry too smart.

Near the end of his life, Sullivan reported that he had problems in lecturing that were "built out of a great deal of experience in being an essentially solitary, overprivileged juvenile, surrounded by numerous people who were not free from envy."[8] The "overprivileged" condition that he speaks of is surely not economic or social; it is clearly the intellectual encouragement that he had from his mother, his Aunt Maggie, and Professor Butts; and it was his precociousness that was envied, as his achievements are still envied by some inhabitants of that small world, as well as by the larger adult world of colleagues and trainees. Some of this envy was induced by Harry himself, as he reported in adult life: "It is possible that I underrate the extent to which one can suffer envy, for I recall few instances in which I felt intensely envious. I think that possibly the capacity for missing the more extreme suffering of envy is, in my own case, an artifact of the particular juvenile era in which I lived, an era in which it was necessary to become quite expert at finding and using defensive tools. One of these tools was to provoke envy, as a minor malevolence toward troublesome people; and I suppose that provoking envy in others is one way of sparing oneself the most acute development of it."[9]

At the school in Smyrna, it seems clear that Harry was often the teacher's pet. Certainly the intervention of Professor Butts in his behalf when he first entered school had made him conspicuous; his early ability to read and to compete meaningfully with the older children in identifying fossils, for instance, placed a special mark on him for the teachers and students alike. The teachers took pride in his ability, but there was a price to be paid for that. Basically most of the teachers—and there were only four or five different teachers during the eleven years that Harry was in that school—partook of some of the culture of the surrounding countryside, in which it was not popular to have an Irish Catholic boy as the brightest student in school. So there was an ambivalence, at best, in some of the teachers' attitudes, to say nothing of the more troublesome reactions of students: "Quite often there are stereotypes of juveniles' relations to teachers; and if one is actually teacher's pet, or simply for some reason the teacher is especially interested in one, one has to act under the aegis of the juvenile stereotype of the teacher's pet, and cannot therefore derive any simple profit from what would otherwise be a fortunate accident."[10]

In later years, Sullivan would consider his own juvenile era and his early experience in school as absolutely essential to his development. The opportunity to compare authority figures, to learn other values, to have access to a peer group was essential in his survival; but he came to understand that there were serious lacks in his own juvenile experience. As his theory developed, his attitude toward these lacks took on a new urgency. He came to feel that his own personal psychoanalysis, undertaken before he had developed a theoretical understanding of the importance of the juvenile era, had been inadequate in dealing with some of his own difficulties in living. It was compromise and cooperation that he saw as the skills ideally learned in the juvenile era; and it was these skills that he found lacking in himself. Old-timers who knew him as a child often use one word for him—an "underling"—and this probably refers to the way he learned to fend off the teasing and bullying that went on in the recess period. At the same time, one glimpses in his writings and in the accounts of other school children his precociousness in the classroom and the somewhat brash and boastful way that he showed off his knowledge at times.

Yet a new day was dawning for him. By his own theory, the emergence of the preadolescent era and the finding of a chum—someone who can be trusted—is the most important era in correcting for the inadequate experiences in preceding developmental eras. In his own life it was certainly a crucial event.

10

The Quiet Miracle

Around the age of eight and one-half, nine and one-half to twelve, in this culture, there comes what I once called the quiet miracle of preadolescence.
—Sullivan, *Conceptions of Modern Psychiatry*

In the fall of 1900, when Harry was eight and one-half years old, he found a friend in the village school when the new year started— Clarence Bellinger, who was thirteen and one-half years old. Although Clarence lived on the next farm to the Sullivans, the two boys did not get to know each other until they went to the same school. The Bellingers' farm was just a mile beyond Harry's house on the same road, which led between rocky outcroppings and over high meadows toward South Otselic. That mile had been important in determining Clarence's schooling, for it meant that the Bellingers lived in another school district and that Clarence had had to go to a nearby one-room country school until he was ready for high school. But Harry's grandfather Stack had anticipated that the village school would be better, so Harry was eligible for village school beginning with the first grade. The superior schooling in the village explained in part the fact that Harry would be only two years behind Clarence in graduating from high school, although Clarence was five years his senior.

In that time and place, only a few farm boys went on to high school; even village boys often dropped out of school before completing high school. Most of the high school graduates were girls. But Clarence, like Harry, was an only child, and his mother had high expectations for him.

In many ways these two boys were an unlikely pair, even in appearance. Clarence was short, fat, and awkward; his mother reported to the neighbors that she had to have three kinds of pudding for supper, because she never knew which kind Clarence would prefer on a particular day. Neighbors link the fact that Bellinger was large-bellied as an adult to his mother's indulgences of him when he was at home. By contrast, Harry was thin and undeveloped for his age, and five years younger to boot.

Their parents, too, were quite different, for the Bellingers belonged to the Anglo-Saxon Protestant tradition in Chenango County, and Clarence's father was a member of the I.O.O.F. like Harry's Uncle Ed in South Otselic. But Harry desperately needed a friend, a "chum," as he later termed it; and Clarence was a newcomer to the village school, without any other ties. Harry had already been in the village school for three years, and he had gained certain skills in turning aside some of the real bullying that was forthcoming from the larger village boys. So it was that over time Clarence and Harry, a strange twosome in a number of particulars, became fast friends.

In those days children might walk as far as four miles to go to high school, and Clarence's house was less than two and a half miles from the village school. But Clarence was considerably "spoiled," according to village lore, so his parents, more affluent than the Sullivans, supplied Clarence with his own horse and wagon to go to school. Some arrangement was worked out between the Sullivans and the Bellingers so that Clarence would pick up Harry as he came along, and they would ride back and forth to school together. Over a period of time, they were given the task of drawing the milk from the hill farms down to the village, where it was deposited at the cheese factory or taken to the railroad depot for shipment to the city. The horse was stabled in the old tannery building by the bridge that ran over Pleasant Brook, and the two boys then walked a few rods to the school building. Even to sophisticated village children, the status of coming to school every day in this conveyance, with important duties, was considerable.

When the snows came, the boys rode to school in a wagon with runners. And on many a winter afternoon, when the snow was right for such sport, Clarence would allow certain carefully selected village children to tie their small sleds onto his wagon as he drove up the west hill out of the village bound for home. When they were at the top of the first hill, before the road dipped down again, the village children would untie their sleds and coast swiftly down the road into the village, by then in the half light of late afternoon. In my mind's eye, I can see Clarence and Harry, his adoring coachman, as they watched the other children race back down to the twinkling lights of the village, and then turned toward home, the lantern lit on the side of the wagon-sleigh, the horse pulling slowly and steadily through the ruts in the road. Such moments of shared triumph must have drawn them close together, so that they could talk with trust of all the hopes and fears that clustered around their lives, restricted and lonely as they were.

In truth, neither of them had anyone to confide in except each other, for they were treated as outsiders by the village children. Although the coming of Clarence to the village school and the advent of the horse and wagon had changed Harry's status drastically, not all of the change was benign. He was no longer the isolated farm boy from the hill; now he was a member of an envied and hated twosome. Even the favors bestowed on classmates who wanted a free ride up the hill were parceled out so carefully by Clarence that resentment against Clarence still lingers on in village lore, for Clarence might deny this favor on a particular evening as punishment for an earlier slight. It was Clarence who made such important decisions; Harry was his willing slave, copying at times some of Clarence's arrogances, but still an underling.

In general, farm children were ostracized by village children in that time and place. Nor was the popularity of Clarence and Harry enhanced by the fact that they were considered "the smartest boys in the village school." And Harry's defensive tendency to arouse envy in his classmates was reinforced by Clarence. A teacher in the lower form at the time when Harry and Clarence were in high school together remembered disdainfully, some sixty years later, their swaggering airs; they would tuck their thumbs under their suspenders—she illustrated the gesture—and brag of the fact that they were both smart, and some day the world would hear from them.[1]

This sense of common greatness was augmented by the near coincidence of their birthdays, for Clarence was born on George Washington's birthday, which obviously destined him for great things; Harry had missed this honor by one day, so that he had to work harder to compensate for his eternal youthful status with Clarence and for the input of the stars. Still, Clarence encouraged Harry early on to dare to hope that he could overcome such preordained handicaps; only later, when Clarence reached adulthood, did it occur to him that his protégé might outstrip him. But in the beginning, the closeness of their birthdays was a bond between them—with an especially important meaning for Harry, who had an Irish love of coincidence and the magic of dates.

Over time, a difference between them could in itself become a bond that cemented their relationship. In the eyes of the community, Clarence's family, like Harry's, were religious outcasts. For the Bellingers did not go to any church regularly, as far as anyone remembers. Some people said that they were Episcopalian, but that in itself was somewhat suspect. There was no Episcopal church in the village. In that remnant of the burned-over district, each child had a clear notion of where the other child went to Sunday School and how often. Was he a Congregationalist, a somewhat resented group and the most snobbish of the various Protestant sects? Or a Baptist? Or a Seventh-Day Baptist, who went to church twice a week? Or a Methodist? But no one knows what church the Bellingers went to: "Don't know as they went to any church," several neighbors report. And Harry's grandparents and his own parents went to the Catholic church in Sherburne—but "not often enough."

Clarence and Harry had to make their own entertainment, for they were both excluded from the cultural life of the village. Certain dramatic, musical, social, and literary events took place each winter in the Opera House in the village, always in the evening; but farm families rarely took their children to them. An eight o'clock performance was an indulgence that could not be allowed when the head of the household on a dairy farm had to arise at four or five in the morning to attend to the animals. Village people do not remember children from the farms coming to an evening's performance in the village before the advent of automobiles. For entertainment, Harry and Clarence depended on reading and endless discussion; books were plentifully supplied by Margaret Stack, who mailed them from Brooklyn where she had gone to teach while Harry was still in grade school. And there was always the daily newspaper, which brought important news of the larger world and supplied grist for the discussion of various plans for the future. One or the other of the boys had an occasional trip to the outside world, although such trips were usually within a small radius. The Bellingers sometimes visited in Madison County where Clarence was born, so that he had a somewhat larger geographic compass than Harry. And Harry of course occasionally visited his Uncle Ed's hotel in South Otselic and brought back news of the bar where his cousin Leo sometimes helped out, waiting on the drummers who frequented the Gothic House. Harry's Aunt Margaret was also a source of information on the ways of the larger world, although visiting her was out of the question. At the time New York City was a far-off dream, although both Clarence and Harry would live there as adults.

From school, they went home each day to quite different households, for the Bellingers were obviously more affluent than the Sullivans. Clarence's father could spare a horse for the trek to school, while Harry's father at best had only one farm horse. The postman, Mance Messenger, pastured his horse in a field owned by Timothy, across from the Sullivans' front door; for this favor, Messenger allowed Timothy to use the horse on Sundays to go to church in Sherburne and for other occasional excursions. At times, Timothy might be without the use of a horse other than Messenger's. But Harry could brag to Clarence of his Uncle Ed's livery stable in South Otselic; and from time to time Uncle Ed would come to visit driving an elegant rig and two fine steeds. The boys' interest in horses was a part of the general interest of the County. Racing was a part of the life there, and even good church people bet on the horses on occasion, although this was not formally condoned. It was rumored in the County that the Catholic priest was sometimes seen at the races at County fairs; this was formally disapproved of, even by farmers who themselves bet on the races.

The direct connection between Sullivan's theory and his own experience in growing up is nowhere more evident than in his early formulation of the specific timing of preadolescence, as cited at the beginning of this chapter. In his later theory, he defined preadolescence in a more operational manner: the juvenile era, which precedes preadolescence, "extends through most of the grammar-school years to the eruption, due to maturation, of a need for an intimate relation with another person of comparable status. This, in turn, ushers in the era that we call *preadolescence,* an exceedingly important but chronologically rather brief period that ordinarily ends with the eruption of genital sexuality and puberty. . . ."[2] He had obviously come to recognize that his juvenile era had been unusually brief and his preadolescent experience unusually early—a deviation related to his isolated position in the school society until the advent of Clarence. His earlier specific reference to "eight and one-half, nine and one-half to twelve" is clearly autobiographical in light of the realities of his life at that time; the "one-half" refers obliquely to his birth date, February 21. School began early in September each year, and Harry reached the halfway point between his birthdays shortly before, on August 21. Old neighbors report that Clarence and Harry got to know each other when they started driving to school together. When Harry was eight and one-half, Clarence began to go to school in the village, beginning in the fall of 1900; but his attendance that first year was spotty and irregular. As an adult, Sullivan may have wondered whether his own relationship with Clarence could have developed more fully in that first year if they had seen more of each other. At any rate, Sullivan is quite certain that by 1901, when he was a year older, he was completely ready to enter into this relationship. In 1901, when Clarence was going regularly to the village school, he was already fourteen and a half; even a year earlier he would have been well past the age of twelve. Thus Sullivan's first formulation excludes Clarence from any significant benefit to be derived from the very relationship that was so crucial to Harry.

At one level, it seems preposterous to suppose that Sullivan set up his timing of preadolescence so as to give himself a relatively good experience, and to exclude Clarence from being able to use the same experience with as favorable an outcome. But after puzzling over this possibility at some length, I think that this is precisely what happened—that Sullivan, without specifically producing his data (gathered from a variety of patients, trainees, and colleagues) is stating that if, by the age of twelve, or *before* finishing grammar school, one has missed out on establishing even a brief relationship of trust with another person of "comparable status," then one is seriously handicapped in profiting from the experience.

Sullivan's technical term for this important relationship is *isophilic,* that is, the love of someone like oneself. He achieved this state with Clarence, and he saw it as crucial in his own survival; however important it was for Clarence at that time, its impact was not as far-reaching as for Harry. On Bellinger's frequent trips back to Smyrna as an adult, he told many stories about Sullivan, "all of them bad," according to old neighbors. As an adult, Sullivan never mentioned Bellinger to anyone, so that even his closest colleagues and his foster son did not know of their relationship as boys until I uncovered the story in Smyrna. Thus Sullivan retained the memory of his chumship unsullied and did not confuse it with Bellinger's general reputation as an adult. Whatever Bellinger's assets were, he did not profit from the experience at anywhere near the same intensity as did Sullivan, as will become clear in the course of this book; and Sullivan's theory offers an understanding of Bellinger's somewhat disappointing life.

In his most moving statement on the relationship of chums, Sullivan writes of the fleeting nature of trust in our society:

In this brief phase of preadolescence, the world as known gains depth of meaning from the new appraisal of the people who compose it. The world as rumored is a wonderful place; the quest of Sir Lancelot rises from the mists of faëry to all but a pattern of life to be lived. Experiences reported from excursions away from home carry a coloring of friendly wonder. The future is constructed in relatively noble terms by the reveries that prepare for tomorrow and that assuage disappointment, take the humdrum out of monotonous tasks.

The imaginary people of preadolescent fantasy may seem to us insubstantial; the imaginary play of the preadolescent may seem but old, romantic folklore crudely adjusted to the spirit of the times. The illusions that transmute his companions—if they be illusions—may seem to us but certain of an early end, a disillusionment. But whatever his people, real, illusory or frankly imagined, may be, they are not mean. Whatever his daydreams with his chum, whatever his private fantasies, they are not base. And as to his valuations of others, here we may take pause and reflect that it may be we who see "as through a glass, darkly."

These young folk are grossly inexperienced. They are often grossly misinformed as to the motives that are prominent in adult life around them. But I surmise that after the measure of their experience, they see remarkably clearly. Also, I believe that for a great majority of our people, preadolescence is the nearest that they come to untroubled human life— that from then on the stresses of life distort them to inferior caricatures of what they might have been.[3]

⊷ 11 ⊶
Only Child

The only child, particularly the only surviving child, or a child whose birth has been long deferred and greatly desired, is almost always pampered and protected in such fashion that he is restrained from development of realistic self-appraisal, and goes on into the era of socialization with characteristics potent against his acceptance by other children. It thus comes to be a very real misfortune to live even for a few years as the only child. The possibility of full development of personality under these circumstances is thereby rendered rather remote. A degree of the same handicap extends to a great many first-born children.

—Sullivan, *Personal Psychopathology*

DIFFERENT as were the occupants of the Bellinger and Sullivan households in certain obvious ways, both Harry and Clarence had to contend as only children with the doting attention of adoring mothers. For each of them, the mother was overly important. Clarence's mother, like Harry's, was not particularly young (about thirty-three) when she had her first and only child. And each of these intelligent, isolated farm women found some consolation in planning a brilliant career for her only child.

The farmer fathers were nondescript figures—to the neighbors and doubtless to the boys themselves. Sullivan has reported that he did not get to know his father until after his mother died in 1926. He describes his father as a "remarkably taciturn man who had become a widower (and his son a physician of some twelve years' experience) before they got well acquainted with each other's views."[1] There is no specific information on Clarence's father, but the lack of such data from either old neighbors or from Bellinger's adult colleagues—when there is considerable information on his mother—seems to admit the possibility of the same patterning.

The distance from his father that existed through all his growing-up years is cited by Sullivan as one of the crippling effects of being an only child. He theorized that all first-born male children—and he thought of only children as special instances of the larger category—had some special problems with their fathers. If the first-born is a boy, "he is apt to grow into morbidly close or morbidly distant relationship with the father."[2] There seems little doubt that he considered his relationship with Timothy as being "morbidly distant." At close range, he could also observe Clarence's similar relationship with his father. Whatever the distance may have been in the beginning, it became greater as the years went by, for both boys would be headed toward university careers by the time they left the village school; and as their vocabularies grew, their conversation took them farther and farther away from the older men in overalls up on the farm. And the womenfolk in both households encouraged them to study instead of helping out on the farm.

Until Harry was eleven, he had one handicap as an only child that Clarence did not share—a grandmother who lived with the family: "If one must be an only child, one might choose to be born of very poor but honest parents who *do not* provide a home for any of their [adult] relatives."[3] It seems clear that as a child he saw the presence of his grandmother as both an asset and a liability. He often felt caught between the three adults who lived with him; in the summer there was usually a fourth adult, his Aunt Margaret. At the same time, he suggests that having "poor but honest parents" may be an asset. The indulged only child in the neighborhood was Clarence, whose parents were certainly *not* poor. The quotation represents a rather thinly disguised comment on both his and Clarence's households.

Mary Stack's importance in the farmhouse where she held sway for half a century cannot be underestimated. Even after her death, she continued to dominate her daughter, leaving Ella Sullivan unable to deal with her own child in an appropriate manner. When, near the end of his life, Sullivan referred to his experience in childhood as "an inexplicably powerful but by no means unpunished minority of one," he implied that his grandmother was a stern disciplinarian, but that he had inexplicable—and confusing—power over his parents.[4] His mother was consistently overindulgent, and his father withdrew from the fray. When Harry was alone with his parents, he could do pretty much as he pleased, according to a cousin, Margaret [Normile] Hannon; neither parent could correct him—they "just couldn't touch him."[5]

A measure of Mary White Stack's matriarchal position in the extended family can be found in the newspaper account of her death and funeral in the *Sherburne News* for July 18, 1903. She died of asthma in the farmhouse, and Dr. Thurston G. Packer, who would later recommend Harry for medical school, filled out the death certificate. It was the first major family event within Harry's memory. James Stack's son Bartholomew, by then a priest in Camillus, New York, officiated at the funeral in St. Malachy's. Stack relatives came from near and far, more than had come for Michael Stack's funeral. Maggie Stack came from New York City, of course, and she would become of increasing importance to Harry as the years went by. She had a different kind of authority over him than his grandmother, and she was a stabilizing force for Ella Stack in advising her about Harry's education. Together they began to plot and plan for the career of this boy who came to belong to both of them.

From time to time, Timothy made attempts to include Harry in the work on the farm. It must have seemed unnatural to him for a boy to grow up spending so much time inside the house with the womenfolk. But all indications are that Timothy's efforts were largely abortive. In the summer of 1907, when Harry was fifteen, Margaret Normile, who was younger than Harry, visited on the farm for a week. She recalls only one occasion when Harry replied to his father in more than one syllable: "His father wanted to know if he was going to do some little chore he had asked him to accomplish, if he was going to finish it that afternoon. And Harry said, 'Well, I'm going to Sherburne to the library.' And his father said, 'Don't you think it's time that you finished your work?' And Harry said, 'Not when I have a ride to Sherburne.' "

In another exchange over Harry's doing farm chores, she reports that Timothy told Harry as he went out in the morning to attend to some farm work: "Remember to feed the hens for your mother." Harry did not look up or answer his father. When Timothy came in for dinner at noon, he said to his wife, "Did Harry feed the chickens?" The incident as recalled by Margaret Hannon goes on: "And Ella Stack Sullivan said, 'Oh, yes, yes, before he went up the hill,' or before he went wherever. I looked up and caught Margaret Stack's eyes on me. And we both knew that she had lied for him. He hadn't fed the chickens at all; she had gone down and done it all."

When the Sullivans went to Norwich in the fall to shop, it was their wont to go to the Normiles' for the noonday meal. On one such occasion, Margaret Normile remembers Harry's unseemly behavior and Timothy's inability to intervene:

My dad was . . . on his mettle [that day] to draw Timothy Sullivan into a conversation, because Timothy Sullivan was *the* most inarticulate man I think I have ever known. . . . He simply could not express himself. He was not stupid; I can remember, the week that I spent up there, he always read the Norwich *Sun* each day. . . . He would come in, have his supper, pick up his paper and go [out on the porch] and read it carefully, and yet never comment on anything. Well, my dad, this noon was . . . trying to get Timothy involved. Ella Stack on the other hand was very easy to talk to, joining happily in conversation. And I could see Dad glancing up every once in a while, with this light scowl, and my father was [usually] the pleasantest looking man. I looked across the table, and Harry had brought a book to the table and was reading it. Well, my dad took it as long as he felt he should, and he finally said, "Harry." And Harry looked up. . . . "I wish you would close the book." Harry slammed the book shut. Neither did he join in the conversation. . . . Timothy Sullivan looked extremely pleased that someone had dared correct his son.

Family memories, on both sides, show that Timothy was estranged from Harry partly because of the boy's interest in learning. When a Sullivan relative asked Timothy how Harry was, on one occasion, Timothy replied, "Harry is well but I can't get any work out of him. I sent him out to pick apples and after a couple of hours I went to the orchard and not an apple was off the tree and there sat Harry under the tree reading a book that no-one else could get any sense out of. He is no good to work, for he has his nose stuck in a book all the time."[6]

Leo Stack's daughter, Dorothy, remembers a similar story, told her by either her mother or her great-aunt Margaret: "Harry would be trying to help his father in the fields and he'd find a bug he didn't know; the next thing his father knew, he'd have to hunt him out; he'd be in the dark living room, in the Smyrna house, on his belly with a book, hunting up the bug. His father couldn't understand it, and I suppose Harry couldn't understand his father."[7] As an adult, Harry would retain the values of his mother and his Aunt Margaret, and he would resent any kind of pointless drudgery that kept him from more important work.

However much Sullivan lamented the "illusions" with which he was saddled by his mother, both her nagging intent on having him achieve intellectually and his Aunt Margaret's knowledge of how best to reach that goal were critical factors in his productive life. And his position as an only child reinforced the intensity of their devotion, however much it may have isolated him from his father. Moreover, his mother provided him with social skills that would serve him in good stead in later years; all of the Stacks were good conversationalists, although Ella reserved this part of her nature for relatives; neighbors considered her, in turn, sharp, withdrawn, and queer.

Before the advent of Clarence, Harry, as an only child, had no way to deal with his father's and mother's reputation in the neighborhood. In Prohibitionist Smyrna, his father was obviously considered a drunk. In his lectures, Sullivan makes occasional references to the problems of a patient whose father is known as the village drunk. A neighborhood story about Harry's mother gives clear evidence of her reputation in Smyrna: Dr. Packer once asked young Harry, in front of a visitor from New York City, how his "ma" was, in order to get Harry to exhibit his brogue. "Oh, she's all right," said Harry, "except that she gets those sweats."[8] The story is told more than a half century after the event, but the storyteller acts out the parts with great hilarity, with an attempt at an Irish brogue.

The clear communication is that Ella's queerness is doubtless related to the menopause, a common explanation for eccentricity in that day. Yet somehow the story puzzles and leaves one with an unpleasant feeling, as one senses the inability of young Harry to deal, as an only child, with these neighborhood stereotypes.

There was, of course, another only child that Harry saw periodically—his cousin Leo. Undoubtedly Sullivan would have included Leo in the category of being "morbidly close" to his father, for everyone in the family—and eventually everyone in the County—would see Leo as a model son. Harry obviously resented Leo in this role, for there is a note of envy in his description of the boy who has a morbidly close relationship with his father. In truth, Leo would remain throughout Sullivan's life an unrealized ideal in many particulars.

❧ 12 ❧
Going to Church

The adolescent of bygone generations often came
promptly to be "religious." He accepted the entrenched regulations of life perforce.... Sexual asceticism was the greatest good, and both organized
and informal opportunities for its achievement were
provided.
—Sullivan, *Schizophrenia as a Human Process*

SULLIVAN'S writings reflect the most minute observation of his daily
encounters at school at a time when most children are engaged in living on a day-to-day level that does not survive in memory. But his observations on going to church are not recorded in any of his lectures. The
omission is significant, for the impact of the Church on his theories seems
unmistakable, and he is quite explicit in defining the sexual asceticism
taught by the Church as posing powerful problems for young adolescents.

During Harry's childhood, loyalty to the Church was the one parental
prerogative that his father continued to assert. However uneven the family's attendance at St. Malachy's may have been, the importance of attending Mass as often as possible was staunchly upheld by Timothy. In
1900, when Harry was in his ninth year, Ella presented Timothy with a
small prayer book for Christmas, appropriately inscribed, and this book
was still in Sullivan's possession when he died; it seems to stand as Ella's
gesture of reconciliation on the subject of going to church.

On October 12, 1904, Harry was confirmed at St. Malachy's, taking as
his own religious name "Francis," doubtless inspired by the life of St.
Francis of Assisi. The Saint's day is on October 4, only eight days before
Harry's confirmation; with Harry's magical love of dates, it would have
been more propitious if it had fallen on the same day, but some compromises are necessary. And Harry, like St. Francis, described his relationships with animals in anthropomorphic terms. As a child, he always had a
dog; and in adulthood, after he had established his own household, he
had a succession of dogs as household pets, often more than one at a time.

The eccentric and close relationship that Sullivan maintained with his dogs will be documented later.

He also had a magical love of horses, but this relationship seemed more remote and legendary than the very real relationship he had with dogs. Yet horses were very important symbolically in his scheme of things, and after he had had some experience with riding, he spoke rather unrealistically of the horse as a "uniquely gifted sub-colleague."[1] He mentioned cats in his writings, but he expressed no tenderness for them, suggesting that when all the data are in, we may discover that sadism is in part a "hereditarily determined tendency" in members of the cat family.[2]

His attitude toward animals was in part, at least, related to being Irish, for beasts and birds played a prominent role in the stories of the lives of the early Irish saints. Beauty or intelligence had to be a characteristic of a beast or a bird before it was included in these stories. Although most of the animals were not endowed with magical characteristics, certain fabulous animals did appear. There were, for instance, beautiful horses of the "water-world" in Ireland, and these fabulous creatures seemed to expedite the tasks of the Irish saints.[3] This seems to have been the function of horses for Sullivan, too, though at times he actually represented himself as one of these magical horses.

It is interesting to speculate that the name of St. Francis of Assisi may have been selected by Harry because of the Saint's "marriage," as it was termed, to "Lady Poverty." In particular St. Francis feared that "Lady Learning" might become a rival to "Lady Poverty," in the teachings of the Church—a fear that as far as I know Sullivan never shared. St. Francis' ideas of poverty clearly expressed one pole of Sullivan's later attitude toward money and material success and made him throughout his life responsive to the needs of the poor; but there was always the other pole, represented by Leo. And this part of Sullivan's character led him as an adult to drink only 100-year-old French brandy even if his bills went unpaid, and to adopt St. Martin as his second patron saint.

By the time Harry was confirmed at St. Malachy's, he probably knew all there was to know about St. Francis of Assisi.[4] Whatever else bored him about going to church, he liked the stories of the saints and had considerable knowledge of them; and he appreciated the ancient beauty of the Catholic liturgy. Moreover, the Latin used in church formed a continuum with his interest in the scientific names for geologic formations.

On the occasion of his confirmation, Harry sat for a picture with the confirmation group, composed of forty-one girls and twenty-four boys, as well as several adults who were sponsors for the occasion. Six of the younger boys sat on the ground in the front row, and Harry was one of these, sitting taller and straighter than any of the younger group, in an aloof, dignified, terribly lonely style, at variance with the soft lines of his face. Although he was late in his thirteenth year, he looks small and cherubic, scared and undeveloped.

The picture was taken on the side of what is referred to as the "old Congo Church." For the thirteen years that Harry went to church in Sherburne, he attended church in this building. It was a discard of the Congregational Church and had been moved from its original site in the middle of Sherburne to the area north of the village, near the part of town where the Utica Mills had a branch factory and the "foreigners" lived. When the building was moved, it was of course consecrated as a Catholic Church—and, it was hoped, all the spiritual taint of the Congregationalists was exorcised; but in truth, the stained glass windows in the clapboard building were unchanged and bore the names of the Protestant parishioners to whom they were dedicated. The Congo Church building was abandoned in 1922, long after Harry had left the County, and a new St. Malachy's now stands near the center of the village—a twin-spired brick building with proper stained glass windows on an impressive site. But the descendants of the Irish Catholic settlers still refer to the previous building as the "old Congo Church"; and one feels that shame and anger are combined in the appellation.

The only firsthand account of Harry at St. Malachy's reveals him as an outsider. Two of James Stack's granddaughters, who also attended St. Malachy's at the same time, remember Harry in a carefully pressed serge suit, with knicker pants, standing alone in the churchyard after Mass, aloof and distant. He seemed miserable, they thought. This standing alone on the edge of a group is a picture of Sullivan that persists. While close friends remember him as merry and witty in a social setting, people who saw him in situations of less intimacy think of him as testy and caustic—and often obviously miserable. Junior colleagues, who saw him usually in seminars, are apt to discount the idea that he could be kind and merry. This kind of dual personification was not unlike Ella Stack's reputation in the family and in the neighborhood.

On the face of it, Harry did not find a community of young people at St. Malachy's with whom he could be friendly and intimate while he prepared for confirmation; his visits there were brief and structured. Even his instruction for confirmation was slight and intermittent because of the multitude of difficulties attendant on getting to Sherburne, whether in summer or winter. The Stack cousins feel that Harry's subsequent drift away from the Church could be explained by the minimal nature of his instruction.

Yet the Church gave him an identity and made him part of an ancient tradition in the service of mankind. Like Saint Francis, who had undertaken self-analysis after a long illness, Sullivan began to analyze his own life very early, and his main insights came from observing what happened to him in growing up, and how and why it differed from what happened to Clarence, to Leo, to the boys and girls in the village school. And his psychological survival during the teenage years depended to an extraordinary extent on his growing ability to analyze the facts of his life in the farmhouse and at school. Traces of the daily struggle to digest the emotional meaning of the events of his life exist in all of his writings: *He was aware.* In this struggle, the identity given him by the Church was important. Throughout his life, Sullivan showed evidence of some strength that emanated from this identity; and the fact that he could have a hand in choosing his own religious name was no insignificant part of this. Thus St. Malachy's gave him the wherewithal for some *rite de passage* to an identity of his own, so that his mother's fierce need for him to become famous was softened for him by the tradition of the saints—the need to make a contribution to mankind.

Another example of Sullivan's inability to deal directly with the impact of the Church and of his ethnic identification on his own early life is his failure to include such factors in his detailed discussion of conducting a psychiatric interview. Thus he lists, as areas for psychiatric investigation, such wide-ranging subjects as disorders in learning toilet training, attitude toward games and partners in them, experience in college, and attitudes toward risqué talk, but he makes no reference to obtaining data on the patient's religious and ethnic orientation.[5] Yet in his clinical papers, he includes extensive information on the conflict between religious teachings and the emergence of lustful feelings, in verbatim excerpts from the productions of his young patients hospitalized with serious schizophrenic disorders.[6] And his theories on love, intimacy, and lust have an important relation to his indoctrination in the Catholic Church in general and, more particularly, to his knowledge, either mediate or direct, of the teachings of Saint Augustine, as followed faithfully by Irish Catholics.

Lust and love were considered by St. Augustine as completely separate emotions: perfect love is directed first toward God and then is reflected in human relationships; but lust can only be excused as a way of begetting children. Although Sullivan's definition of love concerned only human relations, it was influenced by the teachings of St. Augustine: "When the satisfaction or the security of another person becomes as significant to one as is one's own satisfaction or security, then the state of love exists. So far as I know, under no other circumstances is a state of love present, regardless of the popular usage of the word."[7] It is an ascetic definition in many ways, sharply at variance with the Freudian definition of love as given in the *Psychiatric Dictionary:* "Love is pleasure; when the pleasure is directed to oneself it is self-love; the word is annexed by a hyphen to the particular part of oneself that pleases; it may be oral, anal, genital, muscular, dermal, psychic. . . . When love is directed away from oneself, it becomes object-love, which has as many manifestations as self-love."[8] Such a definition would be completely unacceptable to Sullivan, who placed most of these events under the rubric of "lust."

While Sullivan expressed the belief that some sexual experimentation with a chum, in the late stages of preadolescence, could be a normal part of growing up and lead towards a heterosexual mode of interaction in adult life, he seemed to cling to the belief that there was a more perfect love inherent in a chumship that was untouched by lust: "The preadolescent frames of reference are, at least in our culture, about the clearest and most workable ones that we have. They do not include lust as a complicating and distorting factor—generally, a confusing and misleading element. Love is new and uncomplicated."[9] In his final formulation, he was still stressing the difference between intimacy and lust: "I still find that some people imagine that intimacy is only a matter of approximating genitals one to another. And so I trust that you will finally and forever grasp that interpersonal intimacy can really consist of a great many things without genital contact; that intimacy in this sense means, just as it always has meant, closeness, without specifying that which is close other than the persons. Intimacy is that type of situation involving two people which permits validation of all components of personal worth."[10]

Thus Sullivan expresses an ambivalence about genital contact between chums. It might ease the later transition to heterosexuality, he posits, but it is a "complicating and distorting factor" in early intimacy. He implies that nothing afterwards was as uncomplicated for him personally as his experience with Clarence. There is almost a defensiveness about what he did achieve, as if he were saying: *I may be viewed as a caricature of life, but I did achieve the knowledge of what love could be when I was a preadolescent; I wonder how many people have achieved that ennobling experience with any other human being.*

By Sullivan's definition, most people in this society do not achieve more than a lustful heterosexuality. Although Sullivan posits the possibility of lust and love uniting, there is a tinge of sadness about it, as if this were all but impossible, given the culture and the guilt surrounding sexual relations. There is about this whole subject in all of his lectures, both published and unpublished, a contrast between lust and love that seems very close to St. Augustine's beliefs. In his *Confessions,* St. Augustine writes of this sharp contrast:

I want to call back to mind my past impurities and the carnal corruptions of my soul, not because I love them, but so that I may love you, my God. . . . For in that youth of mine I was on fire to take my fill of hell. . . . But I could not keep that true measure of love, from one mind to another mind, which marks the bright and glad area of friendship. Instead I was among the foggy exhalations which proceed from the muddy cravings of the flesh and the bubblings of first manhood. . . . These so clouded over my heart and darkened it that I was unable to distinguish between the clear calm of love and the swirling mists of lust.[11]

In this same passage, he speaks of lust as "forbidden by your laws but too much countenanced by human shamelessness." These ascetic standards for love, as exemplified by St. Augustine in the fourth century, survived relatively unchanged for all Christianity through the Middle Ages. Gradually Protestantism modified this standard; but Catholicism did not consider marriage and the family as a worthy option until much later.[12] And the Irish branch of the Church has continued to maintain the ascetic view that marriage is an inferior option for those who cannot worship God fully. The shadow of St. Augustine's teachings still dominates the lives of many Irish people, including Irish-Americans. Being a "eunuch for the kingdom of heaven" is the most honorable status for a man, according to St. Augustine; and a woman, under the laws of Church obedience, must submit to the sexual advance of the husband almost against her will and only for procreation.[13] This last edict posed a particular problem for women after the famine years, when the necessity for limiting the size of families became apparent. This was partly accomplished by late marriage; after the famine, the average age for marriage in Ireland moved to thirty-two, so that the span of child-bearing years for the woman was considerably shortened.

In his writings, James Joyce adds an Irish dimension to the struggle between lust and love that extends beyond the dictates of the Church in Ireland. In several short stories, for instance, Joyce spells out the tragedy implicit in walling off ascetic love from sexual feeling—a division that Sullivan recognized. In "A Painful Case," Joyce reports on the tragic results of the continuation of this division. An unmarried man meets a married woman at a concert, and over a long period of time they develop a close relationship of the spirit exclusively. Their interest in music unites them more and more, and on one particularly intense evening, she "caught up his hand passionately and pressed it to her cheek." This ends the relationship for him. He sees her once more, and they agree to "break off their intercourse." Two months after his last interview with her, he writes in his journal: "Love between man and woman is impossible because there must not be sexual intercourse, and friendship between man and woman is impossible because there must be sexual intercourse."[14] The story proceeds toward death and meaninglessness for both of them.

Joyce often despairs about the possibility of bringing ascetic love into meaningful relation with life and sexual passion. But usually Sullivan was more hopeful; he is often credited with helping colleagues, friends, and patients to arrive at a more meaningful relation in marriage. In general, he thought that it would require a sexual revolution to arrive at a more benign approach to the dilemma, for guilt in the society was omnipresent. Judged against the teachings of the Church, as filtered through the Irish conscience, his struggle to resolve the dilemma seems all the more significant.

✎ 13 ℘

None Too Happy a
Circumstance

> The juvenile who has been unable to adapt himself
> and be adopted by people of his age and school
> group . . . may develop the preadolescent type of in-
> timacy with a person chronologically still definitely
> his senior, but in personality very late in reaching
> [preadolescence]. That is none too happy a circum-
> stance. . . . But it is the most fortunate thing that can
> happen . . . in this situation, which shows very seri-
> ous warp to personality anyway. Now this particular
> situation of the older boy, who has been fixed in an
> earlier phase of development than the younger boy
> . . . and is gradually reduced to some kind of dis-
> charge of the preadolescent tendencies in this rela-
> tionship, is a peculiarly grim pattern because, re-
> gardless of how disastrous one's development has
> been, there comes the time when the puberty change
> occurs.
>
> —Sullivan, unpublished lecture

WITH no personal references, Sullivan is here describing quite precisely the particular situation that existed for both himself and
Clarence, as their relationship developed. The "quiet miracle" of having
Clarence as a friend in the early years was of crucial importance in res-
cuing Sullivan from spending his life in a mental hospital, or as a rural
eccentric. Yet he viewed the relationship as much less than ideal for him,
and as "grim" for Clarence.

For six years Clarence and Harry participated in a growing intimacy,
until Clarence went away to study medicine at Syracuse University. In
those six years, they had grown together in their intellectual interests and
in their shared goals. Yet the difference in age posed problems for both of
them in the years associated with chronological puberty. There is no
stronger proof of their growth of intellectual intimacy and the limits of

that growth for later development than the simple facts of their adult lives: both became psychiatrists, and neither ever married.

According to Sullivan's theory, the two-group of preadolescence should at some stage begin to merge into gang life in which various two-groups interlock; out of this experience, the model for social organization and in particular "opinion leadership" develops.[1] But it is clear that neither Clarence nor Harry had such experiences of group life in Smyrna, at school or on the farm: "In some small rural communities," Sullivan reports, "there are only a very small number of preadolescents at any one particular time, and therefore the social organization of these preadolescents is very poorly representative of . . . society."[2] Again he speaks of geographic isolation in preadolescence as one form of isolation that can have disastrous outcome: "The only preadolescent in a sparsely settled rural community . . . may secure some socialization of the ordinary preadolescent type in the hours of the country school. On the whole, however, the inaccessibility of his home—and the ignorance of his family of the significant needs of this era of growth—tend to separate him from gang life, if not from having a chum . . . [and] he is more of a participant observer than a unit merged in unthinking cooperation."[3] His own chief tool as a clinician and social scientist was precisely that of participant observation; the outsider, the loner who lived mainly on the edge of things, had definite assets for this kind of observation. But the role of participant observer would not be one that Bellinger could play in his professional life.

There is strong indication that Clarence and Harry did not progress in their relationship to any sexual intimacy; the references are veiled in Sullivan's writings, but the content is clear. Such experimentation in some kind of preadolescent sex play would have come about naturally in gang life; and Sullivan comments on this aspect of so-called normal development in the male:

One finds among some psychiatrists a tacit if not an expressed belief that gang cultivation of sexual pleasures is most unfortunate. Appropriately enough, such students rarely discover that mutual masturbation often becomes a competitive game and that frank homosexual procedures are by no means uncommon in gangs. I have had opportunity to study one community in regard to the alleged evil consequences of these factors and can contribute something perhaps a little more than prejudice to the matter of gang 'sexuality.' In this community—a fair-sized village of the Middle East [U.S.]—a large number of the early adolescents participated in overt homosexual activities during the gang age. Most of them progressed thereafter without let or hindrance to the customary heteroerotic interest in later adolescence. Some of the few boys in this community who were excluded from the gangs as a result of their powerful inhibitions, who missed participation in community homosexual play, did not progress to satisfactory heterosexual development. Judged by objective showing, there resulted a proportion of maladjustive sexual processes per capita very much greater in the nongang boys than in the gang alumni.[4]

The "fair-sized village of the Middle East" undoubtedly refers to Smyrna; the boys who were subject to "powerful inhibitions" were Harry and Clarence Bellinger. The passage appears in Sullivan's first book, written in the late 1920s and early thirties but never published until 1972. In his most complete and final statement on preadolescent groups, when his pronouncements were more public and his words were being recorded, he makes the same basic statement; but he has changed the location of the village to Kansas, and the participants are now in the "terminal phase of preadolescence":

I was once able to find out something about the adult lives of a onetime preadolescent group who had attended school together in a small Kansas community. I first had access to this information through a man who had been one of the preadolescents in the school, and I was later able to follow this up and get rather complete information on the group. This particular man was an overt homosexual. During his preadolescence, he had been distinctly in the out-group, if only with respect to so-called mutual masturbation and other presumably homosexual activity which went on in this group of boys as preadolescent pals; that is, he had not participated in any of the mutual sexuality which went on in the terminal phase of preadolescence in this group. There was one other preadolescent who had not participated in it, and I was able to track him down. I found that he also had become an overt homosexual. Those who had participated in mutual sexuality were married, with children, divorces, and what not, in the best tradition of American society. In other words, relationships of what might be described as 'illegitimate' intimacy toward the close of the preadolescent period had not conduced to a disturbed type of development in adolescence and later; the facts showed something quite different.[5]

The "small Kansas community" may be a disguise for Smyrna; or Sullivan may have acquired confirming data from a patient or a psychiatric colleague.

    In these two passages, Sullivan is suggesting that the lack of gang experience was crucial in the emergence of the patterning of "overt homosexuals." Yet in the first passage he refers to "powerful inhibitions" that excluded the "few boys" from the community homosexual play. It seems clear that these inhibitions, as they can be reconstructed, were crucial in Harry's and Clarence's lives.

    While the circumstances of life in the village school tended to prevent both Harry and Clarence from having any chance encounters with sex in that arena, there seems to have been in addition an enveloping attitude in the home environment that served as a further shield from exposure to sex.

In differing ways, Caroline Bellinger and Ella Stack managed to discourage sexual development in their sons, as if sex had been put on ice. A kind of biological withdrawal set in, so that both Clarence and Harry seem to have suffered some actual delay in the emergence of puberty.

The delay had more effect on Clarence than on Harry. Even as a grown man, Bellinger was described by neighbors and colleagues as a fat, overindulged boy who was subservient to his mother. All the descriptions of Bellinger give him a eunuch-like quality, as if he had been thwarted biologically and had never attained his full growth, psychologically or physically. To the end of his life, he abhorred the name "Clarence," although it was not an uncommon name in the period when he grew up; but he had the air of a fat boy who had been teased unmercifully about his name in school. His adult colleagues would sometimes chide him, "Now, Clarence," when he annoyed them, and this sally would invariably produce in Dr. Bellinger a childish rage.

Obviously the early friendship of Harry—five years younger, thin and eager, catching up to him in school—was not an ideal one for Clarence; it did not compensate for all the handicaps he had when he entered high school in Smyrna. Clarence was chronologically approaching puberty when he first knew Harry, and that inappropriate friendship seemed to hold him in a kind of physical vise, with no way to break through the barriers to any kind of adulthood. And he was in his twentieth year before he went away to college—too late by then to achieve a more suitable preadolescent experience.

The home restrictions on Harry's encounters with sex can be reconstructed with some degree of accuracy. They were complex, but probably somewhat less malevolent than Clarence's. Nonetheless the restrictions were acute enough that puberty was probably delayed for Harry until he was in his seventeenth year and a freshman at college.

In often vivid language, Sullivan refers to the male infant's first encounter with the penis, to illustrate the early training in what he terms "primary genital phobia" by the mother or her substitute. Both Harry's mother and his grandmother Stack had some part in early establishing this area of his body as "not-me," as he would later term it. He was two and a half when Mary Stack took over his care; and her reinforcement of the phobia may have been somewhat greater than Ella Stack's. But the earliest training, "in the cradle," as he envisions it, was undoubtedly Ella Stack's:

> We will take him in the cradle, and here we will see him, after the fashion of all his predecessors, actively and pleasantly engaged in the exercise of such ability as he has discovered. . . . he will have felt of nearly everything, including a great deal of himself, he may have put a good deal of himself in his mouth, or tried to, but in this business of exercising newly elaborated motor systems and gradually clarifying sensory feel, he will

almost inevitably ... have fallen upon a small protuberance in the groin, and in doing this he will have found it handy. It is suited to manipulation. It is astonishingly well located geometrically. A slight curve in the elbow puts it well within reach of the already nimble fingers.

So far nothing of any moment has occurred. But we will now have, let us say, the mother ... encounter this discovery of the infant, and we will make her a person who has been forced to organize the self on the basis of our more rigid puritanic tradition.

Under these circumstances, although in ordinary consciousness she is not wholly unaware of this anatomical peculiarity of the male, in her own infant she will feel that Satan is in the very near vicinity, that here is a manifestation of the bestial nature of man in the very act of erupting in her infant, and she will want to do something about it. She will wish to save this infant.[6]

For a while the infant struggles against this fear of the mother's, but in the end he takes an unusual interest in that area of his body:

After months of struggle there has been impressed upon this infant a type of interest, a mark, if you please—an emotional mark—about the groin area which is so significant that when I was younger and more reckless about language, I called that state "primary genital phobia." ...

One does not fear something of no interest to one. Anything invested with fear must by definition, by the inherent character of our contact with the universe, be of interest to us. And, therefore, because of this taboo the child has interest, unusual interest, an utterly useless interest so far as the development of personality is concerned, attached to the penis.

As a child and as a juvenile he continues to have this interest. Why? Because this thing was precipitated in personality very early, very firmly. All the red flags of anxiety came to attach to it. Moreover, mamma is always watching. Where the devil has shown up once, you may confidently expect him to return—quite unlike lightning.[7]

In these two passages Sullivan seems to be reconstructing his own infancy, not from memory but from the continuity of attitude—the way he felt about his own body as learned from his mother and his grandmother.

Shortly after Harry was three years old, a new alarm about the dangers of sex had been sounded in the Norwich *Sun.* On April 4, 5, and 6 of 1895, the Oscar Wilde case was covered in some detail on the front page of the *Sun.* Many a mother in the County, whether old settler or immigrant, must have shuddered to read of the Wilde trial in which such evil deeds were described that the newspaper had to leave blanks in the reported testimony. The story fed into the pervasive fears of all parents, but Irish-Americans must have had a special fear. Wilde was described in the paper as an Irish playwright, gifted and at the peak of his success, and enticed into the most evil of all sexual activity—the seduction of young males. Wilde's love letters to young boys were described in the newspaper and partly quoted in censored form. Oscar Wilde's crimes were referred to as "unnatural." But what did the word "unnatural" mean? What was natural and what unnatural? The terrible burden of being a mother and deciding what kind of behavior to discourage in a young son was almost too much for many a woman in that community. It is safe to assume that an only child who was male came under particularly careful supervision. Moreover, was a particularly bright child, who seemed destined to be a famous man when he grew up, particularly vulnerable to precocious exploration of the part of the body that was better forgotten?

In Harry's case, the example of Oscar Wilde must have been awesome indeed for the whole family. The Irish who came to America were particularly prone to mental illness; this generally held belief was reinforced by an early United States census report.[8] "Sexual Sin," as Sullivan termed it later, was thought to be the most prevalent cause of mental illness. The fear that mental illness was inherited existed as a full-blown belief at that time; and Harry's mother had had a nervous breakdown of some kind. As one reconstructs the history of the County, of the Irish-Americans in that part of the world, and the particular history of the Stack and Sullivan families, the attitudes of Mary, Ella, and Margaret Stack toward Harry become understandable. After Ella Stack returned to the farmhouse, she needed to reassure herself that her illness was not inherited by her son. She kept close tabs on his activities; and she and Maggie Stack made an effort to see that he was kept busy, largely with intellectual pursuits. The *Sun* warned from time to time that Satan loves idle hands. And the Stack women understood all too well that this child would be watched closely by all the neighbors, that there would be a kind of satisfaction for the old Yankee neighbors in the village if Harry turned out to have problems like his mother—not out of any particular malice but to prove to themselves that the Irish immigrants were somehow unreliable and that the taint of mental illness was obviously inherited.

Yet his training in attitudes about sex was not as one-dimensional as Sullivan indicates at times. There was some variation in attitudes among the adults. For example, there was the experience of the boy of five who saw his father's "semi-erect" penis and reported this encounter to his mother and his "maiden (maternal) aunt," and six months later with different results reported to the same audience the coitus of a bull and a cow. The child learned from these two encounters that such conversation should be suppressed when he was around women. It is not clear whether the child could bring up such matters with his father, although at a nonverbal level—assuming the story to be autobiographical—his father, who would have been present at the time of coitus of the bull and cow, did not prevent the child's witnessing the event.

The accident of being an only child was probably much more important than any other factor for the delayed development of both Clarence and Harry—that and their lack of significant relationships with other boys in their own age groups. Moreover, evasions about sex such as those described above were probably usual in all families in that time and place. It is a vast oversimplification to suppose that some rich and underlying neurosis in Ella, or Maggie, or Mary Stack was responsible for Harry's delay in development. Indeed, this kind of anxiety still survives in a watered-down version in most parts of America. Harry's delay lay more in the complex network of his own isolation as Irish and Catholic and in being considered too smart for his age. His fears had little chance for correction in the school society, or in other social encounters while he was growing up; almost the only chance for any correction was in his relationship with Clarence. And there is a good deal of indication that indeed Clarence had nothing to offer in combating fears and anxieties about sex, however much he remained a gateway for Harry to the idea of college and moving away from the confines of Smyrna.

In their important years in Smyrna, any significant relationship with girls for either Clarence or Harry was out of the question. They were isolates, and they were odd; they never did any farm work; and they were too good in school. There were few boys in Smyrna who persevered into high school in those days, so that the scholarly ones were labeled early.

Harry's plight can be more readily understood by comparing the pattern of his early life with that of his cousin Leo. Since Leo was seven years older, the idea took shape in Ella's and Maggie's minds that the only difference between Harry and Leo was that Harry had not yet caught up to Leo. Indeed it seemed highly probable to them that Harry might surpass Leo, since Leo had spent many of his growing-up years without a mother. But the rules of the game were quite different for Leo from what they were for Harry as well as for Clarence.

Although Ed Stack was never actually affiliated with any Protestant church in South Otselic, Leo and Ed were accepted in the community as Protestants and did not suffer from the kind of ostracism accorded the Sullivans for their church affiliation, or the Bellingers for their non-church-going pattern. Part of this acceptance of the Ed Stacks was related to the affluent position Ed held in the community, and part to his relationship with the Browns, but some of the acceptance was related to the position of South Otselic in the County: it was geographically, economically, and socially different from the villages along the Chenango River and in its hills. In brief, South Otselic, which was situated on the Otselic River, was more self-contained economically than most villages of its size in the County. Its chief industry, the fish-line factory, was never listed in the *Sun* during the 1893 depression as being in financial difficulty, as was true for other factories in the County. Whatever minimal anxiety was felt in South Otselic during that period, no one could blame foreign workers in the factory for the trouble. Even though Ed Stack was seen as Irish-American—and was raised as a Catholic—he was also perceived as an asset to the community, for he ran both a hotel and a livery stable where local people were employed. The foreigners brought in to work on the canal and railroad in the Chenango River valley never came to the Otselic River area; thus the values held by the old Yankees were never challenged in any way. There was a certain relaxation toward religion and the occasional outsider that did not exist in Smyrna at the same time.

Ed Stack's granddaughter, Dorothy Stack, has described the religious background of the Stack and the Brown families:

Michael, my great-grandfather . . . came to this country from Ireland, running away from an older brother who was a priest and wanted to take [him] for the priesthood. So it's quite obvious that he wasn't quite as religious as the rest of the family. However, Michael's family was all brought up in the Catholic Church, of course; this included Ella, Ed, John, and Margaret. But Ed was living in a small town (South Otselic), and Norwich [and the nearest Catholic church] was twenty miles away. . . . South Otselic had two churches, a Baptist and a Methodist church; one was supported by my grandmother Brown, and the other by my grandfather Brown. I don't believe that my father [Leo] was sent to church at all, and since it was such a long way to Catholic Church, by horse and cutter, or horse and buggy, Ed didn't go very much either. There came a time when he wanted to join the Masons, and of course the Church said no.[9] You couldn't do that and be a Catholic, too. And he said, so then, all right, I'll be a Mason. . . . I'm sure that he was motivated by the fact that that was a very outstanding social thing to do as far as that small town was concerned; it had very little to offer socially. So that would be much more important to him than going to Church if he happened to be of not too religious a turn, and that seems to be the case.

Dorothy Stack goes on to report that the priest was sent for when Ed was dying: "The priest told him that if he would say he was sorry, that he could be taken back into the Church and could be buried in holy ground, and [Ed] said, 'I've lived without the Church, and I can die without it.' "[10]

However complex the religious compromises might seem, the social definition in South Otselic of such compromises made them possible. The fact that the Browns, the most prominent couple in town, could amicably support two different churches obviously set a pattern of acceptance of different sects, quite different from the religious tradition in Smyrna.

When Leo was in his twelfth year, the *Sun* carried a story on one of his adventures that further illustrates the disparate nature of his preadolescent experience as compared to Harry's: "The son of Landlord E. J. Stack, . . . received an ugly wound in the hip, from the accidental discharge of a revolver which he was placing in his pocket. In company with two boys of about his own age Master Stack started out hunting. The revolver was an old one and in attempting to put it in his pocket it was dis-

10. The Gothic House, Ed Stack's hotel

12. Leo at college

11. Ed Stack in his Odd Fellow's
regalia

13. Leo's wife, Nina, and their daughter, Dorothy

charged.... The wound is not considered dangerous."[11] For a boy of eleven to have a revolver and to be out hunting with his friends represented a life considerably different from Harry's life on the farm. Moreover, the *Sun* disapproved of even milder escapades of boys of foreign extraction who lived on the wrong side of the tracks in Norwich. But Landlord Stack and his son, "Master Stack," were accorded the respect and concern of an English squire and his son. It was hard to think that all this had taken place anywhere in the County in the space of fifty years—this movement from hated Irish immigrant to success and respect.

The shift from preadolescent experience, to gang life, to heterosexuality can be relatively simple in certain circumstances of life, according to Sullivan's theory. Leo was an example of such successful transitions. At fourteen he began to "go with" Nina Brown, then twelve. Although there was a long waiting period before their marriage—Leo would be past twenty-five before he married Nina—there were undoubtedly more serene and acceptable ways then of handling this long waiting period. At sixteen, Leo went away to college, for he, too, was precocious in his studies. And by the time Leo had graduated from Clarkson Institute in Potsdam, Nina was away at Vassar. When she graduated, they would be married; this was an accepted fact for many years by everybody concerned.

Tales of Leo and Nina must have been part of the continuing conversation at the farmhouse between Ella and Maggie. For Maggie had been an integral part of the life at South Otselic until Ed married his second wife, Marcia, in 1896; and Maggie had been accepted by the Browns and entertained by them. The Brown house is still referred to as a "mansion" in South Otselic. As described by Dorothy Stack, Leo and Nina's daughter, it was a very elegant house with inlaid hardwood floors, oak paneling, and a beautiful oak stairway. There were marble washbowls in the bedrooms, and a marble washbowl by the carriage steps, at the side of the porte cochere. The barn was magnificent, with a cupola on top; even the barn doors had heavy brass fixtures.

By comparison, Ed Stack's hotel was less elegant, but it had its own importance in the community. "My grandfathers [Ed Stack and Ralph Brown] were *the* prominent men in that little town," Dorothy Stack reports. "They were both very fond of horses, very fine high-stepping horses. Grandfather Stack had a livery stable because of the hotel business. ... Both of them were very well-to-do, as it went in that small town, and they were rather rivals about their teams, especially their personal team of horses that pulled their carriages and sleighs."

For Harry, Leo's life became the standard by which to judge the perfect pattern for a young man growing up in that day and age. In the family, Leo was not considered just lucky, but as somehow deserving of all this splendor. And Nina became the model of the ideal fiancée and wife. Much as Harry resented the standard of elegance set by Leo, it influenced him in his adult life. His houses always had symbols of taste and elegance, even though they remained incomplete, with curious evidence of unfinished splendor. His automobiles were always somewhat "classy," as a friend has described them—a yellow Franklin when he was a young psychiatrist, and, near the end of his life, a Lincoln. The famous livery stable of his Uncle Ed was represented in his love of horses, and the expensive cars were a representation of the fancy conveyances of the Browns and the Ed Stacks. When Sullivan acquired his first house, he tacked up over the door an iron symbol of St. Martin on horseback, and all his friends and colleagues, including the attendants on his ward, thought of St. Martin's as a haven—in much the same way that the Gothic House provided food, shelter, and drinks for the weary traveler.

Of all the wonders of the Browns, their two daughters were perhaps the most notable in the eyes of Ella and Maggie. Nina was considered by people throughout the County as one of the most beautiful and elegant of women. Her sister, Jessica, shared some of this acclaim, but she was not considered to be on a par with Nina. The description of Nina's beauty by old-timers in the County is much the same picture as emerges from her daughter's account: "I think that everyone who knew my mother considered her a very beautiful woman. She was extremely feminine. She had a magnificent skin, wide-set, very very black eyes and golden chestnut brown hair. . . . She had nice features too, although . . . her nose wasn't set on quite straight . . . and her mouth was really too big for beauty and so were her ears. . . . But she really gave the effect of great beauty. And almost to the day she died—she was eighty-three, and had been in bed and failing for five years—she was still beautiful."

This was the woman that was set before Harry as an ideal. And there seems little doubt that some such ideal would persist in his mind up to the time of his death. To close friends and colleagues, he would sometimes joke about finding himself a "rich widow." In truth, Nina would be a rich widow by the time Harry was thirty-four.

The evidence for Sullivan's interest in Nina is tenuous at best, but occasionally it seems quite specific. In the midst of a clinical discussion on the meaning of stereotyped verbal communications, Sullivan reminisces: "I am reminded of the young lady whom I admired a great deal when I was a boy; one evening she came along in her sables and jewels with her obviously prosperous escort and looked into the sunset . . . and said, after taking a deep breath, 'My God, how cute!' "[12] The young lady and her escort must have been Leo and Nina, since no other young visitors of such glory came to that modest and remote farmhouse; and the sunset from that hill is indeed impressive. Young Harry was obviously impressed by the richness of the young lady's attire, but he succeeds in conveying an impression of silliness, as if Sullivan as an adult still felt irritated by Leo's romantic success.

In family lore, the Stacks were destined for greatness. Leo achieved real greatness in the eyes of the best families in Chenango County, even if his life was cut short when he was in his forty-first year. But Harry's greatness was more difficult to accept in the County. He and Clarence Bellinger somehow managed to get turned in the wrong direction, according to County history. Retrospectively it seems not at all strange that the boy on the next farm, fat, spoiled, and bullying, would pave the way for Harry's escape from Smyrna village; and that Leo Stack would forever represent an unrealized dream—of acceptance, of wealth, of status in his own community, of a brilliant, happy, and opulent wedded life.

❧ 14 ☙
Aunt Margaret

> Most people learn [early in life, that] the power of
> verbal propositions ... is a function of the person
> who hears [them], that a thing perfectly useful with
> mother does not click so well with father, and that
> some things which are quite effective with both
> mother and father lead to anxiety when tried on the
> maiden aunt who has had some experience in edu-
> cating children and sees that little Willie is becoming
> a rationalizer.
> —Sullivan, *Conceptions of Modern Psychiatry*

In various autobiographical references, Sullivan stresses in an almost
one-dimensional way the plight of the only child isolated on the farm
with an overconcerned mother and a shy father. This same oversimplified
picture appears in a biographical sketch written by his close friend and
colleague, Clara Thompson. As a clinician, Sullivan warns against the
lack of reality in such one-dimensional accounts and recommends that
the therapist look for the missing person, the semiparent.[1] Margaret Stack
was such a semiparent in Harry's life.

In lectures on the early school years, Sullivan makes numerous references to a "maiden aunt," which are wry, half critical and half indulgent.
She is not given much credit in his theory, except in a somewhat negative
fashion, as in the epigraph for this chapter. Here the maiden aunt is unnamed, but she teaches school; elsewhere, she is called Aunt Agatha, or
Aunt Katherine, or whatever. Sometimes her nephew goes unnamed or
he is called "little Willie," but in either event, the aunt is Margaret Stack,
and the nephew is self-centered in his relationship with this aunt:

I've often wondered if I'm the only person in psychiatry or the social sciences who has pointed out the absence of anything properly referable to
as love before preadolescence.... No matter how much your parents
knew you loved them as children, and however dear some teachers of
yours knew you were, and however 'intimate' you were with the members
of your ball team and so on, you mattered most. You mattered actually so

exclusively that only miracles of foresight prevented your showing how terribly self-centered you were to doting Aunt Katherine, who came to you expecting a great enthusiasm and one thing and another on your part, instead of merely curiosity as to what gifts she brought and what favors she would give. In other words, there is no unnecessary concern with other people's satisfactions or securities [before preadolescence].[2]

Although Sullivan does not accord much respect to "Aunt Katherine," it is his own aunt who emerges as the most significant adult in his transition from Smyrna to the larger world. As he was growing up, she continued to move farther and farther away from Smyrna, first to South Otselic, then to Oneonta in the next county eastward, and finally to New York City and environs. But each summer she came back to Smyrna, bringing Harry visions of this ever more distant world. In the end, it was Margaret Stack who would rescue all of them, giving Ella Stack some realization of her dream that Harry would finally become famous and justify all the frustrations that dwelt in her fettered life; furnishing most of the money that would educate Harry; and almost convincing Timothy that—even though he did not understand the strange world of psychiatry and mental hospitals—his only child had become important in that world.

Both the neighbors in Smyrna and Sullivan's colleagues have described his early life as that of a poor farm boy, and many stories in this vein still survive in the Chenango hills. As the most famous resident of Smyrna in the first part of the century, he is still a thorn in the side of some of the old residents, who find comfort in the fact that they knew him when he had nothing. Some of them remind each other that, even though he eventually had an office on Park Avenue in the City, he could not afford to buy markers for his parents' graves in the cemetery in Sherburne. In one familiar reminiscence, Harry as a young boy was delivering eggs at the house of a well-to-do resident, and he paused to admire a map of the world that hung on the wall. "How much did that map cost?" he asked the neighbor. "Fifty cents," he was told. "Wal," Harry said (and the story always includes this "wal"), "I guess it will be a long time before I get one like that." Yet this story is apocryphal; everybody in Smyrna knew, and perhaps resented, that Harry Sullivan got books all the time from his Aunt Margaret in the City, and that his wish for a map would have to wait only until Margaret Stack was informed of it. Harry knew that too. There seems little doubt that no child in Smyrna was kept better supplied with intellectual stimulation from the broader world in which Margaret Stack lived. Doubtless his two uncles, Ed and John, were also generous in their gifts to Harry, but it was his Aunt Margaret who formed the real link between the world of ideas and his life on the farm with two rather elderly parents. With real justification, the Stack cousins still resent the posthumous summations of Harry's early life as being that of a poor farm boy. He had never really wanted for anything, they thought, except for companionship; his Aunt Margaret had seen to that.

In the County, she is still referred to as "Maggie Stack," and that was her name as given in the first official record that is extant—the state census report for 1875, when she was eleven years old. Her Stack relatives— James Stack's children and grandchildren—call her Margaret, or Aunt Margaret. But on official documents, including her death certificate, with information provided by her nephew Harry S. Sullivan, her name is given as "Marguerite." Her birth certificate was destroyed long ago in a fire, so there is no way to determine her official name, which in fact is true for most of the Stacks and the Sullivans. In general, as in other immigrant families, the name was subject to the occasion for which the name was being used. Thus she herself used the name Marguerite when she filled out her application for normal school; she also made herself five years younger on that form, just as Sullivan, for other reasons, would add five years to his age early in his career. Some of these decisions made in a state of anxiety by Margaret Stack and by Sullivan too did not exhibit much foresight and would prove embarrassing later; out of such vain strivings for security, Sullivan would understand the role of anxiety in life—a state that may make a person unable to profit from an unfortunate experience.

As long as Leo needed her, before his father remarried, Margaret spent most of her time in South Otselic at the Gothic House. Part of the time she taught school there—first in the nearby country school, then at the Union School. She was past thirty when that part of her life was over. This was followed by a brief period when she taught at the country school that Clarence Bellinger attended, before he went to high school in Smyrna. Indeed, Margaret may have been the initial link between Clarence and Harry in the plan for them to ride together to the village school.

In 1900, when Harry was eight and one-half and about to embark on his friendship with Clarence, Margaret went away to normal school in Oneonta, in the next county eastward, to be trained as a teacher in a two-year course. Shortly afterwards, she went to Brooklyn, New York, to teach at Public School 164 for the next thirty years.

She was thirty-five years old when she went to Oneonta, but she listed her age at registration as thirty; her "guardian" is listed as Edmund Stack, who probably agreed to be financially responsible. She seems to have had some hesitancy about identifying herself as a Catholic, for her church connection is given as Presbyterian on the entrance form; this was later crossed out, apparently by the same person, and "Catholic" substituted—that is, the handwriting is the same, but a different pen was used. Lucy, one of James Stack's daughters, had preceded Margaret at Oneonta, identifying herself as a Catholic; and Margaret may have been shamed into a declaration of loyalty to the Church. But two years later, when Margaret graduated from normal school, her practice teaching record shows that she is "Episcopal," as if some compromise had been worked out in her mind between Catholic and Presbyterian. In venturing out into the larger world after Oneonta, she must have seen clearly what the penalties would be for identifying herself as Catholic, in that time and place. The picture had been all too clear for her, as she moved back and forth from the hotel in South Otselic, where Ed had money and prestige, to the dark farmhouse in Smyrna where life was frugal in all directions.

At best, Margaret's exposure to formal education was limited, but by comparison with other women of her time in rural areas her accomplishments were impressive. Although she had only a grade school education when she went to Oneonta Normal School, she had begun to acquire certain skills in South Otselic that were important and proper for a young woman of that time. By the time she left Oneonta, these skills were formally recognized in her record there—she could sing, play the piano, and draw. Her marks at Oneonta show the same pattern as Harry's would later show at Cornell: during her first term, her marks were good—14 A's out of 22 grades, in an amazing array of subjects. Thereafter, most of her grades declined, with only one A, in psychology. Many of the subjects in her first term were in the sciences—botany, physiology, zoology, physical geography, chemistry, astronomy; in all of these subjects she received the mark of A. In Latin 1 and Latin 2, she also received a mark of A. Her exposure to Latin and science was undoubtedly a prelude to Harry's early interest in those subjects. When she went to the City to teach, the enriched curriculum of city children played its part in further broadening Harry's interests.

In the task of readying Harry for a career, there was a division of labor between the two women, Ella and Margaret, the oldest and the youngest of the children in an immigrant family. Together they focused their hopes and their lives on Harry, who in reality belonged to both of them more than he ever belonged to his father. Each recognized the importance of the other. It was Harry's mother who stayed on the farm and fussed over the growing child, waited on him, protected him from farm chores, cooked hundreds of chickens and baked innumerable pies in the hot summer months over a wood stove, washed thousands of eggs for marketing, finished tasks set for Harry by his father but abandoned before they were completed—a pattern of devotion that made him forever dependent on someone for the daily routine of living, so that at the end of his own life he was, at some level, as much an invalid as he considered his mother. As an adult he would describe his mother to Clara Thompson as a "complaining semi-invalid with chronic resentment at the humble family situation," but this was only one part of her nature, as he knew full well.[3] When Margaret came in the summer, Harry was exposed to the ready wit and the good conversation that went on between the Stacks. Although the neighbors saw Ella Stack as a recluse—withdrawn and retiring, devoted to her chickens, to her churning, to her housekeeping, and very careful with money—her relatives, including the Normiles on the Sullivan side of the household, saw her as hospitable and generous, almost gregarious at times. It was Margaret Stack who kept this part of Ella alive on her summer visits so that Ella could continue to function for Harry in the long winter months.

In the beginning, it must have been bewildering to the child to observe that his mother could be a different person in certain situations, that when they visited the Normiles each fall in Norwich, his mother wanted to listen to John McCormack on their phonograph and hear again about a concert he had once given in Binghamton. She expressed interest in lectures and concerts, although it is doubtful that she ever attended one either in the Smyrna Opera House or in Norwich.[4] His later formulation of the importance of interpersonal relationships must have taken root early, as he saw his mother change before his eyes on such occasions: "For all I know," he once said, "every human being has as many personalities as he has interpersonal relations."[5]

Margaret's role with Harry was much more rewarding, of course, but Ella seems never to have resented the closeness of her sister's relationship with her son. A picture of Margaret Stack's importance to Harry emerges from Margaret Normile's report of a visit she made to the farm in 1907. Harry at fifteen was about to enter his last year of high school, and his cousin Margaret, who was eight years old, was visiting on the farm to regain her health after a bout with jaundice. Harry appears in his cousin's account as clearly adolescent in appearance. She reports that he was at the gangly stage, very thin, with no interest in food. He wore glasses—an indication of the fact that his extensive reading had already made it obvious that he needed them. In manner he was uncomfortably defiant with his parents and treated his young cousin as if she were "thin air." But his relationship with Aunt Margaret was confiding and close; one gets the feeling that she was more like an older sister, although there was a difference of almost thirty years between them. In one group photograph, Margaret Stack looks enough like Harry as an adult that they could be mistaken for brother and sister.

Margaret Normile slept in a small room, next to Margaret Stack's. After the young girl had gone to bed, she would hear Harry come in to his aunt's room and she would hear them talking in very low tones, very late; he was confiding in his aunt, asking her about schools in the outside world, and so on. His Aunt Margaret was "the only person Harry related to" in the household, according to Margaret Normile; they had a close intellectual relationship, she thought. She describes Harry as having a "barren" life on the farm: "Harry must have been practically closeted with his parents for long months. The only relief came to him summers in the person of his aunt. . . . It was however a female influence, and she, too, adored him [like his mother]. She was more of a sophisticate, more realistic, than his mother. It must have been a barren sixteen years [on the farm], with books and introspection his only pastimes." Yet as Margaret [Normile] Hannon would eventually point out to Sullivan, "You left Smyrna with every book you read, with every publication your Aunt Margaret sent you."

Even as young women, Ella and Margaret Stack had begun to play the roles in which they were cast by fate. A picture of Ella as a young woman shows her as handsome, proud, and determined, as if she were already fighting against the fate of the eldest girl in an immigrant family. The pictures of Margaret as a young woman—and there are several, some doubtless coming out of her sojourn in South Otselic—show a softness and a gentle beauty that are lacking in Ella's picture, and reflect the relative ease of her own growing-up years, cushioned as she was by being the youngest child in the family. The years wrought changes in both their faces, of course. Margaret's gentleness was modified by some of life's disappointments, so that later on her face reflected some of Ella's determination in the early years. Ella's face, when she was in her seventies, appears eagerly accommodating, but it is the face of a person who has given up long since; as she had grown older, the proud neck that appears in her youthful pictures seems to have collapsed in a congenital weakness, and that, too, contributed to the quality of defeat in her demeanor. Margaret was never defeated, and this would be a quality that Harry Stack Sullivan would maintain until the end of his life.

Margaret must also have been high-spirited. Dorothy Stack remembers her that way: "What a knowing heart. Then too she was so full of fun. Once when my ear of corn was too hot to eat, she told me to dunk it in my ice water. Mother watched me in horror, as my manners were always *perfect*. Margaret said, 'I told her to,' in twinkling glee before Mother could say a word. All the Stacks 'twinkled' and were very charming, and that is the way I remember Harry—very much a Stack."[6]

There is little doubt that Margaret was the most sophisticated and charming woman that Harry knew intimately, over long stretches of time, in his growing-up years; as he timidly began to be aware of his emergent sexual feelings, he must have seen her as a threat to his studied composure. His mother was old and fussy, and it was easier to deny her as a sexual being. But with Margaret it was more difficult. Her sheer sophistication from living in hotels—first at the Gothic House and then later at the Hotel St. George in Brooklyn Heights for the last twenty years of her life—was a quality that Sullivan would always admire and try to emulate. Some of her sophistication was superficial, but it was underlaid with wisdom and an acceptance of different kinds of living arrangements, a tolerance for all sorts of people, and a real knowledge of how difficult was the path from a small farming community to the large city. In family annals, Margaret is described as living at the Hotel St. George with a "woman friend," but this is the only note of mild disapproval that emerges from a description of Margaret's accomplishments, with the implication that perhaps her famous nephew had somehow tried to emulate her in this way by living with a male friend. When Margaret was past seventy, she still retained the stance of a "real sophisticate," according to Leo Stack's daughter, Dorothy, who tells of having dinner with her:

She was in her seventies then. Her dear friend, Betty, had died, and Margaret [had been] retired for a number of years from the New York Public School System, but she just fascinated me. . . . We sat in her room and talked, and of course I was still a young girl, and she was an old lady. I expected to find an old lady, because quite a number of years before that, my mother had sent her a very elegant silk-satin nightgown with lace [as] a present, and Margaret had returned it saying that she no longer wore such things. And my mother felt a little sad about it because Margaret had been a very smart woman. . . . Well, when I got to the St. George Hotel, she greeted me in the sheerest of black silk stockings, and beautiful legs, with high-heeled black patent leather pumps. . . . [She had on] a black dress printed with rather bright colors in a rather small pattern—it was a very attractive dress. Her figure was like a girl's—really lovely. Her hair was dyed a sort of caramel color—a very soft, light brown; Margaret's hair was [naturally] very dark and slightly wavy. . . . Margaret also astounded me by smoking a cigarette in a long, long dramatic cigarette holder. This is not at all what I was prepared for. And she tripped down to the St. George dining room on her little high heels like a young girl.[7]

The story of Margaret Stack reflects the story of many a young woman in that day; it is peculiarly the story of unmarried Irish-American women who dedicated their lives to careers as nurses or teachers in the cities of America, so that nieces and nephews could have a chance. At that time, custom and sometimes even law dictated that such careers could not be continued after marriage; only single women, or widows like Ruth Benedict's mother, were allowed to think of having a career. In particular the daughters of immigrants clustered together, like the hired girls in Willa Cather's *My Ántonia,* to brave the trials of living in the outside world, whether city or town. Thus several of James Stack's daughters and granddaughters set up islands of hope and safety in the City; they were loyal to and supportive of each other and of those left behind in the rural areas. Such women gained considerable knowledge of educational opportunities; as women, they did not have equal opportunity with men, but they struggled to make the dream come true for others.

In the Sullivan family, too, there was such an aunt—Ella Sullivan Crandall, Timothy's sister. She became a nurse in Philadelphia and did not marry until late in life. Most of her life was given over to the care of others. She also took an interest in Harry and may have helped him financially and psychologically at one time. Although she was far removed geographically from Harry during most of her life, she was a tower of strength for other young relatives in Norwich; and her reputation among the Sullivan relatives in Norwich is essentially the same as that of Margaret Stack.

For both Leo Stack, the motherless boy in South Otselic, and Harry Sullivan, caught on the farm with rather elderly parents, Margaret Stack was a refuge; she was a semiparent to both of them. She was the extra resource that made a difference to a wide range of people who refer to her as "Aunt Margaret," although perhaps no relationship existed at all, or at best only a second cousinship of another generation. In a formal picture of James Stack's direct descendants and their families, taken in the 1920s, the only collateral relative in this group of nineteen people is Margaret Stack. By then, most of James Stack's descendants were city dwellers and had long since accommodated themselves to America. Michael's children and grandchildren had also moved well beyond Smyrna, except for Harry's mother.

As the years went on, it must have been a burden for both Margaret and Harry to go back to the low-ceilinged interior of the farmhouse, with its discouraged and lonely inhabitants. But Margaret remained faithful to the end, and set a standard here, too, for Harry. When Ella died in the winter of 1926, both Margaret and Harry were in the farmhouse, helping to care for her; he had come from his clinical duties in Towson, Maryland, and she from her teaching duties in Brooklyn. There was no electricity, no plumbing, no central heating. If they had gone to a farmhouse in the west of Ireland, the contrast could not have been sharper.

❧ 15 ❧

Graduating from High School

> The two, who are never so happy as when they are together, unwittingly but assiduously cultivate each other's characteristics, develop identical or complementary interests, and so alter their social values that they come to be in more or less complete agreement one with the other.
>
> —Sullivan, *Personal Psychopathology*

N o matter when the formal decision to become a psychiatrist was made by either Clarence or Harry, the pathway toward that outcome seems almost predetermined by the Smyrna years; and the coincidence must be accepted as more than the spin of chance. For six years, the two of them had grown together in their intellectual interests and in their shared goals. They had obviously discussed various possibilities for a profession that would satisfy the yearnings of their respective mothers. And they had been exposed to an extraordinary debate on the meaning of mental disorders, suicide, and crime in the daily news in the Norwich *Sun.*

In his lectures, Sullivan would comment on the process of sharing goals, beginning with the advent of the preadolescent chum: "If, for example, one of them has some vague interest in chemistry and the other had no interest at all in any particular natural science, the chances are that the relatively uninterested one will be happy to develop an acquaintance with chemistry."[1] Sullivan reports that his own interest when he first graduated from high school was in becoming a physicist, although his "curiosity about people and their relationships gradually took precedence over his curiosity about things. Shortly after graduation he decided to study medicine and psychiatry," according to his own account.[2]

Even before that decision was made, however, it seems more than likely that Clarence and Harry had discussed the career of physician. In another reference to preadolescence, Sullivan seems to be speaking specifically of Clarence and himself as planning together on the possibility of becoming physicians:

Then was the first time that one began to be keenly interested in matters that can properly be called the state of society, the civilization in which one lives, the future that would grow out of the present. Not in terms of, *I will go to school and become a doctor, and thereby get on intimate terms with a great many desirable women, and make money,* and all that sort of thing; but rather in terms of, *Well, what are the responsibilities that a doctor ought really to perform, and will I be able to do a good job in that field? . . . What is the best plan for my future, which will give me a good living and a feeling of self-respect as a worthwhile person among other people?*[3]

It was Clarence who graduated first from Smyrna High School, in June 1906, two years before Harry. Although Clarence had toyed with the idea of studying law, he spent the next four years in medical school at Syracuse University. So eager was he to be both a physician and a lawyer that he would lead his colleagues in later life to suppose that he had been enrolled initially at Syracuse in prelegal training, but no evidence of this exists in the University records. Nor did his specialty in psychiatry show up in his four years at Syracuse. But in the first summer after he graduated from Syracuse, he had a psychiatric residency at St. Elizabeths Hospital in Washington, D.C., under the superintendence of William Alanson White, who had been a staff psychiatrist at Binghamton State Hospital from 1892 to 1903. No record exists of any further contact between White and Bellinger. A decade later, Sullivan, too, would have his first formal training in psychiatry under White at St. Elizabeths, and their association would continue until White's death.

Newspaper accounts of Clarence's graduation from the village high school show that his class was composed of six students, three boys and three girls—an unusually large proportion of boys for that period, representing some older boys who had gone back to school when a high school education had become available in Smyrna. As was customary at that time, each graduate performed at the exercises, but there was a sharp differentiation between the girls and the boys: the girls' contributions were labeled "essays" or "themes," and the boys' "orations." The titles of the essays in general were more contemplative; the titles of the orations were more action-oriented. Clarence chose as his subject "The Influence of Invention on Civilization"—a strangely appropriate title in view of his later career in psychiatry: he would become one of the early advocates of insulin shock treatment, metrazol, and finally electroshock therapy for hospitalized patients—chemical and mechanical "inventions" that Sullivan would never countenance in his own care of patients.

Clarence's graduation was an event of significance for Harry—now he would again be an isolate in the school. Moreover, the graduation of Clarence's class removed most of the older and more accomplished students from the school. The high school as a formal part of the New York State regents' system was relatively new in Smyrna, and several students in the early years represented a backlog of older students in the township who were interested in advanced schooling.

There are two group pictures of students taken in the period after Clarence graduated; in both pictures, Harry, at fifteen or sixteen, seems considerably older than the other students. In one picture, taken in front of the schoolhouse, Harry stands in the back row as the tallest boy in the school picture—spectacled, austere, and flanked on each side by three girls. He could be a teacher by his mien, for he looks almost middle-aged. In his confirmation picture, taken some three years earlier, he had looked undeveloped for his age; but in this picture he looks as if he had glided silently into middle age, with no intervening experience. In the other group picture, taken in the interior of the Opera House at either a birthday party or the graduation class party, Harry stands off to the side of the group, tall and gauche, one eyebrow cocked in a nervous gesture that he retained as an adult. As in the school picture, he is the only person wearing glasses. His suit, ill-fitting and of a lighter color than that of any of the other boys or men in the picture, makes him look as if he is a janitor, or a scarecrow from his father's field. As one old settler of Irish-American parentage has suggested, the Irish in Smyrna were about as popular as a skunk at a Sunday School picnic. Another resident of the County, also Irish-American in origin, said of the picture: "Well, at least, he [Harry Sullivan] made it to one party." The picture illustrates both attitudes. In the last summer of Sullivan's life, he would attend a conference in Roffey Park, near London; in a picture taken of the main participants at that conference, Sullivan stands at the edge of the group and seems equally ill at ease.

Harry's graduation in 1908 ended the two-year period of isolation at the village school. He had seen Clarence on holidays and during summer vacations, when he was home from Syracuse University. Clarence had new and challenging knowledge to report, which for the first time gave him an intellectual advantage over his devoted slave. Two decades later, Sullivan refers to the developmental change in the "isophilic friendship," which may well apply to the gradual change in his relationship with Clarence: "By their [older folk's] fancied approval and disapproval, even the affectional bonds of an isophilic friendship that has survived puberty may be disintegrated in the service of status-pursuit."[4] Some such pursuit must have occupied Clarence in the role of studying to be a doctor, while Harry was still in high school.

But in June of 1908 Harry began a period of unusual glory, to which Clarence was witness. Clarence arrived home for the summer vacation on

14. Harry's confirmation picture, 1904

15. The Smyrna schoolhouse

16. Harry as a high school senior, 1908

17. Harry (standing at extreme right) at a party in the Smyrna Opera House, about 1908

June 2; and on June 6, as reported in the *Sun,* Harry went to Norwich as a candidate for the annual examinations for the State Cornell University scholarship, held in the Supervisors' rooms in the courthouse. There were only three candidates in the County, two from Norwich and "Harvey [sic] S. F. Sullivan of Smyrna." It was a signal honor for the high school in Smyrna, so newly formed. No such honor had been bestowed on Smyrna at the time of Clarence's graduation.

A series of stories on the graduation events appeared in the *Sun.* On June 23, the pastor of the Baptist Church in Smyrna preached the baccalaureate sermon in the Opera House. Two other pastors of local Protestant churches participated in the formal ceremonies for the three graduates, one of whom—the most brilliant—was Catholic. One evening there was a party for all the students in the school.

On June 27, 1908, the *Sun* carried the story of the graduation exercises:

On Wednesday evening the graduation exercises of Smyrna High School were held in the opera house which was tastefully decorated in white and gold, the class colors. A bank of daisies and large anchor of the same flowers were among the chief decorations. The three graduates consisted of Miss Evelyn Eddy, who delivered an excellent theme on "The American Indian," Miss Susie Tackabury, who spoke most pleasing on "Atmosphere," and Harry Sullivan, who delivered an able and thoughtful oration on "Achievements in Science." An orchestra furnished music between the speaking, Rev. Charles Frear delivered the invocation, Hon. G. P. Pudney presented the diplomas in his usual happy manner, and Rev. W. D. Eddy pronounced the benediction.

As the valedictorian, Harry was the last speaker. No matter how grudging the old Yankee settlers were, he was obviously the brightest student and had brought honor to the village. On June 30, he and the two girl graduates journeyed to Norwich to have their pictures taken at a studio.

On July 6, the final glory was achieved. The announcement appears on page 5 of the *Sun,* and indicates some confusion about the order of his middle initials:

Smyrna Boy Wins Cornell Scholarship
Harry S. F. Sullivan Was the Successful Candidate
From Chenango County

Albany, July 6 (Special): State Education Commissioner Andrew S. Draper has just announced the list of successful candidates for Cornell University scholarships. The awards are made annually, after competitive examination, and there is a state scholarship for each of the one hundred and fifty assembly districts in the state.

The successful candidate from Chenango county was Harry F. S. Sullivan of Smyrna. . . .

Harry's registration at Cornell would be in the College of Arts and Sciences. It would be three more years before he entered medical school in

Chicago; and the path by which he arrived at medicine and psychiatry was complicated and considerably delayed.

So it was that neither Clarence nor Harry had any visible commitment to psychiatry when they first graduated from high school. Yet the decision was already in the making, as one reviews the pattern of their lives and the history of mental disorder in the County. Moreover, there was an important link to a psychiatrist in the village itself. The only physician in Smyrna at that time was T. G. Packer, who had attended Ella in her first delivery and had been the officiating physician at the time of Mary Stack's death. Dr. Packer had a son, Flavius, who also became a physician, first defining himself as a neurologist and then as a psychiatrist. By 1905, Flavius Packer, who was twenty-five years older than Harry, had established a small private hospital for mental patients in the Riverdale section of Manhattan. In the summer he sometimes sent patients to his father's house in the village of Smyrna, as part of their recovery; and it is possible that both Clarence and Harry may have seen these patients on the streets of the village. In any event, it is quite clear that by the time Harry went away to college, both he and Clarence were well aware of Flavius Packer's medical specialty and would have perceived him as having a conventionally successful professional and family life.

Yet this professional model from a previous generation does not explain the coincidence of Harry's and Clarence's professional and personal lives over the years. In a history of the village of Smyrna written in the early 1960s, Frederick Sprague, a native of Smyrna, somewhat older than either Harry or Clarence, has commented implicitly on these coincidences, as well as on Harry's getting into "trouble": "Clarence Henry Bellinger, son of Charles of Smyrna Hill and old district four, and born around 1890 [actually, he was born in 1887], became a prominent physician and was at the head of a state hospital for the insane, never married. In 1906 he was in the graduating class from Smyrna High School." Later, Harry's name appears: "Harry Sullivan, born the son of Timothy in Norwich Feb. 21, 1892, got into trouble as a boy charged with using the mails to defraud, yet he became a noted psychiatrist. He died unmarried in Paris, France, Jan. 14, 1949."[5] In the short space devoted to Harry, Sprague, who graduated from Cornell, has managed to touch lightly on the subject of some trouble that Harry got into when he went away to college; but the limited space on Harry's trouble does not do justice to the subject as it is still discussed in the County.

One small item that appeared in the *Sun* shortly after Harry and Clarence left for their respective universities in the fall of 1908 has a kind of symbolic significance for the careers that each would follow. In the Smyrna column for October 30, there is the following item: "Mrs. J. Smith who has made her home with C. H. Bellinger and family, has been adjudged insane and will be taken to the Binghamton State Hospital."

How long Mrs. Smith had lived in the household or who she was is not known; this almost casual personal note was a symptom of a widespread public health problem throughout the County. In the pages of the *Sun* from 1891 to 1910, there is a continuing preoccupation with mental illness, much of it violent, eventuating in suicide, suicide combined with homicide, and murder. The problems were colossal, and the preoccupation with them constituted a mental health problem in itself. The forces driving these two farm boys toward the field of psychiatry were omnipresent.

❧ 16 ❧
Prologue for a Psychiatric Career: Suicide and Murder in the Norwich *Sun*

We might illustrate the power of the press by commenting on its unintended effect of determining the fashions of suicide from time to time. . . . I have lived through three periods in which self-destruction by way of bichloride poisoning enjoyed a typical vogue. Bichloride poisoning is a horrible way of terminating life. The newspapers, without mentioning this, report . . . that some more or less notable person has died of [this] poisoning, self-administered. Shortly afterwards there are little squibs . . . in the newspapers to the effect that this and that person has died by bichloride. The fashion is spreading.
—Sullivan, *Conceptions of Modern Psychiatry*

BETWEEN 1900 and 1910, poison was a popular method for committing suicide in the County—partly because survivors did not have to clean up any blood, as the Norwich *Sun* reported. Thus one of the suicide fashions that Sullivan would have observed in his Smyrna years came from his reading of the *Sun*. The preoccupation with suicide in that part of the world was particularly intense in 1908, the year in which Harry graduated from high school and enrolled at Cornell. The rate of suicide for the County in that year was the highest in a ten-year period and the highest of any rural county registration area in New York State. The national rate shows this same peaking for 1908, partly related to the 1907 depression; but Chenango County had over twice the national rate in that year.[1]

Within the same period, murder also loomed large in the *Sun*. In June 1906, the year and month in which Clarence Bellinger graduated from high school, the *Sun* began an extensive coverage of four murder cases and for the next four years provided a conflicting dialogue on the relation between crime, mental illness, and social class. The first murder, the Thaw case, took place in New York City on June 25, 1906, and became the focus of national attention for many years. The second, the Gillette case, was reported in the *Sun* less than a month later; it impinged on the County more directly than the Thaw case, for the victim, a young unmarried woman pregnant by the defendant, was a County resident, although she was drowned in another county. Eventually this second murder would be fictionalized in Theodore Dreiser's *An American Tragedy*. The third and fourth murders took place in the County itself. The third murder, the Scott case, took place on October 26, 1907, shortly after Harry began his last year in the Smyrna school; and the fourth, the Hill case, took place on August 26, 1908, shortly before he left for Cornell. Both the Scott and the Hill cases eventuated in conviction of first-degree murder—the first such convictions in the County for twenty-five years.

These stories of suicide and murder provided Harry with his first and perhaps most important data on the prevalence of mental illness around him and the role of the psychiatrist in observing the human scene and in acting as an expert in murder trials. Clarence, who left Smyrna two years before Harry, was provided with some of the same influences in the choice of his career. As one reads through these news stories for the critical years, one begins to understand why both of these isolated boys might choose to be psychiatrists.

Specifically for Harry, the stories in the *Sun* also offer an insight into what must have been his own experience at Cornell and how he and others in the County would have viewed the events. Moreover, the stories often included a sexual dimension and so were particularly significant for a boy who belatedly was experiencing the initial urgent onset of sexual feelings.

In the first decade of the century, the high rate of suicide hit many of the rural counties, including Chenango, that had been involved in the spate of religious fervor in the first half of the previous century. Two of these counties showed an even higher rate than Chenango County during at least one of these ten years.[2] Thus, as a new century began, faith in a personal God who would reward the deserving had begun to falter in this part of the world, and suicides on the farms and in the villages expressed the community's sense of abandonment. Even the urban areas in New York State did not show the same high rates of suicide during this ten-year period. What was happening in these rural areas during these years was clearly worse than the impersonality of the big cities as a backdrop for suicide.

In the days before the invention of the radio and television, the weekly newspaper was the window on the world for most people in rural areas. Thus the Norwich *Sun,* as an independent daily in a small rural county, represented an early and unusual example of the impact of daily mass communication on a small community. Only three other villages in the state that were comparable in location and size (less than 6,000 population in the village of publication and located in rural counties) had a daily.[3]

In the pages of the *Sun,* readers found a continuing debate on the meaning of suicide, gradually moving towards a more profound understanding of the phenomenon as potentially extending to all people in trouble, regardless of age, sex, or social class. At the same time, the *Sun* inadvertently promoted a kind of contagion of suicide as a way of exit from trouble and even implicitly recommended the way in which suicide could be best handled so as not to disturb, more than necessary, the relatives and friends who found the body.

In spite of the community's preoccupation with suicide during the pertinent years, the newspaper did not specifically admit the serious nature of this public health problem until 1909, when the rate of suicide had begun to decrease in the County. An editorial in the *Sun* for July 10, 1909, reporting on the increase in deaths by suicide in New York State, implied that Chenango County was a part of this problem. Up until then, there had been an attempt, as there was in 1893 with the economic depression, to locate the trouble in other rural areas—or in cities, or with people who were shiftless, immoral, or whatever. At another level, the *Sun* had struggled for some time to be fair, to understand what was happening, and to make sense out of this serious problem; by 1909, it had begun to admit that the trouble was ubiquitous.

The seriousness of the situation in this early period can be measured in part by my own field experience in the County a half century after this epidemic of suicide. From the time of my first contact with the County, various people volunteered information to me about suicide; this was before I had begun to read the *Sun* or to formulate for myself the intense preoccupation of people in that part of the world with the fear of suicide. The thread of suicide continued to run through all my field work in Chenango County, extending over a period of more than a decade. For example, County residents would spontaneously mention the number of suicides on a particular village street over the years, the human motivations for suicide ("He wouldn't turn Catholic, and she wouldn't give up her Church, so he hung himself in her barn"), and even the question of whether Harry Sullivan's death was a suicide.

Several people in the County suggested to me that the mystery of Ella Stack Sullivan's illness might be related to an attempt to kill both herself and Harry. That she was disturbed and not directly involved with the care of Harry for some time seems more than probable; but the assumption, however correct, that she may have been involved in attempted infanticide and suicide is related to the local belief that a psychological disturbance involving a woman with a young child could be sympathetically and logically explained in this manner.

One can reconstruct the climate of Chenango County in the relevant years of Harry's life in Smyrna by focusing on what is basically an interlocking process. First of all, the pattern of suicide in the County is an index to the prevailing mental health of the community. Another vantage point centers around the murder cases that vastly mobilized the community's awareness of the meaning of murder and of the possibility that murder might be the outcome of mental disturbance. And finally, there are the countervailing forces mobilized in the community as a whole in an attempt to define a more meaningful way of dealing with life than suicide or murder or mental illness. These countervailing forces are also found in particular persons and social institutions. Thus the lawyer Will Sullivan, who was Timothy Sullivan's first cousin, developed an advanced attitude toward crime and mental illness and became an important force in the community. The Norwich *Sun* promoted a dialogue in the County by its own ambivalent treatment of the cause and cure for suicide, murder, and related violence. And the Binghamton State Hospital in Broome County to the south, the main resource for severely disturbed patients in Chenango County, had become over the years a source of leadership in more humane attitudes toward mental illness. Two psychiatrists who were on the staff at Binghamton in these early years would play a crucial role in Sullivan's adult professional life: William Alanson White, who was an assistant physician at Binghamton from 1892 until 1903, when President Theodore Roosevelt appointed him as head of the prestigious Government Hospital for the Insane in Washington, D.C. (St. Elizabeths); and Ross McClure Chapman, who had a post similar to White's at Binghamton, from 1908 to 1916, and then went to St. Elizabeths and served under White. Chapman subsequently headed Sheppard and Enoch Pratt Hospital near Baltimore, where he encouraged Sullivan to do his most famous clinical work with schizophrenic patients.

In his autobiography, White comments on his "introduction to the problem of suicide" at Binghamton: "While I had seen the results of this impulse in my general hospital experience I had never been personally acquainted with people who were depressed and who were headed in this direction."[4] The patients that White knew at Binghamton were sometimes people whose tragedies were reported in the *Sun.* Some of the patients came from Smyrna. In 1896, for instance, a prominent merchant in

Smyrna was forced to sell his business as a result of the economic depression; he was thereafter judged insane and taken to the hospital in Binghamtom. A month later he died there. The links between remote villages and the Binghamton State Hospital were intensified by such occurrences, which often necessitated the visit of a psychiatrist to the patient's home before and after hospitalization.

Sometime during the eleven years that White was at Binghamton, he began to do consultancies in the communities themselves, usually at the request of the local physician who would often anticipate trouble in a family. In slow buggy rides with the country doctor through outlying districts, White came to understand the importance of the family doctor in spotting the presence of trouble and its dynamics.[5] Thus the common sense of the family doctor became a part of White's approach; in later years Sullivan would appreciate White's forthrightness in approaching patients.

Retrospectively, White would summarize his experience at Binghamton as showing that patients "are very much more like the rest of us than they are different from us." And this one-genus postulate would also be basic to Sullivan's thinking. Yet at the time White left Binghamton in 1903, he was as nativistic in his attitude toward mental illness as most of the old Yankees in Chenango County. A few months before he left, he had given a paper before the National Geographic Society in Washington, D.C., in which he reported that 50 percent of the 25,000 insane in New York State are foreign-born—"the off-scourings of all Europe"; this "influx of defectives" will have "a constant leavening effect on the whole population," he predicted, using "leavening" in a pejorative sense.[6] At the same time, his experience at Binghamton had left White with other insights that would gradually overcome his simplistic nativism.

The legend of White as a benevolent physician remains strong to this day in Chenango County; and most people feel that it is logical that Harry Stack Sullivan would name his foundation after White. Somewhat reluctantly, Chenango County was also moving towards a one-genus postulate in the first decade of the century. The enlightenment came in large part from the pages of the *Sun*, which expressed slowly changing explanations for mental illness, suicide, and murder.

Part of the increase in suicide in Chenango County, as documented by the *Sun* for the first decade of the century, was obviously related to the alternatives in cases of poverty, poor health, frequent pregnancies, marital difficulties, financial ruin, and so on. Both the poorhouse at Preston, west of Norwich, and the state hospitals in other counties were far removed from most villages and farms in Chenango County; each of them spelled disgrace. The County Almshouse at Preston offered only a very deprived existence, accompanied by the special disgrace of failing in what had once been judged a land of plenty. Sometimes a man would kill himself just before he was to go to Preston. Often a person committed to the State Hospital would "die" shortly after admission; and one must assume that some of these deaths were accomplished by suicide and not reported as such in the newspaper out of deference to the family.

In the beginning, there were clear-cut answers in almost every suicide case reported in the *Sun*. The most reassuring cause was an inherited tendency. Following the depression of 1893, several prosperous farmers in the area killed themselves because of financial failure, and this, too, was accepted as a reasonable action.

Sometimes there was a spate of suicides in one particular locality that could not be explained in a reasonable way; and these occurrences lent themselves to the frightful idea of an epidemic. In an area that had been witness to many epidemics of both the spirit and the body, this thinking was natural and in many ways realistic. The presence of daily reports in the newspapers of these events helped to keep the idea of suicide and the preferred method constantly before the eyes of the public.

As early as 1890, the *Chenango Telegraph,* reporting on three suicides in and around New Berlin within a brief period, termed it a "suicidal epidemic," although the three suicides are linked together only in time and location, without any supporting evidence. On April 28, 1909, almost twenty years later, the *Sun* reported on an "epidemic of suicide" in Elmira (in an adjacent county) in which three persons killed themselves in a 48-hour period and a fourth tried and failed; in this account, the connection between the three deaths is made explicit.

In the course of this continuous and major preoccupation with suicide over a twenty-year period, the *Sun* published many detailed and insightful stories, some of them sympathetic about the fears of the victim. Yet there is a pattern of denial in what was happening, which only gradually gave way to more enlightened understanding. The main focus was on the belief that the staid, God-fearing, middle-class residents of Chenango County could dismiss what was happening. This dissociation took several forms: the *Sun* generally carried more startling details on suicides that took place elsewhere—in other counties, other states, other countries—or on suicides that took place in the County with the victim from elsewhere; or again, if the victim was poor or engaged in morally reprehensible conduct, the news story was more outspoken. Some geographic distance and an immoral sexual relationship offered the opportunity for detailed coverage of the story, for instance.

In Harry's last year of high school, two cases of suicide by young people struggling with problems of love and sex marked a change in the *Sun*'s approach. In the first case, the victim was a 19-year-old man from Binghamton who was employed in Norwich. The precipitating cause of his suicide was a letter he received from the girl he loved, saying that she was going to marry someone else. In a story carried prominently in the *Sun* for January 16, 1908, the paper makes it clear that a Chenango County girl had narrowly escaped marrying into a family doomed to disaster and possibly carriers of poor genes. The suicide of one son was merely a new disaster in a long series of untoward happenings in a large family that included another son who was under criminal indictment for larceny. Yet the story gives the victim his just due as "a young man of exemplary habits [and] an attendant at Calvary Baptist Church." The story exonerates the young woman from responsibility for having jilted the young man, since her own family had also had "its share of troubles," including the fatal accident of one brother and a second brother who had accidentally shot another young man. The whole story ends on almost a positive note, as if everybody did the best he could under tragic circumstances. There is ambivalence in the story, but the explanation has the air of being human and naturalistic.

The most interesting example of a change in attitude is found in the treatment accorded the second suicide. At the request of the family of the victim, the *Sun* published on March 2, 1908, a long letter written by a young girl to her fiancé shortly before she committed suicide. Both families were highly respected in the County. The girl's family had chosen this way to quiet speculation as to the cause of the suicide and also to express their understanding of the young man's innocence. The letter is not essentially different from those written by mentally disturbed adolescents today; thus blanks (like those indicated by dashes, as printed in the *Sun*) are often magic (and inconsistent) ways for avoiding words that evoke terrible anxiety—in this instance, words relating to marriage and marital sex. The letter and the comments made by the reporter illustrate a beginning public openness in discussing sexual matters. The story carries an implicit recommendation that sexual fears between young couples be discussed openly and reflects some of the reasonable fears held by women in that time and place about childbirth:

"My own true Claude. . . . I have cautioned mother and the rest not to lay any blame at all on my dear old boy because I am leaving you. People will talk but Claude remember, you, God and I know, that you dear heart, and I are innocent of sin between you and I. . . . You know that I love you for you have said that you knew I did, so don't think that it has ceased, only that I have done this to save you a lot of trouble in after years. You know Claude that I am easily discouraged that I am apt to cry any time just as much as I am to laugh. I believe I'm crazy. . . . You know I have cried a great many times when with you, but never could give any reason for it, could I? . . .

"So it would be still harder for you after we were ———, so for the great love I have for you, I'll save you all this trouble won't I dear. . . . Perhaps you will think I never intended to ——— you. Yes certainly I do, or will if I don't succeed in this, as I love you so, but something which seems to me just awful is the cause of this. Allow me to write a little, that I could talk to you if I were your ———. The problem of having children is horrors to me. . . .

"You know I have talked of suicide at times for three years, haven't I? Well that was the cause of it all. . . . Not but what I love children, it is the process. Oh! I know I ought to be willing to go through anything for the love of you but I am crazy or I could and be glad to. . . . Now Claude, in course of time I hope you will find another one, to take the place of Vera. One that will love you as dearly as I have, but not be crazy and foolish like I have. One that will make a lovely wife to you and oh! so loving. Sometime tell your children of Vera, the crazy, foolish acting Vera, that loved you so much that she rather give up her life, than ever cause you any trouble by being crazy. . . . Forgive me, please, for this awful horrid idea has an awful strong power over me. Now imagine Vera's arms around your neck, looking into those eyes so true loving you, with pats on the cheek, with kisses no end, but after a farewell one, X."

The news story included a plea from the parents and the *Sun* for understanding. The exposure of such intimate details by the family marks a new clarity in the approach to a suicide of a member of a County family in good standing. The paper does not attempt to do anything but express sadness. For the young people in the County, including Harry Sullivan, such a news story provided an opportunity to see, often in startling detail, what strong emotions and conflicts governed people's lives. The people whose tragedies appeared in the *Sun* were infrequently people that one knew, but almost always they were *like* people that one knew.

Most newspapers today could not print stories like those in the *Sun*, with so many conjectures about the lives of the principals, without running the risk of libel. Yet these stories began to expose the reader implicitly to the dangers of overly rigid standards for sexual morality, and to the need for rethinking the values of the nineteenth century. The problems emanating from the "civilized" sexual morality of America, as encountered and challenged by Freud in his 1909 visit, may have been recognized earlier by the residents of rural Chenango County than by the educated, upper-middle-class people living in and around Boston and other coastal cities. In a rural area, where people knew each other and their troubles intimately, at least by word of mouth, there had never been the same involuted neuroses that Freud had found in Vienna or that Morton Prince and James Jackson Putnam found in urban, upper-middle-class Boston.[7] The patients who committed suicide or went to Binghamton had succumbed to familiar nightmarish life situations that might have affected anyone's peace of mind. Farm animals kept most of the population in touch with the realities of sex and gestation, even though this exposure raised problems at the same time as to how the sexual behavior of humans should differ from that of farm animals.

In time, the actual crises that had been undergone by so many people in the County opened the door to the necessity for some change in attitude about sexual standards, for instance. Moreover, a kind of voyeurism was implicit in the detailed news in the *Sun,* so that people could begin to understand that their frightening emotions had been experienced by others.

As the infallibility of God diminished as a guiding principle, the role of man-made justice and the necessity for fair-minded experts became subjects of general interest, reflected in the *Sun.* In particular, the role of alienists and lawyers at murder trials had a special interest for both Harry and Clarence. Alienists and lawyers seemed at some level to have more power than judge or jury; and they had to be privy to the secrets of life and love, sickness and tragedy, that dwelt in the minds of murderers. The psychiatrist was obviously an important person in the scheme of things; and he was both revered and paid for being an expert. At the same time, he had a legitimate right to know something about the secret lives of people; if one could not participate in life directly, then one might vicariously observe the most intimate parts of other people's lives. The role of participant observer that Sullivan evolved so critically in his later thinking had some of its beginnings in his encounters with the four significant murder cases as reported in the *Sun.*

In the Thaw case, both the murderer and the victim represented "probably the most famous of murder cases involving America's super rich."[8] The murderer pleaded insanity at the time he committed the murder, with success. In the Gillette case, the murderer and his victim were both of modest backgrounds, and the murderer was eventually electrocuted. In the Scott and the Hill cases, the murderers were both relatively poor local boys and there was some question as to their mental competency; they were both electrocuted. Will Sullivan was appointed by the Court to defend both Hill and Scott, and he did so with dedication and at considerable emotional expense; his effort was, of course, unsuccessful. The outcome of these cases was not decided quickly, so that there was some interlocking of news on them during Harry's last two years in Smyrna and his first and only year at Cornell.

The enlightened position that Will Sullivan came to take on the issues of crime and mental disorder as related to social class must be seen as important in Harry Stack Sullivan's career. By an apparent coincidence, Will Sullivan held many of the same attitudes on crime and mental illness that William Alanson White had begun to espouse in that part of the world in the decade before these particular murders. From the time White first went to Binghamton, he began to take an interest in crime and mental illness, and this interest continued throughout his professional life, eventuating in many articles and two books on the subject. His interest was more than theoretical, for he engaged in various kinds of medico-legal work in these early years.[9]

While the influence of Wiliam Alanson White on Sullivan has been widely recognized, the importance of Will Sullivan is largely unknown, even in the County. The only direct evidence of Harry Sullivan's awareness of the importance of Will Sullivan to his own development is meager. Shortly after Sullivan's death, his unpublished writings were brought to the office of his journal, *Psychiatry*. Only one personal item was found in these files—a newspaper clipping from the *Sun*, on the death of "Judge Wm. H. Sullivan," with the date recorded in Harry's handwriting. Moreover, the record of Will Sullivan's life as obtained from the *Sun* and from innumerable old-timers in the County bears many striking similarities to Harry's career.

For over thirty-five years, William Henry Sullivan was known as "Judge Sullivan" in the County, a title stemming from his early career as a justice of the peace, from 1891 to 1900. In 1894, when Will was twenty-four years old, his career showed enough promise that the *Sun* carried a long article on him, titled "From Farm to Fame." It identifies him as a young man "of Irish parentage," but no mention is made of the fact that he was a devout Catholic; readers are reminded that he was "for many years" a hired man on the Bissell estate. The article ends with a personal and professional evaluation of Will Sullivan that evokes Harry's own lack of interest as an adult in having a fashionable and remunerative psychiatric practice: "Personally, Judge Sullivan is a jovial, big-hearted man whose only fault, if fault it is, is an excess of generosity. It is proverbial among the profession that he does enough legal service for nothing to make many a lawyer wealthy. He cares little for society, saying he does not feel at home there" (March 12, 1894).

From 1894 onward, Judge Sullivan's name often appeared on the front page of the *Sun,* sometimes in the headlines. Early in the century, he became an important figure in the Knights of Columbus, so that his Catholicism became a visible part of his life and eminence. Although his religious affiliation and ethnicity became accepted and acceptable in Norwich over the years, they were never completely accepted in the hill country around Smyrna. There were people in Smyrna who claimed to have actually seen the guns in the basement of his church, the Catholic church in Norwich, and it was quite clear that Will Sullivan was one of the people who would man those guns, when "they" were ready to strike.

During World War I, Will Sullivan was the chairman of the Chenango County Draft Board—a difficult post in that rural community, but one in which he gained new respect. In World War II, Harry Stack Sullivan would play an important role at a national level in establishing mental-health criteria for draftees, and in this way too, his career seems to echo Will Sullivan's.

In the years when Harry was considering a choice of career, Will Sullivan's fame increased, and part of this importance stemmed directly from the two murder trials in which he figured so prominently. There was a growing interest in trials, particularly for murder, in the *Sun;* and this interest was triggered in part by the Thaw case in New York City, which began to claim national and local attention in June 1906. At almost the same time, Clarence Bellinger graduated from Smyrna High School and perhaps regretted that he had committed himself to medical rather than legal training. Both boys must have followed the news avidly, for it was the kind of case that included conjecture about the life of the wealthy, the life of chorus girls, and the life of a famous architect, Stanford White, who had designed the gateway in Washington Square in Greenwich Village.

The first trial of Harry K. Thaw ended in a hung jury on April 13, 1907, with five jurors voting for acquittal on grounds of insanity. There were alienists for both the defense and the prosecution. Psychiatrists who had been connected with Binghamtom State Hospital appeared mainly as expert witnesses for the defense: C. G. Wagner, superintendent of the Hospital; Smith Ely Jelliffe, who had been associated with William Alanson White at Binghamton during an earlier period; and "Dr. W. A. White, superintendent of the government hospital for the insane at Washington, D.C." There were other alienists who appeared for both the defense and the prosecution in probably one of the most garish murder trials that ever took place in this country.

In later years, William Alanson White would report that his participation in this trial was a unique experience: "It probably may be said to be historically the beginning of the modern type of murder trial, and I may say that it and all similar experiences, of which there have been many in this country since then, I believe are not only exceedingly discreditable to our civilization but are decidedly harmful."[10] The problem, as White saw it, was that the so-called experts, often the alienists in a murder trial, could find themselves adversaries, some for the prosecution and some for the defense. In that event, the caliber of the experts might be determined by the wealth of the defendant. In the end, White proposed that a panel of experts make a recommendation in such cases, without representing either side as such.

The pages of the *Sun* showed the same kind of ambivalence and uneasiness about the issues of the Thaw case as had occurred around the issue of suicides. If Thaw were insane at the time that he murdered Stanford White, then he should be accorded the same verdict as the poor man—he was not responsible for an act committed when he was insane. But this thinking was offset by the fear that Thaw was receiving such special jail treatment that it was difficult to know whether he had been able to purchase favorable expert testimony. During Thaw's long stay at the New York Tombs cell, before any decision had been reached, he had his meals catered from Delmonico's.[11]

A second trial of Thaw began on January 6, 1908, and the spectacle of drama, wealth, and national coverage took on a new momentum.

Wagner, Jelliffe, and a London alienist testified. Finally a verdict was reached that Thaw was not sane at the time of the murder, so he was to be sent to Matteawan State Hospital for the criminally insane. Subsequently, Thaw's family used every method to show that he was now sane and should not be kept at Matteawan; and this kind of argument, decision, and counterdecision continued up to the time of Thaw's natural death many years later. On July 16, 1909, the *Sun* reported that Adolf Meyer of the state lunacy commission had testified about a conversation he had had with Thaw as to the reasons that led him to shoot Stanford White; Meyer also would be an important figure in Sullivan's career. Thus over a period of more than three years, the *Sun* had continuous coverage of the Thaw case, and the names of psychiatrists who would become crucial in Sullivan's own development appeared prominently.

While some of the editorials in the *Sun* on the Thaw case represented an informed way of looking at the issues involved, other statements reflected more punitive attitudes toward crime. They also predicted certain attitudes that still exist in the County about Harry Stack Sullivan himself and his own youthful encounter with the law while he was at Cornell. In brief, a new dilemma was posed by the plea of insanity in a murder trial: Would such a plea be used casually in cases of larceny, or lesser offenses, so that the community would become prey to thieves as well as murderers, and indeed to crimes of all kinds? The expert's theory of a "brainstorm," as the *Sun* termed it, could empty the jails into the surrounding countryside. This concern was a crucial prelude to the other murder cases that were already beginning to claim the attention of the *Sun* readers. Rural morality had need to show that it was superior to city morality; it was an old and important theme in rural America, and it would be used in a punitive and tragic way within Chenango County itself.

Less than three weeks after Thaw killed White in New York City, on July 14, 1906, the *Sun* carried its first report on the Gillette murder (the case made famous by Dreiser); in many ways this case superseded the Thaw case in importance for local people. An unmarried County girl from South Otselic, known as "Billie," had been drowned in Big Moose Lake in the northeastern part of the state. Suspicion centered on a 22-year-old man, Chester Gillette, with whom she was last seen. Chester and Billie had been working at a skirt factory in Cortland, owned by Chester's rich uncle, when Chester found out that Billie was pregnant by him. But he had already begun to think of marrying a rich girl who belonged to his uncle's circle. Billie's pressure for him to marry her when she found out about the pregnancy had dictated his taking a hasty trip with her to the Adirondacks, where the drowning took place.

Gillette's case stirred strong sentiments in Chenango County. On the one hand, he came essentially from the same general background as many of the residents of the County. He was considered a poor boy, and his parents belonged to a religious sect, not too dissimiliar to some of the sects in Chenango County. The Gillette family had traveled around the country in a missionary-like tradition; and Chester had eventually hunted up his rich uncle in Cortland, taking a job in his factory at a modest level in order to make something of himself. But sex had betrayed him.

Even today old-timers in the County express pity for Gillette. A distant relative of Billie by marriage noted sympathetically but not for the record that Billie had once worked for a doctor in South Otselic, and if she had told the doctor about her dilemma, "he would have helped her and all the terrible mess wouldn't have happened. . . . How different things are now. That was a long time back."

Although Gillette was not, strictly speaking, an ordinary God-fearing, ambitious poor boy—for he had traveled rather widely and had been at Oberlin College for a while—the *Sun* pictured him as a typical poor boy on his way up the ladder.[12] In the course of a long court case and several appeals, Gillette continued to be pictured as a poor boy who was caught in the machinations of the court procedures. There was an attempt by the newspaper during the long court case and appeal to evaluate the cause of the disaster and the moral meaning of Billie's behavior. The trial took place in Herkimer, seat for the county of the same name and the locale of the murder, but all aspects of the case were covered carefully by the *Sun,* mainly through boiler-plate material. Although the defense tried to prove that Billie had committed suicide, the jury found Gillette guilty of first-degree murder, and in December of that year he was sentenced to die in the electric chair. By the end of 1906, Gillette was in the condemned quarters in the Auburn prison, awaiting a date of execution. Early in 1907 his death was stayed by appeal. Later that year, Gillette, who had become quite a celebrity in his own right, gave advice to his friends, as reported in the *Sun,* not to read "certain kinds of books"; if he had not read such books he would not be in his present trouble (Aug. 16, 1907). There were more appeals and at least one stay of execution in early 1908, but on March 20, 1908, he was electrocuted in the Auburn prison.

In June of that year, Harry graduated from Smyrna High School. The execution undoubtedly formed a grim backdrop for Harry's plans to leave home and go out into the world. There were so many pitfalls; and certainly Harry would have access to many books that were dangerous to read. One can only imagine the anguish with which all these news stories were read in the farmhouse on Smyrna Hill.

In the fall preceding the execution of Gillette, another murder case began to claim the attention of the *Sun* readers. This time the suspected murderer was a Chenango County boy, and the murder had been committed near Norwich. On October 23, 1907, the *Sun* reported that the body of Delia Scott had been found by a search party led by her stepson, William Scott. The authorities gained a confession from Scott through a ruse perpetrated by a family friend, E. Harrington, who promised William his freedom if he would cooperate. The body showed that the woman was shot in the back and "a certain atrocious act committed on [her] after her killing" (May 4, 1907).

From the first, Scott had been a prime suspect, since he had left his parents' house in a wagon accompanied by his stepmother, and she had not been seen since. The *Sun* reported that Scott had shown signs previously of some character defect. He had after all recently been released from the reformatory in Elmira, where he had served a term for grand larceny in the second degree; and his own father stated that he believed that William had intended to kill both parents in order to gain possession of their home on Waite Street, perhaps in preparation for his forthcoming marriage. Waite Street was in a rather poor part of Norwich, only a few blocks away from the house in which Harry had been born. Both Scott's father and the stepmother were "full-blooded Irish," although William's own mother, who was dead, was not Irish.

The very first story in the newspaper reports that "some question has been raised as to [Scott's] sanity." And throughout the stories for the next twenty months until Scott's execution in Auburn prison, questions about his sanity, either explicit or implicit, appear here and there. There seemed to be very little overt motivation for the murder, and no indication that he had been mistreated by his stepmother.

On January 18, 1908, Scott was indicted for first-degree murder. He had no counsel, so the judge appointed Will Sullivan, who, two days later, filed a plea of not guilty, specifying insanity at the time of the commission of the crime. This plea was supported by Scott's friends, who reported that as a young boy he was "incorrigible" and that when he was very young he had been struck in the head by a wagon.

Throughout the trial, Will Sullivan made every effort to show that Scott was not responsible because of his "imbecility," which he cited as a form of mental disease. The drama of the situation is obvious: a poor Irish-American lad, fifteen years junior to Will Sullivan, was charged with murder; and a man who knew what it was to be poor and Irish-American was asked to defend the younger man singlehanded. There was no money for an expert psychiatric witness, so the lawyer must depend upon the best witnesses that he could obtain free of charge.

Throughout the trial, Will Sullivan did not attempt to deny that Scott had killed his stepmother, and he recommended that he be kept in a state asylum for life, claiming that Scott was insane at the time of the murder. The only alienist in the trial appeared for the prosecution. He testified that Scott knew right from wrong, but even he would not swear that Scott did not have some form of insanity.

Four physicians (not psychiatrists) appeared for the defense. All of them testified rather extensively to the fact that Scott had very poor eyesight. Scott's eyes had been operated on for cataracts, and one eye specialist noted that a cataract "weakens the mental facilities and is a mark of degeneracy." Another physician noted that Scott's skull was shaped somewhat abnormally, and such a condition might retard brain growth and cause insanity. In addition, there was expert testimony that Scott's senses of touch, sight, and hearing were defective, and "the senses being defective, transmission to the brain would be impaired and thus the mental faculties weakened" (May 1, 1908).

Near the end of the trial, the paper began to predict that Will Sullivan would probably lose the case; yet in the course of the intense period of the trial that lasted less than a week, public attitudes had been subject to some important changes. There was some beginning awareness that Scott had had a hard early life—that, as Will Sullivan had stated, he "was brought up in the grossest immorality." On May 2, only two days before Will Sullivan would give his summing up, the paper noted that "Attorney Sullivan is entitled to much credit for the work he has done in behalf of the defendant. . . . No one could have put forth greater efforts than Mr. Sullivan. . . . The defendant is without means and Mr. Sullivan is aware that his only reward will be the satisfaction of knowing that he has done his duty."

In his closing speech to the jury Will Sullivan pointed out that the defendant "did not know the nature and the quality of his act. . . . Every doctor sworn on the trial has agreed that the defendant was on Oct. 18th last, suffering from imbecility, which is a form of insanity. 'The only points on which they differ,' he said, 'were upon the degree of his insanity.' " Scott's mother had died when he was very young, and Will Sullivan pointed out that "this young man never knew the ennobling feeling of a mother's caress. He never had any of those influences which would develop a child's brain in the proper channels." Sullivan "also touched on a certain atrocious act committed on Mrs. Scott after her killing and asked 'Was that the act of a sane man.' He said such acts were those of imbecility and moral perverts." Referring to Harrington's deception of Scott, promising him liberty if he would confess, Will Sullivan said that it was a dirty trick. He frequently spoke of Scott as "a benighted imbecile, and a driveling idiot." Most of Sullivan's speech was taken up with listing Scott's acts of insanity and evidence of his hereditary defect. Toward the end, he read "extracts from several medical works." He said that there was no motive, and therefore the murderer was insane; "Sullivan asked for an acquittal on the grounds of insanity, saying that the defendant was no more responsible than would be the favorite horse of any one of the jurors, should he run away and thereby kill a human being" (May 4, 1908).

But the verdict on May 5, 1908, was that Scott was guilty of first-degree murder, although the jurors did not reach this decision until the fifth ballot. The conviction automatically carried with it the death sentence—the first such conviction in Chenango County in twenty-five years. The date of execution was set for June 22, 1908, but Will Sullivan appealed immediately. His appeals at each level would delay the execution for almost a year. These events were perceived in Norwich as being very hard on Judge Sullivan, and there was no criticism of his attempts to save Scott and later Hill, the other man defended by Sullivan and found guilty of first-degree murder. During both crises, Will Sullivan developed serious illnesses, and the *Sun* implied that these illnesses were a result of the tension under which he had operated in these cases.

On May 8, the *Sun* reported that Scott would rather die than go to the asylum—a view generally held in the County; thus the reporter has managed to reassure the formal jury and the larger reading public that Scott's problems would be best solved by death. So the young man with such poor eyesight and an odd-shaped head was disposed of for the moment, until a year later when Scott was executed and the *Sun* carried its largest headline in a twenty-year period.

In the summer of 1908, only a few weeks before Harry would leave for Cornell, there was another murder in Chenango County, called the Hill case. Thus before Scott reached the electric chair in June 1909, a second murder, almost as horrendous as the others, would claim the attention of *Sun* readers. In this instance, the suspected murderer, Earl Hill, was from Oneonta in an adjacent county; but the victim was a fairly prosperous Chenango County farmer, who was murdered on his farm in Bainbridge. Robbery seemed to be the only possible motive, and two suspects were almost immediately fastened upon in public opinion—one named Earl Hill, 19 or 20 years old, "described as reckless and not very bright," who was considered the instigator of the crime; and the other, David Borst, who "does not look like a criminal," and who claimed that he "was not the leader of the pair" (Aug. 27, 1908). "It was a case of getting into bad company," Borst maintained.

Feeling against the suspects was so high in the community that they had to be transferred to the Norwich jail, which was more tightly secured than the Bainbridge jail. On September 1, 1908, the *Sun* printed a story from the Oneonta *Star* which sums up the general attitude of the public: "The story of the events leading up to the crime, the crime itself and the parts which the principals and others have played since, is a strange one and is, it is safe to say, without parallel in the state of New York." Both Hill and Borst are "fairly representative of a type of young man which is to be found in saloons and other resorts" in every rural village in New York, the *Star* reports; they do not work, get support from their parents, and engage in pickpocketing. Borst had the better record, but was easily influenced by the "big, lusty fellow," Hill. "The boys made stealing their trade," according to the *Star*. Hill "did not appear to be worried over his capture, for he rolled cigarettes, nonchalantly, and said but little."

In the early arraignment of Earl Hill, an affidavit asked that counsel be assigned to Hill, and the court again assigned Will Sullivan to an indigent murder defendant. Hill entered a plea of not guilty. Between the arraignment and the trial, which began in April 1909, Will Sullivan was ill, and during most of March, he was in Georgia because of ill health. By now, it must have seemed clear to him that Scott, who was at Auburn awaiting various appeals, was destined to end up in the electric chair; and Hill, if one was to judge by the attitude expressed in the newspaper, seemed destined to become another occupant of death row at Auburn.

On April 27, 1909, the *Sun* commented on Will Sullivan's health, only three days before the Hill case was to go to trial: "Since his return from the south, Attorney Wm. H. Sullivan seems a different man. It is evidence that his sojourn in Georgia has worked wonders in restoring his health, for he is once more the same alert, watchful, capable 'Sully' that the 'boys' all remember. His color is good, he appears fresh as a cucumber and says he is 'feeling fine.' " There is in this item a clear indication that the community is beginning to understand the heavy burden that has been laid on Will Sullivan through these months, and a growing sense of community responsibility to see that a fair trial is obtained even when the community is outraged.

There was a great deal of trouble in finding a jury that was acceptable to both prosecution and defense in the Hill case; there was already an implicit understanding that Hill was a more important defendant than Borst, so that the trial for Borst was postponed. A special jury panel of 100 was drawn to augment the regular panel of 36; eventually, in order to find a twelfth juror, the entire panel, regular and special, was used up. Some of the rejected jurors had had a previous opinion from news stories, or from talking with people involved in the case, and so on; still others were opposed to circumstantial evidence, or the death penalty, or the defense of insanity.

Two jurors were challenged peremptorily by the defense after the judge had denied a challenge for cause, both because of the insanity defense. One of the jurors from Smyrna noted that he believed that the plea of insanity had been abused in some murder cases. Another juror said of the insanity defense: "I haven't much use for spontaneous insanity or brainstorms. To convince me insanity would have to be connected with the defendant both before and after the crime" (April 28, 1909).

In the Hill case, also, the defendant was presented to the court as possibly not responsible because of an injury to his head when he was a young boy (May 5, 1909). Hill's mother and two aunts testified that he had "acted funny" all his life, that he was "absent-minded" and "irratio-nal" and complained of headaches (May 6, 1909).

The alienist who had appeared as the "insanity expert" in the Scott trial again testified for the prosecution. He stated that "in his opinion Hill did know the nature and quality of the act assumed and did know that the act was wrong. [On cross-examination] he said that the acts described by defendant's witnesses did not necessarily indicate a disordered condition of mind. In some cases diagnosing mental disorders is largely a matter of guesswork" (May 6, 1909).

Although the evidence against Hill was largely circumstantial, the jury took only two hours to deliver a verdict of guilty, on May 7, 1909. As soon as the jury made its decision, Will Sullivan was again ready to press for an appeal. He asked to have the jury polled, and he stated that he would make every effort to overturn the conviction. The sentencing took place on May 8, 1909, and Hill was taken to Auburn the same day. While Will Sullivan was working on an appeal for Hill, the governor refused Sulli-van's appeal for Scott on June 7, 1909. On that same date, Will Sullivan visited the Auburn prison to see both Scott and Hill, and told Scott that his last hope was gone (June 7, 1909). The denouement of Scott's case was swift; a week later he died by electrocution. The appeals delayed Hill's execution until April 18, 1910.

In both cases almost the same time elapsed between the actual murder and the execution—about twenty months. But these two murder cases changed forever the character of Chenango County, for it had now moved into another century, and it knew that even in the midst of rural bliss, the worst could happen. For Will Sullivan the world had changed, too. He had been forced to face the reality of defending two losing mur-der cases; there was no money for alienists to testify for the defense, and he now fully understood that the wretched of the earth live by quite dif-ferent rules from the rich. He had identified with the underdog, and the underdog had lost; but he remained identified with the struggle that could not be won in his own generation. And this, too, would become a motif of Harry Stack Sullivan's life.

Two weeks after Scott's electrocution, a Binghamton newspaper car-ried an editorial titled "Chenango County Murders"; it was promptly re-printed in the *Sun,* which prefaced the editorial with its own comment: "Chenango County is getting a wide reputation as a bloody part of America. This morning a Binghamton paper devoted much editorial space to the bloodthirstiness of the people of this county." The Bingham-ton editorial questioned the concept of rural virtue: "Chenango and Broome counties are made up largely of prosperous agricultural sections with a population of a higher standard than the average. Binghamton is the only city in the two counties. But even in Broome county a large majority of the murders during the past quarter of a century have been committed outside the city. In spite of the peace and repose supposed to be characteristic of rural communities, hard cider, bad whiskey, jealousy, lust and bad tempers have been combined with homicidal results altogether too frequently" (June 28, 1909).

In October 1907, Scott had murdered his stepmother. By June of 1909, he was electrocuted. In that twenty-month period, Harry Stack Sullivan had completed his last year in Smyrna High School, graduated with honor, won a state scholarship to Cornell University, entered the University, and been suspended in the spring of 1909. In inexplicable ways, he, too, had gone through a crisis of no small proportions in connection with some purported larceny. The explanation of his crisis, as it still exists in some parts of the County, is worded in such a way that it is bound up with the horrendous murder cases that were reported so extensively in the *Sun*. Some of the neighbors believe that he claimed insanity to keep from going to jail. Others express a more sympathetic viewpoint, seeing him as an underling like Borst, led on by older boys.

❦ 17 ❧
Cornell Crisis

A great many people whose self-esteem has been
somewhat uncertain, depending on scholarship only,
find their standing as students rapidly declining as
they become completely preoccupied with the pursuit of lust objects. Thus they become the prey of severe anxiety, since their only distinction is now being
knocked in half.
—Sullivan, *The Interpersonal Theory of Psychiatry*

O N September 28, 1908, as recorded by the *Sun*, Harry left Smyrna
for Ithaca. For a long time he had yearned to be out in the world,
away from the quiet and dark interior of the farmhouse. Clarence had
been gone from Smyrna for two years, except for vacations, so there was
not much for Harry to say good-bye to. There was his dog who would
miss him. There were his parents, aging and yearning over him—his
mother bothersome in her concern, his father diffident and reserved in his
emotions. And finally at a more remote level there was Jim Yockey, their
closest neighbor, an eccentric bachelor who had come to live just across
the road from the Sullivans and who had become a boon companion for
Harry's father and sometimes a helper on the farm. There was no way to
know at the time that it would be old man Yockey who would understand
Harry's plight when he got in trouble at Cornell—understand better than
anyone else in Smyrna, including his own mother.

Whatever the means of travel, the actual trip from Smyrna to Ithaca
was not an easy one in those years, even though it was only about fifty
miles westward as a crow flies. By train, Harry would have gone south
and west to Binghamton and transferred there to another train going
back north and west to Ithaca. By a horse-drawn conveyance, the journey
would have been more direct, but it would not have been feasible if
the family wanted to go there and back in one day. Since Uncle Ed was
paying Harry's Cornell expenses not covered by the scholarship, he
might have taken Harry over to Ithaca in his new four-cylinder Buick

runabout, but that too would have been at best a long day there and back; undoubtedly it would have been a moment of triumph for Harry to drive up to the campus in the Buick, for there were few cars indeed in those days.

Harry entered as a student in the College of Arts and Sciences; and his subjects in the first semester were chemistry, calculus, physics, and Latin. The choice of subjects indicates that during this period immediately after high school, he still planned to become a physicist. But he was already confronted by new emotions, and studying was not as simple as it had once been. While his marks in the first semester were reasonably good, particularly in view of his modest preparation for these subjects in high school, he was obviously no longer the smartest boy in school.[1] Such a comedown is often inevitable as one moves from high school to college, but in Harry's case his security was considerably bound up in being successful in school. Moreover, he was for the first time in close association with many boys, most of them older than he, who were far advanced in the puberty changes, so that it became impossible to delay longer his own awareness of sex. One of the direct outcomes of less than perfect grades was a loss of face with his parents, his relatives, and the neighbors in Smyrna, who had not always been supportive of his intellectual achievements.

There was at least one poignant sign that those first few weeks at Cornell were hard on Harry. The *Sun* reports that he came home for a visit at Thanksgiving time, which may have been determined by the imminent death of his grandmother Sullivan, whose funeral Harry probably attended. His cousin Margaret Hannon remembers that Timothy and Ella brought Harry down to her house in Norwich so that he could catch the train back to Ithaca. There was some unpleasantness, as she remembers it, and Harry was very unhappy about going back to college: "His mother explained it very briefly, saying that she thought it was homesickness as much as anything; this was his first trip home." Yet, as this cousin notes retrospectively, "You can't imagine Harry being sick for his home up there in Smyrna, because he wasn't that fond of it."[2]

By the second semester, there is clear evidence that Harry's marks had begun to slip more seriously. He dropped Latin and substituted drawing, though this was well within the Stack tradition; several of James Stack's children were relatively good amateur artists, and Lucy Stack had been enrolled at Yale Art School a decade before. By the end of the semester, he was marked as suspended until February 1910. He never returned to Cornell. There is no reason given on his college record for this suspension; Cornell did not enter derogatory information, such as arrests, on a student's record.

A whole series of events—including the emergence of a delayed and stormy puberty—contributed to the denouement of his college career in this second semester, and these events inform the most important part of Sullivan's theory on the schizophrenic process in adolescence. The events are complex and interlocking, some to be inferred and some documented.

The nature of the difficulty that emerged in the second semester at Cornell shortly after he was seventeen years old on February 21, 1909, is spelled out in Sullivan's published and unpublished writings. When he refers to seventeen as the latest age at which puberty can appear, he is undoubtedly writing about himself. "A particularly deviated environment may delay ... the appearance of the genital sexual impulses until after seventeen."[3] The "deviated environment" refers to his whole growing-up experience in which he was cut off from normal contact with his own peer group, and his interest in his own body was kept under sharp control by his mother, reinforced by the teachings of the Church.

Part of the delay in puberty can be examined in light of Harry's almost exclusive association with women in his growing-up years. On the one hand, he had no opportunity to know girls of his own age through school or church; nor did either his mother or his Aunt Maggie encourage such contact. On the other hand, most of his intimate contact with people in the Smyrna school was with women, with the exception of Clarence and Professor Butts. Most of his teachers were women, and he did not participate with his father in farm work, so that he had a particularly close and intimate relationship with his mother and his aunt. Aunt Maggie would have been preferred over his mother, for she belonged to the glamorous life of New York City; she was ten years younger than his mother, and she was intellectually more developed. Moreover, she had a way of life that offered a bridge to the larger world. In writing of the shift to heterosexual interests in adolescence, Sullivan says: "If the heteroerotic impulses focus on a frankly incestuous object, the mother or an aunt, then either the object finally recoils when unable longer to deceive herself as to the nature of the impulse, or a woefully maladjustive life is initiated for the boy."[4] One cannot discount the autobiographical reference here. Elsewhere Sullivan has commented on the importance of sisters in the shift to heterosexual interests; in his own case, the only possible objects in the years at Smyrna were his mother and his Aunt Maggie.

Whatever his fantasies were while he was living in Smyrna, it seems fairly certain that physical intimacies with another person of either sex were nonexistent. But, as Sullivan notes, his hypothetical young person finally "comes to adolescence," after "having stumbled through preadolescence, let us say, carefully avoiding any physical intimacies with anbody.... Even in our particular boy with the puritanical mother, lust swings his attention towards his penis as an instrument in social situations. Along with the coming of this impulse there appears a curiosity as to the stories about it which the social environment produces, and it gets to be frightfully troublesome."[5] Some of this curiosity had been generally encouraged by the suicide and murder stories in the *Sun*.

Several parts of Harry's life at Ithaca encouraged the appearance of genital sexual impulses that were waiting for some expression. In Smyrna, he had had no access to movies, which were beginning to be an important part of the training for adult life in American society. There were three movie houses in Norwich before he left for Cornell, but it is doubtful that he had much chance to go to them. Although the industry was in its infancy, it had already become an important part of the life of college-age students. Movies with romantic titles, such as "Samson and Delilah" and "Western Courtship," were particularly popular with students. Some of the films were moralistic, such as "The Devil," described in Faustian terms by the advertisements. College boys were beginning to collect pictures of stars, mainly female performers. Sullivan's later description of an imaginary youth who discovers the movies includes at least some of his own experience at Cornell:

A young man goes one night to the movies, alone, as usual. He often does this when he finds he cannot "concentrate" on his studies—in which he is doing less and less satisfactory work. He often falls asleep over his books but even with nine or ten hours of sleep, he awakens less and less rested. Sleeping is becoming his major activity; he can't seem to get enough of it. Yet he can't put the books aside and just go to bed; he knows he is not doing good work—and he is very ambitious to be a success. The movie is better than just chucking the book, and it is about the only thing he can do, at night, except an occasional solitary walk. He has long since given up his efforts to be one of the boys, to play games and converse with others. They don't seem to find him interesting; in fact, some of them have made fun of him, quite openly. At least, he is pretty sure that this happened, and that none of them have much respect for him—but he does not think about that if he can help it.

This particular evening, as the platinum-blonde heroine is revealed to the ecstatic audience in a moment of ingenuous helplessness, something happens to our boy. He has an 'electric' feeling; he is jolted out of his all too usual gloomy calm; he realizes that here is the Perfect Woman. He is in "love."

He sits through a second showing of the film, aflame with mounting excitement. He goes out and walks the streets—walks, in fact, far out into the country. Dawn finds him writing a letter to his love. He may or may not mail it. If he does entrust it to the mailbox, in all likelihood the postman ultimately brings him a photograph—straight from Hollywood. But in any case, his life is changed. The gloom is gone. He is warmed by an inner fire. He spends long hours in fantasy about the dear one. Studies cease to have any relevance. And the people who were once sources of self-abasement, are now of no moment whatever. They wonder what has happened to him; he does not notice them at all. The 'affair' may go on for months—as our boy moves on to the schizophrenic dénouement. All the reality of the love-object is photographic. He has no need even for the sloppy 'details' of her life distributed to the hungry world in the movie journals. Everything is provided by his revery processes; other people's view would garble his private perfection.[6]

But movies in Ithaca were not the only access that Harry had to "variations on this theme of the fantastic love affair." Cornell was coeducational; and even though the girl students were not considered appropriate love objects for the average boy at Cornell at that period and town girls were preferred,[7] Harry may have become lost in contemplation of a girl in one of his classes that first semester. "Sometimes, the unwitting object is a classmate," he reports. If "the luckless youth" reveals his feelings "to the astonishment, chagrin, and sometimes horror, of the girl," then what transpires may "do his tenuous self-esteem no good whatever and the psychosis, the severe mental disorder, frequently makes itself manifest in his performances immediately after the shock of the misunderstanding."[8] In another passage, he talks of a classmate in a calculus class—a subject that he took in his first semester:

While he believes that he has become interested in a young lady, has sought her company and has finally got himself noticed so that he can discuss calculus with her, the facts which determine that situation are very much more on the side of the genital lust motive than they are on the intellectual pursuit of calculus. But it is only of the latter that he can be aware, and so he is constantly having difficulties in his interpersonal relations.

The girl has regarded his 'approach' as quite subtle—but he never arrives. She may give him a helping hand, but he somehow overlooks or misinterprets it. If she makes the best of a bad job and they actually discuss calculus problems; even then—as under any other circumstance—he leaves unsatisfied, with a feeling that things have not worked well. That night, he awakens wet with perspiration, from a dream in which he has been kissing and fondling this girl's breasts—and has just bitten one and swallowed the nipple![9]

There was yet another, perhaps more powerful, deterrent to any experimentation with girls; it was most generally contained in the Irish attitude that marriage should be postponed and in the Church's emphasis on the postponement of sex until marriage. All of this was emphasized by the attitude of the community, as reflected in the *Sun,* that it was easy for a young person away from home to get into trouble and ruin his life. In that troubled spring at Cornell, all the newspapers carried anniversary stories of Chester Gillette's death in the electric chair just a year before, on March 30, 1908, because he had drowned his pregnant sweetheart.

In Sullivan's theory, the first appearance of the lust dynamism at the age of seventeen—the latest possible age for its onset—is ominous. It is often accompanied by a psychotic episode, in which the person's sexual awareness, so long kept in abeyance, appears when his peer group is already well informed emotionally on its meaning. If the person does not mature sexually until seventeen years of age, then the disturbances can be "so frightening that even internists talk about the late maturity type." In the next lecture, Sullivan notes that "the person who has not had the security of adequate preadolescent experience," as he is confronted with the appearance, through maturation, "of uncomplicated lust and the desirability of the genital orgasm," at the same time as the appearance of "obscure and warped . . . heterosexual interests, it is that person who develops the psychosis."[10] He seems to be taking note here of the actual inadequacy of his unequal experience with his only chum, Clarence, as preparation for heterosexuality.

Throughout his writings, Sullivan insists that the so-called homosexual has always had some brief look at heterosexuality. Heterosexual interest is universal in the young male:

There seems with the puberty change to come always a movement toward what might be described as the biological genital adaptation, a genuine curiosity and reaching toward some community of interest and mutual respect from members of the other sex. There are all too vastly numerous retreats from that interest in our world as we most intimately know it these days. In other words in America certainly—I think probably in England and perhaps elsewhere in the Western European culture—the change in the status, the social status in the role of women and the place of mothers in the government of the home, has in some cases included elements which just are not consonant with a placid progression through adolescence, and in some children who have been under the influence of the more eccentric varieties of the home situation, you do not easily obtain the history of any such movement toward interest in members of the other sex as I have suggested. You just get a bland story of always having feared and hated women and one thing and another.[11]

As a teacher of psychiatric residents, Sullivan warned them to be skeptical of the patient's statement that " 'I never had any interest in a woman except my mother' which I believe is one of the convictions which can never be substantiated on careful study, when you are talking to a man, and similarly the girl who 'never had any interest in men except my father.' "[12] Such statements were never true in Sullivan's clinical experience; instead there was a history of tentative, however brief, movement toward a person of the other sex, followed by a rebuff.

Whatever his overtures to girls in that winter of 1908–1909, they were in all probability very tentative and highly unsuccessful, so that he was thrown back upon daydreaming in order to avoid rejection. But as Sullivan notes, "Sexual daydreaming becomes definitely dangerous as soon as its content becomes incommunicable to the chum."[13] At Cornell, he was thrown among boys who were, for the most part, considerably older than he was, both chronogically and emotionally, so that he did not have a ready substitute for Clarence. Actually his closeness to Clarence had probably terminated when Harry was fourteen and Clarence went off to Syracuse Medical School. In this way his isolation from his contemporaries grew apace, and he was left alone to pursue his sexual daydreaming. When such daydreaming "occurs in an individual not socialized to the extent of having a chum, it is one of the most destructive of the manifestations of autoerotic arrest," he goes on to say, "leading generally to a paranoid personality, if not to schizophrenia, frequently with suicide."[14]

His loneliness must have been exceedingly great; he describes in his writings the "quintessential force" of the experience of loneliness and notes that it is so great that it almost defies description. "Under loneliness, people seek companionship even though intensely anxious in the performance. When, because of deprivations of companionship, one does integrate a situation in spite of more or less intense anxiety, one often shows, in the situation, evidences of a serious defect of personal orientation."[15]

He seems to have sought some relief from that loneliness in the only model he had—his experience with Clarence; he began to move toward the students in the dormitory, no more removed in age from him than Clarence had been.[16] But he was not acceptable to this group as other than an underling. Out of loneliness, then, and probably in a state of schizophrenic panic, he seems to have become a cat's-paw for a gang of boys in the dormitory.

❧ 18 ❧

The Trouble

> He was selling something illegal through the U.S.
> mail. He was arrested. His choice was either to go to
> jail or declare himself insane. The story is that he
> went insane to avoid jail.
> —Edith Bradley, teacher in the Smyrna School

HOWEVER else the story may vary—and no official record has surfaced—the trouble that Harry got into at Cornell almost always concerns the United States mail. In Smyrna, even now, the United States mail is a sacred institution, not to be taken lightly. Before there were many telephones in the area, the post office and the telegraph operator in the railway station were the only immediate links between Smyrna and the outside world. I myself had an encounter with the sacredness of the postal service in Smyrna in 1964, when for a month I lived in the County, working on Sullivan's early life. One day, I parked my car briefly in front of the post office on the main street in Smyrna, while I visited the office of the Town Clerk. When I returned, a group of men were standing around the car; and when I got into it, there was threatening talk of my "interfering with the delivery of the United States mail." There were parking spaces all around, in front of and in back of my car, and there was no "no parking" sign in evidence. But I had managed to park there in the precise period of time when the mail was brought up from Sherburne; and this action was seen as interference with the delivery of the mail, possibly arising in a curious way from their knowledge by then that I was interested in the boyhood of Harry Stack Sullivan. In subsequent visits, I was careful never to park near the post office.

So it was that the story that Harry had trifled somehow with the United States mail hit with particular force in Smyrna. The news drifted back from Ithaca in various ways, perhaps first from a local boy, Fred Sprague, who was registered at the Cornell School of Agriculture at about the same time. In his history of Smyrna, Sprague reports that Harry as a boy was "charged with using the mails to defraud." In conversation with me,

Sprague has referred to Harry as an "underling" and a "cat's-paw." But Sprague did not have, or choose to give me, any more detail than that. Another source of information at the time may have been Mance Messenger, for many years the rural mail carrier in Smyrna. His job made him somewhat of an authority for people in Smyrna; but whatever he knew was compounded by his sense of loyalty to Tim Sullivan, who had supplied him with powerful cider when he went up the hill in the evening to take his horse to pasture. The information about the cider was cheerfully supplied by Messenger, but he walked away when I asked him about Harry's "trouble" at Cornell.

Nearly half of the boys placed on probation in New York State in 1908 had committed either larceny or burglary, according to a story in the *Sun* for March 16, 1909. In the winter of 1908–1909, the Ithaca newspapers reported several burglaries of post offices in nearby communities, almost as if one robbery had inspired the next. On March 13, 1909, for instance, the post office at Cayuga, at the other end of the lake from Ithaca, was robbed for the sixth time in five years; the *Ithaca Daily Journal* reported that the safe was picked by experts, who left no clues.

There is no mention of any Cornell students being involved in these burglaries. The University then as now made every attempt to protect its students, particularly if, like Harry, they were under the legal age. Yet the opportunities for tampering with incoming mail for students at the University were particularly good. The campus at Cornell is set far up on a hill, and for years students took turns going down to the post office in the evening to pick up mail for other students, since there was no regular evening delivery at the campus. Finally there were so many losses of letters carrying a dollar bill from home, or packages containing a birthday gift, such as a watch, that the post office refused to continue the practice of giving out mail to one student for a group of students. On February 25, 1909, the *Cornell Daily Sun* carried an editorial entitled "The Post Office," which mainly consisted of a letter from a student who signed himself "One Who Likes to Hear from—Home":

Some time ago the postmaster in charge of the Ithaca Office announced that the distribution of the evening mail would be discontinued on account of the "abuse of the privileges on the part of the students." It was said that the many complaints of letters being lost was due to the fact that one man had been permitted to get the mail for as many houses as he desired and his negligence in delivering the same to the parties to whom the letters were addressed had caused much trouble to the office. In a town the size of Ithaca, two deliveries daily are hardly sufficient. The students have submitted to the inconvenience of going downtown for the mail at night for a long time with the hopes that in the near future a third delivery would be inaugurated. Now, however, the only means whereby the mail arriving on the afternoon trains may be obtained has been taken away.

The fact that losses may have occurred through the delivery at the window to the wrong persons is very possible, but it seems that that obstacle might have been overcome by the distribution, by the postmaster, of cards, permitting the bearer to get the mail for the address stated upon the card.

The only coherent account of Harry's involvement with a gang of older boys in the dormitory suggests, without documentary proof, that he became a cat's-paw in a more ambitious attempt to control incoming mail. Perhaps the gang was frustrated by the ruling of the post office that discontinued the informal distribution of the evening mail; in any event, the gang conceived of a plan to obtain "chemicals" illegally. The gang would order supplies for a drugstore in the town proper, using the store's own stationery if that were possible; and subsequently a member of the gang would go around to the drugstore each morning, after the early delivery and before the store had opened, to pick up the package from the doorway when it arrived. The chemicals would then be disposed of through the use of a fence. Finally the gang ran afoul of the law and were about to be apprehended. When the jig was nearly up, the older members of the gang commandeered Harry to perform the task of picking up the loot, and he was the one who was caught. Whether the other boys were apprehended is unclear. There is a general belief, held even by sympathetic neighbors, that Harry was arrested and sent away to some institution, perhaps a jail or a reform school, or to a mental hospital. At any rate, he was suspended from Cornell in the spring of 1909 until the first semester of the 1909–1910 year, and he never returned. For a two-year period, Harry's whereabouts are not known. Then he reappeared in Smyrna briefly before he went away to medical school in Chicago. That is all anyone seems to know for sure.

The legal charge must have been considered somewhat minimal by the authorities at Cornell; the suspension for a semester does not seem particularly punitive, and may in fact have been related more to his failing grades than to the particular events of the trouble, in which he may have been judged as relatively victimized. But his disappearance fanned the flames of prejudice and bigotry that still dwelt in Smyrna. There was a belief that somehow Judge Sullivan may have been successful in getting Harry off, that Harry had always been "smart like a fox" and he had been able to accomplish what Scott had not—he had gotten himself declared insane.

Edith Bradley's interpretation of Harry's trouble at Cornell, as given at the beginning of the chapter, became over the years a commonly held belief in the village. The story gained certain credence from Clarence Bellinger's later accounts of events in Harry's life after he left Smyrna. Most villagers refuse to repeat what Bellinger said about Sullivan's adult life—it was "all bad." Some people believe that the "crime" was committed in Chicago, although this seems apocryphal; an examination of court records there discloses no information of this nature. Again, it would seem more reasonable to some of the neighbors for a boy to get in trouble in a big city like Chicago than in Ithaca, still too close to rural life to be defined by them as a den of iniquity. One woman reports that Sullivan could never practice medicine in the United States after his encounter with the law, with this information supposedly coming from Bellinger. When she was reminded that Sullivan did have a private practice in New York City, she replied, "Yes, but not medicine, psychiatry." Most of the negative stories about Sullivan seem to have originated with Bellinger after he had become the head of Brooklyn State Hospital many years later. By then, Bellinger may have begun to resent the professional success of someone who had once been his underling. Whatever Sullivan would feel about this betrayal by his old friend, he never told anyone about his early friendship with Clarence Bellinger, or gossiped about him. Thus Sullivan remained clearly indebted to Bellinger for what friendship Clarence had offered in the loneliest years.

The Stack cousins, who are well aware of the fact that Harry got into some trouble at Cornell, are more understanding. Most of them realistically minimize the importance of the incident: he was too young to go off alone like that, and his parents finally realized this and took him out of school, afterwards sending him to medical school. There is no mention of the intervening period of at least two years before he went to Chicago. Another version is that Uncle Ed withdrew his financial support of Harry at Cornell after he found out that Harry was using the money to go to New York City and spend time with a chorus girl; but this is obviously a distortion of whatever happened.

Sadly, Ella Sullivan, and to some extent Harry himself, acted as if the disgrace were real and overwhelming. Leslie Hopkins, a neighbor farm boy five years younger than Harry, remembers that Ella would walk away without a word when anyone asked about her son, even after Harry had graduated from medical school. To some extent, the Sullivans tried to cover up for Harry for at least a brief period, for the Smyrna column carried a notice in November 1909 that Harry was home from Cornell for the holiday; he may or may not have come home for a visit, but he was no longer registered at Cornell. However revealing are Sullivan's own writings on the plight of a boy like himself, the descriptions are so veiled that, unless one has the background of the situation, the personal meaning escapes the reader.

There are countless references in Sullivan's writings to the complexity of the situation in which the isolated boy finds himself as he moves into adolescence, and of the great risks to his mental health as he becomes increasingly cornered by the conflict between his need for self-respect, his drive toward companionship, and some adjustment to his sexual needs. Some of the references are obviously derived from his own experience, or are compounded from his own experience and that of patients. It would require a major research effort to evaluate all these references and to sort out—when there is no documentation of Harry's actual experience with the court and the mental hospital—the exact relevance of a particular passage to Sullivan's own life history. Some brief excerpts will illustrate the problem.

In *Personal Psychopathology*, the only formal, full-length book completed by Sullivan himself, he seems to use his own life experience more precisely and with less camouflage than in any of his lectures, which form later books.[1] In that early book he cites three kinds of behavior patterns for the isolated boy who is at a loss in the movement into adolescence, because of his lack of experience in gang life and in his dealings with an appropriate preadolescent chum; two of these patterns, the first and the third, seem particularly relevant to his own situation. His first special case is found in boys who, "because of serious deviation of personality growth, are excluded from gangs and chumships." Such a boy may be

clearly conscious of his 'difference' from the other boys, of his being an 'outsider,' of his being distrusted, if not despised, by the 'regular fellows.' Often, he has earned a nickname cruelly indicative of the most conspicuous social manifestation of his limitation. The drive toward integrating isophilic situations is not diminished by unfortunate experiences. . . . His self-respect is gravely impaired. His authority-attitudes are upset. His schoolwork suffers. If he can he becomes loosely associated with some other 'failures,' often under quasi-leadership of an older, badly beaten boy. . . . It may be that the [younger] boy is so unhappy that he submits to manipulation for criminal purposes. It may be that, while he is incapable of submitting himself thus far, he is glad to participate in activities clearly damaging to those who "belong."[2]

Sullivan's third category of isolation is

. . . primarily geographical. The only preadolescent in a sparsely settled rural community is a classical example. . . . This boy always suffers a prolongation of the adolescent epoch. He usually takes on superficial behavioral patterns of preternatural maturity, for the elders are much more attractive to any preadolescent than are juveniles and children. But this early 'aging' is specious. The working out of isophilic tendencies is not satisfactory and is spread over years of experimentation—usually with caution learned by disappointing, if not actually painful, experience. Fantasy processes and the personification of subhuman objects are called on. Loyalty is developed to abstract ideals, more or less concretely embodied in fanciful figures, rather than to concrete groups. The capacity for sympathy becomes peculiarly differentiated because of the elaboration of its underlying tendencies in loneliness, among fanciful objects.[3]

Thus Sullivan's own account of the problems of the isolated boy seems to be closely allied to the story that I have pieced together of the events at Cornell. This is also confirmed by a critical piece of information that indirectly came from Jim Yockey (who died many years before this study was begun), and that was relayed to me by Leslie Hopkins. As a boy, Hopkins passed Yockey's house on his way to high school in the village. Hopkins, who lived on a nearby farm, gradually became a close friend of Yockey's. Hopkins finally elicited a sympathetic account of Harry's trouble from Yockey, who in turn must have obtained it from his boon companion, Timothy Sullivan. According to Yockey, Harry was innocent; he was framed by the older boys when the police were hot on the trail of the gang.

No one is quite sure when Jim Yockey appeared in Smyrna, but there is a mention of him in the newspaper in the year before Harry left for Cornell. He continues to be thought of as a hobo by the village people, even though he owned a small piece of land and a modest house beside the pond and across the road from the Sullivans. Although his main employment was as a farm laborer, he had been trained in the Midwest as a plumber—a skill that was becoming increasingly important in the County. When he was twelve years old, he had been seriously crippled in a sawmill; his clothing was caught in the wheel, and his body had gone through the mill. Thereafter one of his upper arms had grown to his body, with deep and terrible scars on his trunk. Leslie Hopkins remembers that on his way to school he would sometimes be summoned in to Jim's house to remove painful bits of bone from his body with pincers, these bits having worked through to the surface. Yet Yockey maintained a remarkable agility and was a diligent worker on the nearby farms; he could set out cabbage plants faster than anybody around Smyrna, although this procedure, which required the use of both hands, would often cause blood to stream down the side of his body to which the arm was attached.

Retrospectively, it is clear that old man Yockey, as he was affectionately known, was one of those magic anomalies that exist in one's growing-up years—adults who do not fit into the regular scheme of things, so that they furnish a special glimpse of the splendid caricatures of conventional life that exist in hidden spots all over the earth, at once more intriguing than the well-ordered adults who people most of one's days. He was the butt of village jokes, and an occasional news story would appear in which Yockey was twitted for being a bachelor; in one story, the writer suggests that Yockey should get a bird for his cage on Smyrna Hill. Yet he had a reputation for utter integrity, and however much his radical political ideas were ridiculed, he was listened to with great interest by the "stove committee" in the village general store. Sometimes Jim and Tim Sullivan would disagree on politics rather loudly, according to Hopkins;

Tim was a dedicated Democrat, but Jim was a Socialist, which was even worse than being a Communist.

In neighborhood lore, old man Yockey and Tim Sullivan had a close and convivial friendship. Jim Yockey was the principal cornet player in the Smyrna Band; and Tim could sing. Over Tim's cider, they often collaborated musically. On a summer evening, Tim's singing and Jim's cornet would echo up and down the high meadows on the hill, and farm children would smile as they heard them then and as—fifty years later—they tell about them. For one brief period, Jim could not play his cornet; he had lost his teeth, and the store teeth did not stay in. So he sold his cornet. But then Tim's boy, Harry, a doctor by then, came back on a visit; and he told Jim Yockey that he could keep his teeth in with peanut butter and bought him a fine new cornet. So the singing and the playing of the cornet in unison began again, although Jim never completely recovered his old prowess. Here and there in Chenango County, this act of generosity on Harry's part is still remembered with affection.

Jim Yockey seems to be the only Smyrna neighbor who would figure in Sullivan's adult life and who also had an insightful understanding of what had happened to Harry at Cornell. One glimpses over the years the compassion with which these two friends, Yockey and Tim Sullivan, surveyed the plight of Harry, so removed from the ways of the world when he left Smyrna. After his mother's death, Sullivan would report that he finally came to know his father for the first time; and one feels the importance of Yockey in this rapprochement.

Old man Yockey's independence is still mentioned in the County—his ability to survive and to make do in spite of all his afflictions and his physical and mental oddities. Near the end of his life his independence failed him; too old and too weathered to work anymore, he went to the almshouse in nearby Preston for his last days. In a strange way, Jim Yockey's life-style was close to that of Sullivan as an adult. Near the end of his life, Sullivan would describe himself as a bachelor, when he had given up the idea of ever finding a bird for *his* cage; and his politics were closer to Yockey's than to anybody else's in Smyrna. He must have been exposed to some of the ongoing political discussion—sometimes raised to the pitch of an argument—between his father and Yockey. Like Yockey, Sullivan would lend himself to being the butt of jokes in a whole series of stories that were passed around from one colleague to another; yet at the same time, his clinical judgment and integrity were completely respected. In Sullivan's interpersonal theory, each man finds his own immortality for better or for worse in "a reverberating cosmos."[4] In some such subtle fashion, Jim Yockey achieved his own immortality in Sullivan's concern for each person's dignity and potential.

❧ 19 ❧
The Disappearance of Harry

The focus of my interest from before medical school
[has] been the schizophrenic states.
—Sullivan, *Conceptions of Modern Psychiatry*

WHATEVER the legal definition of Sullivan's episode at Cornell, he himself considered it as his first encounter with "the schizophrenic states." And wherever he went in the next two-year period—when he "just disappeared," according to old neighbors—his life took on a new direction and his life's work began to be mapped out. This can be documented by his own personal communications and by his veiled and sometimes quite definite references in both published and unpublished writings.

As I have reported in the prologue, he once told me almost casually about his schizophrenic break, which in context clearly implied hospitalization; he did not specify the period involved, but he said that he was "young." He told his friend and colleague, William V. Silverberg, that he had spoken as a very young child with an Irish brogue, learned from his grandmother Stack, but that he had repressed it when he went to school because he was teased by the other children; it did not reappear again, he said, until he had an episode of schizophrenic terror during adolescence. He told another colleague, Dorothy Blitsten, that at nineteen or twenty, he believed that he was "mentally retarded," as if he had feared that he was permanently damaged by his illness.

Thus when Sullivan reports that he was specifically interested in schizophrenic states even before he went to the Chicago College of Medicine and Surgery in 1911, when he was nineteen, he implies that he studied his own state. Elsewhere he makes reference to his personal knowledge of institutional care, as early as 1908, although he probably meant 1909.

The record of those years, of where he was hospitalized, has evaded me, although I have searched diligently for over ten years, following up all kinds of leads.[1] Yet the fact of his illness and hospitalization has become more and more credible.

A reasonable story can be constructed from a few known facts, including the Sullivan family's known legal, medical, and psychiatric resources and Sullivan's own references to these years. To begin with, Cornell itself had an enlightened view of the psychological stress that students encountered, particularly in the freshman year. Many of its students came from farming communities and had to skimp for money, particularly in the period following the 1907 depression. In the fall of 1908, when Harry was in his first semester, Cornell opened a "Psychic Clinic" on campus to minister to students with attacks of "the blues." The *Ithaca Daily Journal* for October 29 reported that many students who had "depressed and dolorous views of life are now under treatment." Thus Harry's involvement in a criminal gang would have been viewed with some sophistication by the authorities, with perhaps some sensitive recommendation to the court.

Harry's parents also had access to several significant people in this crisis. Timothy's cousin, Will Sullivan, would have been a strong and sympathetic figure and may have been active in the resolution of the crisis; Smyrna neighbors believe that Will was involved in the outcome. Maggie Stack was loyal to Harry and more knowledgeable about the traps for young people to be found in a relatively urban area; some Stack relatives think that Harry was sent to stay with his Aunt Margaret after he was suspended. And finally, there was Dr. Thurston G. Packer, the family physician in Smyrna, who had a son, Flavius, who was both a neurologist and a psychiatrist by then; it seems inevitable that the Packers were crucial in any plans for Harry.

Although Bellevue Hospital has no patient records at all for the relevant period, a network of circumstantial evidence suggests that Harry may have been on the psychiatric ward there for at least part of this period. A brief examination of the Packers' connection (father and son) with Bellevue will suggest the cogency of this assumption. In addition, Sullivan's later relationship with A. A. Brill, who was also a consultant on the psychiatric ward at Bellevue from 1908 to 1911, will strengthen the basis for this assumption.[2]

Thurston Packer had himself trained at Bellevue Hospital Medical College, graduating in 1881, when he was thirty-eight years old. Born in Jefferson County, near the Canadian border, he had come to Smyrna in the same year as he had graduated to take over the practice of a physician who was nearing his retirement. His son, Flavius, was then fourteen years old. Thus the Packers, like the Fultons in Norwich, were interlopers within the County tradition. Thurston Packer had been trained in a hospital that had an early acquaintance with the dispossessed, since New York was, of course, one of the main points of debarkation for immigrants. From its beginning as a hospital in 1734, Bellevue had a close relationship to the indigent of the city, having grown out of a "Publick Workhouse and House of Correction." For many years, it was the largest city hospital in the world. Thus the senior Dr. Packer, who remained a general practitioner all his life, had an unusual exposure to immigrant populations, and there was a beginning psychiatric service there as early as 1870. Flavius also became a physician, graduating from Albany Medical College in 1893, a year after Harry was born. One of Flavius Packer's closest friends at medical school was a young Armenian student, Menas Sarkis Gregory, who had been born in Turkey. After graduating from medical college, they both went to Kings Park State Hospital for residencies in neurology, which also included psychiatry as it then existed. Flavius Packer was subsequently invited to come to Bellevue to help in setting up a more enlightened psychiatric service, sometime near the turn of the century. Packer in turn recommended that Gregory also come to Bellevue to help him in this endeavor; and between 1904 and 1936, Gregory himself became the guiding light of the increasingly effective psychiatric service at Bellevue, with a special interest in psychotic patients.

Although young Packer went on to become head of three different small private psychiatric hospitals, he and Gregory remained the closest of friends. Thus when Harry Sullivan needed hospital care, Flavius Packer might well have made arrangements for him to go to Bellevue. If so, Harry would have found there a person with special experience and skills for his care. Gregory, who was only five feet tall and remained a lifelong bachelor, had a sensitive feeling for patients, and as an immigrant, a special understanding of the difficulties of transition to another society. It is worthy of note that at the end of the two-year period of Harry's disappearance from Smyrna, it was the senior Packer who acted as one of the two physicians who recommended him to medical school.

However vulnerable this chain of evidence may seem, there is another link to Bellevue that is more significant. Before I had ascertained any connection between the Packers and Bellevue, or knew that Brill was a consultant there in the critical years, I had made note of the strong link between Brill and Sullivan that developed over the subject of schizophrenic patients. Brill tended to downplay his early experience with using psychoanalytic techniques successfully with psychotic patients, in part to minimize his deviance from Freud on the efficacy of such techniques for other than neurotic patients. But Brill had a feeling for Sullivan's life and his work, partly emergent from his own experience of coming as a poor immigrant boy of fifteen to America from Austria-Hungary. Over the years Sullivan was sometimes a discussant of Brill's papers, and sometimes the roles were reversed.

The most important of these interchanges occurred in 1929, when Sullivan was a formal discussant of Brill's paper entitled "Schizophrenia and Psychotherapy." Sullivan's discussion focused on the importance of the hospital attendant in the recovery of schizophrenic patients. "Twenty-one years of observation," Sullivan stated, "have convinced me that therein one touches upon one of the greatest truths concerning the Institutional Care. What the hospital employee is permitted to do to patients often beggars any layman's fancy."[3] The paper was originally given in May 1929, and published in the November 1929 issue of the *American Journal of Psychiatry,* so that, in effect, Sullivan was reporting that he was hospitalized in 1908, and began his acquaintance with institutional care then. That, however, would have been when he was sixteen years old and in his first semester at Cornell—at variance with the Cornell records, which show him still in school at the beginning of the second semester. The slight discrepancy may simply be a mistake in timing, or it may indicate that Sullivan had an earlier brief encounter with the hospital in the first semester at Cornell, and attempted unsuccessfully to continue with school. In any event, the statement in the context of Brill's paper and Sullivan's discussion seems to be a personal jogging of Brill's memory.

There are other instances of such gentle sparring about schizophrenia, with pointed references by Brill to Sullivan's knowledge of the process. Thus in October 1929, Brill as a discussant of Sullivan's paper on the environmental factors in the development of schizophrenia began by pointing out Sullivan's profound knowledge of that process: "Dr. Sullivan has the capacity, I might say the schizoid capacity, to wax wittily and instructively about the nature and meaning of schizophrenia. Whatever he told us about the subject I can assure you is entirely true. . . . There are very few observers in this country who have devoted as much time to schizophrenics as Dr. Sullivan, so that his statements are authoritative."[4] Again, in 1932, Brill specifically commended Sullivan for his clinical observation of schizophrenic phenomena: "I once differed with H. S. Sullivan, who stated that the progress of schizophrenics with olfactory hallucinations is invariably bad. Further investigation has taught me that Sullivan was correct."[5]

Although Brill and Sullivan were almost a generation apart in age, their respect for each other had some common basis that transcends the professional relationship of two psychiatrists. By comparison, Sullivan never achieved the same feeling of camaraderie with White; and White seems never to have commended Sullivan's work in any of his published papers. Coincidentally, Brill, like White, had an opportunity, considerably later, to gain some knowledge of the life of Chenango County and its environs, so that his own insights may have entered into his adult relationship with Sullivan. In 1918, Brill became a prime consultant to Dreiser on *An American Tragedy.*[6]

Within Sullivan's own terminology, the years when he just disappeared might be termed "the fatal years." He would use this phrase to discuss the case of a particular patient in a lecture he gave to psychiatric trainees. In this lecture, Sullivan begins by noting that he has prior information from a referring physician or a family member that the patient was once in a mental hospital for two years, which is coincidentally the same period of time that Sullivan was out of the picture. Sullivan attempts to find a way by which he can elicit the information from the patient directly:

In the course of the interview, I am able to inquire several times whether something that was being discussed ever got serious enough to be genuinely incapacitating. The answer in each case is, "Oh no! No indeed!" There is no suggestion that this man has ever had anything remotely like a mental disorder; the possibility is denied categorically, from every approach. Toward the close of the interview, I take counsel with myself and discover that I am not quite clear on his chronology of employment. I then say, "Now let's track down, year after year, just what you were doing and where." When he comes to *the fatal years* there is a pause, and things don't go so well. I say, "Well, you continued in your former employment through that year?" "No. No, I didn't." I wait for about thirty seconds, and then I say, "Well?" And he says, "As a matter of fact, I had some difficulty with my wife at that time, and had to take some time off from my employment. I was actually so upset by this business that I stopped work for a year and a half and took a trip." I say, "Well, well. Where did you go?" The man tells about the start of a trip, and then suddenly says, "Did you know that I was in a mental hospital?" To this I say, "For God's sake! Tell me about it." And he does. [Emphasis mine][7]

In this instance, Sullivan has collateral information and can finally elicit information from the patient on his "fatal years." Without collateral information, Sullivan's own "fatal years" remain an unfilled gap in his life history.

From the spring of 1909 until the spring of 1911, there is no information in the *Sun* on Harry's whereabouts, except for the one false lead on his being home from Cornell at Thanksgiving time in 1909. Near the end of April, 1911, the *Sun* carried an item in the personal column for Norwich: "Henry Sullivan of Smyrna was a caller in this village Saturday." It is probable that the information came from a relative in Norwich, and perhaps Harry's name had been formalized in order to indicate a fresh start. Again in August of that year, the *Sun* carried a terse statement on Harry's new career, in the Smyrna column, with information undoubtedly supplied by his parents or Thurston Packer: "Harry Sullivan has left for Chicago where he expects to enter the medical department of the Chicago university." By the time he went to Chicago, he was well on the road to studying psychiatry, although lack of money and lack of adequate training at the Chicago College of Medicine and Surgery would delay him. But his choice had been made by events—economic, sociological, historical, psychological—over which he had little control, as he would later theorize.

❧ 20 ❧

The Chicago College of Medicine and Surgery

Consider, again, the effects on the living of the out-
standingly bright boy from a small town when he
enters a great metropolitan university.
            —Sullivan, "Tensions Interpersonal
                            and International"

I N the first decade of this century, the number of immigrants arriving in this country reached an all-time peak of almost nine million, and thousands upon thousands streamed through New York State on their way to Chicago. The Norwich *Sun* for Monday, March 22, 1909, reported that 15,000 people had landed on Ellis Island two days before; and that on Sunday sixteen carloads of immigrants had been shunted through Norwich northward on the Ontario and Western. The interest in Chicago grew as the number of immigrants there increased. Harry Sullivan's journey westward to the Chicago College of Medicine and Surgery in 1911 was only part of that trend. Relatives and neighbors assumed mistakenly that his school was connected with the already renowned University of Chicago; but it was in fact the medical branch of Valparaiso University in Indiana.

Midwestern colleges and universities were beginning to gain a new prestige in the East. In Chenango County, most of the better-heeled descendants of the first settlers still sent their children to eastern colleges. Ruth Fulton Benedict, like Nina Brown Stack, went to Vassar College— the proper place for young women who insisted on advanced education. Although some few of the young men went to the select Eastern universities, most of them went to nearby engineering schools or agricultural colleges. Yet there was a growing feeling, particularly among the young, that Chicago was more exciting and forward-looking than Boston, which was still referred to as "the Hub." The activities of Jane Addams at Hull-House and in the Illinois State Legislature were reported in the pages of the *Sun* after about 1900; and there was a growing respect for this gentlewoman who fought to protect the rights of immigrants and their children. There was a general knowledge that John D. Rockefeller had financed the new beginning of the University of Chicago in 1892 and that its first president, William Rainey Harper, had been found in New York State's Chautauqua Liberal Arts College.[1] Both names, Rockefeller and Harper, carried their own measure of prestige and respect in the County.

All of this general feeling about the Midwest and the new emergent role of the immigrant in the life of the Midwest must have been a part of Harry's implicit approach to Chicago, but it was subdued by his own sense of shame and failure as he began a new educational attempt. In later years he would refer to the Chicago College as a "diploma mill," but this was an inadequate description of the whole tradition of Valparaiso University, and a misunderstanding of the sophisticated decision by his Aunt Margaret—and perhaps the Packers—that this was the best place for him to go.

Beginning in 1873, Valparaiso University had been taken over by two remarkable men, Henry B. Brown and Oliver Perry Kinsey, who set high standards within the experimental and democratic tradition of Bronson Alcott's School of Philosophy in Concord and the liberal arts college at Chautauqua. An open admissions policy was later modified for the more stringent requirements of professional schools, but the general tenor of their philosophy did not change. The catalogues for the Chicago College for the years of Sullivan's attendance there reflect this philosophy: Everyone is to be given "an equal opportunity to obtain a medical education in a high-grade medical school . . . regardless of financial circumstances." The instruction "shall not be inferior" to that of any school in the country, even though their fees may be higher. And "the school shall continue to grow and prosper from the excellence of its work rather than by denouncing the work done by other schools."[2]

In 1911 the Chicago College of Medicine and Surgery had 179 students in its freshman class.[3] Almost thirteen percent of the students were from Europe, Asia, and Africa. First- and second-generation Americans were not designated, of course; Harry Sullivan, the grandson of immigrants on both sides, was listed as coming from New York State.

The admissions sheet gives his name as Harry F. Sullivan, with his correct birth date and age. His nearest relative is Timothy J. Sullivan. He has two required references, B. J. Ormsby of Norwich, who had been the physician in attendance at his birth, and T. G. Packer. The credential for admission was only the New York State Regents Certificate, the mark of his high school graduation. There is no mention of Cornell, although Cornell University received a request, in the spring of 1911, that Sullivan's record at Cornell be sent to an institution not specified in extant files; in any event, the Chicago College did not accept any credits from Cornell, according to its registration form. It is possible that such information had proved fatal at another school.

Sullivan's training at medical school was probably at least average for that period. The location of the College, directly opposite Cook County Hospital, was excellent. Many of the students, like Sullivan, had to work while they were in school, so that the training was interrupted by the student's own financial needs at times. The student could enter directly from an accredited high school, which was then true of many medical schools. In the same general period, the medical school at Syracuse University had accepted Clarence Bellinger directly from Smyrna High School and awarded him a medical degree four years later.

The Flexner report, which set standards for medical schools in the United States and Canada, appeared only a year before Sullivan matriculated at the Chicago College. While most schools moved slowly toward these standards, the Chicago College took note of the new standards very early. In the 1912–13 catalogue, the College announced a combined course "whereby both a literary and medical degree may be obtained upon the completion of a six-year course. . . . Medicine, properly considered, is one of the learned professions." The announcement notes that many high-grade medical schools require a four-year collegiate course preliminary to the study of medicine, which "often becomes a hardship on students. . . . Therefore, this school does not require such an extensive course as a prerequisite, but strongly urges all students who can afford it to take advantage of the combined literary and medical course." If even the six-year program had become mandatory, Sullivan would have undoubtedly dropped out; there was no way for him to acquire the necessary money for additional years. Yet the emphasis on broader education for physicians would have a strong impact on him: during the Chicago years, he began the lifelong habit of reading widely, of becoming on his own initiative a broadly educated person; and he would stress this phase of a good medical education in his teaching of young resident physicians.

Without a scholarship, the financial burden of even four years was great indeed, and it was necessary for Sullivan to work as much as possible. The annual tuition rate was $100, and room and board were about four or five dollars a week, so that with no incidentals the cost would be over $1,200 for the four years. Even though Margaret Stack sent some money "each week" while he was in medical school and his parents sent whatever they could afford, he was still hard pressed to meet the cost.[4] He completed his formal class work in 1915, but his degree was delayed until 1917 while he earned money to pay back fees, according to his own account.[5]

There may have been another reason for the two-year delay: Sullivan's

marks were spotty, his performance uneven. His record appears at times
close to failing, so that he may have had to make up certain work; or he
may even have gambled on the hope that, over time, the requirement
would be waived. Part of his poor performance could be explained by the
necessity to earn money; but part of it could be explained by a growing
irritation with any demand for useless rote learning. His isolated childhood and the lost years when he had to disappear in order to make a fresh
start imposed on him an intolerance for wasting time and an intellectual
curiosity as an adult that made him an expert in such disparate areas as
breeding day lilies or devising electronic equipment for recording sound,
far ahead of his time.

During the first year, he completed only four of the five required subjects, with a B in Anatomy, a C in Chemistry, a D in Physiology, a B in
Materia Medica, and no final mark for the required course in Histology.
During the second year, he completed only seven of the eight required
courses with a B in Anatomy, a C in Chemistry, a D in Physiology (which
he was failing at the end of the first semester), and no grade in Embryology, with a note on his formal record that he had done no laboratory
work in this subject and had a conditional mark on class work at the end
of the first semester that year.

There is indeed a question as to whether he ever completed this work in
Embryology. In the files at Loyola University, which took over the Chi-
cago College in 1917, there is some undated correspondence between two
faculty members concerning H. F. Sullivan's work in Embryology. It
seems probable that this correspondence took place in the period when
Sullivan was trying to qualify for a medical degree. The first letter is from
G. E. Wyneken, M.D., Associate in Surgery at the College, and is addressed to L. F. Bennett, A.M., M.S., Professor of Embryology. Dr.
Wyneken writes: "Will you kindly look up your grade in Embryology for
H. F. Sullivan who took your work (as he says) about 1912–1913. I enclose an addressed stamped envelope for your immediate (if you please)
reply." Professor Bennett answers on the same piece of paper, rather
tersely: "I find that H. F. Sullivan took the examination at the end of the
second semester of 1912–1913 and made a grade of 70%. He did not take
the laboratory nor was he in class."

In the third and fourth year, Sullivan's subjects were varied and he
took more than originally prescribed; this can be explained in part by the
fact that during this period the College changed the program from a
four-year to a five-year course, so that the last two years were somewhat
more intense than those prescribed by the earlier announcement of curriculum. His marks continued to be on the low side. In one two-year
course in Obstetrics, he received a grade of E for both years. The course
was taught by William H. Rubovits, M.D., whose daughter, Dorothy
Blitsten, became a friend of Sullivan's in the 1930s. Sullivan's account of

this course, as reported by Dorothy Blitsten, puts a somewhat different light on Sullivan's grade for the course:

Shortly after I married Lionel Blitzsten* (1932) Sullivan had business in Chicago and stayed with us. Lionel was busy and I was delegated to meet Sullivan at the station. I approached this assignment with some apprehension. Sullivan was reputed to be devastatingly impatient of the wives of his colleagues. Incidentally, in my experience, this proved to be one of numerous false imputations. In any case, we met and exchanged conventional words of greeting. As we got into my car and I was driving home, Sullivan broke the silence that had descended by asking: "You don't happen to be related to William Rubovits, do you?" When I replied that he was my father, Sullivan relaxed visibly and said, "In the medical school I attended there were only two instructors whom we respected. One of them was William Rubovits. Besides, he was probably responsible for my getting through the school at all. As you know he taught obstetrics, which was not a subject that interested me profoundly. Also, I was working nights in the coroner's office and came to his lectures in a somewhat somnolent state. One day Rubovits asked a question and failing to get an answer from the first student apparently proceeded to ask it of each student in turn. As the turn approached me—and he still had no answer—I was roused from my sleep. I don't remember what the question was precisely, but when it came to me, I muttered: 'The psychoses of pregnancy' which, miraculously, was the answer. I have always thought he passed me on the basis of it, since my knowledge of obstetrics remained singularly limited." So I knew that Sullivan had lived in Chicago, had worked his way through medical school, and the medical school he attended. None of this was ever referred to again.[6]

Sullivan's communication about his course in obstretrics and his career at the College in general is noteworthy, since he seldom talked about his past. Rubovits was still alive at that time and did remember Sullivan, as it turned out.

The College's printed list of subjects for each year, on which the grades were recorded, do not indicate that there were any formal courses available in psychiatry, or its equivalent. Neurology is formally listed for the junior and senior years, and Sullivan received a final grade of D both years. In his junior year, a subject, "Psych.," not formally listed on the reporting form, is written in; he got a mark of D on this for the first semester, but no final grade.

In the four years that he attended medical school, Sullivan received only one grade of A as a final mark—in Toxicology—although he occasionally received an A for the first semester's work on a subject. His interest in toxicology and his work in the coroner's office are noteworthy. There seems little doubt that his initial interest in poison goes back to the growing interest in poisons as a way of suicide in Chenango County. Al-

* Dorothy Blitsten has simplified the spelling of her husband's name.

though he had a variety of jobs in Chicago while he was in school, he reported that the one that he liked the best was working for a toxicologist in the coroner's office.[7]

By one of those curious turns of fate, Sullivan's own death would pose sufficient questions about the cause of death—he was found in his hotel room with pills scattered around him—that his body would be taken from the Ritz Hotel to the Paris toxicologist. It is an ironic touch that would have pleased him.

Clearly the choice of the Chicago College of Medicine and Surgery for Harry's education was dictated by financial considerations and by the need to make a new beginning after the crisis at Cornell. The distance from Chenango County was an important consideration, as evidenced by the attempt to make a fresh start by adopting a slightly changed name, H. F. Sullivan—an easy adjustment in a family still disadvantaged by its immigrant status; even in second and third generations of immigrant families, names or ages were often changed in the direction of necessary expediency or supposed conformity to American standards.

It was an adjustment to failure that led Sullivan to Chicago, but ultimately it had the greatest importance to his intellectual development. Here he could shed the illusions that his mother had clothed him in; he was no longer trying to follow in the successful model of Leo Stack, or even of Clarence Bellinger. And that freed him from the Horatio-Alger standard, at least in some dimensions, for the rest of his life. A generation earlier, Chicago had moved Theodore Dreiser in the same direction, so that his most important novels reflect the impact of a great industrial city on a young man, brought up in poverty in a small town in Indiana as the son of a German Catholic immigrant father. Dreiser, too, was familiar with the temptation of crime, having embezzled twenty-five dollars from an employer's accounts when he was about the same age as Harry at the time of the Cornell episode.[8]

During his years in Chicago, Sullivan would have contact with all manner of people, but most of them were working-class people from the four corners of the earth, including industrial workers injured in the steel mills. For the rest of his life, he would grow restive when he had too much contact with upper-middle-class patients or psychiatric trainees. He sought throughout his life to devise some way to avoid psychiatric tragedies in the dispossessed, and like William Alanson White, he saw crime as the mark of a sick society. Young male adolescents, growing up in the slums of a great city, often have only a choice between crime and mental disease, he stated at various times. This great sweep of his thinking was formed out of his own experience as it was enlarged and defined by the immigrant population of Chicago generally and of its hospitals more specifically. It is difficult to think of any location at that period in America that was more widely concerned with digesting the immigrant—not with isolating him as on the East Side in New York City, but with the daily problems of living with him. The impact of Chicago would be felt all his life, eventuating near the end of his life in a paper titled "Towards a Psychiatry of Peoples."[9]

However spotty his education, Sullivan had finished in some fashion the required courses at the end of the term in 1915; but his education in medicine had just begun. Throughout his life, he showed an expert knowledge in various areas of medicine, according to his colleagues. One must assume that this knowledge came from his own experience in practicing medicine, by specialized training after he left medical school, and from his own avid interest in a wide range of subjects, some of which he pursued in the Crerar Library in Chicago. In the next six years before he went to St. Elizabeths in Washington, his experience was diversified and difficult to reconstruct, as he struggled for financial and intellectual security.

✎ 21 ☙

The Struggle for Security

Sadly enough, those to whom life has brought but a
pleasant flood of trifling problems without any spectacular disturbances, who have grown up in quiet
backwashes far from the industrial revolution, within
the tinted half-lights of the passing times—these are
afield in undertaking the schizophrenia problem.
        —Sullivan, *Schizophrenia as a Human Process*

B ETWEEN 1915 and 1921, Sullivan was out of Chicago from time to
time on various assignments; but he continued to claim Chicago as
his home until late in 1921, when he went to Washington, D.C., and
began his work as a civil servant assigned to St. Elizabeths Hospital. The
information on these years is contradictory and confusing; job applications filled out by Sullivan himself show almost a clinical picture of con-
fabulation. But the main outlines of the period in Chicago are clear. He
was struggling to find a job, and he was constantly fighting against a sense
of failure that bordered on schizophrenic panic.

His various references to the time when he began the study of schizophrenic states—dating it first in the year when he was at Cornell, and
later in the Chicago years—locate periods of his own distress rather than
any professional specialty undertaken that early. His decision to begin
the formal study of schizophrenic states would not come until 1922, and
the making of that decision would evoke in him a dream akin to schizophrenic panic. All of the previous references must be understood as retrospective evaluation of what he was experiencing personally in his struggle
for security.

Thus his own encounters with the schizophrenic states began before he
reached medical school, but his understanding of them came, as he has
reported, from his experience with people, mainly immigrants, remain-
dered by the industrial revolution in Chicago. The indoctrination of his

own forebears into a new society, however difficult, was far removed from the harsh realities of those Irish immigrants who, though seeking farm-land, remained in the great cities through financial and physical exhaus-tion. Until Sullivan went to Chicago, he had no knowledge of the realities of either urban or rural transition of the immigrant and his children, other than his own unusual childhood; and he tended to blame his posi-tion of being an outsider on more immediate realities. Most of the hard-ships of his parents, and grandparents, took place before he was born, or before he could remember: his grandfather Sullivan's death while work-ing on the railroad; his father's work in a factory, cut short by the forced cutbacks in the depression years; the deaths of his older brothers as re-lated to the public health problems on Rexford Street; and his mother's despair. During the Chicago years, these kinds of realities came into sharp focus. As he drifted around from one dreary job to another, living with no consistent or traceable housing, filling out application forms with conflicting and exaggerated claims about his age and experience, one glimpses his own encounter with the industrial revolution. He teetered on the edge of disaster constantly, but the teetering itself eventually gave him a command of the terrible loneliness and despair that a young per-son, without any way to define his worth in the larger world, constantly struggled against. He observed that a young person living in the slums of a great city could lose his sense of foresight, could act in a moment of des-peration in such a way that he would end up in a prison, rather than in an institution for the insane. In the slums of a city undergoing great growth and rapid industrialization, the doctrine of freedom of will did not apply; often the only choice was between living and a slow death. Even as one went up the ladder, 'moral' decisions were not always possible. Theodore Dreiser, like Sullivan, would feel that a steadfast conscience was not a universal trait, that people were often caught in situations that weakened the ability to follow the path of duty: "To those who have never wavered in conscience, the predicament of the individal whose mind is less strongly constituted and who trembles in the balance between duty and desire is scarcely appreciable, unless graphically portrayed."[1] From per-sonal observation, both Dreiser and Sullivan felt that only the clear fore-sight of the result of certain actions could restrain the deprived person from acting hastily and ruining his future.

In Sullivan's struggle for security in the Chicago years, he often exhib-ited a lack of foresight, so that retrospectively he understood all too well the narrow precipice on which he had walked. When he stopped going to classes at the Chicago College in 1915, he was not eligible for a degree, as indicated by the final report sheet on his grades. Moreover, the rules of the school required that he pay all back fees and complete a year of in-ternship before the formal degree could be granted. Neither the records at Valparaiso University in Indiana, nor those at Loyola University, show that Sullivan ever received a medical degree. But the diploma, properly signed and executed in September 1917, was found in Sullivan's effects, and a copy of it has now been placed in the files of Loyola University.

This story is as puzzling and as complex as many stories in Sullivan's life. In the same month that the buildings and equipment of Chicago College were purchased by Loyola University, Sullivan received his degree from Valparaiso, signed by many of the same professors who had been his teachers in medical school. In that transition period from one university to another, Sullivan apparently straightened out his credentials and paid his back fees, or as many as he could. Undoubtedly the tradition of Valparaiso University, as set up long ago by its founders, held sway over the decision of the faculty to waive some requirements, probably both financial and academic. Also it seems quite likely that Sullivan himself was persuasive and determined to overcome the irregularities of his record. The decision was obviously wise, whoever made it, and at twenty-five years of age, Harry Stack Sullivan's name was inscribed on the duly certified diploma. It was his first use of the name Stack at medical school. And it seems to have been the last medical diploma issued by Valparaiso University; no other degrees are listed for September of that year, although a list of graduates from Chicago College is given for May 1917.

In the two-year period between the end of his class work at the College and the granting of the degree, Sullivan's activities were diversified. Without his medical degree, he turned first, on August 15, 1915, to industrial surgery, a not unusual activity at that time in Chicago for a young doctor not yet duly legitimatized. For "six and one-half months," as he reports, he worked as an assistant surgeon for the Illinois Steel Company at their hospitals in South Chicago and Gary, Indiana. He is never so explicit and consistent again in reporting length of service, so that one senses the dreariness of the task, as if he had counted the days. He would later use this experience to illustrate for his trainees the tedium of going over the same ground with a patient, and the necessity for establishing a therapeutic goal as soon as possible; otherwise the situation is "painfully reminiscent of the steel plant where I once worked; after a sleet storm, the little narrow-gauge locomotives with their loads of ingots would struggle along the icy tracks and progress would apparently be made, when suddenly everything would slide back to just where it had been before."[2]

The icy winter probably helped to determine his departure from this job, for by the end of February, 1916, he had either resigned or been fired. But there were other considerations: without his degree from medical school, his salary was minimal, and he would later report that he had never liked operative surgery. Moreover, he had difficulty adjusting to any kind of regimentation; as he observed from time to time, he had not been trained in compromise and cooperation in the school society in

Smyrna. Eventually he would have to establish his own school and journal in order to meet this need for freedom.

Although the encounter at the steel mill was brief, it had a discernible impact on his thinking. In the first part of 1941, only months before the United States entered World War II, he would write an article on psychiatry and the national defense, spelling out the elaborate plan, already devised by him, to train general practitioners. In fact this plan was the one used by Selective Service in the task of determining which draftees should be referred on to a psychiatrist. In a section on industrial psychiatry, he commented on the particular problems in industry that dovetailed with the problems of Selective Service, and he noted the impact of recent history—in particular, the depression of the 1930s—in posing special problems for both industry and the civilian army.[3]

For almost four months after he left the steel mill, Sullivan's whereabouts and means of livelihood are unknown. However, late in June, 1916, he enlisted in the Illinois National Guard, at a time when the nation was already beginning to anticipate its involvement in the European war. He was stationed for most of a five-month period near San Antonio with an infirmary attached to the Engineer and Signal Troops of the Twelfth Provisional Division, according to information supplied by Sullivan on a later application to the Army Provisional Division, with a rank of sergeant. His references to these five months are considerably more cheerful than the experience at the steel mill: "The young doctor . . . spent some time in military service with the National Guard mobilized on the Mexican border."[4] In various of his published and unpublished writings, he describes with some delight his experience on the rifle range, when he stuck a "very, very dear friend of mine on one such occasion" with a pin when the friend was concentrating on firing. "And sure enough, as I had expected, it was only after having fired that he reached around to the injured area and gave me the devil. Literally, on the rifle range, things are suspended from any disturbance of one's consciousness until it is time to notice them."[5] He used this experience as a physical analogue for the psychological phenomenon of "selective inattention," which he described as a powerful response to the pain of anxiety, so intense at times that a person cannot profit from a bad experience. Sullivan always told this story with humor and delight, as if the whole experience of the "young doctor" stationed on the Mexican border was of a piece with nothing else up to that time.

During that same interlude he had a chance to ride horses; and the workhorses that he had known on the farm at home became transformed into riskier and more exciting specimens. Later, in a 1918 Army Qualification Card, he reports that he has had some experience or aptitude in "equitation," obtained in the "Infantry and Cavalry," but this must refer to his experience with the National Guard. He once stated that riding be-

came for awhile an important pastime, and he listed it as one of the hob-
bies that is expressive but not demanding of personal intimacies: "Riding,
again often an attenuated participation in a group of like-minded people,
is peculiarly significant because of symbolic investitures of the uniquely
gifted sub-colleague, the horse."[6] He is describing himself when he reports that "people who have but very limited ability for human intimacy
can assuage loneliness through these instrumentalities [such as games and
sports], without any risk of troublesome interpersonal developments."[7]

His riding was interrupted for a while by a fall from a horse in which
he broke his jaw, and he would use this experience much later as a teaching device. In this instance, he discussed his fall from the horse in relation
to "attempted suicides which prove such dramatic failures that we are inclined to suspect the honesty and reality of the attempt." He was also
tackling the fallacy of will power as built into the culture:

On a certain occasion, under certain unamusing circumstances which I
must suppress . . . I ceased to be on the back of the horse. . . . Prior to this
accident I had been somewhat given to jumping horses. Subsequent to
the accident, for over a year and a half, I made no successful jumps. I invariably pulled the horse off as we approached the hurdle, to my great
embarrassment and very considerable loss of prestige. It none the less
happened inevitably, and it was only after about a year and a half that I
succeeded in so 'controlling' my motor apparatus that I and the horse
could get over a hurdle again.
The story is told to illustrate the vanquishing of my desire for prestige
and my satisfaction in such things well done by something which was
quite exterior to my control. In all it was me, but when I say it was me I
mean that it most emphatically was not my self. My self was all set to resume jumping horses with the pleasure that comes from it and that special expansive satisfaction that attends doing something about which
many people are somewhat hesitant and which not too many people do
quite well. . . . My will, to drop into the archaic language, was too weak to
control some base impulse in me that thwarted the horse and me.

He went on to say that falling from the horse "has, so far as I know,
nothing to do with suicide," but the person who fails at an attempted suicide may be showing the same pattern of behavior as Sullivan's balking
at a jump: "The act has been contemplated carefully and the motivation
is there. So far as the person is aware there is no room for doubt but that
he will now destroy himself. But something 'stupid' is done so that the act
fails and he does not die."[8]

According to Army records, Sullivan's career in the National Guard
was terminated on November 9, 1916, by a "physical disqualification." It
is difficult to believe that a broken jaw disqualified him, but there is no
specific information on the termination. In the following winter, he "first
submitted [himself] to some 75 hours of psychoanalysis, as psychoanaly-

sis existed in the winter of 1916–17," as he reported in 1934.[9] In a later lecture, he states that his "first personal experience with psychoanalysis" took place in 1915.[10] The 1915 date may represent a brief encounter with psychological help when he was in his last semester in medical school or subsequently working at the steel mill hospital; or he may simply have been careless about the date. In either case, the 1916–17 date is more precisely stated and fits in with a period of confused information on his activities, as reported on various applications. The question remains as to where he got "75 hours of psychoanalysis" that winter. This statement appears in a paper given before the American Psychiatric Association, as part of a symposium on the relation of psychoanalysis to psychiatry, in which A. A. Brill participated. There is the remote possibility that Sullivan may have been in New York City that winter and that he may have received some help from Brill himself. This kind of special communication with a member of his audience was characteristic of Sullivan; he may have been gently chiding Brill on the nature of psychoanalysis as it "existed" and was practiced by Brill at that early period. Or again, Sullivan may have been exposed to some psychiatric help in Chicago that was labeled psychoanalysis. In that period, the term "psychoanalysis" was often used to refer to any kind of dynamic psychiatry that emanated, no matter how remotely, from Freud and his followers.

One can only speculate as to the impetus for Sullivan's turning to psychoanalysis at that particular time. In spite of his various claims that he had early decided on a career in psychiatry, this seems to be retrospective thinking. Nor is there any evidence that he would have had the money and inclination in that period of great uncertainty to have sought out psychoanalysis as an intellectual interest; its ideas were still controversial at that time and far removed from the practical interests of a young would-be physician. Only a personal disturbance of some intensity would have led him in this particular direction. The disturbance may have been linked to the death of a close friend whose identity is not known. A man "with a French name" was a classmate of Sullivan's in medical school, and his death upset Sullivan greatly; but again, no date for his death has been established, and the one student with an obviously French name cannot be traced in the medical school's annual catalogues beyond Sullivan's first year.[11] The disturbance may have been heightened by the economic crisis of that year before he received his degree, but the termination of his stint with the National Guard because of a "physical disqualification" suggests that he was in psychological turmoil. The Army may have arranged for some psychological help.

There are various clues throughout Sullivan's writings that suggest that he again underwent a schizophrenic experience during this period, but the references are veiled and require wide inference, based primarily on his consistent pattern of mining his own experience for the benefit of his trainees. In 1924, when he presented his first paper on schizophrenia, he stated in essence that since 1917 ("the past seven years") he had "seen and studied a group of brief schizophrenic illnesses which recovered with definite favorable change of personality."[12] At least the first of these cases studied may have been his own, followed perhaps by fellow patients when he was an outpatient or in an institutional setting. And in 1929, he referred to the fact that he had been preoccupied with "problems concerning schizophrenia" for thirteen years, again pinpointing, in essence, the "winter of 1916–17."[13] When Sullivan applied for Federal employment as a psychiatrist in 1921, he stated that in 1916–1917, he had had training at three hospitals, "Illinois State Hospital, the West Side Hospital, and the Clinic of Cook County Hospital." The first listing is not identifiable since there were several state hospitals in Illinois at that time, but it was used to substantiate his psychiatric training; in the same application, he claims psychological training, which obviously refers to his "psychoanalysis" in that winter. He only mentions this particular hospital training on one application. It is possible that he himself was hospitalized at one of these hospitals for some brief period after he got out of the National Guard.

He reports that for a "few months" he tried private medical practice. And in his files, there is a letterhead used to make a carbon copy of a letter dated April 1918; the letterhead carries the information "H. Stack Sullivan/ Surgeon/ 175 W. Jackson Blvd./ Chicago" and two phone numbers. This was undoubtedly in the period before he got his degree in September 1917, a period when, he reports, he was working for "five casualty companies." But the period in which he had his own office as H. Stack Sullivan must have been longer than a few months. As late as 1919, his name still appears in Chicago telephone directories as "H. Stack Sullivan, M.D.," each time with a different address. All in all, there are three addresses given for his career as H. Stack Sullivan. The listing of two phone numbers on the letterhead is the first instance of a characteristic that would follow him for the rest of his days: in adversity, he always kept up appearances. The style of the stationery is also the first clear evidence of his later interest in graphic arts; the lettering is clean-cut, without the serifs that were usual in that period—in truth, it shows the same sense of elegance and readability that would be characteristic of his journal, *Psychiatry,* when it began publication twenty years later.

During the same general period, he began to use the full name, Harry Stack Sullivan, which appears on his medical diploma, as if he were maintaining two identities—one as a surgeon, for purposes of earning money; the other as a physician in search of a rewarding specialty. Using the name on the diploma, Sullivan listed five other addresses on applications made to the Army; in the same general period he had his shingle out as H. Stack Sullivan. All of these eight addresses within a two-year period are in the Loop area of Chicago, except for his use of the address for Loyola University, considerably north of the Loop, when he first applied in 1918 for an appointment in the Army Medical Reserve Corps. But he was slowly finding his way out of exile, now that he had his M.D. degree. On January 8, 1918, the *Sun* reported that "Dr. Harry Sullivan of Chicago is visiting his parents in this vicinity for the first time in several years." So the disgraceful exit from Smyrna had finally been righted; and this, too, must have been a driving force through these years of disgrace and struggle.

A month later, on February 12, 1918, Sullivan made his first application to the Army for an appointment in the Medical Reserve Corps.[14] With this application, he began a certain series of falsifications of his life and experience, as reported in subsequent documents, that are at best confusing when one is trying to reconstruct these years. The changes in names are themselves mystifying for anyone who at a later time tries to put together the person who graduated from high school as Harry Francis Stack Sullivan, the person who disappeared (with perhaps another name) after the Cornell crisis, the person who went to medical school as H. F. Sullivan and graduated as Harry Stack Sullivan, and the person known as H. Stack Sullivan who practiced surgery. Finally he would settle on the name Harry Stack Sullivan, with no M.D. after his name on most letters written after the 1930s.

Perhaps the most clumsy and potentially embarrassing of these attempts to falsify facts is Sullivan's change in the year of his birth. Beginning with the application interrogatory made out on February 12, 1918, for a commission in the Army Medical Corps, he made himself six years older than he was—in fact, he is by this information a year older than Clarence Bellinger and only a year younger than his cousin Leo. All the Army records seem to show this date of birth (1886), so he was probably simply continuing a falsification from information given when he joined the National Guard. The same date is carried on Federal employment records. Between 1918 and 1931, each register of physicians published by the American Medical Association carries the incorrect year of birth, although his changing addresses, professional affiliations, and so on, seem to be correct for the respective years. Finally, when he began private practice in New York City in 1930, he corrected the year of birth, so that the next register (1931) is correct for the first time.

On the Army applications, there are other dates that do not mesh with the 1886 birth date. Thus he did not bother to change the date of graduation from high school in accordance with the birth date, so that he would have been twenty-two years old in 1908 when he graduated from high school, and ten years old when he started school, according to other statements made by him. But the juggling of facts about his experience and training becomes a more cumbersome piece of falsification as time goes on, so that throughout all the official pieces of paper that exist, there is no way to piece together adequately the years from 1915 until he went to St. Elizabeths Hospital late in 1921. In general, the facts and figures were tailor-made for each situation: thus the information on two Army interrogatories changes rather drastically within two months; although the Army in general was the recipient of both documents, they went to two different departments in the Army, and he obviously took a chance. There is a frantic feeling about all of this, as if he were struggling for his very existence, both economically and psychologically.

The first Army application, filled out a few days after Sullivan had been to Springfield to take his examinations for licensing in the state of Illinois, reports that he has passed the examinations, and that he is an applicant to the local medical societies and "thereafter to Illinois State Med. Soc., and to American Medical Association." The last-named affiliation would not take place until the 1930s. He claims only six and a half months' hospital experience, referring to the time at the steel mill; he does not mention his work at the three hospitals in 1916–1917, which he claims at a later time. He stresses his work in industrial surgery, reporting twenty-five months' experience in that field, caring for approximately ten cases per day for the whole period, with "some internal medicine and neurological work." Thus he is including the period in the National Guard in this reckoning. In total, he accounts for thirty-one and a half months after medical school, which would tally with the total time exactly, without allowing for periods of unemployment or for some kind of "physical disqualification." In answering a question on "other educational advantages," he reports that he has had "postgraduate instruction in surgery" with two of his professors at medical school, but he notes that his "ultimate specialty" is internal medicine and neurology. He reports a year's work at Cornell in 1908–09 as "two courses of lectures." In answer to a question on his acquaintanceship with "ancient or modern languages or branches of science," he reports that he has "some knowledge of Latin, French, and Spanish. Acquainted with Physics, Psychology, Biology, Anthropology and Ethnology, Paleontology, and Geology." The fossils near the Smyrna schoolhouse still survive in this description; and physics comes first in the listing—it is a passion that will never leave him.

As a result of this application, Sullivan passed an examination, was recommended for a commission on April 13, 1918, and forthwith began work before the formalization of the commission as first lieutenant, on May 7, 1918. He reports in the letter of acceptance that he has been assisting Major Edmond J. Doering since April 13, "in examining and supplying medical attention to the detachments, National Army, enrolled at institutions here for special training."

But he was already moving restlessly in another direction. On April 6, 1918, a week before he was recommended for the commission, he applied to the Director of the Section of Anthropology, in the Surgeon General's Office of the Army, for a commission in the Sanitary Corps. Sullivan's answers even to some of the same questions are sharply different. He omits his "postgraduate training in surgery" under "other educational advantages" and lists "private tuition in Psychology and Anthropology, and two years research (literary and practical) in Anthropology and Etiology (medical) at Crerar Library and Chicago." His "ultimate specialty" has in the space of a few weeks been realized, for it is now "Internal Medicine and the animal factors entering into this work, as exemplified in Heredity, Psychology, Anthropological characteristics." He states that he has had two years of instruction and practice in this specialty, since he concluded his undergraduate medical studies, "in the field provided by the industries of Chicago." On this application, he does not mention the word "surgery."

His information on two years of study at Crerar Library was probably fairly accurate. His ability to work long hours, including nights and weekends, would follow him for the rest of his life. His "permanent address" during 1918 was 69 W. Washington Street, near the Crerar Library. He obviously spent a great deal of time in the library, particularly when he was unemployed; but two years seems an excessive estimate, given the whole time sequence.

The final document is an Officers' Qualification Card, prepared by Sullivan on July 8, 1918. Here again he goes back to the emphasis on surgery. His principal civilian occupation has been as physician and surgeon in "office and consultation work entirely." His opportunities for instruction or practice in *operative* surgery have been "limited," he reports. During his last year in civilian life he earned $3,600, which would have been a sizeable income for a young doctor at that period who had been licensed for only a few months. His specialization is internal medicine, although he notes that he has spent most of his time in industrial surgery. He has had two years of clinical experience in cardiovascular medicine and in neurology. In the listing of occupations at which he is experienced or expert, and the number of years spent in each of these occupations, there are again data that do not agree with information given on earlier forms. The only occupation in which he claims to be expert is personnel direction, citing a half year of experience. In surgery, he indicates two periods of experience, and this obviously refers to part of his experience in the steel mills and his later casualty company work. Within the field of operative surgery per se, he only claims a half year of experience in "spinal column and cord, fractures, and roentgenology." On this form, Sullivan claims a year and a half at Cornell, with a specialization in "Science (Natural)." Earlier he had claimed only a year at Cornell. In a long list of special military qualifications or aptitude, he lists two: Equitation, under Infantry and Cavalry; and "Operations Section," under General Staff.

Six days after this rating sheet was filled out by Sullivan, in longhand and in ink, someone else rated him, in pencil, on the same sheet. He received 12 points on "physical," 15 on intelligence, 12 on leadership, 15 on personal qualities, and 32 on "Gen. Value," with a total of 86 (apparently out of a possible 100). From this rating scale, it is probable that 15 was the highest possible score on the first four, and 40 the highest on the final item, so that he received the full score on intelligence and personal qualities. The rater (whose name does not appear) has known Sullivan for six months and recommends especially executive and administrative duties. The total effect is to present a picture of a physician who prefers internal medicine to surgery and one whose administrative abilities are in many ways superior to his other abilities.

There is a kind of clumsy exaggeration evident on these interrogatories that communicates an obvious lack of foresight—as if the person making out the forms lacked the ability to see the significance of the falsifications. It is perhaps the clearest indication of Sullivan's psychological instability, stemming from the early years and the trouble at Cornell. Thus he invited a problem when he changed his experience at Cornell from one year to one and a half; and such a risk was not essential. The change in birth date was also an unnecessary risk, although, like the change in name to H. Stack Sullivan, it may have served to camouflage his identity.

Yet some part of the falsifications is only an exaggeration of what we all might do under certain conditions—for instance, in a period of high unemployment, or in trying to get a grant for advanced education. For Sullivan, the difference was in his own ability to observe and remember what he was doing; the clear recognition over time of how such falsifications took place; the knowledge of the anxiety that attached to faulty self-esteem; and the understanding of the necessity for putting one's best foot forward in an uncertain world—particularly if one were poor and a member of a minority group. So this period of uncertainty in his life became an important qualification for his life's work, simply because he examined it endlessly, as if he had found a new and unclassified geologic specimen. His curiosity about the world around him, always including himself in the interaction, was a distinguishing characteristic in his later theory.

As a stranger in a strange land, he would always find something to explore. On the hill in Smyrna, he had lived largely in an Irish world, created by his grandmother Stack and his mother; his encounter with a larger world outside of his own relatives was mainly with Clarence and with an occasional teacher or neighbor who made some contact with him. In many ways, he was not far from the immigrant boat, in psychological and sociological terms, when he went to Ithaca and again when he went to Chicago. His insecurity and diffidence would never rub off, although it would ease; and the self-knowledge of these insecurities would lead to vast areas of extraordinary sophistication and ability.

Sometime in the Chicago period, his fondness for alcohol had its beginning as a way of handling anxiety. It was a fondness inherited culturally from his father and from his grandfather Stack—the odious vice detested by the women of many an Irish family but a necessity for the men who had to face repeatedly the grim realities of famine and migration. The first formal record of Sullivan's use of alcohol is found in the two 1918 Army interrogatories: "Do you use intoxicating liquors or narcotics; if so, to what extent?" In the February answer, Sullivan reports, "Yes, occasionally drink intoxicant before dinner." In the April answer, he states: "Yes, occasionally take appetizer before dinner." As a nephew of the man who ran the Gothic House in South Otselic, which included a "decent" bar, he was aware of the niceties of such distinctions. A man who took only "appetizers" could scarcely be classified as an alcoholic. Yet from his writings there is a clear indication that alcohol served important purposes for him; and certainly among his colleagues there was a running argument as to whether he was an alcoholic or not. He often referred to the importance of alcohol for the psychological survival of the young person in distress. He saw it as one of the necessary evils for dissolving anxiety, particularly in adolescence:

I sometimes think alcohol is, more than any other human invention, the basis for the duration and growth of the Western world. I am quite certain that no such complex, wonderful, and troublesome organization of society could have lasted long enough to become conspicuous if a great number of its unhappy denizens did not have this remarkable chemical compound with which to get relief from intolerable problems of anxiety. But its capacity for dealing with those problems naturally makes it a menace under certain circumstances, as I scarcely think I need argue. . . . Since the self-function, which is, of course, very intimately connected with the occurrence of anxiety, is inhibited and disturbed by alcohol, but one's later recall is not, one experiences the anxiety in retrospect, you see. And the problems that get one all too dependent on alcohol are, I think, the problems of sexual adjustment, which hit hardest in early adolescence.[15]

In another lecture, he commented both personally and professionally on the use of alcohol:

[I am] a person who uses, I think, in the average year far more spirituous liquor than most of you could survive without impairment of your liver (I'm not guaranteeing what the cause of my death will be by any means) [and] a person who has anything but ingrained teetotal tendencies and [who] comes from a particular clan or ethnic group which is notorious for its thoroughgoing familiarity with spirituous liquors (which perhaps can compete only with another ethnic group, the Scots, and I should say could compete with heavy handicap for the Scots). [So] don't think that what I have to say about alcohol in its relation to mental disorder represents a prohibitionist prejudice on my side. There are a number of disastrous aspects of alcohol in relation to human life and, if you please, society. And I feel I must take another very strong position. So far as I know I am the only person who has said that the human race may well owe its continued survival solely to the discovery of ethyl alcohol—so you see, I am anything but a prohibitionist. But, however completely Western society owes its survival to alcohol, alcohol is a very treacherous element in the appraisal of interpersonal difficulties and in the planning of adequate handling [of them].[16]

It seems unlikely that Sullivan had any experience with alcohol at Cornell, but in the Chicago years he definitely began to use alcohol to combat anxiety, as indicated in the Army interrogatories and in his various lectures on the subject. Toward the end of his life, when he was seriously ill, he used it more often, even while he was working, especially to combat the pain of angina. An admiring colleague who regularly went to him for consultation reported that during this period she always tried to see him in the morning hours rather than later: "He would be drinking after lunch." Yet by and large, he appears to have used alcohol judiciously. Although some few colleagues describe him as obviously intoxicated on one or another social occasion, most colleagues do not report ever having seen him more than mildly affected in a work situation, and that only infrequently, during the last few years.

Certainly in the years I worked with him, it never seemed to interfere with his creativity or energy. On Christmas Eve, 1947, about a year before he died, I spent several hours working with him while he sipped 100-year-old brandy through the late afternoon and evening, carefully defining the brandy as medicine. During other work sessions, more often in restaurants, he always offered me a drink, which I usually accepted; this time he did not. The level in the brandy bottle went steadily downward, but I never noticed the slightest abatement of interest in the task or any loss of competence. When I was ready to go, he apologized to me for asking me to work on Christmas Eve. Only much later did I realize that he was lonely on this occasion and that his solitary drinking was a way of denying his loneliness and defining the situation as work-oriented rather than social. He was fifty-four years old when I first knew him; yet he sometimes showed the gaucheness of the shy young men whom I knew as an undergraduate.

Sullivan was on active duty as an officer in the Medical Corps for only about seven months. Shortly after the Armistice, on December 16, 1918, at the "Convenience of Gov't" he was mustered out, with an honorable discharge. Apparently his last official contact with the Army took place

176 PSYCHIATRIST OF AMERICA

two months later, when he received a notice of his appointment as a captain in the Officers' Reserve Corps, but he was never activated to this post. The commission was sent to his latest address in Chicago: the University Club of Chicago, as would befit an Army captain. He had his picture taken as a captain, rather than as a first lieutenant; and this picture shows Sullivan at his most romantic—a young Irish poet in uniform with the intellectual's pince-nez glasses. There is no doubt as one looks at this picture and ponders on all the despair that lay behind him that the Army was, like the scholarship to Cornell, a magic talisman on the road to acceptance. It is not strange, then, that he always had a strong positive feeling about the Army.

For a man of peace, this affinity for the Army seemed odd to his young colleagues thirty years later. But it was in character, and it was in the tradition of the Irish soldier. Two first cousins—John Stack's boys—made a career out of the Marines, moving up the ladder out of their First World War experience and retiring as brigadier generals. And finally, it was the Army that formed the transition to Sullivan's next assignment and that eventually led him to St. Elizabeths Hospital and his career under William Alanson White. In a very real sense, it was the Army that put him on the high road to a productive life.

When the war ended on November 11, 1918, Sullivan was still three years away from beginning his formal career as a psychiatrist. It was not until November 1921 that he became a "neuropsychiatrist," according to Federal Government classification, and was assigned to work at St. Elizabeths as a liaison officer for the Veterans Bureau.[17] In those three years between 1918 and 1921, he again shifted around from pillar to post, not yet able to arrive at his "chosen" profession, as he would later term it.

But the aftermath of the war provided employment and important experience for him. On April 24, 1919, he began work as an Assistant District Medical Officer in Chicago's Eighth District Office of the Division of Rehabilitation for Disabled Soldiers, Sailors, and Marines, a part of the Federal Board of Vocational Education. By October 1919, he had been moved from Chicago to the headquarters of this board in Washington, and by November 2, 1919, he was designated as a Medical Executive Officer in the Washington headquarters. His appointment to the Federal Board was concurrent with a reserve commission in the U.S. Public Health Service, at the rank of "Passed Assistant Surgeon." He entered on active service effective November 1, 1919, by which time he was "Acting Surgeon." He was paid by the Public Health Service from then on, although his work was still with the Board. He was permanently assigned to Washington, with temporary assignments to various offices—Detroit, Chicago, Boston, Philadelphia. One travel order shows that his task was "visiting hospitals, interviewing patients, conferring with employers." In a later application to the Veterans Bureau, he defined his duties at the

Federal Board as being concerned with the "re-examination of applicants" who had cardiac and neuropsychiatric disabilities, for Federal Board assistance; after an examination, he rated the vocational handicaps of the veteran. But he also conferred on statistical reports, in one instance for a month in Chicago. On August 20, 1920, he was authorized to attend the American Legion convention in Chicago.

This experience, varied and challenging, gave him cogent background for his role in the Second World War as a consultant to the Selective Service. It also moved him closer and closer to an understanding of the need for preventive psychiatry, for he had a chance to observe the psychological pattern of stress as it appeared in a wide range of veterans.

His connection with the Federal Board of Vocational Education seems to have come to an end in the fall of 1920. In the application for the Veterans Bureau, Sullivan indicates that he left the Federal Board in November 1920, and this seems to tie in with other secondary information. But during the next twelve months, his employment is uncertain. He reports that he was a "psychiatrist" at the "Public Health Institute." But this seems to be an organization like the "Illinois State Hospital"—too general for identification. During part of that winter of 1920–21 he was in Smyrna, as can be substantiated from the Norwich *Sun,* and in part from Sullivan's own report of his activities. In his autobiographical account, Sullivan reports: "After caring for his father through a grave illness, Sullivan returned to Chicago, arriving only two days before a telegram recalled him to Washington to become United States Veterans' liaison officer at St. Elizabeths Hospital."[18] This implies that his father's illness took place in November 1921, when he went to St. Elizabeths. But the serious illness of his father, mentioned in the *Sun,* took place a year earlier. It is of course quite possible that his father's illness lasted a long time, yet the picture that emerges from the newspaper does not support this possibility. It is more probable that Sullivan was again besieged by anxiety over the lapse in his employment.

On October 26, 1920, at about the time he left his work at the Federal Board, the *Sun* reports: "Dr. Harry Sullivan, of Chicago, is spending several days with his parents, Mr. and Mrs. T. J. Sullivan." On November 5, 1920, the *Sun* states that T. J. Sullivan, who has been on the sick list for several days, is reported as slightly improved. On November 19, 1920, the *Sun* reports: "T. J. Sullivan, who has been confined to his home for the past few weeks does not improve as fast as his many friends would be glad to have him. His son, Dr. Harry Sullivan, of Chicago is with him." On December 31, 1920, the *Sun* reports on Timothy's progress: "T. J. Sullivan who has been confined to his home west of this village for several weeks has sufficiently recovered to be able to pay this place a visit on Thursday. His many friends are glad to see him out again." On February 8, 1921, there is a special item with a brief headline in the Smyrna news column: "Dr. Sullivan Leaves: Dr. Harry S. Sullivan, who has been enjoying a visit with his parents, Mr. and Mrs. T. J. Sullivan, left Friday [February 4, 1921] for Boston, Mass. from which city he will return by way of Washington, D.C., to Chicago." Thus, according to the paper, he was apparently then living in Chicago.

During the spring and summer of 1921, Timothy and Ella seem to have been unusually active and social, according to the *Sun,* but Harry was not in evidence. In a whole series of social items in the Smyrna column about Ella and Timothy and their guests and social activities that summer, there is no mention of Harry's being there. But on October 28, 1921, shortly before he went to St. Elizabeths, there is an item about Harry: "Dr. Harry Sullivan of Chicago has been spending some time with his parents, Mr. and Mrs. T. J. Sullivan. He left for Washington, D.C., on Thursday." This was the eventful trip that took him to St. Elizabeths and, as he noted, "launched" his career as a psychiatrist.

With his trip to Washington in November 1921, Sullivan gave up forever his residence in Chicago. But his experience there would eventually form a link between his own thinking and the social science that was developing at the University of Chicago. He would never be affiliated with that university, but the bond between himself and sociologists like Robert Park and W. I. Thomas would be much more than an intellectual conviction. It had been forged out of his and their observation of life in Chicago at about the same period.

⊷ 22 ⊷

The Impact of St. Elizabeths Hospital

> At last his career as a psychiatrist was launched—
> and under the aegis of the Federal Government!
> What is more, at St. Elizabeths Sullivan made the ac-
> quaintance of ... William Alanson White, famous
> teacher and encourager of psychiatric research.
> —Sullivan, *Current Biography,* 1942

UNTIL Sullivan became a liaison officer for the Veterans Bureau at St. Elizabeths Hospital, the pattern of his life had a linear quality. Even though there remain many questions and gaps in tracing out his earlier years, one can safely assume that he had had few meaningful relationships, either socially or intellectually. Clara Thompson has reported that even after he got to medical school, " his poverty and his feeling of not knowing how to belong kept him still isolated from his contemporaries."[1]

He was almost thirty when he arrived in Washington to take up his new duties, and more than half of his life was over. But in the succeeding twenty-seven years, he would move swiftly and tellingly into the mainstream of American psychiatry and social science. To fully understand the dramatic quality of the change in his life brought about by his brief formal affiliation with St. Elizabeths Hospital, one must review the pattern of his life before and after November 12, 1921, when he assumed his new duties. He had emerged from a life of isolation and struggle, of almost built-in deception in order to survive; he now found himself in a benign setting, where he was accepted by people who shared his interests, and where his curiosity about life was not only tolerated—it was encouraged. As he came to know the people that clustered around William Alanson White, different parts of his earlier experiences were brought into play in rapid and overlapping succession. As he became freer in interchange with a brilliant assortment of clinicians and social scientists over the next ten years, he could watch himself changing gear with each new encounter. Because each significant experience from his earlier life was separated by layers of loneliness, he had never homogenized his experiences into a facade of conforming reactions to new people or new situations. Thus he had an extraordinary ability to watch himself in these new encounters, whether with colleagues or with patients. The actual isolation of his early life forced on him the awareness that one's happiness and one's despair are in a constant state of flux, heavily dependent on the immediate situation and its echo from the past. By 1926, he was able to state in a formal professional meeting that "interpersonal factors seem to be the effective elements in the psychiatry of schizophrenia."[2] It seems to have been his first formal use of the term "interpersonal," but its gestation began in the experience at St. Elizabeths.

Although Sullivan felt that his new job launched his career as a psychiatrist, his actual title at the Veterans Bureau was "neuropsychiatrist," in accordance with the particular problems seen in soldiers who had suffered neurological and psychological damage in the war years. Indeed, his work was probably not too different in its beginning from his earlier work at the Federal Board of Vocational Education. Only a few months before, the Rehabilitation Division of the Federal Board had merged with a part of the U.S. Public Health Service and the War Risk Insurance Board to form the Veterans Bureau, which eventually became the U.S. Veterans Administration. Thus Sullivan's work had not changed in character; the change was in the setting itself and the wide range of people and ideas at "St. E's," as staff and patients familiarly termed it.

Over a period of almost twenty years, White had made the hospital a national institution, famed for its benign care of patients and for its encouragement of staff initiative, particularly in the use of dynamic psychiatry for psychotic patients. He was "the great encourager," as Harold Lasswell has named him.[3] So it was that resident physicians and other staff had a feeling of loyalty to each other long after they had left the hospital and gone on to diverse careers. Many of the staff members from the same period as Sullivan, or just before or just after, remained Sullivan's colleagues and friends for many years. Ernest Hadley, then a young psychiatrist, came to St. E's in the same year as Sullivan. In 1938, seventeen years later, Hadley and Sullivan would inaugurate and coedit (with Thomas Gill) the journal *Psychiatry*. Another staff member, Lucile Dooley, had been at St. E's for five years when Sullivan arrived; she would be one of the cosigners, with Sullivan and Hadley, of the incorporation papers for the William Alanson White Psychoanalytic Foundation in 1933. She was eight years older than Sullivan, and her training was broad and impressive. Originally she had come to the hospital as a lay analyst, with a Ph.D. in psychology from Clark University, where she had studied under G. Stanley Hall. She had recently finished her M.D. degree at

Johns Hopkins while still working at St. E's. Under the direction of a senior psychiatrist, Edward J. Kempf, she had been working with manic-
depressive patients, using modified psychoanalytic methods.[4]

By the time Sullivan came, Kempf was no longer on the staff—he had
left the year before—but he remained an important person at St. E's,
partly through occasional consultation at the hospital and mainly
through his impressive book, *Psychopathology,* which had just been published.[5] Many of Sullivan's most cogent concepts were derived from
Kempf's formulations, which took on different definitions in Sullivan's
later thinking. Thus Kempf referred to "Not-I, Not-me, Not-myself" as
personifications from early life. Sullivan would later use the term "not-
me" as correlative with the experience of "good-me" and "bad-me" in
early personifications of self. Or again, Kempf used the term "preadolescence" to describe the years from three to ten; Sullivan used the same
term, defining it as a developmental phase of relatively brief duration
beginning at about age nine. Moreover, Kempf used the term "social
esteem" in much the same way as Sullivan would use "self-esteem," although Sullivan made the experience much more critical in a person's
mental health. In 1911, Kempf had been one of the first psychiatrists in
this country to use Freud's dynamic psychiatry in the care of psychotic
patients.[6] Kempf's early experience had been in a state hospital, as was
White's, so that Sullivan entered a clinical setting in which elitism in the
selection of patients for intensive care was not tolerated.

In this beginning phase of experimenting with Freudian psychology,
the staff at St. E's had a rather cavalier attitude about its modification for
use with psychotic patients, although Freud himself had frowned upon
this development. Twenty years later, some of the participants in these
experiments, such as Hadley and Dooley, were gathered into the fold of
classical psychoanalysis and tended to discount these more radical years
when ideas were changing rapidly in an exciting intellectual milieu.
White had been impressed by Freud's work for many years; but eventually he, too, would have to make a decision on the tight limits of classical psychoanalysis. When the Foundation named after him and formed
in his honor came into formal operation, White requested that its name
be changed from Psychoanalytic to Psychiatric—a mark of his disaffection for the direction of psychoanalysis in this country. Like Adolf Meyer,
the head of Phipps Clinic at Johns Hopkins University, White would ultimately feel that the transfer of Freudian theory to an American society
would only serve to undo some of the gains that were beginning to be
made in understanding the particular problems of a diverse and new society.

There was one staff person at St. E's who steadfastly maintained a
rather jaundiced attitude toward all this interest in the new psychiatry—
the psychiatrist Roscoe Hall, who was almost exactly four years older

than Sullivan and who, like Sullivan, would remain a bachelor. Hall was valued for his clinical judgment as an admissions officer and for his ability to develop nonthreatening relationships with patients. Hall undoubtedly played an important part in Sullivan's introduction to this somewhat overstimulating environment. His birthday, like that of Sullivan's first chum, Clarence, was on February 22, only one day after Sullivan's, but the relationship was otherwise quite different. For many years, Hall and Sullivan would get together for happy exchanges, over alcoholic beverages consumed with such skill that the sessions could continue for hours without either one showing signs of fatigue or lessening of wit. On one occasion when I shared drinks with them in connection with a rather boring professional meeting in Asbury Park, the conversation was witty, genial, sparring; and Sullivan was more relaxed than I had ever seen him.

Hall had grown up in Millerstown, a village in central Pennsylvania, as an only child of middle-aged parents. His father was a country doctor in this village, which was about two or three times larger than Smyrna. In true WASP tradition his father made elaborate plans for his education—"college, medical college, a year in Germany, $1,000, and then if he did not succeed, it would be his own fault." All of this firm control over Roscoe's destiny was abruptly terminated by the sudden death of his father when Roscoe was about fourteen. As he would report much later, his first reaction when he heard the news was to say to himself: "Now I can ride the white horse." It had been a wish denied him by his father, but it would not be denied by his widowed mother. Thereafter Roscoe, freed from paternal restrictions on an otherwise quite indulged childhood, went on to a happy and carefree existence.[7] The story of the white horse sounds like the stories that Hall and Sullivan would tell each other, guffawing loudly the whole time, while they downed some more brandy. It was the kind of story that then, as now, might have encouraged a colleague to make a psychoanalytic conjecture, but Hall and Sullivan shared an aversion to such easy one-upmanship. A very close colleague, William V. Silverberg, has recalled an incident when he made the mistake of offering Sullivan that sort of off-the-cuff interpretation, while a guest at Sullivan's house in the Sheppard years:

I do not recall how the subject arose, but Sullivan remarked to me one afternoon that as a child he had hated and feared spiders. I commented, quite naively—like the fool where angels fear to tread—that spiders generally symbolized the mother. "Oh, do they now?" said Sullivan in a sing-song, argumentative Hibernian intonation. "And how do you know that?" he asked, so challengingly that I felt warned not to pursue the subject. "Oh, I think I read it somewhere," was my reply, limping rather hastily away from the battlefield. So far as I know, the topic of spiders was never mentioned again by either of us.[8]

Part of this distaste for glib interpretations expressed by both Sullivan and Hall had about it the flavor of rural America—the need to laugh at the city slicker, to make fun of highfalutin ideas. They also had a shared experience in the prominent role of their mothers in their lives. Roscoe's mother lived with him for a time at St. E's, and Sullivan came to know her quite well and to give her a good deal of attention. She was a sweet and gentle old lady, a devout Methodist who did not always approve of Roscoe's cronies and leisure activities, which included a fair amount of convivial drinking. But Sullivan liked her and was able to win her over, and he was always on his best behavior around her. When Roscoe's mother died in the 1930s, a group of doctors, including Sullivan, journeyed with Roscoe to Millerstown for the funeral; it was in many ways a satisfying trip, for while they tenderly laid her to rest, they extolled her virtues afterwards in their usual way, without any danger of upsetting her.

Yet all the friendships that Sullivan formed at St. Elizabeths paled, of course, before the significance of William Alanson White. White was in his heyday by 1921. By walking a tightrope between the needs of patients, who always came first, and the political surveillance of Congress, White had managed to build the institution into a haven for staff as well as for patients, where an extraordinary amount of work was done in a congenial and stimulating atmosphere. In 1918, less than four years before Sullivan's arrival, White had married for the first time at the age of forty-eight. His wife, Lola Thurston, widow of a U.S. Senator from Nebraska, was a person "with considerable grace and charm," and she gave White "a wide entree into the social life" of the city.[9] Sullivan and Lola White early formed a close relationship. Sullivan's remarks about finding himself a rich and charming widow, which he continued to make up to the end of his life, were not entirely facetious, given his admiration of White's success in marriage somewhat late in life.

There were other far more important bonds between White and Sullivan. White invited confidences with his staff, and he apparently came to know a great deal about Sullivan's early life, either from Sullivan himself or through a network extending back to White's stay at Binghamton. Most of Sullivan's colleagues, even those who knew him well, had very little information on his beginnings—not because Sullivan was secretive, but out of his gradual estrangement from his early life, almost as if he had no ability to verbalize it. From scattered references in his own writing, published and unpublished, and from chance remarks by those who knew him best, one glimpses a shy protectiveness about his bleak life in Smyrna. His ability to move back and forth between the two worlds—the world of an apartment on Park Avenue, for instance, and the farmhouse on a dirt road, with no electricity—gradually diminished. After his father's death in 1931, he would never go back to Chenango County. Probably, as time went on, his chief contact with that early existence was vicarious, through the bleak lives of his patients. With them, in any case, his defenses dropped away, as his friend Clara Thompson has reported: "I . . . learned that this man, who in public could tear a bad paper to bits with his scathing sarcasm, had another side—a gentle, warm, friendly one. This was the side he showed his patients. Anyone who has seen him talking with a disturbed catatonic can know that he has seen the real Harry without pretense or defenses. There was nothing maudlin about his tenderness—it rather conveyed a feeling of deep understanding."[10] With White, Sullivan's defenses were partially stripped away in the beginning, for he felt that White had rescued his career and set him on his way.

Part of Sullivan's feeling came from White's attitude about crime. The shame of Sullivan's experience at Cornell—the stigma, the feeling that he had somehow ruined his early glory—was subjected to reality by White. No one in America at that time was more advanced than White in his approach to crime. In White's one-genus postulate, the criminal was not essentially different from the rest of mankind: "The difference between the so-called insane person or the criminal on the one hand and the so-called sane or normal person on the other is only a difference in quantity, a difference in the strength or weakness and the balanced relations of the various tendencies and stimuli with which he has to deal."[11] Sullivan's later formulation was essentially the same: "In most general terms, we are all much more simply human than otherwise, be we happy and successful, contented and detached, miserable and mentally disordered, or whatever."[12] Like Will Sullivan, White had a sociological approach to murder and was therefore an early opponent of capital punishment. Only a small number of murderers were executed, White pointed out; and they were "for the most part youths who are defenceless, without money, friends, or influence, not infrequently mentally defective, or else they are persons against whom there is at the time a prevailing great popular prejudice."[13]

White's attitude about the so-called insanity dodge, a characterization that Harry had been saddled with in Chenango County, was matter-of-fact: "Not only do no criminals get off by the 'insanity dodge' but over 50 per cent of those who are convicted are suffering from mental disease or deficiency."[14] Such statements must have hit Sullivan's ears like a clap of thunder close by. From a sociological stance, White must be seen as Sullivan's most important therapist.

Superficially it might seem that White and Sullivan had somewhat similar childhoods. White considered himself "psychologically" an only child, since his only sibling, a brother, was ten years older and not significant to him in his growing-up years.[15] Like Sullivan, White was awarded a four-year scholarship at Cornell, when he was only fifteen, as compared to Sullivan's age of sixteen. Like Sullivan, White had an early interest in the natural sciences. Several obituary notices at the time of White's death refer to him as a "poor boy," an adjective often applied to Sullivan. In both instances, the term is misleading. By force of the Stack legend, Sullivan would probably have gone to college eventually; and he certainly had access to books, good food, and adequate housing in his early years. White, who seems to have never referred to himself as "poor," stressed the financial reverses of his father when he was quite young and tended to define his years at Cornell as deprived.[16] In truth, he combined two traditions—the New England WASP tradition and the Horatio-Alger tradition of overcoming the financial reverses of his family—that worked in tandem to produce a well-balanced and successful psychiatrist.

White reports that on both sides, his family was "Anglo-Saxon, American and New England," like so many in Chenango County.[17] His mother, a native of Boston and related to seafaring folk, came from a "somewhat superior stratum" than his father. She was concerned with artistic and intellectual matters. His father focused on politics and business, and left his son's rearing largely to his wife. Early in the marriage, the family moved to Brooklyn Heights in New York, where William was born in 1870. The father was a successful businessman in New York City for some years, and the older son was sent to the best private school in the city. William began his education in a private school, but he soon had to transfer to public school because of reverses in his father's business; his mother was very much "disturbed" at this turn of events.

A friend told him of the possibility of getting a scholarship at Cornell University; and he saw this as a way to pay for most of his own education. At fifteen, with no high school diploma, he took an examination for one of the scholarships established under the land grant laws. There was no serious competition, as White has noted, because there were fewer applicants than the quota for the city. Because the minimum entrance age at Cornell was sixteen, White had to "stoutly and valiantly" lie, as he reports, and he gave his age as seventeen. This was a very difficult thing for him to do, he states, since "truthfulness was one of my outstanding qualities." He wanted this to be recorded so that anyone working on his chronology would not be puzzled by this discrepancy. Sullivan could never afford to admit this kind of discrepancy, and this as much as anything else tells something of the difference in the necessity for fabrication from one life to another.

During the entire four years at Cornell, White busied himself with earning money and exploring a whole series of subjects, ranging from the natural sciences to philosophy and psychology. But his difficulty with mathematics forced him to abandon physics. He began by focusing on natural history, but when it was abolished from the college curriculum, he began to study whatever he wanted, registered for as many hours as the college would allow, and "did not graduate because I had not followed the prescribed routine." He then attended Long Island College

Medical School, which was near the house in which he had been born. By that time, the financial position of his father was so bad that the family had moved away from that neighborhood and was living in a boarding house. Some of his family's friends from the more affluent days helped him to get a reduced rate for his two years of medical training.

At twenty-one, White graduated from medical school, having finally managed to graduate for the first time. His cheerful report of his schooling and his subsequent rise to the prestigious appointment at thirty-three to be head of St. Elizabeths is told with the air of a natural winner. White's sympathy and understanding of crime and mental illness had the assurance of one who, after overcoming some temporary adversity, was eager to assume the burden of noblesse oblige. For Sullivan, adversity had been a more permanent part of life. As someone who had been personally involved in mental illness and perhaps crime, Sullivan accepted White as someone who might appropriately bestow favors on him, as one of the dispossessed. But he yearned for a fuller appreciation of himself by White than he ever received. Over time, he came to understand the differences in their views and their early experience; he even respected and perhaps envied White for belonging, but he learned to keep a certain formal distance from White. There was a time in their correspondence, for instance, when White made an effort to be less formal by beginning his letters with such phrases as "My dear Sullivan," but Sullivan never began his letters with anything other than "Dear Dr. White," or "Dear friend."

In particular, Sullivan respected White for his broad interest in the social sciences, which coincided with Sullivan's intellectual interests, and for White's close relationship with significant figures in a wide range of the natural science disciplines. White had maintained an interest in the natural sciences from his days at Cornell, and this had been fortified, while he was at Binghamton State Hospital, by Smith Ely Jelliffe, who became a lifelong colleague of primary importance. Jelliffe had taken a job at Binghamton for the summer of 1896, in order to have an inexpensive vacation for himself and his young family. He had been trained first as a botanist, then as a pharmacologist, and finally as a neurologist and psychiatrist. His interests were catholic, and his rapport with White was almost immediate. It was Jelliffe who, early in their relationship, introduced White to the importance of psychoanalysis, although Jelliffe was skeptical from the first about the importance of sex in Freudian theory. In March 1909, when Jelliffe was in Austria, he wrote a letter to White: "The whole Freud business is done to death. The lamp posts of Vienna will cast forth sexual rays pretty soon . . . I suspect William Tell's apple must have been a pair of testicles."[18]

Yet both White and Jelliffe maintained a dedicated and lively interest in the importance of the new psychoanalytic approach. In 1913, the two of them began the publication of a new journal called the *Psychoanalytic*

Review, originally subtitled *A Journal Devoted to an Understanding of Human Conduct.* Before its inception, White wrote to both Freud and Jung as well as to psychologists, historians, anthropologists, and philosophers, partly to help in the determination of a name. Most of the people consulted, including Ernest Jones, suggested a more general title for the journal, with "Psychopathology" being highly favored as a part of the title, rather than "Psychoanalysis." But both White and Jelliffe settled on the latter as the proper emphasis for the journal. By so doing, they made the word more general than Freud and his disciples wanted it to be; and they elevated its importance for the social scientists who were still skeptical of the Freudian approach.

The model of having one's own publication was important for Sullivan. The prestige of the *Psychoanalytic Review* was considerable from the beginning. Shortly after Sullivan left St. E's in 1924, he wrote his first two papers, one of which was accepted by White for the *Review.*[19] From letters between Sullivan and White, it is clear that publication in the *Review* was very important to Sullivan.

By the fall of 1922, Sullivan was no longer content with being a liaison officer, and he approached White about the possibility of having a full-time clinical post at St. E's. White claimed to have no post available at the time, but there is evidence that he had misgivings about Sullivan. Sullivan then made at least two applications for clinical jobs elsewhere, one to Boston Psychopathic Hospital, under the superintendency of C. Macfie Campbell, and the other to Sheppard and Enoch Pratt Hospital in Towson, Maryland, headed by Ross McClure Chapman. Both Campbell and Chapman asked White for a letter of recommendation. White answered both men with the same letter:

I have your letter . . . inquiring about Dr. H. S. Sullivan. I could not consider Dr. Sullivan's application for this staff because the administrative positions were all filled with no prospects of a vacancy in the immediate future. Dr. Sullivan functioned here for sometime as a liaison officer between the Veterans' Bureau and the Hospital. During that period our relations were eminently cordial and we got along nicely. As regards my opinion as to his availability for a staff appointment, I should say, as I told him once, that I do not feel that I really know Dr. Sullivan very well. He is a keen, alert, somewhat witty Irishman, who has a facade of facetiousness which it is a bit difficult to penetrate. One or two occurrences have made me think that back of that facade was a considerable discontent that might perhaps express itself in alliances with other discontented spirits. However, this is perhaps an unfair presentation of his character. He probably is better equipped than the average State Hospital assistant, has had a considerable experience, is a genial and pleasant individual, and I should have very seriously considered appointing him in some capacity if I had really been in need of assistants.[20]

In spite of White's faint praise, Chapman almost immediately hired Sullivan at Sheppard.

White's letter of recommendation marked an early cloud in the relationship between him and Sullivan. As time went on, Sullivan became doubtful of White's ability to be candid with him, and he would begin to sense that White did not see him as quite belonging to the same elite. Some of the very characteristics that made White so admired by Sullivan—for example, his genial assurance in dealing with congressional investigations of St. E's—were reminiscent of the ruling Yankees in Chenango County, and Sullivan must have become wary about this part of White's nativistic coloration. White seemed more comfortable with those who came from the same background, like Hadley, Kempf, Dooley, and Hall. His catholicity of approaches to mental illness did not extend to placing a "somewhat witty Irishman" in his inner circle. Yet Sullivan did not brood over the disappointment; for the rest of his life, White would remain the switchboard through which Sullivan began his vast network of communications with all the important thinkers in the interdisciplinary field of psychiatry and the social sciences generally.

Studying Schizophrenia at Sheppard

> I had to undergo [this dream] very early in my study
> of schizophrenia, in order to realize that I had some
> grave barriers to the task which the gods had brought
> me.
> —Sullivan, *The Interpersonal Theory of Psychiatry*

S HORTLY before Sullivan left Washington for his new post as an assistant psychiatrist at Sheppard, he had a dream in which the spider of
his childhood reappeared in a terrifying way. He reports that he had the
dream

at the time when it became possible, finally, for me really to start on an
intensive study of schizophrenia, partly by my own efforts and largely by
accident; and I had decided on this study and all the arrangements were
satisfactory. You all recall the geometric designs that spiders weave on
grass, and that show up in the country when the dew's on the ground. My
dream started with a great series of these beautiful geometric patterns,
each strand being very nicely midway between the one in front of it and
the one behind it, and so on—quite a remarkable textile, and incidentally
I am noticeably interested in textiles. Then the textile pattern became a
tunnel reaching backward after the fashion of the tunnel-web spiders,
and then the spider began to approach. And as the spider approached, it
grew and grew into truly stupendous and utterly horrendous proportions.
And I awakened extremely shaken and was unable to obliterate the
spider, which continued to be a dark spot on the sheet which I knew perfectly well would re-expand into the spider if I tried to go to sleep. So instead, I got up and smoked a cigarette and looked out the window and
one thing and another, and came back and inspected the sheet, and the
spot was gone. So I concluded that it was safe to go back to bed. Now, I'm

not going to tell you all about what that meant, because only God knows what I dreamed; I've just told you what I recalled. I'm trying to stress the hang-over, the utter intrusion into sensory perception, which required the shaking off of the last vestige of sleep process, the definite reassertion of me and mine, Washington, and what not, in order to prevent the thing from going on. Fortunately, with some assistance, I guessed what might be the case, and thus escaped certain handicaps for the study of schizophrenia. I might add that spiders thereupon disappeared forever from my sleep—so far as I know.[1]

Such nightmares or "dreadful dreams, with recollectable content [represent] a grave emergency in personality," Sullivan notes, but the competent adult can report such a dream and thereby "make use of interpersonal relations in a curious attempt to validate the nature of the threat." His account of his own nightmare includes this kind of "assistance," which may have come from White as a parting gift. In reporting the dream, he deals again with the fallacy of making a superficial interpretation of dreams: since his fear of spiders began when he was about two and a half, and since "the spider is a mother symbol, . . . one can picture what profound problems I had in repressing my hostility to the mother, or something of the sort. But I prefer to say, simply, that I didn't like spiders, and I disliked them so much that I wouldn't pass one [when I was a young child]."[2] His misgivings concerned his own earlier bouts with alarming schizophrenic processes; the nightmare that persists into waking life is a potential signal of danger, he theorized. Yet there was something that drove him on to try to understand "the lonely ones."[3]

In December of 1922, Sullivan began his work at Sheppard, living first on the hospital grounds in an apartment in a building known as Windy Brae, originally designed as a residence for the superintendent, and later moving to a house on Joppa Road. The Sheppard grounds were extensive and rolling; and from his apartment he could look out on an unspoiled landscape, not too different from the scenes of his childhood. In the end, this landscape would seem most like home to him, and he would live in a Maryland countryside not dissimilar from Towson for the last ten years of his life.

It was in Towson that his most important clinical work was accomplished over a period of less than eight years. He came to Sheppard almost a fledgling in psychiatry; but by the time he left he was a legend in both the clinical world and the world of the social sciences. All of this was basically made possible by Ross McClure Chapman, the superintendent, who gave unprecedented privileges to Sullivan for the crucial years. Like White, Chapman had the rare gift of not having to compete with his own staff, so that Sullivan's experimental approach delighted him. Chapman also had White's interest in devising new approaches to psychotic patients. Near the end of Sullivan's stay, the privileges extended by Chapman were resented by other staff, and Chapman had to withdraw his support. But in the intervening period, Chapman encouraged Sullivan to work in an imaginative and dramatic fashion.

Chapman's own career had essentially followed White's in several particulars, but his family background was more affluent. Born in a village on the eastern end of Lake Ontario and raised in a comfortable environment that dictated certain loyalties, Chapman would remain a Republican, a Presbyterian, and a Mason to the end of his life.[4] Yet he had the ability to unbend, and during Sullivan's years at Sheppard, which coincided with Prohibition years, both Chapman and Sullivan kept bottles at the old Maryland Club on Charles Street in Baltimore. In age, Chapman, who was born in 1881, stood exactly midway between White and Sullivan; in personality he had much the same midway position, so that Sullivan always had a more relaxed relationship with Chapman than with White. Yet all three had a common knowledge of mental disorder in Broome and Chenango Counties, and some consensus about the care of patients.

In 1908 Chapman married and took a junior post at Binghamton State Hospital, five years after White had left. He stayed at Binghamton for eight years, developing an insight into the patient population that was congenial to White's philosophy. In 1916 White asked Chapman to come to St. Elizabeths as his first assistant physician, and Chapman stayed there until a superintendent was needed at Sheppard, in 1920. Chapman's duties at a much smaller hospital were less demanding than White's; and he remained primarily a clinician and an educator. His personal life was saddened by the death of his only child, a daughter, when she was in her teens. Perhaps out of this disappointment, he had no interest in doing his own research. At the same time, he expedited the research of many young psychiatrists over the years, notably of course Sullivan, "one of the two most influential psychiatrists ever associated with the Hospital."[5]

The institution itself was peculiarly fitted for Sullivan's work. Its first patient had been admitted late in 1891, shortly before Sullivan was born, so that it had enough history for stability but not enough for bureaucracy. Although the hospital was privately endowed, the patient population was almost as varied as that of a state hospital. It did not cater to the upper-middle-class patient, as so many other private hospitals did; but it was not bound by the niggardly fiscal policies of the usual state hospital. The original benefactor of the hospital was a Quaker, Moses Sheppard, who had been a warden of the poor in Baltimore and a commissioner of the prison; his concern for the mentally disturbed, who were usually housed in almshouses before the Civil War, was mobilized into social action by Dorothea Lynde Dix in the winter of 1851–52, five years before Sheppard's death in 1857. Within that five-year period Sheppard had set up a fund for the establishment of the hospital, specifying that only the income could be used, so that it was almost thirty-five years before there was enough money to ready the buildings and admit patients. Sheppard specified that the asylum was to care "first, for the poor of the Society of Friends; secondly, for such of the Society as are able to pay; and then for the poor indiscriminately; afterwards the Trustees will use their discretion."[6]

In the first ten years of the hospital, more than half of the patients had only common school education, and less than twenty percent had any college training.[7] The emphasis on serving the poor had been modified somewhat since the hospital had opened its doors, but it was still maintained to some extent when Sullivan began his work there. Thus in his first extensive report on individual patients, published in 1925, only one patient out of the six is specifically described as having been to college.[8] Sullivan did not focus in the beginning on sociological definitions of patients, so that such information might have been omitted from the case reports of the other five. Yet some of the information that is reported on the other five patients suggests that they came out of working-class, rural, or even immigrant families. Thus the parents of the patient in Case 1 were "born abroad," an expression that may have been used by Sullivan to upgrade the patient's status as the son of immigrants. Case 2 reports on a Catholic patient who spent part of his early life in an orphanage. Case 3 contains no information on class, although the patient may have been raised on a farm; by the age of eighteen, his only sexual experience had been with a cow. In Case 4, the patient and his siblings had been to college. In Case 5, Sullivan specifically reports that the patient was "born on a farm, [and] the family was quite poor." The patient in Case 6 had been an ordinary seaman and then had a job, probably as a factory worker. The information included on these last two patients, both of whom clearly did not come from middle-class backgrounds, is considerably longer than on the other four cases. At least four of these six patients had some possible similarities to Sullivan's origins and difficulties as to social class and status. But there is no way to ferret out the actual social class of all his Sheppard patients; nor are the above suggestive references a definitive indication of social class. Although Sullivan kept extensive records on many patients at Sheppard, only a relatively small number of cases are recorded in his papers. Thus in 1927, he writes of Case 75; but only a few intervening cases, by his numbering system, are reported in his papers.[9]

As will become clear, Sullivan's awareness of the connection between social class and mental illness was stirring in him before he left Sheppard; and it must be assumed that he found there patients who clearly illustrated some of the trauma and loneliness, the ostracism and panic, that had haunted his own early life. But a sophisticated knowledge of the importance of these factors was not apparent in most of the case histories, which were mainly based in the beginning on a solid attempt to modify the psychoanalytic approach as little as possible so that it could be used for psychotic patients.

Sullivan's respect for the Society of Friends, which persisted throughout his adult life, was related to the tradition of Moses Sheppard at the Hospital. As a boy, Sullivan had been aware that Quakers had once lived in Smyrna, for there was a Quaker cemetery not too far from the farmhouse. But their significance in the community was not great at the time, so it is doubtful that this early peripheral encounter was of any moment to him. His approbation of Quakers seems to have come mainly from his experience at Sheppard, although Hadley was raised as a Quaker and this may have also influenced Sullivan's attitude. In a lecture given in the 1940s, Sullivan states that the Society of Friends "is the most astonishing demonstration of there being a Christian way of life that I've encountered—in fact, almost the only one." He seems also to have partially identified with its founder, George Fox, who "had a lurid schizophrenic panic and a fairly prolonged schizophrenic illness. . . . Anyway, he was able to maintain, perhaps improving mental health, with recurrences of fairly serious personality disorder."[10]

In accordance with the tradition of Moses Sheppard, Chapman had a specific interest in creating a therapeutic milieu at the hospital, since there were not enough medical personnel to give each patient a great deal of individual attention; and this interest coincided with Sullivan's and with the hospital's tradition. For many years, the hospital had been specifically concerned with training nurses and attendants in specialized procedures for dealing with mental patients. In 1905 the hospital had established a training program for psychiatric nurses; and in 1911, "a less extensive course was established for attendants, leading to a certificate."[11] Thus Sullivan found a hospital already geared to the idea of a therapeutic milieu. But he wanted to control that milieu more carefully than was possible in even a small hospital like Sheppard, which admitted only 210 patients during 1923, the first full year that Sullivan was on the staff. Gradually Sullivan's requirements were put into effect: he wanted a small ward of male patients that would be cut off from the rest of the hospital; he did not want any female staff on the ward; he wanted to hand-pick the male attendants for the ward; and he wanted adequate recording equipment so that he could record and conduct research on schizophrenic thought, at a time when schizophrenic patients were not supposed to produce other than "word salads"—irrational words strung together at random. Thus he eventually established what was essentially a one-class and one-sex society in a research setting. As a physician, he had status greater than either patient or attendant; but he did everything possible to minimize the impact of this status by treating the attendants on his ward as "assistants" and training them in his philosophy and techniques, so that they could act on their own. It is doubtful that any other hospital in America at that period could have tolerated a ward of this nature. Even today, such a ward would be unlikely, although there are of course many one-sex wards in state hospitals staffed mainly by attendants of the same sex; but physicians and psychiatrists do not spend much time with such patients, and the attendants are seldom treated as full-fledged adjuncts to the therapeutic process.

The physical location of Sullivan's ward varied over the years. Originally it was simply an isolated part of the original reception center for male patients. But in the year before Sullivan left Sheppard, a new reception building (now called the Chapman Building) was completed; and Sullivan specifically designed his own ward in this building. It is this ward that he described in his important paper on "Socio-Psychiatric Research":

A six (two 3-bed, intercommunicating) bed ward was used, physically approximating a detachment from all but the occupational and recreational services, and in part from these. In particular, the nursing care was independent. The hydrotherapy and physiotherapy were effectively independent. The administration, supervision, and patient-doctor contacts were segregated and entirely supervised. Specifically, by eliminating supervision of the Nursing Service . . . I was able to grow in the sub-professional personnel a lush crop of self-respect from good accomplished with the patient. The modern nurse is usually so well trained in (a) The Ethics of Nursing—including a tacit "my Profession, right or wrong, but always my Profession"—and (b . . . n) all sorts of valuable words, phrases, conceptions of diseases and treatments (especially for distributing blame), techniques and crafts, that her aptitude for integration into the complex uncertainties of the mental hospital milieu is vestigial, and only by a personal personality upheaval is she apt to come again to that intuitive grasp of personal totalities that was once her property in common with all preadolescents.

The graduate of our medical schools, for somewhat different reasons, is so detached from a "natural" grasp on personality that it usually takes him from 12 to 18 months residence on the staff of an active mental hospital to crack his crust to such effect that he begins to learn "what it is all about." The graduate nurse, however, harassed as she is by upstart internes, inefficient physicians, utterly unmoral male personnel, etc., etc., seems usually too preoccupied ever to make this beginning.[12]

This plan, philosophically and organizationally, made Sullivan's work at Sheppard famous. Its most important ingredient was a sophisticated therapeutic design, and it worked. In the beginning, its fame spread largely by word of mouth. Patients tended to get well—to make "social recoveries," as Sullivan preferred to name the end result.

The ward can be viewed as evolving out of Sullivan's own early life. Thus Clarence Bellinger had made the difference between some life for

Harry Sullivan and no life at all. Brief and unsatisfactory as that relationship was in some particulars, it was crucial; it provided an experience that could be built on later. Yet it had happened by accident, because they were both rejects from the ongoing social structure of the village and school society in Smyrna. Thus the necessary ingredient was a benevolent intimacy, no matter how brief. Sullivan's definition of the word "intimacy" bears repeating: "And so I trust that you will finally and forever grasp that interpersonal intimacy can really consist of a great many things without genital contact; that intimacy in this sense means, just as it always has meant, closeness, without specifying that which is close other than the persons. Intimacy is that type of situation involving two people which permits validation of all components of personal worth."[13]

Out of his own experience, he assumed that the young male patients on his ward had missed out on a relationship of reciprocal trust in the preadolescent period. Thus he tried to create such an experience, to begin with what he considered to be the basic experience of trust—the preadolescent friend. In order to do that, he eliminated people from the ward who represented complications to his own development in preadolescence—people that had to be circumvented if one were to achieve one's own identity. Female nurses, who were counterparts for the women in his youth—his mother, his Aunt Margaret, Clarence's mother, the female teachers at the Smyrna school—were removed from the ward as complications in achieving peer trust. Even other psychiatrists who might be counterparts for Professor Butts or Uncle Ed were unnecessary adjuncts. Life for a young person who had lost his way had to be simple at first. In the beginning of Sullivan's experiment at Sheppard, he may have chosen to work with staff who were low on the totem pole because he himself was more comfortable with them; and he had to be relatively free from anxiety himself if he were to work with disturbed patients. But shortly he came to understand that the patients also experienced less anxiety with lower-echelon staff.

By the end of his stay, the therapeutic design was more specific, and he had a clearer idea of why it worked theoretically. He came to understand that he was selecting employees for the ward who were very much like himself and like the patients—they were "sensitive, shy, and ordinarily considered handicapped employees." These employees were taught that the schizophrenic patient was a person like themselves; and as the employees

ceased to regard [the patient] in more or less traditional ideology as "insane," but instead had stressed to them the many points of significant resemblance between the patient and the employee—we created a much more useful social situation; we found that intimacy between the patient and the employee blossomed unexpectedly, that things which I cannot distinguish from genuine human friendships sprang up between patient and employee, that any signs of the alleged apathy of the schizophrenic faded, to put it mildly, and that the institutional recovery rate became high.[14]

In summary, Sullivan enunciated the theory of *similia similibus curantur* ("like cures like") as the final outcome of his work at Sheppard.[15] Eventually he saw the critical task as one of selecting the right personnel. But he had difficulty in communicating to professional staff at Sheppard and elsewhere how he made the selection. He could not conceptualize past the "age-old classification of the liked, the unliked, and the disliked," he admitted. Other people—" 'really normal extraverts, good 100 per cent people' "—were apt to give a fourth classification to his "chosen ones"; they termed them "peculiar," he reported; yet "not all the 'peculiar' people of my personal experience have aptitude for the socio-psychiatric rehabilitation of schizophrenics."[16] He remained somewhat frustrated by his inability to define more specifically the caliber of the staff that he selected; as a scientist, he deplored his inability to systematically describe human behavior, and he assumed that a way would eventually be found. In his most optimistically prophetic vein, he envisioned a time when all the problems of selection of personnel and training of them would be solved: "When . . . the efficiency of socio-psychiatric treatment has been demonstrated, I surmise that we will be encouraged to develop convalescent camps and communities for those on the way to mental health. In a not too distant time, these socio-psychiatric communities may come to be the great mental hygiene, with a great reduction in the incidence of major mental disorders, at least of the schizophrenic type."[17]

In arriving at an interpersonal solution for schizophrenia, Sullivan used various research tools and clinical techniques along the way; some of these he retained, others he discarded. Thus he tried hypnosis briefly, but eventually he decided that it was too risky because it involved the process of submission of the patient to the therapist.[18] When he arrived at Sheppard, he found a hydrotherapy department already in existence under the direction of J. Ruthwin Evans, who became one of Sullivan's most valued assistants; and Sullivan continued to feel that this treatment was efficacious for patients in panic. In the beginning he advocated the use of chemotherapeutic agencies for patients in extreme "panicky states"; but these were to be used only briefly as adjuncts in order for the therapeutic process to proceed. He reported that ethyl alcohol, in particular, was useful to

impair the highly discriminative action of the more lately acquired tendency systems, and permit the at least rudimentary functioning of the more primitive, without much stress. After from three to ten days of continuous mild intoxication, almost all such patients, in the writer's experience, have effected a considerable readjustment. The *modus operandi* may be indicated roughly by remarking that these patients discover by actual experience that the personal environment is not noxious, and, having discovered this, have great difficulty in subsequently elaborating convictions of menace, plots, fell purposes, etc. It is the rule to have several interviews with the patient during the period of intoxication, and in them to carry out the reassuring technique above indicated.[19]

As time went on and the use of drugs for the control of disturbed patients became more widespread, he would feel apprehensive about the use of all chemical agents, even for panicky patients. Too often they were used as substitutes for the interpersonal relearning that he felt was so important for social recovery. And he would not countenance the use of electroshock therapy or lobotomy. When he spoke of his own schizophrenic illness, he stated angrily that if electroshock or lobotomy had been in use in hospitals when he was growing up, he would have ended up his life as a "vegetable."

In creating an ideal environment for schizophrenic patients, Sullivan also created a world in which he might have grown up without injury to his self-esteem; and out of that clinical world, he evolved a personal life with his assistants, the "chosen ones," that can only be considered restitutive for him also. Some of these assistants became his best friends, and bonds with at least two of them—Ray Pope and J. Ruthwin Evans—remained intact, as he went on to fame.[20] Sullivan's apartment at Windy Brae and later his house on Joppa Road in Towson became the meeting place for staff who worked for him. In particular, Sullivan mentions that five of them were the "most satisfactory employees that I have ever been able to make contact with."[21] Evans in particular seems to have been singled out by Sullivan in a 1947 lecture, although he was not named: "At one time I had a really marvelous assistant—one of those people without any particular formal education whose gifts and life experience had produced the sort of person who automatically reassured terrified people. He possessed no suitable hooks that panicky young schizophrenics could use to hang their terror on, and he reflected in many other ways the naturally estimable personality structure that would be required for dealing with schizophrenics."[22]

Some of the quality of Sullivan's relationships with his assistants can be glimpsed in Evans's reminiscences on the Sheppard days.[23] Evans has told a story about Sullivan's Studebaker roadster, which Sullivan was driving when Evans first met him. Shortly afterwards, Sullivan acquired a new car—a yellow Franklin. But Evans noticed that the Studebaker continued to sit in front of the Joppa Road house, unused, after the acquisition of the Franklin. Evans wanted a car very much, so one day he broached the subject to Sullivan, asking him why he hadn't traded in the Studebaker for the Franklin. Sullivan reported that he couldn't get enough money for it; he wanted $125. Evans told Sullivan that he was not able to pay that much in cash, but he wondered if he could pay for it a little at a time. Sullivan's reply was direct, according to Evans: "I don't know you. You impress me as an honest person. Still I want you to assure me that if you can't continue regular small payments at some later time, you will talk it over with me, not just disappear." This kind of premonition of Evans's possible disappearance was derived from Sullivan's own knowledge of how he sometimes handled similar problems; also it is clear that he feared that he might lose Evans because of some financial embarrassment.

The denouement of the story is also characteristic of Sullivan. Evans was working in the hydrotherapy department at Sheppard when Sullivan first came; and Sullivan suggested to Evans, shortly after the arrangement about the car had been consummated, that Evans give him some treatment for his skin, which was dry and scaly. So Evans gave Sullivan a series of salt glow treatments, in which wet salt, applied to the body, stimulates circulation and leaves the skin pink and moist. At the end of the first month of such treatments, Sullivan, who found his skin much improved, gave Evans a generous check for his work, and asked to have the treatments continued. This arrangement continued for some time, so that Evans was able to complete the purchase of the car, with some money left over for other purposes.

On Sullivan's ward at Sheppard, the roles of patient and staff sometimes blurred, so that people were indeed more alike than different. Thus one patient on Sullivan's ward later became the head of a technical department at Sheppard and worked at the hospital for several decades afterwards. Sometimes an attendant would find himself disturbed and upset about his work; and he would enter another part of the hospital as a patient for a few days' rest. There was no stigma attached to such a change in role. Schizophrenia was a human process; and the more sensitive a person was, the more he was able to recognize periods of stress in himself, when it was wise to retire from the fray.[24] In such an atmosphere, patients felt that they were part of a vast learning process. Thus as patients improved, they would volunteer to go with Sullivan and Evans to participate in case presentations at the University of Maryland Medical School, where Sullivan taught from 1924 until he left the Baltimore area.

Almost as soon as Sullivan arrived at Sheppard, he began his own class for attendants, which was held in his apartment and then at his house. He began the course, which took place twice a week, with a session on prenatal care, and then followed the developing person in basically the same way that he did in his final theoretical statement. Thus Sullivan began his long teaching career by teaching attendants. The professional contact with these assistants was not limited to the seminars; after hours, the attendants would drop by Sullivan's house for informal case conferences on the progress of a patient.

His assistants also spent a considerable number of hours in socializing at Sullivan's house. Evans and the staff member who was an expatient often went to the Maryland Club with Sullivan. On their way home from the Club, the three of them would sometimes stop at a delicatessen and get milk and sandwiches to take to Sullivan's house for a quick supper. Once in a bad rainstorm, when Sullivan was at the wheel, the car skidded and turned over, with all four wheels completely in the air. No one was hurt; they all got out of the car, righted it, and drove on. Forty years later, Evans remembered the occasion with distinct pleasure.

Shortly after Sullivan moved into the Joppa Road house, he placed near the entrance way a small figure of St. Martin on horseback. The saint, who is usually depicted as a young mounted soldier dividing his cloak with a beggar, is the patron of innkeepers and drunkards; the inclusion of drunkards is purely accidental, for St. Martin's day in Catholic history happens to be on the same day as the Feast of Bacchus in Roman mythology. But the inclusion was not accidental at St. Martin's in Towson; in this fashion Uncle Ed's Gothic House in South Otselic was reincarnated.

Whenever over the years anyone has talked about Sullivan at Sheppard, an air of youthful pleasure is communicated. Thus Donald Reeve, the printer at the Lord Baltimore Press who guided the journal *Psychiatry* through its early history, knew Sullivan when he was at Sheppard and drove a jaunty yellow Franklin around Baltimore, blithely collecting estimates on all kinds of projected publications over a decade before his journal became a reality. When I began to work for Sullivan in 1946 and was overawed by his knowledge and prestige, Reeve taught me to understand another side of Sullivan, to see him as a person, with all his charming and delightful eccentricities, for Reeve admired the whole man. In turn, Sullivan treated Reeve with unfailing respect, according him the stature of an expert in his own field, even though, as Reeve would note, he had never even been inside a high school until late in life when he began to teach printing design at a Baltimore high school. In the end Don Reeve would trust Sullivan's journal *Psychiatry* enough that he allowed the journal to fall behind on printing bills. After nine years of publication, it was over two years in arrears. Without Reeve's faith in the journal, it would have folded early on.

In many ways, these were years of fulfillment for Sullivan. He expanded in all directions, trying to make up for the socializing he had missed in Smyrna. Thus at the Joppa Road house, he had a player piano—"a ¾ grand piano (which also played rolls)"—and he acquired his own taste along with many rolls of classical music.[25] And while he continued to be generous to a fault with junior staff—thus the advent of Evans's first child was an occasion for Sullivan to pay the medical expenses of a fine pediatrician for a year—he began to move also into wild extravagances for himself, so that for the rest of his life he was eternally recuperating from a hasty and expensive purchase of some kind or other.

Retrospectively, it seems tragic that Sullivan was not able to institutionalize satisfactorily his major insights at Sheppard, even though William V. Silverberg maintained the ward successfully for one year after Sullivan left.[26] As the years went by, Sullivan despaired more and more of the relevancy of medical education for the "schizophrenia problem." For a long time, he thought that perhaps a new training pattern could be evolved within the university setting for medical students going into psychiatry. Then he began to wonder whether a whole new discipline could be evolved. But the training of staff who could work with disturbed young people—and he felt that most adolescents in this society experience potentially critical stress in arriving at adulthood—had to include a participant understanding of social deprivation, that is, some knowledge of the "industrial revolution," as he termed it.

In the last decade of his life, he moved almost entirely toward preventive psychiatry, recommending some kind of "personal inventory"—that is, an abbreviated training/therapy experience—for anyone who dealt as an expert with other people, such as teachers (particularly nursery school teachers), lawyers, and ministers. And he voiced considerable despair about psychiatrists per se having the necessary humility for the work; too much of their training had to be undone. It was this despair that would arouse some in the psychiatric profession, after his death, to deny the importance of his work, to define him as only a skilled therapist, who acted in an intuitive way, nothing more. So his chief contribution—a theory that made sense—was sacrificed to the status needs of his contemporaries. The brilliant achievement at Sheppard was too often brushed off as an isolated illustration of the brilliant, eccentric clinician at work.

✎ 24 ✐

Clara Thompson,
"Dear Friend and
Colleague"

> It seems to me that from 1923 on, Sullivan was a
> more influential factor in my psychiatric life than
> any other one person. Certainly he has influenced
> my life over a longer period.
>   —Clara Thompson, unpublished lecture

SHORTLY after Sullivan came to Sheppard, he heard a young psychiatrist, Clara Thompson, give a lecture at the Phipps Clinic of Johns
Hopkins University, and he determined that he must meet her. On every
dimension, except probably one—sexual intimacy—this relationship became one of the most important in his life, as well as hers. As a colleague,
she was crucial for him, too. Through her, he gained more than a formal
knowledge, for example, of Adolf Meyer's thinking, for she spent four
years in Phipps Clinic, headed by Meyer; and in the late 1920s, Sullivan
persuaded Thompson to go to Budapest for analysis with Sandor
Ferenczi so that she could come back and teach him what she had
learned, as was the custom of that day. In this latter role, Sullivan referred to Thompson as his "training analyst." Moreover, both of them
had a sympathy and understanding of "the lonely ones," so that Sullivan
could develop his theories on schizophrenia under her gentle, down-to-
earth probing. As a friend, she was capable of withstanding his eccentricities, and she remained publicly loyal to him for the rest of his life, as he
did with her; at the same time, they were free enough to criticize each
other in private.

Thompson has described the occasion of their initial meeting in April
1923:

I was giving the first paper of my life, which was on "Suicide and Psy-
chotics" and I had a temperature of 105 and had typhoid fever, but no-

body knew it. Apparently I looked like hell, and I was scared to death in addition, and Sullivan saw me and he thought, "My God, that woman is schizophrenic—I must know her!" . . . I proceeded to have my typhoid fever which he didn't know about, and a few months later he got in touch with me and found out to his dismay I wasn't as schizophrenic as he thought. (I won't say I wasn't schizophrenic!) . . . When I went to Ferenczi I was already very much oriented in Sullivan's way; and when [Erich] Fromm and [Karen] Horney came along, we also were very much in the same line as Sullivan. In fact, I would not have gone to Ferenczi . . . if Sullivan hadn't insisted that this was the only analyst in Europe he had any confidence in; and therefore, if I was going to go to Europe and get analyzed, I had just better go there. So I went.[1]

Clara Thompson's reference to being schizophrenic is at one level hyperbole; at another level, she is giving full support to Sullivan's dictum that all of us have full knowledge of the schizophrenic process, particularly in the adolescent years. Although her own early life had been somewhat less traumatic than his, at the time they met both of them had handicaps for putting an end to their loneliness. She was then in her thirtieth year, and he was past thirty-one; neither of them had formed any durable relationship with a person of the other sex—at least none that was visible. In Irish lore, a person who is not married by the time he is thirty-two is doomed to a single life. Sullivan's own mother had married only a few weeks before she was thirty-three, and the Stack cousins felt that she had barely escaped being an old maid. In both Stack and Irish lore, Harry himself was fast approaching the age of no return when he met Clara.

Clara's trip to Budapest in 1927 may have had some hidden meaning for both of them—the hope that somehow the confusions of her own earlier years might be righted and then the pathways taught to Sullivan; but by then, it was too late for him at least. Neither would ever marry, although Thompson, at the age of forty-five, would begin to live with the Hungarian artist Henry Major, who was not free to marry; and their relationship endured, although largely as an annual summer idyll at Provincetown. Throughout Clara Thompson's life, she spoke of Sullivan in an adoring way; and she may well have yearned to be more than friend, colleague, or sister to Sullivan, even after the advent of Henry Major.[2]

Sullivan once told a friend that he and a young woman had agreed on one evening to announce their engagement to marry; the next morning, according to Sullivan, they both broke their necks to be the first to telephone and break the engagement.[3] Whether or not the story was apocryphal, the situation rather accurately describes the reluctance of both Clara and Harry to give up any of their independence in the Baltimore years.

Thompson seemed peculiarly reticent with friends and colleagues about her childhood and early adulthood. In a sensitive biographical essay, her friend and colleague, Maurice R. Green, has written of this phenomenon: "Unlike the rest of us, who frequently spoke about our families, friends, and old times in school and hospital work, she seldom referred to the past."[4] Sullivan showed the same reticence. Neither Ernest Hadley nor his wife, who had a close personal relationship with Sullivan for many years, ever heard him talk about his early life; the Hadleys sometimes wondered about this omission. Hadley often mentioned his growing up on a farm, but he never knew Sullivan had.[5] Although the Chicago psychoanalyst Lionel Blitzsten and his wife, Dorothy Blitsten, were close personal friends of Sullivan, they knew little about his early life; in fact, Dorothy Blitsten had assumed erroneously that Sullivan's parents were living in a very poor section of Chicago at the time he was in medical school.[6] Innumerable colleagues, such as Lawrence K. Frank and Gordon Allport, and the artist John Vassos, were astounded to learn many years after Sullivan's death that he had grown up on a farm; they had always assumed he was urban in background.

From available information, supplied mainly by Green, a picture of Thompson emerges that has peculiar poignancy for her relationship with Sullivan. She was named Clara Mabel Thompson when she was born in 1893, but she was known as Mabel during her growing-up years. She had grown up almost as an only child—her only sibling, a brother, was six years younger—in a household in which an extended family on both sides lived together in an armed truce. There was a difference in religious dedication between the father and the mother, in which the relatives in the household took sides, although all of them went to the same Baptist church. Clara's father was a self-made businessman, who eventually became well-to-do as the president of an outstanding drug company; he was less rigid in religious matters than the mother, although he participated actively in church affairs.

Clara's family lived on the edge of Providence, Rhode Island, in an area that was then wooded and rural. "During her years in grade school," Green reports, "she was a typical American tomboy, joining with the boys of her own age in the neighborhood in playing baseball, fishing, hiking over the hills, and exploring the woods. In the wintertime they skated together and sledded down the streets and through the outlying fields. She was very popular with the other children."[7] This period of her life was considerably more rewarding than Sullivan's. Moreover, being a tomboy was not a stigma for a girl in the same way that being a sissy was for a boy; and it is safe to assume that Sullivan was considered a sissy by his contemporaries in the Smyrna school. Two years before Sullivan's death, Thompson published an article on homosexuality in Sullivan's journal, *Psychiatry,* which specifically compares these two epithets in relation to the emerging person:

The different cultural attitudes toward the sissy and the tomboy again shows society's greater tolerance for the female homosexual type. When a boy is called a sissy, he feels stigmatized, and the group considers that it has belittled him. No such disapproval goes with a girl's being called a tomboy. In fact, she often feels considerable pride in the fact.[8]

Sullivan would seem to be indulging in retrospective fantasy when he spoke, in 1945, of the possible favorable outcome of the boy who may be partially rescued from an unsatisfactory preadolescence by an "eccentric girl":

Of all the instances of really disastrous course in preadolescence, I have particularly to emphasize as a curiously fortunate, even though in many ways risky, possibility [at] the end of preadolescence . . . that the person who has been unfortunate in the preadolescent stage, even the person who is arrested in preadolescence, may, as his society, his compeers, go on into adolescence, have the good fortune of finding in feminine society available an eccentric girl who fits in with his peculiar restrictions and goes through the motions of the development of adolescent interest, which eccentric relationship, to be useful, is treated by other adolescents and by any significant adults with indifference or approval. Now this . . . combination of morbidity, the extravasation of preadolescent chumship over the boundary of sex, leads to some of the most wonderfully eccentric relationships it has ever been my privilege to hear of. But if they get no unfavorable attention from the environment, they may be therapeutic. It is quite possible that both parties concerned will ultimately, if they are economically successful, take up the time of a psychiatrist; but still, as queer things go, it is really quite fortunate, and not nearly as bad as many another thing that can happen to people who have disaster in preadolescence.[9]

Within the context of their later lives, these two statements have a common theme. Clara Thompson recognizes that Sullivan's own growing up was more difficult than hers; and Sullivan seems to say that an "eccentric girl" might have been helpful for his transition from preadolescence to adolescence. But if Clara Thompson was this "eccentric girl," she arrived on the scene much too late for him.

Through the high school years, "Mabel" was conforming to her mother's standards for her behavior and career. Early in that period, she announced at a Christian Endeavor meeting that she intended to become a medical missionary. Like Harry, she stood at the head of her class all through high school; but in addition to studying hard, she engaged in many extracurricular activities such as boating, swimming, hiking, basketball, and debating. Within Sullivan's theory, her high school life showed more the behavior of the juvenile than the preadolescent; her own preadolescence seems to have occurred when she went to college.

In 1912 she began her premedical course at Pembroke, the college for women at Brown University, and continued to live at home with her parents much of the time. Classmates at Pembroke have referred to her as "Clara," so it would seem that she made the change in name in those years. "Clara's college years were not happy ones," one close friend of that period reports, and she was "lonely and embittered." Her mother disapproved of Clara's decision to abandon the missionary part of her career; and in the same period she gave up going to church, which precipitated a partial estrangement from her mother that lasted for almost twenty years.

Green reports that a classmate, who occasionally spent the weekend in Clara's home, felt that the mother was a "dominating personality, very religious." On those occasions, Clara and she "dutifully went to the Baptist Church on Sunday, but at night Clara would pour her heart out, trying to express her unsatisfied longings and frustrations. I was quite unprepared for what she seemed to expect of me in support and inspiration, and I was afraid of her intensity, never having known it in any one before, and in few since."[10] Thus Clara seems to have prolonged the cheerful competition of a fairly normal juvenile period until she went to college, so that her own preadolescence was delayed until then. Her chumship took place in college; and her search for her own identity took place at the same time. But all of this was under the watchful eye of her mother, so that a change in religious commitment left her quite alone while still overly dependent on her parents.

The conflict between career and marriage also took place in her years at Pembroke, as Green reports:

Before she graduated from college, she met a major in the United States Army Medical Corps. He fell in love with her and asked her to marry him. She was very fond of him, but she wanted to continue with her medical career, even if she had to give up her missionary aspirations. The young major refused to marry her unless she would give up her medical career; and on that issue they broke off. She was deeply troubled by this decision; she felt very disturbed during her years in medical school, not sure whether she had done the right thing for herself, feeling guilty toward the man whom she had rejected and uncertain of her future as a woman doctor.[11]

Clara had an excellent record at Pembroke, achieving membership in both Phi Beta Kappa and Sigma Xi, and to some extent this may have irked Sullivan. She was a New England WASP, and she had been educated at Brown and at Johns Hopkins; and that was a far cry from his own background. But she had been restive under this conformity. When she left Brown, the yearbook showed that her ambition was "to succeed in my fads and overcome my virtues." Her future plans were "to murder people in the most refined way possible."

While Clara was at Brown, she spent a summer working with mental patients as an aide at the Danvers State Hospital in Massachusetts; although she had this early experience with mental disorder, she had not decided on a medical specialty when she entered Johns Hopkins in 1916. In her second year at Hopkins, she met Lucile Dooley, who persuaded her to spend the summer of 1918 at St. Elizabeths Hospital. In this way Thompson came to know White and Kempf a few years before Sullivan's advent at the same hospital. By the time Thompson graduated from Hopkins, she was fully committed to psychiatry. And after completing her clinical requirements for a medical degree at Hopkins and at the New York Infirmary for Women and Children, she began a three-year residency in psychiatry at Phipps Clinic under Adolf Meyer in 1922.

During the years when Sullivan was at Sheppard and Thompson was at Phipps Clinic and then in private practice in Baltimore, neither of them had the youthful freedom to negotiate some end to their loneliness, and to right all the confusions of their earlier years; and neither of them had much more than a kind of intellectual insight at that time into their difficulties, and a fear—emanating from the new-found Freudian insights—that there was an implicit damage in their developmental years from which they might never recover. Moreover, they both had some handicaps from the family definitions of what would constitute an acceptable marriage for either of them. Certainly the choice of a Catholic husband would have further estranged Clara from her family, unless the husband became Protestant. And even though Sullivan was not wedded to formal religion—and had undoubtedly removed himself from its strict accountability by that time—he had a quiet determination not to deny his identity as an Irish-American who had been raised as a Catholic.

But there were more serious disjunctions for Sullivan in sharing any domicile with a woman. His domination by women in Smyrna had been extreme, and any idea of marriage to a woman must have spread alarm throughout his being. There were also matters of prestige, real and imaginary. The real part of the equation reflected back to his cousin Leo's perfect marriage; Sullivan could not present his family and the neighbors in Smyrna with anything less than the equivalent of Nina Brown. The imaginary part centered around the fantasy that if the ideal mate could be found, he would of course marry at once. This fantasy seems never to have left him; he clung to it, partly in earnest, throughout his life. A few years before his death, he was still talking about finding himself a "rich widow." In those years I was working for him on the journal *Psychiatry,* and he would sometimes request that I have funds on hand in the office to cash a check for him when he came in to the Washington office from his own office and home in Bethesda, Maryland. He would make the check out to me when he arrived in the office, and each time would tell me that he was writing in the left-hand corner "for cash only." He would look amused as he imparted this bit of information, as if it were all a joke; but he would report each time that the advice for this kind of notation had come from a lawyer of his acquaintance, who had recommended that when an unattached woman (as I was then) cashed a check for a man, the man for his own safety should always so mark this check. In other words, the money was not for services performed, or for blackmail, or whatever; however much of a joke this was, the check would always be so marked. At the time, I regarded the remark as merely another eccentricity; but later I understood it as a part of a larger pattern of fantasy and withdrawal about several women of his acquaintance.

At the time that Sullivan first met Thompson, she obviously could not measure up to his ideal. She was rather careless about her dress—still maintaining the stance of the tomboy, with the role of the young professional woman superimposed only casually. Moreover, she herself complained about her "compulsive modesty" as an intellectual, and Sullivan found this annoying. Although he sometimes made feeble protestations about the inadequacies of his own theory, they were not of the same caliber. He had the need to think of women as his intellectual equals, and in this particular he would find Ruth Benedict, whom he met in the late 1920s, eminently qualified as a self-respecting thinker. At times Sullivan was irked by the financial situation of Clara's family, which made it possible for her to go to Brown, then to Hopkins, then to Europe, and he chided her about this from time to time, once defining her as "bourgeois." She once reported rather wryly that Sullivan considered her an important exception to his theory that in this society all of us are but poor caricatures of what we might have been; Thompson had lived up to all her potentialities, according to Sullivan.[12] It is difficult to understand Sullivan's remark as reported by Thompson and out of context; it may express his fear that she, with all her advantages, would leave him behind, or he may have used this fairly harsh remark to discourage any hope she might have about his availability as a full partner.

In particular, he felt estranged from her because she enjoyed competition, at a civilized level. He had indeed lost out on the juvenile era, with its importance for learning competition, compromise, and cooperation as "part of good teamwork towards a more general goal." Nor could Thompson, even after her training with Ferenczi, help Sullivan in that particular area of living which had been so satisfactory for her. In one of his last papers, Sullivan refers to this lack in his development and to the failure of his training analysis, which was conducted by Thompson, noting that he had 'finished' his training "in the days of still rather orthodox psychoanalysis before the methodic implications of the here-indicated theory of developmental stages had been suspected." He goes on to spell out his handicaps emergent from an indequate experience in the juvenile era:

By the time that it became possible to observe the related inadequate and inappropriate processes in which I was recurrently involved in later life—especially, unavoidable situations in which I seemed to see activities of the nature of competition, compromise, or cooperation pursued as sufficient in themselves for the good of the team rather than as part of good teamwork towards a more general goal; and, second, in the encountering of a most troublesome poverty of interest in formulating the developmental sequences pertaining to the juvenile era of development—as I say; by that time intercurrent accidents of existence had made life far too short for probably completing the interesting tasks already undertaken; any effort to fill in the missing experience, however vicariously, was grimly unattractive; and one could but put up as many signs as seemed necessary—"Danger: proceed with great caution in this area." This tedious and on occasion grossly inadequate makeshift seems to be characteristic of *unconsolidated* profit from psychotherapy, a condition still all too frequently to be observed in "cured" people.[13]

Thus from many directions, the continuous and dedicated friendship between Sullivan and Thompson must be viewed as a triumph for each of them. Certain values they held in common, of course—in particular, a sense of mission and a respect for patients. Moreover, they both treasured privacy; and this was one of the characteristics that maintained the relationship and limited it at the same time. As Green reports about Thompson, one could be "puzzled and annoyed from time to time by her apparent invulnerability, seeming indifference, and by her businesslike reassurance," but also responsive to her "warm sense of humor and an affectionate smile."[14] Sullivan's colleagues and trainees often expressed the same kind of puzzlement about him. With both, it was probably a fear of too much intimacy. In a paper given at a 1948 meeting, chaired by Thompson, Sullivan reported that his training psychoanalyst "not too erroneously considered" him "to be an outstanding example of the relatively 'anxiety-proof personality.' "[15] Actually, both of them had early developed techniques in the family situation for bypassing anxiety by appearing imperturbable at times, and this was often confusing to the other person in the situation.

Within a few years of their first meeting, each of them would establish an independent household at about the same time. In the mid-1920s, Clara took an apartment at Eutaw Place in Baltimore and began the private practice of psychoanalysis. She and Adolf Meyer had had a serious difference of opinion about her interest in psychoanalysis, and she had left Phipps because she insisted on continuing with her analysis, over his objections. She was then being analyzed by Joseph C. Thompson, a naval medical officer attached to St. Elizabeths, who had only a rather literal knowledge of psychoanalysis.

18. Captain Harry Stack Sullivan, Medical Corps, about 1919

19. James Inscoe Sullivan, about 1927

20. Clara M. Thompson, M.D., about 1921

At about the same time that Thompson moved to Eutaw Place, where she acquired a black live-in housekeeper,[16] Sullivan set up his household on Joppa Road in Towson; and sometime in 1927 James Inscoe, aged fifteen, and twenty years younger than Sullivan, came to live there. "Jimmie," as he has always been known by Sullivan's colleagues and friends, would constitute Sullivan's family for over twenty years. Sullivan often referred to Jimmie as an "adopted son," but in truth, no such legal definition was ever effected. Through usage, however, his legal name became James I. Sullivan, and he is so designated in Sullivan's will.

There is some mystery about the way in which Sullivan met Jimmie, and Jimmie himself has refused to define the first encounter between them, noting that if he reported on this and their life together, he "would have no reminiscences left for myself to write about."[17] In Sullivan's own account of his life in *Current Biography,* he refers to Jimmie as "a former patient." At the time that Sullivan wrote this, sometime in 1941 or 1942, Jimmie typed the manuscript and objected to the reference to him as a patient, but Sullivan refused to change it.[18] In the strictest sense of the word, Jimmie may never have been Sullivan's patient, but it is obvious that the relationship began in a fashion that defined it operationally in this way for Sullivan.

The most reliable account of how Jimmie and Sullivan met comes from Agnes Hadley, who reports that her husband first saw Jimmie outside the Rochambeau apartment building in Washington, D.C., where Hadley had an office.[19] For two or three evenings when Hadley left his office, he saw a boy standing out in front of the building in some kind of catatonic pose. Finally Hadley took him in to his office; subsequently he took Jimmie over to see Sullivan at Sheppard, since he felt that Sullivan might be able to help him. Hadley got in touch with Jimmie's family, but they had no particular interest in him. Jimmie became an important adjunct to Sullivan's household within a relatively short time. Some of Sullivan's colleagues have referred to him as "the man who came to stay." But his actual role in the household became very important for Sullivan's well-being. For over twenty years, Jimmie was family, household staff, and office staff for much of the time. He became a competent cook, a skilled secretary, a devoted companion. Yet he had suffered considerable handicaps from his own growing-up years, in part because of tension in the extended families over religious differences; his mother was Catholic and his father Baptist. After the marriage, his mother's sister had had nothing to do with the family because of the father's religion.[20]

There are two documents that spell out Sullivan's esteem for Jimmie. Jimmie's copy of *Conceptions of Modern Psychiatry,* an edition published in 1947, is inscribed to James I. Sullivan, "beloved foster son; without the support of whose affection, devotedness, patient forbearance, and good-natured self-sacrifice I would have accomplished little." And Sullivan's will, which leaves everything to Jimmie, refers to him as "my friend and ward in fact." He goes on to state: "Said James Inscoe Sullivan has resided with me since the age of about fifteen years, and has been, in all senses, a son to me, and has my love and affection as such."

So a decision was made at some point in the Baltimore years, largely by default; and Thompson and Sullivan set up two separate households and a pattern of visiting. "Once a week until Clara left Baltimore," Jimmie reports, "we entertained her at Joppa Road and she entertained us at her apartment on Eutaw Place."

In that period, many young intellectuals with a sense of social responsibility, following the pattern already established by American artists, avoided marriage. Thus one cannot view the early life experience of either Clara Thompson or Harry Stack Sullivan as a simple explanation for the pattern of living they adopted. They were indeed in tune with emergent attitudes about marriage as an institution in America, documented in part by Sinclair Lewis's novels. Both of them were affected by the writings of H. L. Mencken in Baltimore; and some of Sullivan's writing in *Personal Psychopathology,* begun while he was at Sheppard, is well within the style of the *American Mercury.* There was, moreover, the damaging model of F. Scott and Zelda Fitzgerald, the darlings of the jazz age. By 1927 the Fitzgeralds were living near Wilmington, Delaware; Fitzgerald was drinking heavily and having serious difficulty in writing. It was probably in that year that he met with Sullivan, although the exact nature of the encounter is not known.[21] Zelda's subsequent breakdown and hospitalization at Oscar Forel's clinic in Switzerland in 1930 were well known in American psychiatric circles of that period. Two years later, Zelda was under Adolf Meyer's care at Phipps, and Meyer was in touch with Oscar Forel on the case. By 1934 Zelda was at Sheppard in a catatonic state. Both Sullivan and Thompson were living in New York City by then, but the interconnections between the Washington-Baltimore psychoanalysts and those in New York were such that the failure of an artist married to a potential artist was defined generally as a tragedy of marriage.

For the intellectual or the artist of the 1920s, there was a growing fear that marriage would wreck both lives. An alternative way of life was developing, and it found a well-known expression in the expatriate life of Gertrude Stein, then engaged in encouraging the "lost generation" of young American writers, including Sherwood Anderson, Ernest Hemingway, Fitzgerald, and many others. Stein's association with dynamic psychology had begun at an early period, for she had studied under William James while she was a student at Radcliffe in the 1890s. After that she had begun a premedical course at Johns Hopkins, but she had abandoned it in 1902 for the life of an artist, though she remained involved with the new psychological insights coming out of Vienna. In the process of trying to come to grips with a meaningful life as a woman artist, she had acquired a companion, Alice B. Toklas, who was defined as her secretary-companion—a relationship that lasted for a lifetime. Under somewhat comparable pressures, Willa Cather, then an arrived artist living on Bank Street in Greenwich Village, had set up a household with Edith Lewis as a companion-secretary; and Lewis also remained a part of the household until the death of Willa Cather.

Such alternative solutions, undertaken in a dignified fashion, were a backdrop for the kind of life established by both Thompson and Sullivan. For Sullivan, there was a role model nearer to home, for in the 1920s his aunt, Margaret Stack, was living in the St. George Hotel in Brooklyn Heights with a woman companion. There is an uneasiness when any of the Stack relatives refer to this woman; in particular Nina Stack, who was very fond of Margaret, disapproved of the living arrangements in Brooklyn Heights.[22] As far as anyone knows, Margaret never brought anyone with her on her annual visits to Smyrna. Nor did Harry ever take Jimmie to Chenango County, although Sullivan himself returned there at least three times after Jimmie came to live with him; and Jimmie often accompanied Sullivan on other trips, including one trip made to England. Relatives and old neighbors in Chenango County refer only obliquely to this forbidden subject; there is an unspoken fear that heredity might have played a part in all this—a fear that Sullivan would have scoffed at.

Regardless of Margaret Stack's own living arrangements, she still retained in the 1920s an active interest in normalizing Harry's life. She had been largely responsible for getting him through medical school; there yet remained the task of engineering an acceptable marriage for him. There is some hint of such an intent in the reminiscences of Margaret Normile Hannon.[23] In the late spring of 1923 or 1924, Sullivan, on a visit to New York City after he had obtained the job at Sheppard, arranged to have dinner with his young cousin, who had been attending Columbia University. She was eight years his junior, and they had not seen each other since he was almost seventeen years old and on his way back to Cornell after a holiday. The encounter encapsulates many stories about Sullivan, in particular stories about his relationships with women, and it sheds light on what must have transpired between Clara and Harry.

Margaret Normile, a cousin on the Sullivan side, had been surprised to get a call from Harry. She assumed, later, that his Aunt Margaret Stack had "bushwhacked" him into asking her to dinner. In any event she agreed to meet him at seven the next evening in the lobby of the Waldorf-Astoria, and she arrived promptly. By half past seven, he had not shown up; she was a "little bothered by Harry's nonappearance. By eight o'clock I was boiling mad, ready to walk out. In fact, I had gathered my pocketbook, was putting on my gloves and ready to leave, when Harry Stack Sullivan walked in and recognized me; I think that I would not have recognized him. . . . We went in to dinner. He ordered, and he ordered most acceptably, a beautiful dinner, right wines, everything." But she had the feeling throughout the meal that she was "on a psychiatrist's couch in the middle of the Waldorf-Astoria dining room. The food was served, course after course; he paid almost no attention to it." Instead he queried her on a variety of subjects, including her knowledge of Galvin family history, as reported earlier. But the climax came near the end of the dinner:

We finished dinner, and he motioned the waiter for the bill. The waiter brought it, and Harry started through his pockets, and he didn't have a penny. He was very fortunate in that in my pocketbook was twenty-five dollars to take me home. I was leaving the next night, and going up on a sleeper to be in Norwich on Sunday morning. So I not only had to pay the bill, and leave the tip, but I had to loan him [money] for a taxi back to where he was staying. And I had to take the subway up to One Hundred and Twelfth Street. . . . He assured me that he would go right back [to where he was staying] and write a check, and take it out and mail it special delivery and I would have it no later than noon the next day. . . . Well, I never heard again about the twenty-five dollars.

Sullivan seems to have made no apology for being late or penniless.

When the money did not come by four o'clock the next day, Margaret Normile called home for emergency financing, and her mother said, "Oh, Margaret, didn't you know better than to depend on Harry?" During the course of the dinner, Harry had promised to keep in touch with her "from now on," but she never saw him or heard from him again.

In the same conversation Harry spoke of his wish to have her work for him at a later time, editing his papers. "Some of my critics say that I do not write clearly, that I write too fluently," he told her. Margaret Normile was then studying journalism at Columbia, and she wanted to work on a big news service for a time before she did anything else. Would she be interested then in collaborating with him at a later date—not on the content per se, which she knew nothing about, but on the style? She thought that she would be very interested.

During the dinner, Harry took on a grandfatherly air about her social life. She was a young, attractive, and popular woman, and Harry asked her quite directly about her relationships with men. He was amazed to see how she had changed, commenting that she looked like any sophisticated New York City girl. "You know you're a very beautiful young woman," he told her. She thanked him but he waved that aside. "Don't thank me," he said. "You've taken good care of yourself. You're a good girl, too, aren't you?" She told him that she hoped she was. He inquired about her love life: was there a man in her future? And when he found out that she was interested in a particular man at the time, he wanted to know all about him; what did she see in him? He would not accept anything as a statement of fact; he had to question each statement. What did she like about the man? What did she find in him? Was she sure that the man was basically sound? And was he handsome? When Margaret Normile answered in the affirmative to the last question, Sullivan felt that that was too bad, because handsome men could not be trusted. "And [Harry's] eyes, his piercing eyes," Margaret Hannon exclaimed as she reported this, "you remembered so little else about him."

There is enough in Mrs. Hannon's report to suggest why Sullivan had backed off from any more intimate contact ever again with this beautiful young woman, eligible in so many ways by Harry's own definition; she was after all intelligent, educated, Catholic, Irish-American, an only child of parents with relatively substantial means, not too closely related for marriage, even by Irish Catholic standards, and approved of by his Aunt Margaret, the arbiter of fashion and good taste, as exemplified by the South Otselic Stacks. Perhaps the shadow of his Aunt Margaret helped to abort the encounter. But more likely it was his simple defensiveness about being caught in an embarrassing situation, without funds. He may have left his wallet at home absentmindedly or with unconscious intent; he may even have come knowing that he had no money to pay; but he was always unable to undo a social mistake he had made. In a broader context, the financial embarrassment may have been fortunate for him, whether or not it was intentional: the embarrassment in itself may have been a way to flee from the sexual fears aroused in him by his attractive young cousin. He was afraid of rejection; and he was sure by then that there was something 'wrong' with him.

"From here on in, we will keep in touch," he told Margaret Normile. "I will always keep in touch, know where you are, and what you're doing. And something will come of this." At the end of the meal came the financial embarrassment and the permanent end of their relationship. Whatever the dynamics were, they reached far back; and they were already beginning to form a pattern. There are other stories through the years of his moving toward intimacy and then withdrawing, often in ways that proved hurtful and puzzling to the other person; they often involved women. There are also stories of financial irresponsibility and, side by side, stories of great generosity.

As Margaret Hannon told me this story, the intonations and words seemed almost verbatim and evoked Sullivan as I knew him more than twenty years after the dinner at the Waldorf-Astoria. We talked of the complexity of Sullivan's attitude toward money, and she felt that it was not a simple story of his acting in an irresponsible or hateful fashion. I told her some of the more dramatic stories of his disdain for money—his working with indigent patients, his dedication to important causes of various kinds for no financial gain. I noted that he liked to give extravagant gifts, that he died with practically no money, that he really yearned to be rich so that he could do all kinds of things for people in need. And Margaret Hannon, in a flash of Irish insight, summed up his money problems: "Greed, so he would have it to give. That's the only good greed, isn't it?"

In the end, the relationship between Sullivan and Thompson was that of good friends and colleagues, intimate in some areas, but each maintaining a certain distance. He had much to offer to her as a skilled clinician-theoretician. And she offered him critical bridges to some of his missed intellectual opportunities—for example, her work with Meyer. Thompson had a facility for introducing people to ideas without intimidating them or overwhelming them. She tended to oversimplify at times, but in this instance, such oversimplification may have moved Sullivan to diligently read and understand Meyer's thinking. Later on, of course, he persuaded Thompson to go to Budapest, arguing that she was the one who had the money; then she could come back and teach him what she had learned from Ferenczi.

She had a keen mind, and they shared many ideas. Yet he recoiled from anyone who would try to control him. Some such control was attempted by Thompson in the 1930s when he was establishing an elaborate residence in New York City. Thompson was working with him analytically at the time, and also attempting to communicate what she had learned from Ferenczi. He terminated this work when she tried to discourage him from extensive remodeling and elaborate plans for decoration, predicting that he would go into bankruptcy. He could not work with someone who had such "bourgeois" values, he told her.[24] In the end, he was financially trapped by his venture, and he did go into bankruptcy. But their friendship and colleagueship survived the whole episode.

Among Thompson's possessions at her death, there was the picture of Sullivan, young and handsome, in the uniform of the U.S. Medical Corps, inscribed "to my dear Friend and colleague, Dr. Clara M. Thompson." So it was that the relationship was defined, as limited in some ways as her relationship, while an undergraduate, with the young major in the Medical Corps. It is a curious kind of inscription, particularly the "Dr."; certainly it could never be used in any legal suit to prove anything more binding than friendship. Two officers in the Medical Corps had rejected Clara Thompson in different ways. The first had rejected her right to intellectual achievement; the other had steadfastly accorded her that right, but he had denied her the love of a man for a woman.

🍂 25 🍂

Smyrna Revisited

On Tuesday, March the ninth, 1926, as the sun sunk
below the western hills of her home, Ella Mary Sullivan tranquilly completed her earthly life in its sev-
enty-third year. At the bedside were her husband,
her brother and sister, and her only son.
—The *Chenango Telegraph,* March 12, 1926

B Y the time Sullivan went to Sheppard in December 1922, his mother
and father were both of an age when life on the farm was often too
taxing for their energies. Timothy was in his sixty-sixth year and Ella almost seventy. The farm was not prosperous enough to support sustaining
help, and Timothy depended on trading off with farmers on adjoining
farms for additional help in peak periods. As Harry's creature comforts
increased at Sheppard, the contrast between his life and theirs must have
been more and more painful to him. Yet he was conscientious in visiting
them and caring for them in times of great stress. In the summer of 1923,
for example, he visited them twice, in June and August.[1] And during the
last illness of each of them—his mother in 1926 and his father in 1931—
Harry was present for some days before death came.

Probably in the summer before Ella's death, a series of photographs
were taken on the front stoop of the farmhouse, when both Margaret
Stack and Harry were visiting. The camera was probably Harry's, for by
that time he was experimenting with amateur photography. His parents
are dressed as farm people, but Harry in his bow tie and Margaret with a
strand of pearls around her neck are obviously visiting from the city.
There is a half-smile on Ella's face in two of her three pictures, but the
rest of them have adopted formal and self-conscious poses for the occasion. Harry, obviously ill at ease, has adopted a jaunty air in a kind of
parody of Charlie Chaplin. There is an adolescent gaucheness about him,
although he was past thirty. In one of the pictures, the farm dog has
begun to walk into the setting—there was always a dog on the Sullivan
farm, just as there would always be a dog in Harry's ménage after he had

acquired his own house, first in New York City and then in Bethesda.

Year after year, the round of life in the farmhouse continued much as it had when Harry was growing up. As the years went by, Ella became more and more stooped until she "carried her face" on top of her head in order to look up at people.[2] But she continued her routine, tending the chickens, collecting the eggs, baking six, seven, or eight pies at a time in the summer on the wood range in the kitchen. There was a swing in the side yard that held four people, and it was pleasant to sit there of a summer evening when the work was done; but winter or summer, the interior of the farmhouse was dark and dismal. In the fall and winter the farmhouse was often unbearably cold, even in October, partly because of the underground stream that ran through the cellar.

At Christmastime in 1925, Harry came home particularly to see his mother; she was not well, and in less than three months she would be dead. Harry, ever the observant internist, probably recognized that her life expectancy was not great. On this holiday visit, the unanticipated death of his cousin Leo took place on January 4, 1926. By coincidence, Harry was dining out with Leo and Nina that night in the Sherburne Inn when Leo had a heart attack and died within an hour or two.

Leo and Nina's daughter, Dorothy, who was twelve years old when her father died, remembers well the events of that evening, although neither she nor her younger brother was included in the dinner party. Harry had called in the afternoon, suggesting that he would like to see Leo and his wife before he returned to Sheppard the next day; because his mother was not well, Harry had stayed on past the usual Christmas holiday. Leo had suggested that he and Nina come by and pick up Harry and his parents in his fine new car, the Grey Goose, and take them to the Sherburne Inn for dinner. But only Harry accepted the invitation. The weather had been particularly cold and stormy for a week or so, and the ice on the ponds was so deep that the annual harvesting of ice had begun somewhat earlier than usual. Afterwards relatives would remember that Leo and his brother-in-law had been stuck in the snow the week before on a business trip and had had a hard time shoveling the automobile out, so that Leo might have strained his heart in that way.

Dorothy Stack's memory of that fateful evening began with her father's dressing, for he was buttoning his shirt when he had quite a severe attack of pain; it alarmed her mother for a few minutes, and perhaps her father too. But the pain went away, and he seemed quite all right. Dorothy Stack remembers that her mother was somewhat indifferent about seeing Harry. She felt that her parents had viewed Harry from "a somewhat provincial viewpoint; they felt that he had sort of rejected and neglected his family—perhaps that he was ashamed of his beginnings on the Smyrna farm. . . . I think for Harry it must have been even more of a dis-

21. *Harry, his mother, and his father, about 1925*

22. *Timothy, Ella, and Margaret*

23. Timothy Sullivan

24. Ella Stack Sullivan

mal deal [to visit the farm than it was for Margaret Stack], uncomfortable and uninteresting—and I'm sure he must have done it only for his mother's sake. Though I really don't know what his relationship with his father was, I have the feeling that they didn't have any understanding for each other at all."

One can imagine the encounter between Leo, Nina, and Harry the night of Leo's death. In January, it would be dark before they arrived at the farmhouse to pick up Harry. The house would be dimly lit, as primitive in many ways as the house that Michael had begun to live in some seventy-five years before. His grandchildren, Harry and Leo, had come a long way since then, and each had achieved in the larger world. But Leo's achievements were easily definable in Chenango County. Harry, away from Sheppard and his clinical duties, had no portfolio. At forty-one, Leo was handsome and accustomed, after three years, to his new role in life as an important part of his father-in-law's lucrative business. Three years before, he had given up his position as a partner in a consulting engineering firm in Pittsburgh, and reluctantly, at his wife's insistence and in the tradition of the Chenango County elite, had come back to South Otselic to learn the fish-line business. Leo had vowed to win over his father-in-law by his charm, for the old man was somewhat eccentric and difficult to get along with, but the price had been high at times. So for the last three years before his death, Leo had tried to get used to living again in South Otselic after living in urban settings for well over a decade. Nina was happy to be back home. As the daughter of one of the wealthiest men in the County, as the wife of a man selected to take over her family's business, and as the mother of two beautiful children, she felt happy to be back in home territory once again. All of this splendor was represented in a picture Leo had taken while they were still living in Pittsburgh; it shows Nina and their young daughter Dorothy, as they were preparing to go out of doors on a winter's day. Nina has on a large, elegant hat, a dark greatcoat, with furs around her face, and white kid gloves; in the picture, Dorothy is a small version of her mother's elegance.

So the three of them rode down to the Inn for dinner that January night, hurrying so as not to arrive too late; on Mondays the dining room at the Inn closed rather promptly. Dorothy Stack has reconstructed the scene at the Inn that night, as she remembers hearing the adults discuss it over and over again in the next few days.[3] Immediately after the first course, Leo lifted his head with a queer look in his eyes and confessed that he had a terrible pain in his chest. Nina was not particularly alarmed, but Harry was, and suggested that Leo lie down. Leo got up to go out into the lounge. When he got to the door, he turned around, surprised, and announced that the pain was gone, that he was all right. Dinner was quite strained, and Harry continued to be alarmed. Just as the dessert was being served, Leo had a "really dreadful pain," and everyone left the table. They went out into the lounge, and Leo and Nina sat on a sofa while Harry questioned Leo about his symptoms. He asked Leo if he might call another doctor. Leo acquiesced, and a local doctor came and made a diagnosis of acute indigestion; the doctor asked Leo if he could empty his stomach. Leo agreed that that would be easy, for "one of his pet tricks at college was to drink with the boys and go outside, put a finger down his throat, get rid of all the liquor, and go back and drink some more." After Leo had returned from the men's room, the local doctor went home. Harry suggested that Leo should get someone to drive him home, so relatives from South Otselic were summoned, and there was a delay. It was not an easy trip in the winter on unplowed roads. Harry seemed dissatisfied with the local doctor's diagnosis; but Leo and Nina were unconcerned. Harry insisted that Leo go somewhere else the next day and get a thorough physical examination, which was not possible in South Otselic or Sherburne. Harry was so insistent that, when he left the room for a few minutes, Nina remarked to Leo: "He's just queer, isn't he?" Leo more or less agreed. When they thought that their relatives would be arriving shortly, Leo got up to put on his coat and pitched forward, over Nina's feet, onto the floor. She turned him over, and subsequently reported: "I never even called to him or spoke to him, his eyes were glazed, and I knew he was dead."

After the lapse of many years, Dorothy Stack tried to sort out the events of that evening and Harry's participation in them:

Harry was upset, because what my father had died of was an embolism, and the symptoms were very typical of the off-and-on clogging of the heart's own circulatory system. My mother has always thought that it was the result of shoveling of heavy snow the week or so before, and she's probably right. But, my father was ... really quite the athlete ... a man in perfect health, and this was certainly very unexpected.

So you can understand how my great impression about Harry—the first time that I ever really remember hearing anything about him—was that he was not a particularly welcome associate, at least as far as my mother was concerned; and that she really thought he was a little strange. And yet, you can understand how he would be acting very strangely, trying not to alarm them unduly, and yet to impress upon them that something serious was happening. And I'm sure he must have been terribly upset by the local doctor's diagnosis of acute indigestion.

More than thirty-five years after his death, old-timers still volunteered information on the event when they discovered that I was assembling material on "Leo's cousin," Harry. In South Otselic, the village high school and all places of business were closed for the funeral, which was held at the family home and conducted by the Methodist minister. Leo had been born in South Otselic, at the Gothic Hotel, and the village proudly claimed him as their own: "Notwithstanding the fact that he was deprived of the care of a mother when very young and reared in the surroundings and influences of country hotel life, he came to manhood clean and a general favorite with old and young. He remained throughout his life clean, loyal, unselfish, and lovable with a family life that was above reproach."

The newspaper summed up Leo's decision to return to South Otselic in an accurate fashion: "He had expected to make consulting engineering his life work and it was with deep regret at leaving this work that in July 1923, . . . at the urgent request of the officers of [the fish-line] corporation and for family reasons, Mr. Stack moved back to his home town and acquired a block of stock in that company. At the time of his passing he was acting in the capacity of mechanical engineer and secretary of the company."

Harry decided to stay on for Leo's funeral, which was delayed until Friday because of the weather. After the service, Leo was buried in an impressive plot of ground that overlooked the village. In time, Nina's father and mother, and Nina herself, would be buried there. But the main marker would read "Brown" at the head; to one side would be a small marker for "Stack" and to the other side one for "Angell," the other son-in-law. Like Timothy Sullivan, Leo was a son-in-law who had married into a more important family.

Leo's father, Ed, had been dead for over six years; but the whole question of Ed's having "turned Protestant" was revived for relatives and friends at Leo's funeral, which was a Protestant service, held at his home. In the culture of Chenango County, Leo's death was entered on the baseball scorecard kept by Protestants and Catholics. The Catholics, according to the rules of that game, would believe that Leo, whose father had turned Protestant and gotten away with it, was finally paying for the sins of his father by his own untimely death. But the Protestants would see Leo's success as related to God's benign care for their religion, and his death not as a punishment but as a singling out of an upstanding man for an early reward.

When Sullivan died twenty-eight years later, his colleagues, who knew that Sullivan had moved far away from formal religion, were mystified and even horrified that he had requested of Jimmie that there be a Catholic service. But within the score-keeping in Chenango County, Harry had taken a stand that must have amused him in contemplation and that somehow helped to even up the score that Uncle Ed and Cousin Leo had thrown off balance.

The medical circumstances of Leo's death were of some significance to Harry. His own failure to save Leo's life rankled in him, and he would talk to Dorothy Stack about it in 1938, when they met each other for the first time at Margaret Stack's funeral. It had been in a real sense his debut in the family as a physician, and he had been helpless. Furthermore, it was against his nature to ever explain; one did one's best, but one did not apologize. But the meaning of Leo's death to Sullivan went beyond that, for the death certificate suggested a congenital weakness, which Sullivan came to think might hasten his own death. Leo's death certificate gave the cause of death as "rupture of aneurysm of arch of aorta" by the embolism. This detail implies that an autopsy was performed, since "aneurysm" ordinarily defines a permanent abnormal condition of a blood vessel resulting from disease or other weakness of the vessel wall, and the location was pinpointed. Since the physician who came to the hotel had left before Leo's death, it seems possible that Sullivan himself may have called for the autopsy.

In March of that same year, Ella died with a diagnosis of "cerebral apoplexy," according to the death certificate. These two deaths coming so close together affected Sullivan's prognosis for himself. Five years later, shortly after his father's death, Harry predicted his own death, in a half-facetious way. Even though he doubted the predictability of specific human behavior under the "eternally changing configuration of the cultural-social present," he went on to predict quite accurately his own death: "Conceivably, it was in some ultimately comprehensible fashion ordained at the moment of the writer's conception that he shall cease to live owing to rupture of the middle meningeal artery at the age of 57 years, three months and five days, plus or minus less than 100 hours."[4] Actually, he died in 1949, aged 56 years, 10 months, 24 days, of a meningeal hemorrhage, as shown on the death certificate; thus he died 4 months and 11 days before his predicted death. Sullivan was familiar with actuarial tables from his work in Chicago, and he had apparently attempted to work out the odds for his own death, depending heavily on Leo's fate. He seems to have disregarded his father's span of years in this prediction. Timothy would be almost 74 when he died and Ella was a little over 73, so it would seem that Harry was entitled to a somewhat longer life than 57 by those facts alone.[5]

Perhaps as a result of Leo's death, Sullivan underwent some medical examinations of his own heart. A colleague reported that Sullivan suffered from pain and exhaustion most of his life because of a defective valve in the heart—"mitrostenosis."[6] There was no open-heart surgery available at that time, so that he had to live with this handicap. But the dramatic ending of Leo Stack's life must have added to the strain of Sullivan's last years,when he had reason to think that he was living on borrowed time.

The circumstances of Leo's death are poignant in other ways. Leo was the magic one for Harry, the cousin whom he could never measure up to. And Harry would die in a hotel, too, suddenly like Leo, but alone and mysteriously, twenty-three years later. There was a difference in the way that the *Sun* carried the notices of these two deaths: Leo's death was front-page news, but the news of Harry's death would appear on page 8 of the *Sun*.

In some ways, Harry could live up to Leo's accomplishments. Shortly after Leo's death, Harry acquired the yellow Franklin, a car which probably cost slightly more than Leo's "Grey Goose" and was considerably more flashy. He also had begun to acquire possessions that bespoke widening cultural horizons; sometime in the same general period, he bought the piano that played rolls, so that he could listen to the music he particularly liked—Wagner and Mozart. And he acquired three original etchings for the walls of St. Martin's in Towson, by a little-known English artist of the period, Edmund Blampield. Like Leo, he experimented with photography, and his picture of Jimmie, taken in 1927, bespeaks some skill. Like Leo, Sullivan had considerable genius with mechanical things, and near the end of his life he collaborated with General Electric in refining recording devices for special clinical research. But Leo's marriage to Nina could not be replicated by Sullivan. She—or her counterpart—was far removed from any possibility as a companion for Harry. To see Nina in that period, widowed with two handsome children, must have aroused in him the realization that such beauty and such an achievement would be permanently denied to him. Yet he could settle for nothing less. Within a year or two after Leo's death, Jimmie would be firmly ensconced at Joppa Road, and they would begin the life of two bachelors, each of whom fantasied from time to time that he would eventually find a wife.

On February 25, 1926—less than two months after Leo's death—Ella had a stroke, and her immediate family was summoned to her bedside. Her brother John came from Washington, her son Harry from Towson, and her sister Margaret from Brooklyn Heights. Nina Stack, so recently bereaved, came over to help out. Ella lay in the bedroom to the west of the house, next to the kitchen—the warmest spot in the house during the winter months. The small house was crowded, and it was very cold at night. Nina and Margaret slept up in the loft room over the kitchen, and John Stack warmed their bed beforehand by putting in large sticks of wood which he heated in the oven of the kitchen range: "He was a lovely person and Margaret and I had fun crawling in with the 'wood pile,' " Nina Stack remembered.[7]

In the twelve days before Ella's death, there was tension in the farmhouse. Margaret wanted to care for Ella, but Harry took care of his mother "almost entirely," according to Nina. "He was very 'short' with Margaret which I mildly resented. He was pleasant to me but I decided after a very few days that I was making more trouble than giving help so I left. . . . I do not remember Uncle Tim during this visit." So again, the Stacks took over, and Timothy remained in the background. The house was so crowded that he may have taken refuge across the road with old man Yockey.

Ella was a difficult patient; Harry reported to Jimmie at a later period that "she was very stubborn [during her last illness] and would not use a bed-pan, withholding her urine and feces till she died, saying if God has taken away my strength to take care of my needs, then he means I shouldn't do anything."[8] Ella's vow of continence must have meant that Harry was beset by serious nursing problems in his self-appointed task. With no electricity, no running water, and freezing weather outside, even laundering and bathing would represent major problems.

Yet when death came, those left behind could define the occasion with dignity and a touch of County Clare. Obituaries in the *Sun* were traditionally written by the family, and the obituary for Ella states that she died "as the sun sunk below the western hills of her home." She had died in the west bedroom, and Harry and Margaret, who undoubtedly composed the obituary together, understood something of the significance of that, for "in ancient Celtic mythology, the heaven at life's end . . . lies to the west in the setting sun."[9]

At a deeper level, whether by Michael Stack's design or by chance, the room in which Ella ended her life was traditional by County Clare lore. Conrad Arensberg writes of the lore of the 'west room,' as he experienced it in a village in County Clare, only a short distance from Michael Stack's birthplace. The west room, always located next to the kitchen, was traditionally connected with ceremony and death and with the fairy-lore that still survived—though partially denied—at the time of his study in the 1920s. It was a room reserved for the old folks as they neared the end of their lives. Fairy paths were supposed to pass by the west room, and none of the outbuildings on a farm were located west of the house, since this would interfere with the comings and goings of these spirits.[10] The west room in the Smyrna farmhouse completely conformed to this tradition. In 1961, all of the outbuildings were to the south and east of the farmhouse, as they were in the earliest pictures.

There is little mention of Timothy in the obituary; he was at his wife's bedside when death came, but it was "her home," as indeed it was considered throughout her life. The occupation of her sister, her brother, and her son are suitably identified, but Timothy's work in Norwich and on the old Stack place goes unnoticed. On the same page of the newspaper, there is a "Card of Thanks," doubtless written by Harry in language that he deemed appropriate for the occasion and with a characteristic use of the semicolon: "In happy accord with her request, and with deep appreciation of the fine generosity and quick sympathy which stirred them, we desire to express our gratitude to the good neighbors and friends of the late Ella May Sullivan; alike for willing and for given services in our period of sorrow and of bereavement." It is signed, in order, by Timothy J. Sullivan, John B. Stack, Marguerite A. Stack, and Harry Stack Sullivan. The lack of consensus about given names for the Stacks appears in the paper on the same page: Margaret in the obituary becomes Marguerite in the card of thanks; and Ella Mary becomes Ella May (with a "y"). By this time the name Ellen, which was Ella's original name, has entirely disappeared. The confusion cannot be blamed exclusively on the newspaper. Ella's age in the obituary also differs by a year from her birth date, supplied by the family, on the death certificate.

Nina Stack remembered that there was still so much snow on the day of the funeral that the casket had to be carried down to St. Malachy's in Sherburne on a farmer's flat work sled. Afterwards, Ella was buried in the Catholic cemetery on the hill above the church—the same cemetery where the two babies had been buried so long ago. But no marker was ever placed over her grave, and both Ella and Timothy still lie there in unmarked plots.

On March 16, a week after Ella's death, Harry left Smyrna to return to Sheppard. On the next day, March 17, the Ku Klux Klan celebrated St. Patrick's Day and the departure of so many Irish Catholics who had come to Smyrna for the funeral by burning two crosses on a hill overlooking the depot. Harry missed that celebration by one day. The crosses would be clearly visible from the farmhouse on the hill where dwelt the last of the Sullivan family—indeed, probably the last Irish Catholic left in the village district. Within a few years, a local boy would "convert" to Catholicism when he married an Irish-American girl from another part of the County; and some of the local residents—mainly members of the Seventh-Day Baptist Church—would boycott his business on the main street of the village out of their fears for the future of the community.

While Sullivan was at Sheppard, he had talked about coming back to the Smyrna farmhouse someday and setting up a convalescent camp for young people showing early schizophrenic disorders, following the tradition already begun by Flavius Packer. But after his father's death in 1931, Sullivan would remove himself from Smyrna and Chenango County forever; and, undoubtedly remembering the Klan's activity, he began to speak in his writings of the virulence of prejudice and of its dangers to the mental health of a whole society.

Most of Sullivan's friends and colleagues focus on his mother as the main problem for him in his growing-up years; and Sullivan himself tended to support this when he complained of his mother's personification of him as a clotheshorse on which to hang her illusions. He also must have criticized her to Clara Thompson; Thompson, who never met Sullivan's mother, reported that Ella Sullivan was a complaining semi-invalid who felt resentful of the family's situation. Yet as one reconstructs the total picture, this description seems oversimplified. Ella and Maggie were Harry's chief adult models at home; and because he had limited access to the teachers in the village school, his mother and aunt loomed larger than they would have for most children. However much he might resent his mother's illusions about him, he had an understanding of the frustration and sadness that lay back of her dreams for him. As an adult, he often pretended an indifference about people to whom he was drawn; and he sometimes showed gruffness to cover his feelings of tenderness.

As his professional life progressed, the importance of his mother in his career becomes more and more obvious. If she hung her illusions on him as if he were a clotheshorse, he also came to share many of those illusions and indeed to make them realities. He felt, at times, an annoyance with her unfulfilled life, her protectiveness of him, but it was an annoyance for someone who was close to him and well loved. She was the person who transmitted to him the myth of the Stack family. And the myth was the crucial ingredient that sent him forth on a quest for mankind. When he tried to "run with the Earth into the future," it was the legend of the West Wind as told to him by his mother that set him on that path and gave him the courage to keep on going. He may have been limited by his overidentification with Ella and Margaret, but he had an intuitive feeling for women that never left him. After his death it was the women in his world who were the most unstinting in their praise of him; the praise centers about his encouragement of them as persons. Male social scientists have also been enthusiastic about him as a person and a thinker, but male psychiatrists and psychoanalysts have generally been ambivalent, if not hostile.

Shortly after Sullivan returned to Towson following his mother's death, William Alanson White sent Sullivan a note of sympathy: "I am dropping you this line now to express my sympathy for your recent bereavement. I know what a serious shock such a loss is and I am counting upon your well developed philosophy to take care of it."[11] But Sullivan continued to maintain distance in this relationship, and his next letters, as before, are ended "Respectfully." It is almost as if he felt apart from both worlds—the world of Smyrna, and his new professional world. Indeed in some ways, he may have felt that most of the solid Protestant residents of Smyrna would be more at home with White than they would be with him.

There was already a discernible pattern in this man so lonely in his early years, so much an outcast in his search for an education and a chance to live productively: he would usually be more comfortable with those who had had the experience of not belonging—with patients, with the uneducated, with women—than with those who were the successful ones. In only one close relationship would this pattern vary significantly. Shortly after his mother's death, he met Edward Sapir, respected and established as a linguist and cultural anthropologist. But hidden beneath the surface of Sapir's brilliance were strands of troubled experience that Sapir would reveal to Sullivan in their first meeting.

↝ 26 ↜

The Influence of
Sandor Ferenczi

> Sullivan had a great advantage . . . in that his begin-
> nings were quite unnoticed. There was no Freud
> around here to know that he was doing something
> unorthodox.
> —Clara Thompson, unpublished lecture

THROUGHOUT his life, Sullivan gave William Alanson White "first
honor for maintaining the healthy eclecticism that has characterized
American psychiatry and that has carried it far beyond psychiatry elsewhere in the world."[1] At Sheppard, Sullivan carried out this tradition at
an accelerated pace, first exploring the way in which European psychoanalysis could be modified for the treatment of young patients who came
on his ward, and then reaching out into the field of preventive psychiatry
as suggested by the social science research developing in and around the
University of Chicago.

One of the chief expediters of the vast changes that took place in
American social science and psychiatry between 1921 and 1940 was
Harry Stack Sullivan. Within the tradition of Bronson Alcott and Walt
Whitman, Sullivan swapped ideas throughout the continent, traveling by
train or by telephone, not counting the cost. He had a growing sense of
collective creativity, and an acute awareness of how one's thoughts and
hopes change dramatically in a new situation with another person. Ultimately he would try to explain this phenomenon to his psychiatric colleagues in a paper entitled "The Illusion of Personal Individuality," in
which he expressed the idea in such a bold fashion that he drew fire from
his listeners: "No great progress in this field of study can be made until it
is realized that the field of observation is what people do with each other,
what they can communicate to each other about what they do with each
other. When that is done, no such thing as the durable, unique, individual

personality is ever clearly justified. For all I know every human being has as many personalities as he has interpersonal relations." He observed that the idea "sounds quite lunatic when first heard," but "there is at least food for thought in it."[2] His listeners found his idea so unnerving that Sullivan put the paper aside, and it was not published until after his death. In a society that prides itself on the uniqueness of each person, this cross-section view of humanity was revolutionary.

Yet this perspective on human relationships as an ongoing and modifying series of influences on a given human organism was peculiarly a part of the American experience. A wide range of American thinkers and philosophers, poets, and novelists had dealt with the importance of a chance encounter with a stranger, the impact of finding a person in one's peer group who could be trusted, and the phenomenon of forming a self from "the reflected appraisals of others," as the social psychologist George Herbert Mead would conceptualize it. Such thinking was not confined to the American scene, but the size of the continent and the diversity of its people produced a fertile ground for the emergence of what is encompassed in Sullivan's interpersonal theory.

Sullivan had been at Sheppard a little over a year when he wrote his first two papers. Both of them showed his careful obeisance to Freud and his wish to study schizophrenia within the words and the dogma of classical psychoanalysis—"in strict conformity to the delineation of Professor Freud."[3] In progressive papers coming out of his experience at Sheppard, his horizons opened up at a speed almost unprecedented by other thinkers in the field of personality study; a selection of papers from this period traces out through historical commentaries the pattern of these changes.[4]

He early acquired the habit of reading in a wide field, borrowing a word or a concept here, changing it to suit his own observation, and then discarding it, if a more precise formulation occurred to him. However lonely he might be in his personal life, he never saw himself alone in the world of ideas. He knew that ideas moved swiftly from one thinker to another in the same historical period; it did not matter whether or not he had read a particular book—the influence could be mediate as well as direct. In sharp contrast, Freud prided himself on discovering his theories independently. "I am indebted for having made a discovery to not being a wide reader," he noted proudly, denying the influence of Schopenhauer on his concept of repression; and "I have denied myself the very great pleasure of reading the works of Nietzsche from a deliberate resolve not to be hampered in working out the impressions received in psycho-analysis by any sort of expectation derived from without."[5]

In his final theoretical statement in 1948, Sullivan traces out the main currents of thought that have influenced him: "Needless to say, behind all this phase of psychiatry are the discoveries of Sigmund Freud." After Freud, he cites, in order, the main tributaries to his interpersonal theory:

Adolf Meyer's psychobiology "is the study of man as the highest embodiment of mentally integrated life . . . a more-or-less conscious integration, which makes use of symbols and meanings," and this approach is "a vast improvement on psychology," as it had existed before Meyer. The next important tributary is the social psychology emergent from the "very original thinking" of Charles H. Cooley and George Herbert Mead, "which included the development of the self . . . on the basis of reflected symbols from others and the learning of roles which one undertook to live." The third tributary is from cultural anthropology, "which is concerned with the social heritage of man"; in that category, Sullivan cites Malinowski, Edward Sapir, and Ruth Benedict. And finally he mentions the writings of the physicist P. W. Bridgman, who differentiated, as did Sullivan, between the private and public mode of human interaction; Sullivan agreed with Bridgman that the psychiatrist or the social psychologist can only study the public mode—what goes on between people, including nonverbal gestures that may negate the actual words that are said.[6]

This is a very precise formulation of Sullivan's intellectual antecedents. But the ideas often came indirectly through people he knew, and not necessarily directly or through readings. For example, there is no evidence that Sullivan ever met Mead, or even read or cited his work until the last decade of Sullivan's life. Thus one is forced to look at the links between Sullivan and the particular people involved in this exchange of knowledge.

Since Sullivan began his list with the influence of psychoanalysis on his own intellectual development, it is appropriate to look at the dynamics of his selecting Sandor Ferenczi as the most important of the European psychoanalysts. By the late 1920s, Freud was past seventy, and most of his early followers were too involved with emerging from their long-term stewardships to offer much more than unrewarding controversy. Partly because of geography, Ferenczi had maintained from the beginning a more autonomous position in the movement, and Freud himself had accorded Ferenczi a much more correct collegial position than any of the others.

There is little in the simple facts of Sandor Ferenczi's personal life to indicate why his thinking overlapped in some particulars with Sullivan's.[7] Ferenczi's parents were urban and well-to-do, and their eleven children had many advantages in growing up. Ferenczi got his M.D. degree in 1894, and he began practice as a physician in the Austro-Hungarian Army. In 1900 he opened an office in Budapest as a neurologist. In 1907 he wrote to Freud, and this began their close friendship, which lasted until a few years before Ferenczi's death. During the First World War, Ferenczi served as a captain in the Medical Corps in a small city in Hungary, so that his experience in this particular seems to have been somewhat comparable to Sullivan's. Certainly Ferenczi's two stints as an Army physician considerably broadened his knowledge of all walks of life. In 1919, at the age of 46, Ferenczi married a divorced woman with two children; the marriage had been long delayed by his wife's unwillingness to end an unhappy marriage until her children were grown.

In the fall of 1926, Ferenczi came to the United States for eight months, lecturing that winter in the New School for Social Research in New York City. On December 9, 1926, Sullivan wrote to White, suggesting that he invite Ferenczi, "the genius of the psychoanalytic movement," to come to Washington for three or four months. Two days later, White wrote denying the request; as usual, he was shrewd in avoiding, for himself and the hospital, financial obligations and intellectual disputes. Without White's sponsorship, Ferenczi gave several lectures in Washington in the spring of 1927.

During this period, Sullivan heard Ferenczi lecture at least twice, once in New York City at the 1926 Christmas meeting of the American Psychoanalytic Association, on the subject "Present-Day Problems in Psychoanalysis"; and again on April 11, 1927, in Washington, D.C., at a meeting of the Washington Psychopathological Society, on "The Genital Theory," with both White and Sullivan participating as discussants. But there is no record of any significant personal contact between Ferenczi and Sullivan. Within the next year, however, Sullivan had persuaded Thompson to go to Budapest and study under Ferenczi so that she could come back and teach him what she had learned. Thus Sullivan's main knowledge of Ferenczi's thinking came through Thompson and through his reading of Ferenczi's book, *Contributions to Psycho-Analysis,* which Sullivan cites as one of a half dozen psychoanalytic books that he read in this early period.[8] This particular book then becomes a way of viewing the impact of Ferenczi's thinking on Sullivan, augmented by Thompson's own report of her part in the interaction.

In the summer of 1928, Thompson made her first trip to Budapest, spending two months in analysis with Ferenczi; she followed the same schedule for the next two summers. In the winters, after each sojourn, she passed on to Sullivan the fruits of her experience. Subsequently, until Ferenczi's death in 1933, she went for longer periods to Budapest.

On Thompson's first visit, Ferenczi "expressed surprise . . . at the similarity between many of his views and those of Sullivan."[9] From then on, Sullivan and Ferenczi were engaged at some level in a dialogue through Thompson. The two men had parallel interests in seriously disturbed patients and, beyond that, in the total human scene as worthy of the new insights of dynamic psychiatry. Michael Balint has summarized Ferenczi's place in the movement: "His fame as an analyst for hopeless cases became worldwide and soon he was regarded all the world over as 'the haven of lost cases.' "[10] At the time of Sullivan's death, young psychiatrists working in mental hospitals up and down the eastern seaboard believed firmly that if Sullivan would supervise a case, no matter how hopeless it seemed, the patient would get better. Again, both men saw the necessity for extending dynamic psychiatry to include people of all classes. It is no coincidence that the first plans for the free care of poor patients in a psychoanalytic institute were made in Budapest during the First World War; although the plans did not come to fruition at that time, the attempt had historical significance.[11]

In his writings, Ferenczi was sensitive to the importance of social class and occupation in reporting on patients.[12] Sullivan also showed a beginning awareness of the importance of social class in the case reports from Sheppard. Neither subscribed to Freud's dictum that treatment for "those patients who do not possess a reasonable degree of education and a fairly reliable character should be refused."[13]

Many of Sullivan's most important insights on sexual fears and preoccupations may have begun with Ferenczi's formulations. During World War II, when Sullivan was teaching physicians and psychiatrists techniques for screening young men in the interviews conducted for the Selective Service, he recommended that any evidence of difficulty in urinating in the presence of another person should alert the interviewer to the possibility of more serious problems. This recommendation may be a reverberation of Ferenczi's discussion of a patient with the same presenting difficulty.[14]

In another paper, Ferenczi suggested that concern about either heterosexual or homosexual behavior may be obsessional in character—a symptom of great anxiety in which the person uses the obsessional preoccupation with sexual performance as a way of avoiding anxiety about something else.[15] Thus either intense heterosexuality or homosexuality may be looked upon as a symptom and not as the prevailing source of difficulty in living. Sullivan uses this insight in his description of an office patient who asked for help with a homosexual problem:

The upshot of the [initial] reconnaissance [interviews] was that I told him that I had no psychiatric time available . . . for his interest in homosexual problems. If, on the other hand, he wanted to find out why he could never hold any one job for more than six months . . . and was always in ever-increasing, terrific danger of being completely discredited and expelled by the organization he worked for, then I thought I could find him a psychiatrist. Believe it or not, the patient was quite content to go to work on the problem of why, in the space of six months or so, each one of his bosses came in to such open collision with him that he left. The curious thing about this story is that in the process of studying his difficulties with bosses, the great homosexual problem sort of caved in.[16]

There was another even more important area of theoretical agreement between Sullivan and Ferenczi: the role of the therapist. In 1928, at the time Thompson first went to Budapest, Ferenczi changed his method of treatment—a change that proved fatal in his friendship with Freud. Thompson has reported that their break began with Ferenczi's "advocating the idea that patients needed to be accepted and loved if they were to get well. Also, the patients needed to know the analyst was not perfect; that is, there had to be some opportunity for the patient to have a reality evaluation of the analyst." Freud's reaction was specific; he "began writing Ferenczi letters about his having been a bad boy and acting like somebody in his second childhood and needing love and that probably what he needed was more analysis."[17] The idea that the transaction between the patient and the therapist contained two areas for study—the patient's and the doctor's input into the therapeutic encounter—constituted a serious threat to Freud and his followers. Transference had been given a high priority by Freud, but countertransference—the effect of the analyst's personality on the patient, either negative or positive—had a low priority. Although Freud had first used the term "countertransference" in 1910, and again referred to it twice in a 1915 paper, "it is hard to find any other explicit discussions of the subject in Freud's published works."[18] In a passage on Freud's lack of sympathy for patients, the sociologist Philip Rieff suggests that this "may be one explanation for [Freud's] strict disavowal of countertransference."[19]

In a paper delivered before the Inernational Psychoanalytic Congress in 1932, Ferenczi pointed out the hypocrisy of assuming that the psychoanalyst is detached and objective. If the psychoanalyst is able to admit his errors to the patient, then he frees the patient "to re-experience the past no longer as hallucinatory reproduction but as an objective memory."[20]

Earlier, Ferenczi had spelled out the single major contribution of psychoanalysis: "It has found that the inner resistances may be fixed in the earliest childhood and may be completely unconscious; it therefore demands of every psychologist who enters on the study of the human mind that he should thoroughly investigate beforehand his own mental constitution—inborn and acquired—down to the deepest layers and with all the resources of the analytic technique."[21] In Sullivan's first published paper, he also refers to "the postulate of the unconscious" as "the great contribution of Professor Freud."[22] Like Ferenczi, Sullivan would recognize the necessity for self-observation by the participant in the human scene, noting in 1937 that "the crying need is for observers who are growing observant of their observing."[23] The Washington School of Psychiatry, co-founded by Sullivan in 1936, would implement this philosophy by insisting that any student who had dealings with the problems of other people, whether lawyer, minister, nursery school teacher, or social worker, should have "a searching scrutiny of his personal history, liabilities, and assets from the therapeutic standpoint."[24]

These and other departures from Freudian psychoanalysis did not prevent Sullivan from maintaining an active role in the American psychoanalytic scene, through participation in the Washington-Baltimore Psychoanalytic Society and its training institute. Yet his own theoretical position, distinctively American, moved very far from classical psychoanalysis, under the influence of another theoretician for whom Clara Thompson had also offered a significant connection—Adolf Meyer.

❦ 27 ❧

The Influence of
Adolf Meyer

The psychobiology of Adolf Meyer is the most distinguished recent effort to find a new locus for problems, a new level of reality and knowledge, and new
conceptual tools. Meyer recognizes the hierarchies of
organization and proceeds . . . to bridge the gap between biology and psychiatry.
—Sullivan, "Intuition, Reason, and Faith"

ALTHOUGH Meyer was born and educated in Switzerland, he provided Sullivan with the first developed theory that fit the American
experience. This theory had emerged in part from Meyer's early exposure
to the "Chicago School of Thought," as William James named the rich
explosion of ideas that began to appear in and around the University of
Chicago almost as soon as it opened its doors.[1] Even more important to
Meyer's theory was his personal and professional experience while he was
working at Kankakee State Hospital in Illinois. From both directions,
Meyer became a critical link for Sullivan to an entire network of ideas,
experiences, and people who had already laid the groundwork for an
American psychiatry.

During the Sheppard years, Sullivan actually had two strong figures
who helped him to view with some objectivity the new Freudian psychology—Meyer and William Alanson White; neither of them was "sold on
Freudian theory," as Clara Thompson observed.[2] Psychoanalysis was an
important new tool that needed to be studied from a variety of directions;
but even earlier than White, Meyer viewed psychoanalysis as subsidiary
to the discipline of American psychiatry. Freud's emphasis on the unconscious as a factor in the symptoms of the neurotic patient represented
a substantive contribution, but the concept was not new to American
psychology, as Meyer would note shortly after Freud's visit to America
in 1909; William James and others had long since described clinical

"lapses"—curious slips of the tongue or the unexpected speaking of that which one wanted to hide.[3] Thus almost as soon as Freud's ideas began to cross the Atlantic, Meyer attempted to avoid the formation of a cult in America that would be centered on psychoanalysis as a new religion, with Freud as the chief priest. Subsequently Freud himself would complain in a letter (1938) about the "obvious American tendency to turn psychoanalysis into a mere housemaid of Psychiatry."[4]

The differing viewpoints in Europe and America grew in part out of the respective patient populations. Most of the patients treated by Freud and his followers were at least middle-class and seen in office practice. White and Meyer had their early initiation into psychiatry on the wards of American state hospitals. Many of their patients were immigrants or the children of immigrants who had lost their way in the transition to the new land. One must make "remedial attempts" in the society generally, as Sullivan would later define the task. The necessity for a preventive psychiatry came early into Meyer's thinking. If one were to catch the mental patient before he became destined for a life in a state hospital, then there would have to be some way to detect his beginning difficulties before he developed serious symptoms; in most instances, the patient reported some curious disorder to his family doctor before his mental illness was fully visible. It was necessary, therefore, that the medical doctor be trained in the early detection of warning symptoms. By 1928, Sullivan was also well aware of the fact that even seriously disturbed people often sought first the help of medical specialists other than psychiatrists: "Schizophrenic youths are frequently seen first by rhinologists or ophthalmologists, or urologists, or something of that kind, for alleged ailments of the throat or the eyes or the genito-urinary tract or the gastro-intestinal tract; only later being identified as victims of grave mental disorder."[5] Eventually Sullivan arrived at the same point that the two older men had reached considerably earlier: Psychiatry (not psychoanalysis) must be the core discipline, and it must be kept in medicine. All three of them recognized that whole new disciplines must contribute to the field of "mental hygiene," a term invented by Meyer; and there was in the offing the possibility of a special new degree in medical school. In the fields of prevention and rehabilitation, new specialties would arise that would be independent of medicine; but a patient was a patient, and some of his rights could only be protected within the medical profession.

From the time of Freud's visit, his psychology became a popular idea in this country, particularly along the East Coast. Meyer increasingly feared this popularity. Faith healing and patent medicines had had an unusual vogue in nineteenth-century America. Mesmerism, particularly as it was made fashionable by P. P. Quimby, and Christian Science, as developed by Mary Baker Eddy, had been important deterrents to public support of medical research. America was made up of people from many lands; and it was prey to any new fad. In Alfred Lief's introduction to a selection of Meyer's papers, he notes Meyer's concern about the "persistence of Barnumism in America" and his observation that "many psychiatrists thought that nothing had happened before they made the acquaintance of Freudianism."[6] New ideas imported from western Europe were often greeted with too much uncritical enthusiasm; thus psychoanalysis could easily end up being practiced by charlatans. Indeed White's letter to Sullivan on the subject of Ferenczi's coming to Washington included his fears that psychoanalysis could be oversold, that the exploration of the patient's early memories could become a dangerous pastime for the uninitiated, who might begin to fiddle with people who were, relatively speaking, going concerns. White, unusually eclectic in his approach, was also eventually made wary.

Thus Freud's appearance at the Clark University Conference in 1909 was seen by Meyer and others as a potential threat to the beginning attempts at establishing standards for the practice of medicine in general and psychiatry in particular. Meyer was one of the three honored at the 1909 conference; Freud, Carl G. Jung, and Meyer each received a doctor of laws degree, and each gave an address, with Meyer as the first speaker. Within a month Meyer was slated to go to Johns Hopkins University Medical School to begin plans for a department of psychiatry, to be followed by the opening of the Henry Phipps Psychiatric Clinic. Both William H. Welch, head of the Hopkins Medical School, and Sir William Osler, the former head, had urged that psychiatry be made a specialty of the Medical School; and Meyer had been selected as the man to head up this ambitious attempt to bring psychiatry into a university medical school setting. So it was that Meyer was in no mood to be overwhelmed by the fame of the two who came from across the sea. For the next forty years, Meyer would attempt to set forth the reason why classical Freudian psychoanalysis had only limited meaning in America, unless it were willing to move out of its narrow and time-consuming preoccupations with sex and the unconscious and its emphasis on the unchanging nature of the pathologies in the given patient. In a new and more hopeful society, one had to work with the assets of the patient and get him moving again.

So it was that from two directions, Sullivan was encouraged to be critical of Freudian psychology. White encouraged him to explore the way in which it might be modified for dealing with psychotic patients. But it was Meyer who offered Sullivan the first full-fledged theory that lent itself to the American scene and that depended on only carefully selected parts of Freudian theory.

Adolf Meyer was twenty-six when he came to America from Switzerland; it was 1892, the year in which Sullivan was born. Meyer had obtained his medical degree that same year from the University of Zurich, and he had come to America to pursue a career in neuroanatomy after a brief sojourn in England. Meyer's father, whose thinking had been shaped by the humanist teachings of Zwingli, was a pastor in the established church of Switzerland; and his mother's brother was a physician. Meyer credited both influences in the shaping of his own career. One of Meyer's students observed that he had a "well-integrated pluralism of outlook" from his early life in Switzerland; he was essentially a family doctor in his approach.[7]

By the time Meyer left home, his mother was a widow and alone for the first time; his older sister had died, and his younger brother had left home. But his mother encouraged her older son to seek a career in America and assumed responsibility for the money he needed. He had been promised professional support by the State of Illinois before he came, but the promises did not materialize. In this manner he found himself at Kankakee State Hospital in 1893 as a neuropathologist, in a less exciting position than he had anticipated. Subsequently he received word from home that his mother had had a serious mental breakdown. Meyer arranged for his former teacher at the Burghölzli in Zurich, August Forel, to care for her, and she recovered. This experience made a lasting impression on Meyer and helped to change the direction of his career: he reports that his interest in mental patients as people "became more insistent when my coming to this country helped with many other factors to precipitate a serious depression of three years' duration in my own mother, who had always appeared as one of the sanest persons in my experience and who recovered against the expectations of my old teacher, giving me many an opportunity to incorporate well-known human facts in my more strictly medical thought of the time."[8]

Meyer's stay at Kankakee gave him the opportunity to look at his mother's experience with mental illness and her recovery in relation to the visible waste of lives in the patients that he found at Kankakee, many of whom came from immigrant families. He had begun with the idea of examining the brains and neurological systems of patients who died at Kankakee; but the answer was not to be found in the tissues of dead patients, but in their lives. Julia Lathrop, Jane Addams's co-worker at Hull-House in Chicago, came to Kankakee frequently as an observer for the state. Meyer's wife would later credit Lathrop with being one of the most formative influences in Meyer's Americanization.[9] Hull-House spelled the difference between life and death for many immigrants in the new world. Meyer himself was able to be a close observer of the experiment for a brief period when he spent a week at Hull-House during his recovery from an illness. Eunice E. Winters, Meyer's editor and commentator, states that although Meyer's "aims of prevention and community responsibility were formulated specifically" years after he left

Kankakee, "they had come within Meyer's purview in Illinois. Hull-House, the Child Study Association, a brief contact with Clarence Darrow, all contributed to his broadening human orientation."[10] In the last analysis, the original disappointment at Kankakee marked the beginning of Meyer's remarkable career in quite different areas—psychiatry and the mental hygiene movement: "There is something intensely human about the transformation of mere aggregates of chances into a vision and use of opportunity," Meyer wrote of himself.[11]

Another significant source of Meyer's thought in this early period came from the group of thinkers centered around the University of Chicago. Meyer's introduction to this group had begun thirty years before Sullivan's, so that he had significant immediate contact with the pattern of ideas that were shaping themselves there before the turn of the century. The patients at Kankakee and the rough-and-ready action research at Hull-House in Chicago gave Meyer the critical American experience; but the well-formulated theories in and around the University offered a bridge for Meyer to American thinking. John Dewey came to Chicago in 1894, and Meyer shortly began a lifelong friendship with him. George Herbert Mead and the sociologist Charles H. Cooley provided additional gateways to American thinking. Through these contacts, Meyer became familiar with Charles S. Peirce's philosophy of chance and William James's pluralism. Eventually, when Meyer went to Clark University in 1895, he became personally acquainted with William James. Meyer considered that Peirce, James, and Dewey represented "the finest upshot of the American pioneer spirit."[12]

The words and concepts of these thinkers were hewn from the rough stone of American experience. Partly through Meyer, they made their way into Sullivan's thinking. Thus William James dealt with the unconscious as "selective attention" in the same way that Sullivan would explicitly deal with it three decades later. Sullivan's concept was a refinement on James, but the words derived from the same unpretentious description of the phenomenon of *changing* awareness. Sullivan described with infinite detail the process of "selective inattention" to explain the lapses and gaps in rational thought. Selective inattention "to a certain extent covers the world like a tent," he said.[13]

It is theoretically of the greatest importance that these men discovered for themselves that in the American society a person did not have to be caught in an endless preoccupation with childhood trauma—that the human being had many experiences all along the developing process and that he could be encouraged to extrapolate some hope for the morrow from whatever good had happened anywhere along the earlier developing process. Meyer carried this tradition into psychiatry almost directly from James. Meyer spoke of "more or less consciousness," so that in his theory neither the psychiatrist nor the patient needs to be held up by exploring indefinitely a hidden domain.[14] Both Meyer and James had been trained as physicians and both had fathers who were students of humanistic theology; in both cases, the profession of physician was secondary to the social commitment to a more creative life for all people. James is seldom even thought of as a physician; and Meyer's part in the founding of the Mental Hygiene movement in America was much more in the role of reformer than physician. Near the end of his life, Sullivan also would state that he was more nearly a social psychologist than anything else. All this was in the broad tradition of Peirce's pragmatism, tempered by careful scientific observation and moving toward the fixed goal of amelioration of human tragedy. The goal was the only part that was fixed; all else was in a continual process of flux.

It is peripherally of some interest that three of the people mentioned here (Meyer, Peirce, and Mead) published little if at all before their deaths. With or without the published word, a whole new American perspective was growing. The task was so necessary, so important for the idea of democracy, that people sought to communicate with each other. Phrases caught on and had a life of their own in another's development. There is a clear and traceable continuum between Charles Peirce, William James, John Dewey, and George Herbert Mead; and the philosophic concepts that dominated their thinking—radical empiricism, pluralism, instrumentalism, pragmatism—informed American psychiatry as exemplified by Adolf Meyer and then later by Harry Stack Sullivan. The pragmatism first enunciated by Peirce and embellished by James remained intellectual and scientific; the ethical standards of American democracy demanded that scientific knowledge be used for the good of the people, but this did not preclude high standards of scientific research.

Gordon Allport, the social psychologist, has credited William James with being one of the early proponents of the collecting of life histories from a wide assortment of people, particularly as exemplified in *Varieties of Religious Experience,* and Allport contrasts James's methodology with Freud's: "Unlike James, Freud does not first present his cases and then draw his conclusions. He seems to use cases as exemplifications of theories previously formed. No doubt his frame of thought is changed by the admission of a new case, but so far as the *present* case is concerned, each patient seems to exemplify and illustrate (and not to create) his theories."[15] It was the very diversity of the people in this country that forced a new kind of theory on those who seriously observed the scene. All kinds of disparate experience had to be looked at, not to prove or illustrate a theory but to evolve theories. Meyer stated the goal clearly many times: "The main thing is that your point of reference should always be life itself and not the imagined cesspool of the unconscious."[16] Or again: "I am not particularly interested in data concerning which I have to accept the fact that the dice have already been cast and that life is practically nothing but the dance of factors largely settled by heredity and constitution."[17] Although Meyer had been trained in neuroanatomy and had begun with a rather narrow definition of the importance of the laboratory, he came to feel that this emphasis interfered with the progress of psychiatry. Meyer reported near the end of his life that his "struggle in this country has been with a false conception of science," depending too much on the test tube and microscope as its symbols: "Psychiatry has to be found in the function and the life of the people."[18]

For both Meyer and Sullivan, it was the patient's assets that had to be mobilized. "To use the patient's assets is a more difficult problem than using something under our control," Meyer stated. "It means that we have to search for and rouse the relatively normal person-functions so that they may be made to digest what is less normal and needs reassimilation."[19] Tapes of Sullivan's case conferences provide telling illustrations of this clinical technique. In one instance, Sullivan is asked to comment on the rather discouraging progress of a young schizophrenic boy who is delusional and has to be tube-fed part of the time. The content of the boy's verbalizations is extremely sparse. The staff knows that he has had a love affair which terminated by the girl marrying someone else. Whenever the boy mentions this girl, it is always in terms of the fact that the affair with her is of no importance. Sullivan notes that "if the psychiatrist swiftly comes back with something like, 'Nonsense, you were happy with her,' he may have opened the patient's mind." If the psychiatrist startles the patient with such a remark, he can then pursue the subject further with the patient, as Sullivan suggests:

"And there's no reason on earth why the pleasure you had in her company should be thrown away just because the relationship didn't last forever." . . . I can then become a bit philosophical and say that in my experience any pleasure one has with anybody, even if it is only for a day, is something that it is good to *treasure.* There will be plenty of pain anyway. . . . Insofar as he was happy with this girl, he has proved that he can be human and enjoy life. Now that is far too important for me to leave it alone. . . . It indicates that the patient has some asset which can then be extrapolated into the future—that he might again be happy with someone, even if again the relationship might end badly. This is immeasurably better than being haunted by obscure, practically transcendental horrors which probably are the most vivid experience that the patient has now.[20]

After Meyer left Kankakee in 1895, his knowledge of patients and their lives expanded considerably in various clinical and teaching posts. He credited his wife, Mary Potter Brooks, with refining his theory through her visits to the east-side homes of his patients in New York City; and she is sometimes referred to as the first psychiatric social worker in America.

As early as 1915, Meyer challenged Freud's stress on "infantile sexuality." The developing human moved through a series of equally important eras, as viewed by Meyer.[21] Sullivan would follow this thinking, delineating many of the same developmental areas and defining them both biologically and culturally—a task that Meyer had begun much earlier.[22] In both Meyer's and Sullivan's schemes, the use of language and signs marks the beginning of childhood. Sullivan's juvenile era, which follows childhood, is coincidental with going to school; and this roughly coincides with Meyer's era of the "Big Injun," a term borrowed by Meyer from the Massachusetts educator Joseph Lee and used for an era of self-assertion that appears between the ages of six and eleven.[23] Moreover, all three of them—Lee, Meyer, and Sullivan—posited an era of development between the early school experience and the adolescent era. Lee speaks of eleven as the "age of loyalty"; and Meyer and Sullivan, as well as Kempf, mention specifically the term "preadolescence." The concept seems to have evolved in part out of the American experience. The term does not appear in the *Psychiatric Dictionary,* for instance, which is slanted toward European psychoanalysis.[24] Sullivan considered this era of development—a peer relationship of trust and love with a person of the same sex—of the greatest importance. The fact that Meyer had made the observation earlier and had recognized its meaning in the clinical situation would indicate that it had a peculiar relevance for the American situation. In a society so heavily laden with diverse cultures, hiding under a self-protective conformity, the evolving person had need for confiding in another person who was biologically and culturally like himself, before he could bear to venture out into the larger social scene or significantly cross the sex line. For the emergent person, there had to be a period of experimentation with confiding, with trusting one's mirror image, so that one could express deep feelings in confidence and thus escape, however briefly, the press for conformity in the culture.

There is basically a hopefulness for the developing human in both Meyer's and Sullivan's theory. By contrast, the Freudian idea of trauma in the period of "infantile sexuality" places a monumental block in the way of future maturity—with intensive and enduring psychoanalytic treatment the only possibility of circumventing the trauma, even partially. Sullivan specifically states that the beginning of each era in the developing human represents an opportunity for significantly correcting the distortions of the preceding era or eras. If the person has survived infanthood at all and has some skill at communication, then the opportunity for psychological growth is present through new experiences.

Sullivan's major theoretical contribution—the interpersonal event as the unit for study of the person—can be seen retrospectively as a natural outgrowth of Meyer's early theoretical contribution of putting together the 'mind' and the body in what he originally termed "psychobiology." Meyer's initial attempt to do away with the duality of mind and body was an important step along the way to a theory of interpersonal relations.

The term "interpersonal" was probably first used by Sullivan in 1926.[25] Five years later, Meyer used the expression "interpersonal relations."[26] Both Meyer and White may well have used the word "interpersonal" before Sullivan. Yet it was Sullivan, building on Meyer's earlier work, who elevated a deceptively simple term into the symbol for a whole theory of personality.

For both Meyer and Sullivan, the democratic sweep of their vision tended to obscure the scientific sophistication of their theories. For instance, in the *Psychiatric Dictionary* Sullivan is listed as "the chief proponent of the so-called dynamic-cultural school of psychoanalysis, which emphasizes sociologic rather than biologic events, present-day contacts with people rather than past experiences, current interpersonal relationships rather than infantile sexuality. Orthodox Freudians consider this a superficial approach that limits itself to a single facet of experience, the cultural."[27] A serious reading of only one article of Sullivan's would demonstrate the superficiality of the entry.[28] Sullivan's model is much more complex; and it covers all phases of the patient's life as they are participantly observed by the psychiatrist in an ongoing situation.

In going over Meyer's papers, one has the feeling continually that there was some explicit collaboration going on between him and Sullivan—as if they were in constant communication, sharing ideas in late-night sessions. In reality they were, of course, a generation apart; and most of their contacts seem to have been formal. Meyer occasionally lectured at Sheppard during the Sullivan years, and Sullivan attended lectures given by Meyer at Phipps.

Yet there is some indication that Meyer felt somewhat personally antagonistic to Sullivan during the Sheppard years, which may be partly related to the fact that Sullivan encouraged Clara Thompson in her wish for psychoanalytic training. Meyer had accorded special honors to Thompson at Phipps, and he expected her to follow *his* advice that a formal analysis was unnecessary. When she persisted in her plans, Meyer ended her affiliation with Phipps. Thompson referred to this period of her life and of Sullivan's loyalty to her: "No matter what your mistakes—and he might point them out to you privately—before the world he was on your side. I once had reason to be grateful for this loyalty in a situation where a lesser man might have been concerned at the possible jeopardy to his own status by defending me. I believe that self-interest never had any weight with him when loyalty to a friend was the issue. In all crises he was at hand."[29]

Moreover, by Meyer's standards there was something brash in the young man at Sheppard who defied so many conventions. During those years, Sullivan began his extravagant buying and flouted the Volstead Act; these traits obviously offended the son of a pastor in the established church of Switzerland, who was a teetotaler. The psychiatrist Edward J.

Kempf, who had earlier trained at Phipps under Meyer, reports that he and Meyer once discussed Sullivan's irresponsibility about money. Kempf had refused to loan Sullivan money shortly before he went into bankruptcy in 1931; Kempf and Meyer both felt that borrowing from friends was a grievous fault, particularly when there was no security.[30]

Yet the younger man, while sensing the older man's disapproval, accorded him a central influence on his thinking. Sullivan recognized that the Swiss-born Meyer had been made into a major American theoretician by a series of chance happenings that mirrored his own experience much more closely than White's did. And Meyer himself was enough of a thinker to recognize his bond with Sullivan, no matter how much he might disapprove personally of the younger man. Meyer once referred to Sullivan as one who "for years [had] been active in bringing anthropology and the study of personality together under a lead of psychiatry."[31] In spite of the fact that Sullivan was obviously pleased by this recognition, he characteristically took exception to Meyer in the very next issue of *Psychiatry:*

So great is the power of [Meyer's] conceptual system that one may easily believe that he has in fact made a great refinement of psychology, has finally emancipated it from its medieval heritage. His primary entity, however, is still the *individual human organism* that in some fashion engages in the wonderfully effective integrative use of symbols and meanings.

This common-sense attitude interpenetrates the culture and is powerfully entrenched in almost everyone. Personality is manifest, however, in interpersonal situations, only. The phenomenal presence of personality *in or about* a discrete living being is not demonstrable and need not be assumed. Personality phenomena are conditional on the relevant personal situation, which always includes at least one other person—who need not be contemporarily real or immediately present as an embodied human organism. Persons (personalities) are the entities which we infer in order to explain interpersonal events and relations.[32]

◆ 28 ◆
Meeting Edward Sapir

> The conceptual reconciliation of the life of society
> with the life of the individual can never come from
> an indulgence in metaphors. It will come from the
> ultimate implications of Dr. Sullivan's "interpersonal
> relations." Interpersonal relations are not finger ex-
> ercises in the art of society. They are real things, de-
> serving of the most careful and anxious study.
> —Edward Sapir, "The Contribution of Psychiatry to
> an Understanding of Behavior in Society"

I N the fall of 1926, Sullivan met Edward Sapir, then professor of cultural anthropology at the University of Chicago. Their remarkable collaboration in the next decade dated from this meeting. Both men found in
the Chicago matrix of ideas an intellectual home where they could explore without restraint the possibility of some new alignment of social science disciplines.

Curiously enough, it was Sapir who expedited Sullivan's introduction
to the Chicago school of thought—curious, since Sapir himself stood on
the periphery of the whole movement at the time of their meeting. He had
come to Chicago from Ottawa only a year before his meeting with Sullivan; and although he had had an interest for a long time in the necessity
for collaboration among all the social sciences, including anthropology
and psychiatry, he had remained largely a specialist in the life and language of the Indians in the Northwest. He had delved into the literature
of psychoanalysis as early as 1917, and like other anthropologists in
America, he had recognized that the new dynamic psychiatry of Freud
had somehow to be made a part of the broader study of mankind; yet he
was concerned about its apparent cultism.

Thus at the beginning of their collaboration, both Sapir and Sullivan
stood as outsiders to the mainstream of social scientists at the University

of Chicago, who by that time had a long tradition of studying hoboes, juvenile delinquents, criminals, immigrants in transition to another culture, immigrant newspapers, and indeed every aspect of life in a big city. Both men had studied personality and language within more confined limits: Sapir in exploring esoteric Indian cultures with languages of their own; Sullivan in determining the relation between the thought and the language of the schizophrenic patient on a mental hospital ward.

According to Sapir's second wife, Jean, it was "tragedy" that first brought Sapir to Sullivan.[1] Sapir's first wife had died after a long and terrible illness, leaving him with three children. Shortly after her death, Sapir had left Ottawa for the University of Chicago; a year later, he had married a psychiatric social worker, Jean McClenaghan, who raised the three children from the earlier marriage and had two of her own by Sapir. Soon after his second marriage, Sapir arranged to meet Sullivan in his hotel room in downtown Chicago, where Sullivan was attending a professional meeting.[2] Jean Sapir reports that Sapir needed to talk to someone about the illness and death of his first wife; and he had read an article by Sullivan that interested him. Sullivan's mother had died only seven months before, and Sapir's story of his first wife's illness and death must have evoked in Sullivan some fresh perspective on his own mother's life on the edge of an alien village.

The original appointment in Sullivan's hotel room was at eleven o'clock in the morning. By seven in the evening, Jean Sapir was apprehensive about her husband, who was supposed to return home after his appointment with Sullivan, so she called Sullivan at his hotel and asked him if he knew where Edward was. "He's right here," Sullivan told her cheerfully. The two men had talked in an almost uninterrupted fashion for eight hours. But Sapir did not return home immediately after the call; the two of them could not stop talking to each other, Sapir reported. They were close friends and colleagues from then on, until Sapir's death in 1939.

Edward Sapir was born in Lauenburg, Pomerania (Germany) on January 26, 1884. His mother was from Kovna, Lithuania, and his father, Jacob Sapir, was an itinerant cantor whose work took him from place to place, so that Edward's birth in Lauenburg was a happenstance. Subsequently Jacob Sapir's work took him to London. When Edward was five, the family came to Richmond, Virginia; and when he was ten, they moved to New York City. Sometime after the family came to the United States, the father disappeared; and the mother became the head of the household. After he was ten, Edward's life seems to have stabilized. In this general period, his mother began to focus her full attention on the education of her only surviving child, her younger son having died somewhat earlier. By the end of the nineteenth century, the New York City school system was providing a nurturing environment for many bright immigrant children; Edward won scholarships at the Horace Mann School, followed by a four-year fellowship to Columbia University, where he did graduate work under Franz Boas in linguistics and cultural anthropology.

Edward Sapir's first wife, Florence Delson (shortened from Seidelson), was also an immigrant, having come to this country from Vilna in Lithuania when she was a teenager. She attended Radcliffe College from 1908 to 1911; before graduating, she ran away with Edward Sapir to Ottawa, where they were married in 1911. Sapir was then chief of the Division of Anthropology in the Geological Survey of the Canadian National Museum. Neither family was happy about the marriage. Edward's mother, who was from Kovna, disparaged Jews from Vilna, but the Delsons were even more disapproving. There was perhaps some reverse snobbery in the attitude of Edward's mother: Vilna was the leading center of Jewish culture in eastern Europe from the sixteenth century until World War II, when the Jews were exterminated; and the university in Vilna had been in existence since 1578. It is likely that before emigration, the Seidelsons had had more status than the Sapirs.

An indication of the high standards of scholarship in the Delson family is Florence Delson's entrance into Radcliffe—a remarkable achievement for a girl who had come to this country as a Jewish immigrant only a short time before. Her obvious abilities as a student did not interfere with her charm and high spirits. Other members of her large family who also came to America at about the same time—including two siblings—considered Florence the "blithe spirit" of the family. One of her sons reports that his mother "was a beauty, and a gay and coquettish spirit, and, I believe, drove Dad near to distraction, with her coquettish ways."[3] Of the situation in Ottawa, the same son writes: "Dad was a brilliant, but very serious, dedicated, hard-working, and totally involved scholar—and a jealous husband, who buried his wife (and himself) in a remote, uncongenial little town in a remote country, with no kinsfolk around." Sapir himself referred to his fifteen years in Ottawa as his "Canadian exile."[4] There was no university in Ottawa, nor any art, music, or literary journals; and Sapir, who was a poet as well as an anthropologist, felt cut off from the world of artists and musicians.

If the situation in Ottawa was stultifying for Sapir, who was already launched on a career, it was even worse for his wife. At the time of her marriage, Florence Delson was still an undergraduate; within five years she had three children. Their social life in Ottawa seems to have been extremely limited. There were probably few if any other Jews there, and she was largely dependent on Edward for making friends in an alien setting. In the early years of their marriage, he expected to make a field trip each summer to study further the Indians in the Northwest, leaving her alone with the children in Ottawa. At home he seems to have been so immersed in his work that he sometimes tended to resent the intrusion of the children on his studies, as evidenced by letters to his colleagues.

Even before the birth of the first child in 1913, the strain of the situation for his wife had begun to show itself. In 1912, she was hospitalized in Boston; and Edward found a room near the hospital, giving the address of the rooming house to a colleague, as if he anticipated a somewhat extended illness.

Again, shortly after the birth of the third child, late in 1916, Florence went away to recuperate from what was recognized as a psychological illness, this time to New York City; illness seemed to provide almost her only escape from Ottawa. Only retrospectively did Sapir understand that she had been emotionally ill for some time; he had thought that she was merely "grumpy."[5] Later he would upbraid himself for his lack of sensitivity about her situation and her illness. From time to time, Sapir's mother took over the care of the family; finally she was permanently ensconced in the household, until after Florence Sapir's death.

In 1921, Sapir finished his only book designed for other than a professional audience—*Language*. He had dictated it in "the space of two months from a few hastily jotted notes."[6] As reported in letters to his colleagues, he regarded it as a way to defray the expenses of Florence Sapir's failing health. It is easy to imagine the pressure in the household as Sapir struggled to complete the book in as brief a period as possible. Only a month after he had finished, Florence had a complete break with reality, and Sapir in despair took her to a psychopathic hospital. There were only brief periods afterwards when Sapir would express hope for her recovery. In 1922 he got in touch with William Alanson White, who recommended Edward Kempf as a therapist. But Sapir did not follow up on this recommendation; he felt that he could not afford a treatment process of this magnitude, and he was skeptical of therapy based on Freudian concepts: "My instinct, to be frank," he wrote his colleague, Robert Lowie, on March 14, 1922, "is to let the analysts alone, certainly for the present." On January 16, 1923, he was entirely hopeful about her mental health, which he described to Lowie as "perfect"; but he was discouraged about her physical condition. She had a serious physical problem—a lung abscess. A year later, she died in a Canadian hospital. In the thirteen years of their marriage, she had lived a lifetime of melancholia and physical illness.

The whole experience had been devastating for Sapir. Even after his removal to the University of Chicago and his second marriage, he could not escape the burden of the tragic years in Ottawa. It was this burden that he presented to Sullivan. Afterwards Sapir would never contemplate an analysis for himself; he could never go through all that pain again, as he reported to Jean Sapir. It is clear that he had relived the experience of

Florence Sapir's illness and death during that first encounter with Sullivan. It is equally clear that the two men who met that day did not dwell on Sapir's tragedy as simply a personal one. They both had minds that reached out in all directions. Sapir's story was not unfamiliar to Sullivan. The details varied—the "career lines," as Sullivan later termed them, were unique—but the reactions of each of the two participants in the emerging tragedy in Ottawa were human and could therefore be understood.

It is unlikely that Sullivan had ever been in such close personal contact with a developed mind of this caliber; moreover, it was undoubtedly one of his first intense experiences with a deeply troubled person who was not psychotic. And Sapir must have been almost overwhelmed by the experience with Sullivan—by the quick shift from the personal to the intellectual significance of the data presented to him. After the soul-searching that had begun belatedly in Ottawa and that continued to haunt his days, the hotel room and its occupant, so versed in light and shadow, must have been life-giving.

The similarities in their life histories were notable, as were the superficial differences. Edward Sapir was an educated person, in the most formal sense of the word. Sullivan, who had had less access to good schools, had become broadly educated by stealing time to read in libraries, and by searching out knowledge in an informal way. Their religious-ethnic orientation was of course dissimilar. Both mothers encouraged their only sons—and only surviving child—to get a good education; but urban living and Jewish sophistication about the implementation of educational goals set Sapir's mother apart from Ella Stack Sullivan. For Harry, the more modest implementation was made possible by the schoolteacher in Brooklyn, Maggie Stack, and by the example of Clarence Bellinger at Syracuse.

Yet the similarities between Sapir and Sullivan outweighed the differences. The experience of being a lonely outsider was familiar to both of them. The pressure of being an only surviving child was similar; and the inadequacy of each father was a bond, although Jacob Sapir offered more of an intellectual model than Timothy Sullivan. In that first encounter, an obvious new bond was established. From long introspection about his own life and a close observation of psychotic patients, Sullivan understood that the differences between people were superficial, compared to their common humanity. And Sapir, who could offer strong cross-cultural support for this thesis from his study of North American Indians, was led, through the tragedy of his first wife, to take a new look at the differences between people within the same culture; he began to see these differences as stemming from the intertwining of persons and events, the accidents of fate that gave a person experiences different from his contemporaries but completely intelligible to the observer who attempted to participate and understand the human reaction to this particular pattern of life. What happened to the person—the position of his family in the community, his ordinal position in the family, his experience with teachers at school, any and all of these accidents of fate—affected the person's relations with others throughout his life; but each subsequent significant encounter with a stranger could modify, benevolently or otherwise, the earlier experiences. If all these data on one person could be disclosed in all their ramifications, such data would produce nearly identical reactions in another person. For both men, this way of thinking became more than an intellectual stand.

One can date Sapir's increasing interest in culture and personality from this meeting with Sullivan. By the same token, Sullivan began to move with greater assurance into the role of social psychiatrist, feeling intellectually sure of himself because of the interchange with a first-rate, trained mind. Sapir's early formulations showed up in Sullivan's thinking and writing throughout his life. For example, Sullivan's idea of the "illusion of personal individuality" had been anticipated by Sapir when he wrote to Lowie, on July 23, 1917: "Of course, philosophically there are only unique phenomena in the world. That does not mean, however, that in the typical natural sciences 'uniqueness' is of any value."

Sullivan was still trying to explain this concept to his medical colleagues in 1946:

That there are particular human lives, each with a unique career line, I no more deny than do I the fact that I am a particular person who has a particular dog. . . . He doubtless acts much more frequently in the private mode than could I think that I do. . . . The immutably private in my dog and in me escapes and will always escape the methods of science, however absorbing I may once have found the latter. . . .

Individual differences, especially those which are principally matters of language and customs in people from widely separate parts of the world, may be extremely impressive and may present great handicap to discovering the significant differences in relative adequacy and appropriateness of action in interpersonal relations, which constitute extraordinary success, average living, or mental disorder.

The therapist or the research psychiatrist, however, participates intelligently in interpersonal relations with his confrere only to the extent that these handicaps are successfully overcome or evaded and finds opportunity to gain skill in this particular in his dealings with any stranger.[7]

Although the uniqueness of the person escapes the methods of science according to both men, the actions and writings of one person are expressions of the self and should not be extrapolated as if derived generally from the experiences of others. Again, Sapir anticipates Sullivan. In a letter to Lowie dated June 30, 1917, Sapir writes: "Why do you object to 'I' and 'you'? Do you believe in impersonal urbanity? Isn't it high time we all recognized clearly that art, criticism, and, to some extent, even science are but expressions of self? I have no patience with the conventional dodging of the personal." Twenty years later, Sullivan would set up standards for the use of "we" and the impersonal in the journal *Psychiatry*. He specified that authors must identify their use of "we." Did it mean we in this society? Or we in a particular discipline? Or we, the reader and the author? In essence, the author had to avoid "we" as a substitute for "I." Under Sullivan's editorship, the author also had to avoid the use of the impersonal as a substitute for "I."

For both men, the dissimilarities of experience in a given person had to be defined in order to locate areas of human understanding. The one-genus postulate as formulated by Sullivan—"we are all much more simply human than otherwise"—emerged paradoxically, I believe, from his knowledge of the meaning of the dissimilarities in the opportunities for development in a given person. It is as if the American experience elicits this concept of similarity of human beings, with dissimilarity emerging from the chance of the life situation. From time to time, the concept is forgotten; and a relative smugness descends on the more successful ones. But the best of American literature and science reiterates this theme, rediscovers it from time to time. Thus at Hull-House Jane Addams, brought up in relative affluence as a WASP, had to discover painfully the meaning of human similarity and to abandon the reassuring concept of social Darwinism. Human survival could not be predicated on the chance of poverty, as if the fit people would somehow manage to find enough to eat and the unfit should be left to starve.

For those who had grown up as marginal people for whatever reason—and both Sullivan and Sapir fit this category—the idea of the essential similarity of people, beneath the veneer of ethnicity or social class, seemed natural. At the same time, there was the clear knowledge that one changes, perhaps throughout life, as one has significant contact with new experiences and, Sullivan noted, "finds opportunity to gain skill . . . in his dealings with any stranger."[8] A boy brought up in a household where the culture and the speech were prevailingly those of Counties Cork and Clare could not be unaware of the different standards for behavior and speech at school, where the language and the behavior were rural American. Or again, a boy shunted from one country to another, and from one city to another, in the first ten years of life could not be unaware of the ways in which he learned to speak and act differently when he began to go to school in New York City. As they compared experiences, both of them arrived at much the same position: It is the uniqueness of the opportunity rather than the uniqueness of a given personality or physical organism that spells the significant differences for every American child as he tries to move up the ladder.

Yet I tend to think that in this meeting of two men with disparate training and some commonality of experience, it was Sullivan who taught Sapir that he, too, was marginal—that is, a person of mixed cultures. Sapir had all the trappings of the accepted intellectual who could hold his own in the higher realms of academia; and he had tended to overlook the risks implicit in his own life history. The sociologist Robert Park has noted that the marginal person is potentially in psychological danger as he makes the delicate transition to another culture; at the same time, as Park observes, the marginal person is "relatively the more civilized human being."[9] By fortuitous circumstances, Sapir had achieved the best outcome while avoiding the dangers. Sullivan himself had been in considerable danger as he made a series of transitions from rural home, almost alien to the world around him, to village, to university, to a metropolitan center; but he had survived. Florence Sapir had made transitions of a different intensity; in the space of little more than a decade she had come to a new country, gone away to college, married and gone to another country, and had three children. The nature of her isolation and loneliness had finally shattered the growing fragility of her mind and body in a way that, with more knowledge, might have been averted. Yet this shattering represented no inherent weakness that might affect her children, although it is this kind of fear that still haunts parents today.

So these two strangers found each other and were bound together from then on. Each affected the other's thinking in ways that can be formally documented. But the human bond fit into the stuff of legend as mirrored in literature. James Joyce has written of it in *Ulysses*—of the meeting between Stephen Dedalus, the young medical student, and the older Jew, Leopold Bloom, probably based on an actual incident in Joyce's life, when he was rescued by a stranger named Alfred Hunter. Joyce's biographer, Richard Ellmann, has reported on Joyce's own experience:

Oddly enough, the very fact that they were so slightly acquainted and of such different backgrounds, was what held Joyce's attention. Up to this time his experience of life had been in his own opinion a gloomy vista of betrayals and alienations. He had gradually been "sundered" from parents, classmates, Irish patriots, Catholics. The experience of breaking with people was one he thoroughly understood. Much more difficult for him to fathom than human unkindness was its opposite, and Alfred Hunter's gratuitous help, so different from the treachery of supposed friends, seemed an instance. "Ulysses" probably grew out of a prolonged meditation on the strange possibilities of cohesion between apparently dissimilar men.[10]

The analogy cannot be carried too far, but the symbolism is valid. For both Sapir and Sullivan, the meeting must have seemed a gift. True, they were slated to meet in some fashion, through their common interest in the social science that had grown out of the Chicago scene. But the nature of their first encounter had stripped away the difference in their disciplines, had exposed the nature of their alliance. So the brilliant young psychiatrist was able to define the tragedy of the man before him in human terms; and the skills of the younger man were recognized and defined by the older man, whose more developed mind flashed with genius and recognized it in another.

🐿 29 🐿

Discovering the
Chicago School of
Sociology

All healthy developments in sociology seem to be intimately tangled with Professor [W. I.] Thomas's
work at the Chicago University, and the Chicago
School of Sociology is undoubtedly the dynamic factor in that field now.

—Sullivan, Report to the American
Psychiatric Association

WITHIN six months after Sullivan's meeting with Sapir in the fall of
1926, he had begun to plan on some kind of interdisciplinary collaboration between psychiatry and the Chicago School of Sociology, and
he had settled on W. I. Thomas as the critical person in that development.
The term "sociology" as it was used at that time in that setting included
social psychology, social anthropology, and political science, and Thomas
himself was involved in all these disciplines and more during his long life.
He was in his mid-sixties when Sullivan first sought him out, but his zest
for life and ideas was that of a youth of twenty.

Thomas's life seems to have been relatively uneventful until he came to
the University of Chicago as a graduate student in sociology in 1893, at
the age of thirty. Born and raised in Virginia, he graduated from the University of Tennessee in 1894. Following a year of study in Germany, he
taught English at Oberlin College until he came to the University of Chicago. After receiving his doctorate in 1896, he taught at the University for
the next twenty-two years. Thomas and George Herbert Mead, who were
contemporaries, came to Chicago at about the same time; together they
became a symbol for generations of students of the necessary collaboration between an American theory and empirical studies. Through

Thomas, Sullivan had firsthand knowledge of the thinking and observing that had produced over the years many important empirical studies of immigrants and other dispossessed peoples in Chicago, including Thomas's own monumental work on the Polish peasants.[1]

It was Sullivan's good fortune to discover Chicago social science at a time when it could most significantly enlighten an American psychiatry. Twenty years before, William James had rather accurately predicted the importance of that school of thought, but in the intervening years it had expanded significantly beyond his prediction: "Chicago has a School of Thought!—a school of thought which, it is safe to predict, will figure in literature as the School of Chicago for twenty-five years to come."[2] James himself had stood halfway between European thought and the new "philosophy" that was burgeoning in Chicago. Yet he needed to fit it into his own order of things, so he suggested that the Chicago School had found a *via media* for Concord transcendentalism, his own brand of pragmatism (derived from Charles Peirce's pragmaticism) and the new Chicago empiricism that had begun to move students out into the urban community. The Chicago School had found a middle way, he thought, almost as if this new philosophy had been forced to adopt a compromise in confronting the realities that beset them in that raw city.

It was to James's credit that he recognized so early that something important was going on in Chicago; but he only dimly perceived that what he was talking about was indeed an American school of thought, with a vitality gained from the acculturation of new immigrants. Up to that time, Boston, Concord, and Harvard University, like the monasteries in the Dark Ages, had been considered somehow the golden cornucopia that kept intact the wisdom of western Europe that must be preserved if America was not to be lost in ignorance.

By the mid-twenties, James's vision of a *"via media* between the empiricist and the transcendentalist tendencies" had largely been achieved through empirical studies. The concern with various philosophical positions that had existed at an earlier time was giving way, in Chicago at least, to a recognition that there was no need to set disciplines and philosophies in opposition to each other. The goal was the amelioration of the human condition through careful studies and collaboration between disciplines. The laboratory was the city itself—especially the natural variations of immigrant population, watched with growing humility through the eyes of the two remarkable women at Hull-House, Julia Lathrop and Jane Addams.[3]

There is no indication that Sullivan had any knowledge of this exciting development in Chicago social science during the years that he lived there. He had first come to Chicago as a youth of nineteen, poor and lonely, rural instead of urban, still not assimilated much beyond his Irish grandparents. Thus the Chicago sociologists whom he came to know in the mid-1920s offered him a chance to digest his earlier experiences in the city, and he came to see himself as partaking of an American experience. His nineteen-year-old fears that he was perhaps not mentally competent, his confused fascination with the strange excitements and dislocations of the inner city, the loneliness that threatened to engulf him—all this was of the stuff that the Chicago sociologists had studied for twenty years.

The fine philosophical distinctions between the transcendentalism represented by the Concord schoolteacher Bronson Alcott, in the early half of the nineteenth century, and the pragmatism and instrumentalism of John Dewey, at the end of that century, had merged into a common goal—the development of a meaningful educational and social experience for all children in a democratic society. Alcott had expressed this goal in terms that met the ethical standards of his day. He had originally been impressed with the Wordsworthian concept of each child entering the world "trailing clouds of glory," and this had fit into his struggle to combat the formal attitude of New England theologians who conceived of the child as essentially evil.[4] But in practice, Alcott had been forced to abandon the absolutism of Truth as conceived by Kant and to modify his own ideas on the education of a child as being primarily a process whereby the adult learned Truth from the child; some discipline was necessary in the classroom, he discovered, and not all wisdom resided in the child. On a more domestic level, his search for Absolute Idealism had to be abandoned in his utopian attempt at Fruitlands, in order to save his marriage and the health of his children; he learned instrumentalism in an empirical way. John Dewey's pragmatic humanism continued the search for a good educational system for a democratic society; and this search kept arriving at ideas, such as the progressive standards for good education, that gradually took on a cast of absolutism and adversely affected some child-care attitudes. The attempt was often short of the goal, but the democratic ideal of Alcott and Dewey remained a continuity in the matrix of the Chicago school of thought.

Sullivan became a part of this community of views on childhood education, ethics, and the social order at a new level of sophistication, defining his terms carefully. Near the end of his life, he began to refer to his interpersonal theory as an "operational statement" within a "field theory." Since his death, these terms have also suffered from the Babel of philosophical discourse, so that one has to examine in simple terms just what he was saying about children and society. Sullivan once said that perhaps the only beginning consensus that might avert worldwide disaster is implicit in the sight of a newborn baby and the wish on the part of most people that that baby might have a good life.[5] Unless the baby is damaged at birth, his potential, according to Sullivan, is in direct proportion to his life opportunities. Thus if all children come into the world "trailing clouds of glory," then what happens to them thereafter is of singular importance; Alcott and Sullivan are close in this thinking, and this was the Chicago brand of sociology in the 1920s. Like Alcott, Sullivan had to deal with the meaning of evil; and his definition was a far cry from his own early training in Catholic ideas of "original sin" and from the not too different thinking of the early New England theologians: "Many years ago, I found myself defining *evil* as the unwarranted interference with life. This was not much of a definition but it seemed helpful in that it made the problem an operational one, and the process of tracing warranties for interference might be something at which one could ultimately become skillful."[6] The consensus about the newborn baby and the definition of evil are both essential for our time if the tragedy of poverty and urban slums is to be tackled in other than a makeshift way. Indeed Sullivan's theory is "incommoding to one's complacency," as a colleague stated.[7]

Thus Sullivan's one-genus postulate was merely a more precise formulation of an idea that had been spoken for over a century by each important American thinker in the area of basic democratic idealism. Yet in the Chicago school of 1928, a scientific empiricism had been added without changing the basic goal—the amelioration of the human condition. On this common meeting ground of scientific tools and democratic idealism, Sapir and Sullivan helped to forge a new interdisciplinary communication that would try to do away with the competition between tight disciplines in the social sciences. Sullivan's task was more difficult than Sapir's, for he tried to find a way to bring this approach into general medicine. Sapir felt free to identify himself with Chicago sociology almost as soon as he arrived at the University of Chicago by becoming an editor of the *American Journal of Sociology,* which was published by the University and included a wide range of disciplines.

By happenstance, there is an amusing record of a beginning rapprochement between Chicago sociology and the thinking of Bronislaw Malinowski, the Polish cultural anthropologist. At a 1926 conference, Malinowski tried to differentiate between social science, sociology, and social anthropology in a discussion with the Chicago sociologist Robert Park. Malinowski stated that in America, social science is "the body of all studies which refers to human culture and to human society." He saw sociology as the general theory "which like theoretical physics, deals with certain principles governing all social process." And social anthropology, he thought, "is the application of social principles to the comparative study of societies at lower states of development, with occasional and cautious intrusions into higher societies." But when he was questioned by the chairman of the meeting as to how he would classify W. I. Thomas, Malinowski stated that he believed Thomas's work on the Polish peasants was that of a social anthropologist: "I certainly would try always to keep as close as possible to W. I. Thomas because I admire his work very much. His work on the Polish peasant—being a Polish peasant myself—I would regard as belonging to social anthropology, and we Poles are savages in many respects, as are all other nations."[8] For Malinowski, who had clung to the earlier notion that anthropology was mainly the "study of societies at lower states of development," this reexamination of Thomas's main work was an admission of no mean proportions. At the same conference, Sapir presented a paper in which he suggested that what was needed was a new kind of social psychology. There was a general fumbling for a term and a definition that would somehow provide a meeting place for all the various disciplines interested in the study of man.

Although Sullivan correctly associated Thomas with the University of Chicago, Thomas had been gone from there since 1918, and was living in New York City when Sullivan met him. For almost a decade, Thomas had been largely an exile from his own profession, only gradually regaining some of his formal professional standing. As a role model, he represented something new for Sullivan, for here was a man who lived the life of a Bohemian in many ways, had dared to defy the academic community, and had maintained an intellectual integrity and prestige in spite of his formal estrangement from academia.

The background of Thomas's situation is somewhat as follows: he and his first wife had been engaged in a movement in Chicago to put brakes on United States involvement in World War I by having the Federal government adopt a pay-as-we-go law to finance the war; it was their hope that American taxpayers would be unwilling to go along with the war if they had a current understanding of the cost. But the Federal government was not happy about the plan; and in 1918 Federal authorities devised a way to trap Thomas into a personal indiscretion—not a difficult task, according to legend. The Chicago police were alerted to the fact that Thomas could be found in a hotel room one night with a young woman who was not his wife, and the police apprehended him according to plan. He was arrested, and the news found its way into the headlines the next morning. His friend Clarence Darrow met him at the morning session of the court, and the case was dismissed. The authorities had obviously achieved their purpose through newspaper publicity. Whether or not Thomas was then asked to leave by the University authorities is a moot question, but in any event he left Chicago forthwith, losing his tenure, and moved to New York City.

For twenty-five years Thomas held sway in his New York apartment, and an army of graduate students and colleagues from all the social sciences beat a path to his door; sometime in the late 1920s Sullivan found his way there, too. Robert Park, Thomas's old friend in Chicago, often came to see Thomas, and the two of them regaled each other with stories that became legendary. According to Park, Thomas's apartment smelled of Thomas—his pipe, his dusty books, his endless piles of papers—"as a lion's den smells of the lion." He was by all accounts "at home in the world," as Sullivan would later describe the ultimate in human development. Convivial, genial, and charming, Thomas lived out his life without acquiring bitterness, even though his financial situation was at times precarious. He taught at the New School for Social Research, he had some income from book royalties, and he participated in various research projects. In the vernacular of today, he survived on "soft money." Because of his lurid exit from Chicago, he was, for a time, in trouble with the American Sociological Society; but eventually a group of young Turks rescued him, and in 1926 he was elected president of the Society for the upcoming year. When he was past eighty, he was invited back to the University of Chicago as a visiting professor.[9]

Thomas's career in New York City served as a model for Sullivan and affected his decision to settle there after he left Sheppard. For Sullivan, Thomas exemplified the person who has the expertise of experience and is undeterred by matters of prestige. It was a pattern that Sullivan attempted to follow for the rest of his life.

Sullivan, like Thomas, would live a precarious financial existence in the years following his time at Sheppard, in part because he was unwilling to compromise his intellectual convictions. Unlike Thomas, Sullivan was not willing to settle into a comfortable if somewhat shabby apartment. As a descendant of the West Wind, he had more extravagant tastes that multiplied as time went on, and he depended largely on friends and colleagues to finance both his expensive tastes and his ambitions and laudable plans for research and development in the broad realm of psychiatry and the social sciences.

As a pattern of freedom from official rules began to emerge, Sullivan's acceptance in his own discipline became more and more ragged; the medical discipline in general is prestige-bound by the very title "M.D."; and the psychiatrist, as well as the psychoanalyst, has remained somehow suspect in the general society, so that their rigidities have exceeded, to some extent, those of other medical or paramedical specialists. Sullivan's eccentricities, his Bohemianism, were tolerated by his trainees and his colleagues only because they needed his knowledge in the anxiety-provoking task of dealing with sick people, but they resented his disregard for their growing need to be respected as members of the medical fraternity. Sullivan did not command the same support from his own discipline as Thomas had from his. The difference seemed to lie in the broad humanism that had infected the Chicago matrix, so that in the end Thomas, within his own lifetime, emerged as a free spirit in good standing with his colleagues. Within his own profession, Sullivan is still a controversial figure. He is often the butt of stories about his eccentricities, told with some condescension. But almost from the beginning Sullivan found genuine admiration, respect, and good fellowship with the Chicago social scientists; and as of now his greatest impact seems to be in the social sciences generally. His impact on clinicians has been for the most part unaware and unsophisticated. A psychiatrist of another generation who never knew Sullivan personally has defined Sullivan as secretly dominating much of clinical psychiatry as it existed in America in 1970: "Nothing is more ludicrous about modern American psychiatric writing than our ability to use Sullivan's observations, ideas, and techniques without even mentioning his name. He would have felt like a bastard at the family reunion."[10]

Many of the young psychiatrists who came to Sullivan for training or supervision after World War II have reported on his abrasiveness and what they saw as his need to humiliate them. My own explanation is that he felt completely identified with the patients on whom his trainees were reporting; and when a trainee showed his arrogance or belittled the patient even indirectly, Sullivan's wrath was instant and devastating. Although he never turned on me in this manner, I have overheard several times his exasperation with trainees. He used to have a seminar on Sunday morning in the front room of the apartment where the William Alanson White Psychiatric Foundation was housed from 1946 until after his death, and I sometimes met him afterwards for luncheon, where we would transact journal business. As I would stand in the hall outside the closed door, waiting for the end of the seminar, I would fairly often hear him launching forth at his young colleagues, bitter and sure. His attack would be met by silence; it was very difficult to defend oneself against Sullivan when he was in such a mood. Finally the door would open, and a silent and subdued group of young would-be psychiatrists would file out, followed by Sullivan. He would be perspiring even in cold weather, agitated and discouraged. He would sometimes lament to me that he could not get his ideas across; it was simply impossible.

When he had left Smyrna School for Cornell, he had wanted to be a physicist. First and last, he found congenial discourse only with other scientists; and the science of man that became his most important interest could not be learned in the medical schools, whether "diploma mills" or elite universities. That is probably almost as true today as it was then. His irritation at this lack in his trainees was at times tremendous. In particular, he found that people with limited formal education but with a capacity for human understanding—the attendants on the ward at Sheppard—could more easily understand what he had to teach about the meaning of interpersonal relations in the care of the mentally ill on the hospital ward; there was something in the selection of the medical specialty and its training that seemed to deaden the normal responses of one human being to another. Medical students had had too much formal rote training to be able to learn at the ward level, and not enough formal knowledge of the insights and findings of social science of the Chicago ilk to make up for their needs for prestige.

As for Sullivan, he had made peace with the place of psychiatry, and Sapir agreed with him. "I think that it would be a very difficult proposition to show wherein psychiatry is more of a medical than a social science," Sullivan stated in 1930.[11] And Sapir explained his own nonmedical use of the terms "psychiatry" and "psychiatric": "I use these terms in lieu of a possible use of 'psychology' and 'psychological' with explicit stress on the total personality as the central point of reference in all problems of behavior and in all problems of 'culture' (analysis of socialized patterns).... My excuse for extending the purely 'medical' connotation of the terms 'psychiatry' and 'psychiatric' is that psychiatrists themselves, in trying to understand the wherefore of aberrant behavior, have had to look far more closely into basic problems of personality structure, of symbolism, and of fundamental human interrelationships than have either the 'psychologists' or the various types of 'social scientists.' "[12] In a memorial statement, Sullivan defined Sapir as "a social psychologist and a psychiatrist," although at the same time he noted his achievements as an anthropologist and a linguist.[13] There was a concerted effort in all of this to flesh out the synthesis that James had called for in 1904, to understand the tensions that beset men and that in the end can lead to war and even to the destruction of civilization. Sapir in one of his last papers summarized conclusively the task that remained, observing that as yet social scientists know very little about Sullivan's interpersonal relations:

If we could only get a reasonably clear conception of how the lives of A and B intertwine into a mutually interpretable complex of experiences, we should see far more clearly than is at present the case the extreme importance and the irrevocable necessity of the concept of personality. We should also be moving forward to a realistic instead of a metaphorical definition of what is meant by culture and society. One suspects that the symbolic role of words has an importance for the solution of our problems that is far greater than we might be willing to admit. After all, if A calls B a "liar," he creates a reverberating cosmos of potential action and judgment. And if the fatal word can be passed on to C, the triangulation of society and culture is complete.[14]

Perhaps the professional definition of Sullivan that best suits him is the one that his friend, student, and colleague—and a sociologist—Dorothy R. Blitsten, formulated: "Harry Stack Sullivan was a social scientist whose specialty was psychiatry."[15]

The only significant record of the informal exchange of ideas between the Chicago group and Sullivan is found in the proceedings of two colloquia on "personality investigation," held in 1928 and 1929.[16] White was the chairman of the first colloquium, but the real reins were held firmly by Thomas, who made the first address. Although Thomas was about thirty years senior to Sullivan and about ten years senior to White, it was Thomas who came across as the young man at the colloquium, vigorous and bold, with the capacity to accept Sullivan's ideas as of equal importance to his own; he never condescended to Sullivan in the proceedings of either colloquium.

Thomas ended his address by suggesting a role for Sullivan that in fact he accepted from then on, although it was not his sole activity: "My experience with conferences leads me to suggest . . . that, whatever shape your projects may assume, their consummation would be greatly facilitated by the designation of a liaison person whose sole function would be visitation, exploration, organization. Perhaps you may be able to divert Dr. Sullivan from a brilliant psychiatric career and convert him into the liaison person."[17] Chairman White did not comment on Thomas's suggestion about Sullivan, but it did not matter, for Sullivan had seen himself through Thomas's eyes; and this coincided with his own priorities and spurred him on in the direction he was already taking. The journal *Psychiatry* was the first significant interdisciplinary journal in America, and Sullivan was the driving force behind its inception in 1938. The goals of the Washington School of Psychiatry, which he was crucial in founding in 1936, also largely emerged from his profound concern for the broadening of insights for psychiatrists and general physicians; as time went on, it became clear that the social scientists also needed psychiatry. Thus the Washington School became interdisciplinary in scope, encouraging as students not only various kinds of social scientists but also lawyers, ministers, nursery school teachers, and social workers.

The blueprint for this kind of broad activity is all incorporated in the two colloquia. As Sullivan's career progresses, it is easy to look back on those early conversations and discern the shape of a great deal that was to come. For Sapir as well, his exposure to the Chicago social science beginning in 1925, his meeting with Sullivan in 1926, and his participation in the colloquia in 1928 and 1929 were critical. The anthropologist Clyde Kluckhohn reported in 1944 that "the growing rapprochement between anthropology and psychiatry" came primarily from Sapir's contribution between 1928 and 1939. It is no coincidence that these dates represent very closely the dates of the collaboration between Sullivan and Sapir, terminated by Sapir's death in 1939. This is indirectly acknowledged by Kluckhohn, who observes: "Sapir had no formal psychiatric training, so far as I am aware, and was not himself analyzed. But he had intimate personal relationships with a number of psychiatrists, notably Dr. Harry Stack Sullivan. While deeply swayed by psychoanalysis, he was highly critical of psychoanalytic theory in many respects."[18] The last sentence could be as easily applied to Sullivan also. One can assume that in their many conversations on the growing cultism of the psychoanalysts, the two men had arrived at a consensus. One might also assume that the initial long conversation between Sapir and Sullivan may have constituted the beginning of a significant informal psychiatric training for Sapir, just as Sapir would subsequently teach Sullivan about the meaning of language and gesture in the emergent personality and lend intellectual support to Sullivan's gropings toward a significant theory of personality. For the purposes of this account, the most significant outcome of Sullivan's exposure to the Chicago matrix, as documented particularly by the colloquia, was the fact that it carried within its tradition the totality of the American experience—its diversity, its common sense, its democratic idealism, and its openness to new ideas. He had finally found an intellectual environment that fit his needs.

✺ 30 ✺

Becoming an Advocate

In our culture, there are roles for which the training of isolation and slow completion of preadolescence is by no means disqualifying. From this background, there may come individuals who *finally* mature a personality that stands out well above the average level of achievement, the more in that the carrier comes to integrate interpersonal situations in which he is more of a participant observer than a unit merged in unthinking cooperation. The force of public opinion on such a personality may remain relatively unimportant.

—Sullivan, *Personal Psychopathology*

As an advocate for important goals, Sullivan was staunch and determined; he almost never lost sight of the goals that he first set for himself sometime during the Sheppard years—to make life meaningful and productive for more and more people. He was a creative participant in projects so long as he was not supposed to go along with "unthinking cooperation." Under the latter pressure—the force of public opinion—he would be obstinate and ungiving; and his early encourager, White, would from time to time remind Sullivan that he must observe the "amenities"—a particularly infuriating concept to Sullivan.

The story of Sullivan's organization of the First Colloquium has significance as a prelude to the pattern of plotting and planning that he carried out with varying degrees of success for the next two decades of his life. It is easier to trace out this first major effort simply because he was engaged in only four or five other activities at the same time; after that, his projects were so widespread and overlapping that it is doubtful that any one person was fully aware of the scope of his interests and activities. As he became appreciated for his skill and integrity, his plotting and planning became more subtle and often surprisingly successful.

Thus I remember my own astonishment at his political skill as evidenced at the 1948 meeting of the American Psychiatric Association, held at the Statler Hotel in Washington, D.C., less than a year before his death. My self-appointed role at the meeting was to find new subscribers for *Psychiatry,* so I took my post for long hours at a publications booth in the lobby of the meeting rooms. I knew that Sullivan was staying in the hotel, but I never saw him. He was conferring with people privately. He was living and working in nearby Bethesda by then, but he did not go home at night; nor did he appear in the hotel dining room. From time to time, rumor would float around that some important psychiatrist or other had been asked to dine with Sullivan in his suite. Near the end of the proceedings, which lasted several days, the decision on the election of officers for the coming year was to be announced at a meeting restricted to the membership. There had been a political fight over the politics of the two chief contenders for the position of president of the Association: one represented the use of dynamic psychiatry as the chief tool in mental hospitals; the other, the head of a well-known private hospital, advocated the use of drugs, lobotomies, and electroshock as a more efficient way to handle patients. The battle was fierce; even an outsider like myself could feel the tension as the members began to go in to the meeting room. The doors were closed and the meeting began. Suddenly Sullivan got off the elevator and moved with a couple of henchmen toward the rear door of the meeting room; as he opened the door, I could see the membership with heads turned, cheering his entry; the results of the balloting had just been announced, and everybody knew exactly who had managed the outcome of the vote. Needless to say, lobotomy had been voted out. It was an Irish victory, achieved for a good cause—an occasion for a triumphal entry, *after* victory had been won. The timing was exact; and he had anticipated the outcome so carefully that he did not risk an arrival as a defeated advocate. No one who was witness to that *tour de force* could doubt that the principal mover that day had experienced considerable enjoyment of his skills as he held forth in his hotel room.

A psychoanalyst, John A. P. Millet, who was one of the participants in this enterprise, has written his own account of this experience. "Harry Stack Sullivan remarked to several of us that it might be possible to nominate a candidate from the floor, in accordance with the time-honored democratic process, and thus to break through the hierarchical methods of determining succession to the presidency of the Association." This small group agreed on a candidate and began to lobby for him, and the "hierarchy's candidate was (most unexpectedly, to me) roundly defeated," Millet reports. "This event marked the transformation of the American Psychiatric Association from a static debating society into a dynamic force for improving the care of the mentally ill and for involving the interest of the general public in the 'new look' of dynamic psychiatry."[1]

Beginning in late 1926, Sullivan's first major political struggle began—to achieve a place for psychiatric research, intellectually and financially, in the scientific community. The date marks his meeting with Sapir, which occurred at about the same time as the beginning of his friendship with the political scientist Harold D. Lasswell; both men were crucial in the struggle.

From almost the beginning of Sullivan's career, he had recognized the need for research in dynamic psychiatry. White encouraged that interest, and Chapman had made Sullivan director of clinical research at Sheppard in 1925. Yet within psychiatry itself, Sullivan could find few people who did other than offer encouragement at best. By force of circumstance, he had to find colleagues for his research in other disciplines; and there was, of course, the eternal need for money.

At Sheppard, he had established himself as a therapeutic agent with young male schizophrenic patients. He had begun by modifying Freudian psychoanalytic techniques for the treatment of psychotic patients; in the process, he had uncovered startling new information on the social conflicts implicit in growing up in America, using his own experience in Smyrna as a measuring rod for what went wrong with others. Yet the question remained: Was this phenomenon—this crisis in the preadolescent and adolescent years—a necessary part of growing up in a diverse society? Could it be avoided? How widespread was the danger? Was it on the increase with the tensions of urban living and the pace of the industrial revolution? Above all, he wanted to rule out the possibility that his clinical success at Sheppard could be explained as some kind of clinical magic gift; from the time when he had first examined the ancient geologic relics near the Smyrna school, he had wanted to be a scientist, and that wish never left him. It was clear to him that he needed, as soon as possible, a wider range of data and access to other researchers in the field of human personality.

His sense of urgency probably began to develop in the years at Sheppard; part of it may have been dictated by his fear of a short life, perhaps occasioned by Leo Stack's untimely death. There are several unverified stories of the reason for his fear—of a physician's diagnosis of a serious heart ailment while Sullivan was still a medical student, for instance. Part of the urgency was also dictated by his lost years of struggle and poverty. He did not honor the tradition that youthful struggle in itself was the key to success; learning was a hard business, attended by necessary anxiety, but it did not have to threaten the whole being. Near the end of his life, he would fear that humanity was threatened (generally) by the same forces that dominated his own early life; and he would begin to make realistic plans for the pooling of knowledge on the training of the young so as to avoid the kind of misunderstandings that produced wars—three within his own life experience. In an article on world tensions, "Whence the Urgency," written less than two years before his death, he would end with a plea to his own profession to cooperate in these necessary plans.[2] But he sensed the urgency of what he was trying to do long before then, and he acted each day as if it were his last. This urgency mobilized his friends to support his hopes with money and time and energy; from time to time, one of them would withdraw, fearing that Sullivan was only an extravagant dreamer. He took these withdrawals hard, but he persevered. In particular, William Alanson White, whose hospital was funded by Congress, would periodically have to weigh his participation in Sullivan's ventures against the damage that might ensue from collaboration with a man who had a tendency to cut through red tape, dangerously at times.

In order to understand the magnitude of Sullivan's plan to find a place for psychiatric research in the larger scientific community, one must begin with an examination of the pattern of funding followed by the big foundations as they began to assume importance in the American scene shortly before World War I. Most of them had been set up by men who had limited formal education and no interest in scientific research as such; they defined their goals in terms of immediate humanitarianism. Shortly after the turn of the century, some informal collaboration between various foundations began, but often the terms of a particular endowment were so limited in concept that there was not room for changed needs. In 1916, as a result of war needs, the National Research Council (NRC) came into being as an emergency organization for the "promotion and integration of research in the physical and biological sciences and their application to engineering, agriculture, medicine and other useful arts." In 1918, this body became permanent. In 1930, Frederick P. Keppel, educator and administrator of various endowments at one time or another, noted that nineteenth-century thinking still dominated the awarding of research monies, particularly in the social sciences: "We must remember . . . that the whole tradition of giving has had to do with the direct relief of human suffering. That is what we thought was charity. And the idea of giving with a sufficiently long view to see that research is necessary as a preventive in social questions is not very widely distributed among the people who give." In particular, it was easier in the beginning of research funding, for foundations to understand spectacular results such as those in the field of medicine. Keppel reports that "after insulin was discovered on a very small grant to the University of Toronto by the Carnegie Corportion, its Trustees would [fund] anything that medical research men offered them."[3]

The NRC did not dispense funds per se, but the big foundations depended on it almost exclusively for recommendations on the allocation of funds to particular projects. Various professional organizations, mainly in the physical sciences (the so-called natural or material sciences) had representatives on the Council, including rather prominently the American Medical Association. But psychiatry was a stepchild in the medical profession; moreover, psychiatry could not produce much in the way of hard science that could be used in a proposal to the Council. Nor could social sciences exhibit much in the way of significant achievements, as judged by foundation trustees.

In the early 1920s, there began to be an organized rumbling among social scientists over the fact that they were not allowed to participate in the allocation of funds and receive their fair share. Significantly, the rumbling seems to have been loudest in the Chicago area; in 1925 the Social Science Research Council (SSRC) was formally incorporated under the laws of the State of Illinois. In the beginning the Council was composed of three members from each of seven national societies, representing political scientists, statisticians, sociologists, economists, anthropologists, psychologists, and historians. Psychiatrists and social workers were not included.

The SSRC acted in much the same way for the social sciences as the NRC had for the so-called natural sciences. It had two major activities: first, to make recommendations to foundations on the allocation of monies to projects; and second, to sponsor each summer a week or two of informal conferences between social scientists of differing persuasions at Dartmouth College in Hanover, New Hampshire, referred to as the Hanover Conference. In the evening sessions of the Conference, there were formal addresses by eminent social scientists, including some from other countries. From 1926 to 1930, these sessions also included a statement by that year's chairman or by a prominent member of the official Council on the emergent standards for research. Verbatim records of these evening meetings show a growing preoccupation with making social science worthy of the standard set by the NRC in the natural sciences.

In this search for respectable research, there evolved a curious reversal of objectives as compared with the idea of "charity" enunciated by the nineteenth-century founders of American foundations: A social science project was *not* really scientific if it had as its goal the amelioration of the human condition; thus psychiatrists and social workers were under special scrutiny.

By the spring of 1927, Sullivan had begun the forbidding task of making psychiatry a respectable scientific member of the SSRC. At the 1927 meeting of the American Psychiatric Association, a motion was made and carried that a Committee on Relations with Social Science be established, with White as the chairman and Sullivan as the secretary. The Committee was appointed without much thought and with no specific funds or agenda for action. White and Sullivan had a common belief that the Association should be granted full participation in the work of the SSRC, and that the most logical place to exert political pressure would be directly on the SSRC. White was reluctant to take any political steps that would endanger his position in the larger world; moreover Sullivan was only too happy to begin his own activities immediately—to move around the country and talk with people, to carry on extensive correspondence, to make many long-distance calls, and, in particular, to act as if he had the full authority of White.

White was early made uneasy by Sullivan's zeal in moving ahead. On June 9, 1927, less than a month after the Committee had been named, White sent Sullivan a short note: "Please keep me informed of any developments so that I may know how to act in conjunction with you." Part of White's anxiety was probably evoked by Sullivan's growing collaboration with Harold D. Lasswell, a young professor of political science at the University of Chicago. Lasswell was a protégé of Charles E. Merriam, head of the department at Chicago, and chairman designate of the 1927 Hanover Conference. Lasswell had attended the Hanover conferences from their beginning, and he had his finger on the pulse of SSRC politics. It shortly became apparent that plans were being made by Sullivan and Laswell to arrange for Merriam to invite White to the Hanover meeting that year as one of the guest speakers. Merriam was slow in acting on this suggestion from his former student, and White was embarrassed by the manipulations of these two eager protégés, both of whom he knew.

Within a week after White's June 9 admonition to Sullivan, Merriam wrote a letter to White exploring in a preliminary fashion some such possibility, with a copy to Sullivan as secretary. On June 17, Sullivan wrote to White, ecstatic about this turn of events, and acting as if Merriam's letter had come out of the blue: "Merriam's letter is thoroughly gratifying, isn't it. It behooves us to do much constructive thinking on 'the relation between psychiatry and social sciences' in case we are called to Hanover this year."

By July 7, 1927, White has turned the task over to Sullivan of getting the APA Committee together for a preliminary discussion of the Conference, "provided the matter goes foward to an actual arrangement for the Hanover meeting." He need not have worried that there would be any hitch; by that time, Sullivan had a mandate for some kind of action, and he had his eye fixed steadily on his goal—making a place for psychiatric research in the SSRC. Yet the actual invitation did not come to White until two months after Merriam's first tentative invitation. On August 9, 1927, White confirmed this invitation in a letter to Sullivan, which came as no surprise to the recipient: "The meeting of the Social Science Research Council, as you know, takes place in Hanover, N.H. this month. After considerable correspondence an invitation has come through to participate and I have been asked to speak on the evening of the 26th. I would appreciate very much any suggestions which you have to offer."

In his keynote address at Hanover, Merriam formulated the central problem of the conference as finding a relationship between the natural sciences and the "unnatural" sciences, as the social sciences were facetiously dubbed. He reported that the members were obviously concerned lest social science be but an "impure" version of the "pure" sciences; and that unless the social sciences could find a way to use statistics rather extensively, it seemed doubtful that they would be adequately funded. In such an atmosphere, White's paper on "The Relation Between Psychiatry and Social Sciences," with Sullivan as the lone discussant, did not evoke much interest. White specifically cited the problem of crime as a prime example of the need for collaboration between sociology and psychiatry. He expressed again the idea, old in a democratic society, that "man as the psychiatrist sees him, although he presents infinite differences is from the very beginning fundamentally much more like his fellows than different from them."[4] This formulation failed to find a responsive audience at Hanover; the audience was largely focused on the need for measuring differences, not in asserting the doctrine of mankind as belonging to one genus. Sullivan's discussion of White's paper was carefully prepared and tightly reasoned. He observed that he and the Chicago sociologist Clifford R. Shaw had independently arrived at the same basic formulation about the structure of small groups of two, three, or four. On the psychiatric ward at Sheppard, Sullivan reported, "the studies of groups of two or three came pretty [near to] giving us for our purposes an understanding of the social forces as they appear in the relation of individuals and as they affect those individuals in relation to each other." He went on to note that Shaw had found out that juvenile delinquents mainly operated in groups of two and three; groups larger than four in almost all forms of delinquency were minimal, Shaw had reported; and individual delinquencies were minimal.[5] Sullivan, as well as Shaw, recognized that the "gang" is usually composed of many more than four members; but the gang is actually made up of interlocking small groups of two, three, or four, the composition of which may change back and forth in certain kinds of specialized action, such as an act of delinquency. This important insight on the potential significance of independent findings by Shaw and Sullivan, with its recommendation for collaboration between psychiatrists and sociologists, also fell on deaf ears at the Conference. The question of SSRC membership for the Association was referred to a committee, and Sullivan's efforts had failed for the time being.

Less than two weeks after this disappointment, Sullivan was eagerly seeking another source of research funding. In a letter to White on September 8, 1927, Sullivan suggested that it might be a good idea for White to invite Bernard Hart of the Commonwealth Fund to address one of the psychodynamically oriented societies then in the process of forming along the East Coast. In his answer, White evaded the suggestion that he issue an invitation, pointing out that Hart was reluctant to talk with societies in general and that his schedule was full: "I suppose the only way to communicate with him would be through the Commonwealth Fund. At least I do not know where he is. He went, I think, to Chicago from here. Otherwise your scheme, of course, would be all right." White's use of the word "scheme" indicates his growing wariness; if he had encouraged Sullivan at all about asking Hart to address one of the societies, he could anticipate the letter that Sullivan would have sent to Hart: *Our esteemed colleague, Dr. William Alanson White, has indicated his profound interest in your participation,* etc. Sometimes White had to draw the line; as time went by, he drew the line more and more.

In December 1927, Sullivan managed to get the APA Committee included in the deliberations of various social science disciplines holding concurrent annual meetings in Washington. It was there that Sullivan began to establish a close relationship with W. I. Thomas and to convince Thomas of the importance of a fusion between social science, as it was developing in Chicago, and the psychiatry that he, Sullivan, represented—a contact that became crucial in setting up the two interdisciplinary colloquia on "personality investigation" in 1928 and 1929. Almost immediately, Thomas and Sullivan began to plan for some kind of a conference, and White, still chairman of the APA Committee, became more and more of a figurehead. Thus on February 3, 1928, Sullivan sent White a letter drafted for White's approval, to be sent to the three other members of the Committee. The letter as drafted was subsequently sent to the Committee members, "By direction of the Chairman," and signed by "Harry Stack Sullivan, Secretary":

As members of the American Psychiatric Association committee on the social science relations of psychiatry, we await word from the Social Science Research Council as to a committee of its Council which was recommended to meet with our committee to consider cooperation and the representation of psychiatry on their Council. We have heard nothing of this projected committee since the meeting at Hanover, last fall. The Chairman of our Committee will interrogate the President of the S.S.R.C. in this connection, in the near future.

In the meanwhile, it may encourage you to know that the American Sociological Society has appointed a committee under the chairmanship of Prof. William I. Thomas . . . to meet with us for discussion of common problems and projects for cooperative endeavor on mutual problems.

In the covering letter to White, Sullivan indicated that his patience with the SSRC was drawing to an end, but "I think we can probably afford to wait a while longer.... I have to be in New York City the latter part of next week, and I may be able to stir something of news up at that time."

Throughout this period, there is evidence that Sullivan was heavily engaged in traveling around and talking on the telephone, with the end in view of legitimizing psychiatric research for the purpose of getting money. Much of this activity was not regularly financed. It would be difficult to trace out how he managed, but it is clear that when he went into bankruptcy in 1931 in New York City, part of the financial difficulty could be traced back to this activity.

In the period between the letter of February 3, 1928, to members of the APA Committee and the meeting of the First Colloquium on December 1 and 2 of that year, Sullivan moved rapidly with two agendas: he continued to push the SSRC to see the light, with the encouragement of Thomas, representing the American Sociological Society; and he prepared for the eventuality of a turndown by the SSRC and the institutionalization of a new group of people. Many of the sociologists from the Chicago matrix were prominent in the SSRC and supported Sullivan. Also the American Sociological Society had full membership in the SSRC, and Sullivan anticipated a genuine raid on that affiliation for support of his plans.

On March 28, 1928, Sullivan wrote to White:

The day of reckoning for the Committee on Social Science Relations of the Psychiatric Association draws near. In the report of the committee, I should like to contemplate not only our representation on the Social Science Research Council, but also at least, nominal reference to a good many of the projects under way in America in social science fields having relationship to our work. This means that someone will have to accumulate the data. Is it me? ... Shall we write to the S.S.R.C. asking them what came of the Executive Committee's recommendation for the committee to meet with us and pointing out to them the short time between now and our annual meeting.

I am writing Thomas, suggesting that he assemble his committee of the Sociological Society, so that we can get together with them in the near future. Kimball Young, a very live social psychologist at the University of Wisconsin, is coming through to spend an hour or so with me around Easter Sunday. I hope that he may be one of Thomas' committee; certainly he is with us thoroughly.

By this time, White has obviously decided to leave the affairs of the Committee in Sullivan's hands: "Yours of the 28th received," he writes. "I think probably the answer is Yes, it is *you*. I do not know any other way to negotiate the situation. Go ahead and write them and see what they have to say for themselves." Sullivan is no longer even pretending to get White's approval on the various activities he is conducting in White's name. And White has succumbed to the vitality and energy of Sullivan's will to force two issues: psychiatry must be able to share in funds available for social science research; and psychiatry *can* conduct research.

Sullivan's letter of April 21, 1928, informing White that there will probably be a "round table" late in that year, is the first indication of precisely what Sullivan has in mind—that is, a bypassing of the SSRC by convening a colloquium between psychiatrists and sympathetic social scientists on an equal footing. He does not ask White's opinion, but he does touch base. In essence, it is a *fait accompli,* and he cites the authority of Thomas as somehow forcing the issue—a political maneuver that he has already mastered: "The Sociological Society has appointed as its committee to confer with our committee, Professor William I. Thomas ... as chairman, and Professors Kimball Young and [Robert] E. Park, as members. The only action so far is a suggestion that they organize with us a round table discussion with psychiatrists at their Christmas week meeting in 1928. ... I shall probably see Professor Thomas next Thursday and will have something more to report to you then. I am submitting herewith a draft of the sort of letter that might be sent to the Social Science Research Council." Since the move toward Thomas and his colleagues is important, Sullivan must gain White's support; but he avoids this question, asking only for approval of the letter to the SSRC. Thus he does not solicit White's support directly for the "round table," as he refers to the projected colloquium; and he somehow manages to convey the feeling that Thomas is very central to this development, although this is never stated explicitly; he is obviously hoping that Thomas's endorsement will impress White.

The basic problem of money to finance the colloquium remained unsolved. In essence the Laura Spelman Rockefeller Memorial Foundation was unwilling to participate in a split of energies; if possible, some way had to be found to effect a reconciliation between the psychiatrists and the SSRC, and to avoid a split between the Chicago social scientists and other members of the SSRC. In the meantime, Sullivan continues to act, using whatever credit and funds he has at hand, to set up a plan for a meeting between the psychiatric association and the sympathetic social scientists. On May 2, Sullivan reports to White on the status of the situation:

I regret to report that the Social Science Research Council has not been able to take final action in regard to psychiatry. ... A Committee of the Council has been formed to establish a policy in this connection and to take action in regard of the American Psychiatric Association. This Committee will report at the Hanover Conference this fall.

I am submitting herewith draft of a blank which is suggested for use in a survey of personnel and projects in American psychiatry and related fields. Will you advise me (a) what you think of such an attempt to dis-

cover the status of psychiatric research and personnel and (b) what modifications you would make in a blank used for such a survey.

The survey proposed in this letter begins Sullivan's effort to determine
if any significant psychiatric research is going on; if he can obtain data
on that, he still hopes that the SSRC will accept the psychiatric association in full membership on the Council. The energy expended in this
whole endeavor was tremendous, particularly when one remembers the
other projects in which Sullivan was engaged at the same time. For instance, he was working on plans for a new reception building at Sheppard, where each new patient would come for evaluation and treatment
recommendation; this procedure would be run and financed as a research
project.

Still another activity is proposed by Sullivan to White in a letter written on the same day as the official letter to members of the APA committee. He begins the letter by announcing to White that he is publishing an
editorial on "Psychiatric Research" in the May issue of the *American
Journal of Psychiatry,* of which he was then acting editor. He expands on
the editorial in the letter to White, outlining a plan to ask the APA at its
annual meeting to begin to work out the details for financing "outside of
the regular philanthropic groups" a permanent executive secretary for the
APA who would begin to deal with the "dearth of financial support
which fundamental research in psychiatry has suffered." This proposed
project, to be run by "a scientist of broad training not only in the gover-
nance of research projects but in handling things among philanthropic
organizations," would have a small advisory committee on psychiatric
research to work with him. Sullivan indicates in his letter that he has already found a suitable person, Leonard Outhwaite; the project should be
funded for five years at $20,000 a year. "The one rub with my scheme is
the necessity of securing money for the support of the secretariat." A
five-year plan would cost about $100,000 in all: "If I am any judge, by the
end of that period we will have a great deal of money flowing into good
research projects if we do not have a Psychiatric Foundation itself. . . .
The only trouble with it is that we do not seem to have anything on which
a bronze plaque can be erected." White answered the letter on May 17,
giving lip service to Sullivan's dream, but noting that the "magnitude" of
the project probably doomed it to failure—a prediction that was true for
the moment. Within five years, however, Sullivan would be involved with
others in incorporating an independent foundation, named after White.
For several years after the formal incorporation, the foundation was only
a piece of paper; but by the end of Sullivan's life, the foundation would
be significantly involved in research and training in the interdisciplinary
field of psychiatry and the social sciences.

Since White was not able to attend the general meeting of the Association that year in Minneapolis, Sullivan volunteered to write the Committee's report, complaining only half-heartedly to White: "It looks as if I shall be the goat." So it was that Sullivan, as secretary of the Committee, appeared on June 6, 1928, at the meeting of the APA to present his report on the committee's activities for the year in which he has obviously carried the main burden. In spite of the disappointment at Hanover, the report sounds as if there has been some real movement toward the goal of full recognition by the SSRC of the importance of psychiatric research: White's address was "very well received"; and the question of accepting the APA as a member of the SSRC has "very wide ramifications, and . . . their Executive Committee will certainly not reach any final recommendations before their meeting this fall."

Sullivan's report to the Association on his activities in Washington in December 1927 is almost triumphant; in truth, he has captured the respect of the Chicago group in the American Sociological Society, particularly in the persons of Robert Park and William I. Thomas:

In December, . . . representatives of [the various organizations] which go to make up the Social Science Research Council, held their meetings in Washington. Your committee was again represented, and certain more specific action was taken. For example, the American Sociological Society . . . has long since identified what it calls the psychiatric approach to the problems. It now distinguishes two methods of research. One is the statistical investigation, and the other is the individual investigation, which is called the psychiatric method. We received all the credit that any one could wish from these sociologists because they have identified their case study methods with our methods.

The sociologic society was sufficiently impressed with what we had to offer, that it immediately appointed a committee of its members to meet with your committee, and to see what could be done toward mutual effort. The most tangible result is that Professor Park of the University of Chicago will speak to you tomorrow, he being one of the committee, Dr. Thomas of New York, Chairman, and Dr. Kimball Young the third member.

This impressed your committee as particularly fortunate because all healthy developments in sociology seem to be intimately tangled with Professor Thomas' work at the Chicago University, and the Chicago School of Sociology is undoubtedly the dynamic factor in that field now.[6]

The same report indicates that Sullivan is trying to move toward a collaborative relationship with cultural anthropology, through Sapir's auspices; but Sapir, in allying himself with the interdisciplinary movement envisioned by Sullivan, may have been moving too fast for his own discipline, as reflected indirectly in Sullivan's report:

The anthropologists . . . have recently developed something which is intimately related to our problem to wit, cultural anthropology, and they have shown a very warm interest in what we had to offer. But . . . anthropologists are by no means certain that we have the solution to everything, [although] they are quite certain we have information which pertains to the natural history of man and to human nature, and they want it. They are very willing to do something about it, and I believe in the comparatively near future we will have a committee of their association equally active with that of the sociologists. . . .

I learned with considerable amazement and no small increase in my natural humility [that] they believe the psychiatrists so far have been the mouthpiece of a profound social movement to which the psychiatrists contribute nothing but perhaps an unfortunate vocalization. We don't know what we are dealing with. We merely stand in the forefront and all too often, most unfortunately, assist people who are being crushed by this machine, by the industrialization of society and women, to throw out human values, which we cannot replace, and we have neglected to know anything about human values. No matter what we say about it, we are pathetically ignorant. We haven't the beginning of a clue to the scientific evolution of ethical standards, morals, and so on, to take the place of those which are being swept aside by profound social movements which we innocently at times mistake for newly discovered conditions of repression and escape from the superego.

Your committee I am sure have become the most humble of all psychiatrists and the most enthusiastic. . . . The thing your committee has been driven to is the perception that there is a huge field, a tremendous demand for an actual social psychiatry, a psychiatry which attempts to correlate our over-individual (and perfectly justifiable over-individual in the past) attitude toward the afflicted, the ailing, the criminal and what not, with the mass movements that are going on underneath, with the budding potentialities of man, with creatively evolved social problems that have never existed before, for which there are no historical parallels and about which I regret to say there are no good prophets.[7]

Since White was absent from the Minneapolis meeting, he did not know until he returned from a meeting in Europe how far Sullivan had progressed in his plans for a meeting between psychiatrists and social scientists. But Sullivan has everything well in hand, as his letter of June 28 to White indicates: "Welcome home. I have more than a few matters that I am anxious to take up with you, chiefly in connection with the Committee. . . . Let me submit to you the following tentative idea: that the Committee . . . convene a First Colloquium on Personality Investigation consisting of a superlatively hand-picked group of 24 others and our committee—representing, in actual fact those of the social scientists that have a real message for the world." He ends the letter on a rare note of his own diligence: "Pardon typography, incoherence, etc.; as usual, I have no stenographer." In the original letter, the word "First" has been inserted before "Colloquium" in Sullivan's handwriting. It is not idle optimism; he plans that the First Colloquium will be successful and that another and another will logically follow, until the colloquia will be able to compete successfully with the SSRC for the money doled out by the big foundations.

In his letter of June 29, 1928, White agrees that the plans for the Colloquium are satisfactory, but he anticipates that he will not be able to attend because sickness in his family "may easily, even at that late date, interfere." Since the meeting was not scheduled until December, White's caution about attending indicates some reluctance to commit himself to the mad hatter at Sheppard. By that time, it is quite clear from the letter that Sullivan is moving too fast and too diligently to suit even "the great encourager."

On July 10, 1928, Sullivan sent a letter to White, as a member of the Committee, announcing the setting up of the Colloquium for December 1 and 2, probably in New York City. He attaches a list of thirty proposed personnel, noting that the names of many have been omitted to ensure a compact enough group. He reports ("For the Committee") in this letter that "the committee undertakes to render verbatim proceedings of the colloquium available to those interested, (a) by publication in the January issue of the *American Journal of Psychiatry,* and (b) by subsequent publication in book form." The very next sentence mentions a small matter: "The matter of financing this meeting is still unsettled. For the guidance of the committee will you indicate the possibility of your participating in this colloquium, and give us a provisional estimate of the expenses for which you would desire refund." Although the Laura Spelman Rockefeller Memorial Foundation has not yet funded the enterprise, Sullivan is proceeding as if it had.

White responds with great affability on July 14, 1928. The list includes names that are impressive, and White, as chairman of the Committee, is beginning to be excited about the whole plan. He proposes an important subject for the colloquium: "How culture may be modified." He explains what he means: "At present we suffer in certain cultural regions from an ultra-conservatism which makes progress, after it is perfectly clear upon what fundamental necessities it depends, almost impossible, and the question of putting new scientific facts into effective operation becomes, therefore, one of overcoming cultural obstacles." Sullivan responds in a judicious way on July 17:

I think that there is nothing more crucial to real psychiatry now than is the question of how culture may be modified.

I think that we should have something on our agenda on the question of technique and methods for influencing culture: There is one reason, however, which militates against this. Some of those that I hope will participate fear that there is an undercurrent in social phenomena that is beyond our understanding and entirely beyond our control at present. To open a discussion which would bring in such quasi-philosophical conception as this will be productive of much more words than of ideas immediately useful to all concerned.

If we can make the first colloquium extremely concrete in its results as published in the proceedings, the second colloquium would not only be insured but will be much more capable of attacking the specific problem that you mention, because of the solidarity of interest and viewpoints which should grow out of the first.

In the meantime Sullivan has sent White a note on July 15 to show off the new letterhead for the Committee, which leads off with the full name of the American Psychiatric Association and its officers. Immediately below this and all in capital letters is the name of the Committee on Relations of Psychiatry and the Social Sciences, impressively and properly set, with the letters considerably smaller than the name of the Association. Sullivan has arranged the names of the Committee members in a way that appears innocent but nevertheless implies that Sullivan as secretary is the central figure. For instance, no address appears on the letterhead except his: "P.O. Box 1, Towson, Maryland." The typography is good, the emphasis is clear; it is obvious that Sullivan designed the letterhead and worked over it, with care and some knowledge of public relations. Even the post office box number has been changed for the occasion: in previous correspondence, his box number at Towson was number 15; now it is number 1.

The note to White carries the weightiness of the occasion: "Am sending you this specimen of our letter-head for comment, if any. I had to get something out, to give body to our epistle to the various people that we want to invite to participate in the colloquium."

Sullivan continued to pursue Leonard Outhwaite and Lawrence K. Frank, both closely associated for many years with the Laura Spelman Rockefeller Memorial Foundation, in an obvious attempt to get funding for the Colloquium. There was still the vain hope on the part of the private foundations that the Hanover Conference would accept the American Psychiatric Association as a full-fledged member of the SSRC, and that no independent funding of Sullivan's plan would be necessary. But Sullivan, ever the astute politician in counting votes ahead of time, feared that the answer would be no; and he went ahead with his plans for the First Colloquium as if the money were in hand.

In August 1928, the Hanover Conference again refused full membership to both social workers and psychiatrists. The American Association of Social Workers was too concerned with "particular selfish or altruistic motive," with research as a secondary aim. The American Psychiatric Association was also suspect: "The Psychiatrists' membership ... is very largely that of administrators of hospitals, and you have this applied, practical sort of research I am speaking about." Both of these remarks were made by a sociologist, William F. Ogburn; he was not necessarily reporting on his own thinking, but he was summing up what he believed to be the thinking of the assembled participants. Ogburn recommended that several groups, including psychiatrists and social workers, be given affiliate membership in the SSRC, with perhaps some upgrading of their standing as time went on if they showed themselves to be deserving researchers.[8] But even this compromise measure seems to have been abandoned.

Sullivan had anticipated the result long before, and he had his plans for the Colloquium so well worked out that he was able to bring them to a brilliant fruition in about three months. When the proceedings of the First Colloquium were published, Sullivan made a passing reference in the foreword material to the difficulty of arranging the meeting: "Circumstances left the fate of this project so long in doubt that several were unable to attend." Yet out of the original thirty people who were invited, twenty-one attended. Many of the participants were distinguished in their own fields, and several universities were represented, in addition to the University of Chicago. The Social Science Research Council and several of the funding organizations were also represented.[9] Only three of the five APA Committee members made it to the First Colloquium—White, Sullivan, and Arthur H. Ruggles. Edward J. Kempf was one of the members of the Committee, but he never became active.

At the Colloquium Sullivan was the most active psychiatric participant, for White remained in the role of chairperson throughout. Thomas, Sullivan, and Sapir carried the burden of the discussion relevant to Sullivan's purposes. The fact that social scientists rather than psychiatrists carried the major responsibility in the proceedings is partly hidden in the published version, since Sullivan, as editor, used "Mr." to introduce each new speaker's remarks, including his own, the only exception being "Chairman White." This procedure showed a modesty about what psychiatry had to offer to social science, as well as covering up some of the failure to live up to the original design—a colloquium between psychiatrists and social scientists.

Retrospectively, it would seem that his plan to promote funding for collaborative research might have worked. The two colloquia were highly successful and are still landmarks for scholars studying the history of the fusion of psychiatry and the social sciences in America. But they did not produce any research monies. The depression intervened, and most of the long-range projects dwindled. Some disappeared forever in the 1930s when philanthropists realized that social scientists had not been able to circumvent the great depression, following the 1929 crash. Research money for long-range studies into the behavior of mankind would not again become available until the Second World War and in the postwar period. Sullivan would have plans for a goodly slice of that pie, and he had already helped engineer a number of grants when he died early in

1949. Some of these projects had just begun and came to important fruition after his death, such as the Stanton-Schwartz study of the mental hospital.[10]

By the end of World War II, most research monies came from the Federal government; but again the cautiousness of those who made policy for the awarding of grants led eventually to some of the same problems that existed years before. Monies were given for too brief periods; grantees had to spend too much time writing grant proposals (or finding skilled technicians to perform such services); and often lengthy, useless progress reports were prepared only for the purpose of obtaining refunding or supplemental allowances. Against the whole history of funding for research in this country, Sullivan's achievements must be measured as indeed remarkable. In the end, with daring and finesse, he was able almost single-handed to begin many important tasks that in one form or another have continued in the mainstream of thought even to this day. The minor financial support that he managed to get for the colloquia ultimately paved the way for some of the major collaboration of psychiatry and social science that he envisioned.

ঙ 31 ৯

Leaving Sheppard

Our Board of Trustees is a conservative body.
—Ross McClure Chapman, letter to Sullivan,
March 18, 1930

A T the end of the First Colloquium, Sullivan seemed to be at the peak
of success. Less than a month later, on December 29, 1928, he sailed
to Europe on an unprecedented eight-week holiday, which would include, as always, some work. On this first ocean voyage, he discovered an
ability to relax that he seemed unable to achieve elsewhere for the rest of
his life. He was away from patients and from the telephone; and a continuing sinus pain that had plagued him for years disappeared in the salt
air. He talked of taking other ocean voyages, but he made only one other,
in 1938.

By the time he left for Europe, Sullivan feared that he might lose out
on taking over an important new post at Sheppard, which he had hoped
would enable him to begin significant psychiatric research. Also he may
have anticipated that some of his other plans might be stymied. Thus his
trip to Europe, made at the suggestion of Harold Lasswell, was part of a
new plan. Lasswell was in Berlin on a fellowship during the winter of
1928–29 and was engaged in an overall strategy for setting up an interdisciplinary group at the University of Chicago. The nucleus of the group
would be Sapir and Sullivan, with Lasswell as the junior member. A decade later, Sullivan would review the plans for this collaboration in a report presented to the William Alanson White Foundation, on April 2,
1939: "Plans for the collaboration of Drs. Sapir, Sullivan, and Lasswell
reach back many years and were quite fully crystallized in the Summer of
1930. Dr. Sullivan was to join the staff of the University of Chicago
School of Medicine that Fall, and the three were thereafter to be active in
conjoint investigations in the Department of Social Sciences of the University. Funds for Dr. Sullivan's accession were not clearly in evidence,
however, and he removed from Maryland to New York City. Dr. Sapir
came to Yale in 1931 and plans were redrafted appropriately."

Lasswell, who took credit for first suggesting the 1926 meeting between Sullivan and Sapir, had been unable to participate or to be active in the First Colloquium because of his prior commitments, including the fellowship arranged by his mentor, Charles E. Merriam, the eminent political scientist at the University of Chicago. Young, bright, and precocious, Lasswell yearned to associate himself with both Sapir and Sullivan, who represented a wide range of sophistication in the field of personality and culture. Sullivan, for his part, was also eager to associate himself with Lasswell, partly because Lasswell had access to Merriam, who in turn had important connections with various philanthropies and could obtain financing for projects at the University. One of Lasswell's students has reported that "Lasswell was able to learn at an early age, and from a master [Merriam], the delicate skills involved in raising money for expensive researches."[1]

In particular, Lasswell wanted Sullivan to come to Berlin to pass on Franz Alexander, then living and practicing in Berlin, as the potential psychoanalyst in residence for the proposed new program at Chicago. Lasswell tended to think that Alexander was conservative enough in his dress and deportment that he would not alienate the faculty at Chicago, who were somewhat skeptical of psychoanalysis per se. Sullivan and Lasswell were still hopeful that a genuine rapprochement could be made between Chicago social scientists and European psychoanalysis, with themselves as intermediaries. Alexander did in fact come to the University in the fall of 1930, as its first professor of psychoanalysis, but he lasted only a year there; Sullivan would later report to a friend that he deserved a stint in purgatory because of his participation in this poor decision.[2]

In all these plans, Lasswell was treated as the youngest of the triumvirate; eighteen years younger than Sapir and ten years junior to Sullivan, he was in a sense the public relations man for the enterprise. Throughout his life, Lasswell acted as an intellectual broker for a wide assortment of people, representing many disciplines in many parts of the world. He had received his doctorate in 1926 from the University of Chicago, at the age of twenty-four; and almost immediately he had begun extensive research on the psychopathology of politics and politicians—an endeavor that was supported by William Alanson White, who undoubtedly made available to Lasswell case histories of patients at St. Elizabeths. By 1930, Lasswell's book on this research, gathered from many sources, was published by the University of Chicago and titled *Psychopathology and Politics*. By then, Sullivan was finishing his first draft of *Personal Psychopathology*, planned as a companion piece to Lasswell's. In his bibliography Lasswell announced the forthcoming publication of Sullivan's book, "in which a systematic treatment of the whole field of psychiatry and sociology is presented. Dr. Sullivan has vastly stimulated a rapprochement between physician and social scientist in the United States." Actually, Sullivan's book was not published until long after his death, but the two books can be read as evidence of the interlocking interests of the two men in that early period.

In contrast to Sapir and Sullivan, Lasswell came from a strictly WASP background, but there were notable similarities in the life histories of all three men. Lasswell was born in a small village in Illinois, to a "fairly humble Presbyterian clergyman" and "his unassuming schoolteacher wife." He has described himself as a "psychological only child," for by the time he was five years old his brother, slightly older, had died.[3] Thus all three men had the experience of being for some period in growing up an only child, because of the death of one or more siblings. Sullivan has written of the handicaps of being an only child—and surely one of them is apt to be a sense of loneliness—but there are also obvious advantages, often including special parental pride and attention.

Lasswell reports that as a boy, he was poor in sports because he was smaller and younger than most of his classmates; and he felt himself an outsider and a loner. Most of his schooling up until he went to college took place in Decatur, Illinois, where the family moved when he was still quite young. Both of his parents were well educated for that period, and two of his teachers in high school provided him with the kind of intellectual stimulation that was a part of Sapir's high school experience in New York City and that was largely lacking for Sullivan. Lasswell, like Sullivan and Sapir, graduated from high school at sixteen, as an outstanding student; he, too, received a university scholarship, in this case to the University of Chicago.

Lasswell was clearly more precocious than Sullivan in the scope of his interests and in his reading. Since he was younger than most of the students at the University of Chicago, he early became a favorite of his teachers, including Merriam. By virtue of this special attention, he became somewhat of an intellectual show-off—a pose that he maintained throughout most of his life. Yet he was meticulous in showing respect for people who were less sophisticated in experience and education; and he early developed the concept of "deference" as one of the inalienable rights in a democracy—an attitude that fit well with Sullivan's respect for even the most seriously disturbed patients.

By the time Lasswell went to college, he was already conversant with some of Freud's writings in German, through an uncle who was a physician. His curiosity about psychoanalysis developed rapidly in conjunction with an equal attention to each of the social sciences represented so brilliantly at Chicago in that period. He began to use the new technique developed by European psychoanalysts for collecting life histories of students, of derelicts from the Chicago Loop, indeed of anybody who was willing to have Lasswell interview him in a psychoanalytic fashion. Although Sullivan's and Lasswell's interest in each other's contributions was immediate, they were somewhat testy with each other from time to time. At first Sullivan seems to have been almost overwhelmed with the breadth of Lasswell's readings and knowledge, but over time, he managed to gain familiarity with many of Lasswell's specialities. Eventually he felt somewhat critical of Lasswell's skill in manipulating symbols and his eternal zest for continuous, often one-sided, conversation. Sullivan once described Lasswell as a "psychosomatic monster," after an all-night session at Sullivan's New York house in which Lasswell had held forth, almost single-handed, on some of Sullivan's developing theory.[4] However small Lasswell was as a youngster, one saw him as an adult as large, indefatigable, and clear-headed after several drinks, an appreciable amount of food—and at a very late hour.

Sullivan's first extended encounter with Lasswell was in Berlin, where Sullivan spent most of his time on his first trip to Europe. Sometime during the eight-week holiday, however, he went to Spain, where he "spent quite a bit of time . . . for me" studying the culture in the northern part of that country.[5] In both Spain and Germany, he was exposed for the first time to cultures completely foreign to him; his beginning understanding of the need for a "psychiatry of peoples," as he would later term it, began to take shape, and Lasswell should receive credit for providing him with some of the necessary intellectual tools for observing these new dimensions for his emerging theory. In Spain he visited several mental hospitals, in part inspired by his growing interest in cultural differences in the emergence of mental illness, as sparked by his association with Sapir. To his surprise, he found little if any catatonia in young schizophrenic patients; the painful withdrawal from life that still afflicts so many of the young in this country was not at all usual in young Spaniards in distress.

He visited at least two cities while he was there—one an unidentified industrial city, "a coal port, quite a big city, but by no means a center of culture in the Bostonian sense." The other city was Oviedo, a provincial capital of the old Asturian Spain, "in its own quiet way a great center of culture . . . not penetrated by the Moorish culture, and very proud indeed of being Iberian." In the port city (and in rural areas of Galicia) "it is a common experience to see boys up to, very definitely, puberty urinate quite simply in the city streets. They may turn slightly from one, as if to avert too clear a view of the process. On the other hand, the younger ones show no evidence of self-conscious preoccupation with the genitals, and so on, but take out their little affairs and have their wee-wee and go their way rejoicing. In Oviedo, nothing like that occurs, even in the very poor section . . . [where I] saw no little boys relieving themselves in the street." But *after* puberty, even provincial Galicians—whom Sullivan terms "practically barbarians" in the highly stratified society of Spain—did not urinate in public. Thus the culture permitted the male "to remain quite oblivious to the, shall I say, odious character of having one's genitals seen . . . well into the second decade." But the provincial capital, including the poorer sections, was an exception in that a rigid attitude toward such niceties existed even before puberty.

Information on Sullivan's stay in Berlin is also scanty. Lasswell reports that Sullivan met most of the analysts then practicing in Berlin.[6] There is a rather general legend that Sullivan consulted psychoanalysts in various parts of Europe on this trip, with the idea of being analyzed by one of them; but there is no evidence to support this. The psychoanalyst William V. Silverberg was also in Berlin at that time, and Sullivan, who could not speak German, spent considerable time in exploring the city with Lasswell and Silverberg, both of whom were proficient in the language. Eighteen months later, Silverberg would take over the running of Sullivan's famous ward at Sheppard; there seems little doubt that this early close relationship with Silverberg was of some moment in Sullivan's recommendation that Silverberg take over the ward.

As for Berlin itself, there is no direct information on Sullivan's impressions of it. Sometime in the same general period, he became enamored of Wagnerian opera and was fascinated by the myth of the Rheingold—a myth that ultimately seemed to mesmerize the German people.[7] In Berlin he was associated for the first time with the elite of a great city. Although he had periodically visited Chicago after his student days, and had contact with prominent people in both New York City and Washington, he had been bound by his professional responsibilities to patients much of the time. Now he had the time and the connections to explore the sophisticated life of a great European city—its intellectual and artistic life—and the growing disparity between that part of society and the plight of the ordinary citizen. It was shortly before the coming of the Third Reich, and already the degrading poverty of the ordinary citizen presented a startling contrast to the people with whom he was associating. Shortly after his visit, psychoanalysts who were refugees from Hitler's Germany would begin to arrive in the United States, and Sullivan would be one of the loyal band of psychiatrists and psychoanalysts who would welcome them.

The total experience in Germany pressed in on him and obviously affected his writing from then on. His concern for the tensions that cause wars had its beginning in the 1930s, and it was stimulated by this visit to Berlin. He began to recognize that the child-rearing attitudes in Germany, in Spain, in America, and in Ireland had their beginnings in the religions and the myths of various subcultural groups—some of them dreadful and confining—and largely determined the fate of each child as he moved to chronological adulthood. He had had an intellectual conviction before, but now it was edged with his own brilliant ability to participantly observe. Even without knowing the language of a people, he had tools for observing gesture, style of life, and the barriers created by wealth and poverty. Some of his experience in Germany undoubtedly occasioned his attack on the prejudices that threatened America as well as Germany, exemplified in his editorial on "Anti-Semitism."[8]

By the time Sullivan returned from Europe, the new reception center for patients at Sheppard was nearing completion; for at least three years, he had been actively engaged in every stage of this project—architecturally and clinically. Soon after he came to Sheppard he had recognized the clinical importance of the first twenty-four hours—even the first hour—of a patient's hospitalization, and he had advocated a reception building specially designed for the initial comfort and security of the patient. He was particularly focused on the young patient who was being hospitalized for the first time in an acute onset of schizophrenic processes, for that patient had the best chance for recovery in Sullivan's opinion. In 1926, the hospital had hired an architect to draw up plans for an admissions building, designed specifically to meet some of Sullivan's suggestions.[9] The whole enterprise was fully supported and encouraged by Chapman and the president of the Board of Trustees, W. Champlin Robinson, so that Sullivan could plan lavishly with great assurance. So closely was Robinson identified with Sullivan's ideas that after Robinson's death Chapman referred to the new reception building as a "monument" to Robinson.[10]

Sullivan had envisioned himself as head of this new reception center, and Chapman had originally given tacit consent to this post for Sullivan. But as time went on, a major battle raged at Sheppard around this decision. After Sullivan realized that he would be denied this post, he focused on two parts of the new building—his own special six-bed ward, and the hydrotherapy room. According to Sullivan's specifications, the new hydrotherapy room, which was to be housed in a special 75-foot-long addition to the main building, was to have a palm tree in the center and special imported tiles on the floor. Not all of these plans came to fruition, but Sullivan's interest in them and his proliferation of ideas as to how the room should be arranged never lessened. He himself had an inordinate love of beautiful things, as if he would finally compensate for the bleakness of his boyhood home; and he reasoned that if he responded to beautiful surroundings, then surely they would be a factor in the recovery of young disturbed patients who had suffered some kind of deprivation. This interest in exquisite possessions, often acquired impulsively, would defeat him personally and professionally from time to time for the rest of his life. No matter how devastating the defeat might be, this pattern would not change.

Ross Chapman had been a staunch supporter and friend from the beginning of Sullivan's career at Sheppard. Yet Chapman had early been confronted by two constant complaints about Sullivan's activities—his casualness about money, and his inability to countenance any interference with his ward from the supervisory part of the hospital. For six years Chapman had stoutly defended Sullivan against all comers, for Chapman was basically an unregimented person himself, and he was completely clear on Sullivan's importance to his hospital. By the time of Sullivan's return from Europe, the pressure on Chapman was mounting to such an extent that he had to begin to further dampen Sullivan's hopes. For some time, Sullivan had seen that his years at Sheppard must come to an end within the foreseeable future. Although he was involved in many interesting and useful outside activities, his major interest was still that of a scientist—to conduct action-research in order to determine whether the techniques that worked with a few patients could be used with a larger number. He was not content to remain a clinical miracle man at Sheppard, bringing fame and honor to the hospital, while his research activities were constantly hampered by lack of funds.

Part of the opposition to Sullivan came from the nursing staff; if he were to train more attendants, as he had done on his own ward, to work at the new center, then the role of the professional nurse would be jeopardized at a time when the hospital's income was already threatened. Sullivan did not help the situation; with his sense of urgency, he could not understand why progress in the care of young disturbed patients should be held back by the traditionally hierarchical structure of the hospital.

On May 18, 1929, the new reception center was dedicated, with both Sullivan and White giving addresses; by then, it was generally known that Sullivan would not head it. In another year he would be through at Sheppard. In the meantime, he was busy in many other directions, so that his dissatisfaction—even his anger—was muted. On November 6, 1929, almost two months before he left for Europe, Sullivan had written to White, asking him to recommend an assistant physician to serve under Sullivan for the next twelve months: "I specify a year in that my own plans after that time are uncertain." He reviews carefully what kind of qualifications the "young man" must have. The applicant should be "deeply interested in psychopathology and not too rigidly adherent to any of the existing schools of thought." Moreover, he should have a "deep interest in introverted personalities. Regardless of how shy and sensitive he may be, he must be naturally kindly and patient in the pursuit of understanding of his selected subjects. I do not believe that any person who has had and still suffers the effects of a strict puritanic training can succeed without psychoanalysis and I do not propose to have anyone who must be analyzed before he can function satisfactorily." He suggests, with personal overtones, the kind of austere life the new staff member can anticipate: "The position includes maintenance and a limited salary sufficient for the actual needs of a single man."

On St. Patrick's Day, 1930, a date doubtless chosen by Sullivan with care, he submitted his resignation in a letter to "Dr. Chapman":

It is with a feeling of profound regret that I submit to you my resignation . . . to take effect not later than 30 June 1930.

Throughout the years of our association, I have learned to depend on your uniform interest and encouragement in my attack upon the problems that seemed important, and have come to owe you a great debt of gratitude for opportunities both abundant and unique. I shall always enjoy looking back over these years during which we have come together so far towards what we believe to be modern care of the mentally ill, and towards the ideals of research in psychiatry.

That I am compelled to leave now, on what might be considered the eve of the harvest of fruits of our labor, seems to necessitate an explanation: I have come to feel that there is a grave disharmony between the purposes that inspire your Trustees and those with which I have been at much pains to identify myself.

It has been necessary that I engage in a broadly conceived program in order to carry into some effect the changes in psychiatric thought and practice to which our research pointed. Far from providing the vigorous backing for this program that I would expect from a modern body of interested laymen, your Trustees seem definitely unwilling to give even the necessary local support. Either, I conclude, they are opposed in principle to the activities and values to which I am devoted, or they are inspired by a narrow commercial view of the Hospital—one perhaps including "research" as a form of advertising. If the latter is the case, however much of a "good thing" I may have been to them, such a conception of my work is extremely offensive to me, and one of which I am sure you have been in ignorance.

Circumstances obviously necessary in the development of our program have committed me to activities costly both in money and in personnel. Besides acute suffering because of utterly inadequate personnel, I am beyond any prospect of easy solution in my own financial commitments—made on a common sense assumption as to your Hospital and Trustees. Having on the one hand no extraordinary expectancy, and on the other no external source of funds; being determined at all costs to further the ends that seem to me to be good in psychiatry; I must immediately seek a secure base for my operations, and therefore separate myself from the Hospital.

A day later, Chapman accepted the resignation, suggesting that the illness of the president of the board of trustees (W. Champlin Robinson) was a factor in the sequence of events:

I was very sorry indeed to find your letter of resignation . . . on my desk last night. I appreciate more than I can tell you the personal note therein. They have been good years and years of great accomplishment for you.

Your decision was, I think, sooner or later inevitable. The scope of your interests and the breadth of your actual practical planning in the fields of psychiatric research and education, in the working out of which I would have delighted to participate . . . would have been for an indefinite period hampered [here].

Our Board of Trustees is a conservative body. The hospital's finances properly constitutes one of their chief concerns. The program of building construction not yet completed together with the reimbursement of their

depleted corpus occupies their attention to a degree which precludes . . .
the serious consideration of the necessary expenditures incident to the development of a research and educational program such as you would
carry out here if possible. Under the considerable disadvantages of lack
of money and personnel you have done magnificently. The solution of
the problem of the greater program must, as things are, depend on the
securing of outside funds. It is not necessary to say that that hope, much
in Mr. Robinson's mind and in mine, was built around you as the technical director of such a plan of research. Such a director of high standing is
necessary to the formulation of a research and educational plan and to
assure its execution in order to secure funds.

It seems obvious, however, from your letter of resignation and from
various conversations of ours in the past that you feel too great an insecurity in the local foundations on which plans must be built to commit
yourself to a period of initial months of uncertainty. . . .

Mr. Robinson's illness has been most unfortunate. I shall always bitterly regret that we three could not make an effort to realize some of the
dreams we have dreamed and that we could not have a go at certain
practical plans of yours which I am convinced are of the greatest importance to psychiatry and to humanity.

And so—Finis! But that applies to your efforts here. Believe me, I shall
watch your work elsewhere, under greater advantages grow and prosper
and there will be nothing but a wish for all good luck to you in my mind
and heart.

The letter spells out Chapman's genuine devotion to Sullivan, but he immediately accepts the resignation.

Two weeks after this exchange of letters, Chapman wrote to Robinson
to tell him of this turn of events. Robinson was very ill at this time, and he
died some seven months later. Thus during the spring when Sullivan was
having trouble with the trustees, the acting president was William Dixon,
who became president, in fact, in October 1930, after Robinson's death.
Dixon stressed a tight fiscal policy within the hospital, particularly after
the stock market crash of October 1929. He exercised great care in controlling all kinds of unnecessary expenses at the hospital; for example,
after Dixon discovered that the hospital purchased 31,000 white eggs
each month, he asked the dietician to purchase brown eggs instead, which
were somewhat cheaper at that time.[11] Such economies particularly annoyed Sullivan. The following letter written by Chapman to Robinson on
April 3, 1930, gives some indication of the tension between Chapman and
Dixon, arising from Dixon's unwillingness to make any exception in his
tight fiscal policy in Sullivan's case; it also offers an important clue to the
serious problems Sullivan was beginning to pose for the established order
of things:

In January it came to my knowlege that Doctor Sullivan for the second
time during his stay of years with us was much involved financially and

inasmuch as I have always had a deep personal interest in him and also on account of his position I sent for him to ask him about it. He laid before me roughly what his situation was and we discussed in addition his obligations to the hospital, which had been creeping up. Travel vouchers in the cash drawer amounting to over $400.00 [were] advanced him, [on] which he had not been able to make refunds of [remaining] balances, and he owed telephone bills, gasoline and coal bills, etc. to the hospital amounting to $150.00 or so. . . .

I was from the administrative point of view exceedingly annoyed and from the general hospital point of view much worried. After thinking it over for sometime I brought the matter to the attention of the Hospital Committee, . . . giving them a straightforward picture of Sullivan, the physician, and his value to the hospital—his value as a man and a friend of the hospital—and on the other side, his peculiar characteristics of personality that would permit him to get into financial jams so far as his personal affairs are concerned. I called to their attention his indebtedness to the hospital and suggested that for his preservation and on account of his value to the hospital, something be done to relieve his burden, particularly the cancellation of some of his hospital obligations.

Both trustees looked at the matter from the usual administrative point of view calling attention to the principle . . . that it is not wise as a business procedure to take steps to relieve the personal obligations of an employee who had shown such bad judgement in managing his personal affairs. . . .

I made no argument, admitted that I could see their point of view and the matter was dropped for the time being. I was pretty intensely annoyed at Sullivan. . . . It was not a pleasant matter to have to take up with the Hospital Committee.

I . . . sent Sullivan a memorandum to the effect that the Trustees felt they could do nothing about the situation. . . . Sullivan knew nothing as to what I hoped to do save my remark that I would take the matter up with the Trustees. . . . What I asked for was a friendly gesture from the Trustees toward an unusual person in an unusual situation. I do not know of what value that gesture I asked for might have been. I shall always regret that the Trustees could not have followed my recommendation and let me deal with a difficult situation in my own way. . . . Mr. Dixon talked the matter over with various Trustees [who thought that] to be of assistance to Doctor Sullivan financially would be a wrong thing to do. I took the news philosophically and would like to state that I am sure Mr. Dixon gave the matter his very earnest consideration. . . . I am sure that all the Trustees with whom he conferred read my letters with care. . . . My worries as to the future were not lessened. I felt that we were dealing with matters too large not to be considered formally and on March first I wrote to Mr. Dixon again. I also enclose a copy of this letter. A few days afterward I talked with Mr. Dixon regarding the matter in his office and told him I heartily agreed and in view of that conversation he need not reply.

About the first of March [actually March 17] Doctor Sullivan sent in his letter of resignation. I did not expect it for some months and I hoped that during those months something might occur to mitigate his difficulties. . . . I know you are disappointed in Sullivan's going. It was my hope that in carrying out the plans you and I had in mind for the securing of money that they might be so developed as to give him a feeling of security and a salary adequate to his scientific abilities. We must not forget that there was always a question as to how long we could count on him. He was always an administrative problem along certain lines on account of his inability to behave patiently toward the average individual. He never has been able to adapt himself with patience to many of the people about him. One thing that hurt him was my regretfully having to cancel plans for his taking over the administration of the Reception Building. That was quite out of the question on account of the impossibility of his co-operating with other administrative departments.

He has not definitely contracted with any institution or group for the future but I imagine he will go to Chicago or New York where there are a good many people interested in him, as you know.

Affairs at the hospital are going quite satisfactorily. We are not going into . . . "the red" and have no intention of doing so.

Sullivan's value to the hospital continued long after he left. Indeed, Sheppard probably still prospers from his connection with it. Thus in a history of Sheppard, published in 1971, Sullivan is highlighted as "one of the two most influential psychiatrists ever associated with the Hospital."[12]

After Chapman and Sullivan's sad sundering in 1930, they remained the best of friends. In the middle of the 1940s, near the end of life for both of them, Sullivan would urge Chapman toward life, even though they both knew that Chapman was terminally ill. J. Ruthwin Evans, Sullivan's former assistant, was summoned from Sheppard to take care of Chapman in this last long illness, and he has described the way in which Sullivan kept up Chapman's morale. At the beginning of his illness, Chapman gave up and stayed in bed. Under Sullivan's insistence, a new program evolved. Sullivan would drive himself over from Bethesda to Towson, carrying an oxygen tank in the car, for by that time Sullivan, too, was in bad shape, and seldom drove himself anywhere. But Chapman's needs superseded Sullivan's own health problems. "You're not dead yet," Sullivan would tell Chapman; and he would get him up out of bed so that they could ride through the Maryland countryside together. Under this kind of unsentimental prodding, Chapman was induced to take several trips to Washington where he would take a room at a hotel and entertain his old friends from the past, many of whom he had known since his days at St. Elizabeths thirty years before. Undoubtedly this kind of activity, liberally spiced with alcohol, prolonged Chapman's life and made his exit take on the character of a pre-death Irish wake.

⤟ 32 ⤠

The Descent of the Axe

The axe has descended on my hope for an immediate
beginning of progress on the psychiatric education
matter.
—Sullivan, letter to William Alanson White,
May 21, 1930

D URING the period when Sullivan was beginning to abandon plans
for research at Sheppard, he was vigorously campaigning for the
improvement of psychiatric education for the general medical student.
He envisioned a new Flexner report on the state of psychiatric education
in medical schools, with recommendations for basic changes. In this pursuit he became immersed in a series of political moves among various
segments of the professional community. His goals were eventually frustrated, especially by White, who had been so important to Sullivan in his
beginning career.

To begin with, White was in competition with Meyer—at a most discreet level—in a variety of forums. One direct clue to this is found in
White's plans for an international committee on mental hygiene. Meyer
had been instrumental in founding the National Committee for Mental
Hygiene (NCMH) in 1907. Although White had been active in this organization, his position was always very much subsidiary to Meyer's; indeed
there was never much recognition of White's contribution within this
group. In the mid-twenties, White began to plan for his international
conclave, variously conceived and titled as time went on. In 1928, realizing that he would be unable to attend the meetings of the American
Psychiatric Association that year, White wrote to Sullivan on May 17, requesting his help in obtaining the support of the Association for his
planned "Congress" two years later: "I hope . . . that you will support my
. . . idea against any subtle destructive agencies." White did not specify in

his letter where the trouble would come from, but Sullivan was well aware that Meyer was the person that White feared. In answering White's letter, Sullivan refers to the current president of the Association, which was Meyer; he encourages White in his plans for an international congress, indicates his support, and states that he "shall certainly do everything in my power to bring it about. I had an idea that the good President might offer some—if not subtle, at least obscure, suggestions, which would not further it markedly. Present indications are, however, that he will concern himself largely with a topic on which he is certainly well qualified to speak, to wit, historic retrospect and prospectus of American psychiatric thought."

With this as a backdrop, it is relatively easy to see that White let Sullivan act as a trial balloon as another territorial battle began over who would be in charge of upgrading psychiatric education in this country. It was a field in which White was enormously interested; at the same time, he knew better than anybody else the necessity of preserving the amenities. But when the political battle was joined in the spring of 1930, White finally withdrew his support of Sullivan in spite of the fact that he had strongly supported Sullivan's activities in this area for almost a year.

Sullivan's first published expression of the scope of the problem had appeared in 1927 as an editorial in the *American Journal of Psychiatry* entitled "Medical Education," written when he was acting editor of the journal.[1] In the same issue, the journal published a paper by the psychiatrist Frankwood E. Williams entitled "Psychiatry and Its Relation to the Teaching of Medicine," originally given as an address at the 1926 Association meeting.[2] Williams cited the experience of the young physician in private general medical practice who finds that most of his patients suffer stress reactions that he is incapable of treating. Sullivan used Williams's address to add his voice to the growing concern about the inferior caliber of psychiatric education in medical schools. In his carefully prepared editorial on "Medical Education," Sullivan reviewed the relevant thinking of Sir William Osler, Alexis Carrel, and Abraham Flexner, ending with a plea for action: "Let us, as psychiatrists and particularly as teachers of medical students, . . . renew our efforts to preserve 'the man as a person' from total extinction within medicine. . . . The teaching of an elementary knowledge of how men live, love, hate, and deceive themselves—yea, of how students in medical school compromise, substitute and evade personal problems—this is still good and useful. As time wings its way, the words of our leading internists and specialists may penetrate to the curriculum-makers. When that happy day is at hand, your graduates will be prepared for the seventy per cent of their patients' troubles with which they now have no ability to cope."

In the summer before the Second Colloquium, held at the end of 1929, when the growing interest in the work of that group was becoming increasingly apparent to a wider circle of social scientists and psychiatrists, Sullivan began to think in earnest about using the Colloquia Committee—formally the Committee on Relations with the Social Sciences, as it came to be named by the Association—as a nuclear organization for tackling the work of planning a comprehensive medical curriculum. Contrary to the record of most of the committees in the Association, the Colloquia Committee, primarily through the diligence of Sullivan, had been active and highly successful. Sullivan began to realize that the problem of psychiatric education might be combined with the work of the group already coalescing around the two colloquia. On August 10, 1929, Sullivan addressed a letter to White as chairman of the Colloquia Committee, raising this possibility. He noted that in 1926, when Williams first called for improved psychiatric education for all medical students, the governing Council of the Association had referred the matter to a committee, where the matter had remained dormant. He ended by proposing that the Colloquia Committee set up a conference near the end of that year, "perhaps in Atlantic City," to begin to look at the problem of improving psychiatric education: "It seems to me that a workable group of real medical and related educators getting together in a location where no university influence is centered and being steered rather resolutely to the expression of its views would give us in the proceedings of that meeting a very important point of departure for actual achievement in the field of psychiatric education."

White answered Sullivan's letter promptly, on August 12, 1929, expressing his "hearty accord" with Sullivan. But in a rather indirect fashion, he reminds Sullivan that other people have a vested interest, including himself, in this particular activity. He goes on characteristically to remind Sullivan that "the proper method of procedure would be to communicate with the [APA governing] Council and with [its chairman] and be sure that all the amenities are observed."

On August 21, Sullivan again writes to White and reports on the thinking of other members of the Committee; he is able to report that one of the Colloquia Committee members has been in touch with Williams, who supports this plan. The enlistment of Williams is important, for he is an active member of Meyer's NCMH. The one part of the plan that seems difficult is securing funds for the holding of the conference; Sullivan reports confidentially that he is "hoping that the Rockefeller interests will feel we are a valuable stepchild of theirs, capable of dissipating their money in peculiarly significant fashions." But he expresses doubt that money can be found for financing psychiatric investigations.

In Sullivan's letter of August 29, he conveys a further note of pessimism about possible funding. He has begun to change his strategy, for he is no longer acting in a sub rosa fashion. He intends to write to the president of the Association and tell him about the plans. And he adds an interesting postscript to the letter: "I am attaching a carbon copy of a communication which I am taking the outrageous liberty of addressing to the Chairman [Adolf Meyer] of the [APA] Committee on Graduate Education in Psychiatry! This is the most that I am willing to do with said Committee, toward preserving the well known amenities."

White and Sullivan exchange some further notes on strategies to preserve "the well-known amenities." But after a White letter of September 10, there is a curious hiatus in Sullivan's files on the matter of psychiatric education until April 1930. In the meantime there are certain indications that the establishment has begun to chafe under Sullivan's prodding and determination. He has assumed the position of a gadfly on too many politically powerful people in the APA, at the Rockefeller philanthropies, and at the National Committee for Mental Hygiene. Apparently the NCMH itself has decided to leap into the problem of psychiatric education and has appointed its own committee to investigate the matter, with White as chairman and with Ruggles (one of the original members of the Colloquia Committee) and Frankwood Williams as members; Sullivan's name is conspicuously absent. White has obviously accepted the assignment as the easy way out of the political tension developing over Sullivan's determination to get something done and his dedication to change—always an intimidating procedure for the established order.

When directly outmaneuvered, Sullivan was usually willing to bide his time, but he did not give up. In veiled references to the matter in letters to White, he is conciliatory and accepting. From some experience in such matters, he realizes that over time he may be able to accomplish something, simply because no one else will have the time or take the time, without guaranteed recompense, to do the endless correspondence and planning that are necessary. Also there is clear evidence in Sullivan's letters to White on the approaching Second Colloquium that the Rockefeller philanthropies have begun to put a tighter rein on the relative freedom of that group; its budget is cut so that the pleasant entertainment that marked the First Colloquium must be foregone, as reported in Sullivan's letter to White of October 10, 1929, and each member of the Colloquium is expected to pay for his travel and hotel expense. Moreover, the Colloquium is to be held jointly by the American Psychiatric Association and the Social Science Research Council, with the latter exercising control over the funding—a curious switch from the earlier reluctance of the Council to accept the APA as a full member. Part of the SSRC's growing interest is obviously related to Sullivan's success in organizing the First Colloquium *and* in obtaining money from one of the Rockefeller philanthropies. The closer control over money in the funding of the Second Colloquium reflects the growing feeling that Sullivan tends to overextend himself, without authority, and then expects to be refunded. Thus the funding group insists that the proceedings of the Second Colloquium should be published but that it is unwilling to pay the printing costs. Subsequently the proceedings were published at great expense in the *American Journal of Psychiatry,* undoubtedly arranged by Sullivan, with or without preliminary authorization by the Association.

As formal chairman of the Colloquia Committee, White announces at the last moment that he is unable to attend the Second Colloquium. Under the guidance of Sullivan and Lasswell as co-chairmen, the Colloquium holds another even more impressive meeting. By the standards of most such gatherings the meeting was a model for the free interchange of ideas. Sullivan, for one, even dared to challenge the training for medical research at Johns Hopkins; although the Medical School had been established as a research training institution, no such organized program existed, according to Sullivan. Under Sullivan's leadership at the Colloquium there began to be talk of a new degree—what Sullivan termed "Doctor of Mental Medicine." Such radical talk obviously was a direct challenge to several people; without any doubt, one such person was Adolf Meyer.

By this time White again begins to feel that he and Sullivan may be able to keep control of the plans for upgrading psychiatric education. On April 14, 1930, Sullivan again opens the subject of psychiatric education in a letter to White. He chides White for the inactivity of the NCMH committee. Two days later, Sullivan submits to White a proposed report to the APA on the work of the Second Colloquium. The Association meeting overlaps with the meeting of White's international congress, so that Sullivan is well aware that if anything is to be accomplished at the Association meeting on the matter of psychiatric education, he, Sullivan, will have to carry the responsibility; technically, of course, White should be the person to make the report. In this draft report, Sullivan makes another plea that the Association take responsibility for working out the curricula and plans for such a program.

In a letter dated April 19, 1930, White gives Sullivan the green light to press for action. Also, he finally takes note of the reality of Sullivan's leaving Sheppard and comments on the importance of Sullivan's work in several fields:

I am sorry to learn that you are about to leave Sheppard, but have been expecting it for some time for some reason or other which is not very definite in my mind. . . .

With regard to medical education, the group that you mention have not done anything as yet, because of the burden of the International Congress, but I expect will do something following that. At the meeting in Washington I think the Association should be advised of the situation, for I believe they ought to be back of any effort that looks to providing psychiatrists by enhancing the curriculum of the medical schools along psychiatric lines or in the way of post-graduate opportunities. The future of the psychiatric field depends so much upon this move that the Association needs very much to be a part of it. . . .

I am much interested in what the census of institutional surveys* will show, that it will show the desirability of graduate work in the social sciences interests me very much, for I am sure there is here a wide field not only for research, but for great usefulness which the social sciences need to appreciate quite as fully, if not more so, than the psychiatrist.

With regard to your own relation to the [Colloquia] Committee, I have the following to say: I think it is exceedingly doubtful, in fact quite improbable, if the accomplishments of the Committee would have amounted to anything like they have except for your own personal interest, activities, and endeavors. Having a real belief, therefore, in the usefulness of the work which the Committee may do, I am very loath to see you leave it or alter your relations to it, unless perchance you take its chairmanship, which I should be very glad to relinquish to you if that would insure your continued activities.

On the surface, Sullivan proceeds as if there has been no change in White's attitude toward Sullivan in the matter of psychiatric education. White has gauged Sullivan's reaction very precisely. By April 30, only eleven days after White wrote this magnanimous letter, Sullivan has acted on the encouragement and sends White a well-thought-out and comprehensive plan for the formation of a "Joint Committee on Psychiatric Education," which he has deftly—and logically—related to the work of the Colloquia Committee. Citing the Flexner report again, he outlines the necessity for the complete independence of this Joint Committee, with social scientists, medical educators, and psychiatrists represented as equals and independent of individual affiliated associations. He is obviously buoyed up by White's full recognition of his importance to the Colloquia Committee; with his characteristic energy and optimism, he sees the old Committee assuming, phoenix-like, a new and more important role, requiring extensive rethinking and replanning. Sullivan makes one radical departure in this proposal: he nominates himself as the chairman of this joint committee. Observing the amenities, he states that White is "utterly indispensable, and should be Chairman. The person who grinds at the job, however, will need any little prestige that he can get from the title." As the story continues, this nomination of himself may have been crucial. The funding foundations may have been alarmed because of Sullivan's growing reputation for financial irresponsibility, although many of the unauthorized expenses came out of Sullivan's pocket and eventually became part of his bankruptcy proceedings. And some of

---

* Through his post at the *American Journal of Psychiatry*, Sullivan had been engaged in conducting a survey of mental hospitals to determine staffing, patient population, ongoing research, and need for social scientists. (This was a survey he had suggested to White two years before.)

the psychiatrists within the Association began to resent his growing reputation as a pioneer in the field of interdisciplinary investigations.

In Sullivan's working papers, which he sent to White with the April 30
letter, he develops lists of proposed members of this Joint Committee. In
his final version, as a mark of political acumen, William H. Welch of
Johns Hopkins, then eighty years old and revered as the father of modern
American medicine, is listed as "(Honorary) Chairman," with Sullivan
still the de facto chairman. The name of Adolf Meyer "at Johns Hopkins"
appears only in a subsidiary position as an "advisory contact." Sullivan
also includes in this subsidiary listing the name of a psychiatrist from the
University of Colorado, Franklin Ebaugh; in a few months Ebaugh
would assume control of the whole effort—a turn of events that Sullivan
could not have anticipated.

Part of White's new hopefulness is related to a conversation White had
had with Barry Smith of the Commonwealth Fund earlier in that same
year; Smith had shown some interest in supporting a project on psychiatric education, as White told Sullivan when they were returning home on
the same train from a New York meeting. So there was fresh money in
sight; that prospect, together with White's encouragement, enlivened
Sullivan to move again with increasing swiftness for some resolution of
the whole matter.

On May 2, 1930, only two days after Sullivan's long letter to White
with detailed plans for psychiatric education, White sent a letter to Earl
D. Bond, the president of the APA:

I think the situation is too urgent for the Association to pass the matter
any longer. . . . Now Sullivan, whose energy and persistency you probably
appreciate, has been doing a good deal of work in a preliminary way on
this thing. He has shown what he can do in the work of the Committee on
Social Science Relations. We have worked up what looks like a feasible
plan for doing something about under-graduate psychiatric training and I
think he is probably the man to do the work.

Chapman will explain why I think that Sullivan should be the effective
head of a joint committee. I think that William Welch will be glad to take
honorary chairmanship. It seems to me that it is a good plan but it will
require some handling in council, and I will be out of the picture because
of the [International] Congress.

As soon as Bond received the letter, he conferred with Chapman on the
proposal. Everything seemed well worked out for the Association meeting, which would begin three days later in Washington, D.C. At that
meeting, Sullivan gave the report of the Colloquia Committee in the
absence of White. He noted the success of the Second Colloquium—a
"more highly integrated" meeting than the First—and reported on three
proposals. The first concerned the life history method, which should be
"subjected to cooperative research investigation" so that it could be more

useful in studying personality. The second proposal concerned data from cultural anthropologists on different societies, values, and rules for acculturation, to serve as a kind of ad hoc control group for studying the values and rules of the American society. The third recommendation emerged from the repeated expression in the Second Colloquium of the pressing need for competently trained psychiatrists in approaching any of the great problems that beset society generally. In an impassioned plea to the Association, Sullivan, speaking for the Committee, issued a call for action:

We are confronted by a matter amounting to a national emergency— one not alone of producing psychiatrists enough to meet the need, but one of producing in large numbers, psychiatrists competent to handle the extremely involved [social] problems for which their aid is more and more insistently requested. Any mistakes and shortcomings in psychiatry are bound to repercuss gravely upon the social situation, and we have come to a time when any recklessness or stupidity on our part represents not only an injury to the persons directly concerned but an event from which radiate evil consequences of the most extraordinary variety.... Psychiatric education thus becomes one of the great issues that we must meet....

Your Committee on Relations with the Social Sciences recommends, therefore, that you consider the authorization of four of your members and an alternate to meet with these medical educators, a criminologist, and a representative of the social sciences generally, with power to form a Joint Committee on Psychiatric Education, to study ways and means for bringing about sound and timely remedy of the existing dearth of psychiatrists, seeking for that purpose such funds, expert advice, and other facilities as it may deem wise and expedient.[3]

The report, approved by White and read by Sullivan at the Association meeting, made a specific recommendation on the method for setting up the Joint Committee on Psychiatric Education. Bond, as president, called for a motion from the floor, and Chapman made the motion; it was passed and the matter was referred back to the Association Council for the selection of the five delegates who would be charged with forming a joint committee of social scientists and medical educators on the matter of psychiatric education in general medical training.

As the chief designer of the whole plan, Sullivan made recommendations to the Council, with White's approval, on the membership of the preliminary committee with the task of setting up the Joint Committee. White would be chairman, but Sullivan, as a member, would do most of the work. But, as it turned out, White was excluded by the Association Council; although Sullivan was included, the other names suggested by Sullivan were disregarded. A political battle behind the scenes had changed the nature of the plans for psychiatric education. The removal of White as chairman had effectively taken away Sullivan's power in any further work.

As one reconstructs the story of what has happened, White has himself become a target of certain factions in the Association. The Association held its meetings that year in Washington at the Willard Hotel between May 6 and 9. At the same time and in the same hotel, White was holding forth as the head of the First International Congress of Mental Hygiene. Some of the Association members were annoyed with White over the juxtaposition of meetings; in the voluminous reports of all kinds of meetings in the general field of neurology and psychiatry, routinely carried by the *American Journal of Psychiatry,* there is no mention in the 1930 or 1931 volumes of this International Congress. Moreover, some psychiatrists favored limiting the task of evaluating psychiatric education to their own discipline exclusively, opposing the inclusion of social scientists and medical educators, as advocated by Sullivan and White.

Characteristically, the funding foundations began to withdraw from the fray. As money for grants became scarcer under the impact of the great depression, foundation members kept clear of fights between warring contenders within a discipline. Sometime during the week when the International Congress was meeting, White had another conversation with Barry Smith of the Commonwealth Fund, in which Smith indicated that he would not fund the plan; but White did not tell Sullivan of this defeat for about five weeks. In that period, Sullivan continued to act in trying to salvage the situation, and Smith, who did not want to give the bad news to Sullivan, set up an impossible deadline for submitting a proposal to the Commonwealth Fund. As Sullivan realized that the whole idea of a joint committee, operating independently of all the various associations and with full representation from the social sciences, was being abandoned, he suggested to White that they cut their ties with the Association and set up an independent committee which would form a "Joint Commission." In a letter to White on May 13, he wonders "whether my calm placing myself at the helm of this venture wipes out its possibilities, especially in the matter of financing, I do not know. If so, out I go. Or out goes the plan." He asks White for his advice in this matter, but there is no word from White. On May 21, Sullivan finally receives the news of the end to his plans from Barry Smith, and he writes to White in a bitter mood: "The axe has descended on my hope for an immediate beginning of progress on the psychiatric education matter, this in the shape of advice from Barry Smith that he has conferred with Dr. White, Dr. Ruggles, and Dr. Williams [as members of the NCMH psychiatric education committee] . . . and does not feel that the matter is sufficiently mature to warrant putting it before the Board of the [Commonwealth] Fund at the present time."

By June 14, Sullivan realizes that White has abandoned any work with him on the matter of psychiatric education. He again writes to White to clear up several matters before leaving Sheppard, "around the middle of July." He reports to White that he has been working "some fifteen hours a day since the meeting, in getting the typescript of my book in shape for consideration by the editorial board to which I have finally submitted it." (This is the book *Personal Psychopathology,* which Sullivan later withdrew from publication on the advice of some of his colleagues who thought that it was a premature statement of his theory—another defeat.)[4] He then confronts White with the fact that he no longer supports Sullivan's plans on medical education: "As to the [independent Joint] Commission on Psychiatric Education; for reasons chiefly intuitive I feel that your active enthusiasm has not attached to this proposition." White has been confronted, and he finally wields the axe himself. In the end, White has accepted the fact that he himself has been defeated in his hopes for an interdisciplinary joint committee, and he dissociates himself from Sullivan. In a long letter to Sullivan, on June 17, 1930, White acts as if he had never fostered or signed the recommendation made to the Association on the formation of the Joint Committee. White has by now identified himself primarily with the education committee set up earlier by the NCMH, after his own defeat in obtaining the chairmanship of the APA committee for forming a joint commission. According to White's letter, he had known, at the very time that the APA Council was acting on Sullivan's and White's proposal for psychiatric education, that the plan would not be financed by the Commonwealth Fund; yet he glides over the fact that he did not inform Sullivan for five weeks. Instead his letter reviews the manner in which Sullivan has failed to observe the amenities, and thereby frustrated himself; White acts as if he himself had never been heavily involved in this particular political maneuver: "You must appreciate that I am in an exceedingly embarrassing position with reference to this whole affair." And "under the circumstances you will see that I naturally have certain loyalties and affiliations which I cannot just simply brush aside, and therefore I am bound to see what develops from that original suggestion and to be prepared to make good so far as my connection in that direction is concerned." In this letter White also manages to put his finger on Sullivan's area of greatest vulnerability—his financial problems: Barry Smith would not support Sullivan personally in this enterprise, White says in essence. In this manner, White is able to avoid any expression of his own political failure.

On July 5, 1930, Sullivan writes to White bitterly about the final disposition of the matter:

As to the matter of psychiatric education, I learn from conference with Dr. Ebaugh that this estimable young man—while he may be somewhat uncertain as to what it is all about, from the standpoint of the Association—has a highly organized plan for action, a feeling that Dr. Ruggles or he should be chairman of the Joint Committee, an inclination to the opinion that he can dispense with the medical educators and the social scientists included in the enacting motion; and finally that he is optimistic about getting Commonwealth Fund money for the study. In view of this most gratifying competence, the general attitude of more or less ubiquitous capability of Dr. Ebaugh; in view of the coolness of the Commonwealth Fund and some others concerned toward myself and my plans; and in continuation of my initial impulse when the good Association indicated that it did not desire to entrust me with the responsibility of picking the Committee—as I say, in view of these sundry factors, it gives me great pleasure to retire from the membership appointed by the Association in connection with the matter of psychiatric education.

In the same letter, Sullivan goes along with White's suggestion that Dr. Bernard Glueck be appointed to the Committee on Relations with the Social Sciences, replacing a member who had died. In White's reponse of July 10, he deliberately disregards Sullivan's resignation from the Committee on Psychiatric Education. The entire message from White reads: "I have your letter of the 5th instant. From my point of view, I think that Dr. Glueck is all right." It is a pointed rebuff—one from which Sullivan never fully recovered.

In subsequent correspondence between the two men there are correct communications from Sullivan on the occasion of White's birthdays; there are expressions of concern for Mrs. White when she is ill; and there are letters on subsidiary professional interests. But the great energy that was expended by Sullivan in getting White's approval for his activities has disappeared. From that point on, Sullivan begins to plan for his own institution and publication in order to focus on the research, training, and theory needed if psychiatry was to be more than a sham. His main working colleague in all this would be Ernest E. Hadley; they had first met at St. Elizabeths in the early days, and Hadley would suggest that the Foundation, incorporated in 1933, be named after their first great mentor—William Alanson White. Sullivan would go along with this suggestion. But there was some irony implicit in Sullivan's using White's name: White did not support Sullivan in his dealings with the Commonwealth Fund, but indirectly White's name on the letterhead of the Foundation would, presumably, help to raise money for Sullivan's ideas on psychiatric education. White would eventually resent the implications of this, and he complained to Hadley from time to time about his name being used for fund appeals. It was "bad taste" he thought, when he had been so "signally honored."[5]

There is a curious footnote to this period of defeat, found in Sullivan's career with the *American Journal of Psychiatry*. During the Sheppard years, Sullivan was for a time acting editor of this journal; the designated editor, Edward N. Brush, was elderly and not well, and he gladly gave the reins over to Sullivan. At the 1930 meeting of the Association, Brush commented approvingly on Sullivan's work in putting together the survey of institutional service, staff, and research needs in the 700 psychiatric hospitals throughout the country. Perhaps the *Journal* had stepped outside of its legitimate field, Brush reported, in sending this questionnaire out, but the results had been good.[6] White too had commented favorably on the importance of this census for getting research money coming into psychiatric institutions. Sullivan had wryly noted in an April 17 letter to White that he had financed most of this mailing and had personally done much of the clerical work, although "the Census . . . is in progress under management of the American Journal of Psychiatry."

A year later, at the 1931 meeting of the Association, Brush resigned as editor of the *Journal,* and in a kind of valedictory address on his career he made no mention of Sullivan's work during the many months that Brush was indisposed. Instead, Brush recommended Clarence B. Farrar as the new editor, who was appointed. Sullivan, who had been the most prominent Associate on the *Journal* for some time, was not considered for the post. At that same Association meeting, the Proceedings record "no report" from the Committee on Relations with the Social Sciences. Sullivan had withdrawn from active participation, and there was no one to take his place. Moreover, the work of the Joint Committee on Psychiatric Education fizzled out. And even today, there is no report for psychiatric education comparable to the Flexner report for medicine generally, as Sullivan had so passionately sought.

Shortly after Sullivan ended his efforts for a radical reexamination of psychiatric education in the medical schools, he published an article, "Training of the General Medical Student in Psychiatry," in which he berated the misinformation that was being passed on to students. He included some incidental remarks expressing a caustic view of the situation he had just come through, addressed to his psychiatric colleagues:

Let us by all means gird our loins—if any—for the salvage of the mentally ill, for the popularization of mentally hygienic procedures, and for the restoration to the medical profession of the ability to function in the capacities demanded of it by its patients. But let us by some sublime means focus in the stillness of our studies,—or bath rooms,—on the present state of psychiatry, psychopathology, and psychobiology, and,—like good psychiatrists, casting aside our compensations, sublimations and defense reactions, retrieving our repressed and dissociated materials, and reversing our regressive tendencies—let us bend our energies toward the assembling and refining of *a sound body of information* that will be the fundamental material for training all students. Voices crying in the wilderness are all right; but I could not find a dozen people, today, that I would unhesitatingly recommend as professors and heads of departments in psychiatry. I know a great many psychiatrists who know a great deal more about various aspects of psychiatry than do I. Many of them have discouraged me as to their suitability for the recommendation by *present-*

ing to me, personally, facts that I know are not facts. In other words, they know too much or too well,—they are propagating errors, superstitions, or religions.[7]

From this sequence of events Sullivan gained a reputation that he would never shake; he was regarded by some as opportunistic, perhaps power-driven, and, of course, as irresponsible about money. His experience at Sheppard, with the Association, with White, and with at least some of the funding organizations hardened in such a way that there was no turning back. From that point onward, he undertook the central responsibility himself; thus he is accorded major credit for the founding of the William Alanson White Psychiatric Foundation, with its two central activities—the Washington School of Psychiatry and the journal *Psychiatry*. Interdisciplinary in scope, charged with making "remedial attempts" in an increasingly disturbed world, these two activities of the Foundation would in the end move significantly toward many of the most important goals that Sullivan had spelled out in his plans for the improvement of psychiatric education and research. Indeed these plans, begun near the end of his stay at Sheppard, contain the blueprint for much of his life's work.

A competitive society—and a highly competitive profession such as medicine—finds it difficult to understand the motivations of a dedicated person who advocates any significant change. The most eloquent statement of Sullivan's selflessness is found in an address by a black man— Charles Johnson, then president of Fisk University, speaking at memorial services for Sullivan shortly after his death: "It is one of the strangest paradoxes of our civilization that the simplest human virtues and those which alone give us the right to call ourselves civilized are precisely those which demand the highest courage to translate into life and honest social action."[8] Johnson had reason to know that Sullivan heard a different drummer, for Sullivan had undertaken work for Johnson at a time of racial crisis in Memphis in 1939—work that was poorly paid, dangerous, and unprestigious.

Sullivan's wings had been clipped by the trustees at Sheppard and by White; indirectly they had also been clipped by Adolf Meyer, and by other men in positions of power, most of whose names and ideas have faded from sight. Thereafter the lack of money annoyed him from time to time. But it did not stop him for long ever again. He was in a wide swing of activity and interests that would expand until he died nineteen years later. By then, a surprising number of people in the larger world had recognized the scope of his work and knew that he was running with the Earth into the future.

ᴇ 33 ᴈ

Uncertain Transition

The development of private practice in the depression of the century has been occasion of no little
stress and tribulation.
—Sullivan, letter to Lola White, October 29, 1931

WITHIN six months after Sullivan arrived in New York City on December 15, 1930, his father died. By the time Timothy's will was
probated in 1932, Harry had filed for bankruptcy in New York City.
Timothy's assets did not pay for his own debts, so that some of the expenses of his last illness and the funeral expenses were part of Harry's
bankruptcy proceedings. Both of them were in part victims of the "depression of the century." Farms in Chenango County, particularly in the
hill country, including Timothy's, went for practically nothing during this
period.

In New York City, there were few private patients who could pay for
psychoanalytic care when Sullivan arrived, heavily in debt. His resignation at Sheppard had taken effect on June 30, 1930, but he had stayed on
in Towson trying to finish up his book, still searching for research monies,
and hoping against hope that the position at the University of Chicago
would open up. For over five months he and Jimmie had had little income, and they had borrowed money for living expenses.

He was having trouble in the writing of his book. The first part of
the book contained his Farewell Lectures at Sheppard. He gave them
that title, expressing his sadness at leaving the task that had begun his
career and the place in which he had first come to wide attention for his
therapeutic insights. About his own writing, he was always somewhat
discouraged. In espousing interpersonal relations as the area for investigation, he was taking a quantum jump in the whole field of psychology
and psychiatry. However obscure his prose is in spots, his ideas are the
stumbling block, for they ask the student to dispose of all manner of pre-
conceptions about human relations. Yet he continued to wonder whether
the fault was entirely his own; he tended to think that somehow, some-

body else could state the ideas more simply so that they could be more readily accepted; and he tried to construct teaching devices that would transmit the ideas more precisely.

By August 11 of that summer, Sullivan had not given up completely on the idea of going to Chicago, as he indicated in a letter to White; but he asked for some help from White, in case he decided to practice in New York City:

I am considering going into practice in either Chicago or New York City. It seems as if I should incline toward the latter, as I wish my work to deal chiefly with preschizophrenic and related problems. The relatively high development of psychiatry in the East seems most favorable to such a specialization.

I find that, if I am to secure a license from New York State it will be only as a result of strong representations in my behalf by my friends, for my medical school was not fully accredited by New York at the time of my graduation. Will you give me a letter, addressed to . . . [the] New York State Board of Medical Examiners, if you feel that I am properly qualified for medical practice in the State and deserving of exceptional treatment. My preliminary education was obtained in New York State, of which I am a native. I took my medical work at the Chicago College of Medicine and Surgery (since absorbed into a Class A school) because I had no money and it was the only school that would encourage my enrollment.

White was, as ever, eager to encourage—as long as all the amenities were observed; and he composed a recommendation for Sullivan, dated only four days later:

I consider Dr. Sullivan one of the outstanding men in this country in the field of neurology and psychiatry. Previous to going to the Sheppard and Enoch Pratt Hospital he served for several years on my staff as a liaison officer for the U.S. Veterans Bureau, and for the past few years he has served with me on several important committees of the American Psychiatric Association where he rendered very excellent service. He is a brilliant young man and has devoted considerable time of late to research work in connection with the study of schizophrenia. I feel that he possesses the required qualifications to place him in that class of professional men who on account of exceptional merit are permitted under your laws to engage in practice without the necessity of an examination. He has contributed much of value to the medical literature.

The official records show that Sullivan was a liaison officer at St. Elizabeths Hospital for only two months more than one year, so White is being more than generous in his recommendation.

Sullivan's move to New York City was heralded by an elegant announcement printed on a heavy buff card, with no mention of his degree or specialty. In this new setting, he began to fulfill a personal need that stood in sharp contradiction to his implicit and explicit mission of giving all his energies toward making a more productive society. The deprivation of the Smyrna years had made a socialist of him—but a socialist who admired extravagantly the better things of life. Thus his first apartment in New York was expensive and well-appointed. In the beginning, the Park Avenue apartment, which was on the top floor of a large apartment house, was used as both housing and office. The entrance room in the apartment was large enough to use as a living room, until Sullivan got a separate office; it held, without overcrowding, a three-quarter size grand piano, two sofas, four chairs, and three tables—all described as elegant.[1] The piano, a Bechstein, was a birthday gift to Jimmie from Harry, and after they moved to New York, Jimmie began to take piano lessons. Unlike some of the other furniture, the piano survived through the years, until Sullivan's death; since it was a gift to Jimmie, it could not be taken over to pay debts when Sullivan went into bankruptcy.

At one end of the entrance room was a large, beautiful room, with "sort of a French atmosphere," where Sullivan saw patients. This room was decorated with an eye to later use as a formal living room, with ceiling-to-floor tieback draperies and valances, made to order in a bright yellow damask and "very expensive," partly because the ceilings in the apartment were at least twelve feet high. There was a full dining room, and the kitchen had cupboards from floor to ceiling, which necessitated the use of a ladder. A bedroom and bath off the kitchen had been originally designed for a maid, but there was never a live-in maid in any of the Sullivan establishments. Jimmie resented the fact that Sullivan's colleagues sometimes considered him a maid; but indeed he did act in the capacity of housekeeper-manager for much of the time, being proficient at cooking, shopping, and managing. There were two other bedrooms in another wing of the apartment, and one of them was used as a secretarial office for Jimmie, another of his self-appointed tasks. Sometime in the interim between his coming to live at Sullivan's house in Towson and the New York years, Jimmie became a capable secretary for Sullivan, skilled at reading Sullivan's sometimes almost unintelligible handwriting.

The demise of this elaborate setup was already in sight when the two of them moved into it. Jimmie has written of the fate of the furniture: "We had to get rid of most of our furniture when the stock market had troubles and the wealthy Jewish patients could not pay their bills." By February 24, 1932, Sullivan had filed a Debtor's Petition—a little over fourteen months after his arrival in New York City—and he lists his address as 7 Mitchell Place, where he and Jimmie had a small two-room apartment. He had salvaged his office furniture out of the upset, and his office address was 60 East 42nd Street in the Lincoln Building, where he saw patients—paying and nonpaying—until May 1936.

In the fourteen months between his arrival in New York and his beginning steps toward applying for bankruptcy, he was involved in the final illness and death of his father. So it was that his farewell to Sheppard was followed in less than a year by his farewell to Smyrna. However sad both of these farewells were, they both were freeing in an ultimate sense.

On June 2, 1931, Timothy Sullivan died in the Chenango Memorial Hospital in Norwich. His final illness seems to have marked the last visit of Harry to Chenango County. Timothy had bragged over the years that Harry planned to come back one day and open a "sanitarium" on the farm; but that plan had no doubt been abandoned some time before, perhaps after the Klan visitation following his mother's death. When he received word in New York City that his father was desperately ill with a gangrenous foot, Harry telephoned and ordered an ambulance to transport Timothy from the farmhouse to the Norwich hospital. Harry then took himself to Norwich, where he stayed until after the funeral. The illness, complicated by a "chronic cardiovalvular renal disease" according to the death certificate, lasted for three weeks, but Timothy was hospitalized for only the last week.

Sullivan had "always had the feeling if he could only reach his father there would be understanding, and that indeed finally occurred after he had reached adult life," Clara Thompson has reported. "But in his childhood his father was a shy withdrawn person whose occasional words of approval the boy treasured."[2] Any meaningful relationship with his father occurred after his mother's death in 1926, according to Sullivan himself. Writing in the third person, Sullivan reports: "His father was a remarkably taciturn man who had become a widower (and his son a physician of some twelve years' experience) before they got well acquainted with each other's views."[3] This would have been two years before his father's death. After Sullivan moved to New York City, he came up at least once on the train to Sherburne, where a neighbor met him and drove him up to the farm. It was a bleak, untended, dreary farmhouse after his mother's death, with his father already past the proverbial threescore years and ten and quite unable to take proper care of his holdings. It was during this period that Timothy took to raising gamecocks—probably a necessity to eke out his slender income. His friend Jim Yockey, poor and ill, had been taken to the County poorhouse, so that Timothy was quite alone.

In one of his lectures, Sullivan reports on a visit to his father in this period, using the incident to illustrate the process of selective inattention:

During my father's period of being a widower, I visited him. On this occasion, we sat and talked in the room which I had always liked best in the house. In the process, I noticed that the old gentleman was getting a bit distracted. In my usual fashion I went over the context of our conver-

sation and found nothing at all offensive to him. And so, in the margin of
my mind, I grew more and more puzzled over what was clear to me as
some unsatisfactory mental state in my father. Finally he said, "Well,
what do you think of the wallpaper?" On hearing this question, I was able
vividly to recall that in an hour and a half's conversation, I had studied
every damned line at which the wallpaper came together. I had not only
observed that it was new wallpaper applied since my last visit, but I had
made a minute study for any poor workmanship or regrettable defects in
its application. But that had in no sense disturbed my consciousness. It
required this intervention by my father to attach any awareness in my
mind either of the new wallpaper or of the great care with which I had
been studying it.[4]

By the time that Sullivan got to Norwich to attend his father in his last
illness, he was already overextended financially in New York City. But he
acted with decorum and respect suitable for the occasion. He stayed in
Norwich with his father's sister, Ella Sullivan Crandall, who had been a
nurse for many years at the Norwich hospital. The funeral was held at his
Aunt Ella's house, with the Mass at St. Malachy's in Sherburne and burial in the cemetery, beside Ella's unmarked grave. As one of the chief
creditors, the funeral director became the administrator in the settling of
Timothy's small estate over a year later. The funeral arrangements, as
made by Harry, resulted in a bill of $546—altogether an impressive fu-
neral for a poor farmer in Chenango County during the depression years.
The list of items on the bill included candles, gloves, and other "para-
phernalia" for the services, the purchase of a Clark grave vault, a floral
spray, and a necktie priced at one dollar.

After the funeral Mass at St. Malachy's, the family returned to Norwich where they were to have lunch at Ella Crandall's house. On the way
there, Harry asked to be let out at the Norwich railway station in order to
send a telegram. He never arrived for lunch at Aunt Ella's house, but
took the train back to New York City, having been foresighted enough to
leave his baggage at the station sometime before the funeral. This quick
exit is still the subject of some speculation among old-timers. There is a
general feeling that Harry abandoned the farm and that this failure to
properly care for the animals and the property was somehow related to
Harry's subsequent bankruptcy, which was duly recorded in the County
proceedings at the time Timothy's estate was settled.

It seems more likely that Sullivan's abrupt departure was a careful
evasion of the necessity for explanation if he were to stay around. He was
always more canny about money than others gave him credit for: he was
well aware of the condition of Timothy's holdings, that indeed there was
probably not enough money to cover his bills; and he was well aware of
the condition of his own finances. He was already being hounded by
creditors from the Sheppard days. And the patients who were supposed to

pay for his extravagant furnishings in New York City had failed to materialize. He never liked to "explain," to use glib verbalisms to cover over his own failures; so he simply left.

Moreover, he was due in Toronto to attend the psychiatric meetings, which began the day after the funeral. Timothy was buried on Thursday, and the meetings began on Friday. The funeral, scheduled only two days after Timothy's death, was undoubtedly timed so that Sullivan could reach Toronto on time. In the published version of the paper given at Toronto, he predicts the date and cause of his own death, reflecting some of his preoccupation with his father's death.[5] His hasty exit from Norwich did nothing to endear him to either his Stack or Sullivan relatives, who had long since defined him as queer, unpredictable, and irresponsible.

For eighteen months after Timothy's death, the estate, so small as to be inadequate to meet the expenses of his illness, the funeral, outstanding taxes, and fire insurance, was in litigation. The farm, still intact in size from the property acquired by Michael Stack and farmed for over thirty years by Timothy, was sold at auction for $910 on November 16, 1932—a farm purchased by him for about $3,500 in 1895. The sale of the farm equipment, tools, furniture, hay, team and harness, and car, together with the rent on the pasture, totaled less than $300.

One piece of personal property escaped the auctioneer's hammer. When I first visited the farm, then abandoned, in 1963, I found a doctor's small black bag near the back door in the farmyard on the way to the barn. As an unauthorized trespasser, I was reluctant to pick it up and examine it. There had been tenants on the farm part of the time since Timothy's death; and I fancied that a child had dragged the bag from the attic and played with its contents in the farmyard. When I revisited the farm, the bag had disappeared. In the early 1970s, two out-of-towners bought the house and started its rehabilitation, connecting it up for the first time with electricity. But that project was also abandoned, and the house continued to stand, lonely and mournful, until it burned to the ground in May 1978.

ᶳ 34 ᶳ
Clarence H. Bellinger

> In any society which has open vertical classes, in
> which the individual is taught to conceive the possi-
> bility of his rising or falling, invidious factors con-
> tribute generally perduring color to the personalities
> socialized at each of the, in the U.S.A., ill-defined
> levels. The child of an unskilled laborer, be he now a
> successful physician, still responds emotionally to
> certain words and concepts that are impotent to
> move many another physician whose career-line has
> been parallel, say, from the second year in High
> School.
>
> —Sullivan, "Propaganda and Censorship"

As late as 1940, Sullivan was still trying to extrapolate theory from his
and Clarence's youthful experiences—a process that he was already
engaged in when he went to Smyrna for the last time in 1931. In his book
Personal Psychopathology, which he was still revising at the time of his father's death, he related the experience of his patients to his own experience with Clarence and the village children in his school years. Yet the
various experiences mentioned in this early book, or later, are not simply
autobiographical. There is a silent interweaving and intertwining of all
the patterns of growing up that Sullivan was aware of from his patients.
At the same time, he was heavily dependent on careful reexamination of
the unfolding scene in the Smyrna school society for the hypotheses that,
with testing, became such important elements in his theory.

Although relatives and neighbors have reported that Sullivan did not
return to the farmhouse in Smyrna at the time of his father's death, he
may have made a quiet and unobserved trip to the village and thence to
the farmhouse—along the road that he and Clarence had traversed together so long ago. Jimmie reports that Sullivan brought home from this
final trip nothing except several snapshots that he had found in the farmhouse. One was of Leo Stack when he was eleven or twelve, sitting beside
a girl cousin in the parlor of Gothic House; Leo sits in almost regal

splendor, dressed in his best bib and tucker. Sullivan identified this picture for Jimmie as a picture of himself in the sitting room of the farmhouse; but it was subsequently definitely identified as Leo by his daughter. Two pictures of the Smyrna farmhouse and its makeshift outbuildings also survived from this final visit to Smyrna; otherwise there was nothing in the farmhouse that Sullivan wanted.

Whether or not Sullivan returned to the farmhouse at this time, the occasion itself must have evoked memories of Clarence Bellinger. Their paths had separated some time before, but retrospectively the entire pattern of their relationship and histories could be encompassed within the clinical theory that Sullivan was developing. Both of them had become "inferior caricatures of what they might have been."[1] Although the compass of their lives varied considerably, Bellinger's was the more unfulfilled; within the scope of Sullivan's theory, Bellinger had had an even more restricted experience in growing up than Sullivan. There were similarities that led them to pursue the same profession; and neither ever married. Yet it was not simply coincidence that caused these similarities, just as there was more than happenstance in the differences that emerged in their ultimate destinies.

By the time of Timothy's death, Clarence's parents had left the farm on the hill and were living in Earlville in the adjacent county of Hamilton. But Bellinger continued to visit in Smyrna, driving down from Utica almost every year in his big car furnished by the State, for he lived out his life as an important psychiatrist in the State system. After 1935, when he became superintendent of Brooklyn State Hospital on Long Island, he came to Smyrna each year in a car driven by his chauffeur; and this made a big impression on the people in these small villages—Smyrna, Sherburne, and Earlville.

Yet Bellinger's annual visits mystified people, for there were few in the countryside who liked him, or could say anything kind about him. Neighbors were awed by him, they respected him, they were even proud of him when, in 1947, the *Reader's Digest* ran a story about his work at Brooklyn State Hospital; but they did not like him. One of his important roles in the County was to bring back word of Harry Sullivan. "Everything we know about Harry after he left Smyrna," old-timers reported, "came from Clarence. And it was all bad."

By the time of Timothy Sullivan's death, Sullivan was already outdistancing Bellinger. This was a bitter pill for Bellinger to swallow. His faithful shadow in the growing-up years, the underling who was five years younger, had managed to gain favor in the precise places where Bellinger had been bypassed. Thus both William Alanson White and Ross McClure Chapman had been benign figures in Sullivan's career; and by a coincidence, Clarence had had some contact with both of these men much earlier in his career than Sullivan. Bellinger's first hospital experience, in the summer after his graduation from Syracuse Medical School in 1910, had been under White at St. Elizabeths Hospital—a decade before Sullivan went to St. Elizabeths.[2] For Bellinger, the experience at White's hospital would be the only time in his life that his career took him outside the New York State Hospital system. Thereafter, he went to St. Lawrence State Hospital for a year. From 1911 to 1926 he was on the staff at Binghamton State Hospital; after this, he served at Utica State Hospital until 1935, when he became head of Brooklyn State Hospital.

At Binghamton he came to know Chapman, some years older than Bellinger and a senior assistant physician at the hospital; in 1916 Chapman was summoned to be White's first assistant at St. Elizabeths. A few years later, Chapman became the medical superintendent at Sheppard-Pratt. And this working relationship between White and Chapman became the nurturing environment for Sullivan's beginning career in the early 1920s. From Bellinger's own particular position of growing power in the New York State Hospital system, he must have watched with increasing envy the even more meteoric rise of his closest boyhood friend.

Over the years, Bellinger earned the reputation of being "bossy" at his various posts, particularly in his final position as superintendent of Brooklyn State Hospital, where he remained until his death in 1952. It is the same word that is used to describe him by old-timers in and around Chenango County. At Binghamton State Hospital, this boyhood tendency was undoubtedly reinforced by the superintendent's willingness to have Bellinger take over many of his own arduous administrative responsibilities. But this bossiness made him unsuited for direct work with disturbed patients.

In the 1920s, both Sullivan and Bellinger began to interest themselves in research—a significant coincidence, since not many hospital psychiatrists at that period had research interests. Bellinger's first paper, published in 1925—the same year as Sullivan's first published paper—was considerably more ambitious than Sullivan's, for it reported on 200 cases of senile psychosis, from data collected while he was still at Binghamton State Hospital. Bellinger made rather sophisticated use of his quantified data, and his interpretations show the kind of insight that Sullivan used in approaching his own clinical data. Thus Bellinger reports that "a careful analysis of the 200 cases considered in this paper showed that mental stress and physical illness or injury are the most common precipitating causes in the development of the senile psychoses." He noted: "In practically every instance the precipitating factor either deprived the individual of the principal interest in life or seriously interfered with the established mode of living."[3] His second paper, closer to Sullivan's interests, was titled "Inadequate Childhood Training, A Factor in Mental Disease." It reflects Bellinger's lifelong interest in mental hygiene clinics which had begun when he was head of a clinic in Binghamton. He observes that "a stern exacting attitude toward the child by the parent of the same sex, with a sympathetic attitude by the parent of the opposite sex was found to contribute to parental fixation in many instances."[4] Some of Bellinger's views reveal the stern puritanical background in his boyhood home. For instance, he reports on a girl who was tempted by a married man and became ill; the temptation was pointed out to her, and she came under the care of good foster parents, so that she subsequently saw the evil of her ways and repented. At the time of publication of this paper, Bellinger had recently come to Utica State Hospital as the first assistant physician. Later that year in the same journal, Sullivan published his tenth paper, "The Common Field of Research and Clinical Psychiatry," with the much more impressive job title of "Director of Clinical Research" at Sheppard.[5]

Although Sullivan had moved to a higher level of theoretical sophistication than Bellinger, both were still dealing with some of the same approaches to mental illness. Thus Bellinger published a paper in 1932 titled "Prognosis in Schizophrenia—Catatonic Form," with the following conclusion: "The results of this study seem to bear out the conclusions of other investigators in this field who are of the opinion that a considerable number of cases of schizophrenia of the catatonic type show an amelioration of their mental condition to the extent that they are able to resume their former places in society."[6] In his bibliography, Bellinger fails to cite Sullivan's work at Sheppard—an obvious omission; by this time, just about everyone in the American Psychiatric Association, of which Bellinger was a member, must have been aware of Sullivan's work with schizophrenics at Sheppard and of his reputation for being successful in effecting the social recovery of young catatonic patients.

In the 1940s, Bellinger participated with others in two statistical studies concerned with the use of insulin and metrazol on disturbed patients. When Bellinger died in 1952, the *Psychiatric Quarterly* summarized his work: "Brooklyn State Hospital under Dr. Bellinger pioneered in the development of insulin, metrazol and electric shock therapies in this country"—all of which techniques had become increasingly unacceptable to Sullivan. Although Bellinger, like Sullivan, had interests in preventive psychiatry—in mental hygiene clinics, child guidance clinics, and in hospital-community relationships—he is remembered chiefly for his efficiency as an administrator, which had an importance for him second to none. Thus when a writer was taken through the wards of the hospital by Bellinger in the late 1940s, she marveled at the relative quiet of the most disturbed ward for women. How is it possible? she queried Bellinger. " 'Through shock therapy,' Dr. Bellinger said. 'We don't let them stay disturbed long.' "[7]

Like Sullivan, Bellinger had a better relationship with attendants and patients than with physicians and nurses. In a rift between an attendant and a physician, Bellinger would almost automatically take the part of the attendant. Both of them had clear concern for the welfare of patients, although their definition of welfare varied, with Bellinger placing more emphasis on a clean ward, quiet patients, and good recreational facilities, and Sullivan more concerned with moving the patient out into the larger world, without benefit of mechanical or chemical agents which he believed dulled the patient. Yet as an administrator par excellence Bellinger clearly accomplished some notable changes in the lives of patients at Brooklyn State Hospital; and the stress of his untiring efforts undoubtedly contributed to his death, three years after Sullivan's. Both men would die in harness, and each of them died many years before the ages attained by their respective parents. Bellinger died at 65, almost twenty years before he reached the age of death for either of his parents; and Sullivan died at approximately 57, about fifteen years before the age of his parents at death.

Over the years, Bellinger's appearance changed little; his picture taken in 1935, when he came to Brooklyn State Hospital, shows a man not noticeably different in appearance from the picture taken in 1910 when he was twenty-three and graduating from medical school. Both pictures show a curious combination of an undeveloped fat boy and a reproving and unpleasant older man; his lips are excessively thin, his eyes shrewd and calculating. A picture of Sullivan taken when he was about twenty-six shows him as slight and wispy, shy and gentle, almost poet-like in his pose, reminiscent of a well-known picture of James Joyce. Throughout his life, he kept some of this quality. Whether by suggestion or otherwise, one can glimpse in these pictures of Sullivan and Bellinger as adults the bossy teenager and the shy boy who rode with him down to the village school. To an extent, one can posit some physiological arrest in both of them, stemming out of the overprotective concern focused on each of them by their respective mothers, and out of their general isolation.

Shortly after Clarence came to Brooklyn in 1935 and took up residence in the penthouse apartment on the roof of the hospital, his mother, then widowed, came to live with him and stayed until her death in 1938. Two snapshots of Clarence and his mother, Caroline L. Lanckton, as she is named on her grave marker, were taken as they stood side by side on the roof outside of the apartment. He stands shyly beside her; they are almost the same height. He is not holding her hand, but in both pictures he looks as if he is about to. "She was the only person he was ever afraid of," neighbors and colleagues report.

The stories about Bellinger that linger on at Brooklyn State Hospital, twenty years after his death, show that he was considered even more eccentric than Sullivan—almost as if Bellinger were an exaggeration of Sullivan. Clearly both of them showed certain eccentricities and egocentricities emergent from their early lives; yet their reputations are different. For example, most of Sullivan's junior colleagues felt that he was a hard taskmaster, but that the initiation by fire was worth the price; but there was no such saving grace for Bellinger's staff. His reputation with staff bears striking similarities to the one in Chenango County. He was unattractive; and he was unable to make friends. His staff respected him, he was a strong person, he accomplished a good deal for patients in trying to improve hospital conditions—but no one liked him. When a colleague reported to me that Bellinger's birthday (February 22) was each year the occasion for a celebration in the rotunda of the main building at Brooklyn State, I commented that he must have been popular with the staff. "Oh, no," my informant told me, "no one liked him." Five minutes later, this quiet, circumspect colleague said, in effect, "You know I've been thinking about what I said a while ago; and it was true. I never knew anyone who *liked* him." My informant, a senior psychiatrist with a private practice, was reluctant to have me take notes on my interview with him, and was extremely careful as to what he said about Bellinger, who had been dead then for almost twenty years. Even in the grave Bellinger's power seemed to be a living thing.

Bellinger let his staff know that he had grown up with Sullivan, but he never had a good word to say about him. Bellinger would simply dismiss Sullivan as "a homosexual and a son-of-a-bitch." In Chenango County, Bellinger related stories of Sullivan as an adult, concerning the misuse of money and activities bordering on criminal misconduct. The psychiatrist Edward J. Kempf has reported that many years ago he met a physician on a train who said he had grown up with Sullivan in a New York State village and that Sullivan had begun writing bad checks at an early period. The man on the train must have been Bellinger. Kempf volunteered this information after he reported that both he and Meyer felt that Sullivan was irresponsible about money.[8]

As an adult Bellinger often spoke of Sullivan; but Sullivan apparently never mentioned Bellinger. After I had discovered their boyhood relationship, I queried Sullivan's colleagues about Bellinger. None of them remembered hearing Sullivan mention Bellinger in any connection; nor had Jimmie.

When I was interviewing one colleague, Alfred H. Stanton, and showing him some pictures I had collected for this book, including one of Bellinger, he stopped me, recognizing Bellinger. He had been interviewed long ago by Bellinger at Brooklyn State Hospital, in connection with a possible psychiatric residency there. He decided "within forty-five seconds" that he could never work under Bellinger, who was a "fully nasty man." Bellinger had spoken to Stanton about his plans for emptying the hospital through the use of electric shock therapy, talking about the patients in an impersonal, hateful way. Bellinger was "the personification of a psychologically effective sadist," Stanton told me, adding that the resident psychiatrists at Brooklyn State Hospital uniformly hated him.

Stanton, who was a particularly close colleague of Sullivan's, was excited about the fact that Bellinger and Sullivan had been boyhood chums, that in fact Bellinger was Sullivan's only close friend in those years. "If I now imagine him with Sullivan as the vulnerable loner, this could have been an unbelievably difficult experience. . . . [Yet] I could easily imagine that Bellinger was a bit needing of people, too. I may have put Bellinger off a bit because at the time I was also considering going to Chestnut Lodge [a hospital in suburban Washington, D.C.], because of Fromm-Reichmann. I'm not at all sure, but I could have made some reference to Sullivan whom I knew of from the organizing brochure of the Washington School of Psychiatry [where Fromm-Reichmann also taught]." In the course of time, Stanton had intensive training with Sullivan, and it was possible, he thought, that he mentioned to Sullivan his encounter with Bellinger or his applying for a residency at Brooklyn State Hospital. Yet over the years of close association with Sullivan, at no time did Stanton hear Sullivan even mention Bellinger.[9]

In a curious way, Bellinger's life underscores Sullivan's theory on the juvenile era and on preadolescence. For Clarence, both eras were distorted far more than Harry's. When Clarence attended the country school, he was even more of an outsider than in the village school; his school associates were farm boys, and they shunned a boy who did no chores on his father's farm and who had more of everything than anybody else. Moreover, he was one of the few children in that country school who went on to high school in the village. In some way he never learned the rough and tumble of a young juvenile, for he was a big frog in a small pond in the beginning of his school career. In that same developmental period, Sullivan was clearly the outsider at the village school; his family was poor and he was modest in his relationships with the other children. In my mind's eye, from many a report of his behavior in the school yard at recess, I see him as slight and removed, careful not to antagonize the larger boys; only in the classroom did he dare to come into his own, sometimes being labeled as teacher's pet—a tendency for which he was often punished in one way or another by social ostracism. With the advent of Clarence at the village school, Harry found a friend; although it was not a fully reciprocal relationship, it must have had its tender moments that were sustaining for Harry. For Clarence, this relationship of trust and devotion on Harry's part had a modifying influence, but it came too late; he was always tempted to take advantage of less powerful people, even though he might regret his high-handed ways later. Thus Harry saw his relationship with Clarence as saving him for a relatively useful life; and while Clarence had some important experience with Harry that helped him to become a useful member of society, he never fully escaped from the temptation to bully other people as he had periodically bullied Harry. And he seems never to have been loved or even fully intimate with anybody on a reciprocal level, whereas all manner of people felt intimate with Sullivan in different ways.

Yet for Bellinger as well as Sullivan, their early relationship was absolutely crucial in what they managed to accomplish—Bellinger as continuing to be a big frog in a small pond and Sullivan as a modest but significant voice in the larger world. It is as if Bellinger had to work out all the developmental tasks of his unhappy early life in that one relationship with Harry. So it was that Bellinger had an affinity with the underdog all his life. There are innumerable stories about his taking the side of attendants in hospital disputes. At the same time, he would bully an attendant from time to time, frighten him, threaten him with loss of his job; in one instance, he actually fired a man on his staff who had worked there for thirty-five years, and then hired him back the next day. His values about ethnicity were confused and temperamental. Thus he often referred to attendants as "wops" or "guineas," but supported them in institutional fights.

Bellinger's final ethnic confusion was written into his will. When he died in 1952, he left most of his money to Syracuse University to be used for "Christian boys" who had graduated from high school in Madison or Chenango Counties. Small bequests established prizes for various achievements of students in the public schools of Smyrna and Earlville, to be named after Bellinger himself and his mother and father; each of these prizes was to be used only for students of "Christian faith."

The will also made careful provision for the disposal of Bellinger's body after death; it was to be placed in a molded zinc or copper casket and interred in his cemetery lot at Sherburne West Hill, and a Clark grave vault of copper was to be provided. Another provision took care of his own marker, which was already in place beside those for his father and his mother; only the date of death had to be added, his name and date of birth having already been inscribed. A further provision was made for the "necessary cleaning and repair of the monuments and headstones on my lot in that cemetery." The husband of a cousin was charged personally by Bellinger with the precise task of making sure that the burial vault was securely fastened at interment.[10] There were also definite arrangements for the funeral made in a codicil to the will: His body in an open coffin would lie in state in the main central hall of the Hospital where Bellinger's birthday had been celebrated each year, before being shipped to Sherburne for services at a funeral home. Provision was made for the clothing to be worn, with different shirts, suits, and ties for different seasons. There is a legend at the Hospital that Bellinger picked out his coffin beforehand and took a colleague with him to the establishment so that he could lie in the coffin and made sure it was long enough; he had heard that sometimes legs had to be broken or cut in order to get a body in, and he wanted to be sure that this did not happen; since he was short for a man, this precaution seems to have been unnecessary.

There was one part of the funeral arrangements that was left unattended to. While Bellinger was alive, he had fresh flowers put on his parents' graves on every special occasion; there was a standing order at the local florist, according to old-timers. But after Bellinger's own funeral flowers had faded, flowers never appeared again.

These elaborate arrangements for burial are in sharp contrast to the simple directions that Sullivan imposed: He wanted a Catholic service, and he requested that he be buried in Arlington National Cemetery—a highly practical suggestion since there was not enough money in the bank when he died, three and a half years before Bellinger, to finance funeral costs. His parents' graves in the Catholic Cemetery on the other side of the Valley in Sherburne remain unmarked.

For some years after Bellinger's death, the term "Christian faith" in his will caused considerable legal difficulty at Syracuse University. The belated solution was somewhat evasive, since by then the University had become part of the New York State system of universities and colleges, and it could not accept the legacy directly because of its restrictive features; the problem was solved by setting up the fund under a legally defensible separate incorporation. Bellinger's stipulation was curious in a number of ways: Brooklyn State Hospital had a number of Jewish refugee physicians on its staff in the years when Bellinger held forth there, and he was heavily dependent on them. There were apparently no Jews at all in Smyrna over the years; if there were, they were well hidden.

Neighbors in Chenango County express by innuendo their puzzlement about this stipulation, pointing out that he left his money "so the Jews couldn't get it." It is stated as a question, as if this strange restriction should be explained. If he had designated the money for Protestants only, the provision would be understandable, for over and over again he showed his distaste for Harry Sullivan. At Brooklyn State Hospital, the puzzlement comes from a different direction. There were many Jewish patients at the Hospital, and their parents were significantly grateful to Bellinger for what he had done for these patients. At the time of his death, two Jewish organizations of parents at the Hospital expressed their respects to Bellinger in the obituary notices in the New York *Times*. But stereotypes and patterns of disparagement are apt to be irrational, as Sullivan came to recognize. He once tried to define why he had managed to avoid most of the stereotyped thinking about Jews:

In my own early years, by a series of irrelevant accidents, I heard things said about Jews, but I didn't know any Jews. Because of an extremely fortunate accident of what seemed to be otherwise a very unpleasant developmental history, I did not have very much interest in these vague rumors that I'd never seen exemplified, and so I did not adopt this stereotype.

Therefore I emerged into the adult world with some curiosity about these people, whom I thought of as extraordinary, since my own acquaintance with them resulted almost entirely from perusing Holy Writ. I am glad that I did not fix in my mind some of the alleged attributes of Jews which I might have found lying around in certain juveniles, which in turn they, having no actual experience with them, had taken over from parents and other authority figures. Otherwise, I am quite certain that I would have been richly supplied with stereotypes. And these would have been much harder to correct later than was my curiosity as to what the devil the people who wrote the Old Testament must have been like.[11]

Clarence also knew no Jews in his growing-up years, so Sullivan's explanation is not all-inclusive. But the pattern of learning to disparage was different in the Bellinger and the Sullivan households. However much the Bellingers belonged to the elite in that area by social and economic class, they did not belong to the tiny clique that controlled Smyrna, all of whom attended the churches in the village, which were fundamentalist and prohibitionist. There were two boys in the village school who did not regularly go to a church in the village. One was a Catholic boy, Harry Sullivan, and his folks took him to mass in Sherburne—not often enough, but when they could; that was considerably better than Clarence, who never went to church at all, as far as anyone remembers. At the same time, there is the clear knowledge that the Bellingers were Episcopalian, and the nearest church of that denomination was in Earlville. As everyone in Smyrna knew, Episcopalians are close to Catholics; and they have real wine for communion. In some ways, the Bellingers were deemed Catholics who had backslid and did not go to church often enough; at the same time, there was an implied snobbishness about being Episcopalian that still exists in small-town America. Thus the Bellingers were ostracized to some extent in the village; and Clarence's mother must have watched with anxious eyes as Clarence suffered rejection and unpopularity at the hands of the children at school. At some level she transmitted to Clarence the concept of being "better than" somebody, as some compensation for his situation. The safest focus for this pattern of disparagement was the Jews, the agreed-upon target in America for many years; to have named the Baptists or the Methodists, or particularly the one Catholic family who were friendly, would have further complicated Clarence's problems.

A pattern of disparagement also went on in the Sullivan household, but Harry's ostracism by village children was more obvious and easier for his mother to explain. She could warn him that he would not be accepted by the other children because he was Irish and Catholic; but in Ireland, the Stacks had been scholars and gentlemen, and Harry would eventually succeed. The more difficult area of disparagement for Harry concerned his mother's attitude toward his father, for she disparaged the Sullivans as being shanty Irish instead of lace-curtain Irish. In other words, the pattern of disparagement was contained within the group: his mother—and Harry was impressed with the fact that he was a *Stack*—was "better than" his father. This family-centered disparagement in minority groups is often safer and wiser than attacking the outside world. But in either case, the child has to pay for learning disparagement, as Sullivan observes:

If you have to maintain self-esteem by pulling down the standing of others, you are extraordinarily unfortunate in a variety of ways. Since you have to protect your feeling of personal worth by noting how unworthy everybody around you is, you are not provided with any data that are convincing evidence of your having personal worth; so it gradually evolves into "I am not as bad as the other swine." To be the best of swine, when it would be nice to be a person, is not a particularly good way of furthering anything except security operations. When security is achieved that way, it strikes at the very roots of that which is essentially human—the utterly vital role of interpersonal relations.[12]

Perhaps Bellinger's ethnic stipulation in the will was not as strange as it might seem at first glance. In spite of the malicious stories told by Bellinger about Sullivan over the years, Clarence had included Harry symbolically in the bequests to schools; as a Catholic, Harry would have qualified theoretically as a recipient of Clarence's money, and perhaps in this way Clarence finally recognized the boy who had once been his only friend in a basically hostile territory.

In one other dimension, it seems clear that their boyhood plans had an echo in their later lives, at different levels. While Bellinger was still at Binghamton State Hospital, he began to frequent courts, appearing as an expert witness. A retired staff worker at Binghamton State Hospital remembers that she worked with Bellinger at night on these court cases; he would give her a fifty-fifty cut on this work, she reported, and he was at his happiest when he was appearing in court. This interest in medicine and the law continued throughout Bellinger's life, and the stipulation in his will for medical students carried the provision that any unused balance in a given year would go to a law student. While he was at Brooklyn State Hospital, he also often appeared in court to testify as an expert; and although his colleagues felt that his testimony was usually rambling and imprecise, his position on a given case was usually benign. Sullivan too was concerned about the social and economic deprivation of the young criminal offender, as evidenced in editorials, usually unsigned, in his journal. For both of them, the interest in crime was obviously related to the stories in the Norwich *Sun,* which in turn were a reflection of the mental distress in Chenango County.

And finally, neither Clarence nor Harry ever married. A neighbor, ten years junior to Harry, remembers both mothers. It was no wonder that neither of them ever married, he stated; they had both had enough of women to last them the rest of their lives. Both women were unpleasant and domineering, he thought. Yet again Sullivan's experience was of a different character than Bellinger's: Sullivan achieved an intimate relationship with a number of women, although he seems never to have achieved any enduring sexual expression of that intimacy with any woman for whom he felt deep affection. Yet each man in his own way tried to create a home for himself and for someone less fortunate. For Harry, there was Jimmie, whom he named in his will as his sole heir, "my friend and ward in fact." He goes on to state the relationship, as of March 9, 1939, the date of the will: "Said James Inscoe Sullivan has resided with me since the age of about fifteen years, and has been, in all senses, a son to me, and has my love and affection as such."

Although the bulk of Bellinger's fairly large estate went to Syracuse University, his will also provided for two children of his chauffeur and his housekeeper, who were Catholic: "While I owe no obligation to said boys, nevertheless on account of my affection for them, and the fact that the first years of their lives were spent in my household, I desire to make some provision for, and contribution to, their security and welfare. I am especially desirous that neither of these boys be ever committed to an institution, but rather if necessary that they be cared for in a foster home, to be approved by the Catholic Charities." The will goes on to bequeath a trust of $15,000 and the income from a two-family residential property. Outside of the funds for Syracuse, it was the largest single provision in the will.

There is an amusing variation in a minor particular of their adult lives. In 1936 Sullivan acquired a five-floor town house in New York City; as part of his elaborate remodeling of this house, he had an elevator shaft installed, but the elevator itself never materialized; he went broke first, as was his wont. After Bellinger came to Brooklyn State Hospital in 1935, he managed successfuly to get a private elevator installed by the State for his penthouse apartment on the roof of the main hospital building. And the elevator worked. Bellinger had a knack for getting things done, as he has reported about himself. In the *Reader's Digest* article mentioned earlier, the writer marvels at the fact that Bellinger was able to obtain, during the war years, metal steam carts for keeping food hot while it was taken to wards where patients were unable to get to the dining room; such equipment was then almost unobtainable. She asked Bellinger how he managed to get these metal carts. " 'Why,' Dr. Bellinger answered impatiently, 'I wanted them!' "[13] Sullivan's methods for obtaining the unobtainable were somewhat less successful at times; but he, too, had a knack for often achieving the impossible. For both of them, it was undoubtedly one of the dividends from being an only child.

❧ 35 ❧

A Problem in Economics

Why do some people show a peculiar disregard for
the traditions of New England economy and thrift?
Why do certain members of the best New England
families, instead of carrying on the family tradition,
become shocking spendthrifts? Why do a great number of those people, strewn here and there in the
United States, lead to a vast expanse of dangerous
credit? That is something like a problem in economics, I suppose. We meet those people in the mental
hospitals and outside of them; in fact, I am one of
them myself.
—Sullivan, *Proceedings, First Colloquium*

O N February 24, 1932, Sullivan filed a Debtor's Petition in the
Southern District Court of New York; on June 8, 1933, the proceedings were completed, and he was declared a bankrupt. But the problem was not over; it embarrassed him for the rest of his life, although he
maintained a rather stoic front on the subject.

In the Colloquium statement Sullivan has identified himself somewhat
indirectly as a member of "the best New England families." Some of the
descendants of these New England families lived in Chenango County,
but neither their financial situation nor their attitudes had much to do
with Sullivan's. In a 1946 lecture, he provided indirectly an insight into
his own early experience in economics. He imagines for his audience a
monologue on the topic of economic class that he, as a psychiatrist, might
have with a hypothetical patient, summarizing for the patient's benefit
what he has learned from him up to that point: "Now I understand that
you were born in the country in central New York—a poor farm in an
area where agriculture had really deteriorated into dairying; that in your
home there was no particular luxury—in fact, circumstances were pretty

25. *Clarence Bellinger and his mother on the penthouse roof of Brooklyn State Hospital, 1936*

26. *Sullivan on a Sunday morning in the Blitzstens' garden, 1938*

27. *Margaret Bourke-White's picture of Sullivan, about 1935*

tight. You recall that you had never actually seen money until you were six or seven; and it is quite clear that most of the running expenses of the home were on credit until the harvest, if any, could be converted into money. So it was anything but a plush, prosperous situation."[1] Sullivan is obviously talking about himself here, although he was not born on a farm. It is likely that he did not see money until after he had started school in the village; and, as in other small farm households of that period, there was no money for cash purchases until after the harvest; the running expenses were taken care of by credit for much of the year. He also suggests in this thumbnail sketch of a patient that his lack of familiarity with money was a serious handicap. But he does not go on to any clinical or theoretical formulation from this sketch, as he is wont to do. And in the Colloquium statement, he has merely singled out a "problem in economics" deserving of research.

The magnitude of Sullivan's anxiety about money can be glimpsed in his inability to make significant theoretical use of a difficulty in living that he clearly recognized. He was a skilled observer of himself; and in other areas of personal difficulty he used his own experience in developing his theory and in his clinical practice, but he offered no solution for this particular problem. He often makes a clear connection between poverty on the one hand and crime or mental disorder on the other; but he viewed his own tendency toward reckless and extravagant purchases as something that he could not solve for himself or for others.

Some of the stories about Sullivan's eccentricities seem less strange when one reviews the level of his anxiety concerning money. Thus his abrupt termination of his relationship with his cousin Margaret Hannon, after he had been unable—for whatever reason—to pay the check at the Waldorf-Astoria, seems more meaningful in this context. His stern admonition to Evans, his assistant at Sheppard, about the sale of the Studebaker, followed by a plan that would make it overly easy for Evans to meet the payments, again underscores his anxiety about money. And finally, his abrupt and permanent leave-taking from Norwich—and Chenango County—after his father's funeral has some of the same dimensions.

At the same time, Sullivan's difficulty with money has to be seen within the historical context of the socialist experiment in Russia and the great depression in the United States as they both began to affect many people in the 1930s. Clara Thompson told of Sullivan's disdain for her middleclass values, while she was teaching him her own insights from Ferenczi; he terminated that formal arrangement with her when she objected to his expensive refurbishments for one of his New York City establishments, predicting that he would go into bankruptcy. Her values were too "bourgeois" for him, he told her; and he proceeded to go into bankruptcy, according to Thompson.

Various colleagues and friends report that Sullivan went into bank-

ruptcy twice, once in the early thirties and again near the end of the decade. While there is evidence that he was in serious financial trouble in
1938 and 1939, only one official record of a bankruptcy in either New
York or Maryland exists—the 1932–1933 bankruptcy in New York. The
1932 Debtor's Petition gives some picture of Sullivan's life in the previous
three years. His debts totaled over $28,000, a sizeable amount of money
then; less than $3,000 of this amount was secured in any way, either with
actual merchandise or by rental advances. Unsecured loans from friends
and colleagues totaled about $12,000. The first name on the unalphabe-
tized list of such creditors in the Petition was Freud's translator, A. A.
Brill, who had loaned Sullivan $550 in November 1930, as evidenced by a
note. Other people who are listed loaned Sullivan more or less than Brill,
earlier or later, so it seems clear that Sullivan put Brill's name first for its
prestige value; a psychiatrist who could borrow $550 from Brill in 1930
on a personal note obviously had some distinction.

The first and largest personal loan made in 1930 was for $3,050 in July,
obtained from Clara Thompson, whose address is given on the Petition as
Budapest, Hungary. Thus in the first month after Sullivan's termination
at Sheppard, but while he was still living in Towson, he began to go into
debt. In the fall of 1930, still without any significant income, he needed
more money for living expenses and for his projected move. In October,
he borrowed $500 from his psychiatric colleague, Lawson G. Lowrey;
and in November, he obtained the loan from Brill. In December, the actual month of the move, he negotiated his first documented loan ($117)
from Ernest E. Hadley, who would for another decade and a half support
Sullivan and his ideas with an extraordinary outlay of time, energy, and
money.

The Petition shows another period of generous participation of friends,
in the spring of 1931. In March, Chapman contributed $500. In June, Sil-
verberg was called upon for $215, during the period when Sullivan had to
make a hurried trip to Chenango County to attend his dying father. In
July, Sullivan made his largest personal loan—probably in the vain hope
of recouping at one fell swoop—by borrowing $7,000 from "Dr. and Mrs.
David M. Levy" of "Croton-on-Hudson."

Of the forty-nine unsecured claims in the Petition, about $5,000 was
spent for residence and office furniture. Other unsecured claims included
the bill for a Frigidaire water cooler purchased in September 1931 for
$325; the Petition even included $2.00 from December 1931 for drinking
water. There were a dozen bills left over from the Sheppard period, including a bill for "merchandise" from a piano company in Baltimore, a
grocery bill, a garage bill, an electric bill for the last month in Towson,
and several bills for printing and engraving services, including one from
the Lord Baltimore Press for $137.50. And finally, the Petition listed all
the debts for his father's last illness and the school taxes on the farm in

Smyrna; the value of the farm and its equipment did not equal his father's debts.

The bill from the Lord Baltimore Press is of some importance in Sullivan's subsequent history; in 1946, when I started work for Sullivan on his journal, *Psychiatry,* the printing bills from the same press were several thousand dollars in arrears. Thus some fifteen years after the Press had lost $137.50, its representative, Don Reeve, who had known Sullivan since his days at Sheppard, was willing to support Sullivan as best he could against the fiscal demands and needs of the Press, and bills for the journal were submitted as long as a year after the work was completed.

In the fourteen months between his move to New York and the filing of the Petition, Sullivan had had a discouraging time. He was still recovering from his defeat at Sheppard, his bills were mounting, and the expected patients did not arrive. On March 25, 1931, White as chairman (in name only) of the Colloquia Committee wrote to Sullivan requesting data from him for a report on the Committee's activities during the preceding year. Sullivan waited until May 4, 1931, to answer White's letter—an unprecedented delay, particularly since White had indicated some urgency in the matter. In an angry letter, Sullivan reminded White that there had been three matters that required some action:

As to the first; namely, cooperation with students of the social sciences, I may say that I know of no material development during the past year. As to the second; namely, the mutual utilization of more comprehensive information on personality phenomena, I know of no development during the past year. As to the third; namely, the matter of the formation of a Joint Committee on Psychiatric Education, I understand that Dr. Barrett, as Chairman or first-named member of the group appointed by the Council to this purpose, has been asked to make a report. I judge, therefore, that this is no longer a matter to be reported upon by your Committee.

In brief, as a result of unnumbered factors only a few of which are known to me, the Committee on Relations with the Social Sciences appears to have lain fallow during the current year.

On October 29, 1931, Sullivan wrote to White's wife, Lola, for whom he had a great deal of admiration and regard, and reported on the dismalness of his affairs since he had resigned from Sheppard:

I hear . . . that you were inquiring for my address. It is a very genuine pleasure to receive this assurance of some surviving interest in my for some considerable time extraordinarily inconspicuous existence. . . .

Circumstances have conspired to make the last year and a half decidedly divergent from my accustomed course. I have committed myself to the writing of a book, for which I have no trace of the incredible talent of Dr. White. It is now in its fifth revision and begins to approximate what I wish to produce. I am beginning to surmise that it may be published sometime in the next six months.

Also, the development of private practice in the depression of the century has been occasion of no little stress and tribulation. As nearly as I can discover, the two hundred fifty thousand schizophrenics in the United States are being cared for to the satisfaction of all concerned, and my services can be dispensed with for the time being. Of course this comes as a great shock to me, but a not wholly unexpected one.

I hope that I may have the pleasure of seeing you both with opportunity to discuss one of my research dreams, not more distantly than the holiday week following Christmas. In the meanwhile, let me repeat the expression of my gratitude for your so kindly remembering me.

The letter affords further insight into the state of Sullivan's practice and his mood by October. The answer to Mrs. White's inquiry about his address is more elaborate than necessary; White and Sullivan have been in correspondence on matters having to do with patients, so White has Sullivan's office address. Mrs. White's letter takes recognition of the fact that Sullivan has had to move his residence from Park Avenue, so he can mention his financial situation to her. Thus Mrs. White's inquiry is interpreted by Sullivan as a renewal of friendly interest after the disjunction between White and Sullivan. Sullivan is indirectly apologizing and testing the waters; and it is easier to do this with Mrs. White.

This method of indirection was often employed by Sullivan when he felt anxious or when he wanted to apologize—something he did not do directly. At the time I knew him—from 1946 until his death in 1949—he often made a kind of apology to a given person by talking about that person with one of his dogs who wandered in and out of his office. In a singsong, soothing Gaelic way he once apologized to me for his annoyance at my inadvertent tardiness in arriving in Bethesda on a Sunday morning, by discussing the matter with Blondie, one of the cocker spaniels that rather dominated the household: "She works very hard, doesn't she, Blondie? And she gets up early and rides out on the bus to do a good turn for us, doesn't she?" and so on and on, with the dog utterly absorbed in Sullivan's communications and beginning to regard me as more friend than enemy. Blondie had a reputation for occasionally nipping at visitors, so I had learned to be rather careful when I came to the house. After one such conversation of some intensity, I was never bothered by Blondie again. Frieda Fromm-Reichmann has reported this same kind of communication when Jimmie and Sullivan visited her with several of the dogs in the summer of 1946 in Santa Fe.

This insecurity about relationships was something that Sullivan was fully aware of. "My attitude towards interpersonal relations is rather pessimistic," he wrote in 1939; "a measure of personal success is, therefore, more frequent than is its anticipation. The attitude was fixed in the early years, not so much by a series of failures as by the continuing danger to my security which a failure due to over-optimism would have entailed."[2]

There seems little doubt that all of Sullivan's financial wheeling and dealing reverberated in the psychiatric community at the time; it still reverberates. More of his psychiatric colleagues have volunteered information about his financial dealings than about any other of his eccentricities. Many of these stories seem accurate, and most of them probably have at least some basis in fact; but some others seem to be purely legend. One colleague reported that Sullivan listed Abercrombie and Fitch as one of the sizeable creditors in the 1932 Petition; and that on the day after Sullivan was declared a bankrupt in 1933, he cheerfully opened a new account with the same firm, with no expectation of ever repaying the earlier debt. Such a transaction may have taken place informally, but there is no record of it in the 1932–1933 bankruptcy proceedings. Yet Sullivan had wiped the slate clean, and he acknowledged no particular debt to his former creditors, particularly commercial firms. As for personal loans, he experienced more anguish. Some of his colleagues who had made large personal loans felt puzzled and hurt as the years went by and no formal restitution or apology was forthcoming. Thus David Levy, who greatly respected Sullivan's clinical judgment, complained to several colleagues about Sullivan's failure to make any attempt to pay back the money he had loaned him.

A serious implication of the bankruptcy is found in Sullivan's increasing reputation as incorrigibly eccentric in all ways. A series of communications between White and Sullivan over the arrangements for a dinner party may serve to illustrate the complexity of this process generally, and of White's growing anxiety about Sullivan's behavior. In the fall of 1932—during the interim between the Petition for bankruptcy and the final proceedings—Sullivan was active in arranging for a testimonial dinner on October 15 at the Waldorf-Astoria for his good friend Emanuel Libman, his own physician for many years and widely recognized as a brilliant diagnostician and internist. Two weeks before the event, Sullivan invited William Alanson White and his wife to be guests at his table, informing White that A. A. Brill, David Levy and his wife, William Silverberg, and several others would also be guests at the same table. Undoubtedly it was Sullivan's anxiety about money that made it seem entirely appropriate to entertain some of his creditors in this fashion at the very time when he was in the process of legally erasing his financial obligations to them; almost anyone might define this behavior as somewhat erratic. White, who was not listed as a creditor in the Petition, accepted the invitation promptly.

On October 7, eight days before the dinner was to take place, Sullivan wrote to White again:

I am chagrined to discover that a few women physicians only are being seated for the Libman dinner. I presume that Mrs. White would not care to participate in an affair that approaches a wholly male aggregation. This newest evidence of my insufferable stupidity in anything remotely social just about sinks me.

Will you present my abject apologies, and express my hope that if Mrs. White accompanies you to New York City on the fifteenth, you will both have dinner, luncheon, or breakfast with me the next day, Sunday.

On the next day, Sullivan sent a telegram to White, with further corrections to the plans for the ladies:

ADVISED LADIES WISHING TO BE PRESENT DURING THE DINNER CAN BE ACCOMMODATED AS SPECTATORS IN THE BALCONY STOP HOPE THAT THIS WILL SUPPLEMENT MY LETTER OF YESTERDAY SATISFACTORILY.

On the tenth of October, White wrote to Sullivan as follows:

I have your letter, your telephone, your telegram, your invitations, your modifications and compensations, defences, et al., to all of which I reply O.K. Don't worry. Everything is all right, and in order to assist you in making the necessary psychological adjustment may I say that if anything had happened that was less complex, contradictory, inconsistent and confusing, I would have known that it did not come from Sullivan. Therefore I hand you, already prepared a thoroughly good alibi, which I am sure will work beautifully, maximate your ego, and on the whole justify everything whatsoever notwithstanding.

The words "complex, contradictory, inconsistent, and confusing" seem unkind in light of Sullivan's embarrassment about disinviting Mrs. White, whom Sullivan greatly admired. The rules for attendance at the dinner were obviously not of Sullivan's making and were narrowly professional even for that period. Thus White did not discriminate between what was indeed eccentric and anxiety-provoking about Sullivan's entertaining his creditors (and White had surely learned of the identity of the creditors by then) and Sullivan's growing disaffection for the false barriers of professionalism, gender, and race.

The interchange seems significant mainly because it demonstrates the interactive process then in force throughout the psychiatric community that would eventually define Sullivan as a radical and a somewhat dangerous professional friend; not all of his psychiatric colleagues participated in this process, but it was a strong surge that would eventually break forth in new irrationalities after his death, when he became as politically suspect as if he had been Karl Marx himself. An illustration of that irrationality can be found, after Sullivan's death, in the unwillingness of the Washington Psychoanalytic Society to include in its library certain relevant books, such as first editions of Freud's early books, if they carried a nameplate identifying them as having come jointly from the Washington School of Psychiatry and the Washington-Baltimore Psychoanalytic Society.

This same fear resulted in a period of probation for the Washington group of psychoanalysts, ordained by the American Psychoanalytic Association, until the local group had divested itself of its association with Sullivan and his radical ideas. This fearsome fight, in which people who had received their most important training under Sullivan would begin to recant—to make a distinction between "the psychoanalyst" Ernest E. Hadley, for instance, and Sullivan, the "superficial" practitioner of a pseudo psychoanalysis—resulted in one of the truly amazing distortions in the intellectual history of psychoanalysis in this country. In this mythical history, there is very little recognition of the way in which psychoanalysts were trained in Europe and America in the early third of this century; and artificial standards for training were set for Sullivan which were not followed by anybody at that period, including Hadley, William Alanson White, and, of course, Freud himself. Thus White is generally considered a "pioneer psychoanalyst," as A. R. T. D'Amore has aptly named him.[3] Yet White's training largely occurred in long conversations between himself and Jelliffe, in which they explored as equals the implications of the dynamic approach represented by Freud's discovery of the place of the unconscious in behavior. By contrast, Sullivan's training, as documented here, was considerably more extensive.

To some extent it is easy to be critical of Sullivan as one views retrospectively some of his financial tribulations over the years, beginning with his exit from Sheppard. Many colleagues have commented on the fact that the fees from only a handful of wealthy patients would have been enough to meet his insatiable need for money. They lamented the ease with which he would go off on a new venture—eager, excited, curious about some new source of data on human beings, and hopeful that his friends would provide. But in a larger sense there were social and historical components of his financial improvidence that force one to be less dogmatic about the meaning of his difficulties.

Almost from the beginning, he had an Irish sense of mission, transmitted primarily from the Stacks but also a part of the tradition of many Irish intellectuals. Thus James Joyce's biographer has commented on the place of money and artistic creativity in Joyce's scheme of things: "The surface of the life Joyce lived seemed always erratic and provisional. But its central meaning was directed as consciously as his work. . . . [H]is disregard for bourgeois thrift and convention was the splendid extravagance which enabled him in literature to make an intractable wilderness into a new state."[4] Again to suggest the Irish nature of Sullivan's 'problem,' he expected people to be as generous with him as he was with others. This

328   PSYCHIATRIST OF AMERICA

was not a reciprocal generosity, but rather a generosity he received from one set of well-heeled colleagues that he tended to pass on to others—patients, friends, and young colleagues. Within the tradition of "cooring" in County Clare, one had the *right* to help someone in need.[5] There are many reliable stories of Sullivan's generosity. Thus when Margaret Bourke-White came to his door for help, she paid the bill by taking pictures of Sullivan—one of which, with no credit to the famous photographer, has been used by others over and over again for, at times, dubious purposes of promotion.

Or again, Sullivan once created a minor job and provided a room for the indigent patient of a young trainee. Sullivan excused his generosity by noting that he had been following the patient's progress for some time through reports from the trainee; and he was unwilling to have the patient, who was still in need of care, stop treatment and therefore deprive Sullivan of research data. In reality, he was dedicated to both patient and trainee.

Near the end of his life, Sullivan once complained to a trainee that he only knew patients, noting that even Jimmie was an ex-patient; indeed most of his colleagues, even senior ones, would feel free to call him late at night for advice on their own marriages, or the crisis of a relative, so that near the end of his life, his skill in all human relationships was such that he was constantly engaged in some kind of therapeutic intervention—even with strangers on trains. When I worked for Sullivan, I opened any of his mail that came into my office; and at least twice I found letters from strangers who said that Sullivan had permanently changed their lives by a brief conversation on a train. "I know you won't remember me . . ." the letters would begin, in essence. As one surveys the tremendous number of people who were beneficially influenced by Sullivan and the depleted state of his financial holdings at the time of his death, it is difficult indeed to find any psychiatrist or psychoanalyst of note that accomplished so much and earned so little money.

From another perspective, however, he managed over time to acquire a fair number of extravagant possessions, for which he had an almost compulsive need. He had little patience for postponing his need for beautiful objects. At the June 1938 meeting of the American Psychiatric Association, held in San Francisco, he was again on the verge of bankruptcy and was no doubt rescued by affluent colleagues. Yet he exhibited a total disregard for what they considered appropriate behavior: he entered a small gathering of some of these colleagues in one of the suites at the hotel with a "handful" of opals that he had just purchased at Gump's; and some of his colleagues watched with dismay while he lovingly examined the colors and exclaimed on the luminosity of the treasures, which they felt had been purchased with their money. A few years later even his most loyal supporter, Ernest Hadley, lost patience with one last demand—that Hadley finance the purchase of substantially grown trees with which to make Sullivan's already secluded Bethesda house even more hidden from the road. Even though there were other more serious estrangements between Hadley and Sullivan by then, Hadley's wife, Agnes Marie—a staunch friend of Sullivan's over the years—felt that the demand for the trees constituted the final straw that terminated the relationship.

Whatever the roots of Sullivan's eccentricities about money, there seems little doubt that personal crises and tragedies increased the level of his extravagances. After the major defeat at Sheppard, his defeat in New York, in the midst of the depression, was devastating, and he became more reckless in his purchases. Again, in 1938, at the time he bought the opals, he was under great stress about Sapir whom he feared was fatally ill; shortly afterward he took the ocean trip to England in which his fees from a wealthy patient (for whom he was making the trip) were largely spent on luxurious traveling expenses for his companions. On several occasions, I myself observed that he was extravagant about tipping cab drivers when he was temporarily upset by some crisis in professional politics.

Finally, he was, like every other intellectually aware person of that period, affected by the great economic experiment in the U.S.S.R. and its implications for Western society. One of his patients in New York, Dorothy Schiff, who later became editor and publisher of the *New York Post,* has reported rather extensively on her relationship with Sullivan.[6] Brought up in a wealthy, Republican household, she led a sheltered and, by Sullivan's standards, meaningless existence until she developed an "anxiety neurosis" of some intensity after the birth of her third child. Schiff was impressed by Sullivan's "socialistic ideas." Although she resented his indifference to her "servant problems," for instance, she made significant and radical changes in her personal life within a short time after she began work with Sullivan. She moved from a splendid and remote establishment on Long Island to a hotel in New York City, where she and her husband occupied one apartment and the children, governess, and nurse occupied another. Sullivan worried about the effect of luxurious hotel life on her children; he referred to it as "pretty fancy living," but he supposed that her "kind of children" would have to live in this style anyway. Within a few months after she began to see Sullivan in the summer of 1934, Schiff enrolled in the New School University in Exile, and she began shortly to become involved in politics of an altogether different nature from that to which she was born. Eventually she became an important part of the Democratic Party in New York State and then, in the summer of 1936, a confidant of Franklin Roosevelt. Almost coincidentally she terminated treatment with Sullivan: "As for me," she wrote, "I was in the real world and had gone on to new interests. I didn't need a psychiatrist now; I had a President."

The termination of her work with Sullivan represented a disappointment of some magnitude for him, for she had insisted on helping to support his research. Schiff reports that a year after she started work with Sullivan, she began to be "impressed by his dedication to socialism." He discussed his work with her, including his association with various colleagues—Karen Horney, and some of his colleagues from his days at St. Elizabeths. She realized that he was having difficulty raising funds for research and training, and she told him that she would like to make a contribution. She reports that he hesitated, before explaining that "it was absolutely not permissible for a patient to give money to anything a therapist was involved with, or words to that effect. He may have used the word 'ethical,' but I'm not sure." She persuaded him that this was ridiculous, that she could afford it and that it would be used to help a lot of people. She reports that he let her send a check to the William Alanson White Psychiatric Foundation for $15,000 (in reality, she gave $22,500 over a four-month period, according to official Foundation records). Dorothy Schiff subsequently wondered whether or not she made a mistake in talking him into accepting the money, but she did not feel that it interfered with their work. In the fall of 1935, shortly before she made her first gift, she joined the Democratic Party, and she felt that "he may have decided I wasn't hopeless after all."

The Foundation records provide more details of this transaction. Various papers document Dorothy Schiff's gifts to the Foundation for the express purpose of supporting Sullivan's research. The first gift of $7,500, was given on December 31, 1935, with a covering letter in which Dorothy Schiff designated this amount for Sullivan's use at his discretion for "research and promotional work for the Foundation." The second one, given on April 6, 1936, a few months before she terminated her treatment with Sullivan, was for $15,000 in securities; $12,000 of this was to be used for salary for Sullivan, according to Schiff's stipulation, "to free him to devote part of his time to research and other activities for the Foundation." In her covering letter, she also states that if the plans for a fellowship training course in New York City materialized, she would try to find "a like sum for this purpose in the next two years."

Schiff's original gift of $7,500 was the first major contribution made to the Foundation by other than the actual trustee members, so that it received a fair amount of attention. Sullivan himself composed a letter for "Dr. White's proposed signature," to be sent to Schiff under date of February 27, 1936. There is no indication as to whether it was ever sent, but its contents are of some interest; Sullivan included a beginning definition of the Foundation, then becoming active for the first time, although it had been incorporated in late 1933: "The exploration of human personality and its distortions, the mental disorders which constitute the greatest public health problem of today, will undoubtedly take large sums of money, expended over a considerable period of time. At the present time, this is undoubtedly a legitimate field for the expenditure of private funds, but we shall look forward to the day when some public appropriations, at least those for the care and treatment of the so-called insane, will carry with them automatically a certain percentage to be set aside for scientific research work."

The announcement of the second gift, twice as large as the first, was made at the meeting of the Foundation on April 11, 1936. The reality of the first gift from Dorothy Schiff and the anticipation of the second had already involved Sullivan in the purchase of the house on East 64th Street. Schiff was surprised and flattered that Sullivan consulted her about the purchase of this house. It seems no coincidence that Sullivan's house was only two or three blocks from the double house built by Sara Delano Roosevelt, one for herself and the other for her son and his bride, for Sullivan was as interested in the Roosevelts and the New Deal as Dorothy Schiff.

Although Schiff had specified that her gift should be used in large part to support Sullivan's work, in the form of a monthly salary of $1,000, Sullivan always envisioned fresh money as being earmarked for new expansion; the house must be seen as an example of this tendency. The arrangements for the purchase of the house stirred up in the Board of Trustees a whole series of anxieties. Sullivan justified it as a necessary office space for the research that he and Edward Sapir would carry out. In a letter to Hadley dated February 28, 1936, Sullivan notes one of his justifications for the transaction: "Certainly, it looks as if we were getting space for the research well below the charges that would be made by an office building; there seems far too great a risk of trouble connected with using gilt edge residential space for a research practice including Negroes and Chinese."

Not all of Sullivan's plans for the Foundation's support of his house materialized, however. The Board of Trustees, in its meeting of April 11, 1936, began to place some restrictions on Sullivan's grand plans; again, there was some confusion as to what use would be made of the money. Was it to be used for Sullivan's salary or for the purchase of the house? There was not enough for both, but Sullivan kept both options open in his mind. White proposed that Dorothy Schiff be asked to sign a specific statement on how her second gift was to be used in the current year; and two of the trustees, Sapir and Brill, supported White's formal resolution, to Sullivan's chagrin. Since Schiff's earlier letter to the Foundation had been quite specific, the formal statement, subsequently signed by Dorothy Schiff, was an unnecessary cruelty to Sullivan. White was again acting on Sullivan's reputation, without knowledge of all the facts, as he later admitted. Whatever Sullivan's difficulties with money, there might have been other ways to trim Sullivan's financial sails without expressing doubt directly to his patient and benefactor.

By this time, Sullivan was frantically trying to establish some financial stability for Sapir, who had a serious heart condition. Sapir felt a continual stress at Yale which he had not experienced at the University of Chicago; in particular, he felt he had been excluded from the Faculty Club at Yale because he was a Jew. Sullivan was already beginning to study in earnest the relationship of stress to heart disease, partly because he believed that he suffered from the same propensity. He wanted to offer Sapir a full-time position; yet the financing of Sapir and his family, particularly if Sapir faced a relatively early death, required a great deal of money. There were three children by the first marriage and two by the second; in 1936, the oldest child was twenty-four and the youngest about five years of age. Thus Schiff's originial proposal to finance Sullivan's salary for 1937 and 1938 meant some security for him while he traveled around trying to drum up a substantial endowment for the Foundation, including salaries for himself and Sapir. Again, Sullivan had put too much faith in the hope that something would turn up, and that it would be possible for him to find support for all the plans he had made.

In the summer of 1936, Dorothy Schiff terminated her treatment with Sullivan, and her financial support as patient and donor vanished. Her story is poignant and tells something about Sullivan's way with patients. In the process of her personal growth, Schiff agreed to make a speech on a national radio hookup for the Democratic Party; she was at that time a shy and insecure woman, and she was very anxious about this scheduled speech; she reports that she did a lot of work on it with Sullivan. In the last part of her speech she spoke of her switch·from being a Republican to working for the reelection of Roosevelt, and of an emergent social consciousness that had some implicit relationship to her work with Sullivan: "And as for class hatred, it grows out of unbearable inequalities—social neglect, joblessness, hunger and despair. More and more I feel how dependent we are, one on another. It is impossible for us or our children to be happy and safe unless women and children belonging to less fortunate groups can be happy and safe, too."

Schiff was so exhilarated by the radio experience that she raced to Sullivan's office to ask him how he thought she had done. He appeared to not know what she meant, and she was outraged. She pointed out to him that he had been working with her on the speech for weeks, so he must have known of her fears about it. He asked her how she felt she had done. She reported that she had managed to get through it; "but you must have heard it," she questioned him. " 'No,' he said, 'It isn't my function to listen to you on the radio. Anyway, the electrician was here, but I never had any doubt that you would be all right.' " She was very upset by what she defined as his indifference to her; she seemed to have been unaware that he had other commitments: "I knew better but I still had to have total dedication. I had to be the only one." She charged him with not being human and shortly left his office. She never saw him again. A few weeks later she received a long letter from him, saying that she had not finished her analysis and predicting what might happen to her without further work. She reports in her book that she did need help twenty years later, and that Sullivan had been right.

The loss of Schiff as a patient must have been a bitter disappointment for him. He was meticulous about not taking advantage of his patients, but he was wise enough to understand that he had helped her find a more productive life, and that his work might have been even more amply supported by her over the years. In particular, his plans for working with Sapir had received a serious and perhaps crucial setback; by 1939, Sapir had died, without ever leaving Yale. As with many other creative people in the society, Sullivan began to question the disproportionate distribution of wealth that continued to place him in the position of supplicant or spendthrift.

✍ 36 ✍

Being Free

It is completely irrational to suppose that love can be
other than a high regard for the satisfactions and security of the partner approaching or equaling one's
feeling for one's own satisfactions and security. Now
when that situation is achieved with the biologically
ordained mate of the human being . . . it represents
maturity to me. Not that there is any magic in love,
but it removes the last of the grave problems connected with growing up, so that one is at long last
free to devote the astounding adjustive capacities of
the human being to things which matter in that day
and age. . . . When I speak of one's finally being free
to devote one's abilities to such contribution as one
can make to whatever the general welfare or the sum
total of good or whatever else you wish to quote as
durable justification for life may be, that comes only
when one has established a relationship of love in
both the biologically and culturally ordained rational
sense.

—Sullivan, unpublished lecture

S ULLIVAN felt deprived and embarrassed at times over his inability to
achieve a "relationship of love in both the biologically and culturally
ordained rational sense." He saw "homosexuality as a developmental
mistake, dictated by the culture as substitutive behavior in those instances in which the person cannot do what is the simplest thing to do."[1]
Love could exist between any two people as long as the other person's satisfactions and security were as important as one's own; but heterosexual
love, expressed biologically, made one "at long last free." Over time he
achieved his own freedom, however flawed. Friends and colleagues of
Sullivan's, by their "direct knowledge," report that he had some sexual
experiences with women as well as with men. But there is no ready label
for how he lived and thought and yearned.

Sullivan did not think that many of his married friends had achieved a loving relationship, and he anguished over them when they threw away golden opportunities for "being free." Some of his comments about them were sharp and wry:

I, as you know, am not a benedict, and so my richest field of observation of me-you patterns has been a pastime for misery when I have been a guest in some of my [married] acquaintances' homes so long that they got used to me and acted natural. And really, the little dramas that they run off between themselves gives one a feeling of simple incoherence. The wife is friend, enemy, mother, daughter, public prostitute, and all sorts of things in the course of an evening. And hubby plays his role in it, and she plays hers, and never the twain shall meet, you know. I am exhausted, but they are not. They go on—they live that way by the year. Certain things call out certain patterns, and the fact that they simply are absolutely contradictory to the patterns that were being manifested fifteen minutes before that does not bother anybody but the observer.[2]

In 1942, Sullivan described himself as a "slight, bespectacled mild-looking bachelor with thinning hair and mustache."[3] But Jimmie and Sullivan only partially accepted their bachelorhood; from time to time, each of them sought escape in fantasy about marriage. Occasionally the fantasy might include an unexpected written proposal of marriage sent to an astonished woman acquaintance.

During Sullivan's early years in New York City, some of his romantic excursions into the idea of marriage seem to have been relatively serious, although he was almost thirty-nine years old when he arrived there. He often spoke of his interest in finding "a rich widow" and expressed great admiration for William Alanson White's wife, who had been a widow of personal and financial grace. White had married for the first time when he was forty-eight years old, so that Sullivan felt he still had some time to emulate White. In New York, he had occasion to meet and know more eligible and attractive women than he had ever had before. For a brief period, he was attentive to Karen Horney; and Jean Sapir remembers Sullivan's pride and delight when he brought Horney with him for a weekend at the Sapirs' New Haven house.

Although he had a grave handicap for sexual intimacy with women, he could be intimate with women in every other way. Throughout his adult life, he seems to have had close and enduring relationships with many women, most of whom were either married or spoken for. Several women interviewed for this book spoke of their feelings for him of closeness and friendliness. One senior psychoanalyst confided in me that she would have left her husband in a moment if Sullivan had indicated any "real" interest in her—although she was generally conceded to be happily married and remained so until her death, many years later. There was a kind of safety for him in relationships with women already married, as if he would not have to reveal his own inadequacies.

On the 1938 trip to Europe, he invited Agnes Marie Hadley to accompany him, Jimmie, and a woman patient to England, with Mrs. Hadley acting as a chaperone for the patient; and Hadley urged his wife to accept the invitation. On the ship going over, they all sat at the captain's table; and during their six-week stay in the west of England, Sullivan spent his days writing and consulting with the patient and the patient's family, while Jimmie and Mrs. Hadley spent their days walking through the countryside. When Hadley and Sullivan came to the parting of the ways in 1945, no one grieved more over the separation of their lives than Mrs. Hadley.

Dorothy Blitsten, the wife of the psychoanalyst Lionel Blitzsten, had an important relationship with Sullivan over a period of many years. Although the Blitzstens were eventually divorced, Sullivan continued to value his friendship with both of them. Sullivan encouraged Dorothy Blitsten in every way to establish herself in a profession; and she eventually became a professor of sociology at Hunter College, where she was a staunch advocate of Sullivan's place in the social sciences. A letter from Sullivan to Dorothy Blitsten written in 1940 sums up his reluctance to see any marriage casually terminated:

Our present knowledge of life suggests that the course of your marital events is determined by a sort of vector addition of sympathetic and conflicting tendencies. In the limited field of sexual intimacy, the course had been away from such intimacies and there is no sufficient determining influence to change its direction. In many other fields of behavior, the course seems to be quite satisfactory. A perfectionist might be willing to forego everything, if there was any imperfection. A person lost in psychoanalytic thinking might feel that the absence of lustful rapport indicated that everything was wrong. Both of these attitudes seem to me tedious in the extreme.

In a brief sentence: It seems to me that you give each other a good deal that is valuable and that it is deplorable that there are verbal attacks and appeals to "will" and "deciding" for the alteration of this relationship to something other than it now is. I almost recommend a monthly reading of Mark Twain's "The Mysterious Stranger."[4]

Mark Twain's posthumous story, The Mysterious Stranger, is a recurring interest of Sullivan's.[5] There is a curious fatalism embedded in this story: The mysterious stranger, a nephew of the original Satan, cannot believe that people around him want to stop a terrible event from happening; he accedes to the wishes of mere humans for such magic intervention, but each time the outcome is much worse than the original disaster. Sullivan seemed to use the story as a parable for psychoanalysts and psychiatrists: They might feel that they have the foresight to advise their patients on what changes to make, but such foresight is human and not perfect, so that the outcome may indeed be much worse than anything that could have been imagined; if a change is to be made, then the person must decide for himself, for no one else has the wisdom to dictate such a change to another human being.

Sullivan's letter to Dorothy Blitsten shows his acceptance of his own lot in life, making it possible for him to deal gracefully with the marital problems of his friends. But earlier—in particular near the end of his years at Sheppard—he had a tragic awareness of his own situation. He had clear evidence from his patients—young males showing acute schizophrenic-like panic—that fear of so-called aberrant sexual cravings in the transition to adolescence was often a prelude to schizophrenic panic; and that early and skilled care within a therapeutic milieu could effect a social recovery, with the patient acquiring an ability to handle sexual needs without interfering drastically with his self-esteem. By then, Sullivan was in the fourth decade of life, and he felt that his pattern of life was already determined; thus his discovery could help others more than it could effect any change in himself. In 1929, he reports on his conclusion from the Sheppard experience: "In brief, if the general population were to pass through schizophrenic illnesses on their road to adulthood, then it would be the writer's duty, on the basis of his investigation, to urge that sexual experience be provided for all youths in the homosexual phase of personality genesis in order that they might not become hopelessly lost in the welter of dream-thinking and cosmic fantasy making up the mental illness." His data and certain considerations which he spells out in the same article "lend pragmatically sufficient justification for the doctrine of a 'normal' homosexual phase in the evolution at least of male personality."[6]

Thus almost two decades before the first Kinsey report, in 1948, on the sexual behavior of the human male, Sullivan had arrived from his own data at one of the major findings of that report. He had located the lack of experience with a " 'normal' homosexual phase" in his own growing-up years, and hypothesized that this lack had occasioned his own encounter with schizophrenic episodes. Throughout the rest of his life, he had frequent encounters with that painful experience; as late as 1947, he confided in a woman colleague that he had had severe schizophrenic episodes early in life and that he still had them.[7] He told her that he liked to live alone and spend time away from people so that few people would realize that he had such episodes; in particular he was afraid that he would be put into an institution and that someone would "tamper with his brain."

He spoke of "living alone," although all through this period he was living with Jimmie, of course. Sullivan and Jimmie did in fact maintain an aloneness with each other, almost as if they were one person. Jimmie provided a protected environment and made it possible for Sullivan to accomplish a tremendous amount of work; whether Sullivan had a need for a paper to be typed or for a glass of brandy, Jimmie seemed to under-

stand, without the necessity of words, as if he were indeed Sullivan; and
he moved with quiet efficiency to meet Sullivan's needs. Conversely, Sullivan gave purpose to Jimmie's life. In his own growing up, Jimmie had
been even more damaged than Sullivan—by several accounts he was
mute when they first met—but his intelligence and dedication could be
invested in caring for an important and gifted person. Over the years,
Sullivan came to feel that Jimmie had been cheated—that he might have
moved further and become more of his own person had he not lived with
Sullivan. He confided his sorrow about Jimmie's plight to Frieda
Fromm-Reichmann.[8]

   The most poignant documentation of Sullivan's early awareness that
life had passed him by at some level and that it was too late for him to
'cure himself' is found in two different published comments by Sullivan
on a book authored by "Anomaly" and titled *The Invert and His Social
Adjustment*.[9] In 1927 Sullivan published a long review of the book in the
American Journal of Psychiatry, in which he makes a detailed and revealing estimate of the book, combining a clinical appraisal with personal references, however veiled.[10] Again, in a brief item written for an annotated
bibliography in 1929, prepared for the Second Colloquium, Sullivan describes the book as "a remarkable document by a homosexual man of refinement; intended primarily as a guide to the unfortunate sufferers of
sexual inversion, and much less open to criticism than anything else of
the kind so far published. An interesting psychopathological document."[11]

   In comments peculiarly germane to Sullivan's own experience, Anomaly asserts that inverts do not have homosexual experience in the school
society and states: "I would not assert that the invert boy is *never* received
into the company of other boys, but I am sure that without a struggle, and
without the exercise of unusual talents and great discretion, he seldom
enters the great Freemasonry of boyhood, and that even should he be admitted, he feels that between him and his comrades there lies a gap which
only extraordinary understanding and devotion can bridge."[12]

   In Sullivan's review, he comments on the importance of some "normal" homosexual experience in the adolescent years and cites, as he does
elsewhere several times in slightly different ways, his "research" in this
area (probably in the Smyrna schoolyard): "The refutation of the doctrine of "first experience," has been confirmed by a study made by the re-
viewer: in the community studied, an astonishing proportion of the boys
had engaged habitually in overt homosexual relations. Only a small number failed of heterosexual adjustment of an average type. Those who
failed and continued more or less perverted homosexuals seemed in the
few cases available for study, to have ample determiners for that course,
in the shape of inter-family factors, and the like." Sullivan and Anomaly
agree that if the "first experience" of a sexual nature were determining of

a permanent way of sexual life, then surely half of the male population would end up as homosexuals.

If a "first experience" is not determining, then the relation between the boy and his mother is. Here Sullivan takes exception to Anomaly's statement that the "invert's peculiarly strong and intimate affection for his mother is an effect, not a cause, of his condition."[13] Sullivan suggests that it is perhaps the opposite—the strong attachment of the mother for the son, "with, as a sequel, inversion in the latter. This is especially the case in unhappy marriages—spiteful or otherwise—where the son is required to satisfy the ungratified love-hunger of the mother."

Anomaly himself doubts that cure is possible for a "true invert." On this Sullivan first takes exception to Anomaly's strict definition for a "true invert." No such sharp discrimination exists between a homosexual and heterosexual way of life, Sullivan asserts; all of us have an emotional and sexual interest in both sexes, although the behavior and the primary involvement usually center in one or another direction. Moreover, Sullivan states that "cure" of a homosexual way of life can only be effected if a person wishes to change the pattern of his sexual behavior: "A psychopathologist would hesitate to attempt the 'cure' of a satisfactory adjustment. (And recall that the individual situation determines *in itself* the satisfactory or unsatisfactory nature of its configuration.) [With] no mandate of theological or other transcendental authority, it is not for the physician to say that one satisfactory adjustment is to be preferred in a particular individual to another. One cannot but recall Mark Twain's 'The Mysterious Stranger.' We generally learn to leave well enough alone."

However, given a person's desire for an alteration in himself, a change in inversion can be effected, Sullivan concludes, but " 'cure' in his [Anomaly's] or any other simple sense ceases to be reasonably probable as the sufferer goes through the third decade of life." When he wrote that sentence in 1927, Sullivan was midway through his fourth decade.

Sullivan particularly commends the chapter on "Women, Marriage, Romance," and quotes a sentence italicized in the original: *"In the whole series of parallels between the invert and the normal man there is none more striking nor more pitiful, than the invert's attempt to find peace and satisfaction in the achievement of a permanent union with some similarly conditioned man.*[14]

One of the more comprehensive and intriguing documents that further reveals Sullivan's personal stand on the subject of sex and intimacy is an article entitled "Observations on the Sex Problem in America," written by Edward Sapir in 1928 for the *American Journal of Psychiatry.* The article was written expressly at the invitation of Sullivan, who was at the time acting editor of the journal.[15] This device of getting someone else to write an article on what Sullivan was interested in—after he had determined through long conversations that a consensus had evolved—was a favorite one that Sullivan used during his career as an editor. Indeed Sapir somewhat resented the assignment, as it turned out.

In the article, Sapir pleads for the recognition of cultural values in the patterning of sexual needs: "The problem of sex is fundamentally like any other social problem in that it deals with the attempt of human beings to reconcile their needs with cultural forms that are both friendly and resistant to these needs." He inveighs against the "artificial divorce [that] has been made between the sex impulse and love." The growth of homosexuality in this society can be partly seen as related to this separation of love and sex: "Love having been squeezed out of sex, it revenges itself by assuming unnatural forms. The cult of the 'naturalness' of homosexuality fools no one but those who need a rationalization of their own problems." American morality about sex is quite different from that in western Europe, Sapir states, stressing particularly the situation in France. The higher divorce rate in the United States is related to the "erotic honesty" of most Americans, who basically believe in the value of love; where love fails, divorce follows. In Europe, marital infidelity is the mark of a sophisticated way of life in certain circles. But "Americans make poor Don Juans," Sapir notes.

In one particular passage, Sapir supports the normality of jealousy in a love/sex relationship: "Sex jealousy is . . . said to imply possessiveness. As one emancipated young woman once expressed it to me, it would be an insult to either her or her husband to expect fidelity of them. Yet what is more obvious than that jealousy can no more be weeded out of the human heart than the shadows cast by objects can be obliterated by some mechanism that would restore to them an eternal luminosity?" It was this remark about an "emancipated young woman" that seems to have occasioned a letter of protest that Ruth Benedict wrote to Sapir; it is clear from reading the entire article that this is the only quotation, direct or indirect, to which Benedict could have been referring in her protest. Benedict's letter has not survived, but Sapir's answer is sufficient to reconstruct her letter: "That you would not care for my sex article I took for granted, hence was not interested in sending you a copy, as I do not wish to have our relations unnecessarily muddied by irreconcilable differences, but that you were outraged by a supposed quotation shocked as few things have shocked me. . . . You will probably not believe me—and yet it is the sober truth—when I say that you were never once in my thoughts when I wrote the paper on sex, which I did, by the way, rather reluctantly at the request of Harry Stack Sullivan."[16] One can infer from this interchange that Sapir has heard someone else, other than Benedict, subscribe to the doctrine of absolute freedom in marriage for each partner.

Throughout the article, Sapir is pleading for a conservative approach in the reform of Victorian standards for sexual behavior; some reform is necessary, but love as an ingredient of human relations must remain in tandem with sexual behavior. In many ways Sullivan agreed with this position, although certainly his statements on love and marriage were considerably more complex.

A short time after Sapir's article appeared in print, Sullivan was in Berlin on his first European trip, where he was exposed to the open advocacy of a homosexual way of life in fashionable parts of the city. From subsequent statements made by Sullivan, it appears that he was saddened by the spectacle of so many young people having settled for what he thought of as a second-best way of life.

A year later he spoke in Washington, D.C., on "The Socio-Genesis of Homosexual Behavior" to an audience composed of law-enforcement people and sociologists.[17] In the transcription of his full statement, Sullivan reports a marked increase in the number of homosexual males, and suggests that each generation is showing an increase in that population. "If any of you have doubts as to this, you would do well to inform yourselves of conditions in New York City and Washington." He stresses here that the person showing homosexual tendencies emerges from influences "not hereditary but none the less inevitable, because they were influences which are applied to him in his formative years with the same consequences, which all of you who have studied the evolution of personality see. Now, if that is true, I think it is equally true that sexual activity when it is carried out in a simple and direct fashion takes up an exceedingly small part of one's life and leaves free the vast majority of one's time and a great amount of energy and interest." More than a decade later, he reiterated this theme: "Sex is important for the twenty minutes it may occupy from time to time, but it is not necessarily behind everything else that fills the rest of the time."[18] Over and over again, Sullivan would stress the tremendous waste of human ability that is consumed with worry about aberrant behavior; it is this waste of time that seemed most to bother him.

In the Washington, D.C., paper, he refers to the etiology of the development of a homosexual way of life as usually emerging from the home situation. From life histories collected on this group of people, he reports that a barrier exists against developing an interest in a member of the other sex; these barriers are most often focused on an "abnormal attachment between the mother and son":

Every now and then, at least in the past generation or the present generation, whatever I belong to, women for various reasons, of spleen, economic factors, or whatever, married men who they discovered, on the wedding night or at least during the course of the honeymoon, to be decidedly false alarms, brutes, and what not. But contraceptive measures were not popular in my generation and so out of these unholy marriages there frequently resulted progeny. If the progeny happened to be a boy, in a very, very large number of cases the mother's aversion to the father was considerably relieved because she found in her son someone upon whom to apply a large amount of positive affection which should have been discharged upon the [father]. As a result of this we find, for example, such boys . . . sleeping with their mothers up to fifteen, sixteen, seventeen, which seems to be conventional in many of these situations; and that is only one instance of the enormous amount of effort which is directed by the mother to fixing the son to her.

Such an experience, Sullivan notes, is a very strong motivation for searching for a sexual partner who is "everything that the mother was not, which you might say is a very excellent way to progress into strong sexual interest in members of one's own gender."

During this same general period, he wrote a paper titled "Archaic Sexual Culture and Schizophrenia" for the Third Congress of the World League for Sexual Reform, which met in London in September 1929.[19] This might well be considered his first major paper in the area of preventive psychiatry, for he is concerned here with preventing the waste of young people who arrive at the mental hospital in a state of panic.

The daring of Sapir's and Sullivan's excursions into these fields at that time can be measured by the inaccessibility of all these papers. Sapir's paper is not included in his *Selected Papers* and is not widely known. Sullivan's statement to the sociologists has never been published, although it was given at a meeting of sociologists and police officials in Washington, D.C. And one of the few copies of the *Proceedings* of the Sexual Reform Congress which exist in this country was kept for over thirty years in a vault in the Harvard Law School Library (where, incidentally, also resided a copy of Anomaly's book) and had to be specially requested for examination.

Some time in the New York years, Sullivan asked his artist friend, John Vassos, to design a symbol for him; and this symbol became the horses' heads which are used on all of Sullivan's books, at his explicit request. It would be risky to speculate on the definitive meaning of this symbol, for its antecedents are complex and contradictory; and there is no direct mention of the symbol per se by Sullivan himself in his lectures. Two years before his death, he turned over to me a cut of this insignia and asked that I have it carried on any book publications of his writings; and this request was honored by the Foundation and by the publisher, W. W. Norton & Company.

Other information on the meaning of the insignia comes from the artist and from Jimmie Sullivan. In 1949, shortly after Sullivan's death, Jimmie prepared a memorandum for use in a memorial issue of *Psychiatry* on which we carried this insignia; the editor and I did not use the memorandum as originally submitted, partly because we could not understand what Jimmie meant. Only after I talked with Vassos fifteen years later did I understand Jimmie's memorandum, which read in part: "This symbol with slight modification was reconverted from the Chinese symbol representing Eternal Life. Studied carefully—by those intelligent, the social scientists, psychiatrists, etc., this symbol represents something else. Follow its lines and you will discover. No further discourse need be necessary. A careful scrutiny will communicate." The heads obviously trace out the letter S, but the figures "6" and "9" are not as easily recognized. Vassos has explicitly stated that this is a central intent of the symbol, as Jimmie also implies.[20]

Within the complex of Sullivan's life and theory, there are certain obvious ways to look at the horses' heads. The horse as a symbol of himself was a recurring theme; within his interpersonal theory, a representation of himself would require at least one other person, even if that other person was only imaginary, so there are two horses. If possible, the two people should be on an equal footing, and the heads seem to be perfect negative images of each other. As the Chinese symbol for eternal life, the opposites yin and yang make up the unity. Traditionally, yang is the male part of the symbol, and it means literally the south or sunny side of a hill, hence, light; yang is beneficent, positive, and bright. Yin is female, negative, dark, and evil. In Sullivan's symbol, yin is at the top as reproduced, and this way of turning it was specifically dictated to me by Sullivan. Yet it is difficult to think that Sullivan meant any differentiation between the character of the male and the female. Again, one might suppose that some kind of homosexual intimacy in early adolescence—and perhaps Sullivan is recommending mutual fellatio—might be a reasonable prelude to heterosexuality, and that the symbol is meant to suggest both stages. One might speculate that the symbol is an idealization of Sullivan's relationship with Clarence Bellinger; for the two horses in the insignia seem coequals instead of unequal partners; and there is the representation of some kind of physical intimacy, overt and tender, that was lacking for the two boys who grew up on the hill away from the gang life in the village.

Sullivan often voiced the opinion that only the person who has the dream has any idea of what its symbols mean. It seems safe to say that whatever the meaning of the insignia was for Sullivan, it was not simple and it changed from time to time. In the myth of the Stack family, the "mythological ancestor" is represented as the "West Wind, the horse who runs with the Earth into the future." Yet in order to live a significant life one cannot be alone; nor can one be simply good, or simply evil. But these are my associations to the symbol; and I do not know, of course.

❧ 37 ❧
The Tempo of Life in New York City

On one evening when I came home quite crippled, barely able to ascend the elevator (that is, to survive the elevator boy's comments and fall into my apartment), the protector of my peace and quiet said, "Oh! You must have seen a new patient." And a great light burst on me, and I realized that the times I came home nearest to giving it all up were when I had seen a new patient. And I am not being humorous at all. I am telling you one of the most serious observations of my life: No human problem in our culture is comprehensible on first contact.

—Sullivan, unpublished lecture

THE "protector of my peace and quiet" is of course Jimmie, and it is an accurate description of Jimmie's importance to Sullivan over the years. From various sources, including Sullivan himself, it is clear that private practice was more exhausting for him than his work in the mental hospital. In general the tempo of life in New York was considerably different from Sullivan's life in Towson. To begin with, he had five different residences in the space of eight and a half years, and three different offices, two of them in his place of residence; and he took a keen interest in the decoration of each of these establishments. Moreover, he was probably more social than he had ever been before or would ever be again; thus he went to Sunday afternoon parties at Clara Thompson's, where he met a variety of artists, writers, patients, trainees, and colleagues. In the fall of 1931, he began to journey on a weekly basis to New Haven to participate in Sapir's seminar on culture and personality. Almost immediately after he arrived in New York, he began to meet with old friends in a speakeasy on Monday evenings, with social and professional interests intertwined; and this group, known as the "Zodiac" group or club, acquired over time some distinction in the world of ideas.

The record of his living quarters, as reported by Jimmie, gives some feel for the nature of his existence in these years. At Sheppard, Sullivan lived either on or near the hospital grounds and associated mainly with attendants, colleagues, and patients; in New York, the drive for his own establishment and an independent existence became explicit, and he made several attempts to establish a beautifully decorated dwelling place as a sanctuary for himself and his close friends. Harold Lasswell remembers one evening in the lakefront apartment of Karen Horney in Chicago, shortly after she came to this country in 1932, when Sullivan wove a fantasy of some small island-like retreat in Manhattan where they could all live in harmony and at peace, learning from each other and expanding their lives in meaningful ways. Sullivan's mood that evening was different from any that Lasswell had ever seen at a social gathering. Sullivan was often the central figure at a small party of close associates, witty and charming—somewhat aloof withal; at larger social gatherings, he would withdraw, sit in a corner, or even leave. But on this particular occasion, as Lasswell remembers him, he was serious and wistful.

After the financial collapse of his first Park Avenue establishment, Sullivan moved his office to 60 East 42nd Street, which he maintained until he purchased a brownstone in 1936; in the interim, he took up residence with Jimmie in three different apartments, adjusting himself to his changing fortunes with a good deal of grace. Indeed he seemed to accommodate readily to a decline in his fortunes after the bankruptcy.

His first move was to a small, modestly furnished apartment at 7 Mitchell Place. By then most of the expensive household furnishings had disappeared in a morass of unmet obligations; but Jimmie notes that the apartment was "just below swanky Beekman Place." The next move was to Washington Place, just off Washington Square in Greenwich Village, "not fashionable, but in a clean sort of Bohemian section." Jimmie has described this apartment in almost a carefree manner, as if it represented some release from the tireless expansion and purchasing that had dominated their lives since coming to New York City. It was called a first-floor "garden apartment" although it was actually below street level; yet there was a garden in back that was exclusively theirs. One entered the apartment through the bedroom; the living room with fireplace was at the back; in the bathroom, soot drifted through a grate in the ceiling as one bathed. The bedroom offered access to stray cats who found their way through the bars of high-up windows and left paw prints on the bed linen; Sullivan had no affinity for cats, so he had screens made to order for the odd-size windows. The kichen was small and "insignificant," but this did not matter since they ate out most of the time, in "wonderful eating places of all sorts, French, Italian, Greek, Spanish, Chinese, etc.—excellent food at reasonable prices."

Shortly they were again on the move—this time to a penthouse in a "first-class apartment" building at 151 East 81st Street, "two blocks from

Clara's." This is probably the apartment referred to in the epigraph. Again in Jimmie's description, one glimpses the elegance of the furnishings: "Warm grey walls, black wall to wall carpet, modern fireplace with small maple mantel around it that HSS had made to order and painted white, [with] a bright copper strip around it. On side of fireplace in a set-back area was a large automatic phonograph (Capehart, I believe)." On the other side was specially designed built-in furniture including a dining table that folded into a cabinet when not in use. The cabinet doors were made of "a large very decorative Chinese scenic screen. On another wall was my Bechstein piano," Jimmie reports. From this penthouse apartment, they could see the Queensboro Bridge and Welfare Island.

Living only two blocks from Clara in this last apartment was of some importance, for both Jimmie and Sullivan enjoyed visiting her. Sometimes she had dinner with them, too, at their apartment, but it was her easy hospitality in her own dwelling place that made it possible for them to enter into an expanded life in New York City. Part of Clara's success as a hostess was related to her delight in her Hungarian friends, many of whom were artists. Largely through them, Clara came to meet many American artists as well. Thus the poet Lloyd Frankenberg and his wife, the painter Loren MacIver, went to Clara's Sunday parties because of their acquaintanceship with the Hungarian artist Henry Major. And it was through Clara that both of the Frankenbergs eventually met Sullivan.

Although Clara was comfortable with Jimmie, some of the other colleagues were not, so that Jimmie was not always willing to accompany Sullivan on other occasions. After Sullivan's death, Jimmie wrote a note for inclusion in a memorial issue of *Psychiatry,* on which he placed his initials, J. I. S. But in an attached memorandum, he changed his mind: "On second thought, I think that my name should be used instead of initials as many colleagues do not know I exist."

In the spring of 1936, Sullivan moved into his own house at 158 East 64th Street; and in the fall of that same year, after most of the heavy renovations had been completed, he moved his office there too, so that again his home and office were under one roof. The house on East 64th Street was even more expansive in design and decoration than the Park Avenue apartment. By 1936 Sullivan believed that he was well on his way to establishing a functioning foundation that would combine all his various dreams and ambitions. The main office was to be in Washington; but there would be a New York office housed in the East 64th Street house where most of the research was to be carried out with his friend Edward Sapir, if money could be found to finance Sapir's family needs.

It is of some interest to reconstruct the expansive nature of this establishment. No detail was overlooked, although many of the plans did not come to fruition. The building, a rather narrow brownstone in the tradition of that part of New York City, had five floors. The entrance floor was three steps down from the sidewalk; there was a vestibule with two beautifully carved original doors which opened onto a long flight of stairs, carpeted in black, that led up to the main floor. As one approached the stairway, there was an enormously wide floor-to-ceiling mirror to the left. Jimmie reports that "the purpose of the mirror was for women to give themselves the once-over to see if evening dress was O.K. etc. before going to the next main floor"; over the years, Jimmie and Sullivan achieved a good deal of consensus about such details. On the ground floor there was also a large waiting room with white walls—"beautiful white and black wall-to-wall rubber tile on floor, two small Chinese chairs and a large black and red teakwood Chinese table (authentic)." Toward the front of the house was a small office used by people who answered the phone and looked after callers and deliveries when Jimmie was out. To the rear of the waiting room was the elevator shaft designed for the elevator that was never installed. The main kitchen, located on this floor, contained a dumbwaiter to the butler's pantry on the next floor and a large hotel range.

On the first main floor, Sullivan's office was at the front of the building and a large dining room toward the back. Once the elevator was installed, the plan was for this main floor to be used exclusively for entertaining, and the offices would be on another, higher floor; but since this plan was never achieved, Sullivan maintained his office on this floor throughout his stay. The ceilings on the main floor were very high, and the rooms were impressively large. The walls in the dining room were painted in a beautiful "chrome green," selected by Sullivan. The Hepplewhite furniture in the room was delicately capacious—an oval table eighteen feet long when all the leaves were in, a dozen chairs to match, a large china closet, a three-tiered stationary serving table, a buffet with two separate auxiliary pieces to hold linens and silverware. The original marble fireplace with an enormous mirror over it and the great window that reached from ceiling to floor added to the air of old-fashioned elegance.

Sullivan's office at the front of the building was completely done over in a contemporary way, with the help of his artist friend, John Vassos, who specifically redesigned the fireplace. The top of the marble mantel was covered with teakwood veneer stained in a brownish-red color; the hearth was of "beautiful orange African marble," which was Sullivan's discovery. Two large windows on the street side had inner windows framed in wood with a Chinese design and covered in a translucent material. Between the windows was a Chippendale table on which sat Sullivan's T'ang Horse, "over 2000 years old," colored "cream and orange"— a piece that Sullivan carried with him through the rest of his life. The floor was of a brownish-red cork, and the modern sofa was of "light tan or faint yellow color."

The landing in the large, generous hallway was done in a "vivid yellow specially made for H.S.S. by Horn Company of New York." The wash-room was given attention proportionate to its size; the lower part of the bathroom walls was covered in a bright red rubber tile—"plain, not grooved"—and the upper part and the ceiling were painted white; the floor was of a plain black rubber tile. The care with which all these details (not all of which are included here) were worked out is reflected in Jim-mie's reconstruction of them, more than thirty years after he left the house.

Over the dining room on the next floor—the second main floor—was Jimmie's room, a combination bedroom and sitting room where his Bechstein piano was housed. The room was in itself quite elegant, with its blue and white Chinese rug, a fireplace, a blue and red convertible couch, and a Chippendale coffee table of dark walnut. Jimmie's private bath-room and closets were redesigned in an expensive manner to hold a hid-den dresser and various storage units. Toward the front of the house was another bedroom and bath, for house guests.

On the next floor—the third main floor—there were two unfinished and unfurnished rooms, and to the rear a small stand-up greenhouse was installed for Sullivan. Here he first began to experiment with the cross-breeding of day lilies to produce exotic and new specimens, an activity that he continued when he moved to Bethesda. If all the plans had mate-rialized, it is quite likely that this floor would have been used for offices for Sapir and Sullivan.

The very top floor—that is, the fourth main floor in the building—was Sullivan's domain, although Jimmie had an office on this floor. There was one room filled with bookcases. Sullivan's own bathroom was all white and "severe," according to Jimmie, and his bedroom is described in al-most monk-like terms: there was a maple bed and bedside table, "a phone, of course," several chairs, a chest of drawers, and "a drawing table he used for a desk and/or work table." It is notable that "Harry's floor," so designated by Jimmie, was three stories up from the office where he saw his private patients and two stories above Jimmie's own floor. Here Sullivan could escape from the eternal need for money that was implicit in his private practice; here too he could read and think, far away from the domestic activities of the household. The austerity of Sullivan's floor provides an important clue to the man. He was at his happiest when he had immediate access to privacy, to his books, to his thoughts; something of the austerity of the Smyrna farmhouse remained on this top floor, just as the Chicago years of loneliness and privation had some representation. However much he was interested in beautiful things, however great was his need at times for luxurious possessions, there remained a core of sim-plicity, a respect for the isolated years that had been brightened only by the access to ideas that came from books.

One can catch another glimpse of this East 64th Street house from the description that the writer Ralph Ellison gives of his observations when he worked half-time for Sullivan for three months at the end of 1936, as a combination receptionist and file clerk.[1] Ellison was an undergraduate at Tuskegee Institute in Alabama, and he had taken a year off in order to earn a little money; a sculptor friend of his had recommended him for what was defined as a temporary job with Sullivan. It was a decade before Ellison would emerge as the author of *Invisible Man;* in 1936 he was planning to be a music major. Ellison had never been in such an elegant house before, although at the time it was still being renovated. He sat in an office near the entrance, so that he could send patients up to Sullivan, answer the telephone, and accept deliveries. The household consisted of Jimmie, a cocker spaniel, Sullivan, and a Negro housekeeper. Jimmie was very kindly, but not much in evidence; he would take the dog out for a walk, bring the dog back, and disappear upstairs; after that, Ellison would often not see Jimmie again that day. Sullivan asked Ellison to join him at the luncheon table almost every day, but Jimmie was absent. Customarily, Sullivan had milk and crackers for lunch—a not uncommon light meal in the rural areas in which he grew up. At such times, Sullivan would show Ellison his writings on interpersonal relations and ask Ellison if he thought the writing was clear, and to make comments. It was difficult for Ellison to believe that Sullivan really cared what he thought about the writing, although he felt flattered by Sullivan's interest in his comments. Ellison reported that Sullivan had a beautiful pink spotted day lily on his desk in a very elegant pot, and this came from his greenhouse. Sullivan seemed very lonely, according to Ellison; but he got a lot of telephone calls from various well-known people, like Karen Horney.

Ellison would sometimes see patients leaving the house in obvious distress after a session; one woman in particular would often be in tears when she left. On such occasions, Sullivan would sometimes say to Ellison at luncheon, "I wish that they'd try to help themselves."

Ellison's description of Jimmie's activities deserves some emendation. By 1936 Jimmie was a well-trained secretary; from the New York years onward until Sullivan's death, he worked with competence and diligence on Sullivan's correspondence and writings and on various complicated scheduling for keeping an involved household going—at times on very limited funds. During the course of his career with Sullivan, he went through five typewriters, he has reported. In the hundreds of Sullivan's letters in the Foundation files, complicated and many of them long, and in reports and papers, one sees Jimmie's clear and careful typing on literally thousands of sheets. His recompense was modest, and his recognition was slight; once in the 1940s when Sullivan was ill and without ready income, Jimmie took a job in a lawyer's office in order to keep them in groceries. One can say in all seriousness that it was Jimmie who managed to keep Sullivan going for over twenty years.

Ellison's description of this New York house fits in with Sullivan's life a decade later. However glamorous Sullivan's life was from time to time in the New York period, there were almost monk-like periods of solitude, of thinking, of writing. The first of several cocker spaniels appeared in the East 64th Street house; and they, too, like Sullivan's friends, colleagues, and their children—as well as patients, of course—were observed carefully and found their way into remarkable insights that are scattered through all of his published and unpublished writings.

Retrospectively, Sullivan reports in 1946 that he had envisioned the move to New York City as a way to broaden his clinical experience and his research data: "By 1927 I had decided that I could not find the dividing line between obsessional neurosis and schizophrenia, and that obviously they were so closely related that I would have to overcome my hesitancy about obsessionals and do my bit with them, which I did, by God, for six years, winding up officially somewhere around the early part of 1937."[2] But he also anticipated that his practice there would be remunerative enough to provide him with time and money to pursue a research career with Sapir. Sullivan cites the years of his work with "obsessionals" as six, until 1937, but he was not engaged in a full-time remunerative private practice even that long. He did consultancies at Sheppard and St. Elizabeths occasionally, and he saw quite a few non-paying patients who were artists and writers, mainly because he was more interested in this kind of work; he seems never to have turned away a patient because he was indigent. In truth, a fashionable practice as a way of financing his research interests was never a reality, although he became "among the four or five best paid psychiatrists in New York," by his own account.[3] As Lasswell reported, Sullivan was extremely ethical about not "using" his wealthy patients for his own needs. Moreover, he found it difficult to change the patterns of the advantaged denizens of an urban culture, caught in endless obsessional devices that often were useful in maintaining a financially safe existence. "The obsessional states," Sullivan observed, "probably manifest in most people very early in life, have an enormous impressiveness as the only way one can live, and represent very tedious therapeutic problems where literally the psychiatrist has to have a long and fairly complicated strategy, or [he] gets nowhere, without noticing it."[4] Furthermore, Sullivan was not content to see such patients for an indeterminate period; he wanted to move them on to a more satisfying life, not alone for their personal fulfillment, but also because they had a duty to society.

Some of his most humorous lectures concern obsessional patients.[5] But he stressed to his students that these patients were deserving of the most careful attention; the psychiatrist had to be able to circumvent the anxiety of an obsessional patient long enough for the patient to glimpse a more satisfying way of doing things. Sullivan observed these patients so carefully that he was able to add new dimensions to his evolving theory, particularly on the juvenile era of development as it exists in a competitive American society. In brief, he was becoming a social anthropologist in a world quite foreign to him: "A certain small section of Manhattan society rise from bed in the late forenoon, dress rather carefully, gather up their husbands or wives—their concessions to social necessity, as it were—and proceed to the bridge club. There they engage in an intensely concentrated performance, almost without speech or with only very highly formalized speech. After a considerable number of hours at this, they go out and retrieve their social remnant—by which I mean their mate—get something to eat, and go through a practically meaningless routine of life until the next meeting of the group." Yet these people are not so unusual; large, prosperous communities that center around a suburban country club go through the same meaningless routines: "One's husband or wife who does something for a living to facilitate this pleasant life is obviously an infrahuman creature and is treated more or less as such." Such an adjustment probably ensures that the person will manage to keep out of a mental hospital or to keep from doing anything that is "horribly abnormal." Indeed this kind of person may never show up for a psychiatric interview except in times of personal or national crisis.

He mentions in passing that people who have had a very stressful experience in the juvenile era are *not* members of "New York bridge circles or suburban clubs." He is obviously talking about himself, in part: "They are likely, in fact, to have a quite restricted interest in games and a very sharply restricted interest in people with whom to play them, but that is another story."[6]

This lecture, given some years after he had left New York City, represents his disaffection for the fashionable practice that might have saved him financially. In the process of studying the obsessional devices by which most people maintain themselves in urban society, he came to question the values inculcated in the child in the juvenile era. He recognized that some of his own disdain for these values stemmed from his early inability to compete in the Smyrna schoolyard at the recess period. Over the years he moved slowly and surely toward the position that indeed he had not been as disadvantaged as he had once thought. He had been unnecessarily unhappy in the juvenile era; but he had translated his lack of competitive success into a larger goal—that all people in a democratic society might move toward a happier and more productive pattern of living.

Throughout Sullivan's adult life, there was a continuum in his daily living between work and play. In the Washington years, after his health became seriously impaired, he would worry about the unfinished tasks that he must somehow complete, and he began to insist that social events

352   PSYCHIATRIST OF AMERICA

had to accomplish something. But in the New York years, he emphasized in his own life and that of people close to him the importance, per se, of beauty, of intellectual excitement, of the theater, music, and art; and he became somewhat of a connoisseur of ancient Chinese art.

Like many other psychoanalysts, Sullivan had significant contact in New York City with artists and scholars, particularly young people who, like the photographer Margaret Bourke-White, depended on Sullivan for varying kinds of psychiatric help but did not represent any dependable income. He defined the dancer Katherine Dunham as his protégé and took some credit for her later career as an anthropologist. Her brother, the young and brilliant philosopher Albert Millard Dunham, Jr., was much admired by Sullivan, and his paper, "The Concept of Tension in Philosophy," was published in the first issue of *Psychiatry* and cited by Sullivan as one of the most important papers that he ever solicited for the journal. At different times, various young artists and scholars found temporary shelter in Sullivan's house—for example, Katherine Dunham; the young Irish-born philosopher Patrick Mullahy, who became an early interpreter of Sullivan's theory; and Philip Sapir, one of Edward Sapir's sons.

One of his more developed friendships was with the artist John Vassos.[7] Some time in the late 1920s, Vassos went to Sheppard to visit a friend who was hospitalized there, and he had his first meeting with Sullivan. Their relationship was renewed when Sullivan went to New York City; and Vassos, whose work remains one of the best examples of the Art Deco period, influenced Sullivan in his excursions into decoration. In particular, the brownstone house on East 64th Street showed the influence of Vassos.

In 1931 Vassos published a book, *Phobia,* that describes and illustrates thirty-two phobias.[8] He dedicated the book to "H.S.S." Vassos reports that Sullivan did substantial work on the introduction, but Sullivan was reluctant to have Vassos use his full name for the dedication; as a clinician, Sullivan avoided focusing on the "obscure, practically transcendental horrors" (which would include phobias) that patients sometimes experienced.[9] Sullivan acknowledged his own part in the book, however, by accepting from Vassos the advance on the book, which Sullivan needed for rent. *Phobia,* which is now a collector's item, caused some stir in psychiatric circles; thus A. A. Brill in a review reported that it was "remarkable how closely Vassos' illustrations delineate the true nature of phobias."[10]

When the *Phobia* book was published in 1931, Sullivan and Vassos were guests of honor at a large party held near Vassos's home in Connecticut, and Sullivan spoke. Afterwards, as Vassos reports, a young girl came up to Sullivan and asked him, "Should one take sex seriously?" And Sullivan said gently and seriously, "Well now, young lady, I

wouldn't worry too much about *that."* The comment was reported by
Vassos three decades later. It was the kind of comment that colleagues,
patients, and friends often remembered; its meaning might be unclear,
but the voice, the cadence, the reassuring quality of the words were memorable.

The charm of Vassos for Sullivan—and vice versa—was implicit in the
early role of being an outsider. Sullivan was country Irish when he arrived in Ithaca in his seventeenth year. At about the same age, Vassos,
who was born in Greece in 1898, had had to flee from Constantinople
where his father was the principal of a private school and editor of a
Greek newspaper. There was a price on young Vassos's head because he
had drawn political cartoons that poked fun at the Turkish senate, and
they had been published in a radical newspaper, quite unlike his father's.
Thereafter John Vassos worked at various duties on board ships with diverse missions, some of them dangerous, until 1919, when he arrived at
the port of Boston on a ship that carried a cargo of scrap iron, and decided to stay in this country. He earned his living in the beginning at various odd jobs, including window washing, finally graduating to a job in
which he lettered tags and displays for penny drugstore sales. He went to
night school at the Fenway Art School in Boston, where he studied under
John Singer Sargent, and he had some experience in stage designing. In
1924 he made his way to New York City and eventually became a top industrial designer. After the publication of *Phobia,* he created "graphic interpretations" of famous writings, such as Wilde's "Salomé" and "The
Ballad of Reading Gaol," and Gray's "Elegy in a Country Church-
Yard."

Vassos remembers three times that Sullivan visited him in Connecticut.
The two of them took long walks in the lovely countryside there; Sullivan
enjoyed these walks very much but he was "not countrified," according to
Vassos. Thus again, Sullivan did not reveal to a close friend anything
about his early life.

Sullivan felt that part of their empathic communication could be understood by looking at the political history of both Ireland and Greece. In
the 1930s and 1940s, Vassos and Sullivan were particularly in tune with
each other politically. As an important participant in the Art Deco movement of the twenties and thirties, Vassos has been compared to the Mexican muralists in his attempt to grapple with social and political themes of
that period in a humanistic way; such an interest was of central concern
to Sullivan. During World War II, both Vassos and Sullivan did some
work for the Office of Strategic Services. Vassos enlisted and was com-
missioned as a major in the intelligence service, finally emerging as a
lieutenant colonel, with duties in the Middle East and North Africa.
Vassos reports that Sullivan had an important part in writing the "Book"
of specifications for testing emotional stability in the staff of the OSS, but

that he never progressed beyond the rank of major.[11] The disparity of rank between them—one a renowned psychiatrist and the other almost a self-made artist—amused both of them.

One glimpses a lack of pretense in their relationship that echoed the role of immigrant who had arrived steerage from the other side. Sullivan was two generations removed from that experience, but he still retained some of the wonder of the poor immigrant who had somehow made good. Both of them were far removed psychologically from the "illustrious immigrants" who arrived in New York in the 1930s.[12]

Long after Sullivan's death, an anthology of Vassos's graphic illustrations, garnered from all his books, was published; and here Vassos is more explicit in naming Sullivan directly and giving him primary credit for his own development, second only to the influence of his wife. This book is dedicated to "the brilliant polymorphic memory of Harry Stack Sullivan," and Vassos states that it was Sullivan who "guided me to the realization of *Phobia* and had a profound influence on my life."[13]

Sometime in 1931, three friends from the Baltimore days—Billy Silverberg, Clara Thompson, and Sullivan—began meeting on Monday evenings in a speakeasy for drinks, dinner, and conversation. The group was not too different in membership and intent from the group that had met earlier in Thompson's apartment in Baltimore—sometimes called the Miracle Club because patients often seemed to improve miraculously after their problems were discussed by the club members. The new Zodiac group in New York was named in accordance with Sullivan's whimsy; each member was supposed to select an appropriate animal as his symbol. Sullivan was, of course, a horse; Thompson, who had an affinity with cats, was a puma; Billy Silverberg was a gazelle; and Karen Horney became a water buffalo when she joined the group in 1934. Erich Fromm also met with this group, but he seems never to have participated in the animal mystique. Jimmie, who sometimes accompanied Sullivan, became a seahorse.

The Zodiac group gradually took on general theoretical problems. Thompson has reported that "the things we started talking about then became more and more organized into Sullivan's thinking."[14] Sullivan's thinking also had an important impact on most of the group members. Yet each of them seemed to maintain an independent course of action; they enjoyed each other, but at that juncture there seems to have been no need for competition. Each of them seemed eclectic and strong, and each had something to contribute. Thompson and Horney combined their knowledge of women patients, emergent from two different societies, and each seemed to benefit, as reflected in their writings; Fromm, the only social scientist in the group, supplied important perspectives on the political situation in Germany and its meaning for the psychological state of its citizens; Billy Silverberg, who had taken over Sullivan's ward at Sheppard for a year after Sullivan left, could compare his findings with Sullivan's earlier experience and could act as a bridge between the European psychoanalysts and their American colleagues; and Sullivan brought to the group his ability to observe scientifically and to put into some sophisticated theoretical form what they were all talking about. Although the original group was perceived as a social gathering, its impact on American psychiatric theory was significant and still continues. It is notable that three members of the 1930 group—Horney, Fromm, and Sullivan—wrote books in that period that are still in print.[15]

The early success of these two European psychoanalysts, so closely associated with Sullivan, eventuated in antagonisms between some of the principal participants themselves, and with the rest of the psychoanalytic community in New York City and elsewhere. Much of the rationalization for this antagonism centered on theoretical differences having to do with the correct interpretation of Freud's theories. But Clara Thompson and others, including Sullivan, saw these theoretical differences as a red herring used to disguise more ambitious plans for influence and status. In the 1940s one of the original "mavericks," Karen Horney, finally opted for power, deciding that Erich Fromm, her former admired colleague and the person she had recommended as a training analyst for her daughter, would have to be read out of her organization because he did not have a medical degree.[16] As one of the more important members of the original Zodiac group, Horney would finally become a symbol of treachery for other members. Whatever its ultimate fate, this original group of men and women began a dialogue on human behavior that is still meaningful. The members of the group are often spoken of as neo-Freudians; but the scope of their work and its ramifications cannot be so easily labeled.

❧ 38 ☙

Inventing an
Institution

> It is worth remembering that Loyola and the other
> young men who founded the Jesuits were in long
> friendly relationship before they hit upon their fa-
> mous project. Not only that: they were anxious to re-
> main in some sort of personal relation through life,
> and they invented many expedients before they hit
> on the final one. What we had here was a friendly
> group which desired to preserve their personal con-
> nections before they knew how they could actually
> do it. It is less true to say that institutions are the
> lengthened shadow of a great man than that they are
> the residue of a friendly few.
> —Harold D. Lasswell, *Psychopathology and Politics*

L ASSWELL'S definition of an institution is significantly interpersonal,
and it applies precisely to the rather haphazard formation of the
William Alanson White Psychiatric Foundation in Washington, D.C., in
1933, at a time when Sullivan was still expecting to make his professional
and personal life in New York City. Yet the Foundation was to become
the context for some of Sullivan's major creative activities—especially the
Washington School of Psychiatry and the journal *Psychiatry*. However,
the initial impetus for incorporating an institution came about, independently and almost by happenstance, from the interest of Ernest E. Hadley, Sullivan's friend and psychiatric colleague, in having a proper legal
entity for accepting an anticipated bequest to be used for psychoanalytic
training. As time went on, Hadley became an essential figure in the actual
operation of the Journal and the School, but his area of interest was never
really the same as that of the original triumvirate—Sullivan, Sapir, and
Lasswell. In 1939, shortly after the School and the Journal became fully
operative, Sapir died, and, for a variety of reasons, Lasswell was also out

of the picture. Thus the actual fiscal collaboration that kept these embryonic organizations going between 1939 and 1945, both financially and psychologically, was mainly the work of Hadley and Sullivan.

But the intellectual task was begun in New Haven, and Yale became the first small beachhead for the kind of collaboration between psychiatry and the social sciences that was envisioned by Sullivan, Sapir, and Lasswell. Beginning in the fall of 1931, Sullivan's trips from New York to New Haven were frequent; Lasswell's visits were more sporadic, for he was still based in Chicago, but his input was characteristically intense and wide-ranging. Whether the face-to-face contacts between Sullivan and Sapir were within the formal setting of Sapir's seminars at Yale, or at Sapir's house in New Haven, or at his summer house in New Hampshire, or in New York City, the two men were engaged in an enduring and special dialogue on the relation of culture and personality in which many colleagues and students participated. The direct influence of this dialogue has been commented on by the social psychologist Otto Klineberg and the anthropologist Hortense Powdermaker. The indirect influence, sometimes not adequately recognized, was probably even greater. Thus Erik H. Erikson, who arrived at the Institute of Human Relations at Yale in 1936, was obviously influenced by the climate there, although he does not directly cite, for instance, any important influence from Sapir and only one from Sullivan in his book *Childhood and Society*.[1]

Klineberg, who had degrees in both medicine and social psychology, met Sullivan late in 1931, through Sapir's insistence on Sullivan's importance: Sullivan "was the person ... who came closest to realizing the value of an integration between the psychological sciences on the one hand, and the science that deals with culture on the other hand," Sapir told Klineberg. And Klineberg sat in on Sapir's seminar on culture and personality, in which Sullivan participated almost as soon as it began. "It was my first opportunity to see Sullivan in action," Klineberg has reported, "and I look back upon those early discussions that Sapir and Sullivan had together, and which they shared with some of their colleagues and students, as perhaps the most important beginning of an interest in this broad area of culture and personality, which. . .has so influenced the field of anthropology, that sometimes it is a little difficult to decide when a given individual is an anthropologist or whether he is really a psychologist or a psychiatrist."[2]

In the summer of 1932, the young anthropologist Hortense Powdermaker spent her vacation with the Sapirs in New Hampshire, getting ready for her important anthropological study of blacks in Mississippi. "I was the first anthropologist to study a modern community in the United States," Powdermaker has reported. She worked out with Sapir the arrangement for a fellowship with the Social Science Research Council, and he backed her application; at an unofficial level, Sullivan had reviewed her proposal and concurred in Sapir's recommendation. In her autobiographical report of her summer with the Sapirs, Powdermaker comments on her first encounter with Sullivan: "One particularly long weekend was memorable when Harry Stack Sullivan, the distinguished psychoanalyst, was a guest and the two men discussed their ideas (still embryonic) about the relationship beween culture and personality. The thoughts of one man kindled those of the other. My impression was that the remarkable flow of conversation between them was due not only to the high quality of their minds and to their mutual interest in the relationship between the individual and his society, but also to their personalities—each man seemed to combine within himself something of the scientist and of the poet. I was excited by listening and participating even slightly in this creative communication."[3] When the summer was over, Powdermaker went to Fisk University to confer with two black sociologists—Charles S. Johnson, chairman of the social sciences department, and Franklin E. Frazier, professor of sociology in the same department—as to the best way to approach her field work in Mississippi. Both Sapir and Sullivan were crucial in arranging for this preparation by Johnson and Frazier, who had been trained at the University of Chicago. Seven years later, Sullivan made his own trip to the same part of Mississippi after conferring with Johnson at Fisk, duplicating in some ways Powdermaker's earlier trip.

In the fall of 1932, Sullivan frequently participated with Sapir in a seminar at Yale on the impact of culture on personality. Sullivan's manuscript, *Personal Psychopathology*, was used as collateral reading for the seminar. In the years that followed, until the fall of 1937 when Sapir took sabbatical leave and lived in New York City, Sullivan continued to travel frequently to New Haven to confer with Sapir. Although Lasswell was not as frequently in New Haven as the other two members of the triumvirate, he was omnipresent whenever he descended on them individually or together. His imprint on Sullivan is clear. Particularly in the years after the Munich Pact, Sullivan began to show in his writing, in his innumerable unsigned editorials in the journal *Psychiatry,* and in his participation in several international meetings a sophisticated knowledge of the relationship between personality and politics.

As early as 1930, the three of them had talked of the necessity for interdisciplinary research. Independently and together, they made elaborate research plans. One such plan for observing the interaction of interviewer and interviewee included the use of various kinds of equipment to measure changes in bodily tension, voice change, gesture change (particularly as it related to the first two), and so on. In part this represented a response to the current ethos of the Social Science Research Council that emphasized hard science and did not recognize the place of psychiatric research. At the same time, it represented the intense interest of all three in precise observation and formulation of data. Their plans required many pieces of equipment, some of it not yet invented. Sullivan had considerable skill in devising such equipment, so that the other two depended on him for consultation with the Bell Telephone Company, for instance, and with other companies engaged in devising new equipment. The money for this kind of research was never sufficient to do any appreciable amount of work. Lasswell did record a vast number of his interviews in Chicago; but his records were all destroyed on his way eastward, when the vans carrying them were in an accident. One of Lasswell's students and colleagues has written of this event: "I think it was God's manifest will that in 1938 a moving van bound for New York, which contained Harold's voluminous reports from the paranoid zones of the world between 1928 and 1938, burned to a crisp. The fire freed him from the prison of his files."[4]

In some such sense, the lack of funding for the research to be conducted by Sullivan and Sapir freed them also for the optimum use of their remarkable gifts as participant observers of the human experience, without benefit of very many technical aids. Some of their shared observations centered around the Sapir children. In his frequent visits to the Sapirs after they came to New Haven, Sullivan came to know the two sets of children well. Jean Sapir reports that he identified with the youngest of both sets of children, and that he took a lively interest in their behavior. As a sensitive observer of his own children, Sapir was of particular use to Sullivan. The Sapirs noted that Paul, the older of the second set of children, took over the duty of teaching his younger brother, David, to identify pictures of animals by words. Paul would show David the picture of a lion and ask him what it was, David would say something inarticulate, then Paul would tell him it was a lion; David would then repeat the word, whereupon Paul would say "Paul's lion" and David would then repeat that. Thus Paul owned the words. The adults did not think of this as being significant at first, until David seemed slow in talking, at which time they noted that Paul was controlling the words. Such episodes interested both Sapir and Sullivan, who were aware of professional fights centering supposedly on control of such words as psychiatry and psychoanalysis.

Sullivan was openly critical of the way Jean Sapir dressed David when he was about eighteen months old; David could not stand any tight clothing, so his mother devised some loose garments, with a kind of smock for a top, made of pastel-colored material. Sullivan was so stern with her about the inappropriateness of this clothing that she went out and bought David an outfit of bright red and also a brown-checked suit, both of which Sullivan applauded.

Sullivan also identified with the youngest child of the first marriage, Philip. Sullivan thought that Philip was over-obedient, in contrast to the oldest child who was more defiant. When Sullivan was at the New Hampshire summer house, he observed that Philip had to hand-pump the water several times a day so that the family would have running water in the house; and Sullivan began a fund to buy an electric water pump so that Philip would not have to do this somewhat onerous task.[5]

There are in the published and unpublished writings other indications of Sullivan's interest in observing children. Thus he tells in one lecture of his concern about the child of a colleague. The parents told him something about the child's behavior, when he was visiting them, that disturbed Sullivan "deeply"; and the colleague, who was a psychiatrist, noticed Sullivan's disturbance and asked him what he was thinking. Apparently Sullivan reported that he was disturbed because "the early peculiarity which this child showed was one that so frequently coincided with rather serious mental states in adolescence." The whole episode was recalled to Sullivan years later by David Levy, a child psychiatrist, "who was treating this boy in late adolescence for a very severe personality disorder." Sullivan remembered the event, but not the particulars; and he reports that he was of no clinical help to Levy.[6]

As this informal and pleasant collaboration progressed in the early 1930s, Sullivan, Sapir, and Lasswell talked from time to time in rather nebulous terms of how this interdisciplinary research could be financed and formalized. But it was not immediately apparent how the incorporation of the William Alanson White Psychoanalytic Foundation (as it was originally named) could be related to their particular needs and goals. When Hadley first approached Sullivan about the Foundation, he mentioned a donor who was ready to make a substantial endowment to a psychoanalytic training program; and Sullivan may have started to think of how the use of the money could be appropriately redefined. Shortly after an informal conversation between Hadley and the prospective donor, who specified that a legally incorporated foundation would be necessary, the donor died suddenly without having made the proper legal arrangements for this endowment in his will. So the Foundation began essentially as a penniless dream—a forerunner of its later history.

On the fourth of December 1933, at 2:27 P.M.—as carefully noted by the first president, Harry Stack Sullivan—a certification of incorporation for the Foundation was filed and recorded in the District of Columbia. The three signers of the certificate were Lucile Dooley, Ernest E. Hadley, and Sullivan. All three of them had known each other in the early days at St. Elizabeths and had served a psychological apprenticeship under White, whom Hadley and Sullivan referred to as "Papa White." Within the tradition of that period, White was at least in part their training analyst. All three of them were active in the Washington-Baltimore Psychoanalytic Institute: Dooley was the president-elect for 1934; Hadley was chairman of the training committee; and Sullivan was a member of the education committee. The Institute, which was not incorporated, had in effect created the Foundation as a holding corporation for endowment monies. In this fashion, Sullivan became a critical link between two groups—the informal threesome in New Haven, and the new Foundation. Although the Foundation would become an umbrella for the Washington School of Psychiatry and the journal *Psychiatry*, two interdisciplinary institutions dominated by Sullivan, the Foundation's beginnings were far removed from any such plans.

Lucile Dooley was the senior member of the Foundation threesome, about a decade older than either Hadley or Sullivan. She had grown up in Tennessee, and received a Ph.D. from Clark University in 1916, eleven years after she had finished her undergraduate work at Randolph-Macon—a remarkable achievement in itself for a woman at that period. After working as a psychotherapist at St. Elizabeths under White, she had gone to Johns Hopkins and received her M.D. in 1922. In 1925, she had begun the private practice of psychiatry in Washington, D.C. And finally she had gone to Vienna for a year as a student at the Vienna Psychoanalytic Institute in 1931. Thus Dooley had the most catholic training of any of the three founding members of the Foundation; and she was the only one who had been trained in psychoanalysis in Vienna. Throughout her stay at St. Elizabeths and at Johns Hopkins, she had quietly exerted an important influence on a number of young psychiatric residents in turning them toward the dynamic findings of Freud, in whom she had been interested since his trip to Worcester in 1909.

Ernest Hadley had a career somewhat comparable to Dooley's. He was usually a quiet, genial person, as thoroughly conservative in temperament as the Kansas plains from which he heralded. His early life had been Horatio-Alger-like. He had earned his way through high school and college mainly by working out as a farmhand to neighbors who lived near his family's farm; he got paid double wages for pitching hay because he could do twice as much work as anybody else. Throughout his life, he was "a horse for work."[7] He had a more conventional education than Sullivan, although he was late in obtaining his degrees—a B.S. when he was twenty-four from the University of Kansas, and two years later an M.D. from the same institution; working farm boys in particular were often late in going to college. Although Sullivan and Hadley became close friends and associates, particularly after Sullivan moved to Washington in 1939, Sullivan never told the Hadleys that he, too, had grown up on a farm—a rather clear indication that their experiences on the farm were not of the same ilk.

There were, however, other attitudes that coincided. Hadley had been raised a Quaker, and his sense of dedication to a worthwhile task was of a piece with Sullivan's; thus both of them were willing to labor in the vineyard without much recognition; and neither of them was ambitious to make a lot of money, although their way of handling money was quite different. Sullivan's admiration for the Society of Friends is substantiated in several of his lectures over the years and was undoubtedly heightened by his admiration for Hadley. Thus in a lecture given in the winter of 1942–43, Sullivan described the Society, in its function as a "social suborder," as being "the most astonishing demonstration of there being a Christian way of life that I've encountered—in fact, almost the only one."[8]

Sullivan's and Hadley's divergencies in areas of interest began very early in their relationship. Both belonged to the American Psychiatric Association and the American Psychoanalytic Association, but their emphasis was different. Sullivan became an active member of the latter association in 1924, even before Hadley. But Sullivan expended most of his energy on the psychiatric association. The reverse was true of Hadley. Some measure of their different emphases can be found in an annotated bibliography of 273 entries prepared by Sullivan as a supplement to the published proceedings of the Second Colloquium (1929). As the secretary of the American Psychoanalytic Association, Hadley, who did not attend either Colloquium, contributed nineteen items under the heading of Psychoanalysis and three entries under Sex. Out of twenty-one classifications ranging from Anthropology to Constitutional Studies, from Child Psychology to Sociology, Sullivan contributed to all but three of the classifications—Economics, Ethics, and Political Science; but Sullivan's focus was on Psychiatry, for which he prepared all twenty of the entries. Over forty percent of the 273 entries in the bibliography were by Sullivan. Thus at an early period, the two men had already drawn apart in their professional interests. Yet for over two decades they maintained a close relationship professionally and socially. In hundreds of letters, one senses the demonstration over and over again of their devotion to each other.

Both went into the private practice of psychoanalysis full time at about the same time—Hadley in 1929 and Sullivan late in 1930. But their interest in private patients was different. Hadley enjoyed working with his private patients, mainly government workers and members of official Washington. Sullivan was interested in private practice primarily as a source of data for improving the application of dynamic psychiatry to the needs of a wide range of problems in the larger society; very early he envisioned the necessity for research on a preventive psychiatry.

In the beginning of the Foundation, Sullivan was easily the dominant member, and his downplaying of the role of psychoanalysis was accepted by both Dooley and Hadley. This can be partially documented by the biographical footnotes on Dooley's and Hadley's articles in the early pages of the Journal; they listed themselves as engaged in the "private practice of psychiatry." Later each of them would define themselves as psychoanalysts, but this was after politics with words had become a big and dangerous game in psychoanalytic/psychiatric circles, particularly along the eastern seaboard.

Yet, from the beginning, Hadley clung to certain imaginative ideas from the new European psychoanalysis. Although he was listed as a Professor of Human Biology in a 1936 prospectus for the Washington School of Psychiatry, his chief course, as remembered by his students, was in dream analysis. A young resident would report a patient's dream, and Hadley would set forth on an adventure of associations. It was a pastime that annoyed Sullivan no end. Year after year, in Sullivan's lectures to the same group of residents-in-training who studied under Hadley, Sullivan would observe that the dream as reported by the patient is only what the patient can remember, or what he is able to report. What the patient reports as an association to the dream is of some interest to the analyst, but the doctor and the patient must avoid being caught in an obsessional interaction in which the patient dreams in order to safely carry on a long fantasy with the doctor as to what the dream meant. In Sullivan's thinking, dream life was important in, for instance, avoiding a schizophrenic episode; and it was crucial in signaling to the person who had the dream that he was moving on dangerous ground. In Sullivan's lectures, he made use of his patients' dreams and of his own in only restricted and precise ways—as signals, rather than as symbols of strange and wonderful stories of oedipal urges.

After reading hundreds of letters exchanged between Sullivan and Hadley, one senses that their difference in approach to psychoanalysis was based on differing early experience with daydreams, with fantasies, and with magic thinking. On the hot plains of Kansas in the summer, life was real and earnest; on the hill farm in Smyrna, only magic dreams and books, and stories of past Stack greatness, kept young Harry hopeful of what lay ahead. Sullivan as a clinician was the scientist more than the therapist; he did not attempt to produce adoring patients, only patients with an improved—even a pragmatic—capacity for productive living. Hadley gloried in opening up for the patient the rich and varied life that was implicit in dreams, of discovering for the patient the same introspective treasures that had excited him in discovering his own unconscious.

There was a paradoxical shift in their attitude toward more material possessions. Sullivan felt a strong need for certain luxuries that he had missed in growing up; Hadley responded to this need in Sullivan and was often supportive of Sullivan's financial needs even when they were unrealistic. Hadley himself spent most of his Washington years in a house in exclusive Spring Valley (next door to the house occupied for a while by Richard Nixon), with staid and conservative furnishings, completely at variance with Sullivan's rather unfinished but artistically ambitious surroundings.

A casual interchange between Sullivan and Hadley will serve to illustrate their different approaches to the new psychoanalytic insights. On October 12, 1935, the first formal annual meeting of the Foundation was held in Washington, at which time White was made honorary president and Sullivan the president. It was a great success: White expressed great joy in the honor conferred on him; afterwards they had a convivial time which Sullivan referred to in a footnote to his letter to Hadley written two days later: "Love to Agnes Marie—it was good to see her, but I'd have preferred less of a festival and more of a visit. All in all, my memories of the evening, fuzzy as they are, are all to the good. I gathered also that Dr. and Mrs. Wm. A. were delighted in general and in particular." In the letter itself Sullivan complained of a physical disability which might be traced to the source of the "fuzziness": "I am searching my soul for psychical factors that might account for the extraordinary looseness of my bowels which continues. Maybe I am overstimulated by the actually undreamed of honor that descended on me. If so, I trust that my soma will soon get another final common path, and one productive of material more useful to psychiatry."

On the next day, mail service between New York City and Washington being very swift in those days, Hadley answered Sullivan and commented on Sullivan's indisposition: "We both hope that you have recovered from the indisposition. I am more inclined to think that the indisposition is related to some feeling of hostility rather than to excitement over the honor to which you refer. And since hostility is uppermost in my mind (I have to give a paper on the subject shortly) I should really like to hear your own definition of hostility for purposes of quotation." There is no record extant that supplies Sullivan's definition of hostility, but it is easy to imagine his annoyance.

From the beginning of the Foundation, there was, then, a difference in the plans for it, with Hadley and Dooley quite close in their feeling that psychoanalysis was the central discipline; and Sullivan seeing dynamic psychiatry as the central discipline, including a significant look at sociology, anthropology, political science, and so on. But from 1933 until 1942, the three of them continued to serve as trustees for the Foundation, they taught in the School, and they all wrote for the Journal from time to time. The first of the original founders to remove herself from membership on the Board of Trustees for the Foundation was Lucile Dooley sometime late in 1941, coincidental with the beginning of a great deal of concern in the American Psychoanalytic Association about the writings of Erich Fromm, who had become an important figure and who had begun to publish in *Psychiatry.* Four years after Dooley's resignation from the Foundation, Hadley also resigned. Both resignations grew essentially out of the same political climate, for schisms of some magnitude had developed within the psychoanalytic community. When Dooley was eighty years old, she reported to Robert Kvarnes, the secretary of the Foundation, her regret at her earlier deviation from classical analysis: "She expressed her feeling that the post-Freudian developments had not added to, but rather had taken away from the psychoanalytic movement. In a somewhat apologetic vein, she indicated it was her recommendation that had brought Dr. Sullivan to his appointment at Sheppard-Pratt Hospital, the site of some of his memorable studies. She deserves to give her intuition more credit!"[9]

Once the Foundation and the Yale triumvirate had coalesced in Sullivan's mind, he began to plan on three major activities. First and foremost was his research with Sapir and Lasswell; second, an interdisciplinary school for training in a wide range of specialities; and third, a journal that would be eclectic but interpersonal in orientation. The Washington School of Psychiatry was the first activity to materialize, with its incorporation in 1936; but in the beginning it was indistinguishable from the local psychoanalytic institute and did not become interdisciplinary until 1943. In 1938, the journal *Psychiatry* began publication under three co-editors: Sullivan, Hadley, and Thomas Harvey Gill, a forester and writer, who was expected to offer a broad practical perspective. Beginning with the first issue, the Journal made visible the thinking and research that motivated Sullivan's plans for the Foundation—plans that had little expression or support elsewhere in those early years.

In the meantime, various attempts were made to find substantial financial backing and to develop more concrete plans for collaborative research, which was Sullivan's main interest. In the summer of 1937, these plans took on a new direction and urgency. The immediate impetus was Sapir's ill health and his growing unhappiness with his post at Yale. This posed the first and greatest crisis in the long history of Foundation crises.

◄ 39 ►

The Research Nucleus

BOARD OF TRUSTEES APPROVES RE-
SEARCH NUCLEUS FULL TIME FOR LIFE
AND APPOINTS FINANCE COMMITTEE EM-
POWERED TO EMPLOY AGENT TO RAISE
ENDOWMENT FUNDS. THIS IS AT LEAST A
BEGINNING.
—Sullivan, telegram to Edward Sapir, April 9, 1938

SULLIVAN'S wire to Sapir suggests somewhat ambiguously that financing for the research group is well under way.[1] The telegram is designed primarily to reassure Sapir that all is well, at a point when Sullivan knew that Sapir was seriously ill.

A year before, in the spring of 1937, Sapir had been told by his physician that he should take life easier, but he continued his usual schedule, planning field work in and around Denver for the summer. In Denver, he suffered his first serious heart attack. In the fall of that year, the Sapirs took up residence in an apartment near Columbia University for a sabbatical year. Sapir was in bed a great deal, but he continued to write and to work with colleagues. His wife spent much of the day away from home, for she felt that she had to renew her professional interests and training so as to be able to support the young children and herself in the event of Sapir's rather permanent invalidism or death. A housekeeper came in at noon to prepare lunch for Sapir. Three or four times a week, Sullivan took a cab or bus across town to be with Sapir for the afternoon; sometimes he would stay on for supper. Jean Sapir felt that Sullivan was critical of her for absenting herself from the apartment during the day, but she felt the pressure of her husband's serious illness.[2]

In long hours of conversation between Sapir and Sullivan that fall, it became clear that Sapir did not want to return to Yale. He saw the climate there as anti-Semitic, and he sensed a competition there that was not a part of his years at the University of Chicago. He had brought one of his former students, John Dollard, to Yale; and both he and Sullivan felt that Dollard was overly ambitious and competitive.[3] Thus Sullivan had acquired a new goal—to finance Sapir permanently and with all kinds of guarantees for his dependents, so that their work could go forward. It was a goal that Lasswell also supported, for he, too, wanted to be included in the research scheduled for the East 64th Street house, or for Washington.

On the seventh of October, 1937, an important meeting of the Foundation's finance committee took place in the Army-Navy Club in Washington, D.C., to consider essentially how a master plan could be devised for raising millions as soon as possible. Sullivan, Lasswell, Hadley, and Gill were present at the meeting. Lasswell had prepared a ten-page report on a plan to put the Foundation on a sound financial basis, and after some emendations from the committee, the report was accepted. Lasswell, as the specialist in the relatively new field of public relations, suggested a wide variety of publicity methods: radio broadcasts, celebrations of various kinds, consultation services, the establishment of a program of awards for outstanding people in the wide area of the Foundation's interests, government proposals, conferences, and so on. Lasswell's report also suggested the use of movies: "It would also be a ten-strike if someone connected with the Foundation were able to invent an idea for a feature picture built around some heroic psychiatric physician."

There was no immediate outcome of the meeting, except for outpourings of money and time from various friends of the Foundation. Lionel Blitzsten, a member of the committee and a dedicated friend of both Sullivan and Sapir, undoubtedly took out his checkbook again, as did Gill and others, although this was a continuous exercise that did not basically solve the problem. In the meantime, Sullivan was busy running around the country, as he found time and train fare, to try and scour up more money. At the same time, he was getting together the first issue of the journal *Psychiatry,* overseeing content, type face, selection of paper; and as often as possible he was at Sapir's apartment, engaged in absorbing discussion of a wide range of subjects—including, for instance, the "myth" of Balaam and the ass, evoked by Sapir's avid reading at that time of the Bible in Aramaic.[4]

There was the slim hope that the Journal would put the Foundation on the map and call forth financial support from many people; in the meantime, the overall plans that Lasswell had proposed remained somewhat in abeyance. By February 28, 1938, with the first issue of the new quarterly still far from completed (although it was scheduled to be published in February), Sullivan began to feel quite frantic about Sapir's health, and he wrote to Hadley outlining several plans for the financial support of the entire Sapir family. Initially, the endowment plan did not include provision for Sullivan's own financial needs, which were also acute; his various activities had precluded any increase in the number of paying patients who found their way to his office. In outlining the first plan for Sapir, Sullivan states: "If we were to seek a principal sum that would cover the annual income we stipulated for him [Sapir] and all the dependent allowances needed now, in his case, it would require $712,500. All but $2,000 per annum of the income from this sum would be freed by 1959." There is a paragraph at the end of Sullivan's letter of February 28 that concerns himself: "Words fail me about the birthday gift. I am full of sentiments—the discovery of the insurance premium due has convinced me that I shall accept it. I am very deeply grateful indeed."

In this increasingly desperate situation, in which Sullivan believed that Sapir's actual survival depended on his not going back to Yale, Lasswell proposed an answer to all their problems; he had found the man for the job—a former student at Chicago. Sometime in this general period, Chapman and Sullivan made a trip to Chicago to meet this man so enthusiastically recommended by Lasswell. Their reaction must have been less enthusiastic than Lasswell's, and the matter lay dormant. Hadley continued to feel that they should act favorably on Lasswell's recommendation. On March 28, Hadley wrote Ross Chapman, a loyal contributor over the years to furthering Sullivan's ideas: "The fact is I cannot get rid of the idea of securing Lasswell's friend as a Public Relations Counsel." But at the same time, Hadley was concerned lest the Foundation might be demeaning itself. He reported that a friend of his at American University, "a staunch, upright idealist . . . and for a long time . . . in opposition to paid money makers" had been converted by the experience of using a paid money maker. He went on to state the seriousness of the problem.

We have to do something. Sullivan is worn down completely with the burdens we have let him carry. I know of no one else who could possibly have had the courage to give up valuable professional time as he has done. If we sleep at the switch much longer I am afraid his patience will really give out. After all he does want to live. The Foundation would fold up like a tent without him. Then there is Sapir. Yale, or a particular department thereof, has let him down at a serious time. Only Lasswell can carry on part of the research work projected and he has to make some kind of a decision shortly. I am afraid we may miss the boat there too. With the first issue of the Journal coming out, it is not only an auspicious time to strike but we have to do so. I wonder if we could not take a chance and if there is any way at all to dig up some funds so that we can take a chance on this fellow to raise some money, pronto.

On the same date, Hadley wrote to Lasswell and began to commit the Foundation to hiring the public relations counsel:

I know that there are some 'resistances' but the facts are that Sullivan is wearing out under the responsibility we have let him carry without any relief in sight. To my mind Sullivan is the Foundation and the funds are being exhausted without any replenishment. Moreover, we need you and Sapir on, let us say, full time professorships so that things can move. Sullivan has to be subsidized. My problem is—confidentially if need be—

where to get sufficient money to pay someone to get the money we need. I haven't made much headway on this problem.

It occurred to me tonight that you might give me some facts and figures on what amount we would have to have to begin securing your friend's services. If you can provide me with a letter on this, together with some useful symbols and slogans I might be more useful all the way round.

Lasswell was euphoric at this turn of events. On March 29, he sent Hadley a letter, mentioning his annoyance at Sullivan for not acting more swiftly in the matter of the public relations counsel. "HSS said he was going to see if he could get some action fast [perhaps as early as March 11]. . . . We heard nothing at this end. This is a hell of a way to conduct important matters. Such slackness is a result of the fact that HSS is over-burdened with things that he has no business being bothered with." The man that Lasswell has in mind "is a brilliant young lawyer here who is gifted with brains, brawn, beauty. He has remarkable gifts which he has transformed into skills; he does athletics, dramatics, cooking, piano, etc., etc., with the greatest of ease." Lasswell suggests that this man be paid $500 a month for six months, "with the understanding that he gives as much of his time to us as he can. I know that he is rarin' to go; because he likes the idea, admires Sapir, and feels attached to me. He also respected HSS and Chapman whom he met here. It would not be fair to ask him to give full time yet." Lasswell promises much: "For $3000 we could probably get several millions in the bag. He knows all kinds of tax tricks that will appeal to big money men." He then goes on to state his own needs: "My own situation is that I must either start at once promoting my own show here, or come East. I can't hold back here any longer as I have been doing. The new Vice President of the U [of Chicago] is very friendly to me and I am in a strategic place to get what I want. But I would much rather cut loose and work with Sapir, Sullivan and you: it is better to start something new and sound than to fiddle with the framework of a crystallized structure."

By this time, Lasswell feels critical of the treasurer of the Foundation: "How many millions has the so-called Treasurer raised? Mebbe it would be a good idea to fire him if he can't cough up fast. There are plenty of rich pricks around if they are properly high pressured." The "log jam" could be broken if only the $3,000 were forthcoming: "This Foundation is one of the biggest promotion ideas of all time and it's been handled like a shy girl selling stolen peanuts. That's because you and HSS don't have time to do everything!!" He ends the letter in a brash mood: "So I recommend murder, blackmail, fornication, counterfeiting: but in any case $3000 on the line." The new public relations expert should be hired by the first of April so that he can "start with a bang as the Journal appears," this being of course the delayed February issue. Lasswell's closing phrase gives the air of expertise: "In haste and in irritation," as if the Foundation had been unusually slow in accepting his expert advice.

On April 2, 1938, Sullivan as president wrote a form letter to the trustees asking for permission to hire "an Assistant to the President to carry into effect the program for raising funds." Three days later, Hadley telegraphed Lasswell that funds had been found for the assistant. On April 9, Sullivan sent Sapir the telegram with which this chapter begins.

From this point onward, the excitement gradually changes to a complete sense of failure and defeat. The financial assistant promises much, but the weeks go by with nothing to show for the monies that the Foundation is sending him. In spite of all the commitments that the Foundation has made to Sapir and to Sullivan, both of them are convinced that the chances for success in this enterprise are dimming. At the end of June, Sullivan leaves for England with Jimmie and Mrs. Hadley. At the same time, Sapir notifies Hadley that he plans to "stall" for a year in notifying Yale of his plans; perhaps by April 1, 1939, he will be able to resign, since the Foundation hopefully will have matured enough by then. Throughout this whole episode, Sapir has been removed from the tensions that Hadley and Sullivan are experiencing.

Lasswell continues to be hopeful. On August 7, he writes to Hadley, outlining his own plans for raising money; they seem considerably more sophisticated and dedicated than those of the financial assistant, but at the same time they seem too cheerful: "It seems to me that one of the purposes of our Foundation is to provide for consultants who are capable of advising individuals of influence on their personal problems." He is concerned as to how the Foundation can "create a demand for this kind of consulting relationship." He continues to express great confidence in his former student. But none of the rest of them have any hope left. Sullivan has committed himself to going to New Hampshire at the end of August to visit the Sapirs, but he delays the trip, hoping against hope that he will be able to report on some vast outpouring of money from the Chicago financial agent. In the meantime, he writes to Lasswell on August 22, expressing his growing disaffection for Lasswell's approach: "In the way that you have written [in the August 7 letter], there might be rather violent objection to what looks like commercial activity of the research group. The demand for professional services seems to me to be an inevitable outgrowth of our work if the world holds together. I feel that there is a great deal to be said for having something concrete to offer to potential large donors to our endowments. The Board and the research personnel cannot sacrifice the great goals to the immediate opportunities without complete miscarriage of the greatest opportunity that I have been able to envisage in my life."

On the same date, Sullivan writes to Hadley about the situation, but he gives a somewhat more candid opinion of Lasswell's proposals: "As I rather expected, Sapir is thoroughly disgusted at the 'get-rich-quick' tone of Lasswell's proposals. I doubt if he would consider associating himself with anything like what Lasswell seems to have in mind. This convinces me that the course which I suggested of having all such activities a natural outgrowth of our real program rather than a hothouse forcing of certain paying trends, is the only sane, wise and dignified policy." He ends the letter with a statement of his own unhappy situation: "I got enough rest and stimulation on my visit [to Washington] to realize clearly that I have gotten myself utterly out on a limb. Unless our research nucleus is financed, and that promptly, I shall have a number of practically insoluble problems immediately."

As one goes through the innumerable letters in this whole period of frantic activity, there is evidence of an approaching climax. The financial distress is acute; the split with Lasswell is imminent, since his recommendations have further handicapped the Foundation; and Sapir's health is deteriorating.

After many frantic reassurances from Chicago, the financial agent finally writes a letter of resignation on November 5, 1938: "In view of the record I have made, which is a great disappointment to you and to myself, . . . my temporary formal connection is at an end." However, he promises to continue his great work without any formal pay or official connection to follow his "prospects to a successful conclusion." On November 21, he sends in the only money that he has managed to raise: $250—"the first olive out of a very tight bottle," as he terms it. In a handwritten note to Hadley, Sullivan comments on this record: "Perhaps we ought to frame this 'substantial contribution' promised for 15 Oct. It is about 8 percent of the cost of the 'Finance Counsel,' I gather. Perhaps it should be distributed as dividend to the Trustees who made the loan." By then, the loan of $3,000 had all been paid to the financial counsel.

Even after the resignation of the "Finance Counsel," the crisis continues. For a rival group has been established in Chicago, purportedly organized *for* the Foundation in Washington, but self-serving and inappropriately using the Foundation's name. After several months, the Foundation finally has to "use the talents of Mr. Morris L. Ernst to restrain the Chicago group from besmirching psychiatry in general."[5]

But in the interim period, Sullivan still tries to determine whether or not some good could come out of the dubious publicity engendered in Chicago. He is troubled, but he still keeps his sense of humor when he writes to Blitzsten in Chicago, on December 14, 1938, noting that it is difficult for him to find out from Lasswell what is really going on: "Lasswell says lots of words but few declamatory sentences." But as the letter proceeds, Sullivan's anger and frustration mount:

I regard Edward with affectionate reverence; Harold, with ancient but now rapidly mounting distrust. I have for years felt convinced that if Edward and I could get ourselves properly endowed, we would really accomplish something of durable value. At best, in my thinking, Lasswell has seemed but a highly talented technician; Edward, a genius. And now—and I know how wretchedly you and Dorothy will feel about this—I greatly fear that Edward's continuing life is a matter of weeks, only;* certainly not to be thought of in terms of years. His heart went very bad two weeks ago, so that the local cardiologist despaired of him. I thought he would pull through, and he showed excellent recuperation until last Wednesday morning when he had what looks like another coronary accident. He continues critically ill, but is faintly better again.

Well, with the fading of my last hopes for collaboration with Edward, one of the great roads into the future disappears. For two years, now, I have lived in apprehension at the prospect. Now that the final disaster is immediately before me, I am accommodating myself as best I can. But I rage and rage at the probability that "our promotional work" in Chicago dropped Edward out of the picture as soon as the color of an excuse could be found, and focused itself exclusively on Lasswell with the White Foundation as a sort of vague back-drop for his career, first as the savior of Business and Democracy, now as the new Messiah. If I confirm these suspicions, the White Foundation will prove an unsalable pedestal, I assure you.

At the end of the letter, Sullivan again tries to be fair to Lasswell and to be more understanding of Lasswell's own frustrations and possible value:

It is necessary that I maintain what objective detachment I can muster in this whole situation. Lasswell has had his troubles and disappointments, too; and I may be reading a good deal of error into my private pictures of the Chicago promotion—as a result of his reaction to my increasing distance and disdain for what looks to me like agile opportunism. In any case, we, Hadley and I, are badly handicapped by lack of collateral information, and we wonder if you can find us some facts. We should be careful lest we destroy something of potential value; even if we get nothing whatsoever for our research and teaching, and only act as auspices for Dr. Lasswell and his crew in a good piece of research in antisemitism or something of that sort, it would really be much better than nothing. We shall try to look after the Foundation. Beyond perchance though, we have gone a long way to help him play his game, the last few months. We have had some useful returns from this—in the way of increased interest in us—but we want to know what it has cost, is costing, and is liable to cost, to go on.

The death of Sapir marked the end of the research nucleus as such. For Lasswell, the experience of being actively involved in a dubious enterprise for making money was professionally humiliating. But Sullivan was personally devastated. Their subsequent "drifting apart," as Lasswell once described the situation, was more definite than that. After Sapir's

* Actually Sapir died seven weeks later.

death, Lasswell did not publish again in the Foundation's journal *Psychiatry*, until after Sullivan's death. His name disappeared from the list of directors of the School; he had never been selected as a trustee for the Foundation. In the annual report of the president to the Foundation in the fall of 1939, Sullivan states: "A proposal from Dr. Lasswell concerning a study of resettled communities for the Department of Agriculture was received and taken up with several of the Trustees. This work is proceeding without our auspices." During the war years, both Lasswell and Sullivan were consultants at the White House.[6] In this period Lasswell sometimes met Sullivan and the writer George McMillan for lunch in one of the downtown Washington hotels; they were all three interested in the uses of propaganda in the war effort, and McMillan remembers that this was their main subject of conversation.[7]

So it was that the research nucleus had a brief life. Yet the early relationship of the three men left an indelible mark on the history of ideas in America, although the careful tracing out of their collaborative effort in the field of culture and personality has been largely neglected. Since Lasswell was the youngest of the three and his life span was much longer, his contributions may be more generally recognized, although his collaboration with Sapir and Sullivan is not thoroughly documented as yet. In 1969 some of Lasswell's colleagues and students published a remarkable collection of essays in honor of Lasswell, titled *Politics, Personality, and Social Science in the Twentieth Century*. The breadth of his impact on almost every conceivable area of the social sciences as related to dynamic psychiatry is outlined in these essays. As the editor, Arnold A. Rogow, noted in his introduction, Lasswell "is without question America's most distinguished political scientist as well as one of our best known and most respected behavioral scientists."[8]

The most immediate record of the collaboration of the research nucleus is found in the early issues of the journal *Psychiatry*. In the fateful year when Lasswell, Hadley, and Sullivan, with many others, were trying to finance the research nucleus under the pressure of Sapir's serious illness, the Journal began to be published. The first issue carries three papers by the original New Haven triumvirate, Sapir, Lasswell, and Sullivan. The lead article by Sapir, "Why Cultural Anthropology Needs the Psychiatrist," sets the stage for the wide scope of the Journal. Lasswell wrote the third article, "What Psychiatrists and Political Scientists Can Learn from One Another," and this is also an important weather vane. And the last article is purportedly a first chapter of a book that Sullivan is planning to write, with succeeding chapters in later issues—a plan that never came to fruition in that particular form. "Chapter one" is titled "The Data of Psychiatry," and it is one of the first lucid statements of how psychiatry could become a science. There are other important papers, including Hadley's surprisingly interpersonal paper, "Unrecognized Antagonisms Complicating Business Enterprise," and an article on homosexuality by Silverberg, one of the members of the Zodiac group. A doctoral dissertation on "The Concept of Tension in Philosophy" by Katherine Dunham's brother, Albert Millard Dunham, Jr., is included, apparently in its entirety; it became crucial in Sullivan's own development as a link to the thinking of the philosopher Charles S. Peirce.

But it was Sapir's contribution that most pleased Sullivan; it spelled out an acceptance of Sullivan's interpersonal theory into the field of cultural anthropology that was most important in the interdisciplinary attempts that would follow. The first article in the second issue of the Journal was solicited by Sullivan from Sapir's colleague, Ruth Benedict—the classic study entitled "Continuities and Discontinuities in Cultural Conditioning."

For both Sapir and Sullivan, their students were in many ways their chief legacy. One of Sapir's students, Weston La Barre, who himself has published several articles in *Psychiatry* over the years, reported in 1961 on Sapir's influence on his students:

It was Edward Sapir, more than any other person, who first effectively imported psychoanalysis into the body of American anthropology. A decade or so ago, I had occasion to make a survey of "Culture and Personality" courses then being taught in American departments of anthropology, and the list of teachers then reads like a roster of Sapir's former students and persons directly influenced by him. At a time when the official anthropological journals were systematically ignoring psychoanalysis and the prevailing climate of opinion was chilly if not hostile, Sapir was giving his students as required reading the works of Abraham, Jones, Ferenczi and other classic writers.... Unfortunately, Sapir never published more than programmatic papers in this area; as one of his colleagues once told me, not ironically, "Sapir wastes himself on his students."

La Barre goes on to say that "Sapir's interest in analysis was fostered by his friendship with Harry Stack Sullivan," but this does not adequately describe their collaboration.[9]

When Sullivan realized that Sapir was dying, he characteristically immersed himself in new plans that would represent a continuation of one of their interests—in this instance, Negroes. He made a hurried trip to Memphis, Tennessee, and then to Greenville, Mississippi, at the request of Charles Johnson, to study some of the problems of the black man in the South. In Greenville, he was treated hospitably by a Southern writer, William Alexander Percy, a relative and foster parent of the writer Walker Percy. The latter Percy has reported on this visit of Sullivan's:

One memorable visitor to my uncle's house, a regular stopover then for South-watchers, was the psychiatrist Harry Stack Sullivan. He had been sent down by some foundation or other for an instant psychoanalysis of race relations.

Being the genius he probably was, he didn't take the project very seriously and spent his entire stay sitting in the pantry sipping vodka Martinis (a concoction unheard of in Mississippi at the time), passing the time of day with anybody who came along, and refusing to utter a single conclusion then or later about the "problem."

His silence and his peculiar way of doing field work I can only interpret now as signifying not that there was not a "problem"—indeed the injustices were gross and grievous—but rather that the human condition, race relations most especially, is a very complex business, shot through with paradox, rights thriving with wrongs, joys in the face of poverty, sufferings in the face of plenty—and that one has to look and listen hard and long before venturing the most tentative impression.[10]

Yet Sullivan did draw some significant conclusions from this trip, and they are represented in Johnson's book *Growing Up in the Black Belt*.[11] His method of observation was participant and not as "peculiar" as Walker Percy suggests. The no-man's-land of the pantry in a white Southern upper-class household was then one of the few places in Mississippi from which a white man could appropriately observe the black man.

Sullivan was in Greenville, on February 4, 1939, when Sapir died. On the next day, he telegraphed Hadley to tell him of a few changes in plans, including the cancellation of a trip to Pensacola, Florida, to confer with the United States Air Force; he does not mention Sapir's death. But Sullivan's salute to his collaboration with Sapir had just been published as an editorial in *Psychiatry,* titled "Anti-Semitism."[12] The editorial established a link between anti-Semitism and the usual way in which a Christian child is introduced to the "story of Jesus." It also made a link, however parenthetically, between the Catholic child growing up in a basically Protestant community, and the Jewish child subjected to intolerance. This significant formulation of prejudice in the society came at the same period when Sullivan first became gravely concerned about the black man in the South.

Somewhat later, Sullivan wrote a more formal obituary for Sapir, which was titled "Edward Sapir, Ph.D., Sc.D. 1884–1939"—a significant lapse in the Journal's policy of not listing titles after a name.[13] After citing all of Sapir's honors and affiliations at the beginning of the obituary, Sullivan goes on to express his loss: "Edward Sapir leaves but shadowy marks of his genius in the distinguished scholars who gained their orientation and inspiration in contact with him. His creative work, begun in 1906 in the analysis of American Indian languages, was but moving towards its zenith in his far flung exploration of the relations of culture and personality when his heart disorganized in the Fall of 1937. The span of his interests was far too wide to let him rest in semi-invalidism, he was too vital to accept the biologically inevitable. He was one of the most articulate of men, a poet, a musician, an intellect that evoked reverence, a personality unendingly charming, a genius largely wasted on a world not yet awake to the value of the very great."

Within six months after Sapir's death, Sullivan made the physical move of his household to Washington, buying a house in nearby Bethesda, Maryland. There was nothing to hold him in New York City any longer. Even Maggie Stack was gone, for she had died the year before; and Harry had gone over to Brooklyn Heights once to supply personal information on "Marguerite A. Stack" for the death certificate and again to participate in the wake and funeral. The medical examiner had listed the cause of death as "Generalized Arterio Sclerosis, Chronic Myocarditis," the latter being a congenital affliction that Sullivan also bore. She had been buried in a Catholic cemetery in Washington, where most of the surviving members of Michael Stack's descendants then lived and where Michael's grandson Harry was to spend the last decade of his life.

40

Expanding the Foundation's Horizons

From the end of the [First] World War, in large measure through the continued sanifying influence of William Alanson White, it was the observer and thinker among American psychiatrists generally who gained the most intellectual perspective from Freud's discoveries. His horizon expanded enormously, while that of the established psychoanalyst, especially with the advent of European colleagues beginning around 1930, often narrowed.
—Sullivan, "How Sweet *Are* the Uses of Adversity"

SULLIVAN'S withdrawal from New York City in 1939 was in part determined by his need to free himself from some of the schisms developing there between psychiatry and psychoanalysis, and, more significantly, between psychoanalysts of one faith and those of another. After he came to Washington and tried to establish an eclectic school for training and research, he became increasingly aware of the stranglehold that some of the 'true' followers of Freud were exerting on anyone, anywhere, who was interested in free inquiry. The journal *Psychiatry,* begun in 1938, had established itself from the beginning as a meaningful interdisciplinary forum. But the Washington School of Psychiatry did not become eclectic and vital until 1943, when the need for adequate training of all kinds of professionals and paraprofessionals, arising out of the stress of World War II, changed the School from just another psychoanalytic institute into an important training center. In the struggle of those years, each psychiatrist/psychoanalyst was finally forced to take sides; and by the end of 1945, the struggle had effectively terminated the important working relationship between Sullivan and Hadley in both arenas—the School and the Journal.

Before the influx of European psychoanalysts in the 1930s, American psychiatry had begun to make significant use of Freud's insights, fitting them into an ongoing discipline that had emerged from a democratic society of diverse peoples. But as well-known analysts arrived in substantial numbers, the climate changed. There was a general feeling that European education was so far superior to American culture and scholarship that the earlier development under Adolf Meyer and William Alanson White, for instance, was irrelevant to the great central discoveries of Freud which were now being carried personally to this country by his disciples. Students who clustered around these disciples were often indiscriminate in their readiness to accept the leadership of a particularly well known person; in time, some of these charismatic figures began competing among themselves for the loyalty of their own students.

A somewhat comparable situation developed in American anthropology. Some anthropologists tended to feel that there was no significant development in America until Franz Boas arrived. Boas came from Germany as a permanent resident in 1886, and by the beginning of the century he had established himself in the eyes of many of his students as the creator of anthropology in this country. In a case history of a nineteenth-century anthropologist, the historian Joan Mark has commented on this phenomenon:

The fact is that when Boas came from Germany in 1886, he joined—he did not create—an ongoing science of anthropology in the United States. Yet a legend has been built up around Boas, partly at his own instigation, which has tended to obscure the contributions of his American predecessors and contemporaries. Boas found his own intellectual forebears in Europe, and American anthropologists ever since have tended to appropriate his antecedents as their own. Yet during the middle and late nineteenth century, there were many ideas travelling in the opposite direction, from America to Europe. American anthropology in the nineteenth century, its methods, concepts, and institutional forms, had a profound impact on contemporary European scholars, and to an unrecognized extent has continued to shape the science of anthropology on both sides of the Atlantic.[1]

In brief, although both anthropology and psychiatry benefited from the stimulation of European thought, as represented by Boas's and Freud's followers, there was some loss of momentum in the development of indigenous disciplines, partly because there was often a failure to recognize the value of the development in one's own country.

By contrast with Freud, the physical presence of Boas in this country made it possible for his students to appraise him more realistically. Thus Sapir, who studied under Boas at Columbia, did not become his devoted disciple; but he was never offered a post at Columbia, so he was punished by Boas for his independence. Unlike the anthropologists, the psychoanalysts were, for the most part, not attached to universities, and they were not able to maintain, in the midst of professional and political upheaval, a spirit of free inquiry. A few took up strategic places in the psychoanalytic communities and were relentless in attacking anyone who challenged their territorial rights. New York City became an early focus of this struggle.

The analyst Marianne Horney Eckardt has written an incisive story of the organizational schisms in this period, mainly as they centered around New York City. She traces these schisms, in part, to Freud's dual role as a scientist and an autocrat. As a scientist, he stressed the need for progressive modification of theory to account for new empirical data. "But there also existed Freud the autocrat, who did not give his followers the license to divine and formulate their vision of the connecting links of the empirical data observed." Eckhardt also gives a disarmingly candid account of the participation of her mother, Karen Horney, in the formation of schisms in New York City.[2] Another psychoanalyst, John A. P. Millet, has written of this same phenomenon as it developed in the 1930s and 1940s; and from a twenty-year vantage point, he has described tellingly and noncontentiously the situation in which the refugees brought with them from Europe an "entrenched hierarchical culture" which inevitably led to "convulsive movements in the process of adapting the traditional framework to the impact of a democratic social order."[3]

It is impossible to summarize or make simple sense out of the confusion that existed in and around New York City in this period of relocation of refugees, not all of whom were political refugees. Karen Horney, for instance, had originally come to this country to escape the more academic restrictions, as she felt them, on her development as an independent and popular teacher. She was brought up as a Protestant; relatively naive politically, she did not particularly understand the significance of the political situation in Germany until after she arrived in this country.[4] Moreover, American psychiatrists who had trained in Europe or who became early students of the refugee psychoanalysts in America also participated in the chaos that began to develop and was in full swing by the 1940s.

The sequence of events has been described by Millet:

As more and more of the refugee analysts became qualified as members of local societies and joined the faculties of the training centers the influence of their authoritarian approach to training became more and more apparent. Regulations as to qualifications for training analysts, minimum duration of training analyses, frequency of analytic sessions, number and frequency of supervisory sessions, etc., became more numerous, more exacting, and spread over more areas of the training process.

By the time the United States entered the war a new pattern of administrative policies was emerging in which the influence of the European group and their American pupils was paramount. The number of analysts whose training had been secured in a local institute was too small for them to pit their experience and ideas successfully against the strength, both in numbers, reputation and experience of their elders. The accolade of knighthood in the order of traditional conceptualists had already been given to a handful of American leaders either in Vienna or in Berlin. Their acceptance of the authority vested in Freud and handed down through the International Association was sustained, fortified, and crystallized through reunion with their exiled colleagues.[5]

Retrospectively it is easy to see that two of the emigrant psychoanalysts—Erich Fromm and Karen Horney—were often singled out for special chastisement. As members of the Zodiac group, they had been associated with Sullivan; and as teachers and writers they had clearly taken the lead in a number of ways. Thompson and Silverberg were also special targets, but Silverberg was more adroit than the others in staying somewhat on the sidelines so as to avoid the central conflict. Subtle pressures on the nonconforming members were only a small indication of the caldron of competitiveness and cultism that had begun to develop in American psychoanalysis in the late 1930s. It would eventually dissolve the collaborative relationship that Sullivan enjoyed with Hadley; but paradoxically it also freed the spirit that had originally motivated the research nucleus. Only by moving away from the orthodoxies of the internecine struggles of the psychoanalytic community could such a dream come to a measure of fulfillment.

By the late 1930s, Erich Fromm had become the red flag for rallying opposing political forces in the American Psychoanalytic Association; he continued in that role for over a decade—in fact probably until he withdrew to Mexico in the 1950s. The attacks on him were illustrative of the irrationalities that appear whenever a group of people try to discredit a person or persons who are in the way of its particular goals for power or prestige. Thus one of the criticisms of Fromm cited by various people was that he was not a physician; but no such criticism was made of Erikson, who lacked both medical and undergraduate degrees.

There is a unique opportunity to trace this developing storm through the pages of *Psychiatry* and the files of letters from the office of the Journal during that period. One example of the conflict concerned a paper by Erich Fromm, entitled "The Social Philosophy of 'Will Therapy,' " published by *Psychiatry* in 1939. This paper considerably annoyed Karl Menninger, who was the "most famous American student" of Ruth Mack Brunswick, who in turn was a favorite trainee of Freud's.[6] From his office at One Fifth Avenue, Menninger wrote to Hadley on June 23, 1939, taking strong exception to the article; and in his reply, Hadley suggested to Menninger that his letter might be published in the Journal. On July 6, Menninger answered Hadley's letter, stating that it was not the views of Karl Menninger that the Journal needed but the views of Sigmund Freud. He chides Hadley: "As a Freudian, I should think that you would want the more egregious errors [in the article] corrected. I have heard a great deal of criticism of the article from those whose opinions I know you respect."

Hadley wrote back to say that he had frequently thought of having a contribution from Freud, but that he had hesitated to ask Freud, since he had just been finishing up a book. "I am wondering if you would care to suggest the idea to him [Freud]. In any event I would be deeply obliged if you would provide this office with his address." He added that the Journal could not publish the letter from Menninger because of a decision against carrying any letters, made earlier and overlooked by Hadley; but he suggested a paper on the subject of Menninger's letter.

Menninger answered by stating that he had not suggested an article by Freud, but the use of *"Freud's ideas."* He observed: "Fromm talks about *other* than Freud's ideas—chiefly Adler's and Horney's I'd guess." Fromm did not mention Adler or Horney by name in his article, but Menninger was assigning Fromm's ideas to these 'revisionists.' Menninger thought that it would be unwise to approach "the Professor" at this time; the letter written on July 11, 1939, predated Freud's death by about ten weeks, so he was quite correct in his surmise. Menninger continued in this letter to warn Hadley that Fromm's article was causing a great many uncomplimentary things to be said about its misrepresentation of psychoanalysis; "and I think it is a pity for your Journal to have such an article appear in it unrefuted."

Finally on July 25, Sullivan himself took pen in hand and wrote to Menninger. Sullivan's letter is important, for it clearly contrasts with Hadley's growing fear of offending the psychoanalytic community; and it illustrates Sullivan's reluctance to participate in any plan that might be afoot to interfere with the "freedom of the press":

Dear Karl:
I am much distressed by your reaction to Dr. Fromm's article. I talked with [Hadley] immediately on receiving your letter of June 23rd. The three of us have talked over the starting of a correspondence department with your letter. We have regretfully abandoned this idea because philosophical controversy takes up much space, is of no interest to many of our readers, and is well provided with a channel in the Journal of Philosophy and Psychology—to which latter journal the appropriate audience may be expected to look. I think that we have to consider the type of discussion which is needed here to be definitely in the field of philosophy. It is a questioning of the character of premises and their meaning. We accepted

Fromm's contribution with the understanding that it was to a considerable extent a statement of social philosophical implications.

It was for this reason that we seriously urged that you use your persuasiveness on Professor Freud to elicit from him, presumably for the International Journal, a clear statement of his basic philosophy as it has crystallized over the years.

I think that the serious formulation of basic concepts and the tracing of their implications ought to be done—perhaps by several people in the near future. Not as a matter of what Dr. Fromm's merits [are] but as a matter of our desire to be useful, I bespeak from you anything you can do to secure us articles of this kind. We are not going to become abstruse in this field; we would like very much, however, to represent the best.

Thus it is apparent that Hadley had committed himself to publishing Menninger's letter, when the three-man committee had not yet established policy on it—a minor matter, of course. But the other matter is more important: Sullivan asks Menninger to encourage Freud to write a clear statement of his basic philosophy for the *International Journal*, and by implication not for *Psychiatry*. This is indeed a clear communication to Menninger that in the gathering storm, the American Psychoanalytic Association will not be able to dictate to the journal *Psychiatry*.

The immediate independence of the Journal came partly from its early success with its subscribers and contributors. But most of its independence came from its accidental history, in that Sullivan was unable over a period of years to establish a publishing connection with the *Psychoanalytic Review,* under the editorship of White and Jelliffe, so he had to begin a new journal. As early as 1934, Sullivan was unhappy about the content of journals in the field generally. On June 13, 1934, he wrote to White, complaining about the inadequacies of several journals then in publication. The *American Journal of Psychiatry* was "unfriendly to analysis," and the *Psychoanalytic Quarterly* was "a private organ of the group here [in New York] with which I am most completely lacking in sympathy." White's and Jelliffe's journal, the *Psychoanalytic Review,* was the only one of the journals "for the expression of the really American psychiatric psychoanalytic views. I wish it might have two sections, frankly, one of them restricted to our American variance derived from Freud. As long as there are so many hostilities in psychoanalysis—which hit my friends, even if not myself—it is hard to resolve the publishing problem raised by an eclectic editorial policy coupled with the feeling in Europe that my friends and I are dangerously radical." Sullivan proposed to White that he share his publication in some way, sell an interest in it or whatever, but White never reacted to this proposal.

On May 26, 1937, only a short time after White's death, Hadley wrote to Jelliffe (with Sullivan's concurrence) to inquire whether or not the

Foundation might make an offer on the purchase of the *Psychoanalytic Review*. Hadley wrote that an anonymous friend was willing to pay $3,000 for the *Review;* the friend was undoubtedly made up of several friends who would be persuaded by Sullivan to make up this amount. But Jelliffe wanted more money, and finally decided to continue the *Review* himself.

Shortly afterwards, Hadley and Sullivan began to plan for their own journal. By July 6, 1937, Sullivan had begun to give a great deal of thought to the title, as he wrote to Hadley in a long letter:

I have concerned myself at intervals over the years with the name of a journal which I would like to edit. The tendency has been toward including my more or less proprietary interest in the term 'interpersonal relations.' It has seemed rather timely to emphasize the relations of personality and culture, but the technical meaning of the term 'culture' is not too widely understood, and its popular meaning is rather profanely unsuitable. The term 'civilization,' on the other hand, is really rather expansive. A journal entitled "personality and civilization" seems to me rather grandiose; "journal of interpersonal relations" seems better as a subtitle; "personality and culture" to the uninformed is definitely misleading. If we were to raid the Greek, my inclination would be toward "nexus; a journal of interpersonal relations," or as subtitle, "for the study of man in society." Specifically, "logos" throws emphasis philologically on the rational formulation of events. I do not know that this is necessarily undesirable. I am afraid that a copyright may be held on logos; even perhaps on nexus. "Demos" may be looked at; "Bios" in its extended sense covers the limits of our field.

The eventual selection of *Psychiatry* as the name of the journal elevated developments in American psychiatry into a major discipline and moved away from the conflict implicit in the belief systems that were developing under the term "psychoanalysis." (The subtitle, which changed twice over the years, has always included the term "interpersonal.")

In this same letter to Hadley, Sullivan began to deal with the emergent struggle between some of the European-trained analysts and the Foundation group; he understood that without delay he would have to test Hadley's willingness to stick with the Foundation in this first battle. A crisis had arisen over Jelliffe's new political power after White's death. Since Jelliffe was trained in Europe, he had wanted to attract to the *Psychoanalytic Review* those analysts who as trustees of the new Foundation were not entirely happy with the Foundation's direction. After Jelliffe decided to continue the *Review* himself, he had asked A. A. Brill, then a trustee of the Foundation, to be its associate editor, and at the same time had asked Hadley to be one of the "collaborators." Jelliffe had issued no invitation to Sullivan, although Sullivan's experience on the *American Journal of Psychiatry* outdistanced the editorial experience of either Brill or Hadley.

Sullivan spelled out this political situation in his letter to Hadley: "My first theory was to the effect that you were being offered the subordinate honor to complicate Brill's self-seeking indifference to our interests. I think the whole matter is of very little real importance, and all the honors that could be showered on you would be useful if we created a new periodical. The various considerations that impinge, therefore, cancel one another, and I am entirely without motivation in the matter." In the end, Hadley did not accept the dubious honor offered by Jelliffe.

Sullivan went on in the same letter of July 6, 1937, to express his distrust of Brill, stating that he wanted "to get rid of Brill as a Trustee." Within two months, indeed, Brill had resigned, supposedly because he was critical of the change in the Foundation's name from "Psychoanalytic" to "Psychiatric," a change initiated by William Alanson White before his death. Thus the battle over ownership of words had been joined, and Brill represented the first direct challenge to the fledgling foundation. In this early encounter, Hadley stood steadfastly with Sullivan.

For both Hadley and Sullivan, the Journal became their pride and joy. Hadley was not a writing psychiatrist; he had published only a few papers before he began to write for the Journal. But he was a born organizer, and he took over Sullivan's ideas for the Journal with grace and dedication. Even after Sullivan and Hadley had reached the visibly angry parting of the ways in 1945, Hadley wrote a letter on November 29 to Arnold Emch, then president of the Foundation, and reviewed their roles on the Journal in a generous fashion, noting that the first issue had been "cradled through the press by Dr. Sullivan."

After first agitating Dr. Sullivan with the idea of purchasing *The Psychoanalytic Review* from Dr. White's estate, I soon discovered that the cost of that publication—if obtainable—would float a new Journal for at least five years. It would doubtless be improper to say that *Psychiatry* was started by Dr. Sullivan and me. The role of *promoter* could doubtless be more properly applied to me; and, the role of *creator* of the general purpose and appearance of *the* Journal to Dr. Sullivan. Third, because of his general experience in the field of publications—both authorship and editorship; and the fact that his advice was more practical than that of any other Trustee on the Board, Tom Gill was urged to complete the three-man committee.

In this long letter, Hadley touches nostalgically on the success of the Journal. He reports that he has been complimented over and over again by both authors and readers on his editing. He mentions the quality of the paper—"the finest readable surface obtainable—Ticonderoga Text Wove Yellow"—and "the most readable type—Paragon." Hadley gave up his eight-year collaboration with Sullivan on the Journal with great sadness. In truth, Hadley's chief claim to immortality is found in its pages; he contributed office space, staff, his own time, and he managed to do all this with such attention to detail that even his hard taskmaster Sullivan could find little to fault.

Creating an eclectic and interdisciplinary journal was easier than developing a training institution. The Washington School of Psychiatry, incorporated in 1936, arose out of specific relationships of the founders with the Washington-Baltimore Psychoanalytic Society, and its autonomy to move in association with the other human sciences was established only slowly and at great risk to the personal relationships of the colleagues. Aside from the political problems presented in establishing the School as an interdisciplinary and eclectic training and research institution, there was no financing for such an enterprise at the time Sullivan moved to Washington.

In the fall of 1939, there was a brief period of euphoria when Georgetown University Medical School offered Sullivan the post of professor and chairman of a new Department of Psychiatry. He was interested, and the Foundation's Board of Trustees gave its approval on October 14, 1939, in the hope that this would offer long-term support for the program. Sullivan immediately went to work on an ambitious plan for integrating various approaches into this new department, including psychoanalysis. That word, and the name Sigmund Freud included in Sullivan's proposal, terminated the arrangement within a matter of days; Georgetown's Catholic orientation toward psychoanalysis at that time called for a swift parting of the ways.

A month later, Sullivan gave his well-known five lectures titled *Conceptions of Modern Psychiatry,* under the auspices of the Foundation, as the First William Alanson White Memorial Lectures. In these lectures, he gave full recognition to Freud, Meyer, and White as beginning a trend towards a "complete psychiatry." He cited the early psychoanalytic books that he had read and considered important, all of which had been translated into English by 1930. He then observed that "my subsequent reading of more *purely* psychoanalytic contributions has fallen under the law of diminishing returns" (emphasis mine).[7] It was his public answer to the move to challenge the integrity and free spirit of *Psychiatry,* which had elected to publish papers that were not "purely" psychoanalytic contributions, such as Fromm's paper. Thus, within the space of a month Sullivan had been turned down by a university because of his connection with psychoanalysis, and he had declared his independence of the direction that psychoanalysis had begun to take.

His sortie back into an established institution had been an unproductive detour, but the task of invigorating the School was not very encouraging either. From 1936 until 1943, the interdisciplinary nature of the School existed mainly in Sullivan's mind; the School was thought of chiefly as a kind of holding company for the Institute. In 1939, 1940, and

1941, the program of study was carried in *Psychiatry* under the name of the School, but the courses listed, with one or two exceptions, were offered under the auspices of the Washington-Baltimore Psychoanalytic Society (and, after 1940, the Institute) and mirrored courses given in other psychoanalytic institutes at that time. The power of the American Psychoanalytic Association was evident in the way in which the more independent-minded analysts were listed and by the sorting out of which colleagues taught required and elective courses. Thus Hadley, Dooley, Fromm-Reichmann, and several others were listed in 1940 and 1941 as both accredited training analysts and accredited supervising psychoanalysts; but Sullivan achieved only the last-named accreditation. Within the hierarchy of psychoanalysis, the highest accolade is even yet reserved for the designation of "training," so Sullivan was in essence not fully qualified. There was also an implicit warning issued to Hadley because of his growing association with Sullivan; although Hadley was given full accreditation in the hierarchical arrangements, he did not participate, in these years, in teaching any of the required Institute courses.

The only two elective courses were taught by Hadley and Sullivan jointly. One of these, designated "Non-Clinical Psychoanalysis," consisted of a round-table presentation of guest authorities and was open to students having a doctor's degree in medicine or the social sciences. In the bulletin for the academic year 1939–40, the guest lecturers included Erich Fromm, Ruth Benedict, Harold Lasswell, and others. Only in this one elective course was there any indication of Sullivan's dreams for the School.

The first challenge to the new Foundation had emerged from the Journal's publication of Fromm's paper. The next challenge came in New York City and centered around Karen Horney, who with Fromm had been one of the members of the famous (or now rapidly infamous) Zodiac group. On April 29, 1941, the New York Psychoanalytic Society met and voted to disqualify Horney as an instructor and training analyst, charging her with "disturbing the students." Horney and a group of her colleagues, including Clara Thompson, walked out of the meeting. The crisis had been anticipated for some time; and a new organization was already in the offing. On the next day, the Association for the Advancement of Psychoanalysis was officially organized. William Silverberg joined the new Association, even though he had remained up to that time a member of the Washington-Baltimore Institute. Fromm and Sullivan became honorary members, with Sullivan still maintaining his association with the Washington-Baltimore group; thus Fromm's and Sullivan's participation was largely in the nature of moral support in a situation in which independent thinking of any kind had become increasingly dangerous. Horney was selected as dean of the training institute connected with the new Association.

As executive director of the Washington School of Psychiatry, which was still mainly the psychoanalytic training center for the Washington-Baltimore Society, Hadley wrote in his 1942 report, dated February 14, 1942, of the fear that had been engendered by Horney's move. The fear focused on whether members of the American Psychoanalytic Association who were also members of the new Association in New York would be asked to make a choice of membership. "Some suspicion," he said, "had always been directed at the connection between the local psychoanalytic society and the Washington School of Psychiatry. Fear had been expressed that the teaching in the local psychoanalytic group was dominated by some other authority [that is, Sullivan] than the Council of the American Psychoanalytic Association." Some people had suggested a severance of the fiscal ties between the School and the local Institute to "alleviate this pressure and suspicion and place the local Society and its Institute on an even political footing with the other groups." Hadley reported that under date of December 26, 1941, officials in the Washington School of Psychiatry had passed a resolution that the Institute and the School be separated "without prejudice"; and Sullivan, as president, and Hadley, as executive director, had concurred in this resolution. Thus the pressure of the American Psychoanalytic Association had begun to be exerted directly on the School.

From 1941 to 1943, the new Association in New York, with Horney as dean, proceeded in an amicable fashion, even though they were an eclectic group. But in April of 1943, a new schism developed in that group, which punished Fromm in the same way that Horney had been punished earlier. Fromm's privileges as a training analyst were withdrawn under Horney's leadership because she felt that Fromm as a lay analyst would jeopardize the relationship of the new Association with the New York Medical College, with which they were affiliating. It was, in essence, a red herring, for there were ways in which his privileges could have been protected, as reported by Eckardt. Sullivan and Thompson were both angry at Horney for subjecting Fromm to the same kind of arbitrary standards that she had been subjected to earlier. On April 7, 1943, Sullivan wrote a letter to Thompson, resigning his honorary post with the Association; he then went on to try to assess what must have been the personal and professional history and experiences that led Horney's group to take its action. In the May issue of *Psychiatry* that same year, Sullivan reviewed this kind of situation in more general terms: "Personal and professional insecurity often find expression in distrust of the judgment if not the integrity of others, particularly of colleagues who are actively discontented with somewhat useful things as they are, and insistent that something constructive can and should be done. These influences have combined with the profit-and-prestige motives to make the road to success in professional practice much easier for the gifted and fortunate young psychiatrist to travel in company with his collegues than [along] the path of critic and innovator."[8]

In 1941, in the interim between the forming of the new Association and the removal of Fromm, he had published his first book in this country, *Escape from Freedom*. It had been greeted with a great deal of acclaim, for it was one of the first attempts made to unravel the psychological meaning of the rise of Hitler and his acceptance by the German public. It was timely, and it became a best-seller. Sullivan immediately arranged a new first in the journal *Psychiatry*—a series of eight reviews of the book, referred to as "a synoptic series of reviews," which appeared early in 1942. The first and last reviews in the series were by two of the members of the three-man publications committee, Gill and Hadley respectively. Other reviews were written by Ruth Benedict, the theologian Anton Boisen, the Baltimore analyst Lewis Hill, the philosopher Patrick Mullahy, the anthropologist M. F. Ashley Montague, and the sociologist Louis Wirth. It was an impressive array, and it was bound to annoy Karl Menninger if no one else.

Two years later, a scathing review of Fromm's book appeared in the *Psychoanalytic Review,* the publication that Sullivan and Hadley had once so coveted. It was written by the European-trained analyst Otto Fenichel, who was to play an unwitting role in the split between Hadley and Sullivan, and who was trying to find his own political base in a rapidly fragmenting political situation. Fenichel ended his assessment: "Does our review mean that everything which is good in it [Fromm's book] is not new, and everything which is new is not good? It seems we have to answer: Yes."[9] Earlier Fenichel had been equally attacking of one of Horney's books.[10]

In the end, it was an article by Fenichel, submitted to *Psychiatry* in 1945, that is credited with severing Sullivan's and Hadley's relationship. By then, Hadley had been named chairman of the Publications Committee, in part to induce him to stay with the Journal, for by 1943 he had left the post of executive director of the School, apparently under prodding from the Washington-Baltimore Institute. Sullivan had been ill at the time that the Fenichel article had been received in Hadley's office, and Hadley had accepted the article without checking with Sullivan, later citing Sullivan's ill health as the main reason for not showing it to him. When Sullivan discovered this action, he demanded that the acceptance be withdrawn—a bitter pill indeed for Hadley. For Sullivan, Hadley's acceptance of the article could be justified only on political grounds and not on the substantive quality of Fenichel's paper. In point of fact, the content of this paper on brief psychotherapy is slight. The last sentence in the paper, as it appears in Fenichel's posthumously published *Final Papers*, is sufficient to have nettled Sullivan: "Do not underestimate the advantage of pure gold," a reference of course to the true faith—psychoanalysis.[11] The political meaning of its acceptance by Hadley is clear when one goes through the history of the psychiatric/psychoanalytic community in Washington and Baltimore; eventually each analyst was asked, in effect, to choose between the true psychoanalysis and association with Sullivan. Because of Thompson's, Fromm's, and Horney's connections with Sullivan, each in turn was subjected to intimidation, although the real pressure on Thompson did not come until after Sullivan's death. Political feelings were so strong that many clinicians who make generous use of Sullivan's theories are still loath to ascribe their insights to him.

The emergence of the School in 1943 as an independent institution and as a partial realization of Sullivan's dream grew, first, out of the political battles over Horney and then Fromm, and, second, from the increasing importance of the School as a national resource during the war years, beginning with Sullivan's central role in the formation of national screening plans for Selective Service.

The political battle had two stages. The first stage came in 1941 when the pressure on Horney caused the School to separate itself from the Washington-Baltimore Psychoanalytic Institute. At the same time, the Foundation's heavy commitment to the training of general physicians throughout the country for examination of draftees, in which Hadley was an important participant, used up the financial and personal resources of the School and the Foundation. The journal *Psychiatry* contained more pages in 1941 and 1942 than in any other years, and many of the articles and editorials reported on the careful planning and the implications of this first intensive psychiatric examination of a vast number of eighteen- and nineteen-year-old Americans. This experience was a unique one for Sullivan, giving him his first overview of the serious mental health problems existing in the nation at large; and it would motivate him at the end of the war to begin a new kind of psychiatry—a psychiatry of peoples. In this period of psychoanalytic schisms and of heavy demands on all psychiatrists for national mobilization, the Washington School of Psychiatry produced no catalogue for the 1942–43 academic year.

The second stage came in 1943, with the blackballing of Fromm by Horney's Association in New York. This freed Thompson from that affiliation, and she began to plan with Sullivan and others on a new kind of institution, still called the Washington School of Psychiatry, with a Washington and a New York branch. These plans were put together with the help of many people in both areas, including an analysand of Sullivan's, Janet MacKenzie Rioch, a pediatrician who had become a close friend and colleague of Thompson's and who was completely independent of the psychoanalytic politics. Her younger brother, David McK. Rioch, a research neurophysiologist, had met Sullivan several times in the New York years. Although he had had a distinguished career in his own specialty at Harvard, Johns Hopkins, and Washington University in St. Louis, he joined in 1943 the staff at Chestnut Lodge, a leading psychoanalytically-oriented mental hospital just outside Washington, D.C., in order to work with Sullivan. As a research scientist, he was an important resource for the new School that was emerging; in 1944, he became the executive director of the School, and Hadley withdrew from an active role in the School.

In the realignment of forces, Sullivan had powerful allies. Fromm was an important colleague by virtue of his growing national reputation as both a sociologist and analyst, and he would teach in both branches of the School. Chestnut Lodge offered critical support for this new enterprise. Its head, Dexter Bullard, recognized Sullivan's clinical genius and needed his consultation at the Lodge. Sullivan's regular consultation at the Lodge began in October 1942, when he launched his famous weekly lectures, attended by senior and junior staff. In the developing plans for the revitalization of the School, Frieda Fromm-Reichmann, the senior clinician at Chestnut Lodge, stood firmly with Bullard and with Sullivan. An astute clinician herself, she understood the value of Sullivan in the training of psychiatrists at the Lodge. By the fall of 1943, the new School was in place, under the aegis of an Interim Committee, which carried Hadley's name. No officers were listed, and Sullivan's name did not appear except as a faculty member. The title of the program on the cover of the School catalogue was "Comprehensive Training and Individual Courses Offered under the New Wartime Program." Classes for New York and Washington were listed separately, but the faculties overlapped. All during the war years, and after, Thompson, Sullivan, and Fromm-Reichmann traveled back and forth by train between the two cities on a weekly basis. Others, like David Rioch and Erich Fromm, came and went less frequently. The list of Fellows was headed by Ruth Benedict.

From that point on, the newly organized School moved ever more swiftly toward the goals originally set in New Haven. A wide range of students were accepted, and the School became the training institute for the Foundation. Whatever mutterings there were behind the scenes, the strength of the School was recognized by the American Psychoanalytic Association at a practical level. Between 1943 and 1947, the Washington-Baltimore Psychoanalytic Institute was not a part of the School; but the main teachers in the School continued their affiliation with the Institute. Students who took courses at the Washington School of Psychiatry and were trained by its faculty in an "Intensive Personality Study—Psychoanalysis" were not threatened by the American Psychoanalytic Association when they set up practice.

The congeniality and cooperation between the New York and Washington schools marked a monumental change from the schisms that had rent the psychoanalytic community earlier. The two schools operated as one enterprise until after the war, when the New York group had to be incorporated separately in order to qualify for training under the G.I. Bill. In examining this history of friendly collaboration and freedom that existed until Sullivan's death, one is captured again by aspects of the early life experiences that held together some of the central members of the organizing group. Thompson and Sullivan had a bond that has already been partially identified which made them relatively immune to prestige needs. Janet and David Rioch had also been outsiders in their growing-up years and came into psychoanalysis after successful careers in other medical specialties. Their mother was English and their father Canadian; both of them were members of the "Campbellite" Christian sect, and attended a sectarian school, Butler College in Indiana. Their mother became a physician before she and her husband went to India to establish a Campbellite mission. Both Janet and David were born in India. Eventually both children also attended Butler University before going to medical school. Whatever the problems implicit in the complexity of their early lives as children of missionaries in India, Janet and David Rioch shared with Sullivan and Clara Thompson the quality of intellectual honesty and relative freedom from status needs. And all four had some firsthand knowledge of escaping from the restrictions of rigid belief systems.

In a strange bureaucratic twist, the Washington-Baltimore Psychoanalytic Institute, which had responded to the strictures of the national association in 1941 by withdrawing from any connection with the School, was forced back into a business relationship with it in 1947. During World War II, the courses taught by the Institute had disappeared from the School catalogue, as published in the Journal. But after the war the courses reappeared, so that the Institute could take advantage of the School's status under the G.I. Bill of Rights. Physicians who were veterans could get their full postgraduate training paid for through veterans' benefits, including their training analysis; and the Institute made a temporary truce so that its students would qualify to get the benefits through the School that they could not get directly through the Institute.

In 1946 the New York branch of the School became separately incorporated as the William Alanson White Institute of Psychiatry, so that similiar benefits to G.I. students became available there too. After Sullivan's death, the American Psychoanalytic Association renewed its attack on the so-called deviationists in both schools. In New York, students were threatened with permanent discrediting if they did not immediately sever all course work and analytic training with the disfavored teachers. This threat was in fact a violation of the antitrust laws and, upon legal advice, was shortly withdrawn. Yet the national association over a period of years would continue to exert a constricting effect on both schools, and some of the intellectual freedom to develop a science of the interplay of human emotions would be impaired after Sullivan's death.

❧ 41 ❧

The Bethesda Style of Life

> One way or another, I feel that I have grown too old
> to waste my energy carrying the vast overhead of my
> present way of life. It distracts almost continuously
> from concentration on any of the things in which I
> have enduring interest.
> —Sullivan, letter to Ernest Hadley, August 22, 1938

L ESS than a year after Sullivan wrote this letter to Hadley, he moved to 9003 Bradley Boulevard in Bethesda, Maryland, which became his home and office for the rest of his life. The house was remote from the city in a countryside not unlike the setting in Towson. In other ways, too, his life took on some of the character of the Sheppard period, for he again became an important adjunct to the head of a mental hospital—Dexter Means Bullard at Chestnut Lodge in Rockville. In this last decade of his life, Sullivan concentrated more on "things in which I have an enduring interest" than in any other ten-year span of his life, in spite of his recurrent illnesses and a wide range of activities which sometimes involved extensive travel. But he had given up on the wide sweep of plans that he had made earlier with Sapir and Lasswell; and the financial stress of the New York years was largely over, mainly because Bullard and others treasured his clinical brilliance and his abilities as a teacher.

His most strenuous activity in the early part of the 1940s centered on the war and setting up psychiatric standards for Selective Service. When Congress passed the Draft Act in 1940, Sullivan was asked to serve as psychiatric consultant to the Selective Service Director, Clarence A. Dykstra, effective as of December 5, 1940; but initially this was an unpaid post, and the Foundation arranged to provide for some of Sullivan's services to the Selective Service System through a grant from the Carnegie Corporation of New York. In February 1942, Hadley as executive director of the Washington School reported on Sullivan's activities for 1941;

he had lectured in the principal cities in the United States as well as
holding Selective Service psychiatry seminars covering practically every
area of the country. Yet there was never enough money to give Sullivan
an adequate travel allowance, according to Hadley: "With some minor
exceptions ... Dr. Sullivan has defrayed such expenses from salary.
Travel expenses alone during several months have exceeded income, and
the Foundation has not always been able to provide the salary." Sometime in 1942, Sullivan's relation with Selective Service was terminated,
with the advent of a new director, Lewis B. Hershey, who took "pride in
being an amateur psychologist" and who had little patience with any part
of psychiatry.[1] But as the newspaper columnist Albert Deutsch would
write, Sullivan had already "outlined a magnificent plan for psychiatric
screening of draftees [before] his persistent, courageous fight for a decent
psychiatric program led him to an open break with Gen. Hershey. Most
of the basic principles of his screening plan were adopted later."[2]

In an editorial published at the end of this effort, Sullivan reported in
detail on its history and commented on the failure within the society itself: "With one out of four of our citizens either significantly deficient in
intelligence or so distorted from an optimum development of personality
that the vicissitudes of life are a considerable risk for him, the social system certainly comes very near being impeached."[3]

By the fall of 1942, he became convinced that he had best lend his efforts to more and better teaching, as a basis for formalizing his theory of
interpersonal relations; and he concluded that he was no good in any bureaucratic setting or, for that matter, in raising money for the Foundation. On September 17, he submitted his resignation as president to the
Board of Trustees, noting that in the "seven years of my presidency,
the Foundation has moved no whit nearer to becoming a Foundation,
in the sense of possessing a capital fund." He observed, however, that the
Journal had been successful in establishing a high level of workmanship,
largely through the personal sacrifices made by members of the Board.

Less than a month later, in October 1942, he began his series of lecture-discussions at Chestnut Lodge, which eventually totaled 246 sessions. For several years, when his health permitted, he met twice weekly
with professional staff. Bullard gave Sullivan great freedom in these lectures, and Sullivan developed at a leisured pace some of the theories he
had begun to formulate in five public lectures, given in 1939 and titled
"Conceptions of Modern Psychiatry." Without Bullard's continuing support financially and professionally, Sullivan would not have had the
leisure and motivation to press on in the development of theory and technique. The ideas for all his subsequent courses given in the Washington
School of Psychiatry and the New York branch had their beginnings in
these lectures.

At the Lodge, Sullivan began to have his lectures recorded, and this procedure continued for his classes in the Washington and New York schools. Shortly he began to organize notebooks to use for his formal courses. After his death, three books were put together from these recordings, with guidance from the notebooks; yet only a small percentage of the recordings have been published. Sullivan had a clear view of his debt to Bullard and to Chestnut Lodge in helping him to establish this new freedom. When the 1939 lectures were first put in hardback in 1947, Sullivan inscribed Bullard's copy to "the friend who salvaged the psychiatrist and the psychiatry." Moreover, Frieda Fromm-Reichmann, who was the chief resident psychoanalyst at the Lodge, always expressed her admiration for Sullivan's clinical judgment, and this also contributed to his sense of being appreciated. For the first time since he had left Sheppard, he was more in command of his own life than at any other time, and that made a difference. A writer, H. E. F. Donahue, credits Sullivan with inventing a "deathless couplet" which expressed his delight at finally having some basic income with no strings attached: "I'm in charge/ Because I'm at large."[4] Whoever actually invented the couplet, it was peculiarly Sullivan's view of things at that time.

In an introduction to a published selection from the series of lectures given at the Lodge, Bullard has described the scene when Sullivan gave these lectures, held in the recreation room in Bullard's house on the grounds. Sullivan insisted on having Bullard's Great Dane in attendance, and the dog would lie down on the hearthrug in front of an open fire in the winter months: "At times the dog would be used to illustrate a point, and on these occasions Sullivan might take time out to pat his head, as if asking his opinion too."[5] In this leisured setting, Sullivan began to make use of any and all of his observations, accumulated over the years, at a new level of informality.

Some of his observations concerned his own cocker spaniels. At a half-humorous level, he began to push his listeners away from standard psychoanalytic belief systems and toward the power of observation. One of his favorite targets was the elaborate mystique that had grown up around the psychoanalytic meaning of human feces. His cocker spaniels both in New York and Washington offered a clever way to comment on this:

My boy, Jimmie, acquired the first of our cocker spaniels, and he was a very small and terribly anxious, if you please—that is, extremely timid—puppy, presumably because he traveled half way across the United States while very, very young into the great city of Manhattan, and finally to our very narrow and very tall house [on East 64th Street] in which I had my being in those days. And I was working hard—needless to say, incommunicado even to cocker puppies most of the time—but I would ultimately wander up from my office to the floor above where the puppy had his being. And it became noticeable very early after his coming to our house that when I came in in the late afternoon, puppy did his business. . . . You see, I did not have very much trouble when he did his business—somebody else had the problem of cleaning up and so on. . . . I was glad that things went on all right, you know, since he was so frightened of things on the street so that [there] wasn't any very easy way of promoting good toilet habits. And so, I became practically a cathartic; in fact, when I was out of town, I think there were usually difficulties about bowel movements. . . . Well, now that may sound funny, but as it is the durable characteristic of my relations with all young puppies in our household, it is worth thinking about. You see, it is fully as worth thinking about as that the feces are a gift that the puppy gives me.[6]

In a later lecture, Sullivan returned to the topic as observable in a litter of puppies, fathered by the original cocker spaniel, and born some six and a half years later in Bethesda. In the meantime, the mother of the litter had been acquired as a puppy by Sullivan after he came to Bethesda. The mother as a puppy, as well as her own puppies, initially showed the same behavior as the original puppy in New York City; that is, the occasion of Sullivan's entrance into the appropriate area of the house would mark the puppies' prompt relief of the "accumulated waste products." This remarkable coincidence in two, or actually three, generations of puppies was of considerable interest to Sullivan:

Why I was picked on for this distinctive show of something or other, had to be thought of because I'm a psychiatrist and have, in fact, had a great deal to do with psychoanalytic theory. And one of the things that many of you know all too well, because I think probably it's a mistake, is that the infant makes a present of the feces to the parent; you see it's a kindness that the infant feels he's doing. Well, to a dyed-in-the-wool psychoanalyst, here are my puppies doing the same thing, you see, one after another. Now the latest arrivals also greet my appearance with this enthusiastic hygienic measure. And, of course, those of you who are really humorous might have a quite unpsychoanalytic theory for that, but when a thing happens again and again and again, one has to think, and when one thinks—that is, when one reviews one's observations, which I think is ever so much better than the more dangerous form of thought where you ignore your observations—the reason for these dogs' singling me out is not nearly as wonderful as the psychoanalytic doctrine of the fecal gifts would make out.

In the first place, I believe that the young *will* have difficulty arranging their sphincter control to suit our convenience. I am quite sure, for example, that puppies, for the first eight months of their life, have pretty nebulous ideas of what would be our convenience. And when a person [Jimmie] is around them a good deal and busy with this and that, and [is preoccupied with] perhaps how to get the plumber to fix something or other [and when he] discovers two wet spots here and there on the most treasured rugs, the puppy is not a source of unmitigated joy, and feels, I think, some faint suggestions of that drop in euphoria which, I say, is the parent of all anxiety in the human. And when [the puppy] gets a little bit older he gets occasionally a cuff or two for choosing a particularly inappropriate place or time. I, on the other hand, having no concern for the rugs as long as they aren't seriously damaged, and not being around, when I come in am glad to see the dogs, and pay some attention to them, and as soon as the well-known squatting posture is taken, hurry over with my little pledgets of Kleenex, and the dog after his first experience or two discovers that there is no injury in having a bunch of Kleenex chucked under him; and, almost at once, thanks to my reassuring remarks which don't convey exactly the meaning I may put in the words, but do have an effect in so far as the tone is friendly and appreciative, arrange that these little creatures literally, as soon as is convenient after my showing up, go about their business, looking up at me gaily, you see, for approval, at least to be sure that I'm appreciating it.

And it has become a gift in a way, but not a gift in the sense that gets woven into this all too easy analogical thinking that some people pluck out of psychoanalysis—which I would like to do Freud the honor of saying, I think, Freud never intended should be in psychoanalysis.[7]

In somewhat the same manner, Sullivan tackled the task of discounting empathy as a magic ability of humans, by examining the appearance of the same kind of so-called magic in his original cocker spaniel. He reported that while he was living in the brownstone house in New York, he arranged for a patient of one of his supervisees to act as a receptionist on the ground floor of the house; the patient received a small fee for this service. Sullivan explained his action to the patient as determined by his research interest in the patient, who had no money and would have terminated his treatment without some slight income. Sullivan himself avoided the patient as much as possible, and Jimmie had the task of paying him. Sullivan became disturbed by the fact that the cocker spaniel then in residence "sternly disapproved" of this patient. Even when the dog was separated by two doors from the patient, he would growl and snarl. One day, Sullivan noticed a slight difference in the sounds emanating from the dog, and he asked Jimmie about it. Jimmie reported that the dog was interested in the patient; Sullivan expressed great surprise. "Oh, yes," Jimmie said, "he not only sniffed at the hall door, but I opened to see what would happen and he went in and sniffed the inner door . . . and didn't growl at all." Much to Sullivan's astonishment, he discovered subsequently from the patient's analyst that the abrupt change in the dog's attitude followed by a matter of hours the patient's report to his analyst on the death of his only pet when he was growing up—a dog who was killed in the patient's presence for killing sheep—whereupon the patient reported that he had said to himself: "That's the last time I'll ever love anything." In this account, Sullivan goes on to observe that his own dog became increasingly friendly with the patient. He notes that one might explain this change in the dog's behavior as related to a change in the sweat of the patient, so that its odorous quality changed as he abandoned his "infantile hatred," if one were to use psychoanalytic terminology. But the explanation is not that simple: the change is

pretty miraculous and the more plausible explanations seem to me to degrade the astounding character of the event. As long as you recognize it as astounding and in need of explanation because it's astounding, well and good, but just to rattle off a lot of talk and to feel better about it I think is unscientific and not helpful. . . . Shall we insist that there is an empathic linkage between us and our pets? I hope we won't, and why we won't is this: that I've never been ingenious enough and have never heard of anyone ingenious enough to set up an experiment which would rule out other types of linkage; namely, by sound; by odor; relatively dimly, in the spaniel group, by sight; and so on.[8]

After David Rioch came to the Lodge in 1943, Sullivan's interest in animal behavior as an adjunct to the study of human behavior took on a more systematic character, and his early interest in doing research with Sapir on anthropoids found some fulfillment. Rioch himself had done extensive research on animals, particularly cats; and although Sullivan had no affinity for cats, he valued Rioch's research. Rioch has reported that his own interest was in Sullivan's "commitment to trying to develop a scientific approach to psychiatry with an operational terminology," and he observed that Sullivan "had no trouble getting along with people who presented and discussed data"; but many of Sullivan's colleagues "then and still talk beliefs and interpretations."[9]

In one interchange between Rioch and Sullivan on animal behavior, Rioch stated that animals sometimes showed obsessional behavior. Sullivan denied this vehemently, although later he reported on obsessional behavior in one of his dogs and gave Rioch credit for first calling this to his attention.[10] In his last complete lecture series, Sullivan gave an example of such behavior, including a look at sibling competition as a source of fear and timidity in one of his puppies. Elsewhere, however, he made a distinction between the fear experienced by animals and human anxiety as it appears when a person's self-esteem is threatened; human anxiety may produce a feeling almost akin to physical fear, and it often produces obsessional behavior not unlike that shown by his dog, as he reported in a lecture given shortly before his death.

He began by describing the behavior since birth of the youngest dog in a litter of six, who by the time of the lecture was over two years old. Only two others of the original litter were still in the house. From the beginning, one of the dogs, a rather large male, and the other, "a very shrewd and, shall I say, domineering female," had made life difficult for the runt of the litter. As a result, this small female had learned to escape some of the unpleasant attentions of her brother and sister by "very diligently digging great holes and trenches in the environment." She had a regular ritual about doing this, digging vigorously and then running around to inspect the material from the excavation. But as she grew older, she managed to reach the point where she could more than hold her own with her siblings; indeed she began to treat them rather roughly.

As is quite often true of dogs, all three dogs were afraid of the trash man and upset at the noise surrounding the arrival of the large truck. But the only one of the brood that approached the trash man was the digger, who barked furiously at him: "But she stops, after almost every third bark, to dig frantically, and to rush around and examine the dirt again, and then she goes back and roars furiously at him again. It is not, I think, too much to infer that this dog is really very timid, having had excellent reasons for being afraid in the past, but that she became so accustomed to being saved in the past by being preoccupied with her digging that the excess of fear in this situation leads to the reappearance of her preoccupation with digging."[11]

Sullivan's scientific interest in animals rested on what they could teach about humans, and it was easier to study them than it was to study babies—and he often referred to his lack of experience with babies. Thus his final formulation of infancy in which he postulates "the good nipple," "the bad nipple," "the wrong nipple," and even "the evil nipple" as one of the first differentiations of experience in the human infant—completely unrelated to the one person who may from time to time produce this entire range of nipples—is derived in part from his very careful study of his litter of dogs as they tried to feed from the bitch, avoiding one nipple rather consistently, or fighting over a particularly "good" nipple. In his description of this phenomenon, he cites evidence from other mammals—cats, cows, and mares—all of which he had some knowledge of. Although he had an actual aversion to cats, he certainly observed them often in Clara Thompson's apartments over the years—she always had cats as pets. In several unpublished lectures and in one published paper, Sullivan reports on his brief study of skunks, in which there was clear evidence of fear when they were in "a sufficiently new and unfamiliar environment." Elsewhere he describes this in a more facetious way, as if in some youthful experimentation he had tampered with the dwelling place of some young skunks, perhaps bringing them home as pets, and found that even the very young could react appropriately to the fear of the new.[12]

There are many humorous and less humorous stories about Sullivan's dogs. Occasionally a psychoanalyst arriving for a consultation with Sullivan at the Bethesda house would be nipped rather seriously. Sometimes the colleagues would try to make interpretations to Sullivan of such events, to their later regret. One remarkable story concerns a large New Year's Eve party at Sullivan's house in Bethesda. As one of the guests entered the dining room, two of the dogs jumped up on her; she was concerned that they would dirty her dress, so she hastily reached for a bowl of shrimp on the table and gave each of the dogs one shrimp. Sullivan paled and then disappeared with the dogs for about an hour. He had taken the dogs into the back yard where he pumped out the stomachs of both; he was apparently concerned that the shrimp would make them ill. The astonishing thing about this story, of course, is that the dogs would submit to this rather distressing treatment; but Sullivan had a way with dogs—they adored him, and they defined his various actions as benign.[13]

When Sullivan became seriously ill early in 1945, the poet Lloyd Frankenberg was working at Chestnut Lodge as an attendant, at the suggestion of his friend, Janet Rioch, in this way fulfilling his obligations as a conscientious objector to the war. Sullivan had refused to go to the hospital in spite of medical advice, and Jimmie was exhausted from taking care of him at home. Some time after Sullivan first became ill, Frankenberg was assigned to go to Sullivan's and help Jimmie in any way that he could, on a twenty-four hour basis. Frankenberg received his assignment from Ray Pope, the attendant in charge of the ward on which he worked; Pope, who had been an assistant to Sullivan on the Sheppard ward, believed that Frankenberg would be able to handle what was at best a difficult assignment. Pope had already assigned one attendant to the same task, an ordinarily reliable man who after two days had just disappeared and gone on a "bender" in Washington.

Frankenberg took over the task with good humor and great interest in knowing better this psychiatrist whom he had first met briefly in New York. Frankenberg's wife, the artist Loren MacIver, had already achieved a casual and almost playful relationship with Sullivan on their first meeting at a party, when she had sat on his knee and asked him to remove his thick yellow glasses, saying, in essence, "You're going to be famous one day, and I want to know the real color of your eyes." She reports that they were undoubtedly grey-green around the large dark pupils—an observation completely at variance with the belief of others, including Jimmie and Sullivan himself, that his eyes were very dark brown. But MacIver's careful observation must be given some credence. Behind the thick yellow lenses of his glasses, his pupils always seemed enormous to me; perhaps the iris was narrowed and scarcely noticeable with his glasses on.

As a poet, Frankenberg gained a more global understanding of Sullivan's theory, and a review he wrote two years later for the New York Times on Sullivan's first published book represented the most rewarding public recognition that Sullivan received during his lifetime. Frankenberg has written a memoir of his stay at Chestnut Lodge and his assignment to Sullivan's house, which gives a meaningful glimpse of life at both places.[14]

He describes graphically the stillness of the house in Bethesda, silenced as it was by the careful vigilance of Jimmie. Not even a vacuum cleaner was used, in order to maintain the quiet. When Lloyd arrived, David Rioch met him at the door, greeting him "with a glance of relief," for Rioch had been filling in until he arrived. Sullivan's bed had been set up in the dining room, for he was unable to walk upstairs. Jimmie insisted on giving the medication himself, which meant that he set the alarm for medication during the night; then in order to avoid the actual ringing of the alarm, he would try to wake up just before it went off so that the alarm itself would not disturb Sullivan. Even the dogs seemed to keep unusually quiet. Frankenberg was somewhat skittish about Blondie at first, but after a proper introduction Blondie began to sleep on his bed. At the end of two weeks of uninterrupted assignment, Rioch came to the house one evening to spell him. "Take the car," Rioch told him, "and when you get far enough from the house, yell your head off! Good therapy for all this silence."

One of the main problems for Frankenberg, as outlined by Ray Pope in advance, was that neither Jimmie nor Sullivan liked to make direct requests, so that it would be necessary to anticipate their needs. The lack of direct communication between Jimmie and Sullivan is illustrated in Frankenberg's account. One morning when he was making up Sullivan's bed, while Sullivan was in the bathroom, he found a note intended for the physician who was coming that day: "Tell Jimmie, for sweet Jesus' sake, not to go tiptoeing around the outside of the house to get to the kitchen. Much more disturbing than if he strode straight through here." Later, Frankenberg heard the physician telling Jimmie: "Don't be so concerned about giving your father his medicine at night when he's asleep. Sleep is much more important for him than any pills." On another occasion, when Clara Thompson paid them a visit, she told Frankenberg later of a brief conversation she had had with Jimmie and Harry about the problem of communication: "Why, when you want something, don't you ask for it straight out?" she asked them. " 'Oh *no!*' they both answered."

As Sullivan gradually improved, he began to be more active in the affairs of the house. As word began to spread around in the psychiatric community that Sullivan was improving, he began once more to be in demand. Frankenberg reports one such demand: "One time in the middle of the night the telephone rang. I went to the head of the stairs. Dr. Sullivan already had it in the study. I could hear his voice soothing, reassuring. 'No, no, she's not hostile,' he was saying, it seemed over and over. Half an hour later I heard his voice in the hall, talking to the puppy. 'People conspire against us, Groucho. They want to get us down.' " Groucho was Sullivan's favorite at the moment and was always in the dining room with his master. At that time, there were only three spaniels in the house, "Nebuchadnezzar, the patriarch, all black; his tawny wife, Blondie, and the one son they have kept from the last litter, Groucho, also black."

Finally, as Sullivan was beginning to improve, Frankenberg reports that the tension of the situation was affecting him too. As a condition of his assignment at the Lodge, he was undergoing analytic therapy, so that he became aware one evening that he was severely and unaccountably agitated. Out for a walk to try and calm down, he suddenly said to himself, "After all, there's an analyst in the house," and immediately returned to see Sullivan. An excerpt from his account follows:

I tap rather timidly on Dr. Sullivan's door. "Come in," says his musical voice. Dr. Sullivan is getting undressed. He has taken his shirt off and is walking, [with his] back to me, to put it on a chair.

"I'm sorry to disturb you, Dr. Sullivan, but I'm having unaccountable sensations."

Under the T-shirt and suspenders, his spine is alert. The straight spine is empathy made visible. I have come to the right man.

According to Frankenberg, Sullivan briefly explored the immediate onset of his "sensations," was able to reassure him for the moment, and had him telephone for an appointment the next day with his therapist. Later Frankenberg was to write a poem, "The Plate Glass Window," about the upset he had gone through.[15]

After Sullivan improved enough, Frankenberg came to the house only part time. Eventually Loren MacIver paid a visit to Frankenberg at the Lodge and went to call on Jimmie and Sullivan: "They seem to have added her to their small list of tolerable females," Frankenberg reports. "Dr. Sullivan, she tells me, has spoken glowingly of me. 'He's so human,' he said. This, from him, is the highest accolade I can imagine."

Some two years later, Frankenberg's knowledge of Sullivan's theory had remarkable repercussions in the larger world, when his review of Sullivan's *Conceptions of Modern Psychiatry* appeared in the New York *Times* Sunday Book Review section. The story of this book and of the review is a happy one. When I first came to work for the Journal in 1946, Frankenberg had already returned to civilian life, so that I did not meet him for several years. One of my first recommendations to the Board of Trustees was that the 1939 lectures, titled "Conceptions of Modern Psychiatry," be reprinted in monograph form from the issue of the Journal in which they had appeared. The Lord Baltimore Press still had standing type, and the lectures were much in demand by students in both schools. The remaining copies of that issue of the Journal were held in order to keep stock in balance, but students were disappointed when they could not buy that issue. Some of the Board members feared that Sullivan would rest on his laurels if more copies were made and distributed and that he would be even slower about finishing his eternally promised "new book." In the end, a relatively small reprinting was authorized, which would also include a critique of the theory written by Patrick Mullahy for the Journal, and also in demand by students. At the last moment, Donald Reeve at the Press, who had admired Sullivan for almost two decades, suggested that the reprint be bound in hard cover. Thus the first of the Sullivan books was born, printed on the Journal's yellow paper.

At Patrick Mullahy's suggestion, I sent a review copy of this home-made book to Frankenberg, who sometimes did reviews for the *Times*. On Sunday, August 3, 1947, Frankenberg's review appeared. When I called Sullivan early that Sunday morning to tell him about the review, he was wistful: "Is the review favorable?" he asked me. I told him that it was, without giving him any details. I wanted him to see it for himself. He asked me to mail him a copy. As soon as the mail arrived, he called me; he was almost lyrical about the review. He spoke of having a special copy of the book made for Lloyd, with illuminated letters for the large capital letters used at the beginning of each section of the book; it was, of course, an expensive thought, which never came to fruition.

It seems more than coincidence that the person who first brought Sullivan's ideas to the attention of a wide audience was a poet. Like Edward Sapir, Lloyd Frankenberg understood the excitement of this "gnome-like man," as he once described him, and he communicated this excitement in his review: "Harry Stack Sullivan is one of the least widely known of great men. Within his own profession his name is legend. . . . Sullivan is not among the writing psychiatrists. He belongs rather to a bardic tradition . . . his ideas have spread more rapidly than his fame. . . . By a trained awareness of his own processes ('The wounded surgeon plies the steel,' said T. S. Eliot), the psychiatrist is qualified to recognize distortions in the patient's behavior, caused by unresolved past situations."

Before Frankenberg's review appeared, the sale of the reprints had been substantial, and the first printing was almost exhausted. After the review, a second printing was immediately authorized by the Board of Trustees. For this new printing, Sullivan designed a dust jacket, again on yellow paper, quoting from the Frankenberg review and using the horses' heads as his own symbol for the first time. This second printing was a remarkable success. Over a period of five years it sold over 13,000 copies, and Sullivan became a major figure in the larger world, in large part through Frankenberg's review.

The Frankenbergs saw Sullivan six months later when they attended a lecture given by him in New York City on February 2, 1948. He had never gotten around to writing a letter to tell Lloyd of his keen appreciation of the review. Lloyd writes of this meeting: "Afterwards he was coming down the center aisle, acknowledging greetings. Loren and I were standing at the end of the aisle. Through his thick yellow lenses, his eyes caught sight of us. It was as if he had turned on suns in them. . . . I was rewarded before a word had been spoken."

❧ 42 ❧
After Hiroshima

The bomb that fell on Hiroshima punctuated history.
—Sullivan, "The Cultural Revolution to End War"

RETROSPECTIVELY, many of us can agree with Sullivan, after thirty years, that history was changed by Hiroshima—that the quality of life on this planet took on a more fragile character. Yet, at the time, Hiroshima brought relief to many of us who had grown weary of death and war. There was no such respite for Sullivan; nor was there for his friend and colleague G. Brock Chisholm, the Canadian psychiatrist, an infantryman in the First World War and destined to become the first head of the World Health Organization; in 1945, and particularly after Hiroshima, Sullivan and Chisholm collaborated in a remarkable fashion in their concern about the fate of mankind.

During 1945 Sullivan suffered his most serious illness, bacterial endocarditis, and for weeks he was in bed constantly. By the fall he had begun to recover somewhat, and in October Chisholm paid him a visit; his report of that night, written much later, gives a picture of Sullivan's determination:

During the war a severe heart disability threatened to reduce [Sullivan's] activities to a very low ebb. Indeed, in 1945 he had been under great medical pressure to retire from all strenuous activities. Since all his activities were strenuous and he had no facility for passivity or resignation, this was a time of great trouble and frustration for him.

One night in October 1945, Harry Stack Sullivan faced this problem and reached a decision which has affected the lives of many people and over the coming generations will affect the destinies of many millions. During that night, in his home in Bethesda, he wrestled with all his own particular angels and devils. The context, however, was never personal but astoundingly universal. He surveyed the state of the world, the stature, the level of development, the potentialities and the limitations of the human sciences, particularly psychiatry, psychology, social anthropology, and sociology. His basic question was whether one man could do anything significant, or worth doing, in relation to this total immediate situation; whether, in fact, what was left of his own life could be invested best in long-term academic work at relatively low tension; or whether, on the other hand, he himself, with his particular equipment of training, experience, and relationships, could reasonably hope that he could do anything to help toward a solution. He could hope to live perhaps many years if he would confine his activities within narrow bounds, avoiding the tensions, turmoil, and frustrations inherent in active campaigning for a great cause; or on the other hand he could throw everything he had into a perhaps quite futile effort to get done some of the things he believed needed so badly to be done. He felt that he could not compromise between these two courses; they simply would not mix. It was an "either-or" proposition.

He had become convinced that, if the place of the human race is to be maintained in the great experiment of evolution, drastic and very extensive changes in the usual patterns of human thinking and behaviour would have to be made, and quickly. Also he believed that any real hope of such necessary changes lay in the possibility that adequate leadership might come from the human sciences. During that night Harry Stack Sullivan decided that that possibility was worth betting his life on—in the most literal terms. In the knowledge that his decision would certainly cost him his life, at any moment, but with only faint hope of any useful result, he chose martyrdom—because he was that kind of person, because he could not turn his back on a real need, no matter what the cost to himself. Here was the finest example of social responsibility, unselfish devotion, and true maturity that any of us is likely ever to see. His own comment on his decision was typical Sullivan: "It appears that I'm about to make even more of a fool of myself than usual, but, by God, I'm going to try it!"

From that moment Harry Stack Sullivan paid no more attention to his heart, or to his medical advisors. No physical conditions, of bodily symptom or fatigue, of time, or of space, were allowed any importance. He took on responsibilities and activities which would have appalled a young and healthy man. He drove himself, and everyone else he could get at, as he had never done before. This was not in the least an act of faith; from the beginning he discounted what he was doing as almost certainly useless, but mountains were indeed moved and very much was done.[1]

Sullivan's collaboration with Chisholm after World War II was of a piece with his earlier appreciation of other psychiatrists who had concerned themselves with the broader field of preventive psychiatry, particularly as it pertained to war and its aftermath. After World War I, Sullivan had observed firsthand the enormous casualties of war, both in the disturbed veterans that came under his purview and in the civilian disturbances that increased after that war; and his observations had been heightened by White's experience and thinking on the same subject. Ferenczi, too, had been exposed to the casualties of war in 1894–1895, when he had been a military physician in the army at the age of twenty-two. After that experience he had turned to a formal study of nervous and mental diseases, becoming in 1900 chief neurologist for the Elizabeth Poorhouse.[2]

But Chisholm's experience was even more compelling for Sullivan than that of White and Ferenczi. Chisholm was only four years younger than Sullivan; and he was born in Oakville, Ontario, a small town not too distant in size and feeling from the villages in Chenango County. He graduated from high school in Oakville; and in 1914, at the age of eighteen, he enlisted as a private in the Canadian forces. He served as an infantryman in World War I at Vimy Ridge, the Somme, and in other memorable engagements, collecting several medals for gallantry, and emerging from service with the rank of captain. When he returned from the war, he began his college education at the University of Toronto, from which he received his M.D. in 1924 at the age of twenty-eight. After a year's postgraduate work in London hospitals, he went back to Oakville and engaged in the general practice of medicine there for two years. He then spent two years on the psychiatric staff of Yale's Institute of Human Relations (1931–1933), followed by a year at a mental hospital in England. At Yale he must have been acquainted with some of the work of Sapir and Sullivan.

Subsequently Chisholm returned to Canada, practicing "psychological medicine" in Toronto. By 1938, he was well aware of the threat of Nazism to world peace; he rejoined the Canadian army that same year, and was soon placed in command of the entire North Canadian area, setting up and supervising training camps and defense posts. In 1941 he was placed in charge of Army personnel selection. Although Chisholm and Sullivan had seen one another at psychiatric meetings before 1940, they became close colleagues and friends only after 1940 because of their common interest in the problems posed by selecting a civilian army, in maintaining civilian morale in the war crisis, in the postwar problems of psychiatric disabilities and the rehabilitation of veterans, and in the conviction that war did not have to be inevitable for each generation. Both of them had been exposed to the overwhelming general problems in the society, partly through the examination process for the draft, but also by traveling through their respective countries and by obtaining reports from industry and from various social agencies. Thus they were both aware that the general public would need new and better resources for mental health after the war.

In the February 1945 issue of *Psychiatry,* published shortly before V-E Day, there were three items entitled "The Soldier's Return." The first one was the transcript of a Canadian radio talk given by Chisholm in December 1944; the second one was part of the same series of radio talks, given by Clarence M. Hincks, director of the National Committee for Mental Hygiene for Canada; and the third was in the form of an editorial by Sullivan, an early formulation of the tasks that he would outline as critical after Hiroshima. He worried whether "conservative" sectors in America for whom the war was simply a "dislocation of their affairs" would receive support in refusing the responsibilities of the postwar period; but he saw a hope:

It must be remembered that there was no essential difference in the economic situation of the German worker and professional man in the years of the most severe depression and that of his confreres in these United States. The great difference in the two social areas lay in the ideologies and traditional roots of ideologies that formulated and had formed the social equilibrium of the two nation groups.

The *common man* mattered in the United States—not universally, perhaps not greatly; but significantly. We may have been and still continue to be the most guardedly superficial in interpersonal relations of all the peoples of the earth, but we stem from traditions which emphasize the worth and dignity of human beings, and our inadequacies are matters of deficiency in the understanding and technique of interpersonal intimacy, rather than matters of fundamental cleavage between master and man, between an hierarchy of traditional ruling caste and their vassals and slaves.

Later in the same editorial, he formulated the basic political problem of the next twenty years: "How many in our national legislature can be expected to 'represent' an indifferent and uninformed electorate in the service of universal welfare, against the political pressure of powerful and 'respectable' well-organized and well-informed minorities intent on protecting their respective self-perpetuating interests from changes needed for the common weal?" Later on he wondered specifically of the veterans: "If the veterans and others who have participated in the war are too slow in coming to grips with events, if they become confused and disgruntled early in the postwar reorientation, whence is to be expected to come the pervasive and durable influence which will realize great good for great numbers of people from the appalling wastage of this war?"[3]

Immediately after Hiroshima, the Foundation announced the second of its Memorial Lectures—to be given in Washington, D.C., and in New York City by "Major-General G. B. Chisholm, C.B.E., M.C., E.D., M.D., Deputy Minister of National Health, Canada," entitled "Some Urgent Problems of Psychiatry." For a journal that supposedly never listed the title of M.D., or any other title, after an author's name, this formidable display gives some indication of Sullivan's love of military titles and his respect for Chisholm. The two lectures, one given in Washington on October 23, 1945, with a panel discussion the following evening, and the other in New York City on October 29, were issued in monograph form afterward under the title "The Psychiatry of Enduring Peace and Social Progress."

It is almost impossible to recapture the impact then of these lectures and the panel discussion by various distinguished commentators—Henry Wallace, Abe Fortas, and others. Sullivan, still too ill to participate in the panel discussion, managed to attend the Washington lecture and the panel; later he wrote a memorable editorial (including the sentence with which this chapter begins) which appeared in the next issue of the Journal (February 1946), where the lectures and discussion were first published. Unfortunately this editorial was not included in the monograph reprint that received such wide attention. It was in this period that I began to work for the Journal, and part of my task was to distribute the monographs and answer the many hundreds of inquiries from across the United States. Chisholm's simple but dramatically presented message— that it was possible to gain and use knowledge for the humane raising of children everywhere and that peace and social progress would depend upon raising children to value and achieve those goals—hit a responsive chord in the months after the end of the war.

At the 1947 meeting of the American Psychiatric Association, Chisholm, then the executive secretary of the Interim Commission of the World Health Organization, stated that the International Congress on Mental Health to be held in London a year later, in August 1948, could well be critical in the affairs of the world. But the success of this meeting would require that for the year ahead, informed people throughout the world would meet in preparatory sessions, preferably interdisciplinary, to pool their information. In the August 1947 issue of *Psychiatry,* Sullivan began a specific plan for regional meetings of psychiatrists to pool information from their own training and experience; these meetings should be held regularly, he said, in the year preceding the Congress. While interdisciplinary meetings would be necessary before the end of the year, psychiatrists should at first meet with each other, for indeed they should have the relevant knowledge on the harm wrought by improper child training: "The great hope for the future lies . . . in so reducing the effectiveness of certain vicious elements in current faiths that the young who grow up under the influence of these elders will have much greater freedom to observe and to understand and to foresee correctly than had their parents and teachers and the others under whose authority their abilities for interpersonal relations were moulded."[4] The article in which this call was set forth was titled "Remobilization for Enduring Peace and Social Progress." Its demands exasperated some of Sullivan's colleagues who had collaborated with him and generously given of time and money during the war years; some of them even called his new plan "megalomaniacal." But he anticipated these complaints in his article; in a famous dictum, he forced his colleagues to face the choice of action or inaction: "I say to you with the utmost seriousness of which I am capable that this is no time to excuse yourself from paying the debt you and yours owe the social order with some facile verbalism like 'Nothing will come of it; it can't be done.' "[5]

* * *

In the last summer of his life (1948), Sullivan set forth with both trepidation and high hopes to participate in three international meetings in Europe. In preparation, he wanted special cards made for him at the Lord Baltimore Press: one would list him as editor of *Psychiatry: Journal for the Operational Statement of Interpersonal Relations;* the other would list him as chairman of the Council of Fellows of the Washington School of Psychiatry. He asked me to design these cards and to have Don Reeve at the Press make them up, with tissue between each card. "If that's what Harry Stack wants, that's what he'll get," Don Reeve told me, laughing and explaining that he had never put tissues between printed cards before. Sullivan was well pleased with the results.

He went first to Paris, where he had been summoned to participate in the UNESCO Tensions Project with seven other specialists from various parts of the world. They had been brought together for a two-week period to compose a common short statement on the causes of nationalistic aggression and the conditions necessary for international understanding. Afterwards each participant was to write a more extended statement of his own views; and all of these papers, together with the Common Statement, were brought together a year later in a book, *Tensions That Cause Wars,* edited by Hadley Cantril.[6] Cantril did not participate actively in the meeting, but he was present throughout and has described the procedure used for the meeting. John Rickman, a psychiatrist and editor of the *British Journal of Medical Psychology,* proposed at the beginning of the first session that the group spend three hours in a general introductory period with "each man indicating briefly the story of his life, the influences he thought had determined his point of view and his interests, together with an implicit evalution of his own qualifications for being a member of this particular group." They all felt that this procedure had saved much valuable time. Indeed it fitted the requirements of participant observation. Some of the information supplied was astounding, as reported by Cantril: "Four of them had been in jail sometime during their lives for refusing to give up points of view they thought were right; two of them had had to leave their mother country; two of them had been physically tortured during World War II." At the end of the two-week conference, two hours were spent in "discussing quite bluntly and frankly the tensions we had felt during our two weeks together: the things we had wanted to say but didn't for fear of offending someone, the irritations we had experienced from another's remark, the inadequacies of our discussion."[7]

Sullivan was very proud of the Common Statement issued by this group, and he had it published in *Psychiatry* as soon as he returned from Europe. It has some of the historical perspective of our own Declaration of Independence and some of the economic perspective of the Communist Manifesto. It remains cogent and relevant today:

Man has now reached a stage in his history where he can study scientifically the causes of tensions that make for war. The meeting of this little group is itself symptomatic, representing as it does the first time the people of many lands, through an international organization of their own creation, have asked social scientists to apply their knowledge to some of the major problems of our time. Although we differ in the emphases we would give to various parts of our statement and in our views as to its comprehensiveness and implementation, no one of us would deny the importance of any part of it.

We agree to the following twelve paragraphs:

(A) To the best of our knowledge, there is no evidence to indicate that wars are necessary and inevitable consequences of "human nature" as such. While men vary greatly in their capacities and temperaments, we believe there are vital needs common to all men which must be fulfilled in order to establish and maintain peace: men everywhere want to be free from hunger and disease, from insecurity and fear; men everywhere want fellowship and the respect of their fellow-men; the chance for personal growth and development.

(B) The problem of peace is the problem of keeping group and national tensions and aggressions within manageable proportions and of directing them to ends that are at the same time personally and socially constructive, so that man will no longer seek to exploit man. This goal cannot be achieved by surface reforms or isolated efforts. Fundamental changes in social organization and in our ways of thinking are essential.

(C) If we are to avoid the kind of aggression that leads to armed conflict, we must among other things, so plan and arrange the use of modern productive power and resources that there will be maximum social justice. Economic inequalities, insecurities, and frustrations create group and national conflicts. All this is an important source of tensions which have often wrongly led one group to see another group as a menace through the acceptance of false images and oversimplified solutions and by making people susceptible to the scapegoating appeals of demagogues.

(D) Modern wars between nations and groups of nations are fostered by many of the myths, traditions, and symbols of national pride handed down from one generation to another. A great many current social symbols are still nationalistic, hindering the free movement of thought across political boundaries of what is, in fact, an interdependent world.

(E) Parents and teachers find it difficult to recognize the extent to which their own attitudes and loyalties—often acquired when they were young and when conditions were different—are no longer adequate to serve as effective guides to action in a changing world. Education in all its forms must oppose national self-righteousness and strive to bring about a critical and self-disciplined assessment of our own and other forms of social life.

(F) The development of modern means of swift and wide range communication is potentially a great aid to world solidarity. Yet this development also increases the danger that distortions of truth will reach a great many people who are not in a position to discriminate true from false, or to perceive that they are being beguiled and misled. It must be a special responsibility of U.N. organizations to utilize these means of mass communication to encourage an adequate understanding of the people in other countries. This must always be a two-way traffic. It will aid the cause of peace if nations are enabled to see themselves as others see them.

(G) The prospect of a continuing inferior status is essentially unacceptable to any group of people. For this and other reasons, neither colonial exploitation nor oppression of minorities within a nation is in the long run compatible with world peace. As social scientists we know of no evidence that any ethnic group is inherently inferior.

(H) Many social scientists are studying these problems. But social scientists are still separated by national, ideological, and class differences. These differences have made it difficult for social scientists to resist effectively the emergence of pseudo-scientific theories which have been exploited by political leaders for their own ends.

(I) Objectivity in the social sciences is impossible to achieve whenever economic or political forces induce the investigator to accept narrow, partisan views. There is urgent need for a concentrated, adequately financed international research and educational programme.

(J) We recommend, for example, the cooperation of social scientists on broad regional and international levels, the creation of an international university and a series of world institutes of the social sciences under international auspices. We believe that international scientific fact-finding studies could contribute useful information concerning the cultures of all nations and bring to light dangerous insecurities and sources of tension, as well as legitimate aspirations of people all over the world. Equally certain to be rewarding are studies of educational methods in the home, the school, and in youth organizations and other groups by which the minds of the young are oriented toward war or toward peace. From the dissemination of the information resulting from these studies, we may anticipate the emergence of concrete proposals for the guidance of national programmes of education.

(K) The physical and biological sciences in recent years have provided impressive demonstrations of the effect of research. Some of the practical results have been rather to dismay and disquiet the civilized world than to reduce its tensions. The scientists whose research has been used in the development of atomic and biological warfare are not themselves responsible for launching a curse upon the world. The situation reflects the forces now determining the uses to which science can be put. While other factors are concerned, we hold that the chances for a constructive use of the potentialities of scientific and technological developments will improve if and when man takes the responsibility for understanding the forces which work upon him and society both from within and from without.

(L) In this task of acquiring self-knowledge and social insight, the social sciences—the sciences of Man—have a vital part to play. One hopeful sign today is the degree to which the boundaries between these sciences are breaking down in the face of the common challenge confronting them. The social scientist can help make clear to people of all nations that the freedom and welfare of one are ultimately bound up with the freedom and welfare of all, that the world need not continue to be a place where men must either kill or be killed. Effort in behalf of one's own group can become compatible with effort in behalf of humanity.

GORDON W. ALLPORT
Professor of Social Relations, Harvard University.

GILBERTO FREYRE
Professor of Sociology, University of Bahia, Brazil;
Professor at the Institute of Sociology, University of Buenos Aires, Argentina.

GEORGES GURVITCH
Professeur de Sociologie, Université de Sorbonne;
Administrateur du Centre d'Etudes Sociologues, Paris.

MAX HORKHEIMER
Director of the Institute of Social Research, New York City.

ARNE NAESS
Professor of Philosophy, University of Oslo.

JOHN RICKMAN, M.D.
Editor, *British Journal of Medical Psychology.*

HARRY STACK SULLIVAN, M.D.
Chairman, Council of Fellows, Washington School of Psychiatry;
Editor, *Psychiatry, Journal for the Operational Statement of Interpersonal Relations.*

ALEXANDER SZALAI
Professor of Sociology, University of Budapest;
President, Hungarian Institute of Foreign Affairs.

At the time that the statement first appeared, it was dismissed by many social scientists as too idealistic. The journalist Genêt, writing for the December 11, 1948, issue of the *New Yorker,* commented on the way in which it was more generally overlooked: "A remarkable UNESCO report, signed by eight distinguished international scientists, treats of the causes of the social tensions that lead to war. To date, apparently, no distinguished generals or admirals or parliamentarians anywhere have troubled to read it."[8]

By the time the book *Tensions That Cause Wars* was published, Sullivan was dead; but the other participants had had a chance to make comments on each other's papers and on the experience itself. Some of them commented on Sullivan's importance at the meeting and on the significance of his theory in particular. The only representative from a Communist country, Alexander Szalai, Professor of Sociology at the University of Budapest, had several sharp comments on Sullivan's paper, but he lamented his death: "He was a wise man, he was a good man, he was a knowing man."[9] John Rickman wrote of Sullivan's paper: "One cannot read this contribution without a feeling of sadness at the death of a colleague who was so friendly and forward looking. In particular his early acceptance of field theory—a theory incommoding to one's complacency—puts him among the pioneers. At the UNESCO discussions he quietly introduced this and other views on the problems before us with his native generosity of spirit and humor."[10] Gordon Allport commented in one footnote on Sullivan's place in the social sciences generally: "During his productive lifetime Sullivan, perhaps more than any other person, labored to bring about the fusion of psychiatry and social science."[11]

On July 24, 1948, Sullivan began his work with the International Preparatory Commission (IPC) meeting in Roffey Park in Sussex. The assignment was almost impossible: this group of twenty-five men and women had to prepare in a two-week period a statement for the International Congress on Mental Health, which would meet in London at the close of the meeting in Roffey Park; and the statement would include a recommendation to the United Nations. The statement had to represent at some level the results of the work of about 5,000 men and women of varying professions who, through the previous year, had been working in discussion groups in twenty-seven countries. Not all the statements from the various countries were on hand at the beginning of the work—a considerable handicap. Yet considerable progress was made; and the group came up with the recommendation that a permanent organization, the World Federation for Mental Health, be established—a recommendation that was subsequently followed.

Sullivan was given a great deal of credit for his part in writing this statement, with its recommendations; but some members of the IPC were critical of his participation as well as of the participation of others. Sullivan immediately began to publish in the journal *Psychiatry* anonymous comments solicited from the members of the IPC shortly after their work was completed. One of the criticisms of Sullivan centered around his removing himself from the grounds at Roffey Park and working for a day with his own favorites at a local bar. One of the members of the IPC, A. Querido, a psychiatrist from Holland, later wrote an evaluation of his feelings about several cliques that emerged: "One body, the strongest, assumed characteristics of the true gang: it isolated itself in an aura of secrecy, it even separated from the rest of the members by disappearing a whole day, and came back after a prolonged absence surrounded by tales of great deeds done."[12] Sullivan cheerfully published all such evaluations—many directed at him, as one of the important members of the writing team—in *Psychiatry,* and invited all the other members to submit suggestions and criticisms in the hope that future conferences would be more productive. Some were published before Sullivan's death; but after

his death the Editorial Board abandoned this project, somewhat regretfully.

The UNESCO seminar on childhood education towards world-mindedness was the last of the three conferences that Sullivan attended that
summer. Held in Poděbrady, Czechoslovakia, it lasted for five weeks,
while forty participants representing fifteen different nationalities tried to
communicate their thinking in this central area of work. Both Ruth Benedict and Sullivan attended this conference for at least part of the time. It
was the last summer of life for both of them; and they were working on
ideas that had come to dominate their thinking. If one could but understand by what avenues of circumstance and human influence the thinking
of Ruth Benedict and Harry Stack Sullivan had developed in this direction from their earliest days in Chenango County, then one would
have a fuller grasp on how children could be trained for world-mindedness.

Sullivan returned home from these conferences, full of ideas and plans,
but weary. On September 17 of that year Ruth Benedict died, and Sullivan wrote a memorial account of her life for the Journal, mentioning her
early schooling in the Chenango Valley. On September 24, his old friend
and beloved "chief" at Sheppard, Ross McClure Chapman, died; and
Sullivan published only a brief notice in the Journal, with a promise of a
"suitable memorial in the next issue"—but Sullivan would be dead before he could keep that promise. In December we had a Christmas party
at the Foundation office, and Sullivan came, full of good cheer but frail
and dreading the rigors of his trip to Europe to attend a meeting of the
World Federation for Mental Health. It was the last time most of us ever
saw him.

❧ 43 ❧
Paris, January 14, 1949

> In a loud and frightened world, the quiet passing of a
> quiet man who made a science of the interplay
> of human emotions could easily escape the attention
> of the multitude. But this multitude, as surely as the
> coming of death itself, must inevitably feel the influ-
> ence, if it never learns the name, of one who pointed
> through a confusing maze of human elements to a
> way of survival.
> —Charles S. Johnson, "Harry Stack Sullivan,
> Social Scientist"

IT was his last day of life, and it was his mother's birthday; she would
have been ninety-six years old. He rarely forgot a birthday of someone
who was close to him, as Clara Thompson would remember. "Anniver-
saries were important to him," Clara said. "If he forgot a friend's birthday, he was deeply disturbed."[1]

Now he was on his way home from a discouraging trip to Europe. He
had come for a meeting of the founders of a new organization, the World
Federation for Mental Health; they had assembled in Amsterdam where,
in the course of their talks, he had begun to fear again that old patterns of
prestige and competition were out in force to frustrate the goal of moving
toward a science of man. Still he would never give up. On this trip, he had
had a side errand in West Germany—an informal reconnaissance for the
United States Government; some colleagues would later report that it
was an errand performed at the instigation of the White House itself. He
had met with General Lucius Clay in Frankfurt to try to evaluate what
chances there were for communication between East and West. He was
worried, he wrote a colleague then, about how well Clay was prepared by
life to handle the persisting tensions in Berlin, now four months after the
end of the Berlin airlift.[2]

Within a few short years, the "brave heroes of Stalingrad" had undergone a metamorphosis in the American consciousness into a fearsome

28. Sullivan, about 1948

29. P. J. Mène's bronze sculpture, kept on Sullivan's desk for many years

30. *The abandoned farmhouse, destroyed by fire in 1978*

31. *The County's clinic, renamed for Sullivan, October 12, 1977*

subcategory of human monsters. So men feared in both East and West, as Sullivan had told me when I questioned him about a trip behind the Iron Curtain the summer before: "It is the same as it is here," he said. "Men fear. Over there, they call it the Pentagon; over here we call it the Kremlin." There was so little time, so much to be done.

Most of his close friends and colleagues knew of his repeated insistence on how much he had to accomplish yet. Dorothy Blitsten remembers how Sullivan would periodically express his "rage" at the idea of dying before he was 100; there was so much that he wanted to do. During his serious illness in 1945, he was wakened hourly during the night for medication, and he became interested again in the phenomenon of sleep and the problems implicit in interrupting it too often. In describing this interest to Dorothy Blitsten, he told her that he would not have enough time to study sleep, even if he lived to be "150" years old. She observed to him that he had raised his ante. "I'm older and sicker," he told her. In the fall of 1948, only a few months before his death, he mentioned again his love of life and its opportunities in a lecture given in the Washington School of Psychiatry: "In this game, the further you go, I think, the more you regret that death must be approaching somewhere, because the field of interest and of problems steadily expands, the most exciting field in the world, I am sure, on the basis of its complexity."[3]

For him, it was an indulgence to bemoan what was—what is. The gods had long ago assigned him a task. And one simply lived out the task. Humankind must live more usefully, more productively in a creative, a happy union of mankind's great potential as pushed against the boulder of ancient prejudices. His task was to help push that boulder, however feeble his shove.

From the beginning he had been forced to travel extensively in order to gather together the fragile cohorts of informed people who could help in the task he had taken on. Yet he had always needed a haven, a home where he could contemplate his observations, the tasks before him. Even on Smyrna Hill, there had always been some corner where he could escape from the yearnings of his mother and his aunt Maggie—such powerful yeast in his destiny, however frightening at times. Under a bush in the farmyard, or on the floor in the dark parlor, he could withdraw and cogitate, read, cogitate again, digest all the human incoherencies and sadnesses—his own and others'. Through the years he had depended on home, wherever it was, for such withdrawals, and when he traveled he sometimes took a talisman from home; the chiming clock that the Blitzstens had given him made the trip to Santa Fe one summer and chimed throughout the night on the transcontinental train—a mystery to the passengers in the next compartment. In the course of things, he had traveled hundreds of thousands of miles, mostly by train, and stayed in countless hotels. But it was always hard for him. He needed home.

Now he was in the Hotel Ritz in Paris, and he was on his way home.

There was still one more day of work—to meet again, as he had the day before, with some of the people in the UNESCO office. Hope still dwelt at UNESCO. He had planned to spend two days with the people at UNESCO, as he told Jimmie in his last note, written from Frankfurt, two days before his death.

Frankfurt, 12 Jan

Dearest Jimmie:
   This is the furthest I shall go in Germany. I take the sleeper tonight for Paris—it's much the easiest way or one has to fly back to Brussels and then to Paris. I have to spend two days at UNESCO on some plans about the Tensions project—they are starting some of the research I recommended last summer. Then I shall be on my way home; I trust without the 'flu' which is getting to be a great epidemic in France.
                                            Much love,
                                            Harry S.S.

At the same time, he had written a note to Dorothy Blitsten:

Frankfurt 12 Jan.
I'm getting a chance to profit to the full from the gloves which you sent me for Xmas. While it is by no means Berlin winter here, it's quite a change from the Netherlands.
   Off to Paris and UNESCO by sleeper tonight, and then, after two days, for home. I'm more convinced than ever that war is hell.
                                            Love,
                                            Harry S.S.

He ordered his breakfast, and while he waited, he began to read the newspaper. The day before it had been cold and clear with a maximum temperature of 43; today would be milder, about 50 degrees as a maximum and "mainly fine." The newspaper mentioned the advent of the full moon. The epidemic of flu in Paris was continuing; he hoped to avoid *that,* as he had written to Jimmie.

When the *valet de chambre* had brought him breakfast, he was still clad in his pajamas, sitting at the table reading the newspaper. After the waiter left, the pain must have hit him. An hour later when the waiter returned to remove the tray, the food was untouched, and Sullivan lay dead, outstretched on the floor, with pills scattered around from his case of pharmaceuticals which always went with him on a journey. He was an important "foreigner," and the death was sudden, so the body was turned over to the authorities for an autopsy; and the presence of "poisons" scattered around dictated that an analysis of the contents of his stomach should be made by a toxicologist.

The fact of Sullivan's death carried more swiftly across the Atlantic than it did in Paris. Most Paris newspapers made no mention of it for four days, although it eventually received a good deal of attention. As stipulated on Sullivan's passport, James I. Sullivan was notified by cablegram on the day of Harry's death; and Jimmie drove from Bethesda to the reception building at Chestnut Lodge in Rockville and insisted on seeing Dexter Bullard, then president of the Foundation, in person; Bullard had to come from his house on the grounds of the Lodge over to the main building. Jimmie announced the news simply: "Harry died." Late that night, Theodore Dukeshire, executive director of the School and secretary of the Foundation, called me at home: "I have bad news for you," he said. I interrupted him, "Is Dr. Sullivan dead?" It was no surprise to me. Dukeshire then asked me to get out a press release for the wire services that night. So I went to my office and prepared a release, giving no official cause of death but mentioning his history of severe heart trouble, which Dukeshire had suggested should be included. Most of the major newspapers in the United States probably derived their copy from this release, and actually published stories a day before anything appeared in the Paris newspapers. In this way, only the barest account of the death itself appeared in the United States newspapers; the stories focused on his posts and accomplishments and some few facts of his early life and training as were then known.

On January 18, *Le Monde, L'Humanité,* and *Le Figaro* all carried stories on the death, giving rather full reports on the circumstances. The Paris edition of the *New York Herald Tribune* also reported the death on the same day and noted that there had been a false rumour of suicide: "Failure of the American Embassy to release prompt information, however, apparently contributed to speculations of possible suicide which were played up yesterday in a Paris afternoon newspaper." Nevertheless, "as a double check, [a further] examination was being made by toxicologists." The scattered pills had raised questions. Thus the newspapers in Paris had delayed publication of the story until Dr. Charles Paul, the police surgeon, had determined that Sullivan's death was undoubtedly natural, caused by meningeal hemorrhage with lesions of the liver and kidney, as reported by *L'Humanité.* Because of the presence of "numerous toxic medicines, the organs were sent to the Institute of Toxicology." It would be another week before these final reports were in and the official cause of death, as provided in the U.S. Department of State official document, would be defined, on January 25, as "meningeal hemorrhage as certified by Dr. Paul, medical expert, 52 bis rue de Varenne, Paris, who performed the autopsy." On that same day, the body was released by the toxicologist for cremation and shipment to the United States, eleven days after Sullivan had died. There was a further delay of seventeen days between release of the body and the date of the funeral (February 11), which remains unexplained. Since the ashes were flown to the United States, the delay was perhaps necessitated by the process of obtaining dispensation for a Catholic funeral. Both the reality of the cremation and the possibility of suicide had to be considered before a decision could be made by the Catholic authorities; Jimmie had specified by then that Sullivan had wanted a Catholic funeral.

Suicide had flashed through people's minds on both sides of the Atlantic. Early in the following week, there was a local radio broadcast in Washington, D.C., that mentioned the possibility of suicide—a speculation picked up perhaps by someone on the scene in Paris or from some other source. One of the Washington newspapers called my office to check on this information, and I was righteously indignant, since I was well acquainted with Sullivan's heart condition. I dismissed this event from my mind, and no one mentioned it to me again until more than a decade later when I discovered that Chenango County neighbors and some relatives assumed that he had committed suicide. Then I systematically read the accounts in the Paris newspapers as they were reported at the time. Some of the reports were fairly explicit; *Le Monde* mentioned that there had been no visitors to his room after his breakfast was served, even implying that there had been some question of homicide.

The idea of suicide was almost routinely considered in Chenango County, for people there were all too familiar with the possibility. Moreover, there were probably people in the County who recognized that he had died on Ella's birthday, and this, too, was a not unfamiliar pattern. The first time that I, myself, gave any credence to the idea of suicide was the day, fifteen years later, when I searched out Ella Stack's death certificate, hunting for it in the Town Clerk's book of records; the birth date was one of the items. As I copied down the information, I had a sharp realization that the date was familiar, and I began for the first time to seriously wonder—was it possible?

Once I began to examine the possibility, I found that the same possibility had emerged immediately after his death in the minds of some of his friends and colleagues. His trainees, in particular, had dreaded the impact that suicide would have on their own training and, somewhat secondarily, on their patients' progress. Lloyd Frankenberg, who had lived in France for many years, reminded me that in Catholic France there was always some reluctance about assigning the cause of death as suicide—it makes so much sadness for the family and creates a difficulty in the religious service and place of burial. In the United States another kind of fear temporarily paralyzed some of his colleagues: suicide in the psychiatric profession is always difficult to explain, in spite of the fact that medical doctors in general have the highest rate of suicide of any profession.

Several ideas and questions have absorbed my attention over the years since I entertained the possibility of his suicide. To begin with, I cannot discount the possibility that his will to live had weakened for a moment: he was far from home and he was at least temporarily discouraged by the task he had set for himself; and I had seen him twice suffering the pain of an angina attack. Did he remember that it was his mother's birthday? And was he particularly missing Edward Sapir's wise counsel as the tenth anniversary of that loss approached? Did he remember that in 1931, he had predicted that he would die owing to "rupture of the middle meningeal artery at the age of 57 years, three months and five days, plus or minus less than 100 hours," and that this span of days was fast approaching? Did he think of Leo Stack's death on a January day in a hotel in Sherburne, after the same kind of sudden assault? For a brief moment, he may have turned aside from his will to live; and in his frail condition, the very act of turning aside may have been enough to decide the outcome— even in not using his medication promptly.

His work was so widespread and so extensive that only gradually would colleagues begin to count all the ways in which his death had left them an unbelievable load of tasks. Some of the tasks were so urgent that they had to be assigned to someone immediately. First, of course, there were the patients who were affected. Frieda Fromm-Reichmann estimated that he was an ongoing consultant on 150 cases at the time; that is, trainees or colleagues would discuss a series of ongoing cases with him from time to time, and in this way he was carrying some therapeutic responsibility for this many patients. Moreover, he was teaching a large lecture class at the School and several seminars. He was also consulting on various research projects undertaken in the Washington School of Psychiatry, notably one on stress responses in naval officers.

And then there was the Journal, which loomed large for me particularly. When he had gone to Europe the summer before, he had made provision for certain tasks in case he would not return. He had arranged with me that a member of the editorial board of the Journal, Sarah S. Tower, would take over final decision on rejection or acceptance of manuscripts; and he had indicated to me that she was his choice for his successor on the Journal. He had also discussed his doubts about a man in the psychiatric community who might conceivably want to be editor of the Journal; and in a gentle way, he had indicated that this man had a useful contribution to make to the School and should be encouraged to focus his energies there. His discussion had a strong impact on me, particularly when, within a few months, this colleague acted out Sullivan's prophecy and did make a somewhat strange and abortive attempt to take over the Journal. Sullivan had also planned on which of the colleagues in the School should fall heir to his notebooks that contained carefully worked out outlines for two of the courses that he regularly taught in the School. All these plans presented problems in implementation, and in the end most of the plans were aborted.

But the impact of his death went beyond these formal connections.

"Sullivan died with his boots on," as Albert Deutsch, the newspaper columnist wrote, mentioning the meeting in Amsterdam a few days before, his work at UNESCO, all his varied interests and concerns. There was a sense of a vacuum that permeated the psychiatric and social-science community and even the larger world.

No better illustration of Sullivan's theory could be found than in the different repercussions his death had on Jimmie, on his colleagues, on the Sullivan and the Stack relatives, and on social scientists here and abroad. The Norwich *Sun* published its story on his death on Monday; the AP story originated in Paris, with information obtained from the American Embassy there, and it reported that he died of "natural causes" and that he had been in Germany—a fact that never appeared elsewhere immediately after his death. But the old-timers in the County did not accept "natural causes" as correct. The survivors in the area of Norwich are listed in the *Sun;* they are all Sullivans, although there were also Stack cousins living in the general area. In the metropolitan newspapers on the East Coast, the only survivor is listed as James, described as either an adopted son or a foster son. The notice of the funeral and memorial services to be held in Washington four weeks after his death lists only his Washington Stack cousins—"Brig. Gen. Frederick E. Stack, USMC (retired), Col. Vincent Stack, USMC, and Mrs. Clara Stack Mess."

There was a difference in the reactions of the two sets of Stack cousins. The ones in Washington, all descendants of Harry's grandfather Michael Stack, who had raised his children as "heritage" Catholics, were mainly concerned about Clara Thompson's statement at the memorial service that Sullivan's family was "poor." They had the pride of the Stacks, and they felt that the word indicated a social disadvantage that did not adequately describe the distinction of the Stacks. The grandchildren of James Stack, Michael's cousin, who had maintained a strong religious identification with the Church, were worried about the nature of the religious rites peformed at the burial services. Fifteen years after his death, two of these cousins questioned me rigorously about the funeral and burial. In an interview situation arranged for me for the purpose of discussing what they knew about young Sullivan, they began by interrogating me sharply for several minutes on the nature of the funeral. Was I sure that it was a Catholic funeral? Yes, I told them, I had been there myself. But since I was not a Catholic would I have known? There had been something a little wrong, they thought, and it was doubtful that he could have been buried a Catholic. Besides, he was not a churchgoing Catholic, they pointed out. Indeed, as a child, he had lived so far away from Sherburne that he did not receive proper instruction before he was confirmed, and they blamed Ella for that. The Sullivans were always late for church *when* they came—which was not often enough; Ella would always have to leave the kitchen neat and tidy before she went off to church, and according to Timothy this was what delayed them. Behind all this were two unspoken questions: Had he committed suicide? And was it true that his body had been cremated in Paris before it was returned to the United States? At the time I talked to them, I did not myself realize the import of the questions about the funeral.

In Washington, D.C., the executor of Sullivan's estate, the lawyer Muriel Paul, had had other problems. Upon completion of the report from the toxicologist, she had issued orders to the U.S. Embassy in Paris that the remains should be cremated and shipped back to the United States. She had not realized at that time that Sullivan's request for a Catholic burial would require that the body be left as intact as possible. Hence she found herself in the embarrassing position of having to convince the Catholic authorities in Washington that her order had been given in error; the authorities finally agreed that the Catholic service could proceed, but the burial urn shipped from Paris would have to be placed in a coffin by the local undertaker, in Bethesda. The psychiatric colleagues were upset at the idea of a Catholic service; they argued that Sullivan was not a practicing Catholic, that indeed he had expressed misgivings as to the effect of much of Catholic teachings, that he had not been able to teach at the Catholic Georgetown University because of his intellectual stands—particularly his identification with the agnostic Freud and the whole psychoanalytic philosophy, which was so pagan. Colleagues in the Foundation began to plan for a memorial service to be held the evening of the funeral—a completely nonreligious ceremony in which his colleagues would attempt to place him back in their own urbane tradition. Jimmie, who continued to insist that a Catholic service was necessary in order to follow Harry's explicit instructions to him, found himself caught in the interrogation of esteemed colleagues who over and over asked the same question: Did Harry really want a Catholic burial? And if so, why? Finally Jimmie decided to make a brief published statement about Sullivan's attitude toward religion:

A WORD TO DR. SULLIVAN'S FRIENDS AND COLLEAGUES
To all who may be surprised at the church services for the late Dr. Harry Stack Sullivan, let them be reassured that he was not an overly religious man, and that his views—whether they have appeared in print or were just uttered to some people—still remain the same.

As Dr. Sullivan often said: "Of all the church services, I prefer the Catholic because that service is the most unemotional, most impersonal, and beautiful"; he appreciated the austerity of the rites.

The late Dr. Emanuel Libman—a very good friend of Dr. Sullivan's—and Dr. Sullivan at Dr. Libman's urging used to attend mass at Christmas when Dr. Sullivan lived in New York City. Of course, all of you know that Dr. Libman was Jewish but he too appreciated the austerity and quiet emotion.

Like psychiatry, religion has its use in the world and, again, like psychiatry it sometimes does more harm than good.

J I S

27 January 1949

But the Foundation decided not to publish Jimmie's statement.

The Foundation wanted to send flowers for the burial services ($60 worth), and they asked Jimmie to designate the kind of flowers that were appropriate. He specified orange day lilies. It was February, and as Jimmie would note, it was difficult to find these flowers. But Adolph Gude, the local florist in Bethesda, who greatly admired Sullivan, managed to find a large number of perfectly matched orange day lilies "costing much more [than $60], out of respect for H.S.S.," as Jimmie reported. "I chose the orange day lilies because they were H.S.S.'s favorites, and lemon yellow ones next. I should have chosen the yellow instead of orange, the *faux pas* being that orange is the Protestant color and yellow is the Catholic color."

There were, of course, humorous grace notes that invaded the whole ceremony. Jimmie commented that Sullivan could never get anyplace on time for an appointment—that he, Jimmie, always had to lay out all his clothes for the Doctor, if he were to make an important appointment or an airplane. One time in exasperation, he told Sullivan, " 'The time you take, I wouldn't be surprised if you were late to your own funeral.' He said, 'I guess so.' And, damn it, he was." He was of course buried four weeks after his death. Students, who knew that Sullivan had been cremated and that the coffin contained an urn, speculated that the undertaker would return in the night and remove the coffin in order to save money for the Foundation. Most students felt that Sullivan had been treated as a stepchild by the Foundation, that it had no real recognition that he *was* the Foundation. Patrick Mullahy observed with true Irish wit that Sullivan would turn over in his urn if he knew all the various intricacies of the situation. On the morning of the day of the burial and memorial, Alfred Stanton came back to the Foundation office after the funeral, and we all tried to find the origin of an Irish fairy tale, often told by Sullivan, that Stanton wanted to use at the memorial service. A press release was to be issued on the memorial service, and we needed in advance the text of what would be said. We followed up numerous suggestions and called various reference rooms in libraries, but we could not identify the story. After so many years, I am still not able to identify it, but I have learned since that Sullivan's renditions of all stories, including that of "The Mysterious Stranger," bear only slight resemblance to the original; it is in essence always Sullivan's own story.

The Foundation took great care in arranging for the memorial service. It was held in Sternberg Auditorium at Walter Reed Hospital, where

Sullivan had given his last lectures on "Conceptions of Modern Psychiatry."[4] The auditorium had excellent acoustics, and he had wanted to give his lectures there for that reason. Five members of the National Symphony Orchestra played some of Sullivan's favorite selections—two movements of Mozart's Clarinet Quintet, two movements from Mozart's Serenade in G, and the Adagio from Brahms's Clarinet Quintet. After the music was over, three of his colleagues commented briefly on Sullivan, gathering together some of the diverse strands of his life and work: Clara Thompson spoke first of his early life, as she then knew it, and of the man who had emerged "a hard-headed scientist" with "much poetry in his nature." A younger colleague and student, Alfred H. Stanton, spoke of Sullivan's ability to teach "his students the nature of psychotherapy by living it with them in innumerable ways and in many situations." At the time, Stanton was principal investigator for a research project envisioned by Sullivan almost twenty years earlier to carry forward his work at Sheppard. And finally, the sociologist Charles S. Johnson spoke of Sullivan's work for world peace: "It is tragically fitting that he should have reached the end of his life and work in Europe where the last bright fires of his zeal and skill have been devoted to the analysis of those tensions between nations and groups that lead men to war and to futile killings, that are leading the nations of the world into a new and perhaps last remaining great effort at mutual self-destruction." It had been a long road for both of them, from Johnson's first call for Sullivan's help in dealing with racial tensions in the South, to their knowledge that all peoples were threatened by dangerous tensions, that the task reached out to all corners of the world.

Afterwards there were groups of people that gathered in different areas of the city to discuss the events of that day. Junior students stayed together; young psychiatric colleagues stayed together; and the officers of the Foundation and senior colleagues got together. The junior students felt that it was the best memorial service they had ever attended. They speculated on the music and tried to identify it. Someone suggested that one of the pieces was "The Girl with the Flaxen Hair"; and I, who was a member of this group, have nostalgically listened to this bit of music over the years, so that the music itself became an important part of my symbolization of Sullivan before I thought to check back on the facts.

There was another more serious concern, which has been discussed for years in my presence, mainly by social scientists. Why would Sullivan have specified a military burial, with taps, with a caisson that carried the coffin from the chapel at Fort Meyer to the graveside? He was a man of peace; he was on a mission of peace on his last trip. Yet his military burial is of a piece with all the incoherencies in our society. He chose to be buried in Arlington, I suppose, because he was entitled to it, and neither he nor the Foundation had much money, as usual. He had served in two wars, and there was some pride of that in his gesture, so that in nostalgic moments I think of him as a kind of "Danny Boy"—he had done his duty for his country, he had remained faithful to the faith of his fathers, and he had come back to the symbols of his youthful beliefs. He had opened the way for vast changes in the human condition, but he had not abandoned the vessels of the past that had determined so much of his life, just as it does for all of us.

Many years later I revisited his grave site to look at the marker. It is small, in accordance with the tradition of Arlington Cemetery, and there is an encircled cross cut into the top of it, to indicate that the plot has been consecrated by the Church. The inscription is simple:

Harry Stack
Sullivan
New York
Capt. Med.-Res.
World War I
Feb. 21, 1892
Jan. 14, 1949

He had written his own epitaph in the summer of 1947 in a call to his psychiatric colleagues to remobilize for "enduring peace and social progress":[5]

Begin;
and let it be said of you,
if there is any more history,
that you labored nobly
in the measure of man
in the XX century
of the scientific Western world.

Notes
Acknowledgments
Index

Notes

Abbreviations for Sullivan's published writings

Books written before Sullivan's death

CMP   *Conceptions of Modern Psychiatry: The First William Alanson White Memorial Lectures,* with a foreword by the author and a critical appraisal of the theory by Patrick Mullahy (New York: W. W. Norton & Company, 1953). [First given as five public lectures in October and November 1939, and first published in *Psychiatry* (1940) 3:1–117. Reprinted in book form by the William Alanson White Psychiatric Foundation in 1947.]

PP   *Personal Psychopathology,* with introduction by Helen Swick Perry (New York: W. W. Norton & Company, 1972). [Completed by Sullivan in 1932–33. First published by the Foundation in 1965.]

Books published after Sullivan's death

ITP   *The Interpersonal Theory of Psychiatry,* edited by Helen Swick Perry and Mary Ladd Gawel, with an introduction by Mabel Blake Cohen (New York: W. W. Norton & Company, 1953). [Taken mainly from a series of lectures given in the Washington School of Psychiatry in 1946–47, and titled "Conceptions of Modern Psychiatry."]

PI   *The Psychiatric Interview,* edited by Helen Swick Perry and Mary Ladd Gawel, with an introduction by Otto Allen Will (New York: W. W. Norton & Company, 1954). [Taken from two lecture series given in the Washington School of Psychiatry in 1944–45 and 1945–46, and titled "The Psychiatric Interview."]

CSP   *Clinical Studies in Psychiatry,* edited by Helen Swick Perry, Mary Ladd Gawel, and Martha Gibbon, with a foreword by Dexter M. Bullard (New York: W. W. Norton & Company, 1956). [Taken from lectures given between April and November 1943 at Chestnut Lodge, Rockville, Maryland.]

Books of selected papers, covering Sullivan's professional career

SHP   *Schizophrenia as a Human Process,* with introduction and commentaries by Helen Swick Perry (New York: W. W. Norton & Company,

428   NOTES TO PAGES 5–14

1962). [A selection of papers written and published between 1924 and 1935, with additional papers on schizophrenia published between 1943 and 1947.]

FPSS   *The Fusion of Psychiatry and Social Science,* with introduction and commentaries by Helen Swick Perry (New York: W. W. Norton & Company, 1964). [A selection of papers written mainly between 1937 and 1948.]

Abbreviations for Sullivan's unpublished lectures

UL   Unpublished lecture

WSP   The Washington School of Psychiatry

NY   The New York City branch of the WSP (incorporated in October 1946 as the William Alanson White Institute of Psychiatry)

Con. Lecture series given in designated years at WSP and NY and titled "Conceptions of Modern Psychiatry"

Adv. Lecture series for advanced students given in designated years at WSP and NY and titled as the theory of interpersonal relations in therapy and research

CL   Untitled series of 246 clinical lecture-discussions given at Chestnut Lodge between October 1942 and April 1946

Prologue

1. From untitled, unnumbered, unsigned first page of volume 2 (1939) of *Psychiatry.* Sullivan, as one of the three coeditors in the first eight years of this journal, wrote most of the unsigned editorial material; and this particular piece is his, as verified by correspondence.

2. Sullivan, "Discussion of the Case of Warren Wall" (1940) in *FPSS,* p. 107.

3. Sullivan, "The Cultural Revolution to End War," *Psychiatry* (1946) 9:81–87; p. 85.

4. G. B. Chisholm, "The Psychiatry of Enduring Peace and Social Progress," The William Alanson White Memorial Lectures, Second Series, 1945. (See *Psychiatry* [1946] 9:19–20.)

1. The First Moon

Epigraph: *CMP,* p. 14. Single quotes, as in the word 'marked,' appear throughout Sullivan's papers to

indicate a philosophical or linguistic meaning.

1. Cecil Woodham-Smith, *The Great Hunger: Ireland 1845–1849* (New York: Harper & Row, 1962).

2. *Current Biography* (1942), entry for Sullivan, Harry Stack; p. 812. Wording was supplied by authors during this period, as I verified with the publisher.

3. *ITP,* p. 379; see also pp. 242–243.

2. Ella Stack's Family

Epigraph: "Towards a Psychiatry of Peoples," *Psychiatry* (1948) 11:105–116; p. 109n.

1. *Current Biography* (1942), entry for Sullivan; see p. 813.

2. *ITP,* p. 339.

3. From Neil Stack, "History of: Family of Stack," mimeographed, completed in 1964. His record of the Stacks coming to Ireland from England in the fourteenth century agrees with Edward MacLysaght's

book, *Irish Families: Their Names, Arms and Origins* (New York: Crown Publishers, 1972); see p. 301.

4. See Woodham-Smith, *Great Hunger,* pp. 38, 195. Most information on the famine used in the book is derived from this study.

5. Joel Hatch, Jr., *Reminiscences, Anecdotes and Statistics of the Early Settlers and the 'Olden Time' in the Town of Sherburne, Chenango County, N.Y.* (Utica, N.Y.: Curtiss & White, 1862); see pp. 98–99.

6. Interview with Louise S. Shinners, Norwich City historian, October 4, 1964.

3. Timothy Sullivan's Family

Epigraph: *Current Biography* (1942), entry for Sullivan; pp. 812–813.

1. Usually referred to as "soupie," but given as "souper" in the Oxford English Dictionary.

2. *The Chenango Telegraph,* May 20, 1891.

3. Woodham-Smith, *Great Hunger,* pp. 188 ff.

4. Ibid., p. 205.

5. *The Chenango Telegraph,* June 11, 1874. This story, headlined "Frightful Railroad Accident: Two Men Instantly Killed," appeared on page 3.

6. See, for instance, Thackeray's *Irish Sketch Book of 1842* (Boston: Estes and Lauriat, Handy Volume Edition, n.d., p. 43.

7. See *Book of Biographies: Biographical Sketches of Leading Citizens of Chenango County, N.Y.* (Buffalo, N.Y.: Biographical Publishing, 1898), pp. 506–507.

8. *CMP,* p. 16.

9. Taped interview, Margaret [Normile] Hannon, January 4, 1972. She is a second cousin of Harry's on the Galvin side of Timothy Sullivan's family.

10. In a Utica newspaper, name undetermined, December 26, 1908.

4. Rexford Street

Epigraph: *PI,* p. 73.

1. On the baptismal record, the parents are listed, apparently in error, as Timothy Sullivan and Margarita Stack, with the sponsors as Michael McMahon and Ellina [Ella] Stack. Margaret Stack was probably the godmother, and the names of the mother and godmother were reversed.

2. Louise S. Shinners, "Norwich Golden Anniversary, 1914–1964" (official history, published by the City of Norwich, n.d.), p. 20.

3. *Current Biography* (1942), entry for Sullivan; see p. 813.

4. Personal communication, R. F. Smith, September 30, 1964.

5. Interview with Louise S. Shinners, October 4, 1964.

6. Interview with Ann and Dexter Bullard, February 1971.

7. Interview with Dorothy Blitsten, March 17, 1971.

8. See *Book of Biographies,* pp. 463–465.

9. The Catholic Church in America took a stand on the chief American secret societies, including even the I.O.O.F., in 1894, forbidding membership for Catholics who wished to remain in good standing. See Fergus MacDonald, *The Catholic Church and the Secret Societies in the United States* (U.S. Catholic Historical Society, 1946), p. 211.

10. Norwich *Sun,* August 30, 1895.

5. The Disappearance of Harry's Mother

Epigraph: *ITP,* p. 335.

1. *ITP,* p. 33.

2. Conrad M. Arensberg and Solon T. Kimball, *Family and Community in Ireland* (Cambridge, Mass.: Harvard University Press, 1968), p. 110.

3. Registered as Land Contract in "Chenango Deeds," Liber 195, p. 326.

4. Clara Thompson, "Harry Stack Sullivan, the Man," in *SHP*, p. xxxii. This was an address given at memorial services for Sullivan, February 11, 1949.

6. The Imprint of Chenango

Epigraph: Carl Carmer, *Listen for a Lonesome Drum: A York State Chronicle* (New York: David McKay, 1936), p. 263.

1. Carmer, *Lonesome Drum*, p. 263.
2. Whitney R. Cross, *The Burned-over District: The Social and Intellectual History of Enthusiastic Religion in Western New York, 1800–1850* (New York: Harper & Row, 1965), p. 62.
3. Most of the information on Smyrna is taken from James H. Smith's *History of Chenango and Madison Counties, New York 1787–1890* (Syracuse, N.Y.: D. Mason & Co., 1880), pp. 468–473.
4. From the *Oxford Gazette*, November 1823, cited in Smith, *History*, p. 92.
5. Cross, *Burned-over District*, p. 62.
6. Smith, *History*, p. 94.
7. All quotations in this paragraph are from an unidentified newspaper clipping published in 1946 entitled "Ballad of the Midland," from a feature column "Chips and Shavings" by George W. Walter, a local historian.
8. Norwich *Sun*, May 26, 1896; report given by the superintendent of schools in Chenango County, at a teachers' institute held in Norwich at the end of the school year.

7. The Growth of Nativism

Epigraph: *FPSS*, p. 79.
1. From a map on population distribution for the western part of New York State in 1845, in Cross, *Burned-over District*, p. 68.
2. Hatch, *Reminiscences of the Early Settlers in Sherburne*, pp. 898–899.
3. "Report of Factory Inspection for

1893," published in the Norwich *Sun*, August 22, 1894.
4. Shinners, "Norwich Golden Anniversary," p. 13.

8. Two Chenango Childhoods

Epigraph: *ITP*, p. 230.
1. Interview with Ernest G. Schachtel, April 16, 1970.
2. *PI*, p. 73.
3. *CSP*, p. 134.
4. *ITP*, p. 206.
5. *SHP*, p. xxxii.
6. *ITP*, p. 222.
7. UL 19, CL.
8. Ibid.
9. Letter of Nina Brown Stack to the author, August 15, 1962.
10. *ITP*, p. 226.
11. From Ruth Benedict, "The Story of My Life ...," in Margaret Mead, *An Anthropologist at Work: Writings of Ruth Benedict* (Boston: Houghton Mifflin, 1959), p. 100. Some of the dates used in this section on Ruth Benedict do not agree with dates used by Mead and Benedict. I have relied on personal items in the Norwich *Sun* for the dates of comings and goings of Benedict's family.
12. *Current Biography* (1941), entry for Benedict, Ruth; pp. 65–66.
13. Most of my information on the Fulton grandparents and family has been obtained from the obituary for Harriet Fisher Fulton in the *Sun*, dated June 8, 1897.
14. From Benedict's "The Story of My Life," pp. 98–99.
15. Ibid., p. 99.
16. Mead, *Anthropologist at Work*, p. 83.
17. *CSP*, pp. 107–108.
18. Ibid., pp. 109–110.
19. *SHP*, p. 330n.
20. From Benedict's "The Story of My Life," pp. 102–103.
21. Sullivan, "Ruth Fulton Benedict, Ph.D., D.Sc., 1887–1948," *Psychi-*

atry (1948) 11:402–403. This issue of the journal was published late and did not appear until after Sullivan's death in January 1949.

9. Going to School in Smyrna

Epigraph: *ITP,* p. 226.
1. *ITP,* p. 227.
2. UL 11, Con., WSP, 1945.
3. *PI,* pp. 156–157.
4. *CMP,* p. 111.
5. Paper read at the Chenango County Teacher's Association on December 4, 1909, by Stanford J. Gibson, superintendent of the Norwich schools, and printed in the Norwich *Sun,* October 17, 1910. Most of the information on Butts comes from this source.
6. *Current Biography* (1942), entry for Sullivan, p. 813.
7. Interview with Mary [Wedge] Lasher, October 1, 1964.
8. *ITP,* p. 239.
9. *CSP,* p. 138n.
10. *ITP,* p. 238.

10. The Quiet Miracle

Epigraph: *CMP,* p. 41.
1. Interview with Edith Bradley, July 1962.
2. *ITP,* p. 33.
3. *CMP,* p. 56.

11. Only Child

Epigraph: *PP,* p. 114.
1. *Current Biography* (1942), entry for Sullivan; p. 813.
2. *PP,* p. 324.
3. Ibid., p. 114n.
4. Sullivan, "Towards a Psychiatry of Peoples," *Psychiatry* (1948) 11:109n.
5. Taped interview with Margaret [Normile] Hannon, January 4, 1972.
6. Letter from Agnes Bissell Sullivan to her daughter, Harriet, November 22, 1942.
7. Taped record, Dorothy Stack, April 1972. This tape recording comprises a lengthy family history made expressly for this book.
8. Interview with Mrs. John Widger, October 7, 1964. Mrs. Widger was nine years older than Harry and remembered him in school as "the cutest little boy with curly blond hair."

12. Going to Church

Epigraph: *SHP,* p. 341.
1. *CMP,* p. 224.
2. *PP,* p. 130.
3. Sister Mary Donatus, "Beasts and Birds in the Lives of the Early Irish Saints" (Ph.D. dissertation, University of Pennsylvania, 1934); see especially p. 218.
4. *Butler's Lives of the Saints* was probably the source of his information on the saints; for two centuries, it has been the standard authority on saints familiar to English-speaking Catholics. See *Butler's Lives of the Saints,* edited, revised, and supplemented by Herbert Thurston and Donald Attwater (New York: P. J. Kenedy and Sons, 1956).
5. See "A Suggested Outline for Obtaining Data" in *PI,* pp. 147–178.
6. See, for instance, *SHP,* pp. 35–66 passim.
7. *CMP,* pp. 42–43.
8. Leland E. Hinsie and Robert J. Campbell, eds., *Psychiatric Dictionary,* 3rd ed. (New York: Oxford University Press, 1970).
9. *CMP,* p. 55.
10. *ITP,* p. 246.
11. *The Confessions of Saint Augustine,* trans. Rex Warner (New York: New American Library of World Literature, 1963), pp. 40–42 passim.
12. See, for instance, Rosemary Radford Ruether, "The Cult of True Womanhood," *Commonweal,* November 9, 1973, pp. 127–128.
13. *Confessions,* p. 41.
14. James Joyce, *Dubliners* (New York: Viking Press, 1961), p. 112.

13. None Too Happy a Circumstance

Epigraph: UL 14, Con., WSP, 1945.
1. *ITP*, pp. 249–250.
2. UL 15, Con., WSP, 1945.
3. *PP*, p. 180.
4. Ibid., pp. 170–171. I have retained Sullivan's original use of quotation marks in this passage, a use not retained in the 1972 edition.
5. *ITP*, pp. 256–257.
6. *CMP*, pp. 59–60.
7. Ibid., p. 61. In this 1939 lecture, Sullivan indicates that he has abandoned the phrase "primary genital phobia." But in his last complete lecture series, given in 1946–1947, he still uses the same concept. See, for instance, *ITP*, p. 267.
8. See U.S. Bureau of the Census Special Report, "Insane and Feeble-Minded in Hospitals and Institutions, 1904" (Washington, D.C.: Government Printing Office, 1906). In 1900 only 15.6 percent of all foreign-born in the nation were Irish-born, but 29 percent of the foreign-born in mental hospitals at the end of 1903 were Irish-born. In summary, the report states: "Relative to their numbers the Irish furnish a much larger proportion of the white foreign born insane in hospitals than any other nationality" (p. 24).
9. The Odd Fellows had an organization in South Otselic, and a picture of Ed Stack shows him in an I.O.O.F. uniform, rather than that of the Masons.
10. Taped record, Dorothy Stack, April 1972.
11. Norwich *Sun,* November 6, 1896.
12. *PI*, p. 192.

14. Aunt Margaret

Epigraph: *CSP*, p. 229.
1. *PI*, p. 75.
2. UL 20, CL.
3. Clara Thompson, in *SHP*, p. xxxii.

4. Taped interview, Margaret Hannon, January 4, 1972.
5. *FPSS*, p. 221.
6. Letter from Dorothy Stack to the author, April 2, 1972.
7. Taped record, Dorothy Stack, April 1972.

15. Graduating from High School

Epigraph: *PP*, pp. 163–164.
1. UL 11, CL.
2. *Current Biography* (1942), entry for Sullivan; p. 813.
3. UL 27, CL.
4. *PP*, p. 201.
5. Frederick Burdette Sprague, "Some History of Smyrna," unpublished manuscript, excerpted here by permission of the author.

16. Prologue for a Psychiatric Career: Suicide and Murder in the Norwich *Sun*

Epigraph: *CMP*, pp. 48n–49n.
1. All statistics on suicide are taken from U.S. Bureau of the Census, *Mortality Statistics, 1909; With Revised Rates for the Intercensal Years 1901 to 1909 Based Upon the Census of 1910* [Tenth annual report] (Washington, D.C.: Government Printing Office, 1912).
2. If one arbitrarily chooses the rate of 30 suicides per 100,000 population as representing an unusually high rate (twice the national average for most of the ten-year period), then one finds that 15 of New York's 57 rural counties exceeded that rate for at least one year during that period. And 14 of these 15 rural counties are among the 28 included in Whitney Cross's map of the burned-over district.
3. Statistics on newspapers are taken from *American Newspaper Annual* (N. W. Ayer & Sons, 1905).
4. William A. White, *William Alanson White: The Autobiography of a*

Purpose (Garden City, New York: Doubleday, Doran, 1938), p. 58.

5. Ibid., pp. 270–271.

6. William A. White, "The Geographical Distribution of Insanity in the United States," *Journal of Mental and Nervous Disease* (1903) 30:257–279. See also *National Geograhic Magazine*, October 1903, pp. 361–378.

7. For an excellent description of the state of sexual morality, in New England specifically, in the same period, see Nathan G. Hale, Jr., *Freud and the Americans: The Beginnings of Psychoanalysis in the United States, 1876–1917* (New York: Oxford University Press, 1971); especially pp. 24–46.

8. Jay Robert Nash, *Bloodletters and Badmen: A Narrative Encyclopedia of American Criminals from the Pilgrims to the Present* (New York: M. Evans, 1973), p. 542.

9. White, *Autobiography*, pp. 182–184 passim.

10. Ibid., pp. 185–186.

11. See, for instance, numerous stories in the *Sun*, and Nash, *Bloodletters and Badmen*, pp. 542–545.

12. The information on Oberlin College comes from Ellen Moers, *Two Dreisers* (New York: Viking Press, 1969), p. 200. Moers's book contains a full account of the original tragedy and Dreiser's changes.

17. Cornell Crisis

Epigraph: *ITP*, p. 273.

1. Information on Sullivan's career at Cornell is based on his record in the Registrar's office, as orally reported to me in 1962. Since then, it has been impossible to obtain further and more specific information.

2. Taped interview, Margaret Hannon, January 4, 1972.

3. *PP*, p. 89.

4. Ibid., p. 174.

5. *CMP*, p. 62.

6. Ibid., pp. 100–101.

7. Personal communication, 1962, C. H. Swick, who was a student at Cornell in the same general period, graduating in 1907.

8. *CMP*, p. 101.

9. Ibid., p. 68.

10. UL 7 and 8, Con., WSP, 1943–1944.

11. UL 5, Adv., WSP, 1943–1944.

12. UL 7, Con., WSP, 1943–1944.

13. *PP*, p. 177.

14. Ibid., p. 177.

15. *ITP*, pp. 260–262.

16. For a variety of reasons, I have assumed that Sullivan lived in a dormitory during his stay at Cornell. Indeed his age may have dictated this housing, as one official in the Registrar's office told me.

18. The Trouble

Epigraph: Interview with Edith Bradley, July 1962. She was a teacher in the lower form of the Smyrna School, when Sullivan was in high school.

1. *Personal Psychopathology* was finished by 1933, but it was not published in book form until 1972, in the W. W. Norton & Company series of posthumous works.

2. *PP*, pp. 177–178. I have retained Sullivan's original use of quotation marks in this passage and in the next. For an explanation of Sullivan's use of "isophilic," see *ITP*, p. 292.

3. *PP*, p. 180.

4. See Edward Sapir's description of the meaning of Sullivan's theory in "The Contribution of Psychiatry to an Understanding of Behavior in Society," *American Journal of Sociology* (1936–37) 42:862–870.

19. The Disappearance of Harry

Epigraph: *CMP*, p. 179.

1. The   following   on-the-spot

searches have been made for the critical years: Binghamton State Hospital (for both Ella Sullivan and Harry); Brooklyn State Hospital. Correspondence with institutions has established that no records for Sullivan exist at the Elmira Correctional and Reception Center. Records for the pertinent years do not exist for Bellevue Hospital or for the White Oak Farm in Pawling, New York, headed by Flavius Packer.

2. Information on the Packer family, Bellevue Hospital, and Menas Sarkis Gregory has been pieced together from several sources: Thurston G. Packer is listed in George A. Munson's *Early Years in Smyrna, and Our First Old Home Week* (Chenango Union Presses, 1905), p. 138; additional information on the medical training and experience of both father and son is in various American Medical Association directories. The beginning of a close, long-time relationship between Flavius Packer and Gregory was mentioned by Gwendolyn Daniels, a niece of Flavius and granddaughter of Thurston Packer, in a letter to the author, December 10, 1973. Information on the history of Bellevue was obtained from various encyclopedias; specific information on the establishment of a revised psychiatric service, under both young Packer and Gregory, is contained in John Starr's book, *Hospital City* (New York: Crown Publishers, 1957); see index entries for both names.

3. A. A. Brill, "Schizophrenia and Psychotherapy," *American Journal of Psychiatry* (1929–30) 9:519–541; see especially the discussion by Sullivan, p. 539.

4. Brill's discussion of Sullivan's paper entitled "Environmental Factors in the Etiology of Schizophrenia," in *Journal of Nervous and Mental Disease* (1930) 71:46–56; see especially p. 49.

5. A. A. Brill, "The Sense of Smell in the Neuroses and Psychoses," *Psychoanalytic Quarterly* (1932) 1:7–42; see especially pp. 38–39.

6. See Moers, *Two Dreisers,* for a detailed description of the relationship between Theodore Dreiser and A. A. Brill and its influence on *An American Tragedy* (pp. 262–270 passim).

7. *PI,* pp. 63–64.

20. The Chicago College of Medicine and Surgery

Epigraph: *FPSS,* p. 321.

1. See, for instance, Theodore Morrison, *Chautauqua* (Chicago: University of Chicago Press, 1974); especially p. 260.

2. Floyd W. Reeves et al., "A Survey of Valparaiso University," manuscript distributed by the Bureau of School Service, University of Kentucky, January 1929; on file at Widener Library, Harvard University; see especially pp. 4–5.

3. Information on the Chicago College of Medicine and Surgery during the relevant years is taken from catalogues and files furnished by Loyola University, which took over the Chicago College in 1917. I am indebted also to the faculty and staff at Loyola for their cooperation in explaining various problems incidental to the interpretation of the data—in particular William B. Rich, M.D., Associate Dean for Academic Affairs at the time of this research (1971). I am also indebted to the University Archivist of Valparaiso University for certain documents and information.

4. Interview with Lillian and Helen Stack, July 1963.

5. *Current Biography,* (1942), entry for Sullivan; p. 813.

6. Unpublished memoir, Dorothy Blitsten, undated.

7. Interview with Dorothy Blitsten, March 17, 1971.

8. Moers, *Two Dreisers;* see especially p. 124.

9. See *Psychiatry* (1948) 11:105–116.

21. The Struggle for Security

Epigraph: *SHP,* p. 290.

1. Theodore Dreiser, *Sister Carrie* (New York: New American Library, 1961), p. 245.

2. *PI,* p. 93.

3. *FPSS,* pp. 140–141.

4. *Current Biography* (1942), entry for Sullivan; p. 813.

5. *CSP,* p. 40.

6. *CMP,* p. 224.

7. Ibid., p. 223.

8. Ibid., pp. 27–28.

9. *SHP,* p. 312.

10. *CMP,* p. 178.

11. Personal communication, James I. Sullivan, ca. 1971.

12. *SHP,* p. 14. In 1924, he had had only 30 months' formal experience with patients at St. Elizabeths Hospital and at Sheppard and Enoch Pratt Hospital.

13. Ibid., p. 186.

14. Most of the following information is based on three documents, with information supplied by Sullivan: application for appointment in the Medical Reserve Corps, U.S. Army, February 12, 1918; application for a commission in the Sanitary Corps, U.S. Army, April 6, 1918; and an Officers' Qualification Card, dated July 8, 1918.

15. *ITP,* pp. 273–274.

16. UL 13, Con., WSP, 1943–1944.

17. Information on federal employment, taken directly from Veterans Administration personnel records, was furnished by Dave Stone of the VA Personnel Office, Washington, D.C., in a telephone interview on December 19, 1974.

18. *Current Biography* (1942), entry for Sullivan; p. 813.

22. The Impact of St. Elizabeths Hospital

Epigraph: *Current Biography* (1942), entry for Sullivan; p. 813.

1. Clara Thompson, in *SHP,* p. xxxiii.

2. "The Onset of Schizophrenia," *SHP,* p. 104.

3. Personal communication, Harold D. Lasswell, May 7, 1963.

4. Biographical data on Lucile Dooley are drawn from Douglas Noble and Donald L. Burnham, "History of the Washington Psychoanalytic Society and the Washington Psychoanalytic Institute," 1969 (privately circulated monograph, on file with the Institute office).

5. Edward J. Kempf, *Psychopathology* (St. Louis, MO: C. V. Mosby, 1921).

6. Ibid., p. 295 and passim.

7. Letter from Mrs. Aubrey Patterson to the author, March 28, 1965.

8. Letter from William V. Silverberg to the author, March 9, 1963.

9. Smith Ely Jelliffe, obituary on White, *Journal of Nervous and Mental Disease* (1937) 85:626–634; see p. 633.

10. Thompson, in *SHP,* pp. xxxiii–xxxiv.

11. William Alanson White, *Crimes and Criminals* (New York: Farrar and Rinehart, 1933), p. 31.

12. *CMP,* p. 16.

13. White, *Crimes and Criminals,* p. 178.

14. William Alanson White, *Insanity and the Criminal Law* (New York: Macmillan, 1923), p. 5.

15. White, *Autobiography,* p. 8.

16. Thomas Harvey Gill, review of White's *Autobiography,* in *Psychiatry* (1938) 1:272–274.

17. Most of the information on

White's life comes from his *Autobiography;* see especially part I, passim.

18. Nolan D. C. Lewis, "Smith Ely Jelliffe: The Man and Scientist," *Journal of Nervous and Mental Disease* (1947) 106:234–240; see p. 239.

19. Sullivan, "The Oral Complex," *Psychoanalytic Review* (1925) 12:31–38.

20. Letters of November 14 and November 21, 1922, as quoted in *William Alanson White, The Washington Years, 1903-1937,* ed. Arcangelo R. T. D'Amore (Washington, D.C.: Department of Health, Education and Welfare, publication no. 76–298, 1976); see pp. 78–79.

23. Studying Schizophrenia at Sheppard

Epigraph: *ITP,* pp. 334–335.

1. *ITP,* pp. 335–336.

2. Ibid., p. 335.

3. Clara Thompson, in *SHP,* p. xxxii.

4. The information on Chapman included here comes mainly from two obituaries: William J. Tiffany's in the *Archives of Neurology and Psychiatry* (1949) 61:317–319; and H. M. Murdock's in the *American Journal of Psychiatry* (1949) 105:718–719.

5. Bliss Forbush, *The Sheppard and Enoch Pratt Hospital: 1853-1970* (Philadelphia: Lippincott, 1971); see p. 80. The identity of the other "most influential psychiatrist" is not clear.

6. Ibid., p. 18.

7. Ibid., p. 35.

8. "Peculiarities of Thought in Schizophrenia" (1925), in *SHP;* for patients' education, see particularly pp. 35, 38, 42, 45, 50, and 74. "Case 4" (p. 45) is the only one described as having been to college.

9. *SHP,* pp. 130–136, 178.

10. UL 15, CL.

11. Forbush, *Sheppard and Enoch Pratt Hospital,* p. 64.

12. *SHP,* pp. 263n–264n.

13. *ITP,* p. 246.

14. *SHP,* p. 223.

15. Ibid., p. 262.

16. Ibid., p. 262–263.

17. Ibid., p. 269.

18. Ibid., p. 282.

19. Ibid., p. 287.

20. My earlier contacts with Pope and Evans are reported in my introduction to *Schizophrenia as a Human Process.* I never interviewed Pope formally, and he has now been dead for many years; but I specifically interviewed Evans for this book, in the spring of 1974. Regrettably, no extensive study has been made of Evans's sophisticated knowledge of this ward. None of these highly trained assistants to Sullivan are identified in the Forbush book on Sheppard, and their importance on the ward is noted only in a peripheral manner (Forbush, *Sheppard and Enoch Pratt Hospital,* p. 107).

21. *SHP,* p. 265.

22. *ITP,* p. 336.

23. Unless otherwise specified, most of the following material is derived from a 1974 interview with J. Ruthwin Evans.

24. Personal communication, Ray Pope, ca. 1950.

25. Personal communication, James I. Sullivan, ca. 1971.

26. *SHP,* pp. 290–291.

24. Clara Thompson, "Dear Friend and Colleague"

Epigraph: Clara Thompson, "The History of the William Alanson White Institute," mimeographed report of a lecture given on March 15, 1955, before the Harry Stack Sullivan Society in New York City.

1. Thompson, "History of the White Institute."

2. Personal communications, Maurice R. Green and Mabel Blake Cohen.

3. Interview with Agnes Marie Hadley, September 25, 1968.

4. Maurice R. Green, "Her Life," in Clara M. Thompson, *Interpersonal Psychoanalysis* (New York: Basic Books, 1964), p. 348. See also my entry for Thompson in *Notable American Women: The Modern Period* (Cambridge, Mass.: Harvard University Press, 1980).

5. Interview with Agnes Marie Hadley, September 25, 1968.

6. Interview with Dorothy Blitsten, March 17, 1971.

7. Green, "Her Life," p. 349.

8. Clara Thompson, "Changing Concepts of Homosexuality," *Psychiatry* (1947) 10:183–189; see esp. p. 186.

9. UL 15, Con., WSP, 1945.

10. Green, "Her Life," p. 351.

11. Green, in Thompson, *Interpersonal Psychoanalysis,* p. 205.

12. Personal communication, Clara Thompson, ca. 1947.

13. Sullivan, "Towards a Psychiatry of Peoples," p. 109n.

14. Green, "Her Life," p. 348.

15. "The Meaning of Anxiety in Psychiatry and in Life," in *FPSS,* p. 233n.

16. Personal communication, Maurice R. Green, 1978.

17. Letter from James I. Sullivan, December 3, 1971.

18. James I. Sullivan. All information supplied by him here and elsewhere in this book comes either from a series of informal memoranda that he prepared expressly for the author in 1971, or from various personal communications before and after 1971.

19. Interview with Agnes Marie Hadley, September 25, 1968.

20. James I. Sullivan, materials previously cited.

21. James I. Sullivan has reported that he once met F. Scott Fitzgerald, "probably around 1927." Since he was living with Sullivan at that time, it is safe to assume that he met Fitzgerald through Sullivan. James Sullivan supplied this information in connection with this biography, so I assume that he was indirectly reporting on some professional contact between Fitzgerald and Sullivan. James Sullivan has been particularly careful *not* to divulge information on Sullivan's patients, except occasionally by indirection.

22. Letter from Dorothy Stack to the author, April 2, 1972.

23. Margaret [Normile] Hannon, taped interview, January 4, 1972, and letter to the author, January 17, 1972.

24. Personal communication, Clara Thompson, ca. 1947.

25. Smyrna Revisited

Epigraph: Obituary in the *Chenango Telegraph* for March 12, 1926. Ella Stack's age is given here as a year younger than the age on the death certificate, made out at the same time.

1. From the Norwich *Sun,* June 12, 1923, and August 30, 1923. In connection with obtaining other essential biographical data, Sullivan's cousin, Mrs. Gertrude Nash, searched the *Sun* between September 1922 and September 1923. I am indebted to her for the information on the visits during that year.

2. Taped record, Dorothy Stack, April 1972.

3. Shortly before her death, Nina Stack also described the night of Leo's death (letter to the author, August 15, 1962). Dorothy Stack's oral account (taped record, April 1972) is fuller, but in essential agreement with her mother's. Both accounts agree with the medical findings and with newspaper reports at the time.

4. *SHP,* p. 274.

5. By a curious circumstance, Sulli-

van's age at death was about one month less than the average of the death ages of his mother and his cousin Leo. His prediction may have been made by actually averaging the two life spans and then giving himself a few extra months (3 months and 12 days) to allow for the longevity of the Sullivans.

6. Personal communication, Winfred Overholser (Superintendent of St. E's from 1937 to 1962), 1963.

7. Letter from Nina Stack to the author, August 15, 1962.

8. Jimmie Sullivan reports that "this is pretty much the exact quote" of what Sullivan told him about Ella's last illness (from materials previously cited).

9. Conrad Arensberg, *The Irish Countryman* (New York: American Museum of Science Books, 1968), p. 40.

10. Ibid., pp. 38 ff.

11. Letter from William Alanson White to Sullivan, March 20, 1926.

26. The Influence of Sandor Ferenczi

Epigraph: Clara Thompson, "The History of the William Alanson White Institute," mimeographed report of a lecture given on March 15, 1955, before the Harry Stack Sullivan Society in New York City (with minor editorial changes).

1. *CMP,* pp. 177–178.

2. *FPSS,* pp. 220–221.

3. See "The Oral Complex," *Psychoanalytic Review* (1925) 12:31–38.

4. See my introduction and commentaries in *SHP.*

5. Sigmund Freud, "On the History of the Psycho-Analytic Movement," (1914) in vol. 14, 1957, of *The Standard Edition of the Complete Works of Sigmund Freud,* trans. and under the editorship of James Strachey in collaboration with Anna Freud, assisted by Alix Strachey and Alan Tyson (London:

The Hogarth Press and the Institute of Psycho-Analysis), pp. 15–16.

6. *ITP,* pp. 16–24 passim.

7. Most of the information on Ferenczi's life comes from Izette de Forest's book, *The Leaven of Love: A Development of the Psychoanalytic Theory and Technique of Sandor Ferenczi* (Hamden, Conn.: Archon Books, 1965). De Forest was analyzed by Ferenczi, and as a lay analyst was especially concerned with artists and writers.

8. For Sullivan's other readings in psychoanalysis, see *CMP,* p. 178. Sullivan would have read the first English edition of Ferenczi's work: S[andor] Ferenczi, *Contributions to Psycho-Analysis,* trans. Ernest Jones (Boston: Richard G. Badger, 1916). In 1950 a new edition of the same translation was published, with a short introduction by Clara Thompson, under the title *Sex in Psychoanalysis* (New York: Basic Books, 1950). With the same plates but without Thompson's introduction this was reprinted in England using still another title, *First Contributions to Psycho-Analysis* (London: The Hogarth Press and the Institute of Psycho-Analysis, 1952). Then in 1956 Dover (New York) reissued the book, using the plates of the original Badger edition but under the title *Sex in Psychoanalysis.* For clarity, the pages I cite in this chapter conform to the Badger edition.

9. Maurice R. Green, "Her Life," in Clara M. Thompson, *Interpersonal Psychoanalysis* (New York: Basic Books, 1964), p. 357.

10. Michael Balint, "Sandor Ferenczi, Obit. 1933," *International Journal of Psychoanalysis* (1949) 30:215–219; see p. 217.

11. Freud, "Dr. Anton von Freund," (1920) in vol. 18, 1955, *Standard Edition,* p. 268.

12. Ferenczi, *Psycho-Analysis,* pp.

11, 25, 64–65, 133–139, 155, and 166–167, for example.

13. Freud, "On Psychotherapy," (1905 [1904]) in vol. 7, 1953, *Standard Edition,* p. 263.

14. Ferenczi, *Psycho-Analysis,* pp. 11–20.

15. Ferenczi, *Psycho-Analysis,* pp. 250–268.

16. *PI,* pp. 91–92. For Sullivan's explanation of the reconnaissance, see *PI,* pp. 85 ff.

17. Thompson, "History of the White Institute."

18. Freud, "Observations on Transference-Love," (1915 [1914]) in vol. 12, 1958, *Standard Edition;* see editors' footnote, pp. 160n–161n.

19. Philip Rieff, *Freud: The Mind of the Moralist* (Garden City, N.Y.: Doubleday [Anchor edition], 1961), pp. 10–11; see especially p. 11n.

20. Ferenczi, *Final Contributions to the Problems and Methods of Psycho-Analysis,* vol. 3 of Selected Papers (New York: Basic Books, 1955); see p. 160.

21. Ferenczi, *Psycho-Analysis* (1916), p. 217.

22. *SHP,* p. 9.

23. *FPSS,* p. 27.

24. Bulletin for the Washington School of Psychiatry, 1944–45.

27. The Influence of Adolf Meyer

Epigraph: "Intuition, Reason, and Faith," in *FPSS,* p. 64.

1. William James, "The Chicago School," *Psychological Bulletin* (1904) 1:1–5.

2. Thompson, "History of the White Institute."

3. Adolf Meyer, "A Discussion of Some Fundamental Issues in Freud's Psychoanalysis," published first in *State Hospital Bulletin* 1909–1910, reprinted in *The Collected Papers of Adolf Meyer, Vol. 2: Psychiatry,* ed. Eunice E. Winters (Baltimore: The

Johns Hopkins Press, 1951), pp. 604–617; see especially pp. 612–613.

4. Ernest Jones, *The Life and Work of Sigmund Freud, Vol. 3* (New York: Basic Books, 1957), p. 301. Jones himself published an article entitled "Psychoanalysis and Psychiatry" in 1930, in which he observes that "America has actually created a new profession." See *Mental Hygiene* (1930) 14:384–385.

5. *Proceedings: First Colloquium on Personalilty Investigation,* held under the auspices of the American Psychiatric Association: Committee on Relations with the Social Sciences, December 1–2, 1928, New York City (Baltimore: The Lord Baltimore Press, 1929 [?]); see p. 46.

6. *The Commonsense Psychiatry of Dr. Adolf Meyer,* ed. Alfred Lief (New York: McGraw-Hill, 1948), p. ix.

7. Henry Fox, "Adolf Meyer—A Personality Sketch," *Psychiatry* (1942) 5:159–164.

8. Meyer, *Collected Papers, Vol. 2,* p. 15.

9. Eunice E. Winters, "Adolf Meyer's Two and a Half Years at Kankakee: May 1, 1893–November 1, 1895," *Bulletin of the History of Medicine* (1966) 40:441–458; see p. 444.

10. Ibid., p. 458.

11. Meyer, *Collected Papers, Vol. 2,* p. 15.

12. Lief, *Commonsense Psychiatry,* p. 552.

13. *ITP,* p. 304.

14. Lief, *Commonsense Psychiatry,* p. 614.

15. Gordon W. Allport, *The Use of Personal Documents in Psychological Science* (New York: Social Science Research Council, 1951); bulletin 45, 1942; p. 10.

16. Lief, *Commonsense Psychiatry,* p. vii.

17. Ibid., p. ix.

18. Ibid., p. viii.

19. Adolf Meyer, *Psychobiology: A Science of Man,* ed. Eunice E. Winters

and Anna Mae Bowers (Springfield, Ill.: Charles C Thomas, 1957), p. 157.

20. *CSP,* pp. 377–378.

21. Meyer, *Collected Papers, Vol. 3,* p. 40.

22. *ITP,* pp. 33–34.

23. Joseph Lee, *Play in Education* (New York: Macmillan, 1921); see p. 65.

24. Hinsie and Campbell, eds., *Psychiatric Dictionary,* 3rd ed.

25. *SHP,* p. 104.

26. Meyer, *Psychobiology,* p. 163.

27. Hinsie and Campbell, eds., *Psychiatric Dictionary,* 3rd ed.

28. Sullivan, "The Study of Psychiatry," *Psychiatry* (1947) 10:355–371.

29. Clara Thompson, in *SHP,* p. xxxiv.

30. Personal communication, Edward J. Kempf, spring 1970.

31. Meyer, *Collected Papers, Vol. 3: Medical Teaching,* p. 452.

32. *FPSS,* p. 64.

28. Meeting Edward Sapir

Epigraph: Edward Sapir, "The Contribution of Psychiatry to an Understanding of Behavior in Society," *American Journal of Sociology* (1936–37) 42:862–870.

1. Interview with Jean Sapir, August 17, 1972.

2. Sullivan was attending a meeting in Chicago, probably the Illinois Society for Mental Hygiene (October 19, 1926), where Sapir gave a paper on "Speech as a Personality Trait."

3. Letter from Philip Sapir to the author, October 9, 1957.

4. See Robert Lowie's introduction to "Letters from Edward Sapir to Robert H. Lowie," privately published by Mrs. Luella Cole Lowie, 1965, and presented to the Library of the Peabody Museum (now the Tozzer Library of Harvard University). The Lowie letters cited in this chapter are from this collection.

5. Interview with Jean Sapir, August 17, 1972.

6. See the editor's introduction to *Selected Writings of Edward Sapir in Language, Culture and Personality,* ed. David G. Mandelbaum (Berkeley and Los Angeles: University of California Press, 1958), p. xi. Mandelbaum is reporting on information from Diamond Jenness.

7. *CMP,* p. xii–xiii.

8. Ibid.

9. Robert E. Park, introduction to Everett V. Stonequist's *The Marginal Man: A Study in Personality and Culture Conflict* (New York: Scribners, 1937).

10. Richard Ellmann, "Odyssey of a Unique Book," *New York Times Magazine,* November 14, 1965, p. 56.

29. Discovering the Chicago School of Sociology

Epigraph: *American Journal of Psychiatry* (1928) 8:378–379.

1. W. I. Thomas and Florian Znaniecki, *The Polish Peasant in Europe and America* (New York: Knopf, 1918).

2. William James, "The Chicago School," *Psychological Bulletin* (1904) 1:1–5.

3. In an earlier published statement, I have put together a brief history of Chicago social science (or sociology), including the importance of Hull-House. See the introduction to *FPSS,* pp. xiii–xxxii.

4. See Odell Shepard, *Pedlar's Progress: The Life of Bronson Alcott* (Boston: Little, Brown, 1937); especially pp. 80–83.

5. As I have reported in a commentary to an article in *FPSS,* p. 292.

6. *FPSS,* p. 239.

7. John Rickman, as reported in *Tensions That Cause Wars,* ed. Hadley Cantril (Urbana, Ill.: University of Illinois Press, 1950), p. 81.

8. Proceedings,   Hanover   [N.H.]

Conference, mimeographed, 1926; p. 62. (Available at Widener Library, Harvard University.)

9. Most of this account is based on a conversation in the spring of 1976 with Everett Hughes and Helen Hughes, both sociologists trained at Chicago. They did not agree on whether or not the University had forced Thomas to resign.

10. Leston Havens and Justin A. Frank, Jr., review of Patrick Mullahy, *Psychoanalysis and Interpersonal Psychiatry* (New York: Science House, 1970) in *American Journal of Psychiatry* (1971) 127:1704–1705; see p. 1705. Havens is widely credited with using the phrase "secretly dominates" to describe Sullivan's influence, but Havens is unsure as to where this phrase originated, although the idea is the same as in the review.

11. Proceedings, Hanover Conference, 1930; p. 91.

12. Mandelbaum, *Selected Writings of Edward Sapir,* p. 579n.

13. "Edward Sapir, Ph.D., Sc.D.: 1884–1939," *Psychiatry* (1939) 2:159.

14. Edward Sapir, "The Contribution of Psychiatry to an Understanding of Behavior in Society," *American Journal of Sociology* (1936–37) 42:862–870.

15. In the introduction to Dorothy R. Blitsten, *The Social Theories of Harry Stack Sullivan: The Significance of His Concepts of Socialization and Acculturation, Digested from His Various Papers and Integrated as a Selection for Social Scientists* (New York: The William-Frederick Press, 1953), p. 11.

16. For a record of these meetings, see *Proceedings: First Colloquium on Personality Investigation,* held under the auspices of the American Psychiatric Association: Committee on Relations with the Social Sciences, December 1–2, 1928, New York City

(Baltimore: The Lord Baltimore Press, 1929[?]); and *Proceedings: Second Colloquium on Personality Investigation,* held under the joint auspices of the American Psychiatric Association, Committee on Relations of Psychiatry, and the Social Science Research Council, November 29–30, 1929, New York City (Baltimore: The Johns Hopkins Press, 1930).

17. *Proceedings: First Colloquium,* p. 11.

18. Clyde Kluckhohn, "The Influence of Psychiatry on Anthropology in America During the Past One Hundred Years," in *One Hundred Years of American Psychiatry,* compiled by the American Psychiatric Association (New York: Columbia University Press, 1944); see especially pp. 597 and 601.

30. Becoming an Advocate

Epigraph: *PP,* p. 180. For readability in this excerpt, the last sentence of the original version has been placed first.

1. John A. P. Millet, "Psychoanalysis in the United States," in *Psychoanalytic Pioneers,* ed. Franz Alexander et al. (New York: Basic Books, 1966); see pp. 564–565.

2. *Psychiatry* (1947) 10:244.

3. Proceedings, Hanover Conference, 1930; p. 3.

4. Ibid., 1927; p. 245.

5. Ibid., 1927; pp. 265–266.

6. *American Journal of Psychiatry* (1928) 8:378–379.

7. Ibid., pp. 379–380.

8. Proceedings, Hanover Conference, 1928; pp. 11 and 15.

9. The published proceedings of the First Colloquium lists the participants and their affiliations as follows: F. H. Allport, Syracuse University; G. W. Allport, Dartmouth College; E. W. Burgess, University of Chicago; Z. C. Dickinson, University of Michigan;

George Draper, Columbia-Presbyterian Medical Center; L. K. Frank, Laura Spelman Rockefeller Memorial; Sheldon Glueck, Harvard University; E. R. Groves, University of North Carolina; William Healy, Judge Baker Foundation; F. E. Knight, University of Chicago; M. A. May, Yale University; Elton Mayo, Harvard University; Samuel Orton, American Psychiatric Association; Leonard Outhwaite, Laura Spelman Rockefeller Memorial; R. E. Park, University of Chicago; G. E. Partridge, Sheppard and Enoch Pratt Hospital; Edward Sapir, University of Chicago; C. R. Shaw, Institute for Juvenile Research; Wm. I. Thomas, New School for Social Research; L. L. Thurstone, University of Chicago; Kimball Young, University of Wisconsin.

10. Alfred H. Stanton and Morris S. Schwartz, *The Mental Hospital* (New York: Basic Books, 1956).

31. Leaving Sheppard

Epigraph: Letter from Ross McClure Chapman to Sullivan, March 18, 1930.

1. Bruce Lannes Smith, "The Mystifying Intellectual History of Harold D. Lasswell," in Arnold A. Rogow, ed., *Politics, Personality, and Social Science in the Twentieth Century: Essays in Honor of Harold D. Lasswell* (Chicago and London: University of Chicago Press, 1969); see p. 54.

2. Personal communication, Dorothy Blitsten.

3. Smith, "Harold D. Lasswell," pp. 42, 44–48. Much of the biographical information on Lasswell has been obtained from Smith's essay and from Leo Rosten's essay in the Rogow book, "Harold Lasswell: A Memoir" (especially p. 6). Other information, as supplied by Lasswell, comes from *Current Biography* for 1947 and from several

long conversations I have had with Lasswell beginning in May 1963.

4. Smith, "Harold D. Lasswell," p. 44.

5. Information on the trip to Spain is largely gained from a fragmentary transcription of a 1943 lecture given at Chestnut Lodge (UL, CL 21) in the early 1940s and from the author's conversations with Harold D. Lasswell, June 21–22, 1963.

6. Information on Sullivan's stay in Berlin comes from Lasswell, 1963.

7. *ITP*, p. 341.

8. *FPSS*, pp. 76–84.

9. Bliss Forbush, *The Sheppard and Enoch Pratt Hospital, 1853–1970* (Philadelphia and Toronto: Lippincott, 1971), pp. 88–90.

10. Ibid., p. 100.

11. Ibid., p. 114.

12. Ibid., p. 80.

32. The Descent of the Axe

Epigraph: Letter from Sullivan to William Alanson White, May 21, 1930.

1. *American Journal of Psychiatry* (1927–28) 7:837–839.

2. *American Journal of Psychiatry* (1927–28) 7:689–700.

3. Proceedings of 1930 Association meeting, *American Journal of Psychiatry* (1930–31) 10:323–327.

4. According to Harold D. Lasswell, the sociologist John Dollard was crucial in convincing Sullivan to withdraw the book, stating that Sullivan would later regret its publication (personal communication, 1963).

5. Letter from Hadley to Sullivan and others, January 29, 1937.

6. See Brush's report in APA Proceedings for 1930, *American Journal of Psychiatry* (1930–31) 10:301.

7. *American Journal of Orthopsychiatry* (1931) 1:371–379; see p. 378.

8. Charles S. Johnson, "Harry Stack Sullivan, Social Scientist," in *FPSS*, p. xxxv.

33. Uncertain Transition

Epigraph: Letter from Sullivan to Lola White (Mrs. William Alanson White), October 29, 1931.

1. Descriptions of dwellings in New York City have been provided mainly by James I. Sullivan, materials previously cited.

2. Clara Thompson, "Harry Stack Sullivan, the Man," in *SHP*, p. xxxii.

3. *Current Biography* (1942), entry for Sullivan; p. 813.

4. *CSP*, p. 172n.

5. *SHP*, p. 274.

34. Clarence H. Bellinger

Epigraph: Unsigned memorandum, "The William Alanson White Psychiatric Foundation Memorandum: Propaganda and Censorship," *Psychiatry* (1940) 3:628–632; see especially pp. 628–629. Although this is unsigned, Sullivan lists himself as the author in subsequent bibliographies.

1. *CMP*, p. 56.

2. From an article in the Norwich *Sun* for June 16, 1926, at the time that Bellinger went to Utica. This information about St. Elizabeths does not appear in any other biographical information on Bellinger. The later censoring of this information by Bellinger may be partly an expression of his growing envy of Sullivan's relationship with White.

3. Clarence Bellinger, "A Study of the Underlying Factors in the Development of Two Hundred Cases of Senile Psychosis," *State Hospital Quarterly* (1925) 11:18–25.

4. *Psychiatric Quarterly* (1927) 1:96–107; see especially pp. 98–99.

5. *Psychiatric Quarterly* (1927) 1:276–291.

6. *Psychiatric Quarterly* (1932) 6:475–487; see especially p. 486.

7. Edith M. Stern, "He Brings Hope to the Mentally Ill," *Reader's Digest*, June 1947, condensed from *This Week Magazine*, April 6, 1947; see p. 49.

8. Interview with Edward J. Kempf, spring 1970.

9. Taped interview, Alfred H. Stanton, January 7, 1974.

10. Letter from Mary Fargo to the author, May 8, 1974.

11. *ITP*, p. 237.

12. Ibid., p. 242.

13. Stern, "He Brings Hope," p. 50.

35. A Problem in Economics

Epigraph: *Proceedings, First Colloquium*, p. 62.

1. UL 8, Con., WSP, 1946.

2. *CMP*, p. 198.

3. Arcangelo R. T. D'Amore, "William Alanson White—Pioneer Psychoanalyst"; see pp. 69–91.

4. Richard Ellmann, *James Joyce* (New York: Oxford University Press, 1959); see p. 756.

5. For an explanation of this phenomenon in Ireland, particularly in County Clare, see Arensberg and Kimball, *Family and Community in Ireland*, pp. 72–75.

6. Jeffrey Potter, *Men, Money and Magic: The Story of Dorothy Schiff* (New York: Coward, McCann & Geoghegan, 1976); see pp. 124–127, 132–134, 136, 137–138, 181, 242–243, 244. I am indebted to Patricia Walsh for calling this book to my attention. It contains an interesting account of Schiff's work with Sullivan.

36. Being Free

Epigraph: UL 6, Con., WSP, 1943–44.

1. *PI*, p. 237.

2. UL 7, Con., WSP, 1945.

3. *Current Biography* (1942), entry for Sullivan; p. 814.

4. Letter from Sullivan to Dorothy R. Blitsten, November 27, 1940.

5. Mark Twain, *The Mysterious*

Stranger and Other Stories (New York: Harper and Brothers, 1916). See, for instance, *ITP,* pp. 341-432.

6. "Archaic Sexual Culture and Schizophrenia," in *SHP,* pp. 206-215; see especially pp. 211 and 212.

7. Interview with Kate Frankenthal, May 1970.

8. This information came from the May 1970 interview with Kate Frankenthal, who had been told it by Frieda Fromm-Reichmann. I myself did not have a chance to interview Fromm-Reichmann formally for this book, since she had died before I contemplated writing it.

9. "Anomaly," *The Invert and His Social Adjustment,* with an introduction by Robert H. Thouless (London: Bailliere, Tindall & Cox, 1927). In 1929 the book was reissued by the Williams & Wilkins Company in Baltimore, Md., probably on Sullivan's suggestion; he had close connections with that company.

10. See Sullivan's review of "Anomaly," *The Invert,* in *American Journal of Psychiatry* (1927-28) 7:532-537. Quotations from this review, in the following paragraphs, appear, respectively, on pp. 534, 535, and 536.

11. *Proceedings, Second Colloquium;* see Appendix C, p. 180.

12. "Anomaly," *The Invert,* p. 143 and p. 48, respectively.

13. Cited by Sullivan from "Anomaly," *The Invert,* but not identified by me.

14. "Anomaly," *The Invert,* p. 98.

15. Edward Sapir, "Observations on the Sex Problem in America," *American Journal of Psychiatry* (1928-29) 8:519-534. References to this paper, in the following paragraphs, appear, respectively, on pp. 520, 521, 529, 532-533, and p. 530.

16. Margaret Mead, *An Anthropologist at Work: Writings of Ruth Benedict* (Boston: Houghton Mifflin, 1959), p.

195. The quotation used here follows Mead's with one slight emendation, which I have taken from the original letter as supplied by Vassar College. In the second sentence, the word "probably" follows the original.

17. This paper has never been published; it was given in Washington, D.C., on December 27, 1929, and seems to have been a part of the annual meeting of sociologists; an abstract, which is not communicative, was published in *American Sociological Society Papers* (1930) 24:281-282.

18. *PI,* p. 169.

19. *SHP,* pp. 206-215.

20. Letter from John Vassos to the author, March 2, 1964.

37. The Tempo of Life in New York City

Epigraph: UL 9, Adv., WSP, 1943-1944.

1. Personal communication, Ralph Ellison, spring 1970.

2. UL 6, Con., WSP, 1946-1947.

3. *Current Biography* (1942), entry for Sullivan; p. 814.

4. UL, WSP, March 29, 1947 (not otherwise identified).

5. See, for instance, *CSP,* pp. 229-283 passim.

6. Several excerpts used here are from the same lecture; see *PI,* pp. 153-154 passim.

7. Material on John Vassos is based on correspondence and interviews with Vassos (beginning in 1964) and on a foreword by P. K. Thomajan to John Vassos, *Contempo, Phobia and Other Graphic Interpretations* (New York: Dover Publications, 1976).

8. John Vassos, *Phobia* (New York: Covici-Friede, 1931).

9. *CSP,* p. 378.

10. Thomajan mentions Brill's review in his foreword to Vassos, *Contempo, Phobia and Other Interpretations;* p. viii. I have been unable to

locate this review in Brill's bibliography; nor does Vassos know where it appeared.

11. I have been unable to verify Sullivan's career with the OSS; his grave marker in Arlington Cemetery carries only his rank of captain from his service in World War I. Again it would be quite in character for Sullivan never to mention such an assignment, and for the Army record to be incomplete in this particular, partly because Sullivan may never have bothered to send in the proper information.

12. Laura Fermi, *Illustrious Immigrants: The Intellectual Migration from Europe, 1930-41* (Chicago: University of Chicago Press, 1971).

13. Vassos, *Contempo,* p. v.

14. Clara Thompson, "The History of the William Alanson White Institute," mimeographed report of a lecture given before the Harry Stack Sullivan Society, New York City, March 15, 1955.

15. I am assuming here a normal time lag between writing and publishing. The three books, still in print in 1979, are: Horney, *The Neurotic Personality of Our Time* (Norton, 1937); Fromm, *Escape from Freedom* (Holt, 1941); and Sullivan, *Conceptions of Modern Psychiatry.*

16. For an insightful description of the story of the "mavericks," as the author terms them, see Marianne Horney Eckardt's paper, "Organizational Schisms in American Psychoanalysis," in *American Psychoanalysis: Origins and Development,* ed. Jacques M. Quen and Eric T. Carlson (New York: Brunner/Mazel, 1978), pp. 141-161, passim.

38. Inventing an Institution

Epigraph: Harold D. Lasswell, *Psychopathology and Politics* (originally published separately by the University of Chicago Press, 1930), in *The Political Writings of Harold D. Lasswell* (Glencoe, Ill.: Free Press, 1951); see p. 187 of the 1951 edition.

1. Erik H. Erikson, *Childhood and Society* (New York: Norton, 1950). The reference to Sullivan is in the Foreword: "Neither terminological alignment with the more objective sciences nor dignified detachment from the clamoring of the day can and should keep the psychoanalytic method from being what H. S. Sullivan called 'participant,' and systematically so." The index entry in the first edition of the book carries the name as *Henry* S. Sullivan. In the 1963 edition, the index entry for Sullivan has been omitted entirely, although the one sentence in the Foreword is unchanged.

2. Otto Klineberg's discussion of Charles S. Johnson's paper in Patrick Mullahy, ed., *The Contributions of Harry Stack Sullivan* (New York: Hermitage House, 1952); see pp. 215-216.

3. Hortense Powdermaker, *Stranger and Friend* (New York: Norton, 1966); see pp. 131-135.

4. Rosten, "Harold Lasswell," p. 10.

5. Interview with Jean Sapir, August 17, 1972.

6. *CSP,* pp. 358-359.

7. Information on Hadley's early life has been supplied by his wife, Agnes Marie Hadley, in an interview, September 25, 1968.

8. UL 15, CL.

9. Address (mimeographed) by Robert G. Kvarnes at the graduation exercises of the William Alanson White Institute in New York City, January 24, 1964.

39. The Research Nucleus

Epigraph: Telegram sent to Edward Sapir in New York City on April 9, 1938, from Sullivan, then in Washington, D.C.

1. The first research project approved by the Board of Trustees early

in 1938 was designed as a "Preliminary Investigation of Vocal Behavior," to be conducted by Sapir, Sullivan, and a linguistic psychologist, Stanley Newman. The project was only a small part of an all-encompassing and carefully thought out proposal. But significant monies were never found for any Foundation research until several years after Sapir's death; then the funding came not from philanthropies but from government grants.

2. Interview with Jean Sapir, August 17, 1972.

3. Ibid. Also personal communication, Harold D. Lasswell.

4. See *ITP,* pp. 339–340.

5. From Abstract of the President's report, approved and suffixed to the minutes; annual meeting, October 14, 1939.

6. Personal communication, Harold D. Lasswell.

7. Interview with George McMillan, August 16, 1972.

8. Rogow, ed., *Politics, Personality, and Social Science;* see p. x of editor's preface.

9. Weston La Barre, "Psychoanalysis in Anthropology," in *Psychoanalysis and Social Process,* vol. 4 of the series *Science and Psychoanalysis,* ed. Jules Masserman (New York: Grune and Stratton, 1961).

10. Walker Percy, "A Doctor Talks With the South and Its Young Heroes," in *The National Observer,* week ending September 16, 1972; p. 14.

11. Charles S. Johnson, *Growing Up in the Black Belt: Negro Youth in the Rural South* (Washington, D.C.: American Council on Education, 1941); see also *FPSS,* pp. 85–95.

12. First published in the November 1938 issue of *Psychiatry,* which was characteristically late and did not appear until just before Sapir's death. See *FPSS,* pp. 76–84.

13. Sullivan, in *Psychiatry* (1939) 2:159.

40. Expanding the Foundation's Horizons

Epigraph: Sullivan, "How Sweet *Are* the Uses of Adversity," *Psychiatry* (1943) 6:217–240; see especially p. 230.

1. Joan Mark, "Frank Hamilton Cushing and an American Science of Anthropology," from *Perspectives in American History,* vol. 10, 1976, copyright 1976 by the President and Fellows of Harvard College; see p. 450. See also Mark, *Four Anthropologists: An American Science in its Early Years* (New York: Science History Publications, 1980).

2. Marianne Horney Eckardt, "Organizational Schisms," pp. 141–161; see especially p. 142.

3. John A. P. Millet, "The Changing Faces of Psychoanalytic Training," in *Modern Concepts of Psychoanalysis,* ed. Leon Salzman and Jules H. Masserman (New York: The Citadel Press, 1962), pp. 127–139; see especially p. 128.

4. See Jack L. Rubins, *Karen Horney, Gentle Rebel of Psychoanalysis* (New York: Dial Press, 1978), pp. 103–104.

5. Millet, "Changing Faces," pp. 131–132.

6. Paul Roazen, *Freud and His Followers* (New York: Knopf, 1975), p. 430.

7. *CMP,* pp. 8 and 178–179n.

8. Sullivan, "How Sweet *Are* the Uses of Adversity," p. 219.

9. Otto Fenichel, in *Psychoanalytic Review* (1944) 31:133–152.

10. See Fenichel's review of Horney's *New Ways in Psychoanalysis* in *Psychoanalytic Quarterly* (1940) 9:114–121.

11. Otto Fenichel, *Final Papers* (New York: Norton, 1954), second series, pp. 243–259.

41. The Bethesda Style of Life

Epigraph: Letter to Ernest Hadley from Sullivan, August 22, 1938.

1. Albert Deutsch's column in *PM* for August 13, 1942.

2. Albert Deutsch, "A First-Rate Psychiatrist Passes On," *Washington Times-Herald,* January 17, 1949.

3. "Completing Our Mobilization," *Psychiatry* (1942) 5:281. This long editorial is unsigned, but clearly most of it is written by Sullivan.

4. Letter from Lloyd Frankenberg (whose wife, Loren MacIver, was a friend of Donahue's) to the author, December 3, 1972.

5. See Dexter Bullard's introduction to *Clinical Studies in Psychiatry;* p. xi.

6. UL 6, Con., WSP, spring 1945.

7. UL 5, Con., WSP, 1943–44.

8. UL 5, CL.

9. Letter from David McK. Rioch to the author, February 19, 1979.

10. Interview with David Rioch, March 8, 1971.

11. *ITP,* p. 210.

12. See discussion of paper by Sullivan, "Multidisciplined Coordination of Interpersonal Data," in *Culture and Personality,* ed. S. Stansfeld Sargent and Marian W. Smith (New York: Viking Fund, 1949); see p. 193.

13. Interview with Ann and Dexter Bullard, February 1971.

14. Frankenberg's account of his experience at the Lodge and at Sullivan's house is taken from his unpublished manuscript entitled "The Interperson." I am grateful to Loren MacIver for permission to use and quote from this manuscript.

15. This poem is published in a selection of Frankenberg's poems titled *The Stain of Circumstance* (Athens, Ohio: Ohio University Press, 1974); see pp. 117–124.

42. After Hiroshima

Epigraph: Sullivan, "The Cultural Revolution to End War," *Psychiatry* (1946) 9:85.

1. G. Brock Chisholm, "New Vistas of Responsibility," *Psychiatry* (1949) 12:191–195; see especially pp. 192–193.

2. Sandor Lorand's article on Ferenczi, titled "Pioneer of Pioneers," in *Psychoanalytic Pioneers,* ed. Franz Alexander et al. (New York: Basic Books, 1966); see p. 15.

3. *Psychiatry* (1945) 8:112–113.

4. *Psychiatry* (1947) 10:239–252; see p. 244.

5. Ibid., p. 245.

6. *Tensions That Cause Wars: Common statement and individual papers by a group of social scientists brought together by UNESCO,* ed. Hadley Cantril (Urbana, Ill.: University of Illinois Press, 1950).

7. Ibid., pp. 9–11.

8. Cited by Cantril in his introduction to *Tensions That Cause Wars,* p. 12. Janet Flanner, who wrote for the *New Yorker* under the name of Genêt for fifty years, was born in the same year as Sullivan, and her writings were much admired by Sullivan.

9. *Tensions That Cause Wars,* ed. Cantril; p. 9.

10. Ibid., p. 81.

11. Ibid., p. 135. With Allport's permission, I used his phrase, "the fusion of psychiatry and social science," as the title for one of the posthumous collections of Sullivan's writings.

12. A. Querido, "Notes on an Experiment in International Multiprofessional Cooperation," *Psychiatry* (1948) 11:349–354; see especially p. 352.

43. Paris, January 14, 1949

Epigraph: Charles S. Johnson, "Harry Stack Sullivan, Social Scientist," in *FPSS;* see p. xxxiii. This was an address given at memorial services for Sullivan on February 11, 1949.

1. From transcript of proceedings at memorial services for Sullivan, February 11, 1949; these two sentences were

omitted, unfortunately, in the published version (see *SHP,* xxxii–xxxv), probably at my suggestion and with Thompson's concurrence, at the time that I edited it for the journal *Psychiatry.*

2. I have been unable to locate the note or to identify the recipient, but I remember seeing it at the time and being shocked at the information, new to me.

3. Sullivan, "The Study of Psychiatry," lecture given in the fall of 1948 and published posthumously; *Psychiatry* (1949) 12:336.

4. These lectures were published in the posthumous book *The Interpersonal Theory of Psychiatry.*

5. Sullivan, "Remobilization for Enduring Peace and Social Progress," *Psychiatry* (1947) 10:239–245; see p. 245. Lines arranged by me from conventional prose lines. The semicolon is the one I referred to in the Prologue.

Acknowledgments

In a project of this kind, the encouragement and interest of a few people over many years are essential ingredients. The four people who were most important are listed on the dedication page of this book. Shortly after Sullivan's death, my sister, Eunice Tertell, used her skills as a librarian to organize and code Sullivan's unpublished writings and recordings and to set up standard procedures for editing posthumous papers; her delight at the richness of the material sustained me in mining the papers for this biography. My collaborator on the posthumous papers, Mary Ladd Gavell, made the task of editing Sullivan's papers an exciting rather than an impossible one; she read the first summary of my proposed biography in 1965, and wrote me wise and encouraging comments. For over a decade, my publisher and long-time friend, Arthur Rosenthal, never deviated in his determination that I would write a biography of Sullivan. And finally, Stewart Perry took major responsibility at every stage of the book—searching through old newspaper files, refusing to allow me to abandon the whole thing on four or five occasions, doing most of the content editing on the final manuscript, collaborating in the cutting of over 70,000 words from the working manuscript, and indexing the book.

Several people lent assistance to me in my early and completely unsuccessful attempts to obtain financial support for this project—in particular, Victoria Wentworth Arrington, Jean Evans, Donald Fleming, Martha Gibbon, and Philip Sapir. Their interest was in itself supporting.

Permission for the use of various documents and Sullivan's published and unpublished writings was generously granted by the William Alanson White Psychiatric Foundation in Washington, D.C., and by James Inscoe Sullivan. Mabel Blake Cohen, formerly editor of *Psychiatry* and chairman of the Committee on Sullivan's Writings, was instrumental in securing early access to the Foundation's files. Robert G. Kvarnes, as Secretary of the Foundation, facilitated the final process of formal permissions on the use of correspondence written by early officers of the Foundation, especially Sullivan and Ernest E. Hadley. Katherine Henry, a member of the staff of *Psychiatry*, helped me in locating relevant material in the Foundation files and preparing summaries of them. Permission to use letters of Harold D. Lasswell was furnished by Luis Kutner, Lasswell's executor.

Five people in particular provided extensive and important information: Dorothy Blitsten, a long-time friend of Sullivan's, gave me access to her unpublished memoir on Sullivan and allowed me to use personal letters from Sullivan on file in the Archives of Psychiatry of the New York Hospital at the Cornell Medical Center. Lloyd Frankenberg and his wife, Loren MacIver, did fieldwork for me in Paris and supplied me with many reminiscences from the New York City days; after Lloyd's death, Loren gave me permission to quote from Lloyd's unpublished memoir on Sullivan. Margaret Hannon, as the only person I found on the Sullivan side of the family who knew Sullivan both as a boy and as an adult, gave me essential insights in a long taped interview and in letters. Dorothy Stack furnished me with a long and charming taped history of the Stack family and with many pictures that furnished crucial clues to the family tradition.

Other family members helped me in many different ways. For granting me interviews in person and by telephone and for sending me family pictures and written reminiscences, I am indebted to Marian Crowley, Marjorie M. Gerry, Jane Sullivan Kenific, Clara Stack Mess, Edward Stack, Frederick E. Stack, Helen Stack, Lillian Stack, Nina Brown Stack, and Wickliffe Stack. Neil Stack sent me a Stack family genealogy.

My early introduction into Chenango County in 1961 was made possible by Lucy Horwitz, who located a long-time Irish-American physician in Norwich, Dr. Thomas F. Manley, who, in turn, directed me to a second cousin of Sullivan's, Gertrude (Sullivan) Nash. She was the first person in the County to lend a sympathetic ear to the idea of this biography, and over the years she has helped me in ways past enumerating; she had never met Sullivan, but as a former librarian in the Guernsey Memorial Library in Norwich for many years, she had followed his career closely and helped me to understand the scope of the story that existed in the social history of the County. The staff of the Norwich library—particularly Charlotte I. Spicer, reference librarian on local history—cooperated with me throughout the project, making their files of the daily Norwich *Sun* available to me in the beginning and later arranging for microfilming these newspapers, which made it possible to complete the search of issues from 1891 through 1911. Unfortunately, some of the issues had been mutilated over the years as people apparently cut out articles that concerned them; some such snipping may have taken place on items about the Stack and Sullivan families. Since the *Sun* did not begin publication until late in 1891, earlier social and family history came mainly from items in the *Chenango Telegraph*, which was also available in the Norwich library.

Although I am indebted to scores of people in Chenango County for permitting me to interview them formally and informally, I want to express my gratitude in particular to Edith Bradley, Vaughan Fargo, Mr. and Mrs. Leslie Hopkins, Anne Kehoe, Mary (Wedge) Lasher, Loretta Macksey, Agnes Rexford, Grace Steere, Mr. and Mrs. R. F. Smith, Frederick B. Sprague, Beatrice Sweet, John Tackabury, Edmund P. Tobey, Mrs. John Widger, and Esther R. Woodward.

Many colleagues and friends who knew Sullivan as an adult were interviewed by me, or supplied information by letter or telephone; I particularly want to mention the help of the following people: Hilde Bruch, Dexter and Ann Bullard, Ralph Crowley, Ralph Ellison, J. Ruthwin Evans, L. K. Frank, Kate Frankenthal, Thomas H. Gill, Agnes Marie Hadley, Edward J. Kempf, Harold D. Lasswell, George McMillan, Margaret Mead, Ruth Moulton, Patrick Mullahy, Winfred Overholser, Aubrey Patterson, Muriel Paul, David McK. Rioch, Jean Sapir, Philip Sapir, Ernest G. Schachtel, William V. Silverberg, Alfred H. Stanton, Edward S. Tauber, Robert Trier, Herman Weinberg, Benjamin I. Weininger, and Otto Allen Will, Jr.

Many institutions accorded me essential courtesies in my inquiries, and they are acknowledged for the most part in the notes. I want to thank particularly the faculty and staff of the William Alanson White Institute of Psychiatry, Psychoanalysis, and Psychology in New York City for their sustained cooperation; and the Sheppard and Enoch Pratt Hospital for making administrative correspondence available to me.

James Inscoe Sullivan prepared many useful memoranda for me on Sullivan's life in Towson, Maryland, in New York City, and in Bethesda, Maryland, and helped me on many levels. Research memoranda reviewing batches of data were written for me by Guillemette Caron-Simmers, Linda Hink Harrington, Sylvia Pellini MacPhee, Sue Perry, Susan Tertell, and Patricia Walsh.

Various people supplied me with special assistance: help on legal problems and searches came from Frank Smith, Edward O'Connor, Seymour Farber, and John Van Dusen. A Cambridge neighbor, George McMillan, enlisted the help of William H. Wright, an expert on the behavior of horses. In 1963, Robert Kleiman, then a CBS correspondent in Paris, obtained critical information from authorities in Paris on Sullivan's death. Also, Micheline Fort Harris queried the personnel of the Ritz Hotel in Paris on Sullivan's death there and determined that nothing could be turned up, since the staff denied that Sullivan had died in the hotel, as reported on the death certificate. Ruth and Frank Young helped me in background research in Ithaca. Margaret Adams introduced me to Abraham Glenn, a psychiatrist long associated with Brooklyn State Hospital, who assisted me in checking records there.

From first to last, librarians and local historians have been a source of dedicated detective work. Their names are many, but I shall mention only a few here. Mary Fargo, Smyrna historian for many years, has been indefatigable in collecting old pictures and reams of data, including the records of attendance at the village school for the years when Harry Sullivan and Clarence Bellinger were students there. Louise S. Shinners, town historian in Norwich, furnished important material on the social and economic history of Rexford Street. Librarians at nine different Harvard University libraries helped me in tracking down obscure references, illustrating for me anew the interdisciplinary character of Sullivan's work. In this vast network of Harvard librarians, I particularly want to mention Sheila Hart, who has supplied intelligent guidance for a decade. The reference librarians at Cambridge Public Library have saved me hundreds of trips and hours of work by their skill at finding just what I needed at the particular moment; and I would like to express especially my gratitude to Ann Porter for her interest over the years.

In addition to works cited in my bibliographic notes, my knowledge of the immigrant experience came from the writings of Oscar Handlin and my exposure to Irish folkways from the stories of Frank O'Connor. Although neither is cited in the book, both have been important checkpoints for my own observations—some made in Ireland and some in Boston. In 1971, I made a field trip to the west of Ireland to research parish records and to experience that culture firsthand, and I had an unexpected encounter with Irish "cooring" as a patient in the Orthopaedic Hospital in Croom, County Limerick; the staff under the direction of Sister Mary Gregory and Mr. J. P. Kelly, orthopaedic surgeon, exposed me to the special facility of the Irish for humane and insightful care, including a flask of brandy provided by Sister Gregory for my trip by ambulance to Shannon Airport and thence home. Earlier I had learned to recognize the phenomenon of cooring at Boston Psychopathic Hospital where I did some ward research early in the 1960s and understood for the first time that hospitals in Boston had become world-famous partly through their staff nurses, hired on annual trips to Ireland. Such ability to identify with people in distress is of course a significant clue to Sullivan's life and work.

Another book not cited has also been crucial. M. Harvey Brenner's *Mental Illness and the Economy* (Cambridge, Mass.: Harvard University Press, 1973) gave systematic evidence of the relationship between mental disorder and the social and economic structure of the society—particularly in New York State.

The following friends have read shorter or longer sections of the working draft of the book and made excellent suggestions: Grace M. Clark, Grace Dingee, Maurice Green, Edith Helman, Katherine Henry, Joan Mark, John O. Perry, Sue Perry, Arthur Rosenthal, Calvin Saxton, Suzanne Strickland, and Patricia Walsh. Margaret and Harold Tepper gave valuable assistance in the reading of the final manuscript.

Editorial staff at the Harvard University Press gave critical assistance. Catherine Bayliss was an efficient and considerate mentor; Virginia La-Plante did the overall evaluation of the original working manuscript; and Mary Ellen Arkin tried to create—against substantial odds—some consistency in spelling, grammar, and punctuation in a manuscript that covered, in all, a century of varying rules for writing (some few rules being idiosyncrasies implanted in me by Sullivan himself) and a curious conglomerate of rural and technical language. I am grateful to each of these participants. In the complicated task of preparing the final manuscript, Grace M. Clark caught a significant number of gaffes that had managed to survive through previous versions. In the last year, Suzanne Strickland has provided me with the impetus for completing the final and endless chores; the excitement of a young person about the significance of Sullivan's ideas as applied to current social problems has made my work more meaningful.

Cambridge, Massachusetts
November 1981

Index

DATE DUE